HELEN AND NEWTON HARRISON CALIFORNIA WORK

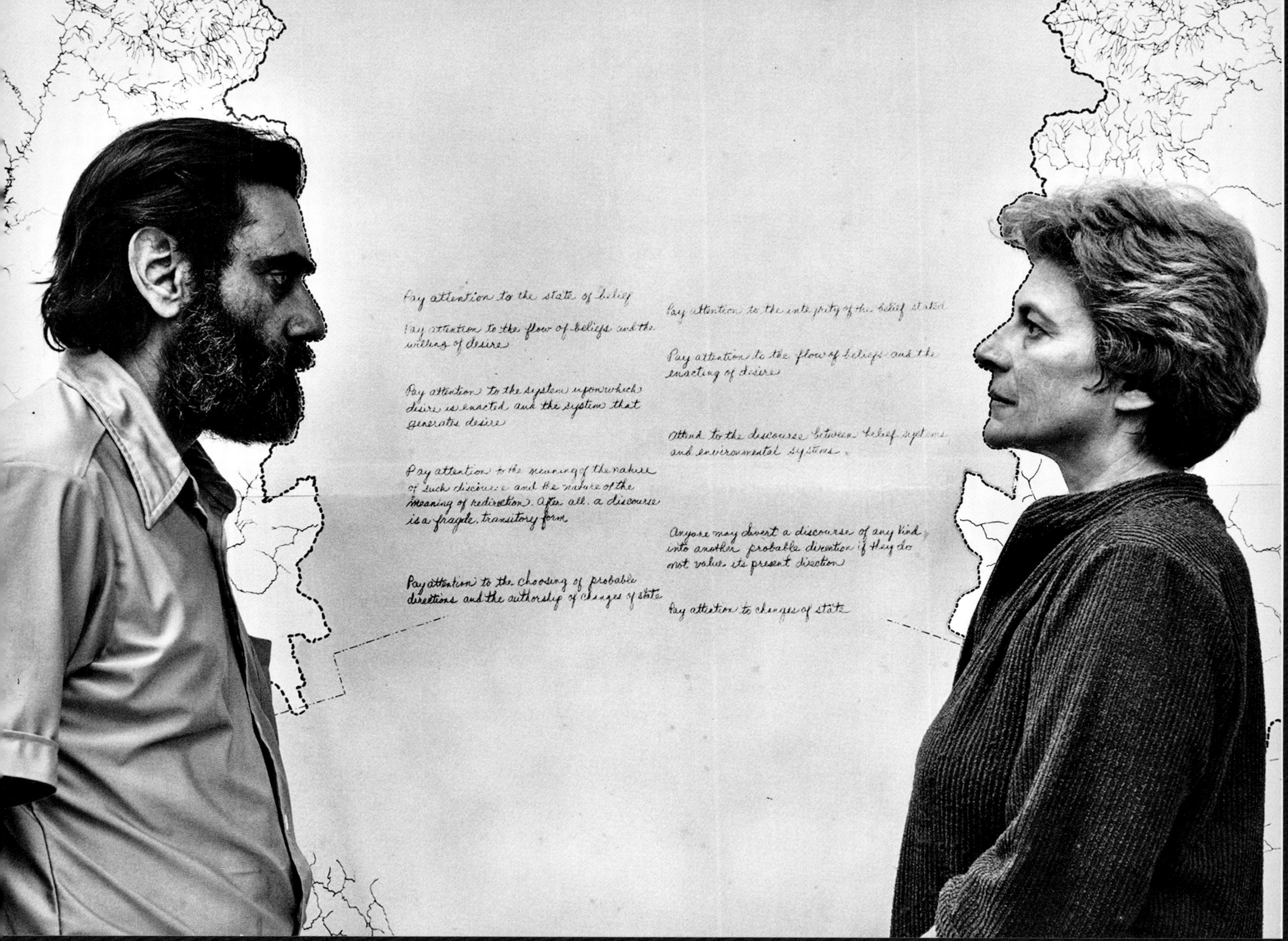
Pay attention to the state of belief
Pay attention to the flow of beliefs and the willing of desire
Pay attention to the system upon which desire is enacted and the system that generates desire
Pay attention to the meaning of the nature of such discourse and the nature of the meaning of redirection. After all, a discourse is a fragile, transitory form
Pay attention to the choosing of probable directions and the authorship of changes of state
Pay attention to the integrity of the belief stated
Pay attention to the flow of beliefs and the enacting of desire
Attend to the discourse between belief systems and environmental systems.
Anyone may divert a discourse of any kind into another probable direction if they do not value its present direction
Pay attention to changes of state

Helen and Newton Harrison California Work

EDITED BY

Tatiana Sizonenko

TEXTS BY

Monica Manolescu
Edward Shanken
Tatiana Sizonenko

Deutscher
Kunstverlag

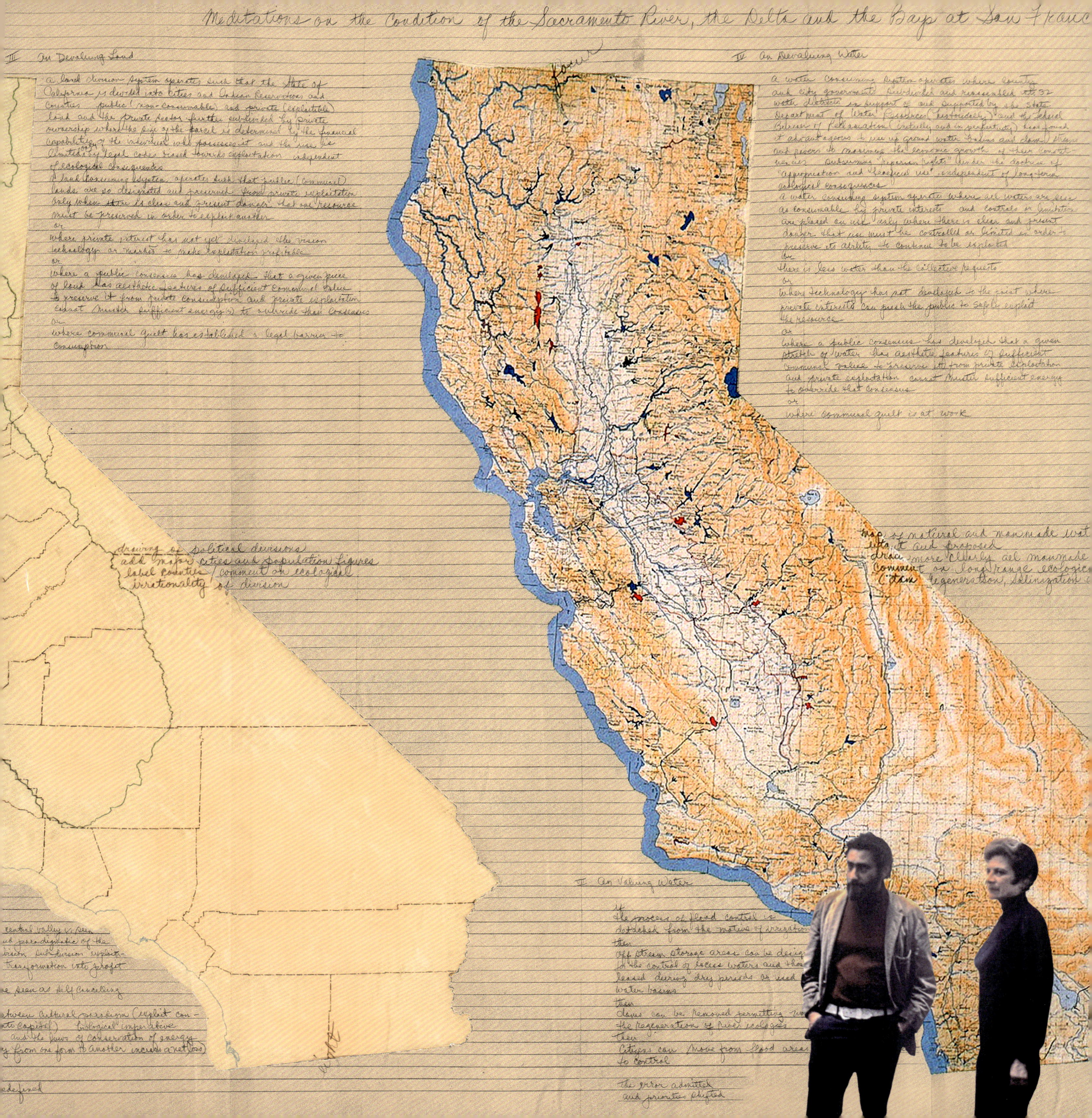
Meditations on the Condition of the Sacramento River, the Delta and the Bay at San Franc
III On Devaluing Land
a land division system operates such that the State of California is divided into cities and Indian Reservations and counties public (non-consumable) and private (exploitable) land and the private sector further subdivided by private ownership where the size of the parcel is determined by the financial capability of the individual who possesses it and the use is limited only by legal codes biased towards exploitation independent of ecological consequences
a land consuming system operates such that public (communal) lands are so designated and preserved from private exploitation only when there is clear and present danger that one resource must be preserved in order to exploit another
or
where private interest has not yet developed the vision technology or market to make exploitation profitable
or
where a public consensus has developed that a given piece of land has aesthetic features of sufficient communal value to preserve it from private consumption and private exploitation cannot muster sufficient energy(s) to override that consensus
or
where communal guilt has established a legal barrier to consumption
IV On Devaluing Water
a water consuming system operates where county and city governments subdivided and reassembled into 32 water districts in support of and supported by the State Department of Water Resources (historically) and the Federal Bureau of Reclamation (initially and in perpetuity) have found it advantageous to use up ground water basins and dam streams and rivers to maximize the economic growth of their constituencies subsuming "riparian rights" under the doctrine of "appropriation and beneficial use" independent of long term ecological consequences
a water consuming system operates where all waters are seen as consumable by private interests and controls or limitations are placed on use only where there is clear and present danger that use must be controlled or limited in order to preserve its ability to continue to be exploited
or
there is less water than the collective requests
or
where technology has not developed to the point where private interests can push the public to safely exploit the resource
or
where a public consensus has developed that a given stretch of water has aesthetic features of sufficient communal value to preserve it from private exploitation and private exploitation cannot muster sufficient energy to override that consensus
or
where communal guilt is at work
drawing of political divisions
add major cities and population figures
label counties / comment on ecological irrationality of division
VI On Valuing Water
if
the process of flood control is detached from the motive of irrigation
then
off stream storage areas can be desig
for the control of excess waters and thos
leased during dry periods or used
water basins
then
dams can be removed permitting
the regeneration of river ecologies
then
citizens can move from flood areas
to control
the error admitted
and priorities shifted

Contents

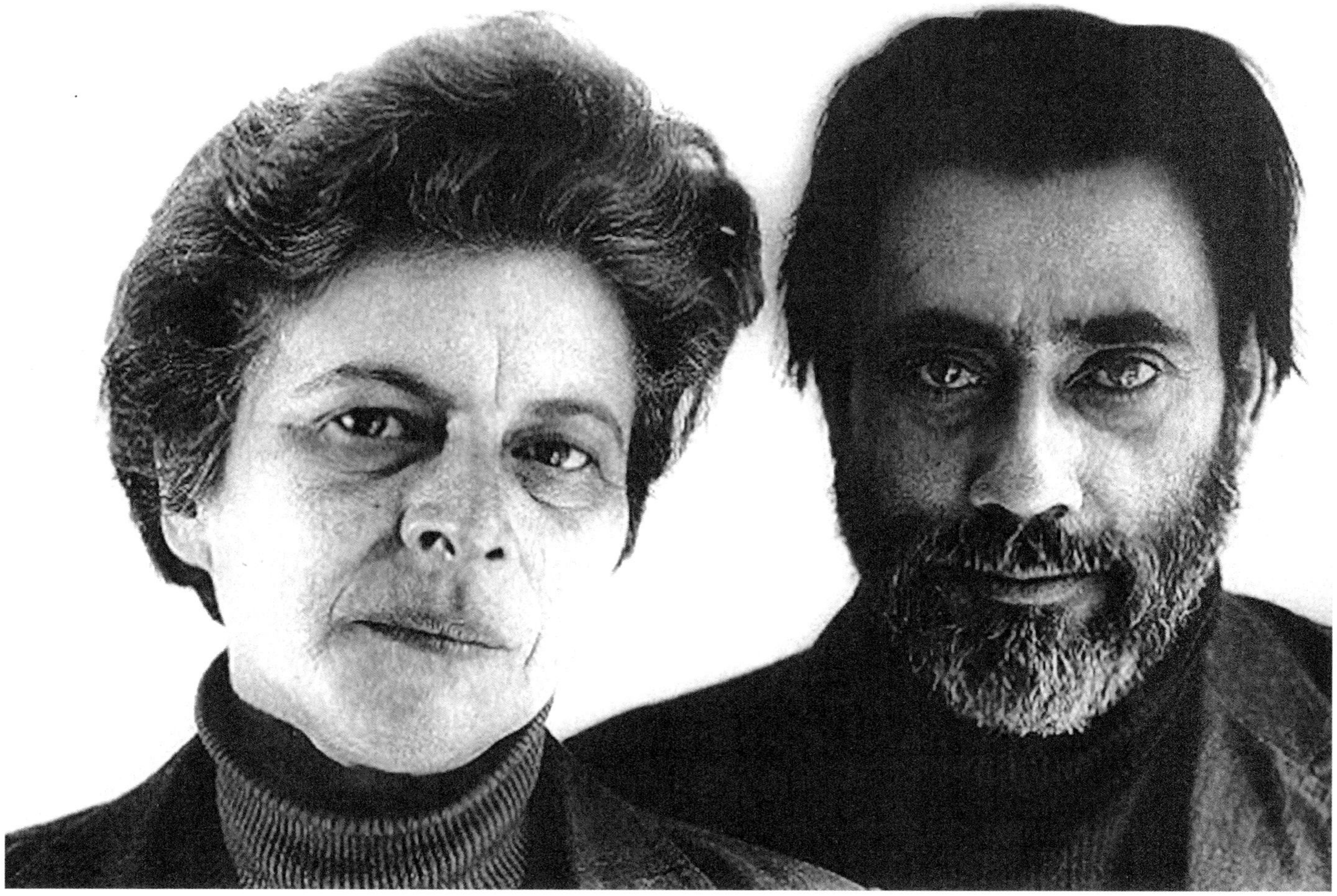

LA JOLLA
HISTORICAL SOCIETY

Helen and Newton Harrison: California Work
is organized and presented by the La Jolla Historical Society with partner venues California Center for the Arts Escondido, San Diego Central Library Art Gallery, and Mandeville Art Gallery at the University of California, San Diego.

PST ART ART & SCIENCE COLLIDE

This exhibition is made possible with support from Getty through its PST ART: Art & Science Collide initiative.
Helen and Newton Harrison: California Work is among more than 60 exhibitions and programs presented as part of PST ART. Returning in September 2024 with its latest edition, PST ART: Art & Science Collide, this landmark regional event explores the intersections of art and science, both past and present. PST ART is presented by Getty.
For more information about PST ART: Art & Science Collide, please visit pst.art

Funding for **Helen and Newton Harrison: California Work** provided by Joan and Irwin Jacobs, the M&I Pfister Foundation, The Seth Sprague Educational and Charitable Foundation, Michael Bernstein and Patti Harp, and Heath and Terry Fox. Additional Support provided by Monica and Charles Cochrane.

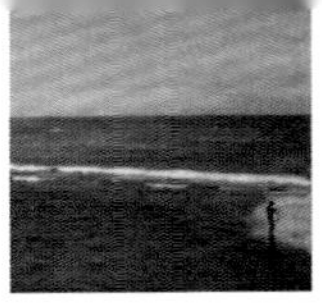

Executive Director's Foreword LAUREN LOCKHART

The La Jolla Historical Society is proud to present the first comprehensive retrospective of the work of Helen Mayer and Newton Harrison, known as the Harrisons. We are grateful that this ambitious project provides the opportunity to return their work and legacy to the seaside village of La Jolla, where their groundbreaking partnership began at the University of California, San Diego (UCSD), and where they presented works that would be forerunners of the ecological art movement, like *La Jolla Promenade*. Presenting their practice on this scale will increase awareness of the Harrisons' prescient work addressing issues of climate change, social justice, and art and technology. The discourses they engaged with since the 1970s have only become more urgent, making all the more timely both their theoretical and practical solutions to the challenges our species faces.

Helen and Newton proposed a relationship between humans and nature that aligns with Indigenous ways of thinking wherein coexistence and gratitude are prioritized over dominance of the land. It is our hope that this project will inspire a new generation to feel empowered to create change, and to live more harmoniously with the environment by listening more closely to its needs, just as Helen and Newton encouraged us to do.

Tatiana Sizonenko, PhD, envisioned and organized this exhibition over the course of nearly five years of thoughtful research and close dialogue with Newton Harrison. Before his passing, we were incredibly fortunate to benefit from Newton's wisdom and guidance on this exhibition and book. Tatiana joins me in offering our sincere appreciation to the Harrison family for their generous collaboration and counsel on this project, without which the scope and depth of this endeavor would not have been possible.

I am humbly indebted to Project Director and former La Jolla Historical Society Executive Director Heath Fox, who has lent his time, talent, and remarkable organizational skills to this project. Along with Tatiana, Heath shared a vision for a project that would inspire greater appreciation of the Harrisons and create opportunities for meaningful regional collaborations across San Diego County, for which I am very grateful.

I am thankful to Edward Shanken and Monica Manolescu who authored thought-provoking new scholarship and perspectives on the Harrisons through their original essays for this publication. I also want to recognize the important contributions of Chris Fremantle and Anne Douglas, who have been instrumental in developing public programming to accompany this exhibition that reflects the Harrisons' commitment to active audience engagement with their work. Thank you as well to Kai Reschke and Petra Kruse for their excellent design work on this book.

I want to acknowledge our partners at each host institution, who have been tremendous collaborators; thank you to Ceci Moss and Ricardo Dominguez of the Mandeville Gallery at UCSD; Gina Lopez, Beth Marino, and Rokhsane Hovaida at the Center for the Arts, Escondido; and Bonnie Domingos at the Central Library Art Gallery in Downtown San Diego. Thank you also to the lending institutions and our colleagues there: Kathryn Kanjo, Jill Dawsey, and Karin Zonis-Sawrey of the Museum of Contemporary Art San Diego; Ann M. Wolfe and Brian Eyler of the Nevada Museum of Art; Ariel Pittman and Michelle Kang of Various Small Fires Gallery, Los Angeles; and Bernard Blistene, Raphaële Bianchi, Karine Jonneaux, Rania Moussa, and Sophie Frouchart of the Centre Georges Pompidou in Paris.

The Getty Foundation appreciated the need for an expansive approach to this exhibition concept to appropriately recognize and celebrate the Harrisons. We owe Heather MacDonald and the Getty Foundation an expression of deep gratitude for their incredible support from the beginning.

A project of this scale and complexity would not have been possible without considerable financial support. We extend our deepest gratitude to Joan and Irwin Jacobs for their lead sponsorship gift, and to the M&I Pfister Foundation for their generous contribution. We are grateful for support from The Seth Sprague Education and Charitable Foundation, Michael Bernstein and Patti Harp, and Heath and Terry Fox. Additional support was provided by Monica and Charles Cochrane.

An exhibition of this scope requires organizational assistance at all levels. The Board of Directors of La Jolla Historical Society have championed this project since its inception; we are very grateful for their continued support. The talented staff have been vital in realizing varied aspects of this project, from program development and additional research to installation planning and artwork transportation. I am immensely grateful to Office and Events Manager Karla Cook; past Deputy Director and Collections Manager Dana Hicks; current Collections Manager Colette Militello; Historian Carol Olten; and Education and Public Engagement Manager McKenna Clifford Yahyai.

The Harrisons offer important lessons for our organization and others through their demonstration of impactful interdisciplinary and transhistorical collaborations. I expect that we will continue to look to their work for guidance and insights about how to better serve and repair our relationship with the Earth for generations to come.

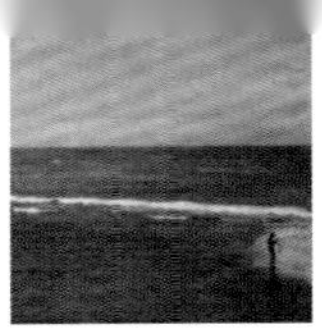

Curator's Statement TATIANA SIZONENKO

Ideas for *Helen and Newton Harrison: California Work* were first discussed during my several visits with Newton in Santa Cruz in the summer and fall of 2019. Serendipitously, Heath Fox, the Executive Director of La Jolla Historical Society at the time, invited me to contribute an exhibition proposal as part of the grant competition for the Getty Foundation's Pacific Standard Time: Art & Science Collide 2024. With the encouragement from the Getty's PST ART staff, the preliminary application was modified to become a four-part retrospective exhibition about Helen Mayer Harrison and Newton Harrison – known as the Harrisons – who, as a couple, played a pioneering role in ecological art.

Helen and Newton Harrison: California Work explores the collision of art and science, art and ecology, and art and social activism in the work of the Harrisons, offering a critical reappraisal of their California-based works through an exhibition catalogue and interdisciplinary public programming with leading scholars, artists, and scientists. By focusing for the first time on their California works produced between 1968 and 2022, the exhibition showcases the formulation and progression of concepts, artistic techniques and strategies, and design solutions that occurred as the Harrisons developed their own model for what it meant to practice art: as research project, as call to action, and as bioregional planning to bring about systemic change, whether social, political, or – most important of all – ecological. *California Work* highlights the innovative ways in which the Harrisons engaged with science and how, grounded in prescient concerns about the issue of climate change (a topic they first addressed in 1974), they took on an increasingly planetary frame of reference.

Helen and Newton Harrison: California Work is presented simultaneously in four locations in or near San Diego, including at the La Jolla Historical Society (the organizer of the exhibition), the California Center for the Arts (Escondido), the San Diego Central Library Art Gallery (downtown), and the Mandeville Art Gallery (UC San Diego). The exhibition examines the California works chronologically and thematically: *Urban Ecologies*, *The Prophetic Works*, *Saving the West*, and *Future Gardens*. Across its four venues, *California Work* explores the potential for the Harrisons' art to generate vital new meanings by engaging viewers in dialogue about the unfolding environmental crisis, perhaps the greatest challenge of our time. We hope to reach out to a wide cross-section of audiences comprising ethnically and economically diverse populations, from urban to suburban, from student to elder adult, as well as local and international visitors.

Helen and Newton are towering figures in American art, in which they viewed themselves as post-conceptual artists. They re-introduced the ethical dimension into contemporary art by deciding that they would do no further work unless it benefitted the ecosystem. The Harrisons' commitment to bettering the world by bridging art with science, social policy, and the environment resulted in founding a new interdisciplinary artistic practice known today as ecological art, which they actively practiced as Survival Art. California Work spotlights the Harrisons' belief that art can change the world for the better, not just by enrichment and engagement, but by proposing new solutions to problems uncovered by artists in collaboration with scientists, engineers, and social planners. Aesthetically, their California works served as a laboratory and a playground for trying out, developing, and mastering many unique artistic ideas and strategies that they would later employ elsewhere around the world.

This exhibition would not have been possible without the generous support and commitment of many people who brought this exhibition to fruition. I especially wish to thank Lauren Lockhart, Heath Fox, and all participating museum directors and staff for embracing the project from its inception. I am also grateful to Heather MacDonald and her colleagues from the Getty Foundation's Program Department and from PST Art for their encouragement and support of this ambitious project.

I owe special thanks to Newton for his active role in this exhibition from the beginning, for his heartfelt friendship and guidance, and for welcoming me into his home, showing me artwork and archival material, and answering my many questions. Many thanks go to the Harrison Family, to Josh (Joshua) and Gabe (Gabriel), for their tireless support of the project, and the Harrison Studio, including Dr. Ruby Barnett, Rachel Smith, and Justin Lane Lutter who helped in different stages while working on this exhibition.

My deepest thanks go to Dr. Petra Kruse and Kai Reschke who successfully brought this exhibition catalogue to fruition despite some delays in the original schedule. Without their profound knowledge of the Harrisons' work and their senior expertise in the publishing industry, this catalogue would not have been possible.

I extend my gratitude to the staff at the Stanford University Special Collections for granting me the necessary access to the Helen and Newton Harrison Papers at a time when COVID restrictions were still in place, and for assisting me with all materials related to the exhibition artworks.

Research for the exhibition catalogue has also benefited from the the winter workshop "Listening to the Web of Life," held on March 17–18, 2022, which I organized in collaboration with Newton, Heath Fox from the La Jolla Historical Society, and Dr. Alexander Gershunov from the Scripps Institution of Oceanography. My sincere thanks go to Heath Fox, Sasha (Alexander), and the workshop participants who came to La Jolla from far away, shared their knowledge, and then contributed their essays to the special edition of *FIELD, A Journal of Socially-Engaged Art Criticism*. I am deeply grateful to Dr. Grant Kester who was instrumental in dedicating the winter issue of the journal to publishing the workshop proceedings in 2023. I also thank Grant for sharing his deep knowledge of contemporary art during my time as a PhD student at the Department of Visual Arts at UC San Diego.

My sincere thanks also go to Dr. Monica Manolescu and Dr. Edward Shanken who accepted my invitation to contribute to this catalogue. The results of their rigorous scholarship are the thoughtful and inspiring essays included here, which are essential to our understanding of Helen and Newton Harrison's work.

I would also like to acknowledge Dr. Jack Greenstein (Emeritus), my dissertation advisor and dear friend, who personally introduced me to Newton Harrison and other UC San Diego founding faculty in the Visual Arts Department. Jack and I had many illuminating conversations during my PhD studies and more specifically while working on the series of exhibitions celebrating the 50th anniversary of the Visual Arts Department and the Mandeville Art Gallery at UC San Diego in 2011–2012 and 2016–2018.

My heartfelt gratitude goes to my husband Dr. Gareth Davies-Morris whose love has supported me and whose expert knowledge of languages and humanities was beneficial for this project as well.

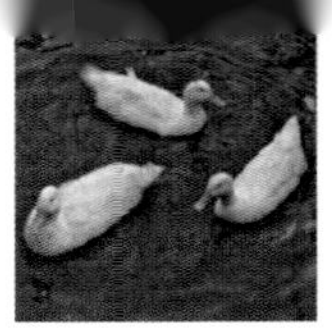

"I am the Lorax" or "What does the Life Web Want?"

The Harrisons, Systems, Speculative Design, and Healing the Earth

EDWARD SHANKEN

I am the Lorax. I speak for the trees.
I speak for the trees, for the trees have no tongues.
And I'm asking you sir, at the top of my lungs ...
Dr. Seuss, *The Lorax*

Ask not what the Life Web can do for you,
Ask what you can do for the Life Web.
Newton Harrison

To spread Helen and Newton Harrisons' ideas more widely, I once proposed to Newton that we collaborate on a news column entitled, "Ask the Lorax," which would combine the character of the syndicated advice column "Ask Abby" with that of the Lorax. Newton Harrison was the Lorax. Or maybe the Lorax was Newton Harrison. Both spoke for the trees. The Lorax spoke for the Swomey-Swans, the Brown Bar-ba-loots, and the Humming Fish. Helen and Newton spoke for the Web of Life in which all beings, sentient and non-sentient, are interconnected and interdependent. The Harrisons and the Lorax were both East Coast transplants to La Jolla.[1] They were highly opinionated, disarmingly direct, deeply aware of the systemic and inextricable interrelatedness of the elements of a biome. They were fiercely committed to preserving biodiversity and to saving the environment. Things really mattered to them. They cared deeply and were driven by an unabating responsibility to make a difference. Apathy was not an option and they worked tirelessly to make the world a better place.

Dr. Seuss children's story has enchanted generations. This fanciful cautionary tale warns of the dire environmental consequences of unchecked extraction and pollution. The Onceler's entrepreneurial greed has decimated a beautiful forest, fouled the air, and poisoned the waters. As a result, the beautiful, imaginary Truffula Tree has become extinct. The Swomey-Swans, the Brown Bar-ba-loots, and the Humming Fish can no longer survive there and are forced to migrate. The extractive business has collapsed in the wasteland of its making. However, there is hope: a lone Truffula Seed remains and we are presented with the opportunity and responsibility to recover the lost species.

Guided by the Jewish tradition of Tikkun Olam (םָלוע ןוּקִית), "repairing the world," Newton's solo work with process, technology, and living systems led to the Harrisons' collaborative work addressing the question, "What can be done?" By 1970, they decided to only make work that served the biosphere. Ecological thinking was in the air. The awareness shared by the Harrisons and the Lorax converged with the passage of the National Environmental Policy Act, the first Earth Day, and the founding of Greenpeace in 1971. The impact of greenhouse gases in the atmosphere was a hot topic (no pun intended) and warnings about the disastrous effects of global warming and the limits of growth became increasingly common. The Harrisons' Survival Series, including key works sited and/or presented in California, emerged at this time. Artworks related to the seven *Survival Pieces* are exhibited as part of *Urban Ecologies* at the La Jolla Historical Society, in the retrospective four-venue exhibition series, *Helen and Newton Harrison: California Work*.

Of particular local interest is *Survival Piece #3: La Jolla Promenade*, first shown as a solo work by Newton in a four-person exhibition at the La Jolla Museum of Art in 1971. This work must be interpreted in the larger frame of the central ambition of the *Survival Pieces* as a whole: to explore the practicality of artistic approaches to food cultivation as an alternative to the highly destructive practices of corporate farming. Newton was disappointed that critics and audiences had failed to recognize the pragmatic value of his two prior *Survival Pieces*, *Shrimp Farm* and *Portable Fish Farm*, as artistic models for sustainable food production. He emphasized that *La Jolla Promenade* offered a practical solution to a local problem: the infestation of gardens by snails, which eat homegrown crops and decorative plants. In addition, the work created awareness of an ancillary problem: the use of harmful pesticides by La Jollans to eliminate the snails. Newton's proposal attempted to solve both problems with a simple and ancient technique. Instead of polluting the Earth with pesticides, *La Jolla Promenade* deployed ducks to feed on the snails, thereby controlling them without harming the environment. Gardeners would benefit from the homegrown vegetables no longer consumed by the snails, as well as from the ducks and duck eggs, sources of high-quality protein.

For all of its brilliance and good intentions, *La Jolla Promenade* was flawed. "The great irony of this experiment" notes son Josh Harrison, was that "ducks will eat snails, but it's not a great delicacy for them. They much preferred the flowers and leaves of the plants the snails also enjoyed."[2] Some solutions developed by engineers and industrial designers are also flawed, and with much higher stakes. *La Jolla Promenade* may not have provided an effective solution to a real-world problem, but it succeeded as a visionary work of art nonetheless. It effectively promoted a 180-degree shift of perspective. What was once perceived as a pest came to be appreciated as a valuable resource to support nontoxic agricultural production.[3] On the other hand, some of the Harrisons' proposals have yielded practical solutions that were implemented on a large scale. For example, the core ideas in *A Vision for the Green Heart of Holland* (1984) became incorporated into the Dutch government's regional development plans and successfully helped preserve what the European Regional Development Group declared in 2005 to be "one of the … most valuable open spaces" in northwest Europe.[4] In the context of art, the *Survival Pieces* share "the strategic convictions of avant-garde artists throughout history: the perception, conception, envisioning, and representation of alternative realities and systems of meaning."[5] By thinking outside the box and, moreover, by thinking out loud in public artworks that go beyond representation to actualization, *La Jolla Promenade* and the other *Survival Pieces* stimulated audiences to also think outside the box, to dream up alternative scenarios, and to take action themselves to realize their dreams.

The Harrisons' collaborative work is characterized by hope balanced with healthy skepticism. Driven by an ambition to offer practical solutions, they use unabashedly poetic means to articulate unexpected insights and to propose visionary

14 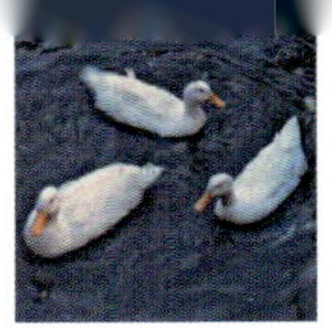 "I am the Lorax"

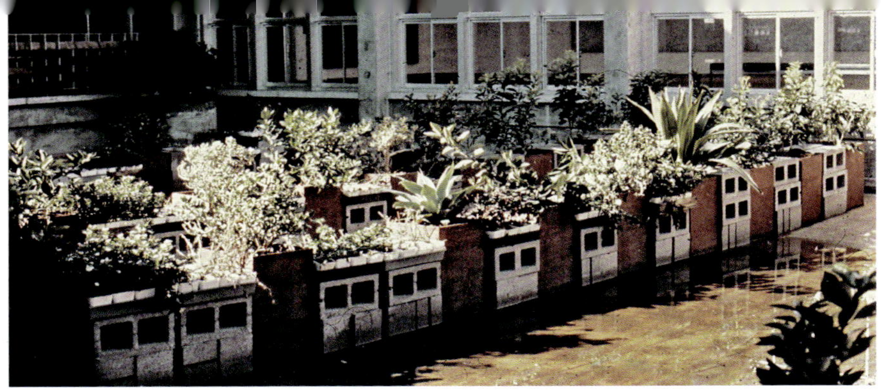

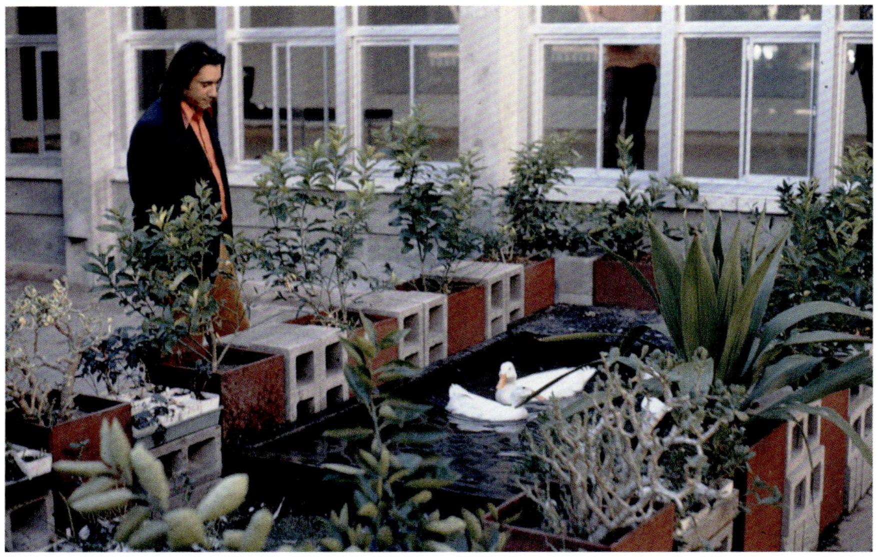

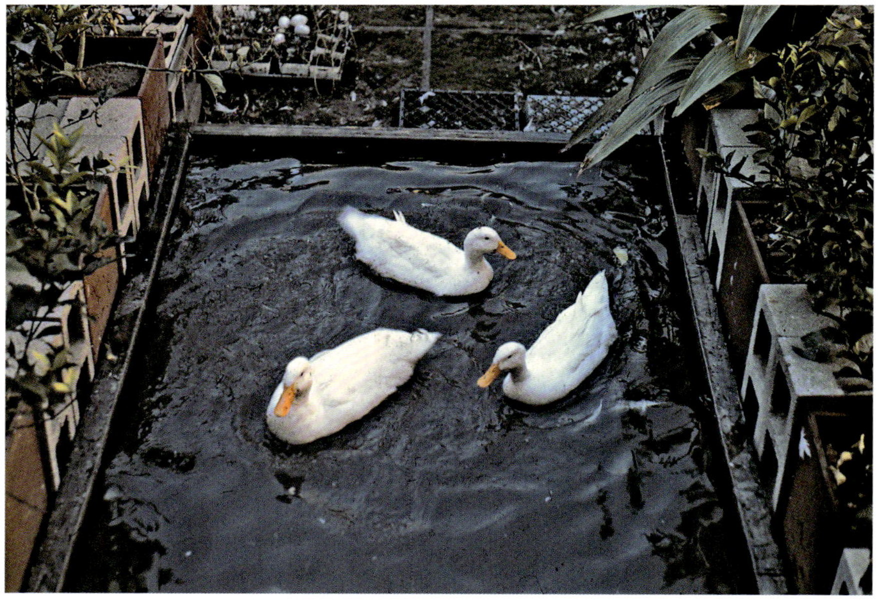

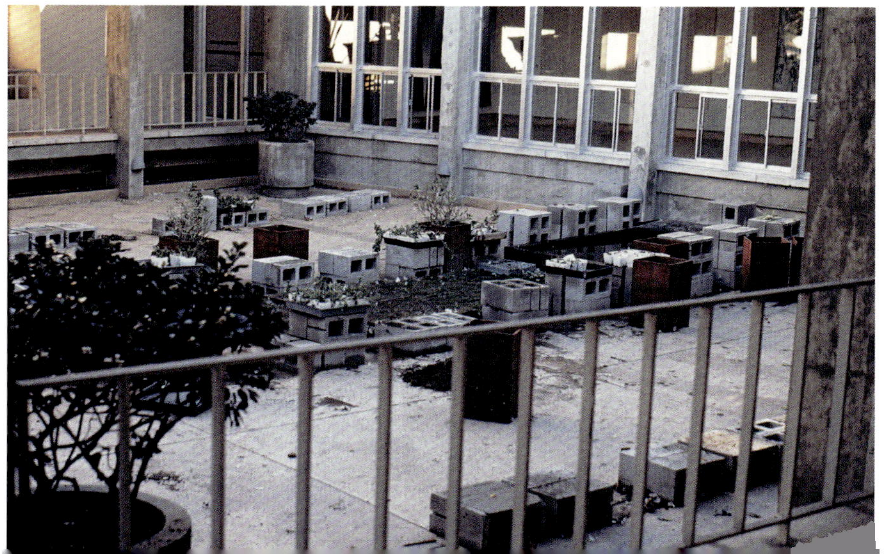

Survival Piece IV: La Jolla Promenade

1971 Museum of Contemporary Art

San Diego, La Jolla, CA

The original garden

A new garden is installed and inspected by Newton Harrison

The ducks before the pond is polluted

The cinder blocks remain

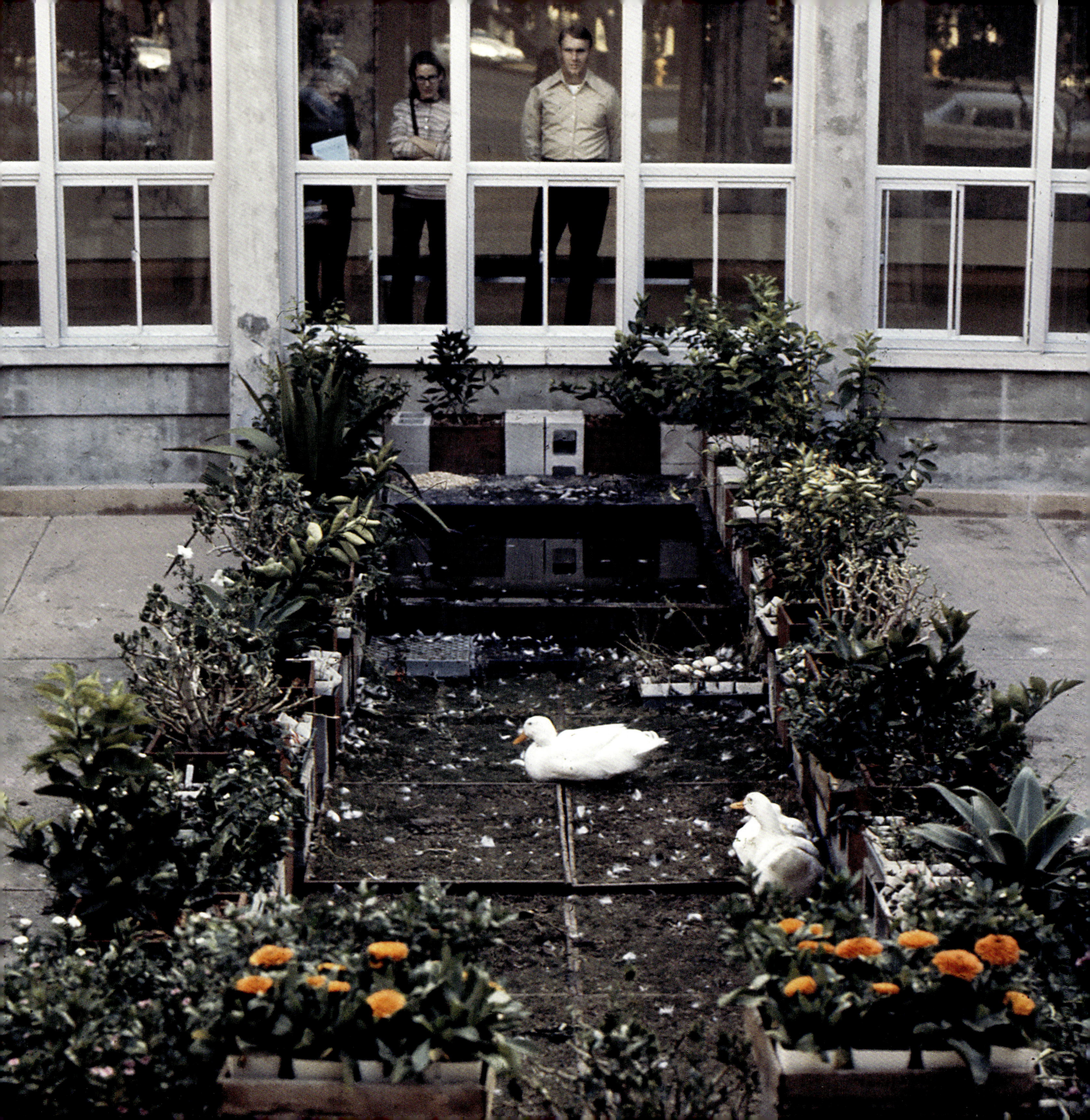

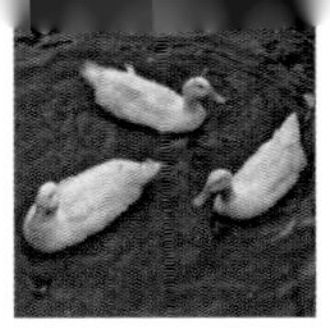

approaches to solve gnarly ecological problems. Their poetic narratives often appear as a dialogue between two voices, as in the exchanges between the Lagoon Maker and the Witness in their landmark *Lagoon Cycle*. One element of the cycle, *The Fifth Lagoon: From the Salton Sea to the Pacific; From the Salton Sea to the Gulf*, proposes a solution (questioned by the Witness in italics) to the inevitably catastrophic effects of the increasing levels of salinity, herbicides, and pesticides in California's largest lake, which reached critical levels in the 1970s.

If
the salinity of the Salton Sea is decreased via an
ongoing exchange of waters with the Pacific or the gulf
....
then
the Salton Sea can be turned to productivity as a
360-square-mile low-intensity aquaculture system
with yields up to 1,000 pounds an acre.
....
Indeed you can transform the Salton Sea but where did
such a curious notion come from
As I tipped the map in another direction looking at
the Salton Sea in relationship to Baja and the
mainland and the gulf an image emerged of the
Salton Sea as a diseased bladder for a moment I
imagined myself as a surgeon inserting a catheter
and generating an artificial urethra
But if your metaphor is extended the ocean becomes a
septic tank
True but all waters finally flow to the ocean
which in one way or another processes all the wastes
that come to it I thought that's what ocean-
watershed relationships were all about
Not at this scale
Not at a single point
Not all at once
and over and over[6]

This excerpt includes several striking elements: 1) the scale of the proposal, which involves creating two-way water exchange systems spanning from the Salton Sea to either the Pacific or the Gulf of California, approximately 160 miles in either case; 2) the ambitious idea to transform a highly polluted, highly salinized body of water that can no longer support marine life or even serve recreational purposes, into a massive and highly productive aquaculture farm; 3) the serendipitous way in which a metaphorical visual experience of an unhealthy bladder perceived by looking askew at a map, catalyzed the conception of a solution modelled on a medical procedure; and 4) the enthusiasm, positivity, and apparent naiveté of the Lagoon Maker and the more stoic skepticism of the wise Witness.

Like many artists and intellectuals of their generation, the Harrisons were deeply influenced by systems theory, which undergirded their approach to aesthetics and environmentalism. Systems theory offers a powerful method to consider phenomena as emerging from complex relationships between many elements. It provides a framework to understand how altering one element, or altering any of the relationships between elements, impacts the whole system. A popular and extreme example is the Butterfly Effect: that the fluttering of a butterfly's wings might ultimately cause a tornado. My many discussions with Newton were always engaged with systemic approaches to art and the environment, and in particular, to mitigating the effects of climate change. The fundamental question that he consistently raised was, "What does the Life Web want?" The Harrisons are widely recognized as pioneers of ecological art and they are equally pioneers of art-science and art and technology, exemplified by *Artificial Aurora*, included in this exhibition.[7] As such, their work weaves together diverse strands of theory and practice, always mindful of the system connections between art, science, technology, and ecology, and always in service to the Life Web.

Critic Jack Burnham's essay "Systems Esthetics" (1968) championed the application of systems theory to art. A two-way dialogue emerged between the Harrisons and Burnham. The latter's essay, "Contemporary Ritual: A Search for Meaning in Post-Historical Terms" (1973) discusses the Harrisons' work with ecosystems, including rituals of food cultivation, preparation, and sharing. "Contemporary Ritual … " also discusses Newton's *Western Salt Works with the Inclusion of Brine Shrimp* (1971), included in the Art and Technology exhibition at Los Angeles County Museum of Art. This work, and Newton's other salt-related works produced in California, undoubtedly inspired the title of Burnham's collection, *Great Western Salt Works: Essays on the Meaning of Post-Formalist Art*. The conversation between the Harrisons' artwork and Burnham's theoretical writings fertilized (organically) the emerging aesthetic awareness of the systemic interrelatedness of phenomena, particularly with respect to art, technology, and the environment, in the 1960s.

Physicist Fritjof Capra's *The Web of Life* (1997) was one of the most important influences on the Harrisons' thinking about art and ecology, especially Newton's in his later years. The book offers a systems theoretical explanation of the physics of environmental sustainability. Capra names the Web of Life as an entity to be honored and protected. He explains how, according to the Second Law of Thermodynamics, which establishes the concept of entropy, closed systems tend towards diminishing levels of energy and order. In other words, the deterioration of a system can be explained in terms of increasing entropy. In the environment, high levels of biodiversity are characterized by high levels of complexity. An ecosystem is comprised of a complex and specific array of entities, substrates, inputs, and outputs. Despite variations in these elements, the system coheres and self-complicates in ways that tend to sustain biodiversity. Because the Earth is an open system and benefits from, among other inputs, a steady source of additional energy from the Sun, certain local systems can resist entropy, and levels of complexity and order, such as biodiversity, can increase in them.

Newton delighted in the realization that if nature is left to itself, the Life Web will produce a surplus. In other words, nature makes more than it needs to sustain itself. As long as we humans do not take more than that surplus, biodiversity will be maintained. As indigenous cultures learned thousands of years ago, if we sensitively and wisely steward the land, we can actually help the Earth to flourish even more fruitfully than without our assistance, and we can draw more from it while minimizing despeciation and sustaining biodiversity. Indeed, following biologist Lynn Margulis's theory of serial endosymbiosis – that organisms mutually support and coevolve with each other[8] – Josh Harrison observes that this "'surplus' is baked in to provide nourishment. We humans need to plug back into being part of the system and rely on those surpluses to nourish ourselves."[9] Perhaps Thich Nhat Hanh said it best, "We are the Earth. The Earth is us."[10] *This is what the Life Web wants.* Monocultural farming, on the other hand, diminishes biodiversity and complexity. When it involves the use of synthetic fertilizers and pesticides, irrigation from distant rivers and dams, the destruction of forests and meadows, and other harmful interventions, monocultural farming significantly increases entropy. In this model, humans take, and take, and take from the environment, extracting resources, depleting and poisoning topsoil, fouling rivers, and polluting the air, without giving anything back. *This is not what the Life Web wants.*

Newton and Capra both reached the conclusion that capitalism is at odds with the Life Web (as Seuss suggested in *The Lorax*) and they proposed that the Earth needs an alternative economic system that is not predicated on maximizing corporate profit but rather is based on maximizing the health of the Web of Life. In contrast to Gross Domestic Product (GDP), a metric used to compare a country's economic success with that of other nations, in the 1970s, Bhutan developed the metric known as Gross National Happiness (GNH). Newton's yardstick was the health of the Life Web, which leads me to propose Life Web Happiness (LWH) as an evaluative metric. In contrast to GNH, LWH is neither anthropocentric nor nationalistic, and takes into consideration the happiness of all beings, sentient and non-sentient, the happiness of the planet (Gaia) as a whole.

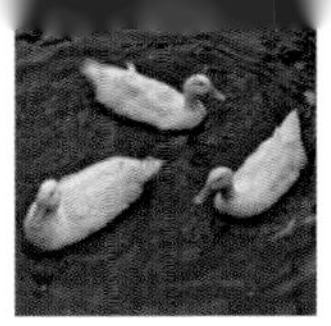

The Life Web was the centerpiece of the Harrisons' eco-aesthetic theory and practice. Like many artists and intellectuals whose positions are informed by scientific evidence, they believed that unless the rise in global temperature stays below a manageable level or, better yet, can gradually be drawn down, the Earth may be facing a mass extinction event, resulting in the loss of 75 percent or more living species in a relatively short period of geological time. The term "Anthropocene" has been ascribed to this potential Sixth Mass Extinction. In the Anthropocene, "humans have become the major force [or Force Majeure in the Harrisons' lexicon] determining the continuing livability of the Earth. The word tells a big story: living arrangements that took millions of years to put into place are being undone in the blink of an eye."[11] Indeed, scientists believe that the current rate of extinction is hundreds if not thousands of times greater than the natural baseline rate, determined by analysis of the fossil record, lending credence to the Sixth Mass Extinction argument.[12] Again, the question is, "What can be done?" Or, in other words, "How can we repair the Earth?"

The field of speculative design offers some useful insights and offers a fruitful frame for considering the meaning and significance of the Harrisons' work with respect to repairing the Earth. Speculative design may be especially well-suited to addressing the Anthropocene because it fosters "critical thinking about how we relate to technology and science, how we organize ourselves politically and socially, and how we define ourselves in a broader ecological assemblage."[13] Anthony Dunne and Fiona Raby, the primary theorists of speculative design, define the practice as "an activity where conjecture is as good as knowledge, where futuristic and alternative scenarios convey ideas ... "[14] Speculative design is anti-pragmatic and anticapitalistic. It intends to identify problems, not to provide solutions. It shuns designing objects for near-term commercial production and aspires to formulate future-oriented design questions that stimulate critical debate. The pragmatic intentions behind the Harrisons' work might arguably disqualify it from the field of speculative design. Artist Kayla Anderson, for example, argues that "Anthropocene narratives coming from the art world seem to be most potentially destructive when they propose to do something, further reinforcing an attitude of human dominance over the planet."[15]

Anderson's point is well taken. However, this perspective imposes a binary opposition between artists and designers who envision problematic future scenarios and propose pragmatic (and often provocative) solutions to stimulate change and artists and designers with anti-pragmatic intentions who envision problematic future scenarios and design provocations to spur critical debate and stimulate change but without offering pragmatic solutions. I do not see these two courses of action as mutually exclusive. Instead, I claim that they can complement each other in a mutually supportive way. Indeed, the Harrisons' work functions on multiple registers. It proposes visionary solutions that contest traditional design responses to the global impact of the Anthropocene. It challenges the viability of capitalism in the battle against climate change. It stirs debate by suggesting provocative approaches to repairing the Earth that appear to be counterintuitive, if not outlandish, and often on a continental and oceanic scale. It engages people as thoughtful partners with their environments to create food and economic systems in which "the harvest preserves the system."[16] The Harrisons' future-oriented works to mitigate the effects of global warming are speculative by nature. In contrast to commercial design, rarely are their projects paid for by corporate clients. Rather, they are developed "on spec," as artistic designs that propose alternative ways of thinking about critical problems, that envision alternative scenarios of what might be, and that suggest innovative approaches to getting from a precarious present to a healthier, more stable future.

The Harrison Studio has created multiple speculative design works works in California. Some of these projects have been cultivated under the aegis of The Center for the Study of the Force Majeure, a research center founded by the Harrisons together with current director, Josh Harrison, at University of California, Santa Cruz. For example, *Living Forests* is a transdisciplinary art-science collaboration across multiple institutions and indigenous tribal groups in several counties. It addresses the California wildfire crisis by joining contemporary fire analysis and management tools with Traditional Ecological Knowledge (TEK). There are two *Future Gardens* in the state, one at the UCSC Arboretum and Botanical Garden and one at the UC Berkeley Sagehen Creek Field Station, with several more under development. These artistic research experiments in species migration are designed to generate scientific data and insight that will help facilitate plant survival (and provide sustenance for animals, including humans) as climate change impacts a plant species' viability in their current locales.

Perhaps the most audacious of the Harrisons' California proposals, the one that is most aligned with speculative design, and that remains the most speculative, is *The Bays of San Francisco*, initiated in 2013. This work addresses an anticipated future scenario in which sea level rise, combined with storm surges, cause the San Francisco Bay to flood, forcing sea-water eastward towards the Sacramento-San Joaquin Delta.[17] Flooding on this scale will overwhelm the 1100-mile system of levees that protect this 738,000-acre expanse of reclaimed marshland, creating a massive estuarial lagoon from Sacramento at the north to Stockton at the south. If that happens, one of the most fertile agricultural regions in the world, responsible for one-quarter of the food in the US, will be devastated; two major cities, including the state capital, will be under water; hundreds of thousands of people will be displaced, and countless species will perish or be forced to migrate. The impact on the California economy will be staggering and US food security will be imperiled. As horrific as this scenario sounds, it can also be seen as the Earth reclaiming those marshlands, recalibrating the relationship of land and water in a way that is arguably closer to what the Life Web wants. Ironically, this revision is precipitated by the Anthropocene, by the very force that disrupted the Life Web in the first place. For the Harrisons, this scenario raises the question, "Can we adapt to this scale of change in a way that benefits a changing culture while collaborating with an evolving ecosystem?"[18]

For many centuries, building levees has been the traditional design approach to controlling encroaching waters. This approach exemplifies the "potentially destructive … attitude of human dominance over the planet," of which Anderson warns. The Harrisons offer an alternative: allow the waters to flood, creating a 400,000-acre brackish waterbody that can be utilized for low-intensity aquaculture, generating up to 2000 pounds of protein-rich food per acre. Even if flooding is taken out of the equation, as temperatures are predicted to rise disproportionately in the Central Valley, and as sources of fresh water become more precious, the future of traditional farming in the region is precarious at best. A massive estuarial lagoon for aquaculture may be a blessing in disguise. As the title of a related Harrison work intones, *Only Fools Pick a Fight with the Ocean: Wise Folk Dance with the Rising Waters*.

We humans are averse to change. Conventional "affirmative" design typically applies technological solutions to maintain the status quo. That is precisely the knee-jerk response that speculative design attempts to challenge. Predictably, the prominent mainstream solutions proffered for the anticipated flooding of the bays of San Francisco call for the construction of levees. There are significant local precedents, including the eight-mile, thirteen-foot-high levee and system of embankments that were constructed in hand with the development of Foster City in the 1960s to protect that vulnerable bay-side real-estate. As is commonly the case, sea-level rise demands increasing the levee's height. To this end, the city issued a $90 million bond to raise it eight additional feet, which will provide protection only until 2050. SFO and OAK airports are also building levees to stave off the rising waters of the bay, with a final tab of over $1 billion for SFO alone. The cost of constructing, maintaining, and periodically increasing the height of these ramparts is astronomical. That does not mean that it is impossible, and it may even be the best of several evils to choose from. But these localized protections do not address the Harrisons' concern about the flooding of Stockton and Sacramento. *The Bays of San Francisco* identifies a problem and demands that we think beyond immediate local concerns and consider the broader effects of sea-level rise in the region.[19]

The Harrisons pose this as a question:

"Can an estuarial lagoon, brought into existence by the Force Majeure [the Anthropocene] and coupled with nature's will to self-complicate and human creativity, generate energy available to do work in this region as great as or greater than those that were dispersed by its transformation into an irrigated farming system?"[20]

Their logic stems from the Second Law of Thermodynamics and from the concept of exergy – the amount of work that can be produced from a system under a given environment. If the loss of entropy (increase in complexity) and the increase in exergy in the envisioned estuarial lagoon is greater than that of irrigated farming, and if the costs are less than or equal to protecting the status quo, then a strong argument can be made to support the Harrisons' proposal. Indeed, they claim that if exergy can be increased, even if that happens incrementally, place-by-place, then "planetary resilience has the possibility of being restored."[21] The theoretical conclusion of the *Bays of San Francisco*, and what remains an enduring provocation beyond the specifics of this particular project and this particular region, is the idea that, "bioregional entropy and energy balance can be regulated by research and human collaboration with the Life Web, always assuming that nature itself has been given agency."[22]

The Bays of San Francisco, like many of the Harrisons' visionary works of art-science, proposes an alternative future that looks very different from the present, especially in terms of topography and land use. It would demand that local populations make dramatic changes and sacrifices (for which they should be fairly compensated) for the good of the state and region, and for the good of the Life Web. It suggests that we dance with the rising waters rather than fight them. And it offers a conceptual framework for thinking about and for thinking through gnarly ecological problems and pending catastrophes stemming from climate change in the Anthropocene. The Harrisons' work predates speculative design by many years and performs its work while not being limited to it. It identifies problems and instigates debate by designing provocative yet pragmatic solutions. In addition to their pioneering work in ecological art and art-science research, the Harrisons should also be recognized as pioneers of speculative design – a form of speculative design that is not engaged with the discourses of design per se, but that is engaged with serving the Life Web.

The "Gaia Hypothesis," co-developed by Margulis and James Lovelock in the 1970s, conceives of the Earth (Gaia) as a living organism – a complex, synergistic, self-regulating system that has co-evolved in ways that maintain the conditions for planetary life.[23] In the mid-1990s, Margulis infamously wrote, "Gaia is a tough bitch – a system that has worked for over three billion years without people. This planet's surface and its atmosphere and environment will continue to evolve long after people and prejudice are gone."[24] Like Margulis, the Harrisons recognized that in terms of geological time, *homo sapiens* are just a blip in the fossil record. For them, however, the inevitability of our own extinction was not a cause for despair or nihilism. Rather, the damage that we are causing Earth/Gaia was a call to action. Driven by compassion for all beings and an unshakable sense of responsibility, the Harrisons worked tirelessly to minimize the impacts of the Anthropocene, to mitigate the effects of climate change, to diminish suffering and despeciation, and to engage us all in the process of healing the Earth.

SO ... Catch! Calls the Once-ler. He lets something fall. It's a Truffula Seed. It's the last one of all! You're in charge of the last of the Truffula Seeds. And Truffula Trees are what everyone needs. Plant a new Truffula. Treat it with care. Give it clean water. And feed it fresh air. Grow a forest. Protect it from axes that hack. Then the Lorax and all of his friends may come back.

Dr. Seuss, *The Lorax*

1 Josh Harrison, Helen and Newton's son and collaborator, recounts that during the time when *The Lorax* was being promoted, Theodor Geisel, aka Dr. Seuss, invited Harrison's whole 6th grade class to his house for readings. Email correspondence with the author, January 1, 2024.

2 Harrison, Josh, email correspondence with the author, January 1, 2024.

3 Rogers, Laura Cassidy, "The Social and Environmental Turn in Late 20th Century Art: A Case Study of Helen and Newton Harrison After Modernism." PhD diss., Stanford University, CA, 2017, pp. 236–238.

4 Harrison, Newton, and Helen Mayer Harrison, "A Vision for the Green Heart of Holland," *The Time of the Force Majeure: After 45 Years Counterforce is on the Horizon*, edited by Petra Kruse and Kai Reschke. Prestel, Munich, London, New York, 2016.

5 Shanken, Edward A., "From Cybernetics to Telematics: The Art, Pedagogy, and Theory of Roy Ascott," *Telematic Embrace: Visionary Theories of Art, Technology, and Consciousness*, 2003, p. 88.

6 Harrison, Helen Mayer, and Newton Harrison, *The Lagoon Cycle*, Herbert F. Johnson Museum of Art, Cornell University, 1985, p 87.

7 *Artificial Aurora,* also known as *Plasma Chamber*, was created in collaboration with the Jet Propulsion Laboratory as part of the Art and Technology program organized by the Los Angeles County Museum of art and presented at the US Pavilion at the World Expo in Osaka and at LACMA in 1971.

8 Margulis, Lynn, *Symbiotic Planet: A New Look at Evolution*. Basic books, New York, 2008. Margulis first published the theory foundations of endosymbiosis in 1967, which were experimentally demonstrated in 1978.

9 Harrison, Josh, email correspondence with the author, January 1, 2024.

10 Hanh, Thich Nhat, *Love Letter to the Earth*, Parallax Press, Berkeley, CA, 2013, p. 46.

11 Gan, Elaine, et al, "Haunted Landscapes," *Arts of Living on a Damaged Planet: Ghosts and Monsters of the Anthropocene*, edited by Anna Lowenhaupt Tsing, et al. University of Minnesota Press, 2017, G1.

12 Extinction Over Time | Smithsonian National Museum of Natural History (si.edu).

13 Anderson, Kayla, "Ecology, and the Future: Art and Design Face the Anthropocene," *Leonardo*, Vol. 48, No. 4 (Special Issue: SIGGRAPH 2015 Art Papers and Hybrid Craft Art Gallery), 2015, p. 338.

14 "Speculative Design," Wikipedia, accessed December 22, 2023.

15 Anderson, *op. cit.* p. 339.

16 Sizonenko, Tatiana, "Helen Mayer Harrison and Newton Harrison: Meditations on Climate Change," *FIELD*, Issue 23, Winter 2023.

17 This 738,000-acre expanse of reclaimed marshland, some of which is twenty-five feet below sea-level, is protected by an 1100-mile system of levees, some of which are fragile and vulnerable to earthquakes and flooding.

18 Harrison, Helen Mayer, and Newton Harrison, *The Time of the Force Majeure: After 45 Years Counterforce is on the Horizon*, np.

19 The predictions about the flooding of Stockton and Sacramento were based on existing scientific data and substantiated by a report from Climate Central, a not-for-profit organization of climate scientists and communicators who "research and report the facts about our changing climate and how it affects people's lives." Climate Central website, https://www.climatecentral.org/what-we-do, accessed December 22, 2023.

20 Harrison, Helen Mayer, and Newton Harrison, *The Time of the Force Majeure: After 45 Years Counterforce is on the Horizon*, np.

21 Ibid., np. Costs must, of course, take into account not just economic costs, but the costs of human and non-human suffering.

22 Ibid., np.

23 Lovelock, James E., and Margulis, Lynn, "Atmospheric Homeostasis by and for the Biosphere: the Gaia Hypothesis," *Tellus,* No. 26, Issue 1–2, 1974, pp. 2–10.

24 Margulis, Lynn, "Gaia is a Tough Bitch," *The Third Culture: Beyond the Scientific Revolution*, edited by John Brockman. Simon & Schuster, New York, 1995, p. 146.

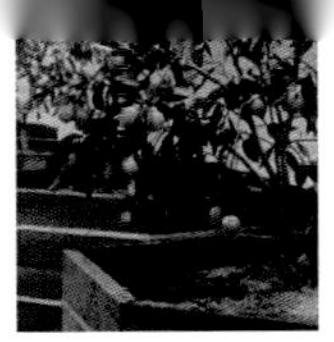

Urban Ecologies TATIANA SIZONENKO

For us, everything started with a decision made in the late 1960s to deal exclusively with issues of survival as best we could perceive them. Each body of work sought a larger or more comprehensive framing or understanding of what such a notion might mean and how we, as artists, might express it.
Helen and Newton Harrison.[1]

Helen Mayer Harrison and Newton Harrison, simply known as the Harrisons, were California-based multidisciplinary artists who became widely recognized for their ecological work. Underpinned by the astute commitment to "listening to the Web of Life," in Newton's words,[2] the Harrisons' pioneering art-and-science collaboration not only ignited the field of ecological and environmental art, but also helped to establish ecological art as a distinctive sub-category that focuses on the biological interdependencies in ecosystems. According to the artist and writer Janeil Engelstad, the Harrisons synergistically employed "empathy and research, ideation and collaboration, and the tools and mindset of the explorer – mapmaking, innovation, curiosity, and the courage to follow their instincts into areas unknown" in their nearly fifty-year collaborative practice.[3] Working in the domains of art and science, the artists engaged a wide range of media, including drawing, painting, sculpture, photography, mapping, poetry, architectural design, technological experiments, land reclamation, watershed and ecosystem restoration, and re-terraforming practices.

The issues of survival and betterment of ecosystems became a central concern for the Harrisons when they began articulating a framework for ecological art in the late 1960s. The ten years between 1970 and 1980 were highly formative for them. In that crucial decade, they redefined their careers and artistic practice completely, developed their first eco-works, and turned their studio into a research laboratory, "a place of experimentation informed by the knowledge and expertise of other disciplines."[4] Their first eco-pieces *Making Earth* (1969–70), *Then Making Strawberry Jam* (1969–72), and the *Survival Pieces* (1970–73) were investigative and exploratory in nature, deeply rooted in their prior artistic and research practices, and revealed the principles and strategies that informed and shaped their joint artistic endeavors for subsequent decades.

THE BEGINNING

Helen Mayer (1927–2018) and Newton Harrison (1932–2022) were from greater New York City and came of age in the years following World War II. Laura Cassidy Rogers' history of this period reveals that they married in 1953 "with ambitions to develop and use their respective abilities in a way that would benefit society."[5] San Diego became their home in 1967, when the founding chair of the Visual Arts Department at UC San Diego, the abstract expressionist painter Paul Brach, recruited Newton to join the faculty as Assistant Professor of Painting. By 1980, the Harrisons secured a joint full professorship in the department, retiring from UCSD in 1993 and opening the Harrison Studio. In 2004, they moved to Santa Cruz to continue the Harrison Studio collaboration. Soon thereafter, they were reappointed as research professors at UC Santa Cruz in 2010, thus achieving a greater than fifty-year career in the UC academic system.[6] Their work in Santa Cruz led to the founding of the Center for the Study of the Force Majeure, an international educational and research center, established by the Arts Division of University of California, Santa Cruz in 2012. After Helen's death in 2018, Newton started several California art projects, including *Apologia Mediterraneo*, *Future Gardens*, and *Sensorium for the World Ocean*, among others.

It is important to recognize that prior to their collaborative work, Newton had a vibrant artistic career as a sculptor and abstract painter that he abandoned in favor of making art that "maintains the world," as Tim Collins describes it in his assessment of this period.[7] In 1965, at the age of thirty-two, Newton graduated from Yale with both a bachelor's and master's degree in fine art, having studied color theory with Sewell Sillman and abstract hard-edged painting with Al Held. Newton began his training in 1948 with an apprenticeship, arranged by his parents, with the celebrated WPA-era sculptor Michael Lantz; continued art studies in Antioch College, Ohio, and, later, was a BFA student in sculpture at the Pennsylvania Academy of the Fine Arts. His training as a sculptor showed great promise, with a Rodinesque approach to the human figure, but it was interrupted by the Korean War draft and the experience of living abroad in Florence from 1957 to 1960. In her dissertation, Laura Cassidy Rogers reaffirms that the stay in Italy was crucial in cultivating his creative freedom and solidifying his ambitions to become a professional artist.[8] Indeed, Newton's direct experience of Renaissance art and culture informed not only his independent work as an artist but also his later artistic moves and strategies in such pivotal works as the *Lagoon Cycle*, the *magnum opus* of the Harrisons' joint artistic practice.[9] In his final interviews with this author, reflecting on his

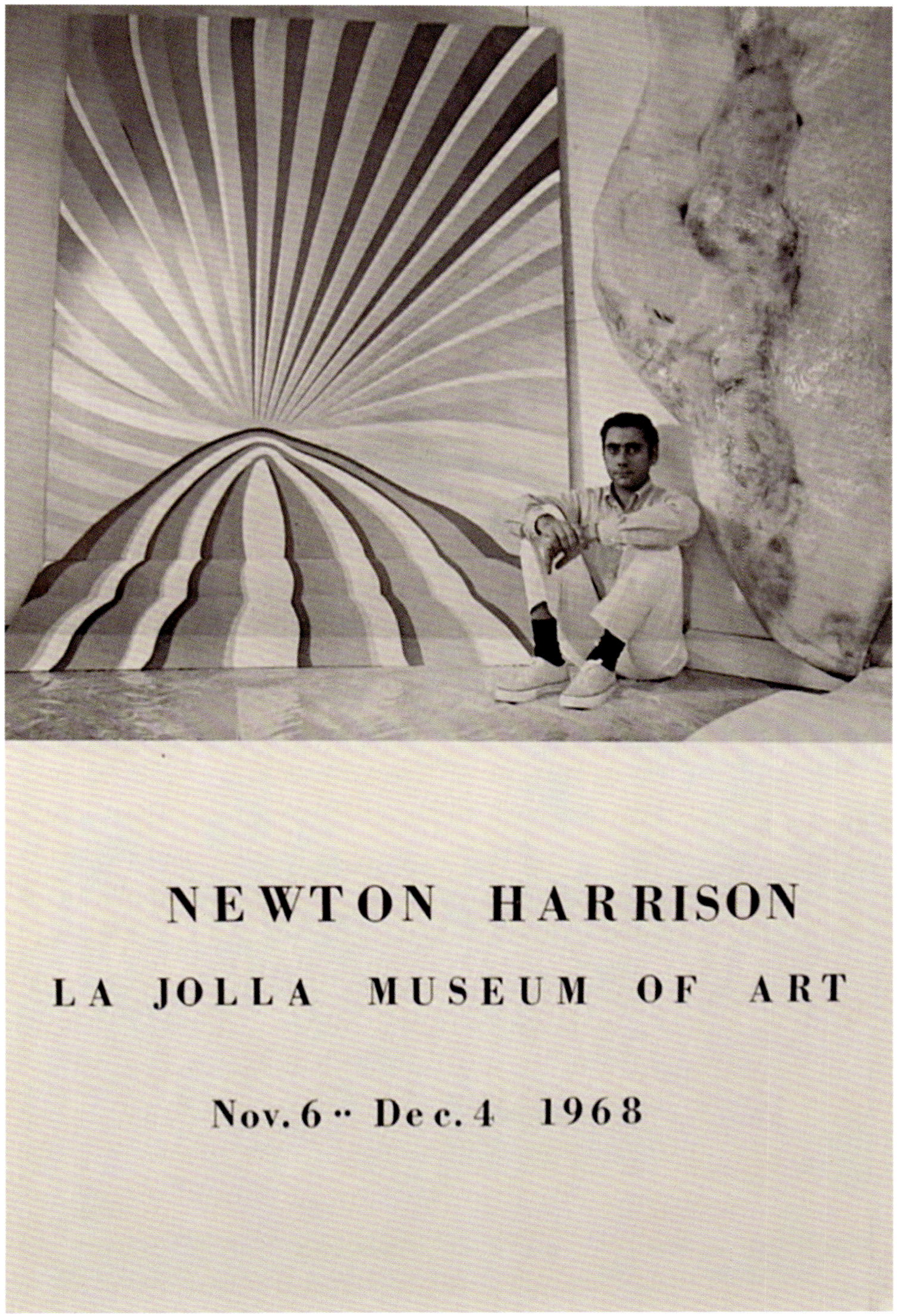

lifelong career in art and ecology, Newton underscored the formative influence of Giotto di Bondone, Donatello, Leonardo da Vinci, and Michelangelo Buonarotti on his own aesthetics and conceptions of art.[10] However, after his return from Florence, rather than completing a BFA in sculpture, Newton put aside the conventions of figure modelling. Finding himself in the dynamic experimental and conceptual art scene of New York City in the 1960s, he entered Yale's BFA program and focused on the exploration of intensity, vibration, and plasticity of hues in abstract painting. Newton painted original, boldly shaped canvases that appeared as pigmented sculptures set in relation to architecture, which helped him to secure his first faculty position teaching visual fundamentals at the University of New Mexico (UNM) in 1965.

Newton's artistic development and the Harrisons' artistic partnership were deeply influenced by Helen Mayer Harrison, a gifted writer and scholar with expert training in language, literature, and education. After high school, she earned a full scholarship to Cornell University in Ithaca, majoring in psychology. Although interrupted by her first marriage, lasting from 1945 to 1952, her college career continued after returning home to New York. Helen graduated with a Bachelor's in English from Queens College, followed by a Master's in the Philosophy of Education at New York University (NYU). Marrying again "a more suitable young sculptor" named Newton Harrison in 1953, Helen embarked on the career path of the educator, when she served as Director at the International Nursery School in Florence in 1958–1960 (while also tending to sons Steven and Joshua; soon the Harrisons family also welcomed Gabriel and Joy). After relocating to New Mexico with Newton, Helen was offered a teaching position at UNM. She became known for her teaching and research-based work in literature as well as activism concerning the issues of social justice and equal access to education at every level of society.[11] Moving to La Jolla with Newton and their four children in 1968, Helen joined UC San Diego Extension as the Director of Educational Programs and was tapped as the next Director of UC Extension in 1970.

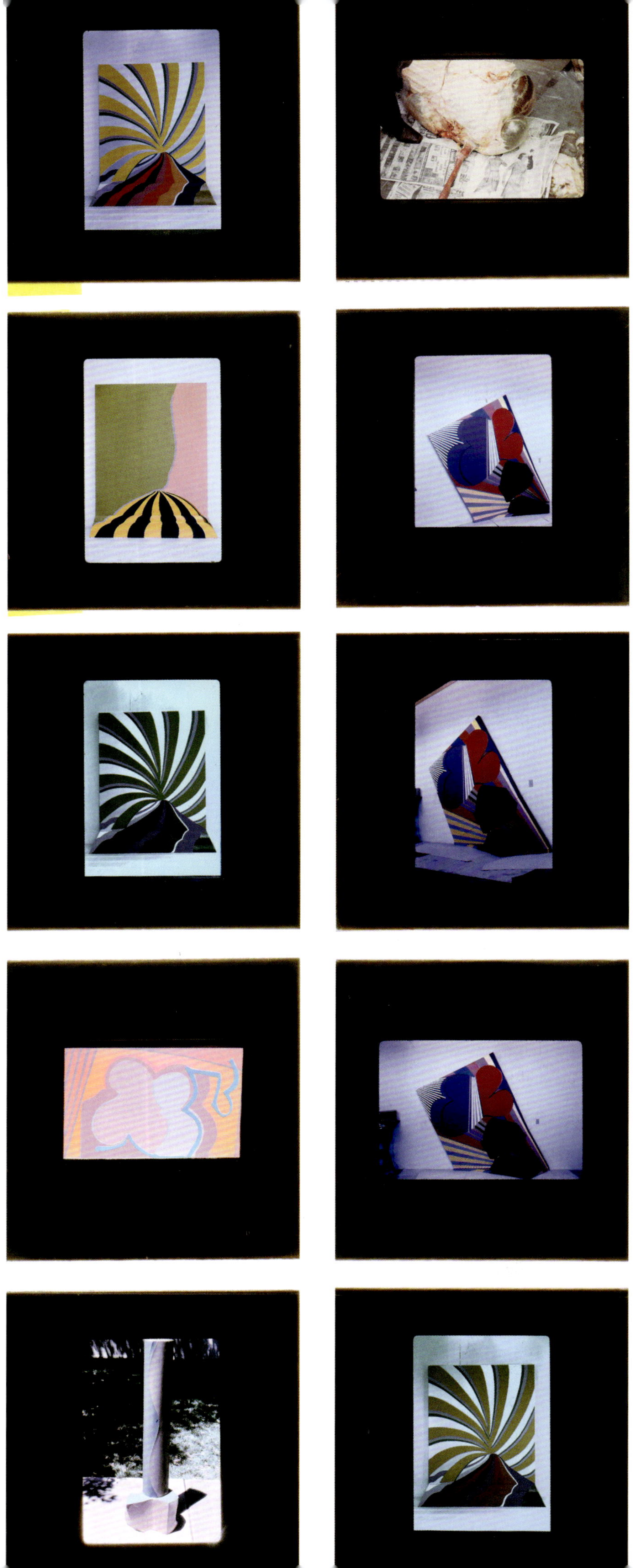

However, she chose to dedicate herself to the Harrison collaboration instead, leaving the field of education after her successful artistic debut, which was marked by a series of fruitful exhibitions in the field of conceptual art, feminism, and activism.[12] In 1972, she fully merged her expertise and passion for language, research, and psychology with art and activism to become a full-time artist.

FINDING A NEW FIELD OF PLAY

The independent artistic practices of Helen and Newton in the late 1960s at UC San Diego laid down the foundation for a collaboration that would last half a century. Helen explored issues related to human and social psychology, equality, and justice. Newton worked in the expanded field of painting and sculpture,[13] experimenting with color in the environment and with technological systems, while also collaborating with physicists, engineers, biologists, and politicians. From oral histories, literature, and interviews with the artists, Newton emerges as the "alchemist" and "builder," and Helen as the scholar and theorist, activist, and "nourisher."[14] The trajectory of their artmaking led them to the discovery of a new kind of artwork that was a complex, transmedia research-based practice, presented in galleries as organic, interactive, ecological systems art.

Instead of solitary artworks appreciated for their aesthetic properties, Newton became keenly interested in hybrid art-objects that challenged the traditional approaches to fine arts. This new direction was in part influenced by his participation in Johan Wilhelm "Billy" Klüver's *Experiments in Art and Technology* (E.A.T.) (1966–1970)[15] and in Maurice Tuchman's Art and Technology Program at the Los Angeles County Museum of Art (LACMA) (1966–1971).[16] In her dissertation, Laura Cassidy Rogers pinpoints concrete moments in Newton's artistic practice of that time when he shifted from experiments in color and shape in his abstract "shaped" paintings to living organisms and physical phenomena as a new artistic medium for his projects.[17] On the one hand, *Newton Harrison*, a solo exhibition of paintings (also known as *Path Series*) displayed at the La Jolla Museum of Art in 1968, remained in dialogue with the abstract expressionism developed by Clyfford Still, Barnett Newman, and Mark Rothko in the 1950s–1960s. On the other hand, new works developed in 1968–1971, such as *On Growth Form and Dissolution*, *Some Beginning Thoughts on the Ocean as Field*, *Plasma Chambers*, *Artificial Aurora Borealis*, and *Brine Shrimp* (*Survival Piece II*), signified his transition to bridging art and science through the organic and interactive behavior of living and technological systems. In these works, Newton broke down the established boundaries of art, going beyond the technical application of known principles by creating novel hybrids in which art and science became mutually reinforcing.

Newton's alchemical transmutations of art from that period are noteworthy for showing the direction in which his and Helen's artistic practice would unfold in the future. Art and science appear to merge as fluid interchangeable categories, feeding upon each other in a powerful fusion driven by the Harrisons' desire for exploration and thus discovery of alternative pathways for generating new forms of knowledge. Schematic drawings for a series entitled *On Growth Form and Dissolution (A Time Piece)*, which also included *Fluorescent Seascape*, *Time Module*, *The Slow Growth and Death of a Lily Cell*, *Mushroom Gradient and Forest Smells (A Landscape)*, and *Wall (A Landscape)* (c. 1968),[18] showed his interest in the process of cyclical growth, transformation, and decay of aphids, algae, calluses, fungi, and mushrooms in controlled environments. However, in contrast to a scientist, Newton carried over the sculptor's reverence for materials when describing proposed components for imagined installations. The central point of his investigation was the living cell as a primary artistic medium that allowed him to explore the idea of time through the life cycle in a carefully proportioned and arranged space. Living cells were depicted as bottled up and treated as sculptural growth forms. The progress of their growth was to be duly observed during the show, constituting both a work of art and of science.

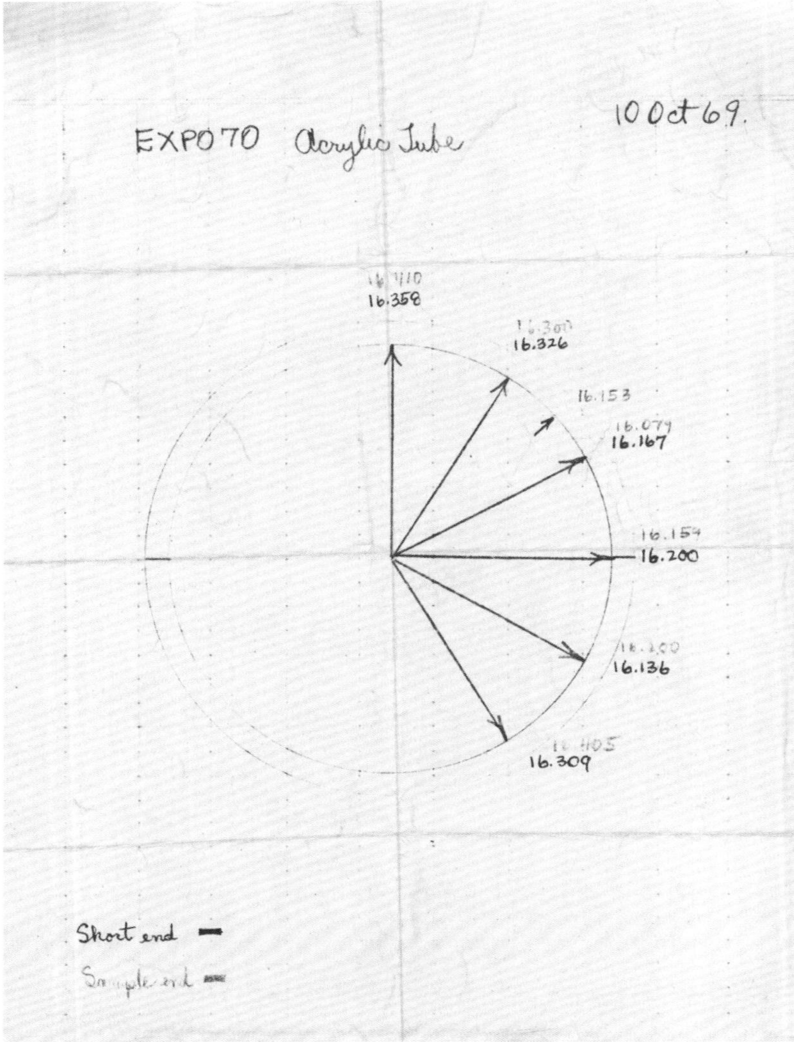

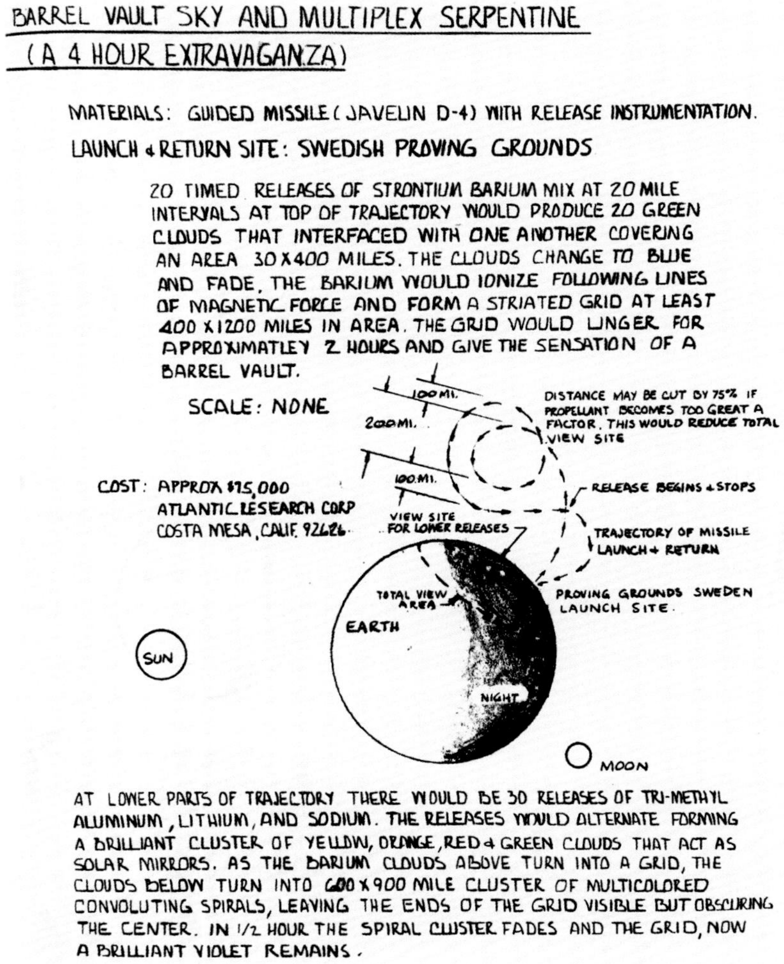

The series *On Growth Form and Dissolution (A Time Piece*, see pp. 34–35*)* was most likely presented in conceptual design drawings exhibited during 1968–1970, though no evidence exists that any were actually ever built. However, there is a small possibility that *The Slow Growth and Death of a Lily Cell* was displayed at the Howard Wise Gallery, as mentioned in the artist's many conversations, including his published interviews documented in the archive.[19] On many occasions, Newton enjoyed recalling that he had a crazy, iconoclastic idea to propagate his own liver cells "to make a feast out of his own liver like a Eucharist."[20] Thus he approached the Biology Department at UC San Diego, where the biologists rejected his speculative proposal but agreed to supply a lily cell with instructions on how to propagate it inside a glass container as represented in the drawing.

In the late 1960s, Newton actively contributed to art and technology experiments to explore his interest in the natural environment. So-called plasma chambers or "glow discharge tubes" became one of the most critically acclaimed and distinguished examples of "techno-art" from the E.A.T. and LACMA programs.[21] In his ambitious project, Newton proposed to recreate the *aurora borealis* – the high latitude atmospheric effect commonly known as the Northern Lights – but encapsulated in vacuum tubes. Featured in the LACMA's *Art and Technology* exhibition in 1971, five 12-foot high, vacuum-sealed, Plexiglas tubes, each 18 inches in diameter, were designed in collaboration with engineers at Pasadena's Jet Propulsion Laboratory (JPL).

5 CLOUDS 5 BANDS

MATERIALS:
1. NIKE APACHE ROCKET
2. NOSE CONE PRODUCED BY THIOKOL CORP.
3. TIMER WITH 5 RELEASE SETTINGS
4. 1 LB. BARIUM STRONTIUM MIX (MATERIALS TO BE IONIZED AND DIVIDED INTO 5 EQUAL PARTS
5. THERMITE CHARGES ATTACHED TO 5 PARTS OF STRONTIUM BARIUM MIX AS VAPORIZING AGENT

REFERENCE: AT 90 TO 150 MILES 1/4 LB OF BARIUM STRONTIUM MIX WAS RELEASED. A GREEN CLOUD OF VAPORIZED BUT UNIONIZED MATERIAL APPEARED, AS IONIZATION TOOK PLACE, A PURPLE BAND APREARED AND TRAVELED AT A SPEED OF 500 MILES AN HOUR REACHING A LENGTH OF 1200 MILES ALONG MAGNETIC LINES OF FORCE. THE CLOUD TURNED BLUE AS THE STRONTIUM IONIZES AND REMAINED STATIONARY. (A CLOUD 20 MILES IN DIA. WAS VISIBLE FOR 2 HRS)

COST: $12,000 - EXCLUSIVE OF LAUNCHING

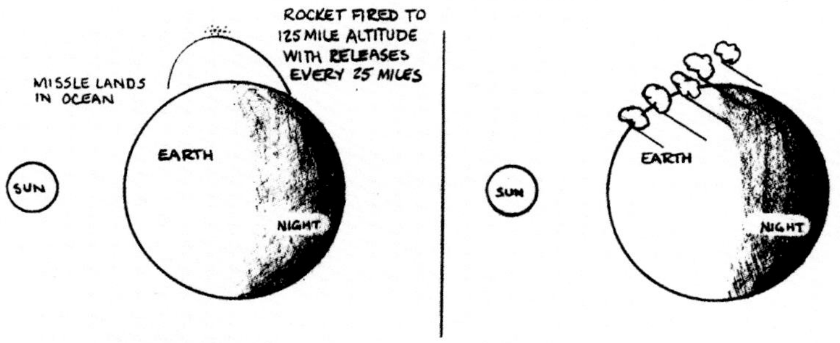

TO BE INVESTIGATED:
1. DIRECTION OF MAGNETIC LINES OF FORCE OVER CHOSEN SITE
2. SAFE OCEAN LANDING FOR ROCKET.
3. BALLISTICS
4. APPROPRIATE POSITIONS OF SUN - MOON - EARTH

NOTE: THIS WORK IS PART I OF A SERIES ON THE AURORA BOREALIS 5 ROCKETS SENT UP FROM OCEANS SURROUNDING EUROPE WOULD BE SEEN FROM EUROPE AND PARTS OF RUSSIA.

THE BIG O - THE GREAT SPIRAL HALO [BOTH WITH MOVING CENTERS]

(2 SKY PIECES TO BE DONE ON CONSECUTIVE DAYS)

SIX JETS WILL LAY A RING MADE OF REFRACTING OR COLOR PRODUCING PARTICLES AROUND THE SUN DURING THE DAY AND THE MOON AT NIGHT FOR A PERIOD OF 15 MINUTES EACH.
A LUMINOUS RING OR HALO WILL APPEAR AND REMAIN IN THE SKY FOR AT LEAST 30 MINUTES.
THE SECOND DAY 6 JETS WILL FOLLOW THE SAME PROCEDURE BUT THE FORM WILL BE IN THE SHAPE OF A SPIRAL.

TESTS: SET UP SIMULATION CHAMBER TO INVESTIGATE MATERIALS FOR POLLUTION CHARACTERISTICS, OPTICAL EFFECTIVENESS AND POTENTIAL FOR DURATION. WATER VAPOR WOULD BE THE CARRIER. NOZZLES, TEMPERATURE AND ALTITUDE WOULD NEED TO BE WORKED OUT USING SMALL CIRCLES AND A SINGLE AIRCRAFT.

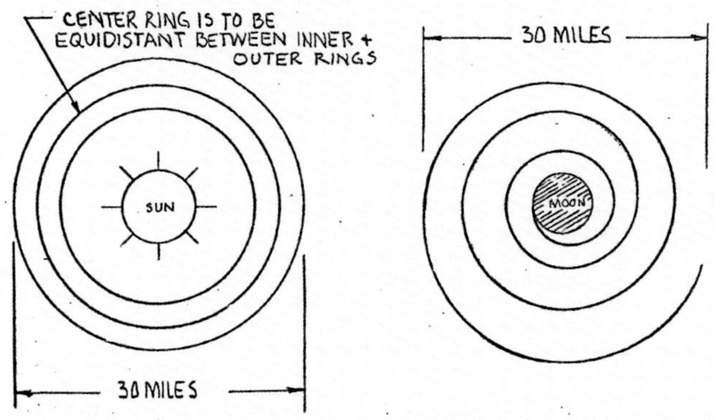

NOTES:
1. JET VAPOR TRAILS ARE THE SOURCE FOR THIS WORK AND THEY ARE WELL DOCUMENTED.
2. A 30 MILE HALO WAS CREATED IN ONE MINUTE USING HELIUM
3. THICKNESS OF RING HAS TO BE DETERMINED AS A FUNCTION OF THE DISTANCE FROM THE OBSERVER.
4. FINE PARTICLES CAN BE RELEASED BY CROP DUSTER ATTACHMENTS TO MAKE MULTI-COLORED RINGS.
5. CLOUDS CAN BE MADE IN THIS WAY AND THERE IS THE POSSIBILITY OF OPTICAL FOCUSING WITH A LENS EFFECT.
6. AT NIGHT ABOVE 55 MILES A SODIUM LITHIUM MIX WILL PRODUCE A 20 MILE HELIX. (FOR MECHANICS REFER TO DRAWING 5 CLOUDS 5 BANDS)

LIGHT PIECE (OPERATES ON A 4 HOUR CYCLE)

* GLOW DISCHARGE LIGHT IS BOTH DIM AND BRILLIANT. UNLIKE USUAL LIGHT IT DISCRIBES ONLY ITSELF. IT IS ALL AT ONCE COLOR, FORM, AND ACTIVITY

A KEYBOARD IS CONNECTED TO GAS INJECTION SYSTEM, POWER SUPPLY, AND PUMPS. BY LEARNING TO PLAY THE BOARD THE VIEWER CAN DETERMINE THE THE EVENTS IN THE INDIVIDUAL CHAMBERS AND MAKE CHAMBERS DIALOGUE WITH EACH OTHER. I FANTASIZE A SECOND SET OF CONTROLS BY USING AN E.E.G SET UP PERMITTING THE VIEWER TO OPERATE THE WORK BY MIND ALONE.

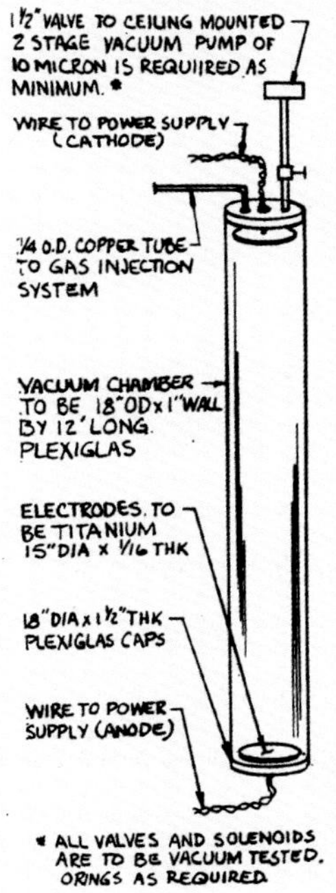

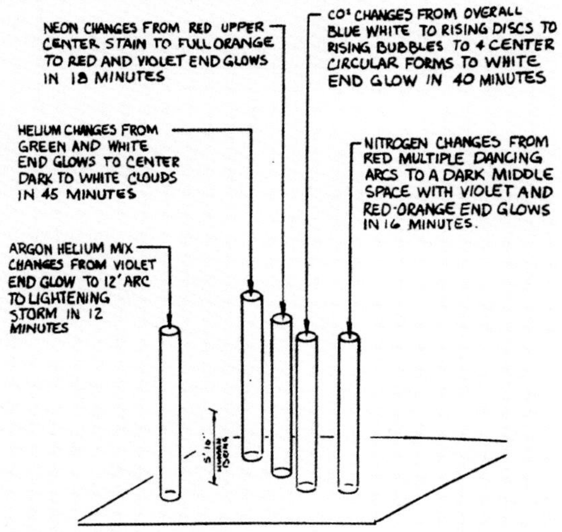

THE CHAMBERS ARE SET UP TO BE SEEN EITHER AS MANY OR AS ONE DEPENDING ON THE VIEWER'S POSITION. EACH CHAMBER GIVES OFF ONLY 5 FT CANDLES SO A DARK SILENT SPACE OF AT LEAST 700 SQ FT IS REQUIRED. ALL COMPONENTS ARE TO BE HIDDEN.

LIGHT PIECE (OPERATES ON A 4 HOUR CYCLE)

GLOW DISCHARGE LIGHT IS BOTH DIM AND BRILLIANT. UNLIKE USUAL LIGHT IT DESCRIBES ONLY ITSELF. IT IS ALL AT ONCE COLOR, FORM, AND ACTIVITY.

A KEYBOARD IS CONNECTED TO GAS INJECTION SYSTEM, POWER SUPPLY, AND PUMPS. BY LEARNING TO PLAY THE BOARD THE VIEWER CAN DETERMINE THE THE EVENTS IN THE INDIVIDUAL CHAMBERS AND MAKE CHAMBERS DIALOGUE WITH EACH OTHER. I FANTASIZE A SECOND SET OF CONTROLS BY USING AN E.E.G. SET UP, PERMITTING THE VIEWER TO OPERATE THE WORK BY MIND ALONE.

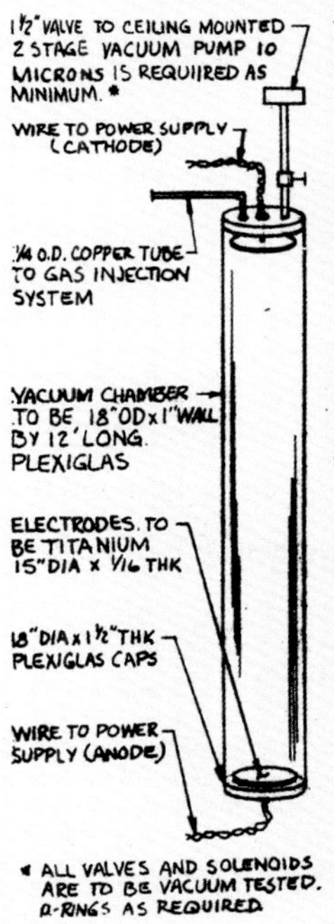

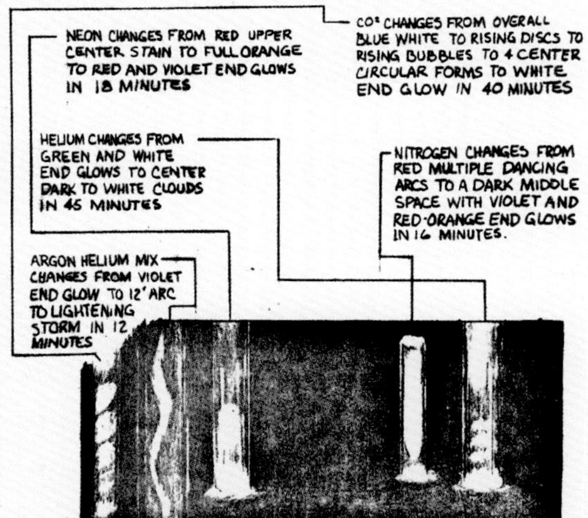

THE CHAMBERS ARE SET UP TO BE SEEN EITHER AS MANY OR AS ONE DEPENDING ON THE VIEWER'S POSITION. EACH CHAMBER GIVES OFF ONLY 5 FT CANDLES SO A DARK SILENT SPACE OF AT LEAST 700 SQ FT IS REQUIRED. ALL COMPONENTS ARE TO BE HIDDEN.

THIS WORK IS BOTH SKETCH AND PROVING GROUND FOR THE ARTIFICIAL AURORA BOREALIS (SEE SKY PIECES)

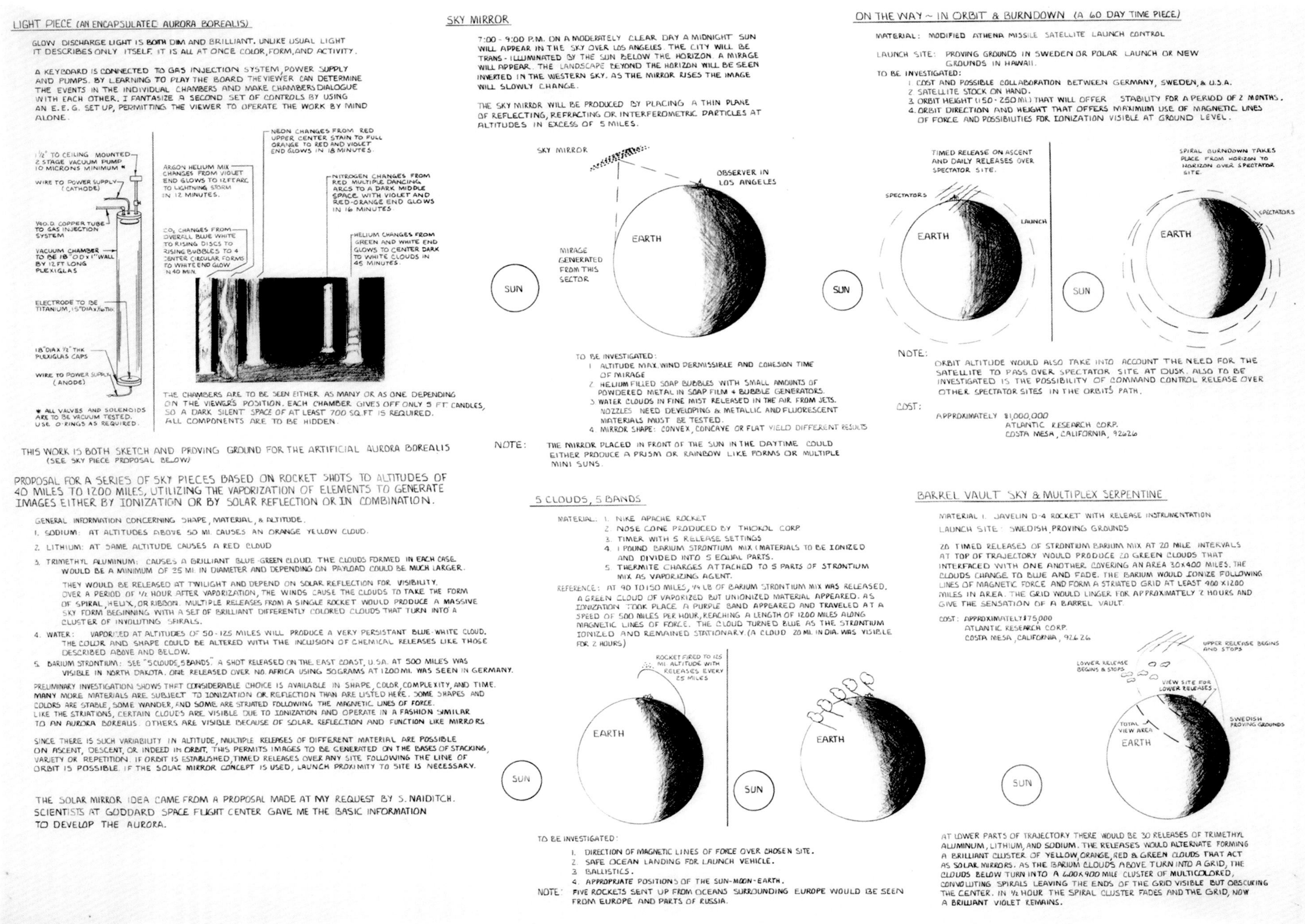

The original idea was first discussed in the experimental design course that Newton taught at UCSD in the fall of 1967.[22] Keith Carter, then a student from the physics department, suggested to Newton to use the laboratory equipment to experiment with the glow discharge inside a bell jar. Through the Art & Technology program at LACMA, Newton met plasma expert Ray Goldstein and Donald Bartz, the manager of JPL's Propulsion Research and Advanced Concepts Section, who together took the project under their wing. Maurice Tuchman was so impressed with *Plasma Chambers* that he included them in the American Pavilion of the *New Arts Exhibition* at the 1970 World Exposition in Osaka (Expo '70), preceding the official opening of the *Art and Technology Exhibition* at the LACMA on May 16, 1971. In his critical review

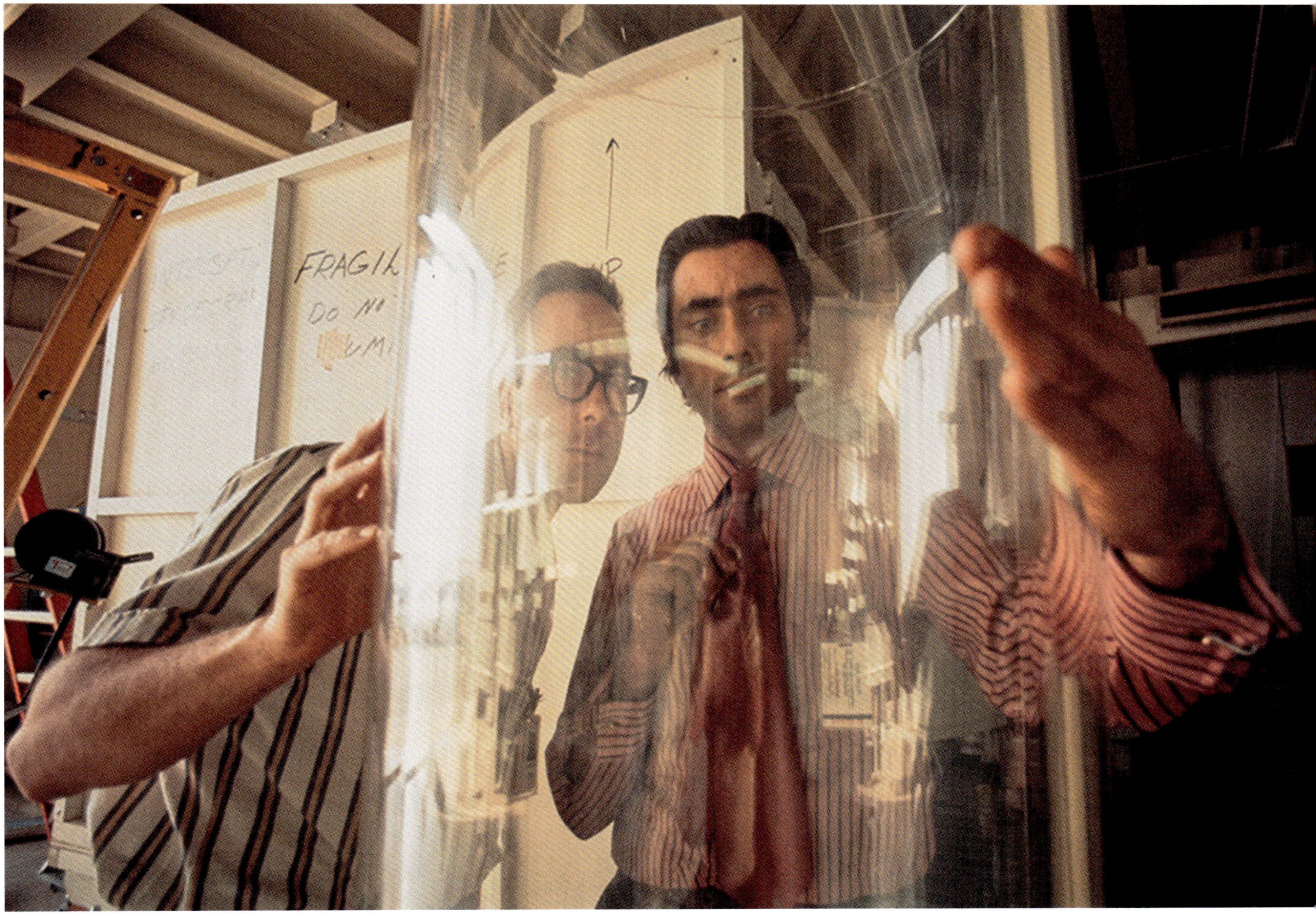

of the LACMA's A&T exhibition, Jack Burnham, an American expert and writer on art and technology, singled out Newton's glow-emitting plexiglass columns as "the most beguiling example of Techart."[23] Burnham wrote that the ceiling-high neon tubes, with their ionized gases of helium, neon, and argon emitting a wide variety of spectral effects, were "mysteriously evocative" of color-field painting. It can be argued that they were nearly perceived as hybrids of sculpture and painting by contemporaries. As Newton said in his conversation with Burnham, his *Plasma Chambers* were a private tribute to Rothko:

" ... just what Rothko was dreaming about. I knew what he was doing ... He was trying to make paint do what paint could never do, although he got his work to cast a light. The

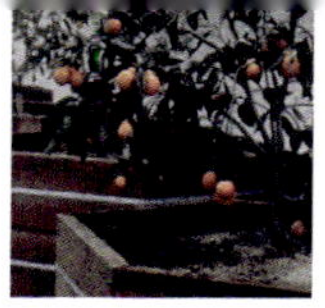

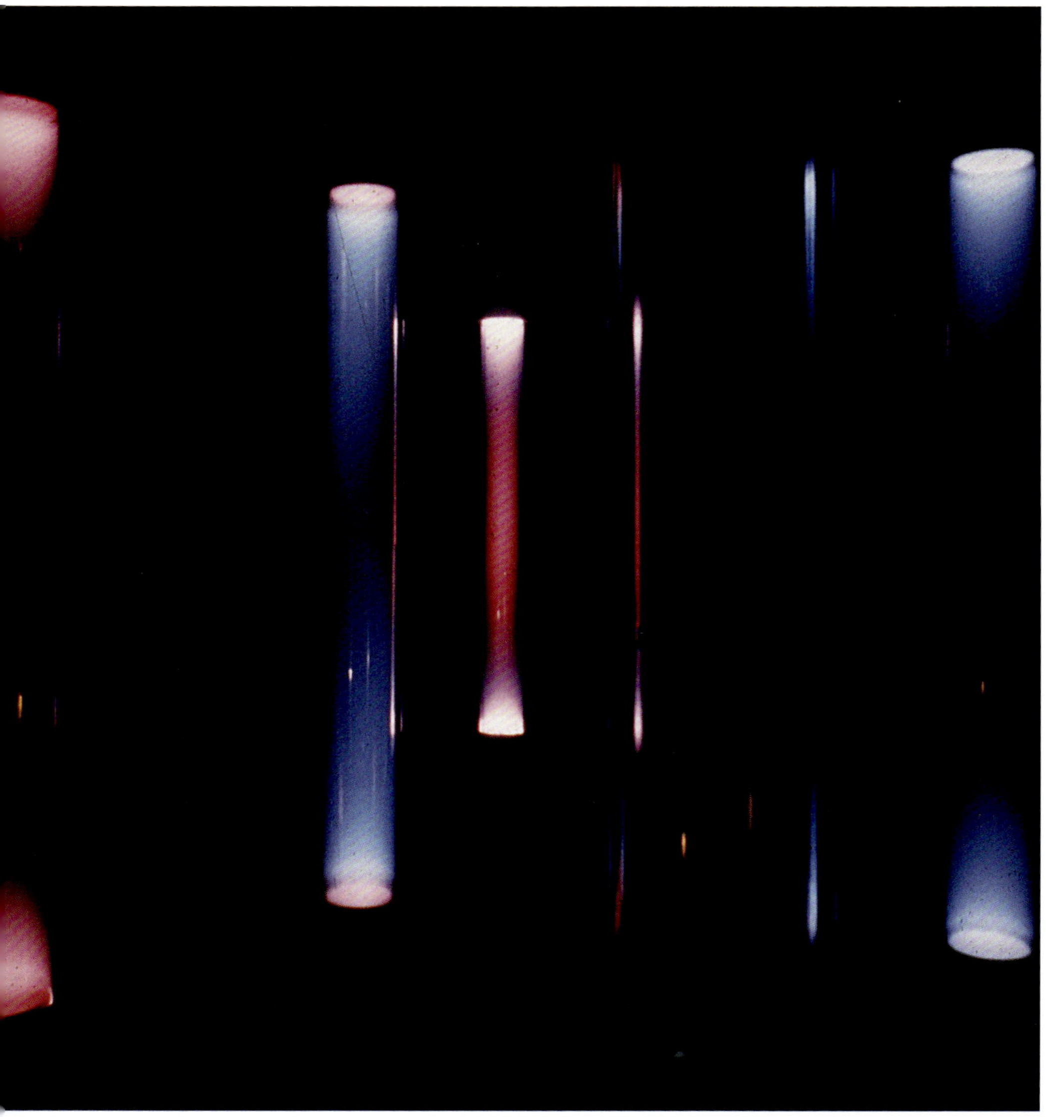

far tube to the right I really made a sort of private homage to Rothko … If you looked at the shape on the top, it was a Rothko type shape, a Rothko color shape, a Rothko intensity shape and it was surrounded by a dark field."[24]

Although Burnham was charmed by Harrison's created environment, he could not quite resolve for himself whether it was art. Burnham's hesitation about how to categorize *Plasma Chambers* was due to the rather technology-savvy design. Goldstein, Newton's enthusiastic collaborator at JPL, pushed him to expand the proposal into our planet's atmosphere, which resulted in conceptual drawings of *Sky Mirror*; *Five Clouds, Five Bands*; *On the Way In Orbit and Burndown*; and *Barrel Vault Sky and Multiplex Serpentine*.[25] The instructions, handwritten on vellum, specified that these pieces would be created by "rocket shots to altitudes of 40 to 1200 miles, utilizing the vaporization of elements to generate images either by ionization or by solar reflection or in combination." Even though the project caught the attention of JPL's highest administrative levels, as evidenced by extensive correspondence in the archive, this last stage of the project was never carried out by Harrison, as permissions and funding were not secured. If realized, it would create a luminous sky spectacle while also potentially gathering vital data about magnetic lines and winds in the ionosphere.[26]

In all, the light pieces, collectively known as *Artificial Aurora Borealis*, reveal Newton's deep fascination with the overlap of art, technology, and science that would positively inform his future collaborations with scientists and engineers. Evidently, it also taught him about the misdirection of Billy Klüver's E.A.T. and LACMA's A&T programs.[27] In a discussion with Janeil Engelstad in 2016, Newton stated retrospectively: "Klüver had it all wrong … and I told him thus … Artists and engineers should not be focused on creative experiments exploring the impact of technology on the individual and society. But rather they should focus on how technology can be of service to ecology and the planet."[28] Was this experience at the A&T exhibition what ultimately influenced Newton's decision to turn away from technocratic and megalomaniac designs to the realm of land and Earth art or art of life-support systems? Certainly, *Plasma Chambers* would earn him both admiration and criticism, as stated by another important art-and-technology writer, Max Kozloff, who described him as a potentially *dangerous* "techno-artist" in the 1971 *Artforum* review of the "Art & Technology" show.[29]

It is against the backdrop of such ambitious and lavishly supported art-and-technology experiments that Helen and Newton created their first series of eco-centered works, known

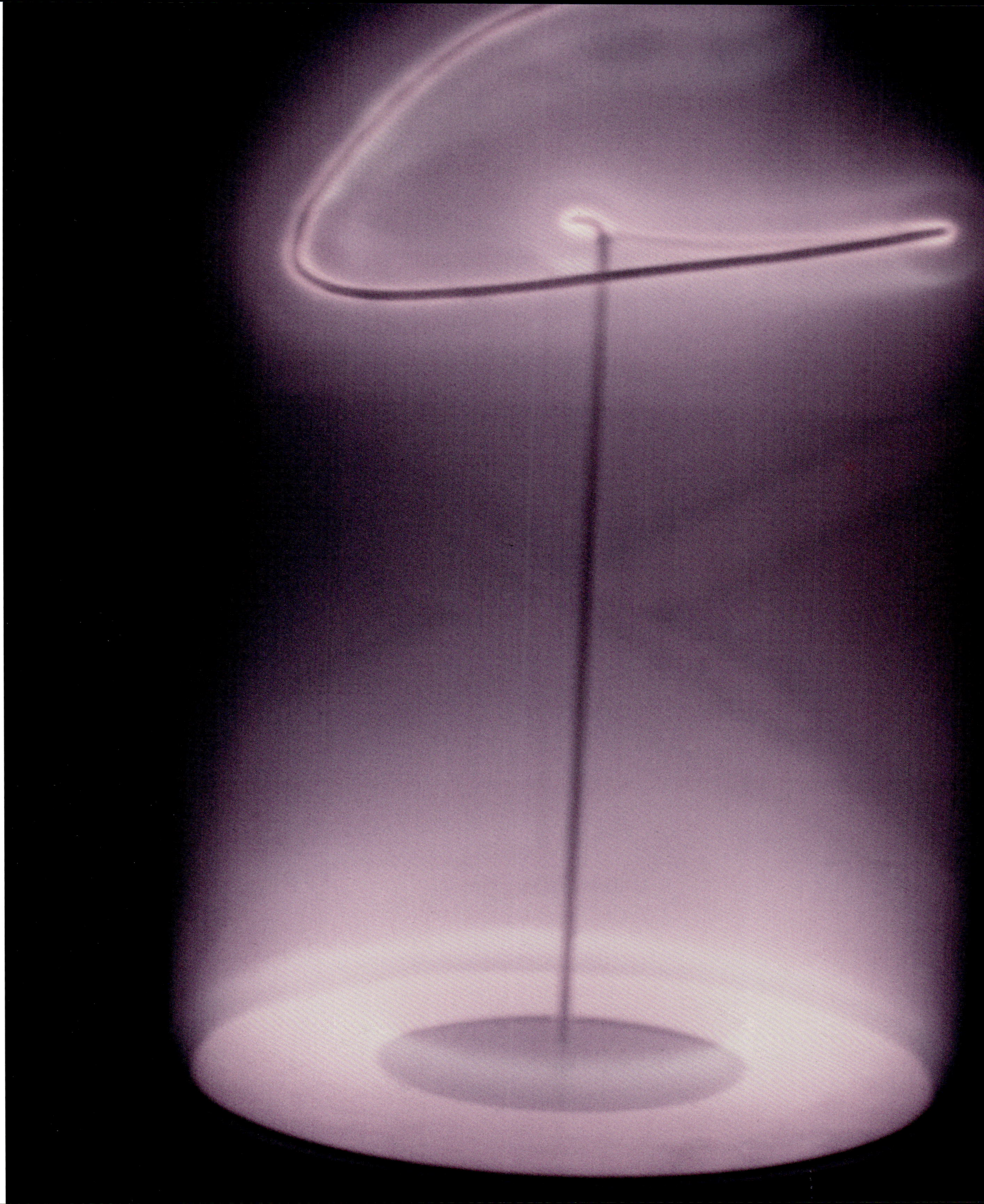

Making Earth

Simplified Wall Text from Revered Earth

By Helen Mayer Harrison & Newton Harrison

The world of soil is bizarre
Communication is chemical and physical.
Worms are its giants.
Movement is slow.
Fungi move through it at rates measured in centimeters per month.
Bacteria move through it at rates measured in centimeters per year.

The world of soil is ancient and magical
contradictory and complex
Mostly solid and opaque to light,
still it acts as a sea to thousands of species
that travel through it horizontally and vertically.
It is the biological filter that detoxifies a large portion of the poisons
that are applied to the environment.

Consider the dynamism of healthy soil.
Consider that soil covers most of the land surface of the planet.
Consider that soil plays a fundamental role in stabilizing the
biosphere.
Consider that new soil formation has been arrested in many places.
Consider that it can take up to a thousand years to make one inch of
topsoil.

Healthy soil is a living system
Healthy soil needs to interact with the air and water
Healthy soil needs access to the products of plants and other
surface organisms

Therefore, feed this earth to a place where the soil is poor. Of
course, you may choose to keep this earth. Then over time it too
will become lifeless and poor.

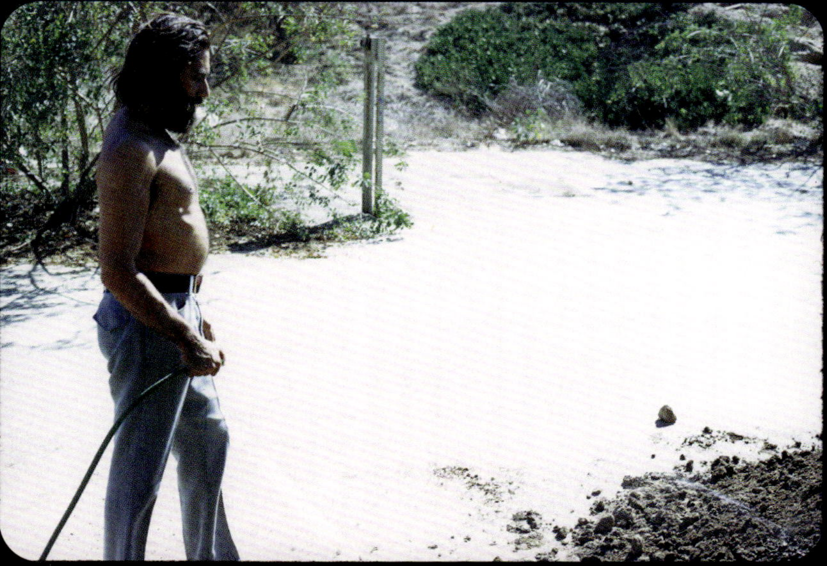

Watering earth

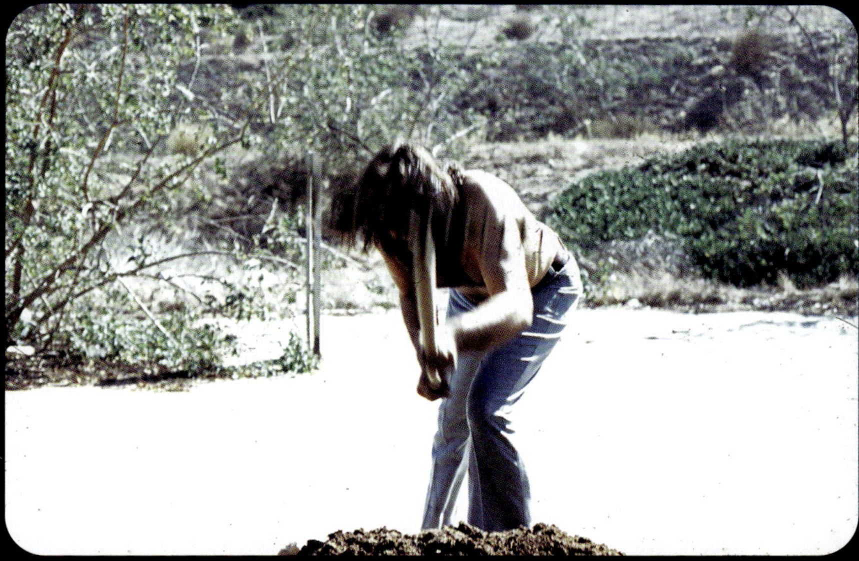

Shoveling and shoveling

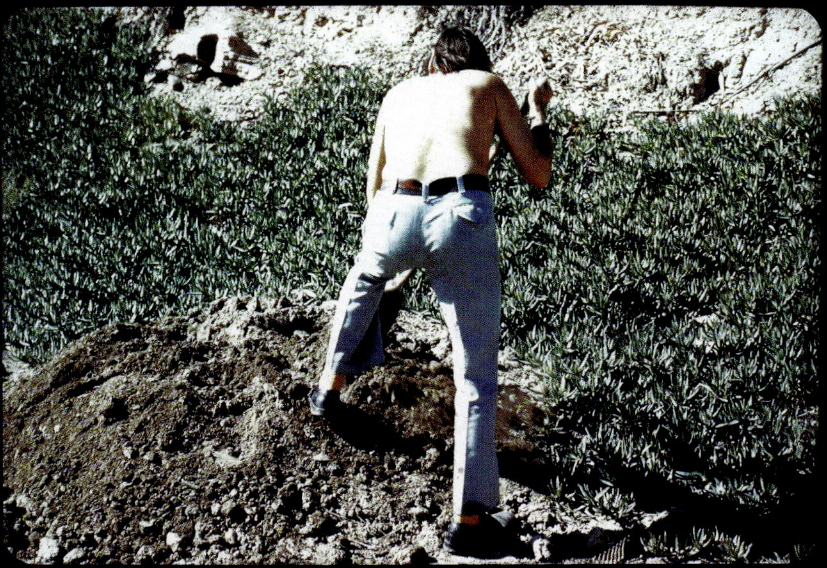

Turning earth

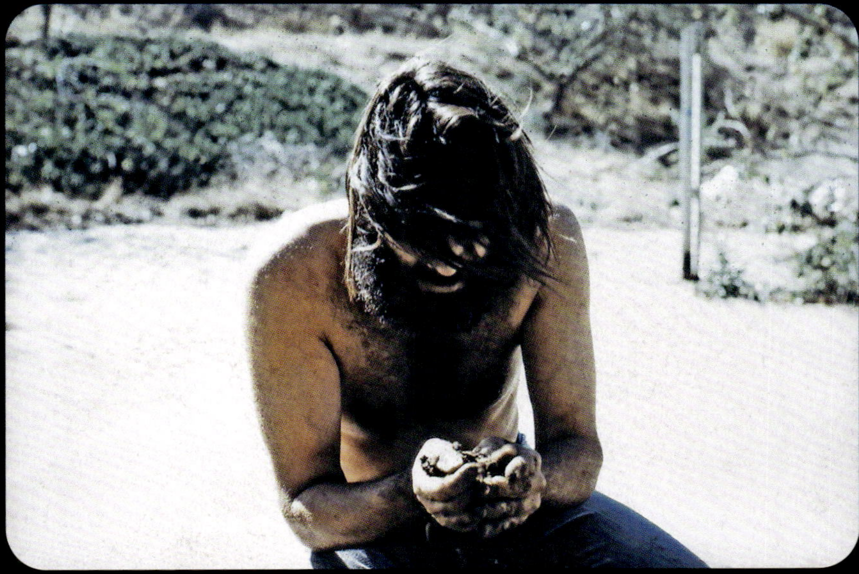

Feeling and crumbling

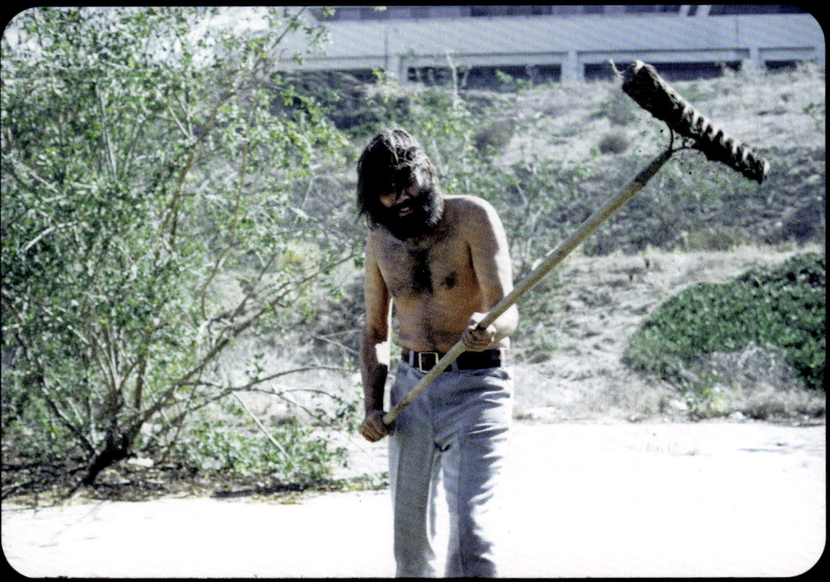

Hoeing earth

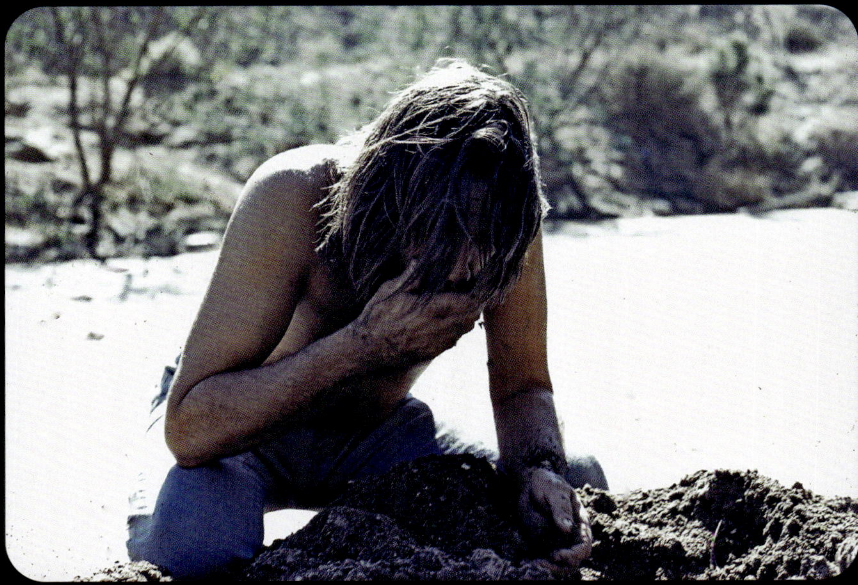

Smelling and tasting

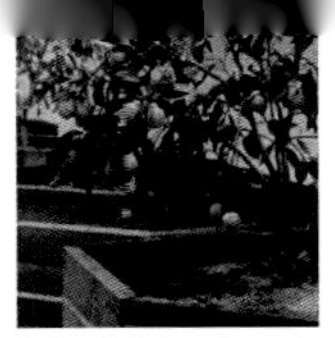

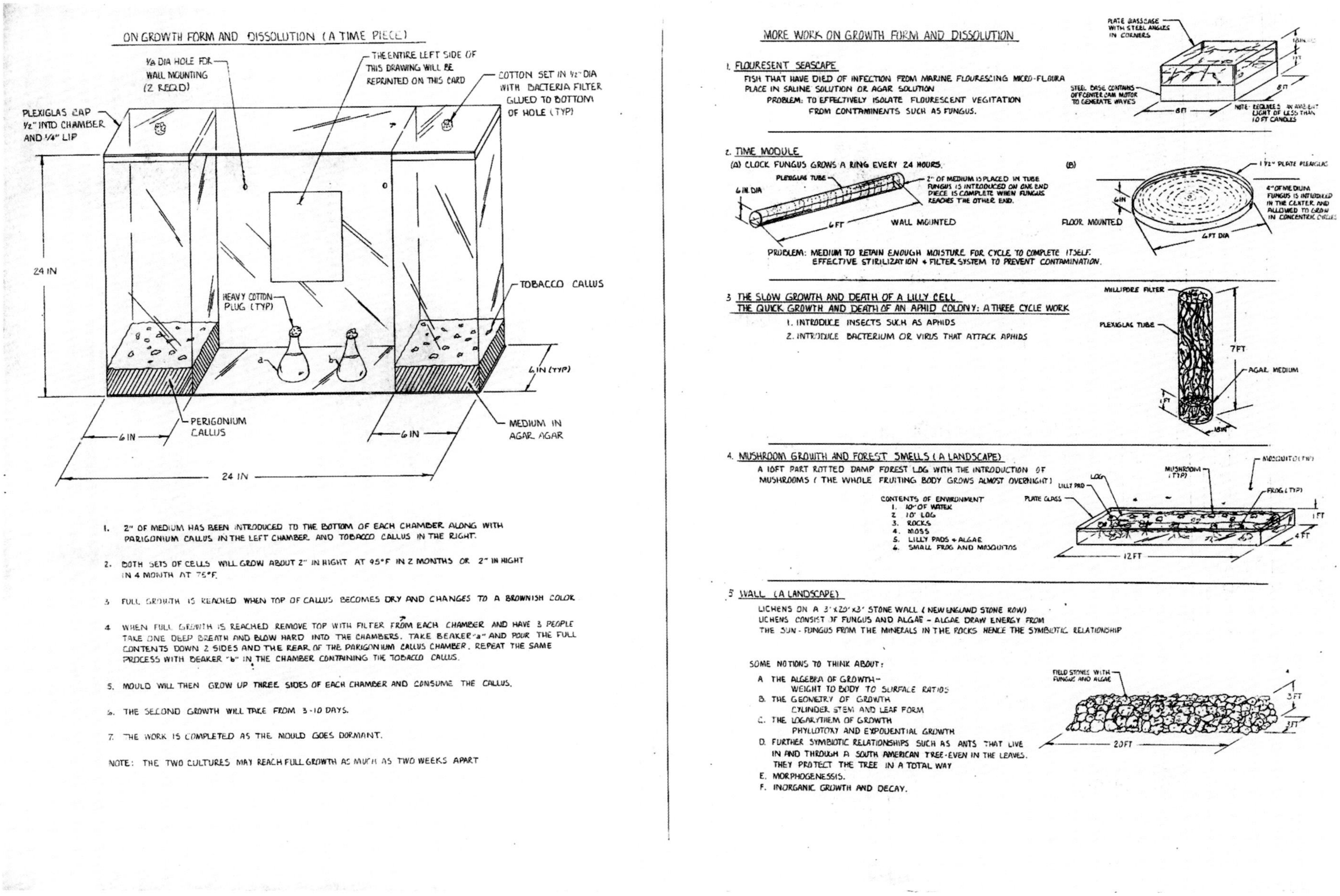

ON GROWTH FORM AND DISSOLUTION (A TIME PIECE)

1. 2" OF MEDIUM HAS BEEN INTRODUCED TO THE BOTTOM OF EACH CHAMBER ALONG WITH PARIGONIUM CALLUS IN THE LEFT CHAMBER AND TOBACCO CALLUS IN THE RIGHT.
2. BOTH SETS OF CELLS WILL GROW ABOUT 2" IN HIGHT AT 95°F IN 2 MONTHS OR 2" IN HIGHT IN 4 MONTH AT 75°F.
3. FULL GROWTH IS REACHED WHEN TOP OF CALLUS BECOMES DRY AND CHANGES TO A BROWNISH COLOR
4. WHEN FULL GROWTH IS REACHED REMOVE TOP WITH FILTER FROM EACH CHAMBER AND HAVE 3 PEOPLE TAKE ONE DEEP BREATH AND BLOW HARD INTO THE CHAMBERS. TAKE BEAKER "a" AND POUR THE FULL CONTENTS DOWN 2 SIDES AND THE REAR OF THE PARIGONIUM CALLUS CHAMBER. REPEAT THE SAME PROCESS WITH BEAKER "b" IN THE CHAMBER CONTAINING THE TOBACCO CALLUS.
5. MOULD WILL THEN GROW UP THREE SIDES OF EACH CHAMBER AND CONSUME THE CALLUS.
6. THE SECOND GROWTH WILL TAKE FROM 3-10 DAYS.
7. THE WORK IS COMPLETED AS THE MOULD GOES DORMANT.

NOTE: THE TWO CULTURES MAY REACH FULL GROWTH AS MUCH AS TWO WEEKS APART

MORE WORK ON GROWTH FORM AND DISSOLUTION

1. FLOURESENT SEASCAPE
FISH THAT HAVE DIED OF INFECTION FROM MARINE FLOURESCING MICRO-FLOURA PLACE IN SALINE SOLUTION OR AGAR SOLUTION
PROBLEM: TO EFFECTIVELY ISOLATE FLOURESCENT VEGITATION FROM CONTAMINENTS SUCH AS FUNGUS.

2. TIME MODULE
(A) CLOCK FUNGUS GROWS A RING EVERY 24 HOURS.

PROBLEM: MEDIUM TO RETAIN ENOUGH MOISTURE FOR CYCLE TO COMPLETE ITSELF. EFFECTIVE STIRILIZATION + FILTER SYSTEM TO PREVENT CONTAMINATION.

3 THE SLOW GROWTH AND DEATH OF A LILLY CELL
THE QUICK GROWTH AND DEATH OF AN APHID COLONY: A THREE CYCLE WORK
1. INTRODUCE INSECTS SUCH AS APHIDS
2. INTRODUCE BACTERIUM OR VIRUS THAT ATTACK APHIDS

4. MUSHROOM GROWTH AND FOREST SMELLS (A LANDSCAPE)
A 10FT PART ROTTED DAMP FOREST LOG WITH THE INTRODUCTION OF MUSHROOMS (THE WHOLE FRUITING BODY GROWS ALMOST OVERNIGHT)

CONTENTS OF ENVIRONMENT
1. 10" OF WATER
2. 10' LOG
3. ROCKS
4. MOSS
5. LILLY PADS + ALGAE
6. SMALL FROG AND MOSQUITOS

5 WALL (A LANDSCAPE)
LICHENS ON A 3'x20'x3' STONE WALL (NEW ENGLAND STONE ROW)
LICHENS CONSIST OF FUNGUS AND ALGAE - ALGAE DRAW ENERGY FROM THE SUN - FUNGUS FROM THE MINERALS IN THE ROCKS HENCE THE SYMBIOTIC RELATIONSHIP

SOME NOTIONS TO THINK ABOUT:
A THE ALGEBRA OF GROWTH - WEIGHT TO BODY TO SURFACE RATIOS
B. THE GEOMETRY OF GROWTH CYLINDER STEM AND LEAF FORM
C. THE LOGARYTHEM OF GROWTH PHYLLOTOXY AND EXPONENTIAL GROWTH
D. FURTHER SYMBIOTIC RELATIONSHIPS SUCH AS ANTS THAT LIVE IN AND THROUGH A SOUTH AMERICAN TREE - EVEN IN THE LEAVES. THEY PROTECT THE TREE IN A TOTAL WAY
E. MORPHOGENESSIS.
F. INORGANIC GROWTH AND DECAY.

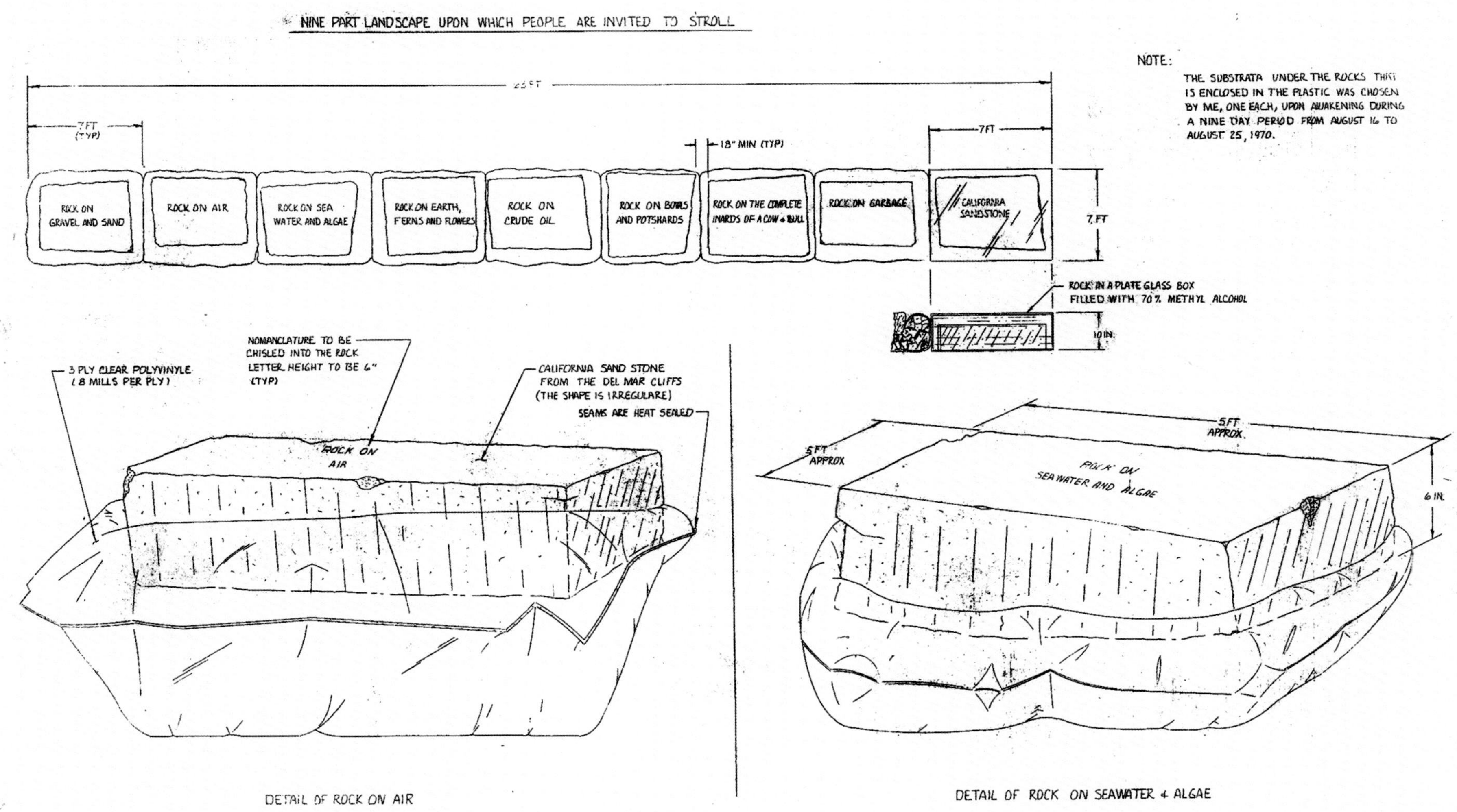
NINE PART LANDSCAPE UPON WHICH PEOPLE ARE INVITED TO STROLL
NOTE:
THE SUBSTRATA UNDER THE ROCKS THAT IS ENCLOSED IN THE PLASTIC WAS CHOSEN BY ME, ONE EACH, UPON AWAKENING DURING A NINE DAY PERIOD FROM AUGUST 16 TO AUGUST 25, 1970.
7 FT (TYP)
18" MIN (TYP)
7 FT
ROCK ON GRAVEL AND SAND
ROCK ON AIR
ROCK ON SEA WATER AND ALGAE
ROCK ON EARTH, FERNS AND FLOWERS
ROCK ON CRUDE OIL
ROCK ON BOWLS AND POTSHARDS
ROCK ON THE COMPLETE INARDS OF A COW + BULL
ROCK ON GARBAGE
CALIFORNIA SANDSTONE
7 FT
ROCK IN A PLATE GLASS BOX FILLED WITH 70% METHYL ALCOHOL
10 IN.
NOMANCLATURE TO BE CHISLED INTO THE ROCK LETTER HEIGHT TO BE 6" (TYP)
3 PLY CLEAR POLYVINYLE (8 MILLS PER PLY)
CALIFORNIA SAND STONE FROM THE DEL MAR CLIFFS (THE SHAPE IS IRREGULARE)
SEAMS ARE HEAT SEALED
ROCK ON AIR
DETAIL OF ROCK ON AIR
5 FT APPROX
5 FT APPROX.
6 IN.
SEAWATER AND ALGAE
DETAIL OF ROCK ON SEAWATER + ALGAE

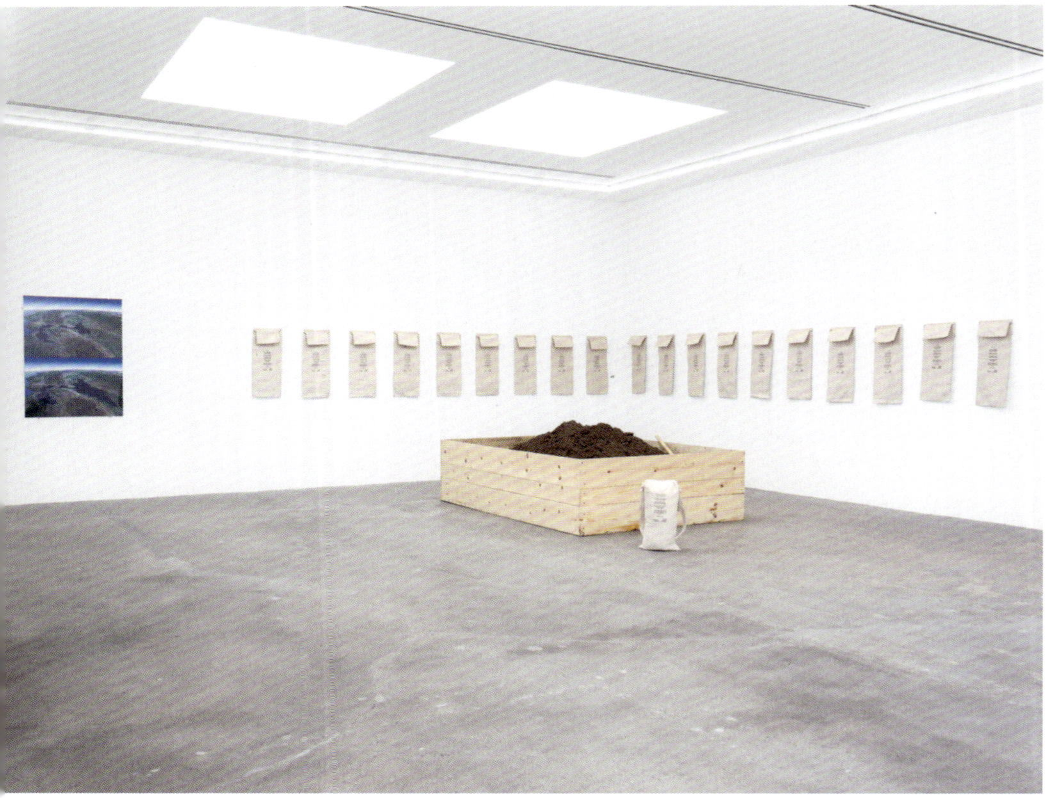

Making Earth, recreation, 1969–ongoing, 2019 Various Small Fires, Los Angeles, CA

as *Survival Pieces*, in 1970–1973. The seven *Survival Pieces* were overarchingly concerned with the total survival of ecosystems and the planet itself from existential threats posed by the abuses of harmful pesticides, exploitative systems of resource management, and failures of the scientific establishment to act in the public interest.[30] The *Survival Pieces* mark a clear turning point in Newton's career, as he would abandon the traditional studio practice with its narrow focus on object making and instead begin focusing on self-enclosed and localized ecosystems, owing to his interest in the complexity of natural processes.[31] Rather than utilizing expensive engineering systems (as in the *Plasma Chambers*), the Harrisons worked with minimal technology and relied on basic shop fabrication. In his review, Burnham noted that *Survival Piece II* included in the *Art and Technology Exhibition* at the LACMA, was one of a "few really interesting" and inexpensive "art and industry" projects.[32]

SURVIVAL PIECES: DESIGNING AND PERFORMING LIFE-SUPPORTING SYSTEMS

The *Survival Pieces* grew out of Newton's initial personal effort to make topsoil, which was becoming endangered in many places. *Making Earth* (1969–1970), a private performance that took place over a period of four months at Pepper Canyon Outdoor Studio, UC San Diego, is well-known today through photographs documenting the piece. The ritual-like outdoor daily "happening" involved a potent assemblage of organic matter, including "sand, clay, sewage, sludge, leaf material, and chicken, cow and horse manure," and followed a set of prescribed moves and gestures.[33] Newton gathered, mixed, watered, and further mixed the matter until it had a rich, forest-floor smell that could be tasted, as he recalled: "The mixture combines with time, and our touch, becoming literally a living element, a medium for growth ... every morning I spend ten minutes of my time with a shovel, ten with a hoe, ten with my hands – and one minute with a hose ... I notice that I breathe in when I pick up a shovel full of earth and breathe out when emptying it. I notice that I make three hoe strokes on inward breathing and three strokes on outward breathing ... In the beginning when the mixture smells vile, I take very deep breaths, drawing in air slowly, but letting it out quickly. At that point my behavior is almost gluttonous. I become very possessive, running my hands through the earth to break up small lumps. This behavior seems compulsive to me. Yet it is very necessary that I touch the soil all over, as a form of ornamentation."[34]

One series of the *Making Earth* performance photographs capture Newton shirtless, wearing blue jeans and looking natural with his long hair and overgrown beard. Framed against the backdrop of the coastal La Jolla landscape, with a tool in his hands (a rake, shovel, or watering hose), he is shown busily shoveling, touching, smelling, and tasting the earth. With his gaze directed inward and his face looking down or away, Newton is represented as a primeval man in relation to a larger environmental space. He later reflected on this performance: "I saw a hand shovel as a metaphor for creating

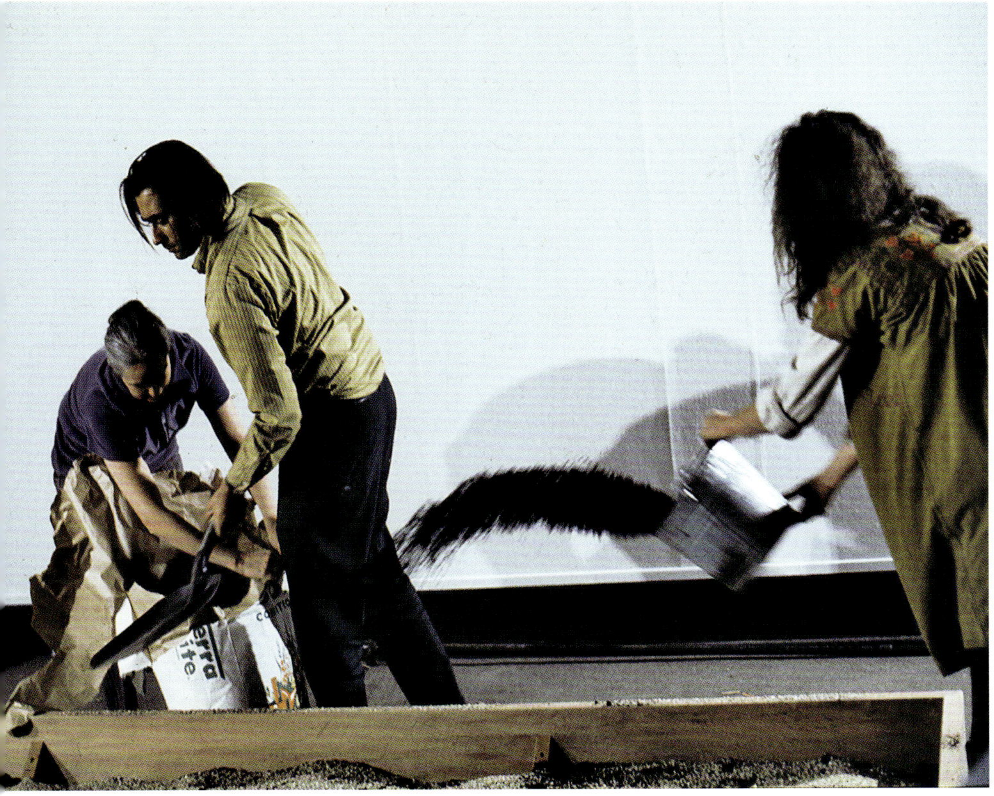

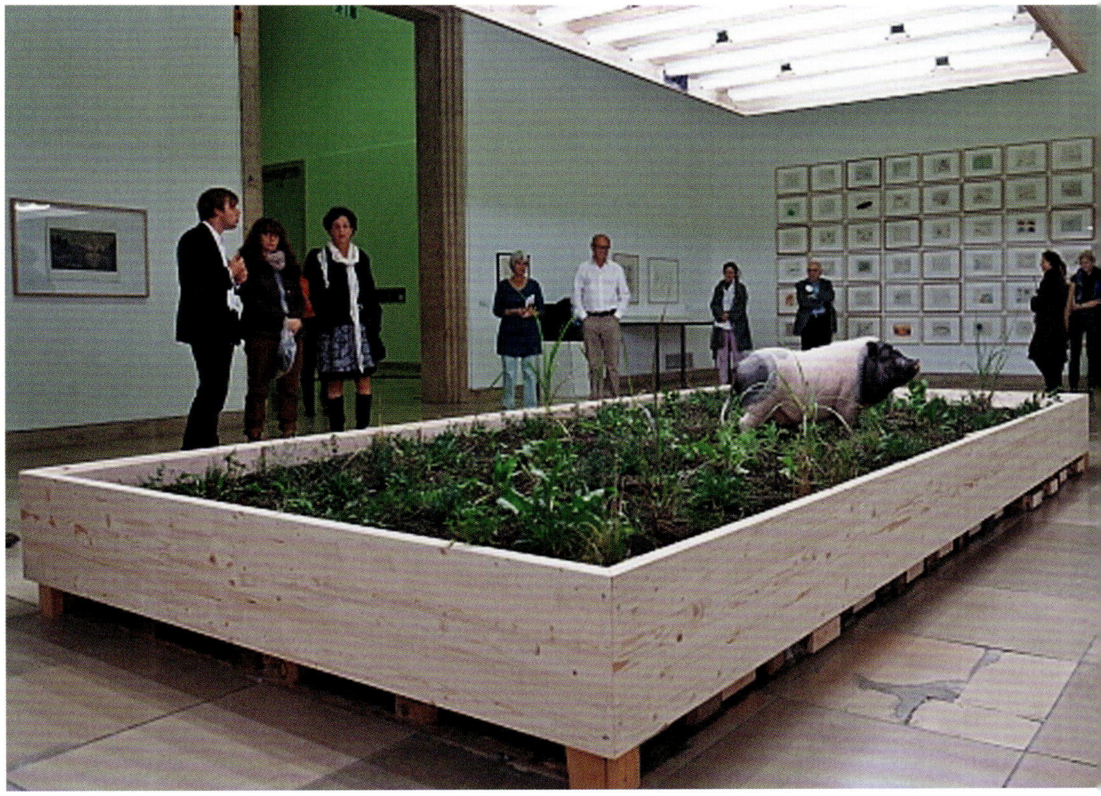

Survival Piece I: Air, Earth, Water, Interface – Annual Hog Pasture Mix, 1971 Museum of Fine Arts, Boston, MA ■ 2012 Museum of Contemporary Art, Los Angeles, CA

earth (as opposed to an overreaching steam shovel, a tool for destroying earth)."[35] As Amanda Boetzkes insightfully writes, Newton rediscovered the Earth and its elements as the basic support of natural life, "turned back" technology "to discover the condition from which it has sprung forward," and created an alternative agricultural technology "through its return to a fundamental bodily relationship with Earth," based on the senses of touch and smell, and ornamented with personal artistic gestures.[36]

Making Earth and the *Survival Pieces* emerged in the context of and in response to alarming headlines, TV and radio broadcasts, and "a flurry of exclamatory books and pamphlets" that professed impending apocalypse due to overpopulation, the planet's environmental fragility, and even the economic challenges arising during Jimmy Carter's time in the White Office.[37] Upon coming to San Diego, the Harrisons became aware of Rachel Carson's *Silent Spring* (1962), one of the most influential books among environmentalists and often discussed in academic circles. Carson spelled out scientifically the far-reaching consequences of pesticide use and the moral bankruptcy of scientists working for chemical companies, and her book urged the public to take the land and the food production into its own hands out of profit-driven government. Another principal book that they also came across was *The Population Bomb* (1968) by the Stanford University biologist Paul Ehrlich, whose central argument (since debunked) was that uncontrollable population growth would soon lead to millions of people starving to death. Well before other artists, the Harrisons reacted to this array of existential threats by prompting the audience to return to basic questions about food production and consumption and by proposing solutions in response.

On many occasions, Newton and Helen stated their position. "I had been thinking about the issue of survival as subject matter," Newton explained in one of several interviews. "My first response was to ponder earth – literally the ground

I stood on. I asked myself what earth meant to me, and what I knew about it. And, to find out, I decided to make earth." Helen commented in turn: "And I began to utilize the piles of earth by containing them and then growing things. So, openers in earth art for us was to make earth, to plant, to grow, to harvest, to do it consciously, to change ourselves

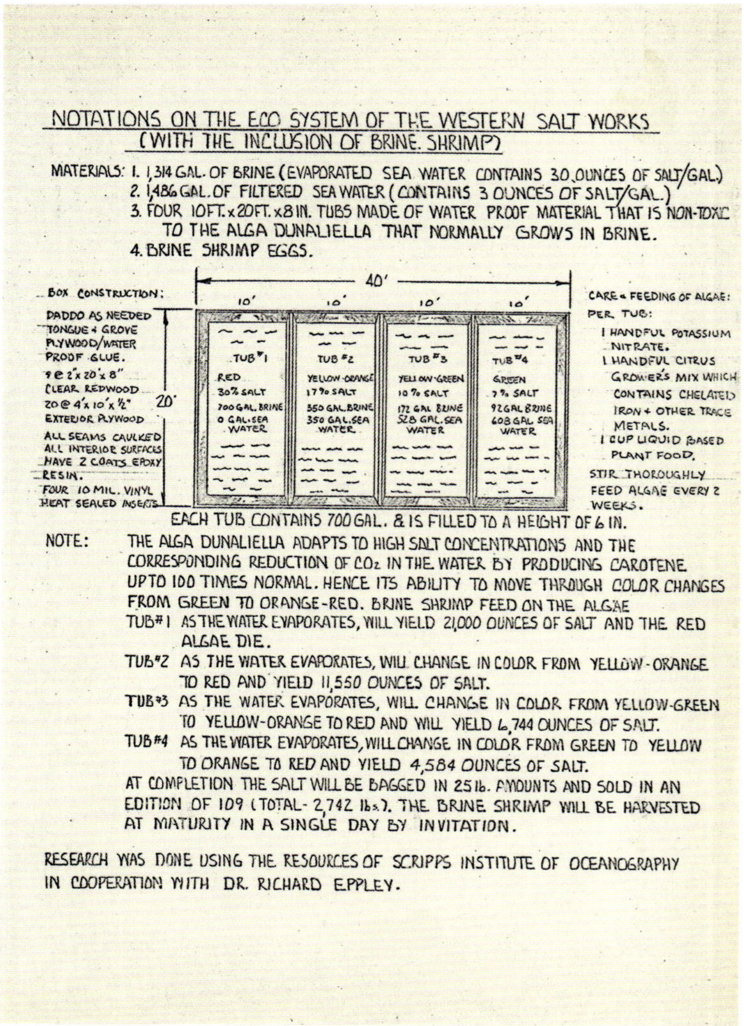

thereby. We did not consider it either interesting or valuable to use earth to make forms on unusual sites."[38]

The Harrisons commenced their collaboration as artists by constructing portable pastures, fish farms, and orchards in various museums and galleries across the United States and Europe. The objective of their installations was to create self-sustaining ecosystems in a controlled artificial setting, marrying natural and scientific processes. The successive *Survival Pieces*, seven in total, are experiments with localized self-generative environments, featuring different kinds of natural growing processes. Because of their ecological concerns, these works already differed from those of other artists who worked with earth as material such as Walter De Maria, Hans Haacke, Michael Heizer, Nancy Holt, Robert

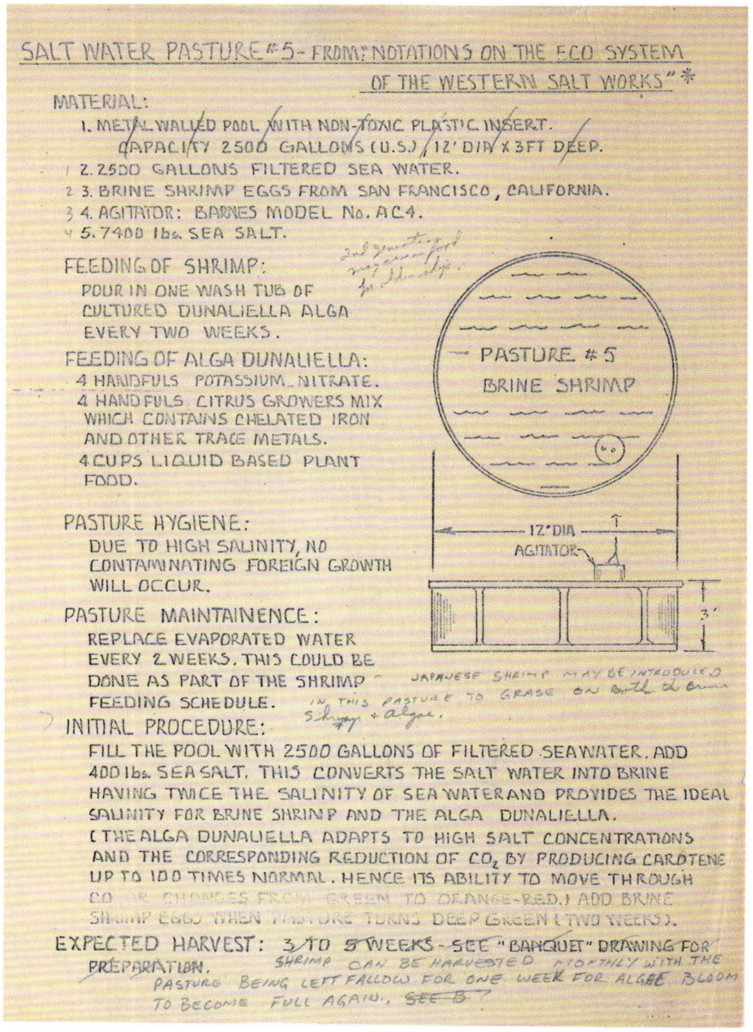

Smithson, Alan Sonfist, and James Turrell. Instead of a simple emphasis on the formal qualities of earth, on light boxes and wooden containers in their installations, the Harrisons put "the utilitarian aspect back into the form" in realizing their food-growing ecosystems.[39] The Harrisons also felt that Earth art was ethically deficient and that "Earth artists damaged or destroyed the immediate environment without serious regard for its plants and animals."[40]

Installation, courtyard of the Los Angeles Museum of Art, Art and Technology Exhibition

The first of these installations – initially titled *Air, Earth, Water, Interface* – was originally commissioned in 1971 by the Museum of Fine Arts in Boston for an exhibition called *Earth, Air, Fire, Water: Elements of Art* that opened in February, three months before the LACMA's *Art and Technology Exhibition*. Later, Newton retitled the work *Annual Hog Pasture Mix*, after the name of the seed mixture he had purchased from a garden catalogue.[41] The handmade soil filled a large 8′ by 6′ planting bed beneath overhead light boxes and was quickly transformed into a lush and beautiful indoor pasture that smelled delicious, as Newton recalled. Archival photos documenting the installation emphasize his performative actions – sewing seed and raking the composted soil. *Annual Hog Pasture Mix* served as a model for life-supporting systems and showcased how sufficient food for all of society could be produced without degrading the Earth. In a comic footnote, the Harrisons requested permission to include a live pig to naturally nourish the crop field but the Fine Arts staff refused, arguing that the pig was a destructive and messy animal rooting the pasture and soiling the museum. *Annual Hog Pasture Mix* was reenacted in 2012 as part of *Ends of the Earth* at the Museum of Contemporary Art, and this time MOCA granted the Harrisons permission to bring a pig, Wilma, to the museum for the closing weekend of the exhibition.[42]

Also in 1971, Newton completed a piece called *Brine Shrimp Farm* (later recognized as *Survival Piece II*) that was displayed as part of the *Art and Technology Exhibition* in the LACMA's outdoor plaza. Subtitled *Notations on the Ecosystem of the Western Saltworks with the Inclusion of Brine Shrimp*, it was informed by conversations with marine biologists Richard Eppley and Michael Mullin from the Scripps Institution of Oceanography in San Diego.[43] The scientists advised Newton that a small crustacean called Artemia – commonly known as brine shrimp – could exist in very salty water alongside algae that would change color as the salinity of the ambient water varied. Assisted by Helen in the research, Newton built a shallow pond of four 10′ by 20′ redwood sections,

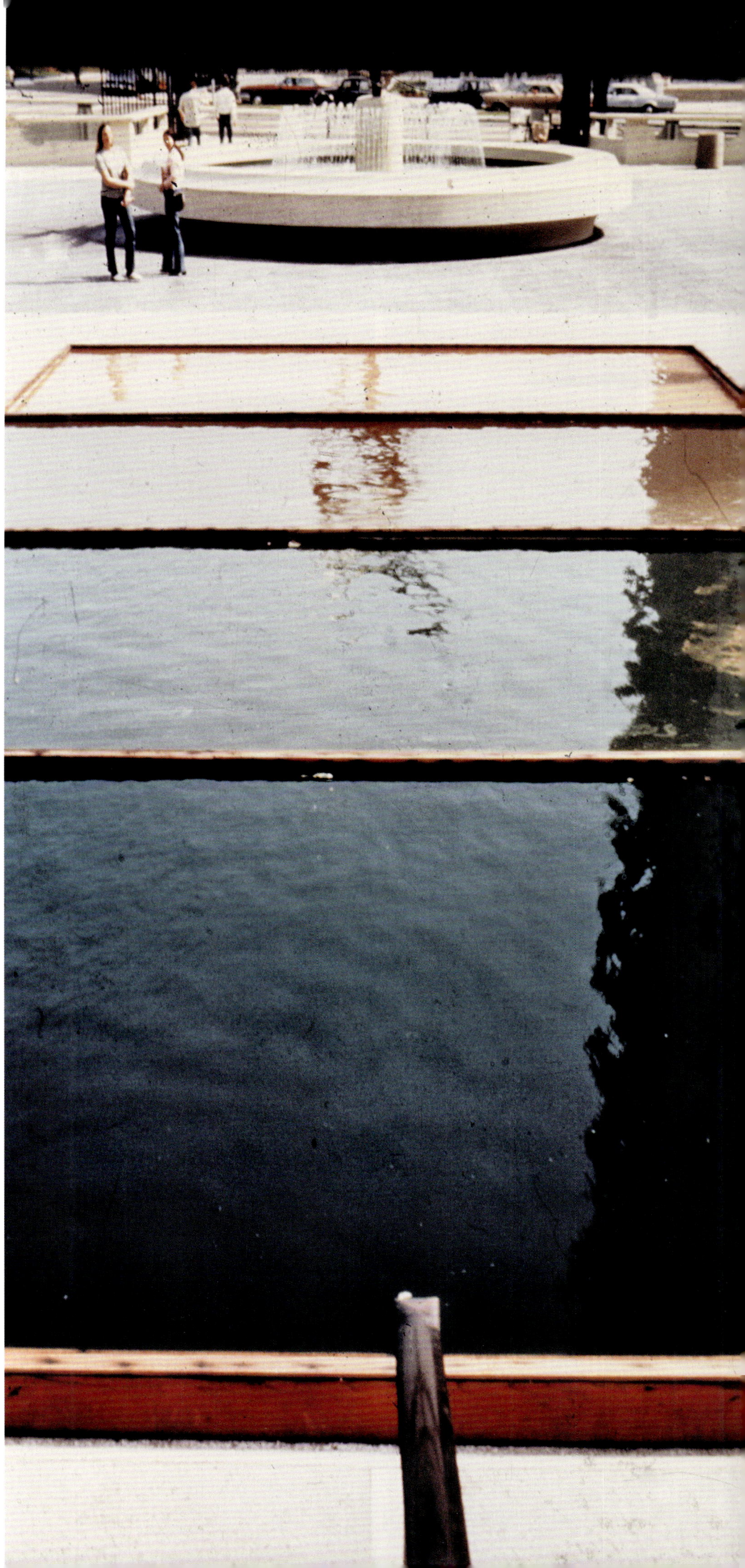

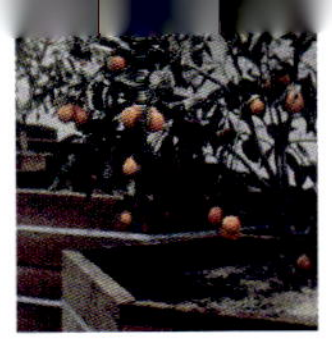

all filled with water of varying salinity. To each rectangle was added brine shrimp and algae, which together were forced to adapt to the different environments. Gradually throughout the summer the water in the tubs turned red, yellow-orange, yellow-green, and green, respectively, due to the effects of the salt on the algae. The result was a living "color field" painting. Besides its striking aesthetic qualities, *Survival Piece II* turned out to be a very successful and productive ecosystem: the artist harvested and sold salt at the end of the summer and used the brine shrimp to make a fish stew. However, it tasted terrible so nobody ate it and thus, unintentionally, the *Shrimp Farm* excluded humans from this functioning ecosystem.[44]

Survival Piece II presented a remarkable contrast to other pieces in the exhibition for its utilitarian and minimal technology of "farming" and "harvesting." The shrimp farm cost only $700, barely more than one percent of an average A&T installation at the LACMA.[45] Although Newton fashioned a new kind of art object that functioned as a closed ecosystem, based on a natural growth cycle, Burnham noted that "the Art World would dismiss it as simple ecological experimentation."[46] Thoughtfully, Burnham added that Newton's profound commentary on the technical hopes and failures of our culture went virtually unnoticed.

Although Newton was the one commissioned to do the works and was listed as the artist of installations at that time, Helen's contribution to research, discussion of works, and design of public feasts (the meal that would often accompany these events) was substantial. Their artistic collaboration was strengthening and growing, and she was finding her way forward as an equal partner. After completing the first two *Survival Pieces*, they developed a quick series of installations over the next six months: *Survival Piece III* or *Portable Fish Farm* at the Hayward Gallery in London, *Survival Piece IV* or *La Jolla Promenade* at the La Jolla Museum of Contemporary Art, *Survival Piece V* or *Portable Orchard* at California State College at Fullerton, and *Survival Piece VI* or *Portable Farm* at the Contemporary Arts Muse-

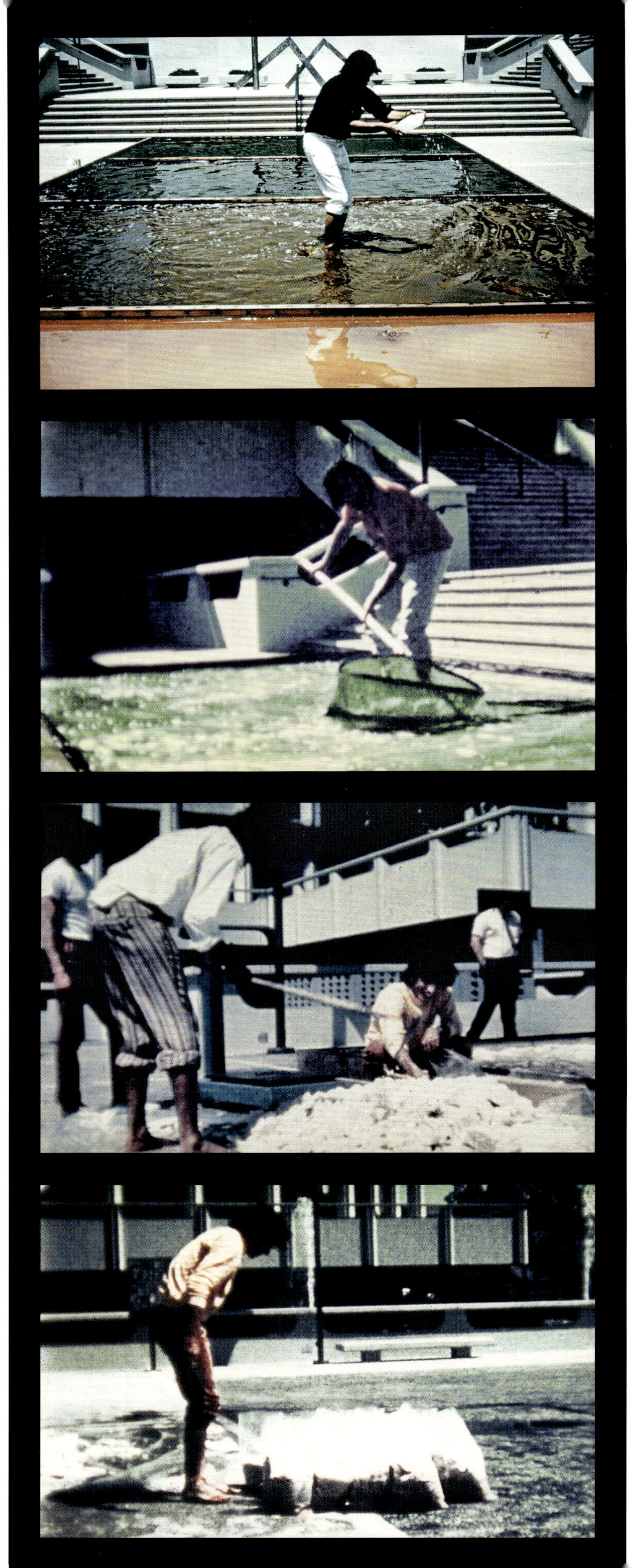

um in Houston. *Survival Piece VII* or *Full Farm* was sketched out conceptually but never exhibited. The Harrisons investigated what could potentially be grown in one's backyard, a smorgasbord including shrimp, oysters, and fish in tanks; citrus trees in planter boxes; and a variety of vegetables in pastures, including beans, peas, carrots, potatoes, and lettuces, thus offering "whole-system backyard farming."[47] Results were presented through conceptual design drawings, which comprise a series of simple steps or "survival instructions" to be reenacted when desired. The works encourage viewers to think about what they would need to survive imminent environmental collapse.

As experiments with closed ecosystems in urban contexts, the *Survival Pieces* were not equally successful in achieving their projected outcomes. Some results were unintended and demonstrated serious inconsistencies. Anne Douglas and Chris Fremantle argue that such contradictions were generative and central for the Harrisons' practice and consider the most provocative to be *Survival Piece III* or *Portable Fish Farm*.[48] This consisted of six rubber-lined steel tanks, three filled with catfish at each stage of their life cycle, another holding brine shrimp and algae once more, and the remaining two tanks housing oysters and lobster. Thus, the tanks served as habitats for catfish and other bottom feeders at different stages of development. An uproar occurred when it was announced that the catfish in the farm were to be publicly killed (electrocuted per Humane Society of America standards) and then served at the opening and subsequent public feasts planned at the Hayward Gallery in London. The gallery and the artists greatly underestimated the difference between American and British values around catfish. Catfish farming was a growing industry in the United States, but in the United Kingdom they were aquarium pets, not food. When the public outcry showed no signs of abating, the Harrisons agreed to have the fish killed privately.[49]

Portable Fish Farm, one of the earliest examples of a more complex closed ecosystem that the Harrisons designed, had both philosophical and practical implications about the food we grow and eat. The artists considered fish farming a means of producing protein, central to their concept of backyard farming. Newton wrote that the intention of the work was to have a system in which catfish would reproduce. Thus, in the strictly ecological sense, *Portable Fish Farm* failed, as the fish did not mate and reproduce as hoped, while the journey was so stressful for the fish that many died *en route* to England from California.[50] Nevertheless, as an artwork, it was over-

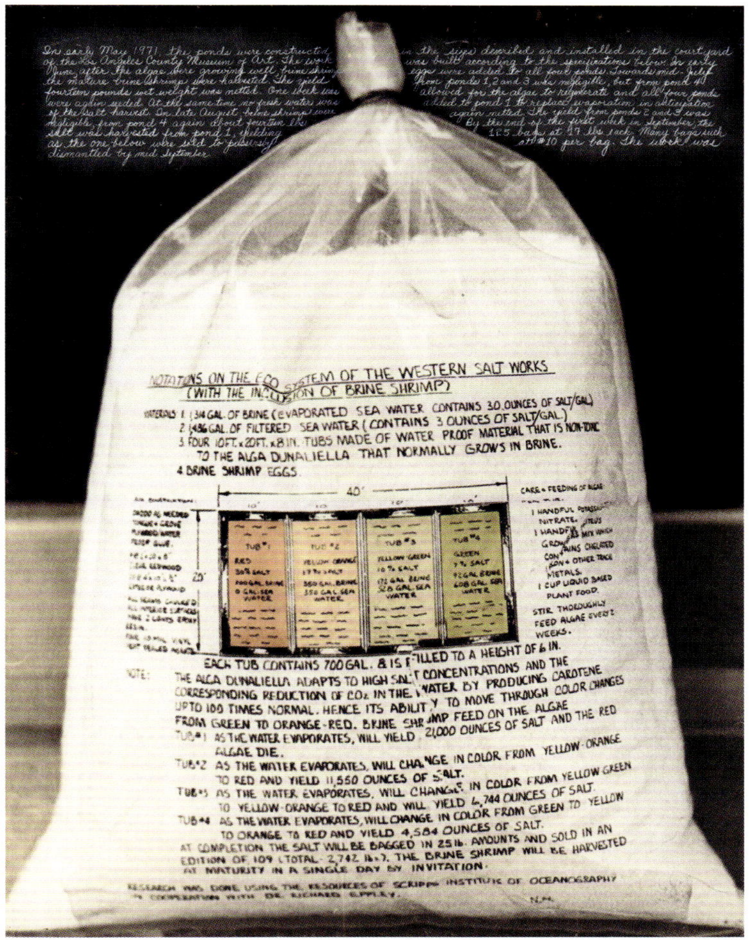

whelmingly successful, stirring up enduring discussion among art curators, critics, and writers about its strong poetic, conceptual, and moral edge. The artists, meanwhile, took note of the mistakes, applying the lessons they learned when creating future ecological works. In keeping up with the Harrisons' focus on communal feasts, the work also resulted in detailed instructions for preparing a series of fish meals (including dispatching the main course in private, one assumes).[51]

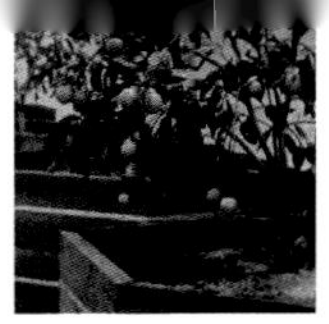

Survival Piece III:
Portable Fish Farm
1971 Hayward Gallery
London, Great Britain
Design drawings

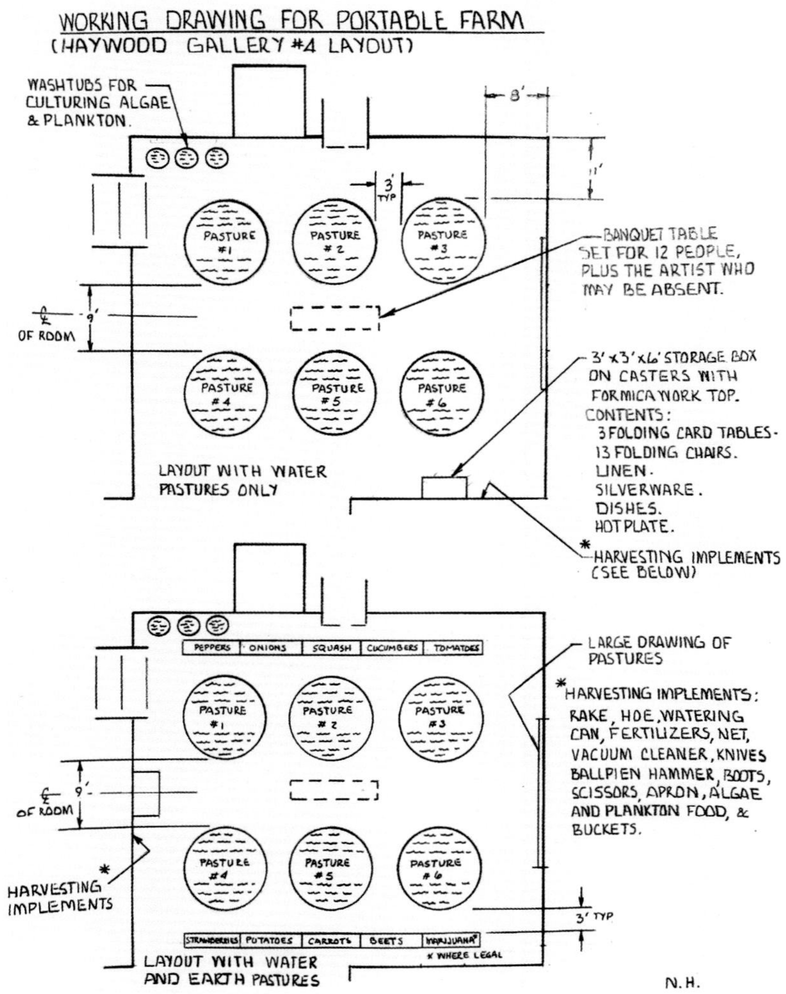

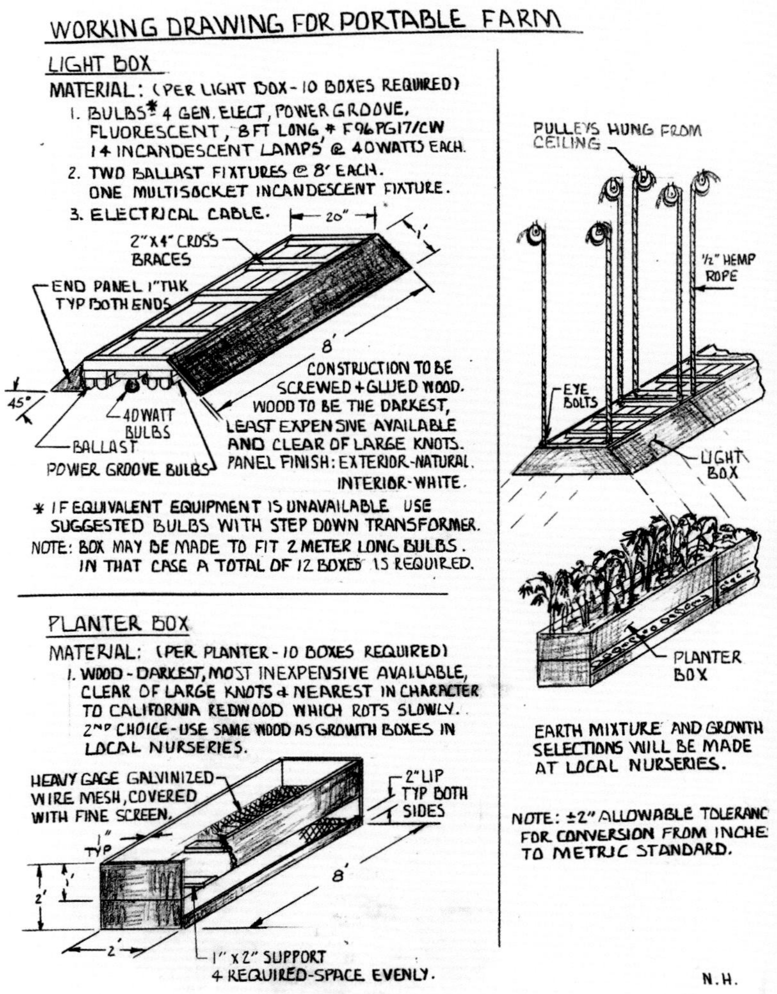

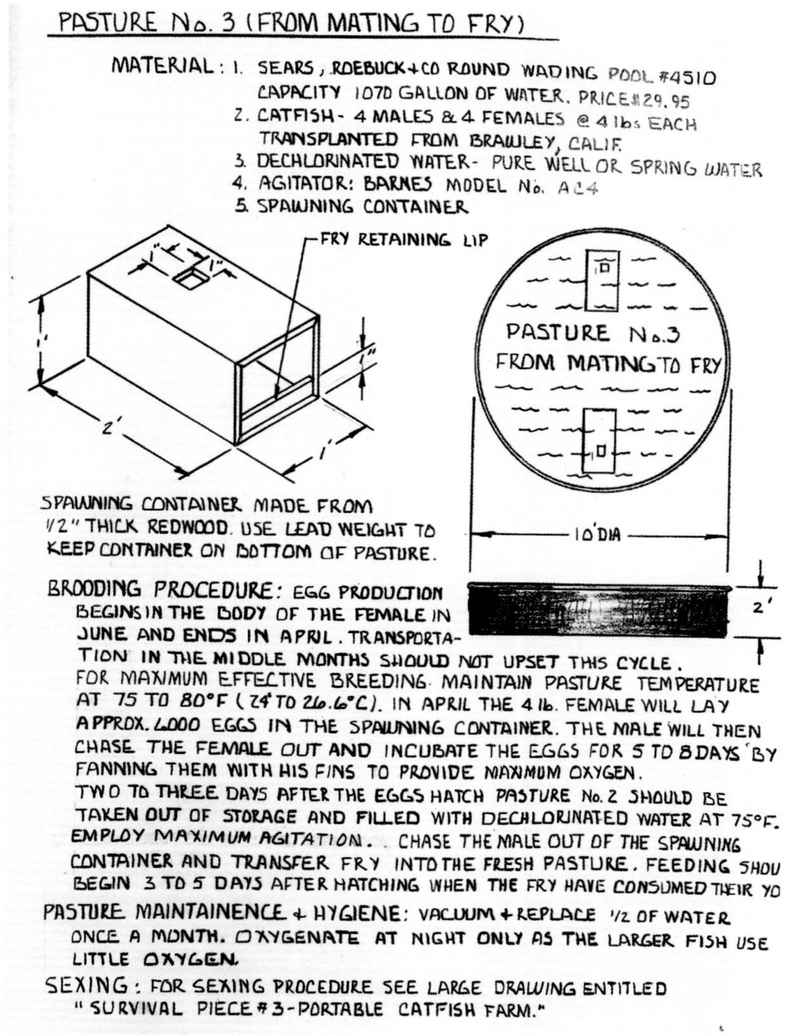

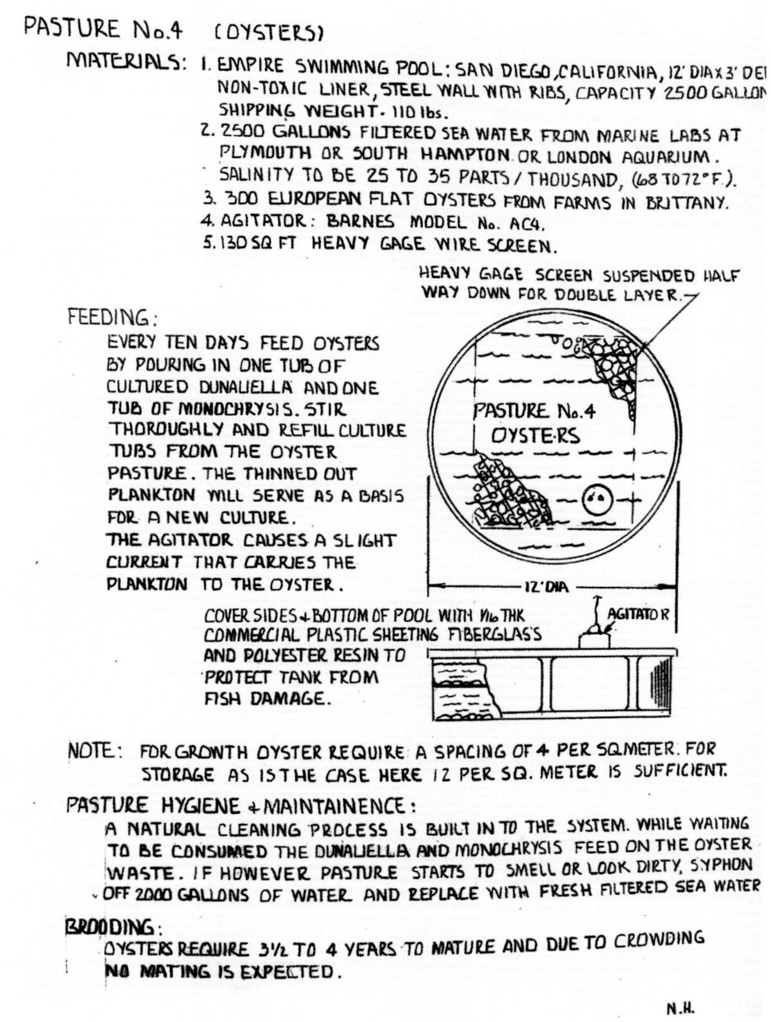

PASTURE No. 1 (FROM FRY TO FINGERLINGS)

MATERIAL: 1. SEARS, ROEBUCK & CO. ROUND WADING POOL #4510 CAPACITY: 1070 GALLONS OF WATER PRICE $29.95
2. CATFISH - 500 FRY TRANSPLANTED FROM BRAWLEY, CALIF.
3. DECHLORINATED WATER - PURE WELL OR SPRING WATER MAINTAINED AT 72°F TO 75°F (22°C TO 24°C)
4. AGITATOR - BARNES MODEL No. AC4

FEEDING: FIRST TWO WEEKS - 1/3 TEACUP PURINA CATFISH STARTER FOOD PER DAY. THERE AFTER FISH SHOULD BE FED 3% OF THEIR WEIGHT DAILY. AFTER 3 MONTHS FISH SHOULD BE FED 4% OF THEIR WEIGHT DAILY AND POOL TEMPERATURE RAISED TO 75 TO 80°F.
NOTE: CATFISH GAIN 1 lb. FOR EVERY 1 1/2 TO 2 lbs. OF FOOD CONSUMED.

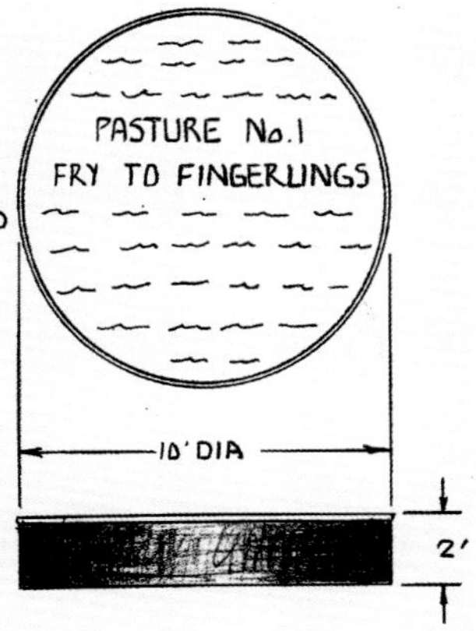

EXPECTED GROWTH: 1 INCH/MONTH

EXPECTED HARVEST: IN 9 MONTHS FISH WILL BE 9 INCHES LONG AND WEIGH 1/2 TO 3/4 lb.

PASTURE HYGIENE: CLEAN WITH SWIMMING POOL VACUUM CLEANER ONCE MONTHLY. AFTER CLEANING REMOVE 1/2 OF WATER AND REPLACE WITH FRESH DECHLORINATED WATER.*

POOL MAINTAINENCE: MAINTAIN MAXIMUM OXYGEN WITH AGITATOR. OXYGEN CONTENT TO BE 7 PARTS PER MILLION.

* ALTERNATE CLEANING SCHEDULE: IF WATER BLOOMS WITH PLANKTON AND/OR ALGAE, PLACE HAND AND ARM INTO THE WATER UP TO THE ELBOW, TWIST HAND SO THAT THE PALM IS UPWARD. IF YOU CAN SEE YOUR PALM THE WATER IS ALRIGHT. IF NOT, APPLY PASTURE HYGIENE PROCEDURE.

PASTURE No. 2 (FROM FINGERLING TO HARVEST)

MATERIAL: 1. SEARS, ROEBUCK & CO. ROUND WADING POOL #4510 CAPACITY - 1070 GALLONS OF WATER. PRICE $29.95
2. CATFISH - 200 @ 1/2 lb EACH TRANSPLANTED FROM BRAWLEY, CALIF.
3. DECHLORINATED WATER - PURE WELL OR SPRING WATER MAINTAINED AT 80°F (26.6°C)
4. AGITATOR: BARNES MODEL NO. AC4

FEEDING: 4% OF FISH BODY WEIGHT PER DAY PURINA CATFISH CHOW. CATFISH GAIN 1 lb. FOR EVERY 1 1/2 TO 2 lbs. OF FEED CONSUMED. IN 2 WEEKS THE INITIAL STOCK OF FISH WILL HAVE GAINED FROM 25 TO 30 lbs. DEPENDING ON HOW FAST THEY RECOVER FROM TRANSPLANT SHOCK.
NOTE: GRADUATE FEED UPWARD WEEKLY.

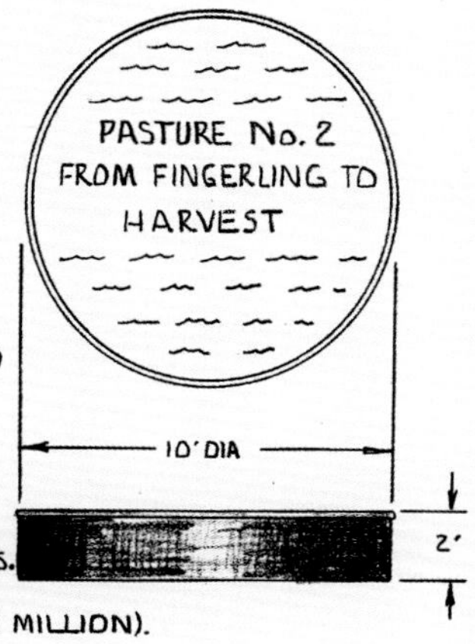

POOL MAINTAINENCE & HYGIENE: DUE TO HEAVY CONCENTRATION OF FISH, POOL SHOULD BE VACUUMED EVERY TWO WEEKS AS LONG AS STORAGE CONTINUES. MAINTAIN MAXIMUM OXYGEN WITH AGITATOR (7 PARTS PER MILLION).

HARVEST PROCEDURE:
1. NET FISH ONE AT A TIME.
2. WHILE THEY ARE STILL ENTRAPPED IN THE NET, RAP THEM NEATLY BETWEEN THE EYES WITH A BALLPIEN HAMMER OR A LEAD PIPE.
3. GUT AND WASH WITH FRESH WATER
4. CLEAN AND STORE POOL.

NOTE: WHEN THE FISH IN PASTURE No. 1 ATTAIN A WEIGHT OF 1/2 lb. THEY MAY BE GROWN FURTHER OR STORED IN THIS PASTURE AS LONG AS NEEDED BEFORE HARVEST. SIZE CONTROL IS MAINTAINED BY PROPER WATER TEMPERATURE AND FEEDING RATIO. GROWTH RATE MAY BE RETARDED BY REDUCING WATER TEMPERATURE TO 60°F AND REDUCING FEED TO 1% OF BODY WEIGHT. FISH STOP FEEDING AT 55°F.

SALT WATER PASTURE #5 - FROM: "NOTATIONS ON THE ECO SYSTEM OF THE WESTERN SALT WORKS" *

MATERIAL:
1. METAL WALLED POOL WITH NON-TOXIC PLASTIC INSERT. CAPACITY 2500 GALLONS (U.S.), 12' DIA X 3 FT DEEP.
2. 2500 GALLONS FILTERED SEA WATER.
3. BRINE SHRIMP EGGS FROM SAN FRANCISCO, CALIFORNIA.
4. AGITATOR: BARNES MODEL No. AC4.
5. 7400 lbs. SEA SALT.

FEEDING OF SHRIMP:
POUR IN ONE WASH TUB OF CULTURED DUNALIELLA ALGA EVERY TWO WEEKS.

FEEDING OF ALGA DUNALIELLA:
4 HANDFULS POTASSIUM NITRATE.
4 HANDFULS. CITRUS GROWERS MIX WHICH CONTAINS CHELATED IRON AND OTHER TRACE METALS.
4 CUPS LIQUID BASED PLANT FOOD.

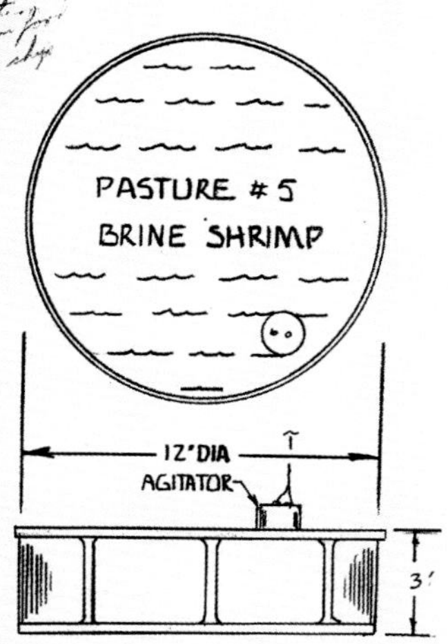

PASTURE HYGIENE:
DUE TO HIGH SALINITY, NO CONTAMINATING FOREIGN GROWTH WILL OCCUR.

PASTURE MAINTAINENCE:
REPLACE EVAPORATED WATER EVERY 2 WEEKS. THIS COULD BE DONE AS PART OF THE SHRIMP FEEDING SCHEDULE.

INITIAL PROCEDURE:
FILL THE POOL WITH 2500 GALLONS OF FILTERED SEAWATER. ADD 400 lbs. SEA SALT. THIS CONVERTS THE SALT WATER INTO BRINE HAVING TWICE THE SALINITY OF SEA WATER AND PROVIDES THE IDEAL SALINITY FOR BRINE SHRIMP AND THE ALGA DUNALIELLA. (THE ALGA DUNALIELLA ADAPTS TO HIGH SALT CONCENTRATIONS AND THE CORRESPONDING REDUCTION OF CO_2 BY PRODUCING CAROTENE UP TO 100 TIMES NORMAL. HENCE ITS ABILITY TO MOVE THROUGH COLOR CHANGES FROM GREEN TO ORANGE-RED.) ADD BRINE SHRIMP EGGS WHEN PASTURE TURNS DEEP GREEN (TWO WEEKS).

EXPECTED HARVEST: 3 TO 5 WEEKS - SEE "BANQUET" DRAWING FOR PREPARATION.

PASTURE No. 2 (FROM FINGERLING TO HARVEST)

MATERIAL: 1. SEARS, ROEBUCK & CO. ROUND WADING POOL #4510 CAPACITY - 1070 GALLONS OF WATER. PRICE $29.95
2. CATFISH - 200 @ 1/2 lb EACH TRANSPLANTED FROM BRAWLEY, CALIF.
3. DECHLORINATED WATER - PURE WELL OR SPRING WATER MAINTAINED AT 80°F (26.6°C)
4. AGITATOR: BARNES MODEL NO. AC4

FEEDING: 4% OF FISH BODY WEIGHT PER DAY PURINA CATFISH CHOW. CATFISH GAIN 1 lb. FOR EVERY 1 1/2 TO 2 lbs. OF FEED CONSUMED. IN 2 WEEKS THE INITIAL STOCK OF FISH WILL HAVE GAINED FROM 25 TO 30 lbs. DEPENDING ON HOW FAST THEY RECOVER FROM TRANSPLANT SHOCK.
NOTE: GRADUATE FEED UPWARD WEEKLY.

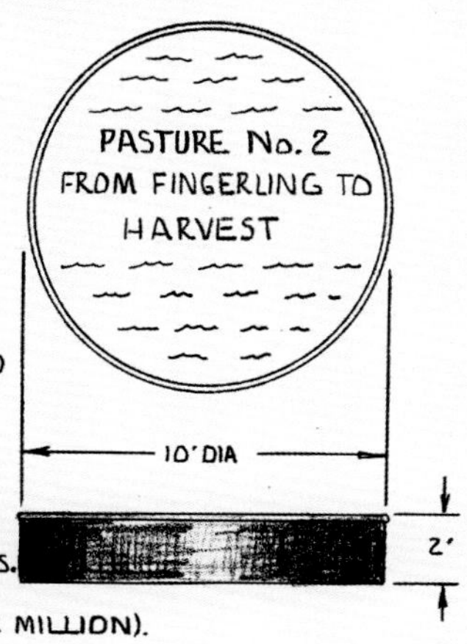

POOL MAINTAINENCE & HYGIENE: DUE TO HEAVY CONCENTRATION OF FISH, POOL SHOULD BE VACUUMED EVERY TWO WEEKS AS LONG AS STORAGE CONTINUES. MAINTAIN MAXIMUM OXYGEN WITH AGITATOR (7 PARTS PER MILLION).

HARVEST PROCEDURE:
1. NET FISH ONE AT A TIME.
2. WHILE THEY ARE STILL ENTRAPPED IN THE NET, RAP THEM NEATLY BETWEEN THE EYES WITH A BALLPIEN HAMMER OR A LEAD PIPE.
3. GUT AND WASH WITH FRESH WATER
4. CLEAN AND STORE POOL.

NOTE: WHEN THE FISH IN PASTURE No. 1 ATTAIN A WEIGHT OF 1/2 lb. THEY MAY BE GROWN FURTHER OR STORED IN THIS PASTURE AS LONG AS NEEDED BEFORE HARVEST. SIZE CONTROL IS MAINTAINED BY PROPER WATER TEMPERATURE AND FEEDING RATIO. GROWTH RATE MAY BE RETARDED BY REDUCING WATER TEMPERATURE TO 60°F AND REDUCING FEED TO 1% OF BODY WEIGHT. FISH STOP FEEDING AT 55°F.

N.H.

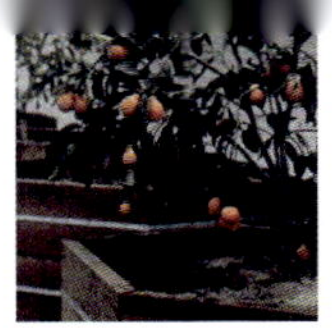

Survival Piece III: Portable Fish Farm, 1971 Hayward Gallery installation views

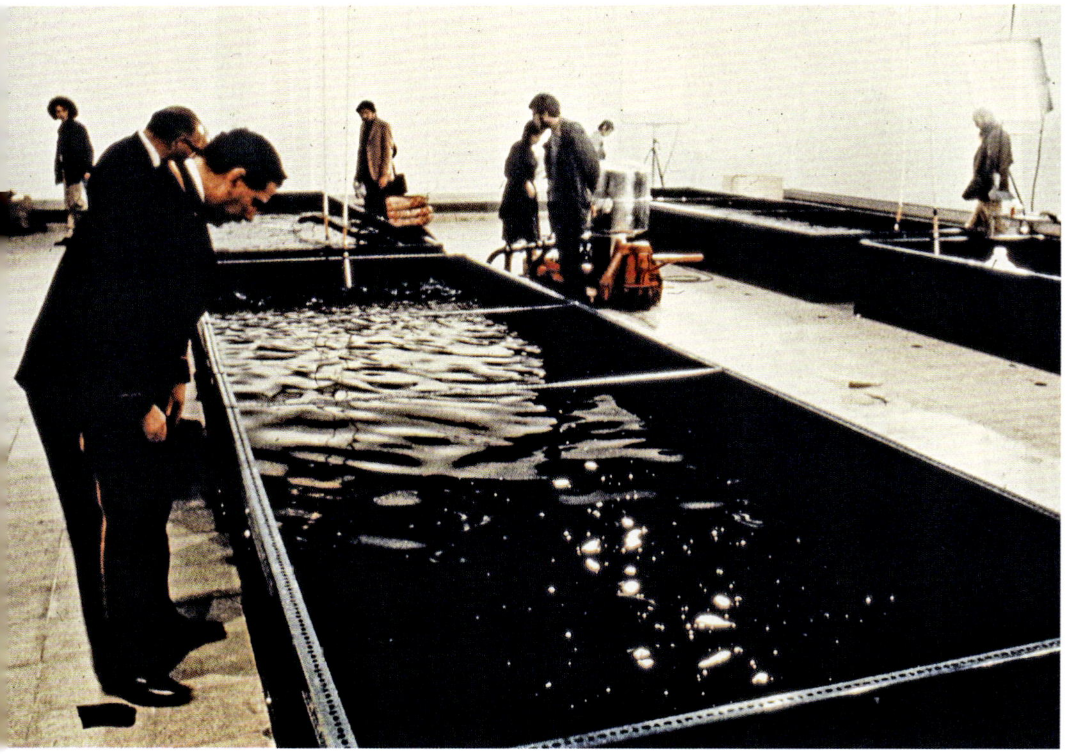

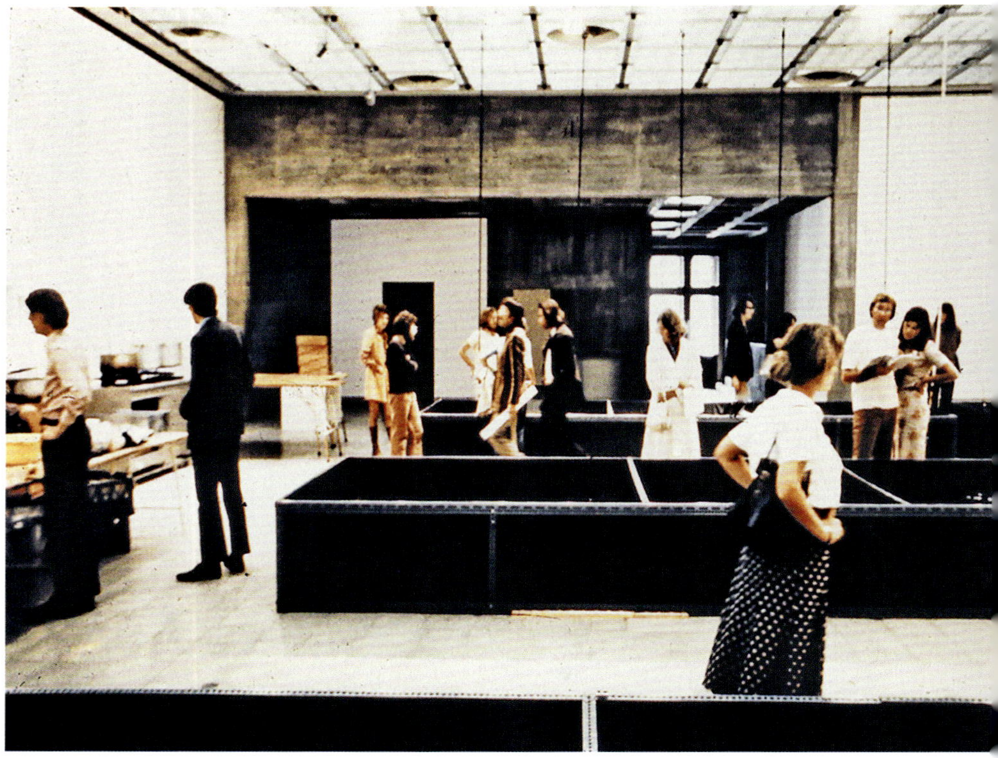

Other *Survival Pieces*, such as *La Jolla Promenade*, offered additional lessons in understanding ecosystems. For the exhibition *Earth: Animal, Vegetable, Mineral*, Newton proposed *Duck and Snail Piece*, an ecosystem of ducks and snails to address the snail infestation in California at the time. At the Museum of Contemporary Art San Diego, the Harrisons put white Peking ducks in the courtyard, a square open space of forty feet on each side, installing a quickly-made garden with a duck pond around which the birds walked – hence the "Promenade" of the more familiar alternative title. Snails were to be collected from the gardens of La Jolla and fed to the ducks to alleviate the snail problem. The shortcomings of the project emerged rapidly: the ducks polluted the garden and ate the snails faster than they could be collected for the exhibition, and therefore they also ate from the actual museum garden, shredding plants, flowers and bushes before the conclusion of the installation. Although Newton had hoped to avoid the earlier pitfalls of *Shrimp Farm* and *Portable Fish Farm*, *La Jolla Promenade* presented him with another unanticipated problem. The Harrisons later reflected that the piece taught them about the limitations of the single cause-and-effect solution of using ducks as snail control from an ecological perspective.[52] Thus they were encouraged to implement whole-systems thinking in their later ecological artworks.

Despite the controversies of *Portable Fish Farm* and *La Jolla Promenade*, the Harrisons continued their critique of industrial exploitation of the land and their quest for alternatives to agrobusiness. Observing the disappearing orchards in Orange County caused by rampant suburban and industrial development as well as air pollution, they decided to make "a Noah's Ark of citrus trees" – the last local orange tree garden, "a memorial of sorts"– as an act of criticism.[53] *Portable Orchard* was an installation with harvesting and feasting commissioned by the Gallery at California State University, Fullerton.[54] The work was composed of eighteen hexagonal redwood boxes, four feet in diameter and three feet deep, planted with assorted citrus and avocado trees,

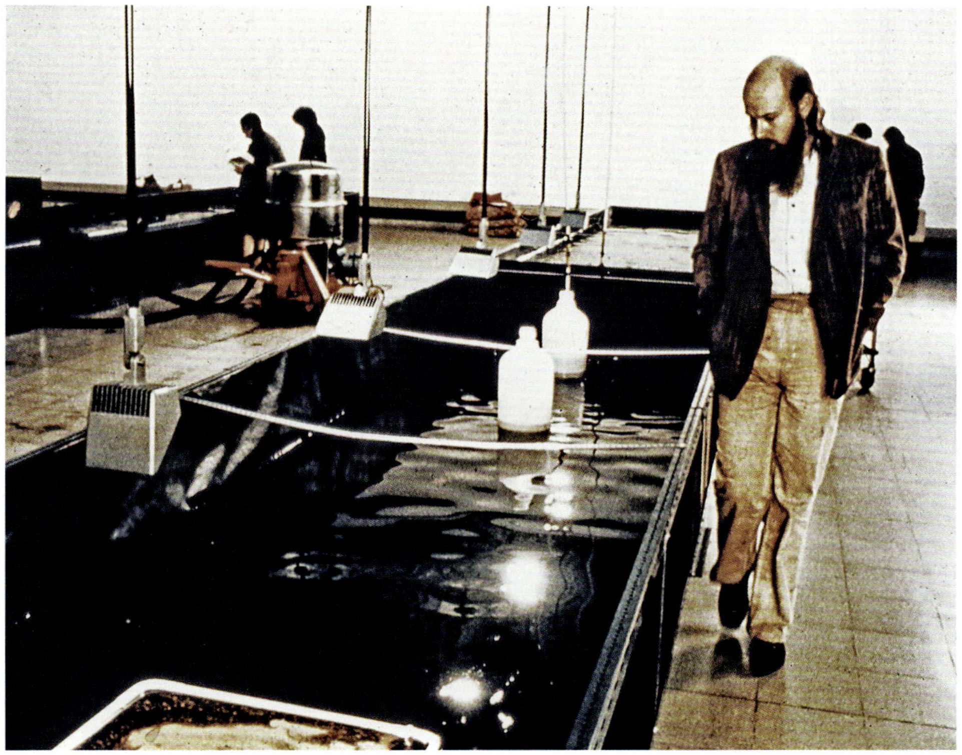

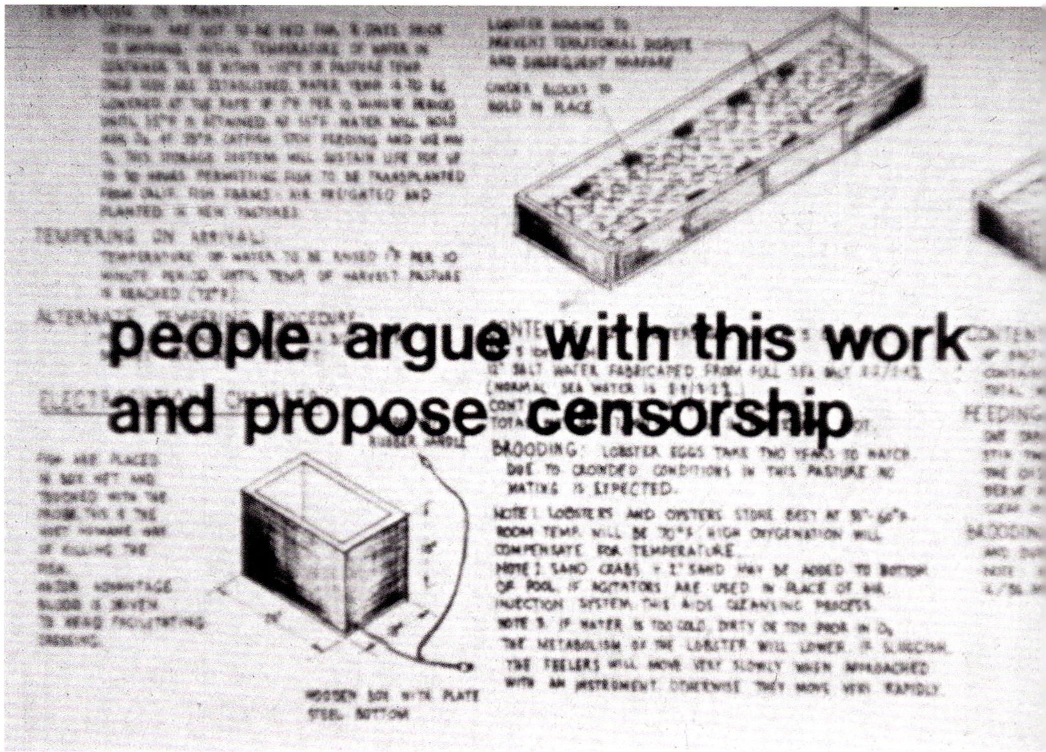

each in a cubic yard of earth, topped by hexagonal redwood artificial light boxes. Newton also harbored a personal reason to build a portable orchard: his prior attempts to grow lemon trees in his own backyard had failed. With the help of horticulturalists and CSU Fullerton students, Newton selected the species of trees, studied root structures, and experimented with possible spacing and watering patterns back at UC San Diego. Based on historical and horticultural studies, Helen designed a public feast with a three-course menu called *Citrus Board for 300*.

Grounded in ecosystem research, *Portable Orchard* was another experiment that imagined a radical lifestyle reorientation to assume personal responsibility for one's own food production in order to protest harmful and exploitative industrial agriculture and ultimately to survive. Demonstrating the Harrisons' mature commitment to functional ends, this project anticipated their vision of portable ecosystems and assisted species migrations occurring within the context of widespread future ecological restoration. Given the evident manifold effects of climate change, *Portable Orchard* assumes an even larger role today, suggesting alternative harvest-producing solutions for surviving the temperature increase caused by global warming.[55] Therefore, *Survival Pieces* can be understood as paths for action, serving as potent metaphors while also revealing scenarios of a changing planet in an altered future.

The *Survival Pieces* belong to the category of the Harrisons' first eco-critical urban works, which visualized self-generating ecological life cycles as art objects. These experiments in urban farming revealed the artists' approach: they made ecology their artistic practice, accepting what natural phenomena could teach them, rather than trying to dominate or impose their will upon nature. They took risks, improvised, and learned from different emerging priorities as they went forward. Anne Douglas and Chris Fremantle correctly observe that the *Survival Pieces* were central for formulating the Harrisons' practice, as through these works they embraced the process of open-ended experimentation and

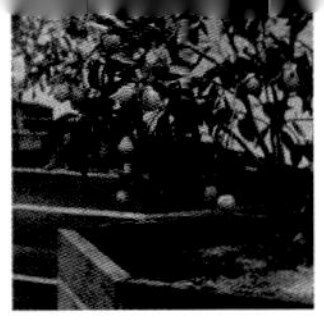

Survival Piece III: Portable Fish Farm, 1971 Hayward Gallery, design drawings

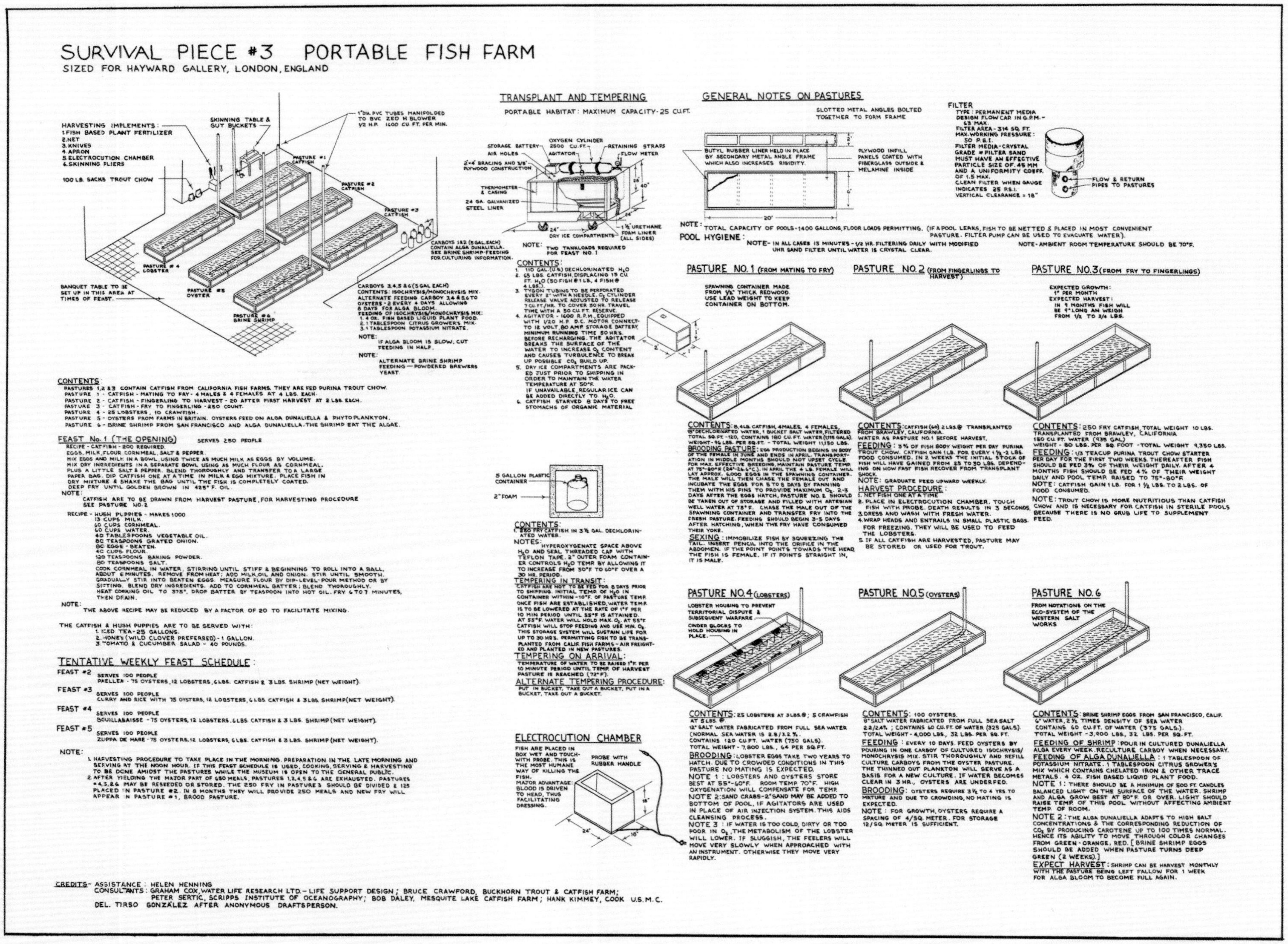

Newton explaining the work

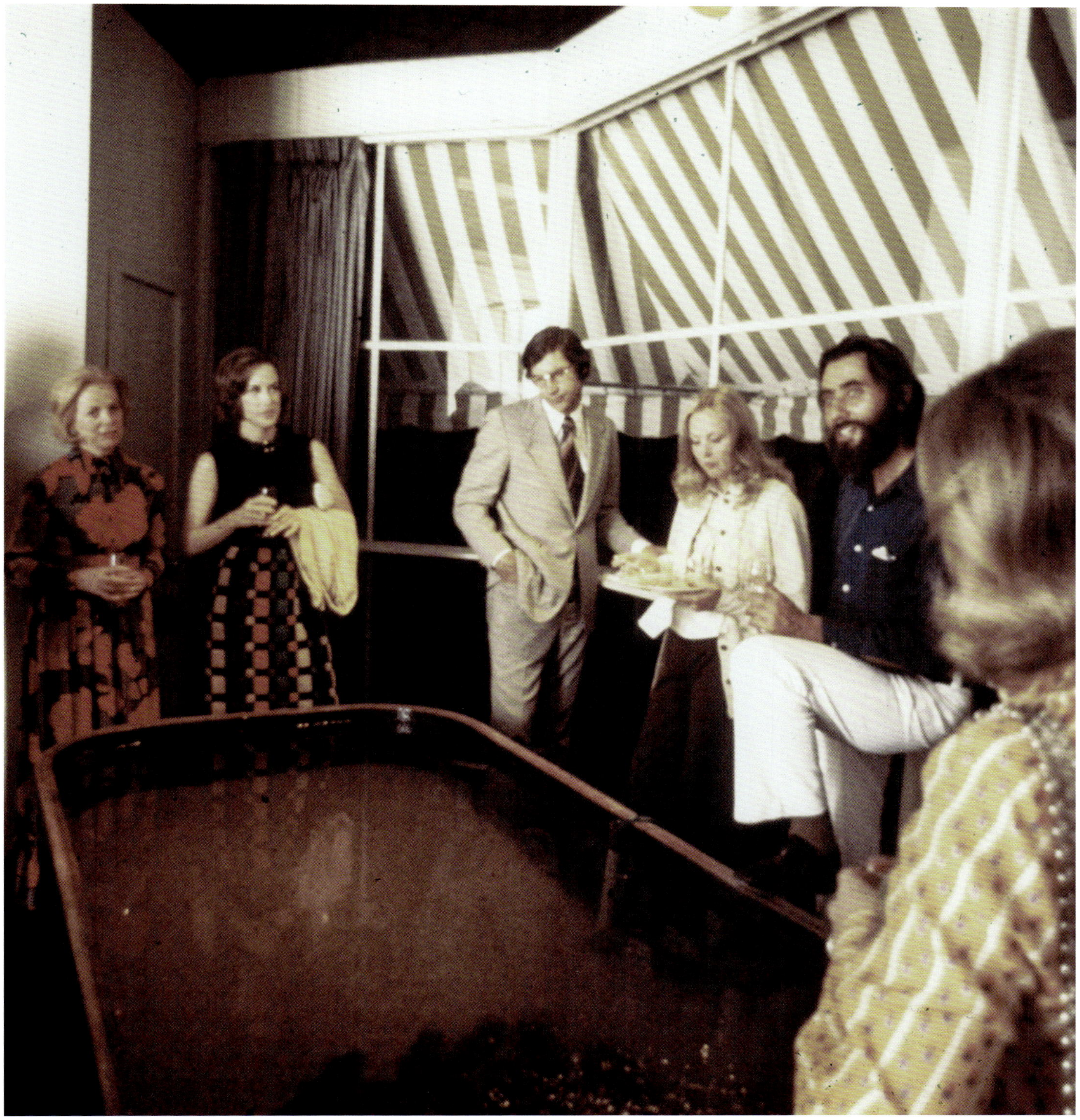

THE FEAST *

MATERIAL: 1. FRIED CATFISH - 200 REQUIRED - PREPARE AS FOLLOWS:
INGREDIENTS: EGGS, MILK, FLOUR, CORNMEAL, SALT + PEPPER.
MIX EGGS + MILK IN A BOWL USING TWICE AS MUCH MILK AS EGGS BY VOLUME. MIX DRY INGREDIENTS IN A SEPARATE BOWL, USING AS MUCH FLOUR AS CORNMEAL PLUS A LITTLE SALT + PEPPER, BLEND THOROUGHLY AND TRANSFER TO LARGE PAPER BAG. DIP CATFISH ONE AT A TIME IN MILK AND EGG MIXTURE, MAKING SURE THAT THE INSIDE OF THE FISH GETS COATED AS WELL AS THE OUTSIDE. PLACE FISH IN DRY MIXTURE AND SHAKE THE BAG UNTIL FISH IS COMPLETELY COATED. DEEP FRY IN 425° OIL.

NOTE: CATFISH (1/2 TO 3/4 lb EACH) ARE TO BE DRAWN FROM HARVEST PASTURE (FOR HARVESTING PROCEDURE SEE PASTURE No. 2 (FROM FINGERLINGS TO HARVEST)).

2. AT LEAST ONE PROFESSIONAL DEEP FISH FRYER.

3. HUSH PUPPIES - 1000 REQUIRED - PREPARE AS FOLLOWS:
13 CUPS MILK.
60 CUPS CORNMEAL.
60 CUPS WATER
40 TABLESPOONS VEGETABLE OIL.
80 TEASPOONS GRATED ONION
80 EGGS - BEATEN.
40 CUPS FLOUR.
120 TEASPOONS BAKING POWDER.
80 TEASPOONS SALT.
COOK CORN MEAL IN WATER, STIRRING UNTIL STIFF AND BEGINNING TO ROLL INTO A BALL, ABOUT 6 MIN. REMOVE FROM HEAT; ADD MILK, OIL AND ONION. STIR UNTIL SMOOTH. GRADUALLY STIR INTO BEATEN EGGS. MEASURE FLOUR BY DIP-LEVEL-POUR METHOD OR BY SIFTING. BLEND DRY INGREDIENTS. ADD TO CORN MEAL BATTER; BLEND THOROUGHLY. HEAT COOKING OIL TO 375° F. DROP BATTER BY TEASPOON INTO HOT OIL. FRY 6 TO 7 MIN. DRAIN.

NOTE: THE ABOVE RECIPE MAY BE REDUCED BY A FACTOR OF 20 TO FACILITATE MIXING.

4. ICED TEA - 25 GALLONS.

6. HONEY - WILD CLOVER - 1 GALLON

7. TOMATO + CUCUMBER SALAD - 40 lbs.

* SERVES 250 PEOPLE.

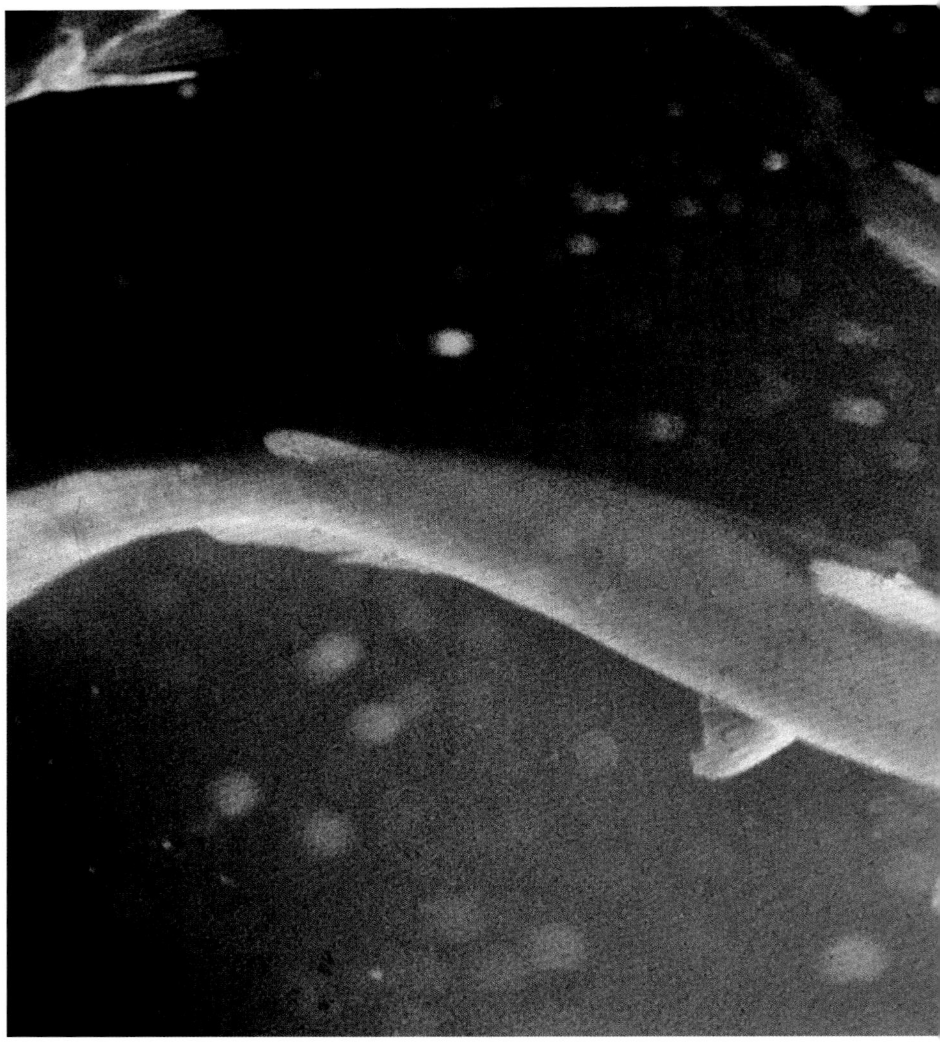

invention: "Each work is concerned with how we feed ourselves and attempts to reveal co-dependence in natural systems in the way organisms live, reproduce and die, enabling the energy of the system to continue to work."[56]

Nonetheless, it took years of research before the Harrisons fully discovered the conditions necessary to sustain an ecosystem. Helen and Newton started at the right time, when ecology was just becoming a new field of research. Their work was strikingly different in scale and method from Sol LeWitt's dematerialized instruction-based art or from monumental works in the land art genre, such as Michael Heizer's *Double Negative* (1969) or Robert Smithson's *Spiral Jetty* (1970). Like no other artists, the Harrisons made a distinction between ecology and growable, nourishable (and nourishing) materials like soil, as Newton explained: "We feel that our works were among the first to deal with ecology in the full sense of the term. The key test for ecological art is the concept of the niche…. We mapped out the basic terrain of the kind of work we still believe in. At that time, we were especially interested in primitivity and strength in ecosystems."[57] Inspired by their own discoveries and intuition, they then made the collective decision to do no work that did not benefit ecosystems.

The Harrisons undoubtedly pushed the framework of late-sixties conceptual and land art in a new direction. The portable orchards, vegetable gardens, and fish farms, initially installed

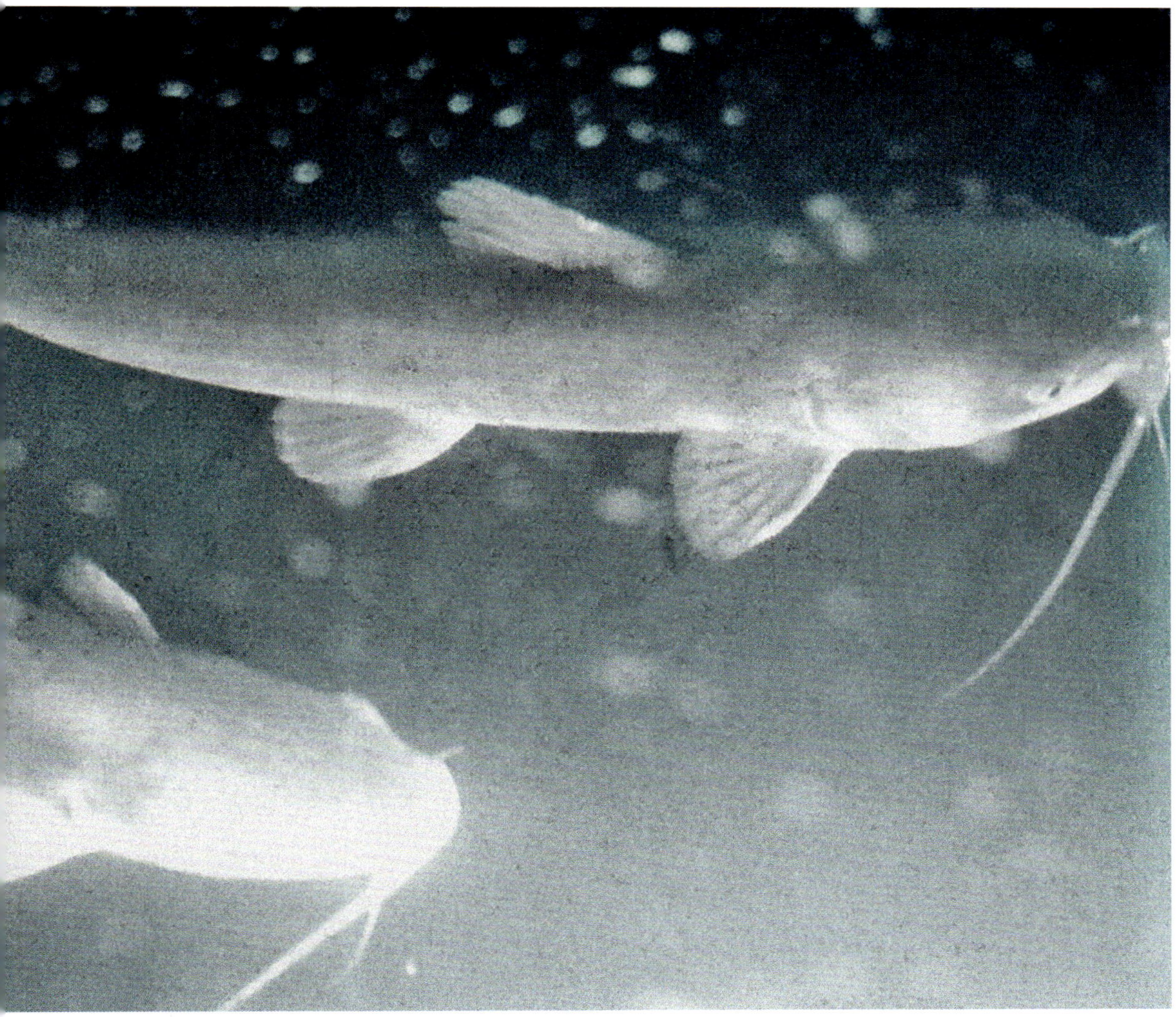

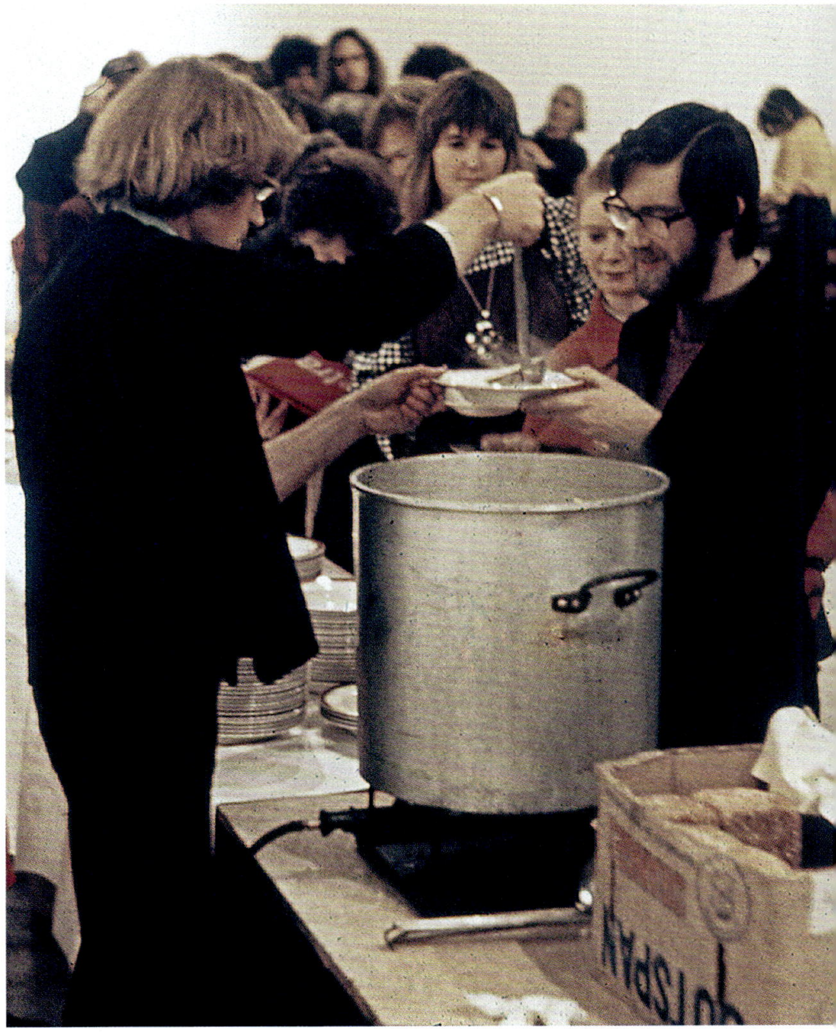

in galleries, set the precedent for their subsequent complex ecosystem work in urban contexts. The *Survival Pieces* both functioned as an early warning system for environmental catastrophe and offered suggestions for surviving calamitous times. As design prototypes for indoor and backyard farming, the *Survival Pieces* called for a transformation of the industrialized food system with its inherent pollution. Over time, the growing impact of climate change not only deepened their commitment to environmentally focused work but also fully confirmed their ethical departure from Billy Klüver's *Experiments in Art and Technology* (E.A.T.) (1966–1970) and Maurice Tuchman's *Art and Technology Program* (1966–1971).

The *Survival Pieces* opened the door for the Harrisons to produce works of art that engaged real-world ecological situations throughout the 1970s, 1980s, and 1990s. The artists developed a range of innovative projects that combined exhibition presentations and performances in galleries, museums, and city halls with field-based research work that sought to inform and influence governmental policies and planning. With a focus on art and ecology, they collaborated extensively with politicians, members of the scientific community (including figures such as John Isaacs at the Scripps Institute of Oceanography) as well as urban and regional planners, utilizing a complex systems perspective.

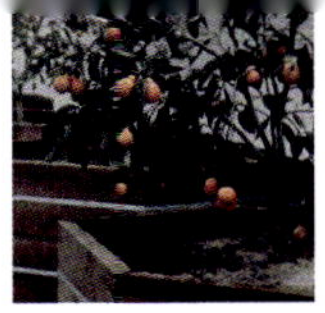

Survival Piece V: Portable Orchard, 1972 installation at California State University, Fullerton, CA

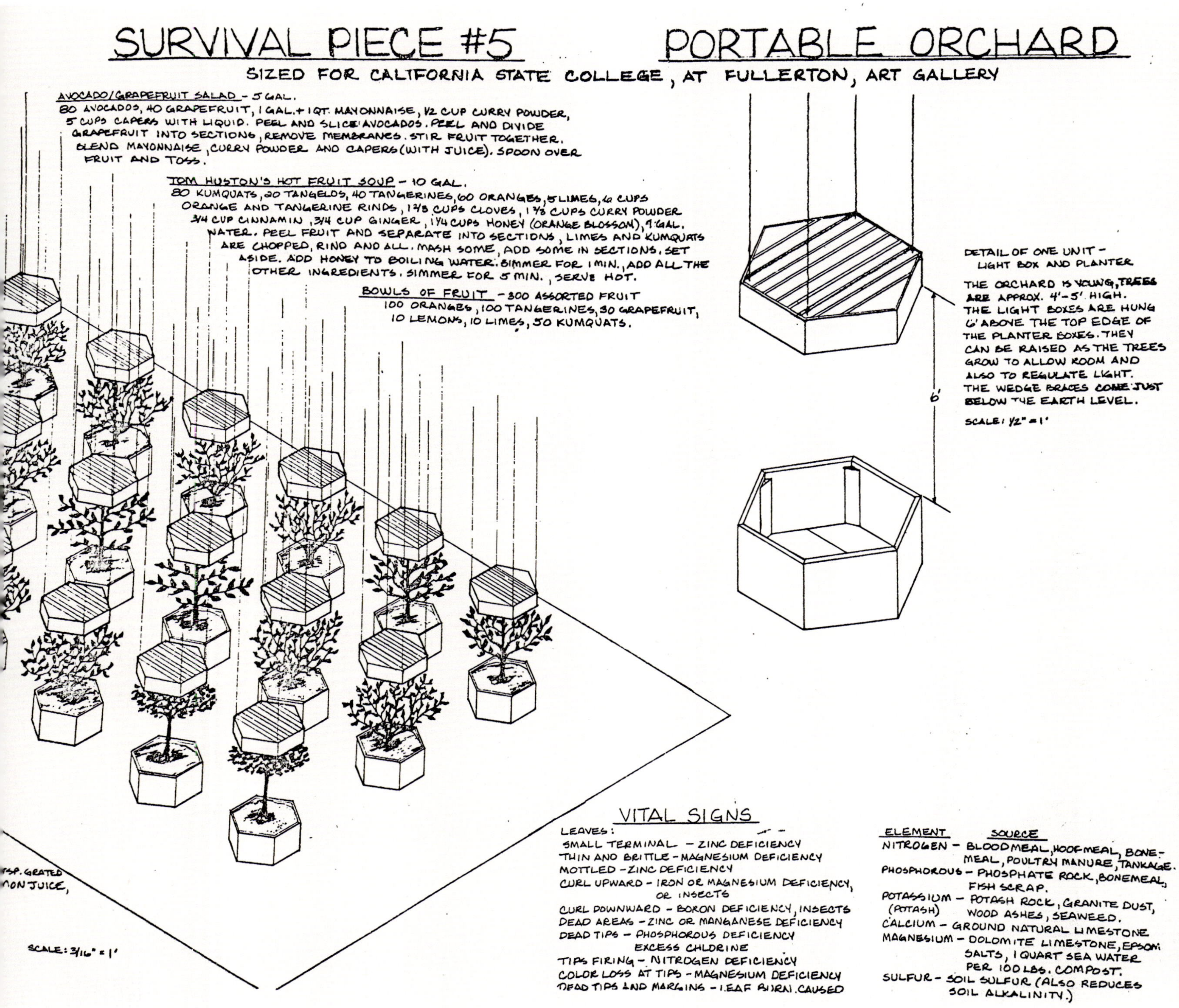

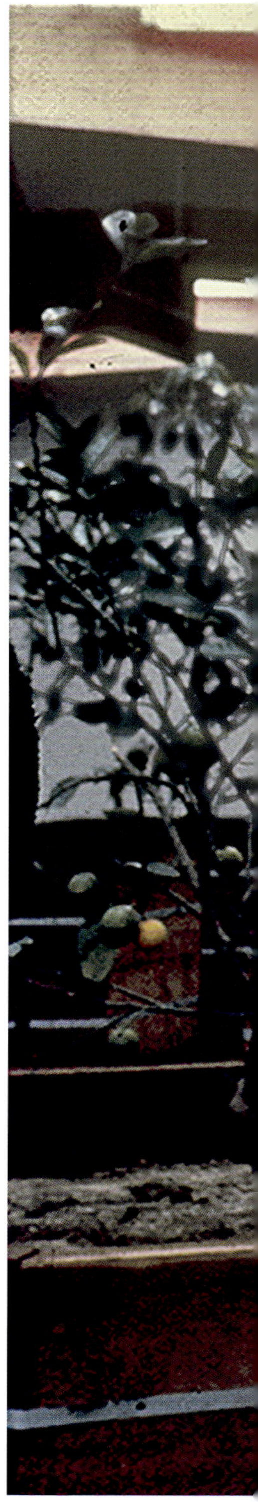

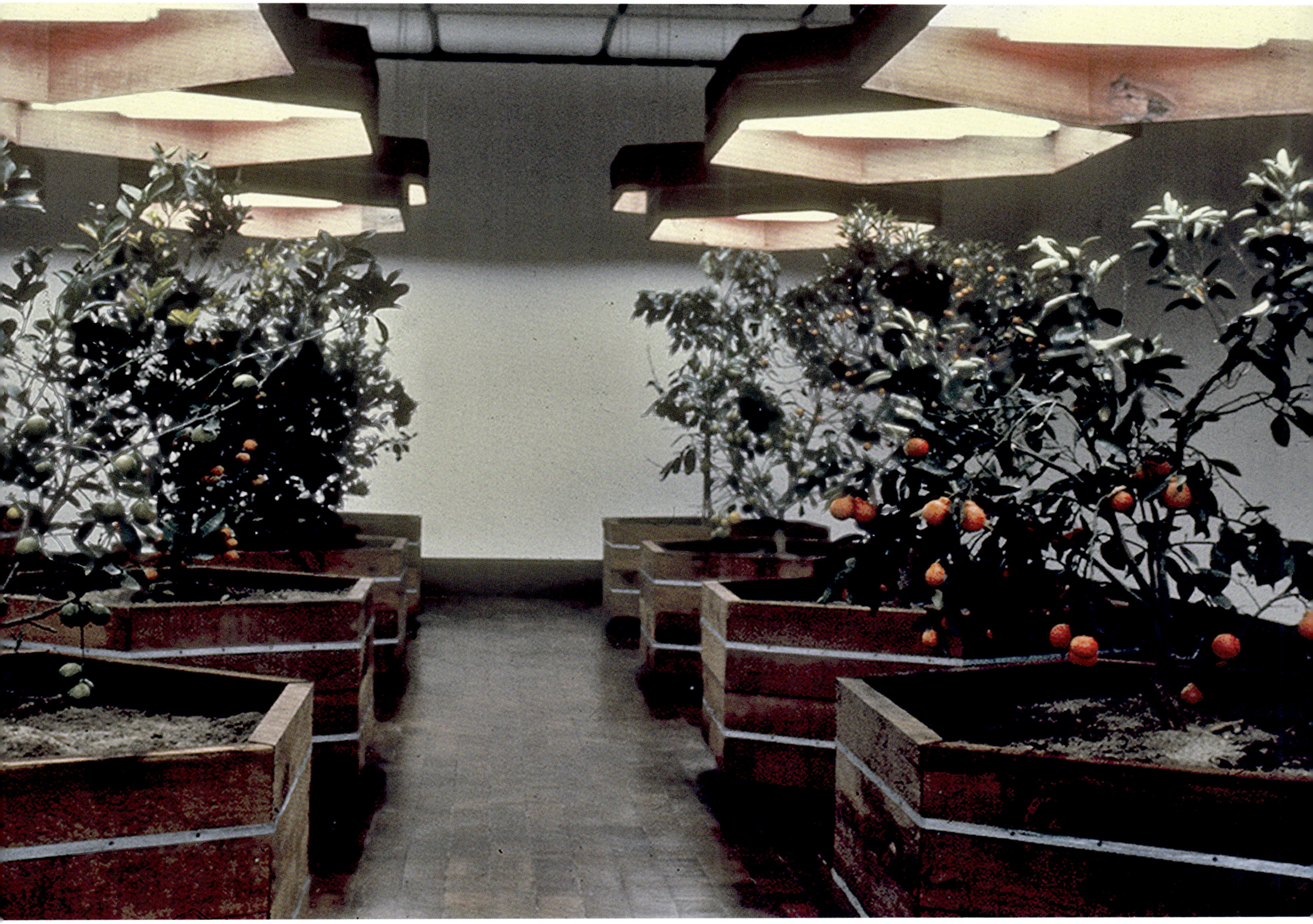

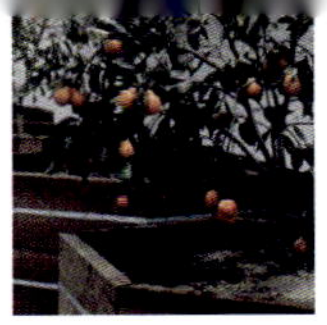

Survival Piece V: Portable Orchard, 1972, drawings and instructions for the installation at California State University, Fullerton, CA

Survival Piece 6: Portable Farm, 1972 Contemporary Arts Museum Houston, TX Installation sketch Helen planting Upright and flat pastures

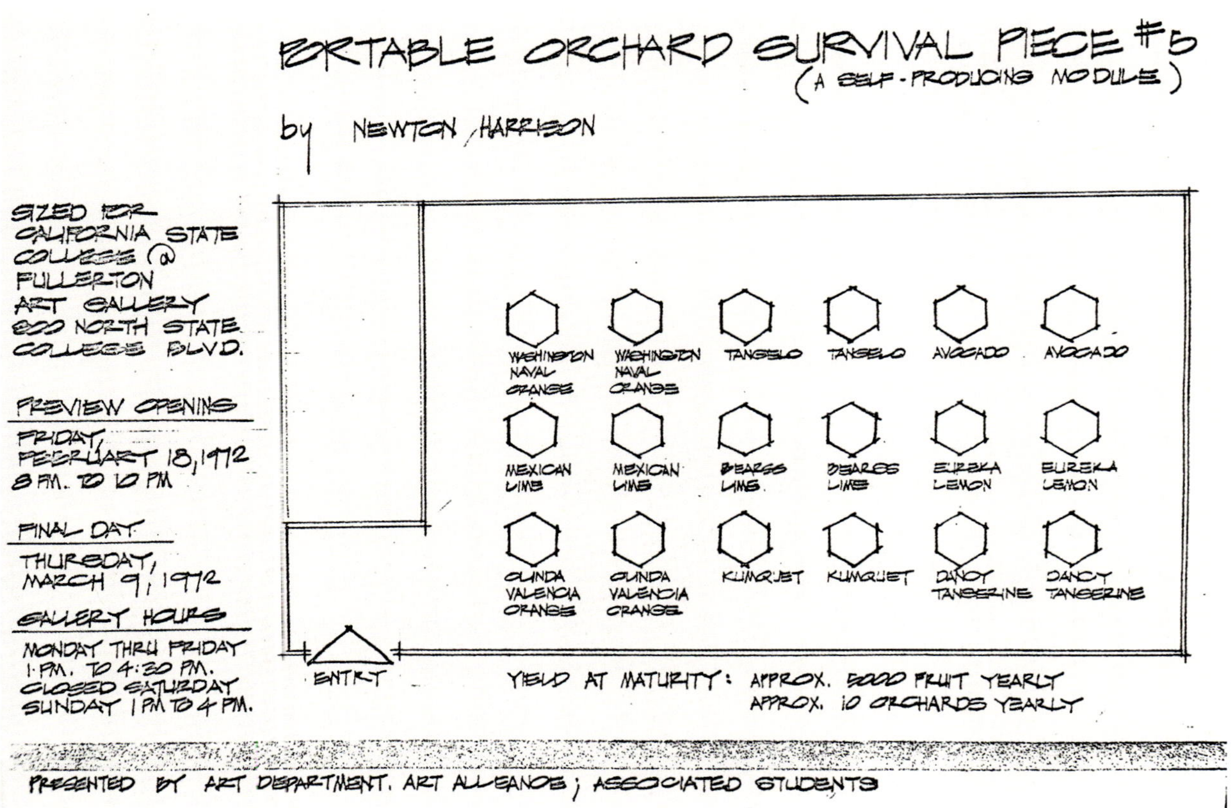

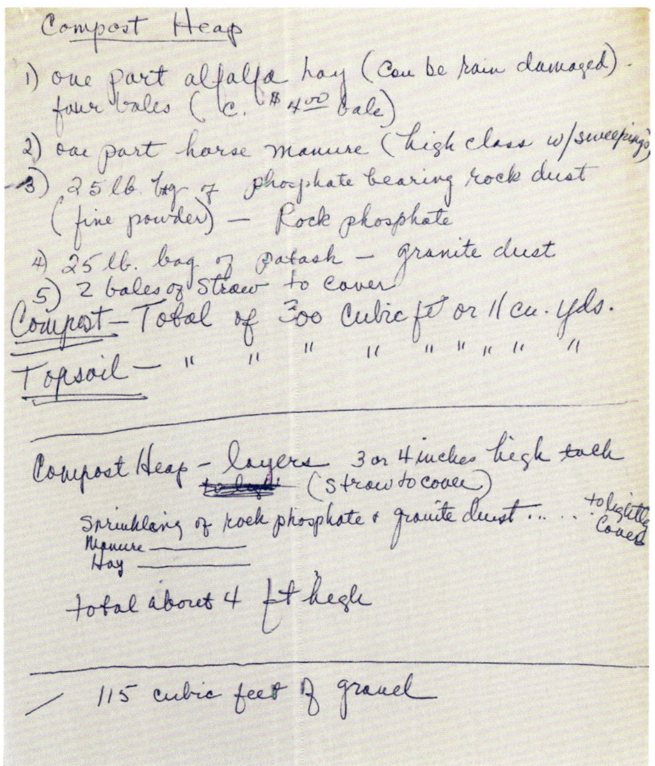

Compost Heap

1) one part alfalfa hay (Can be rain damaged) four bales (c. $4.00 bale)
2) one part horse manure (high class w/sweepings)
3) 25 lb bag of phosphate bearing rock dust (fine powder) — Rock phosphate
4) 25 lb. bag of potash — granite dust
5) 2 bales of straw to cover

Compost — Total of 300 cubic ft or 11 cu. yds.
Topsoil — " " " " " " " "

Compost Heap — layers 3 or 4 inches high each (straw to cover)
Sprinkling of rock phosphate & granite dust ... to lightly cover
Manure
Hay
total about 4 ft high

/ 115 cubic feet of gravel

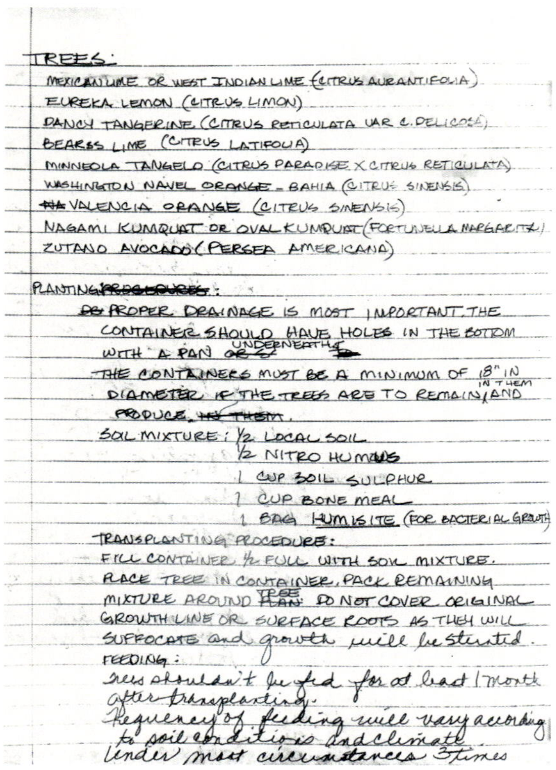

TREES:
MEXICAN LIME OR WEST INDIAN LIME (CITRUS AURANTIFOLIA)
EUREKA LEMON (CITRUS LIMON)
DANCY TANGERINE (CITRUS RETICULATA VAR C. DELICOSA)
BEARSS LIME (CITRUS LATIFOLIA)
MINNEOLA TANGELO (CITRUS PARADISE X CITRUS RETICULATA)
WASHINGTON NAVEL ORANGE - BAHIA (CITRUS SINENSIS)
~~NA~~ VALENCIA ORANGE (CITRUS SINENSIS)
NAGAMI KUMQUAT OR OVAL KUMQUAT (FORTUNELLA MARGARITA)
ZUTANO AVOCADO (PERSEA AMERICANA)

PLANTING ~~PROCEDURES~~:
~~DO~~ PROPER DRAINAGE IS MOST IMPORTANT. THE CONTAINER SHOULD HAVE HOLES IN THE BOTTOM WITH A PAN ~~OR~~ UNDERNEATH.
THE CONTAINERS MUST BE A MINIMUM OF 18" IN DIAMETER IF THE TREES ARE TO REMAIN IN THEM AND PRODUCE. ~~IN THEM~~.
SOIL MIXTURE: 1/2 LOCAL SOIL
1/2 NITRO HUMUS
1 CUP SOIL SULPHUR
1 CUP BONE MEAL
1 BAG HUMISITE (FOR BACTERIAL GROWTH)
TRANSPLANTING PROCEDURE:
FILL CONTAINER 1/2 FULL WITH SOIL MIXTURE.
PLACE TREE IN CONTAINER, PACK REMAINING MIXTURE AROUND TREE. DO NOT COVER ORIGINAL GROWTH LINE OR SURFACE ROOTS AS THEY WILL SUFFOCATE and growth will be stunted.
FEEDING:
Trees shouldn't be fed for at least 1 month after transplanting.
Frequency of feeding will vary according to soil conditions and climate
Under most circumstances 3 times

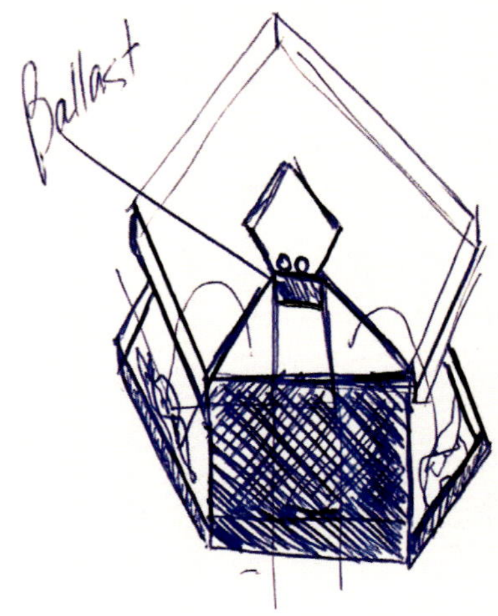

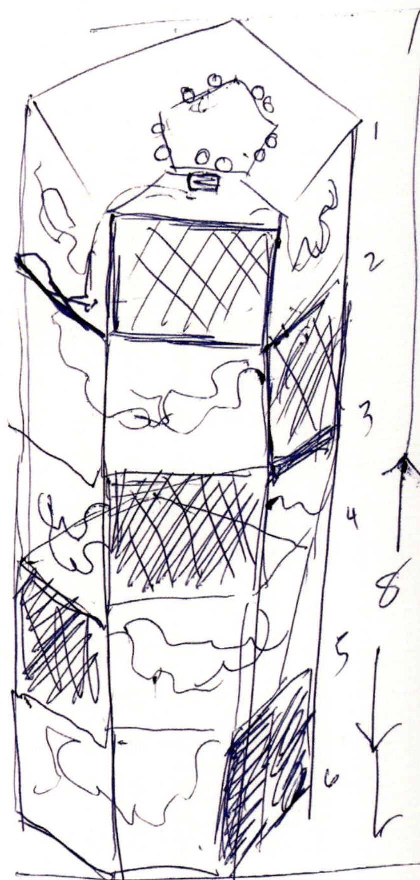

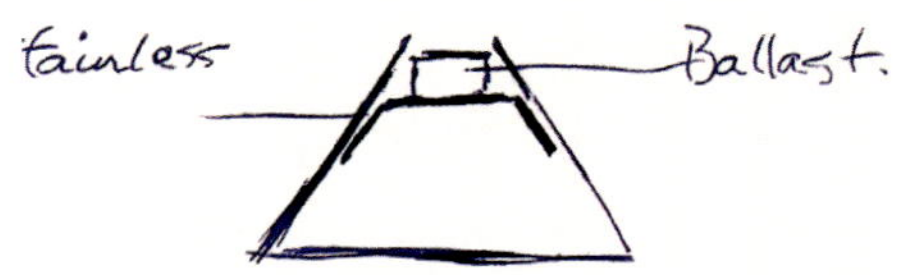

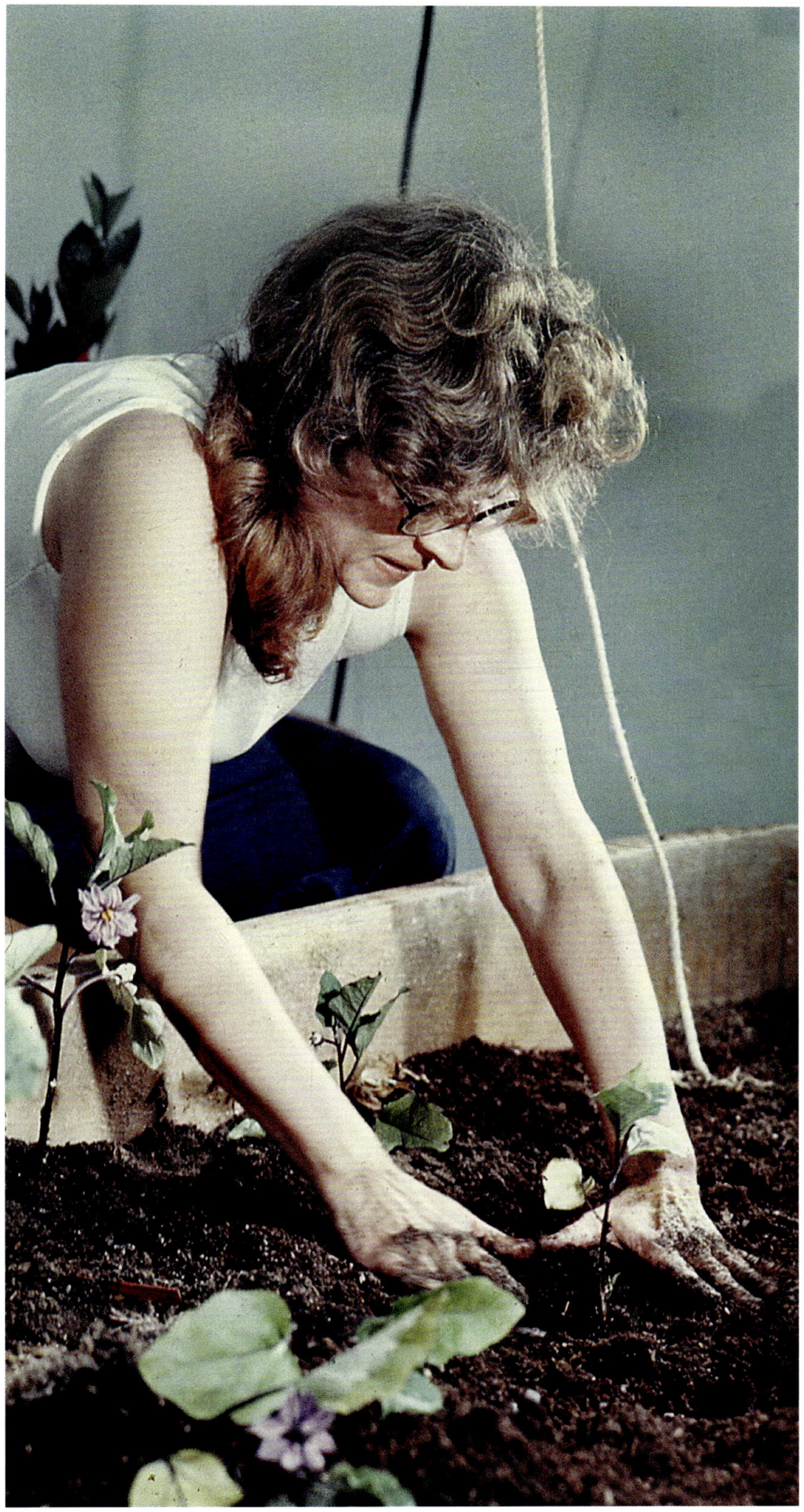
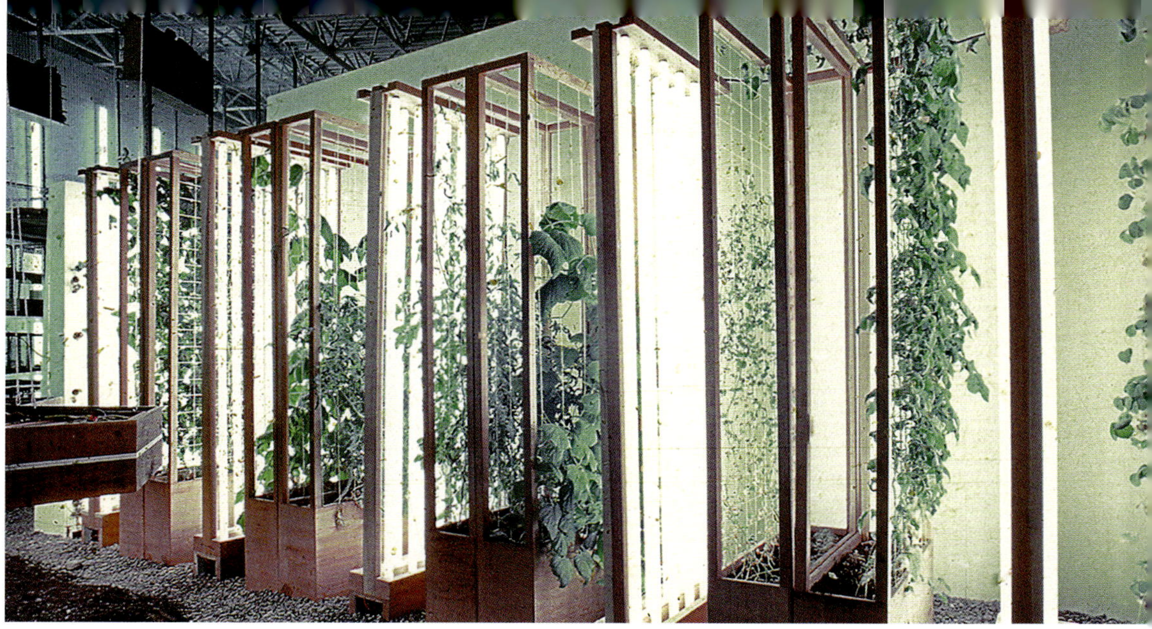
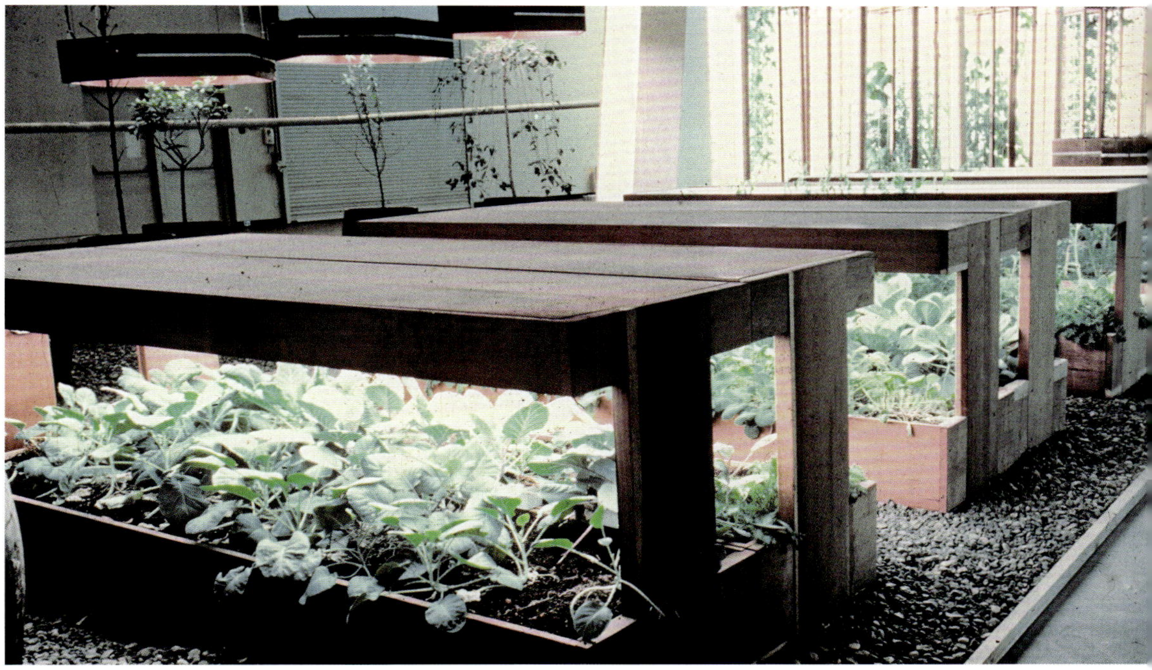
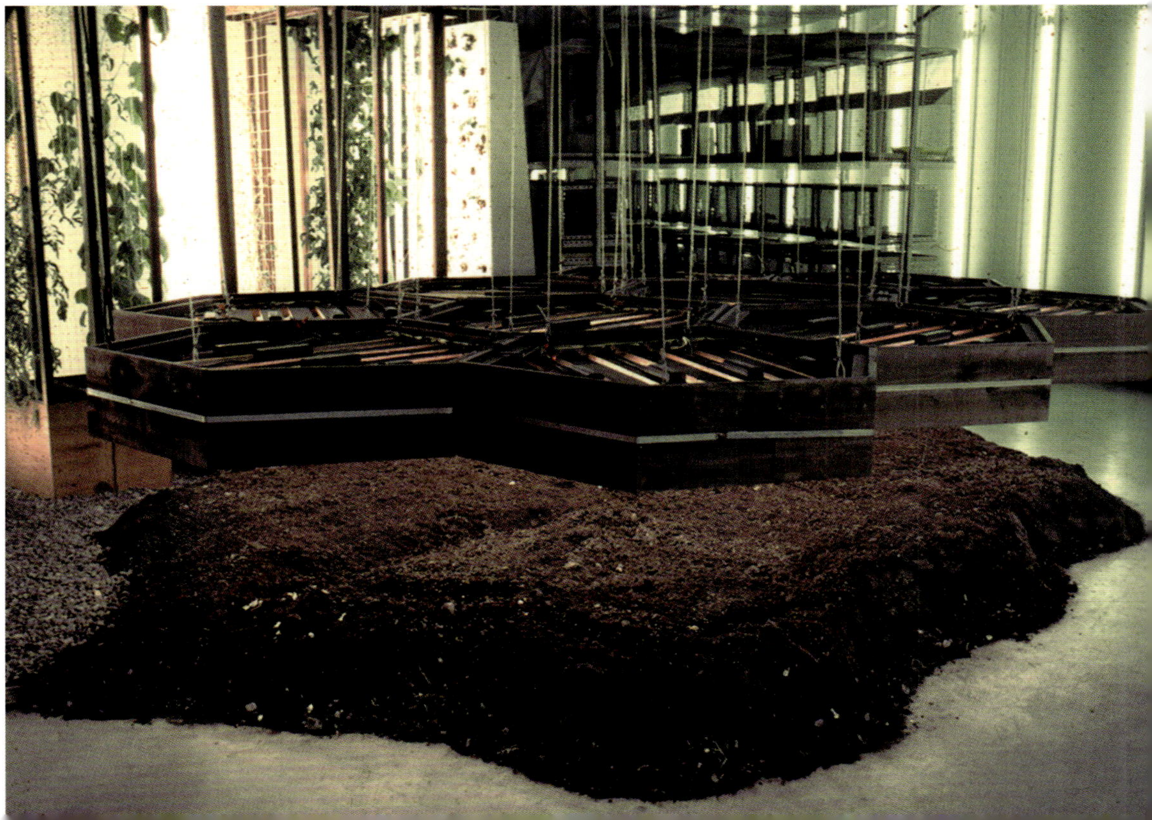

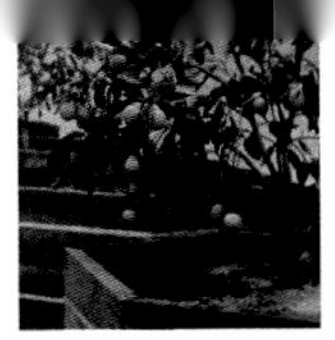

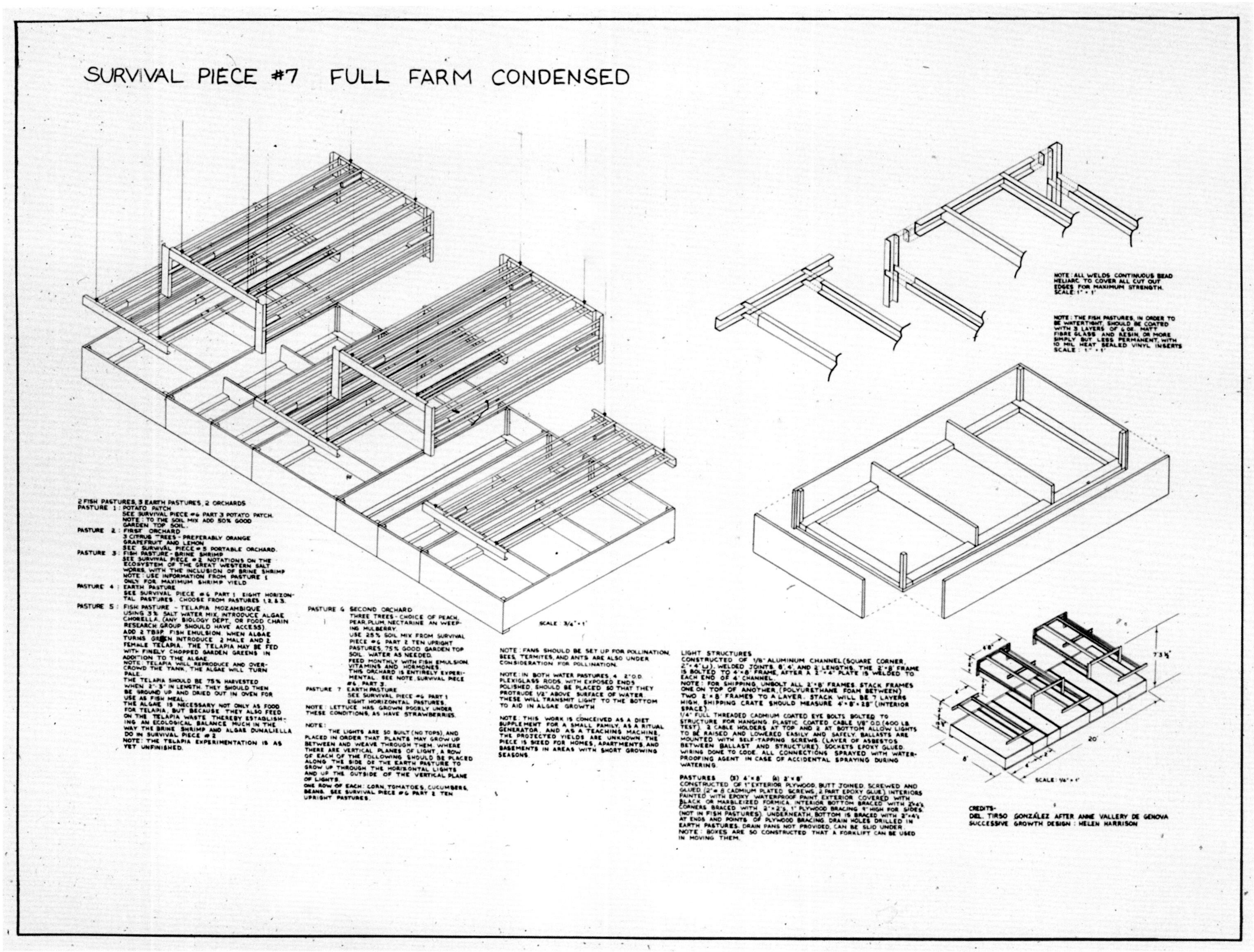
SURVIVAL PIECE #7 FULL FARM CONDENSED
2 FISH PASTURES, 3 EARTH PASTURES, 2 ORCHARDS
PASTURE 1: POTATO PATCH
SEE SURVIVAL PIECE #6 PART 3 POTATO PATCH.
NOTE: TO THE SOIL MIX ADD 50% GOOD GARDEN TOP SOIL.
PASTURE 2: FIRST ORCHARD
3 CITRUS TREES - PREFERABLY ORANGE GRAPEFRUIT AND LEMON
SEE SURVIVAL PIECE #5 PORTABLE ORCHARD.
PASTURE 3: FISH PASTURE - BRINE SHRIMP
SEE SURVIVAL PIECE #2 NOTATIONS ON THE ECOSYSTEM OF THE GREAT WESTERN SALT WORKS, WITH THE INCLUSION OF BRINE SHRIMP
NOTE: USE INFORMATION FROM PASTURE 1 ONLY FOR MAXIMUM SHRIMP YIELD
PASTURE 4: EARTH PASTURE
SEE SURVIVAL PIECE #6 PART 1 EIGHT HORIZONTAL PASTURES. CHOOSE FROM PASTURES 1, 2, & 3.
PASTURE 5: FISH PASTURE - TELAPIA MOZAMBIQUE
USING 3% SALT WATER MIX, INTRODUCE ALGAE CHORELLA. (ANY BIOLOGY DEPT., OR FOOD CHAIN RESEARCH GROUP SHOULD HAVE ACCESS).
ADD 2 TBSP. FISH EMULSION. WHEN ALGAE TURNS GREEN INTRODUCE 2 MALE AND 2 FEMALE TELAPIA. THE TELAPIA MAY BE FED WITH FINELY CHOPPED GARDEN GREENS IN ADDITION TO THE ALGAE.
NOTE: TELAPIA WILL REPRODUCE AND OVERCROWD THE TANK, THE ALGAE WILL TURN PALE.
THE TELAPIA SHOULD BE 75% HARVESTED WHEN 2"-3" IN LENGTH. THEY SHOULD THEN BE GROUND UP AND DRIED OUT IN OVEN FOR USE AS FISH MEAL.
THE ALGAE IS NECESSARY NOT ONLY AS FOOD FOR TELAPIA, BUT BECAUSE THEY ALSO FEED ON THE TELAPIA WASTE THEREBY ESTABLISHING AN ECOLOGICAL BALANCE MUCH IN THE WAY THE BRINE SHRIMP AND ALGAE DUNALIELLA DO IN SURVIVAL PIECE #2
NOTE: THE TELAPIA EXPERIMENTATION IS AS YET UNFINISHED.
PASTURE 6 SECOND ORCHARD
THREE TREES - CHOICE OF PEACH, PEAR, PLUM, NECTARINE AN WEEPING MULBERRY.
USE 25% SOIL MIX FROM SURVIVAL PIECE #6 PART 2 TEN UPRIGHT PASTURES, 75% GOOD GARDEN TOP SOIL. WATER AS NEEDED.
FEED MONTHLY WITH FISH EMULSION, VITAMINS AND HORMONES.
THIS ORCHARD IS ENTIRELY EXPERIMENTAL. SEE NOTE, SURVIVAL PIECE #6, PART 3.
PASTURE 7 EARTH PASTURE
SEE SURVIVAL PIECE #6 PART 1 EIGHT HORIZONTAL PASTURES.
NOTE: LETTUCE HAS GROWN POORLY UNDER THESE CONDITIONS, AS HAVE STRAWBERRIES.
NOTE: THE LIGHTS ARE SO BUILT (NO TOPS), AND PLACED IN ORDER THAT PLANTS MAY GROW UP BETWEEN AND WEAVE THROUGH THEM. WHERE THERE ARE VERTICAL PLANES OF LIGHT, A ROW OF EACH OF THE FOLLOWING SHOULD BE PLACED ALONG THE SIDE OF THE EARTH PASTURE TO GROW UP THROUGH THE HORIZONTAL LIGHTS AND UP THE OUTSIDE OF THE VERTICAL PLANE OF LIGHTS.
ONE ROW OF EACH: CORN, TOMATOES, CUCUMBERS, BEANS. SEE SURVIVAL PIECE #6 PART 2 TEN UPRIGHT PASTURES.
SCALE: 3/4" = 1'
NOTE: FANS SHOULD BE SET UP FOR POLLINATION, BEES, TERMITES, AND ANTS ARE ALSO UNDER CONSIDERATION FOR POLLINATION.
NOTE: IN BOTH WATER PASTURES, 4 2" O.D. PLEXIGLASS RODS, WITH EXPOSED ENDS POLISHED, SHOULD BE PLACED SO THAT THEY PROTRUDE 1/2" ABOVE SURFACE OF WATER. THESE WILL TRANSMIT LIGHT TO THE BOTTOM TO AID IN ALGAE GROWTH
NOTE: THIS WORK IS CONCEIVED AS A DIET SUPPLEMENT FOR A SMALL FAMILY, AS A RITUAL GENERATOR, AND AS A TEACHING MACHINE. THE PROJECTED YIELDS ARE UNKNOWN. THE PIECE IS SIZED FOR HOMES, APARTMENTS, AND BASEMENTS IN AREAS WITH SHORT GROWING SEASONS.
LIGHT STRUCTURES
CONSTRUCTED OF 1/8" ALUMINUM CHANNEL (SQUARE CORNER, 2" × 4" ⊔), WELDED JOINTS 8', 4', AND 2' LENGTHS. THE 2' × 8' FRAME IS BOLTED TO 4' × 8' FRAME, AFTER A 2" × 4" PLATE IS WELDED TO EACH END OF 4' CHANNEL.
NOTE: FOR SHIPPING, UNBOLT ALL 2' × 8' FRAMES. STACK FRAMES ONE ON TOP OF ANOTHER, (POLYURETHANE FOAM BETWEEN) TWO 2' × 8' FRAMES TO A LAYER. STACK WILL BE 7 LAYERS HIGH, SHIPPING CRATE SHOULD MEASURE 4' × 8' × 28" (INTERIOR SPACE).
1/4" FULL THREADED CADMIUM COATED EYE BOLTS BOLTED TO STRUCTURE FOR HANGING. PLASTIC COATED CABLE 1/8" O.D. (400 LB TEST). 2 CABLE HOLDERS AT TOP AND 2 AT BOTTOM ALLOW LIGHTS TO BE RAISED AND LOWERED EASILY AND SAFELY. BALLASTS ARE MOUNTED WITH SELF-TAPPING SCREWS. (LAYER OF ASBESTOS BETWEEN BALLAST AND STRUCTURE). SOCKETS EPOXY GLUED. WIRING DONE TO CODE. ALL CONNECTIONS SPRAYED WITH WATERPROOFING AGENT IN CASE OF ACCIDENTAL SPRAYING DURING WATERING.
PASTURES (3) 4' × 8' (4) 2' × 8'
CONSTRUCTED OF 1" EXTERIOR PLYWOOD, BUTT JOINED, SCREWED AND GLUED (2" × 8 CADMIUM PLATED SCREWS, 2 PART EPOXY GLUE) INTERIORS PAINTED WITH EPOXY WATERPROOF PAINT. EXTERIOR COVERED WITH BLACK OR MARBLEIZED FORMICA. INTERIOR BOTTOM BRACED WITH 2"×4"s CORNERS BRACED WITH 2" × 2"s, 1" PLYWOOD BRACING 9" HIGH FOR SIDES (NOT IN FISH PASTURES). UNDERNEATH, BOTTOM IS BRACED WITH 2"×4"s AT ENDS AND POINTS OF PLYWOOD BRACING. DRAIN HOLES DRILLED IN EARTH PASTURES. DRAIN PANS NOT PROVIDED, CAN BE SLID UNDER.
NOTE: BOXES ARE SO CONSTRUCTED THAT A FORKLIFT CAN BE USED IN MOVING THEM.
NOTE: ALL WELDS CONTINUOUS BEAD HELIARC TO COVER ALL CUT OUT EDGES FOR MAXIMUM STRENGTH. SCALE: 1" = 1'
NOTE: THE FISH PASTURES, IN ORDER TO BE WATERTIGHT, SHOULD BE COATED WITH 3 LAYERS OF 6 OZ. MATT FIBRE GLASS AND RESIN, OR MORE SIMPLY BUT LESS PERMANENT, WITH 10 MIL HEAT SEALED VINYL INSERTS SCALE: 1" = 1'
4'8"
7'3 1/2"
20'
8'
SCALE: 1/4" = 1'
CREDITS-
DEL. TIRSO GONZÁLEZ AFTER ANNE VALLERY DE GENOVA
SUCCESSIVE GROWTH DESIGN: HELEN HARRISON

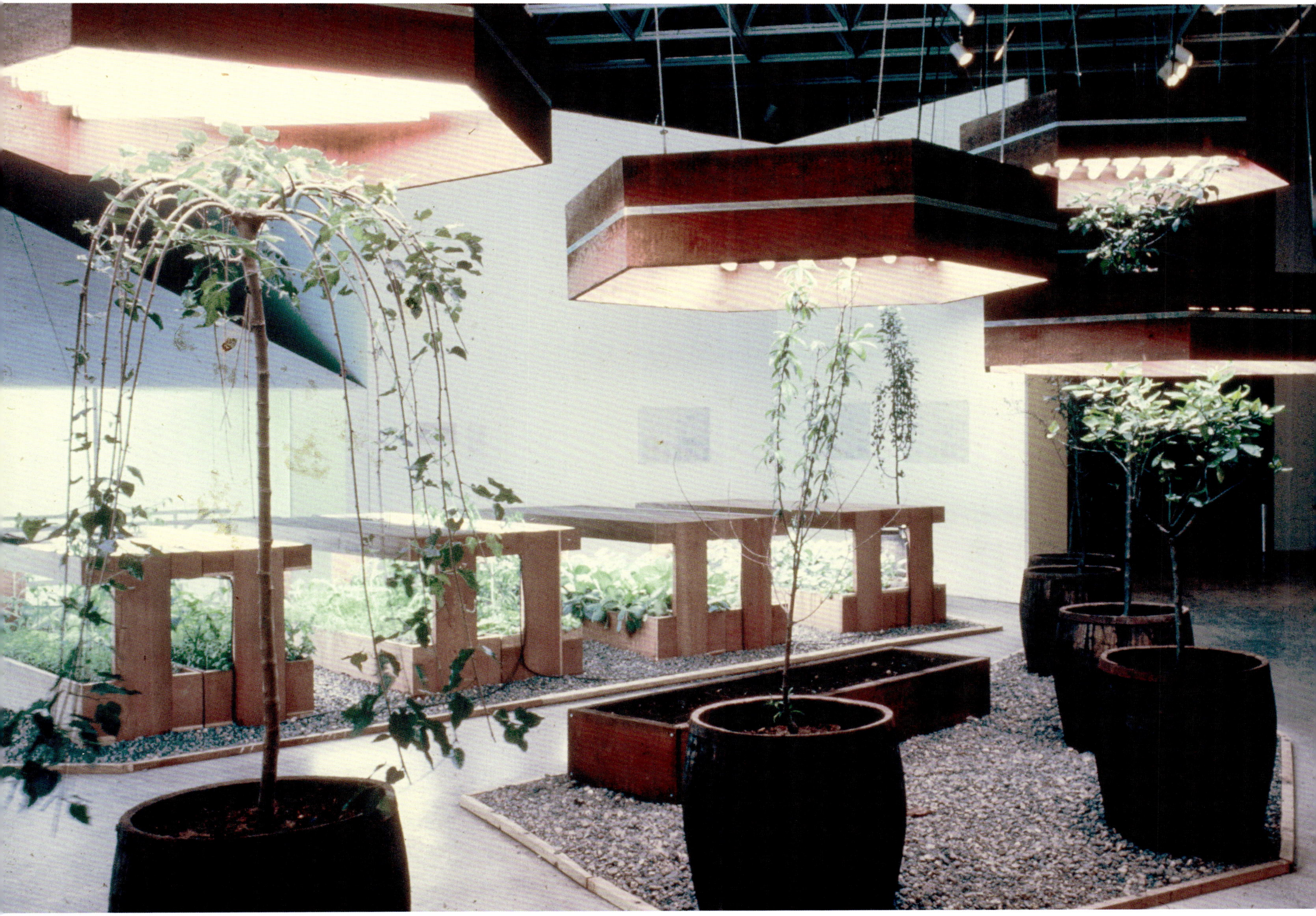

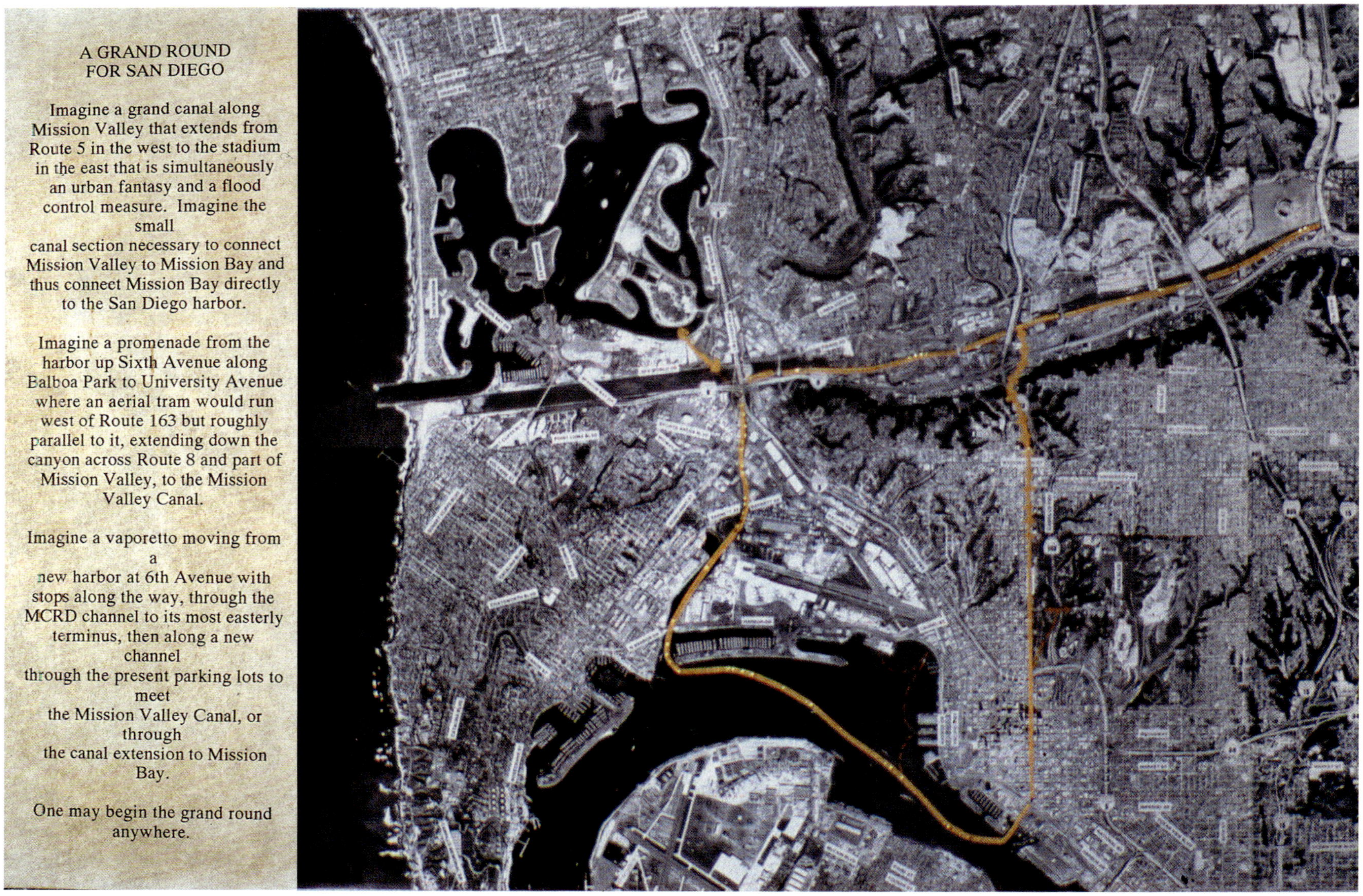

RECLAIMING AND VISUALIZING NEW URBAN ECOLOGIES

The Harrisons produced art in the form of installations, comprising recognizable media: diagrams, maps, photographs, plans, conceptual design drawings, and poetic descriptions. These materials were mounted, framed, and hung like artworks in museums and galleries, and they behaved like works of art. However, they were real-life design proposals dealing with factual ecological and environmental issues. Written in poetic form, the Harrisons' "eco-cultural" visions spoke volumes to government agencies and the broader public about issues concerning modern society's ecological impact on specific locales such as *Arroyo Secco Release* (1985) and *Devil's Gate Debris Basin* (1987–1991) in Pasadena, as well as land reclamation such as *Miramar Landfill* (1992) in San Diego.[58] The eco-critical works from this period showcase the Harrisons' key ecological concerns: how to restore endangered rivers, watersheds, and canyons that were fragmented in California by dams and flood control channels. These works anticipated major questions of the future and tested a range of viable ecological approaches that became central to their later works, which were developed in a global context.

Arroyo Seco Release, A Serpentine for Pasadena (1985) was of one of the principal projects that pointedly mapped out urban ecologies compromised by widespread use of flood control channels in Greater Los Angeles.[59] According to the artists' research, 90 percent of Los Angeles rivers were channel-

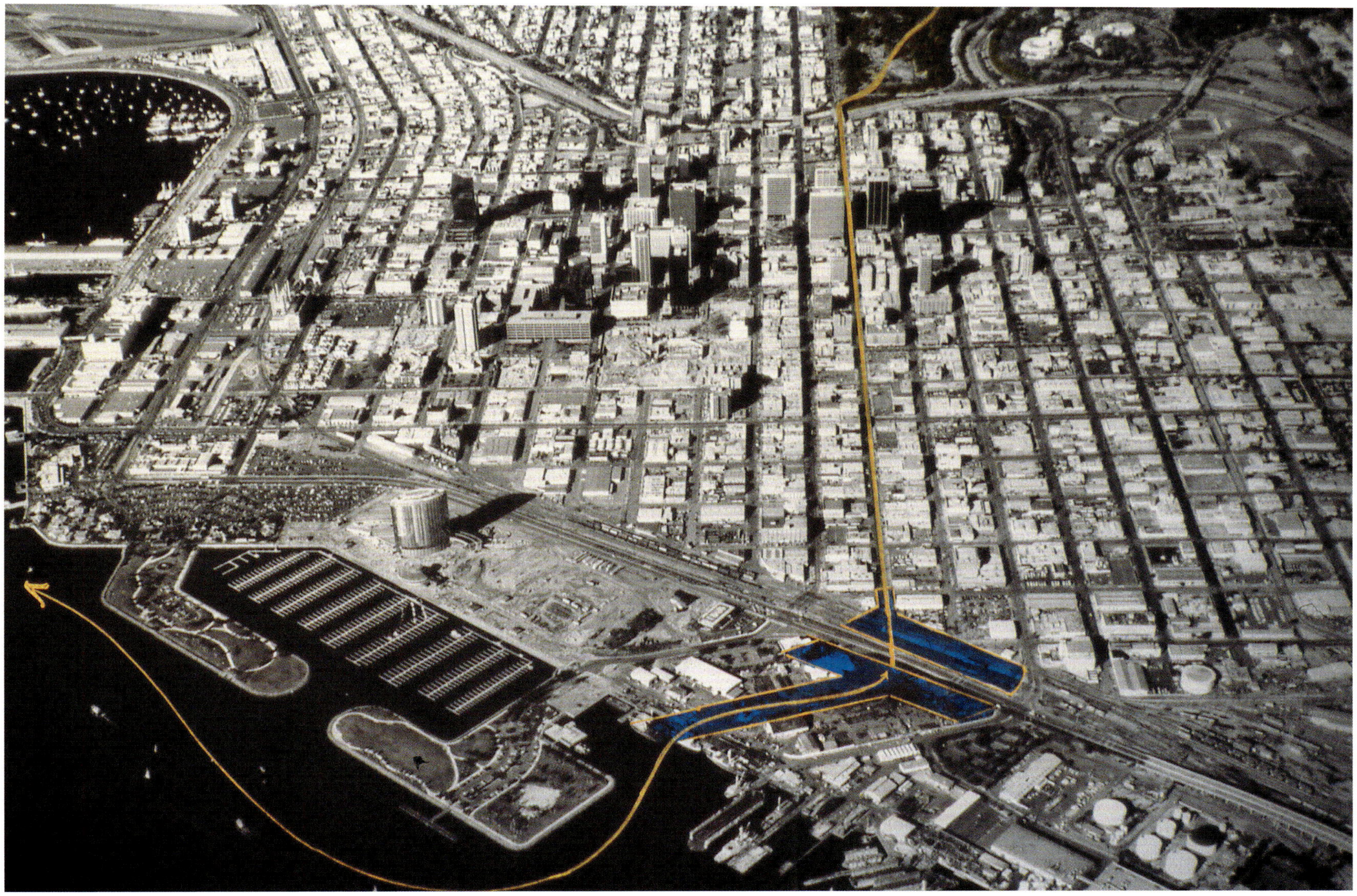

ized without any conservation considerations. Invited by the Pasadena Garden Club, the artists investigated ecological conditions in the lower Arroyo, which had been turned into a ten-foot-deep concrete flood control channel that caused ecosystem fragmentation and the destruction of the original habitat.[60] Maintaining close ties to the local community, the artists explored the possibilities of converting the Arroyo Seco to better uses. Ideas were developed during a visit to Pasadena to address the Western Regional meeting of the Garden Clubs of America, and the work was supported by funding from the Pasadena Art Alliance. The *Arroyo Seco Release* was exhibited and performed initially in the Baxter Art Gallery at the California Institute of Technology, while a shorter version was displayed in the Council Chambers of Pasadena City Hall. Reviewing the Harrisons' exhibition, writer Sam Kaplan called the proposal "the foremost imaginative piece of landscape architecture that deserves serious consideration."[61]

Through a series of convincing conceptual design panels, photographic illustrations, and poetic texts, Helen and Newton visualized a new model in which the concrete spillways were transformed into a park land with a beautiful stream running through it. However, before any work could be started, Devil's Gate Dam, above the Arroyo Seco, had to be repaired. Employing metaphors, the artists spoke of a need to heal the "wound in the land," referring to "the concrete flood control channel surrounded by ten-foot fences topped with

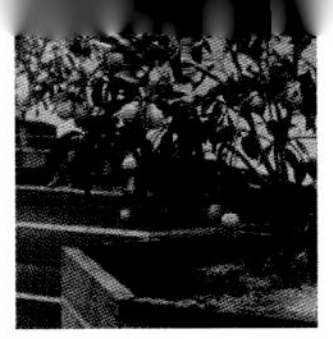

Devil's Gate, a Refugia for Pasadena, 1987 Downtown Gallery, Los Angeles ArtCenter College of Design, Pasadena, CA

barbed wire in which the small local river, the Arroyo Seco, is contained."[62] The Harrisons' proposal aimed to conceal the existing channel with a concrete cap, covered by earth and planted with native grasses and shrubs. The flood control channel would continue to function as an underground conduit, taking the periodic floodwaters to the sea.

The artists estimated that Pasadena would gain an 84-acre park in a densely packed urban-suburban environment. They also hoped that one day, the *Arroyo Seco Release* could be used as a new model for reclaiming all the rivers in the Los Angeles Basin. In the exhibit catalogue, Jay Belloli wrote that the artists intended to reconstitute nature, while also employing up-to-date technology: "Ultimately, the *Arroyo Seco Release* is a model for using technology to help return a natural system to its original appearance and function ... The technology remains, but it is placed underground. What is visible is a metaphor for the environment."[63] The Harrisons wrote in their drawings that the river became continuous, the banks were continuous, and the Arroyo was made whole again:

Imagine every channel in the LA Basin
Covered
And land remade green
And low-flow streambeds established
Where the logic and the will exist

Then new walkways to the sea could be developed
Land added easing crowded terrain
And new public space engendered

Then ribbons of green will run down to the sea
And birds and small life return
As sanctuaries are formed here and there ...[64]

The artists projected that an associated cost of ten million dollars would be needed to reestablish the stream and to bring this unique public space into existence.

The Harrisons' work in Pasadena anticipates the future rehabilitation of the Los Angeles River, which has yet to be done, by ripping up ugly concrete flood channels and taking down nasty fences, re-terraforming the land into a magnificent natural reserve made with the spine of continuous parks instead of open sewers. Other cities in the nation, such as Boston, Denver, New York, Phoenix, and San Antonio, paved the way by landscaping their own rivers into attractive public amenities with the gentle flow of waters. The press and public expressed disappointment when the Harrisons' proposal was not funded due to the lack of, as Kaplan put it, "a sympathetic understanding of the region's varied ecology among the planning and engineering officials of the city."[65]

Devil's Gate, A Refuge for Pasadena,[66] later retitled by the Gabrielino Indians the *Hahamongna State Watershed Park* (1987–1998) was a separate project that further highlighted the artists' commitment to the restoration of natural habitats, regional parks, and watersheds near the Jet Propulsion Laboratory in Pasadena. This project was initiated in order to address the repair work needed to the dam to move forward with *Arroyo Seco Release*. Ernie Messner, a Pasadena resident who was working as a state land acquisition lawyer, was instrumental in making the city take a new look at the area. Messner's efforts also helped to secure city funding necessary for the Harrisons' $30,000 "environmental sculpture." Other support came from the National Endowment for the Arts. In the project development stage, the artists prepared and exhibited a series of area photographs, conceptual design drawings, and a 15-foot clay model. Helen and Newton formulated a new narrative for the region with the proposed lake, waterfalls, and natural habitats while also recommending how to improve the flood control properties of the Devil's Gate Dam. This work alone shows the Harrisons' novel approach to land reclamation of specific watersheds in California.[67]

The 15-foot clay model, now lost and existing only in photographs, was made by Newton and first presented at the Los Angeles Art Center/Downtown Gallery on Colorado Boulevard. In her report Ashley Dunn called Newton's proposal "a vision

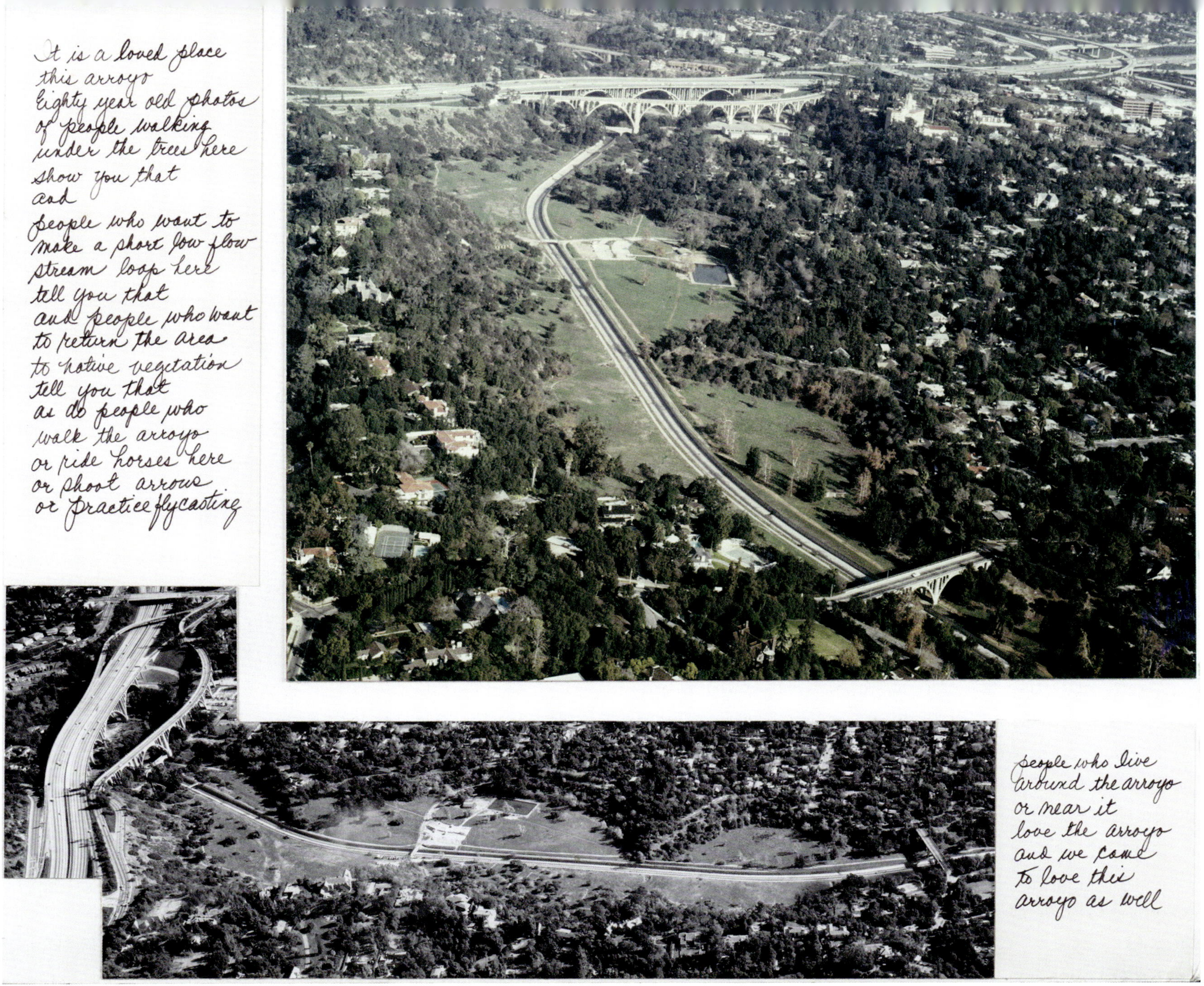

of a sculptor, engineer, and ecologist."[68] The desolate Devil's Gate Reservoir was destined to become an enlarged Oak Grove Regional Park, a public amenity blending, as Newton explained, "a variety of uses, including recreation, wildlife preservation, and water conservation"... and, most important, "wedding the urban and natural ecologies."[69] In her interview with the *Los Angeles Times*, Helen concurred with Newton, stating that the whole purpose of the project was "to reinvent the ecology" there.[70] The Harrisons planned to replace piles of gravel and debris with a pair of winding streams, fed by a two-mile-long pipeline tapped into a Metropolitan Water District that would nourish reeds and trees and would also replenish the reservoir. Parking lots would become wildlife habitats, accessible through a web of nature trails, and a 10- to 15-acre green stretch of land near Oak Grove Park would accommodate a restaurant and playing fields.

The Harrisons' vision was a dramatic departure from the way most people regarded the area. On maps, the Devil's Gate Reservoir appeared as a cool, blue expanse of water, but in reality, the flat area between La Canada Flintridge and Altadena, just north of the 210 Freeway, was a large debris basin full of toxic waste: rocky silt washed down from the mountains and mixed with debris, waste from illegal dumping, and carcinogenic organic chemicals originating from JPL. The area's ecology declined due to the dam and flood control channels that were built in 1920 to impede the flow of water during the rainy season. In the 1970s, the Devil's Gate Dam was declared earthquake-unsafe and the county abandoned maintenance of the area altogether, which led to ecological decline and further contamination.

Central to the Harrisons' plan was the construction of a two-mile pipeline that would restore the reservoir and provide a system to preserve water in the area during regional water shortages. The other important component of the design was its terraforming efforts, consisting of the removal of 3 million cubic yards of dirt, silt, and debris accumulated behind the 68-year-old dam, as well as the reshaping of stream beds, hills, and embankments. The total cost of the Harrisons' vision was estimated at $40 million, according to Thomas K. Underbrink, a city Water and Power Department engineer, who served as project manager. Despite the admittedly high cost, Underbrink argued that it would be worthwhile to fund the project as the restored reservoir would serve well in the future.

In the final conceptual design *A String of Pearls* (1987), the artists drew the Devil's Gate Dam relieved of stress, a 25-acre percolation lake in wet seasons, habitat islands for the lake, a new stream running through the debris basin, a new woodland riparian habitat, and a new percolation basin to create a refuge for wildlife. The largest planned geographic feature was Butterfly Hillside, a 20- to 30-foot-high mound to be planted with flowers such as wild lilacs to attract butterflies, and therefore birds, the foundation for a new ecological system, according to the artists. Just south of Butterfly Hill, the Harrisons envisioned a riverbank environment with plants, animals, and trees such as willows, sycamores, and cottonwoods, which had disappeared over the years. The accompanying poetic text articulated the Harrisons' vision, prophetically insisting that it was absolutely necessary to "separate the process of flood control from the destruction of rivers" in California:

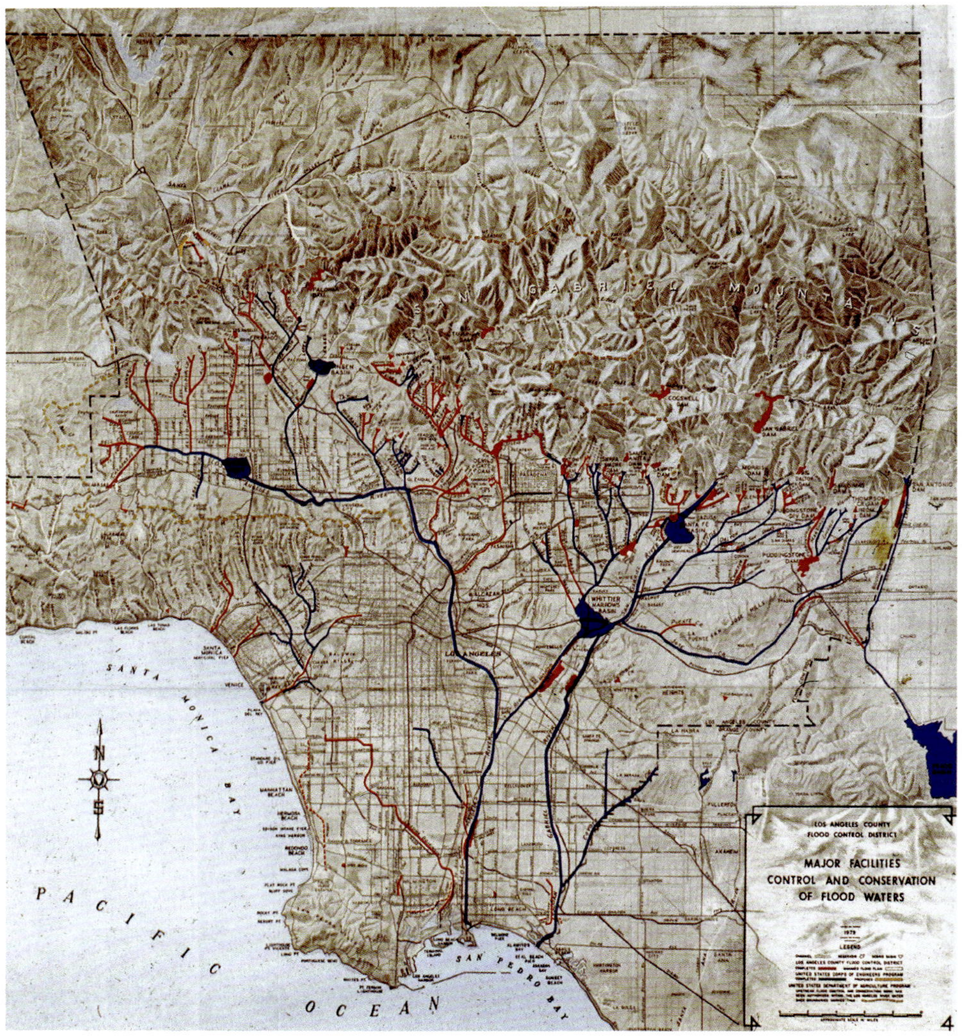

4

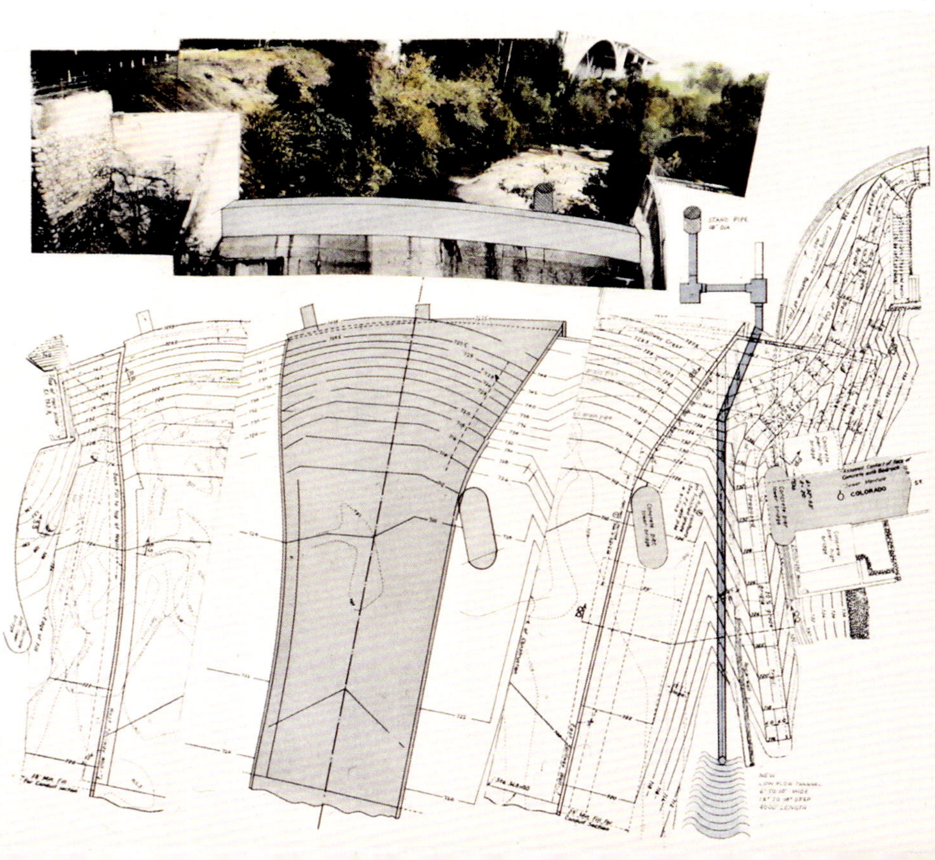

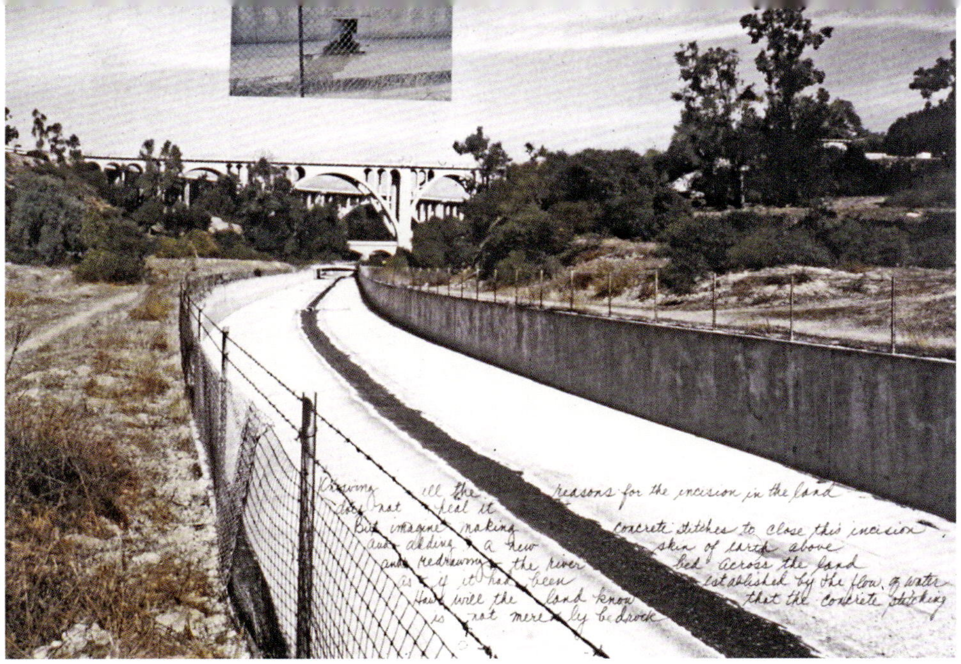

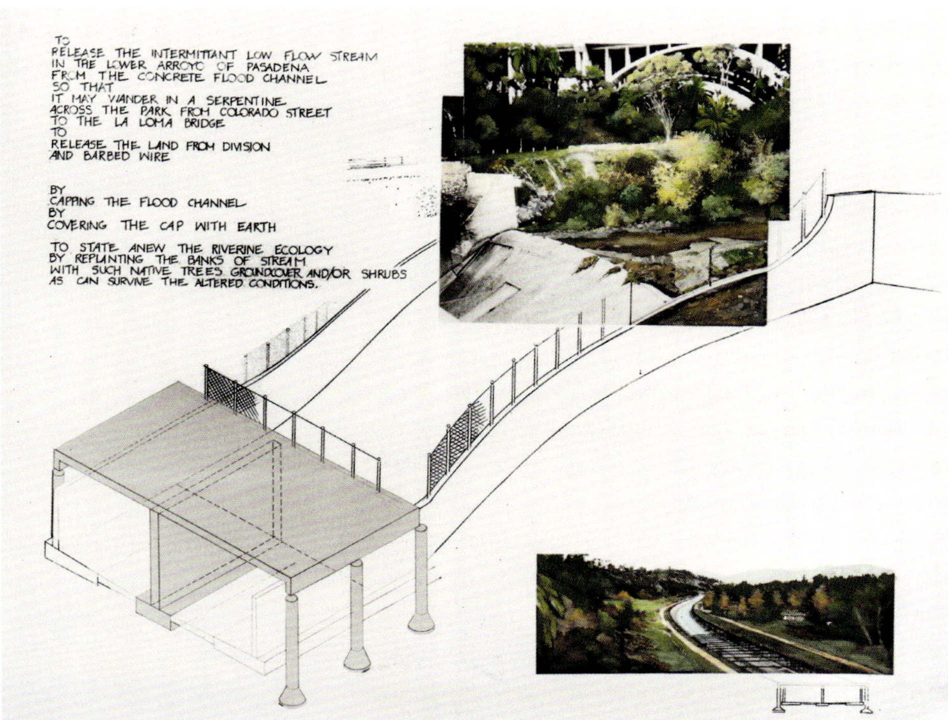

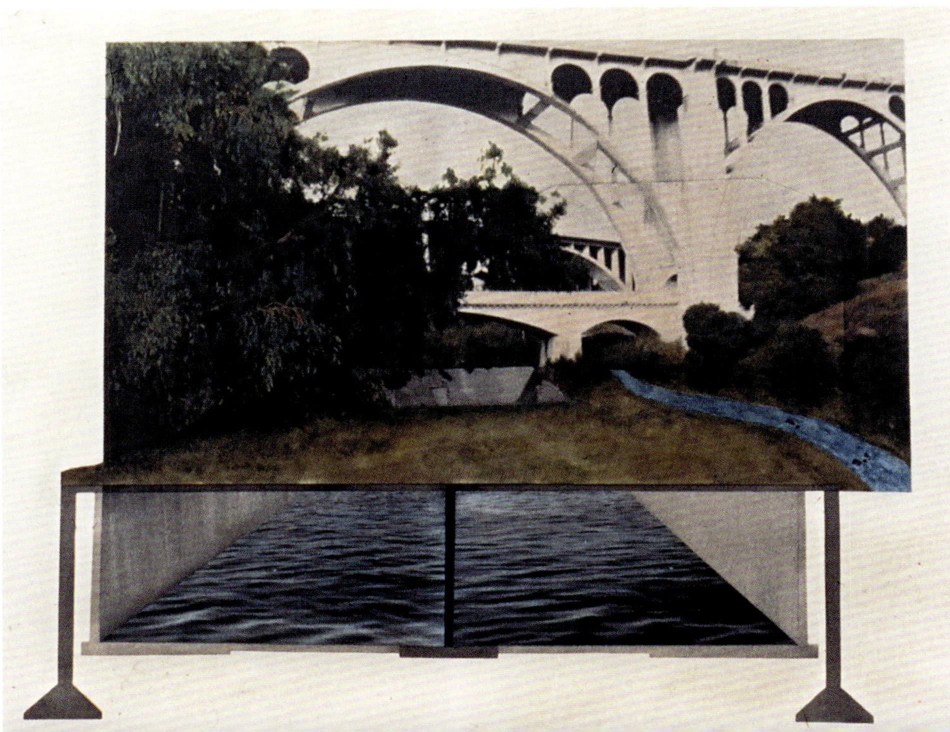

But,
It is possible to separate
the process of flood control
from the destruction of rivers
and riverine ecologies

It is possible to separate
the process of flood control
from the creation of debris basin dumps

It is possible to reconstruct debris basins
bringing back habitat

It is not difficult to combine
the process of flood control
with the generation of new semi-wilderness
and urban ecologies

Nor is it difficult to combine
the process of water conservation
with the generation of new riparian habitats
If
we value generating a new state in nature
that co-joins the urban
and the semi-wilderness ecologies
while benefiting flood control
and storing waters against future need
protecting habitat endangered elsewhere
and adding parklands

Then
It is neither difficult in the short run
nor expensive in the long run
to put these ideas into effect in
Devil's Gate Basin

That basin and dam
designed to catch debris
hold water
and percolate water down
to the Raymond Basin Aquifer underneath.

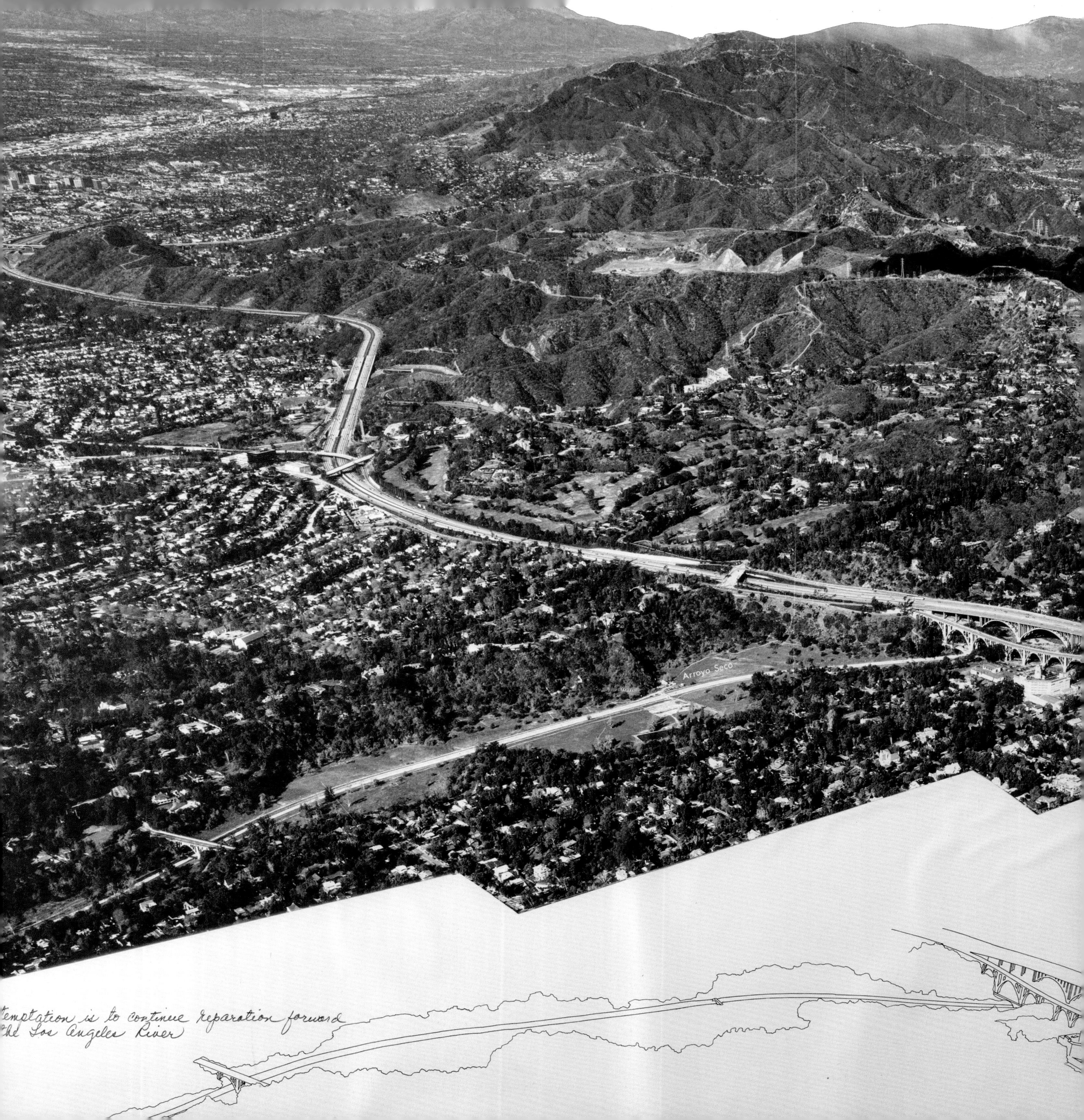
Arroyo Seco
temptation is to continue reparation forward
the Los Angeles River

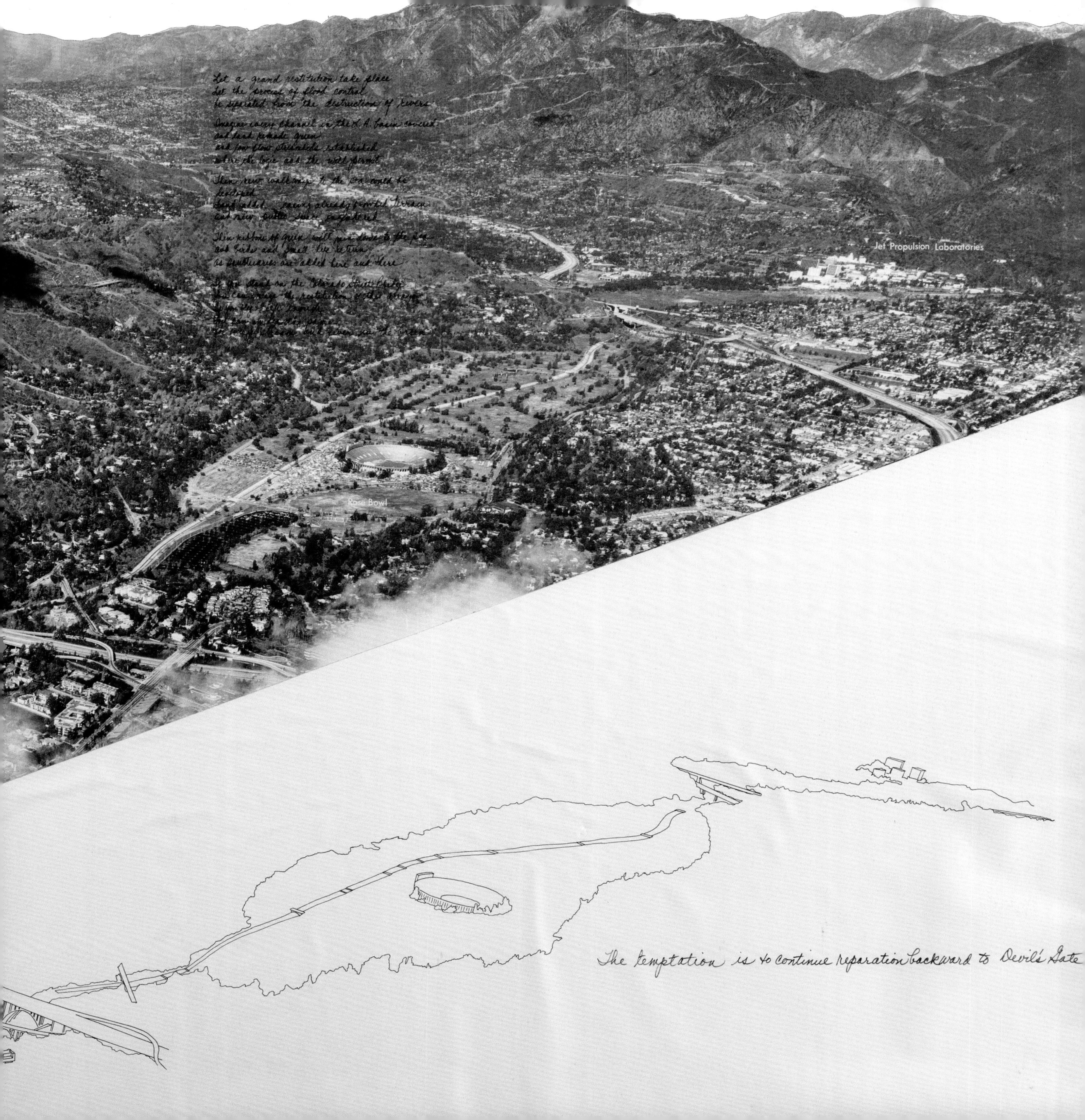
Let a grand restitution take place
Let the process of flood control
be separated from the destruction of rivers
Imagine every channel in the L.A. basin covered
and land remade green
and low flow streambeds established
where the logic and the will permit
Then new walkways to the sea could be
developed
and new public space engendered
Then ribbons of green will run down to the sea
and birds and small life return
as sanctuaries are added here and there
Jet Propulsion Laboratories
Rose Bowl
The temptation is to continue reparation backward to Devil's Gate

▲▼ Devil's Gate Refugia for Pasadena: A String of Pearls (Retitled by the Gabrielino Indians Hahamogna State Watershed Park), 1987

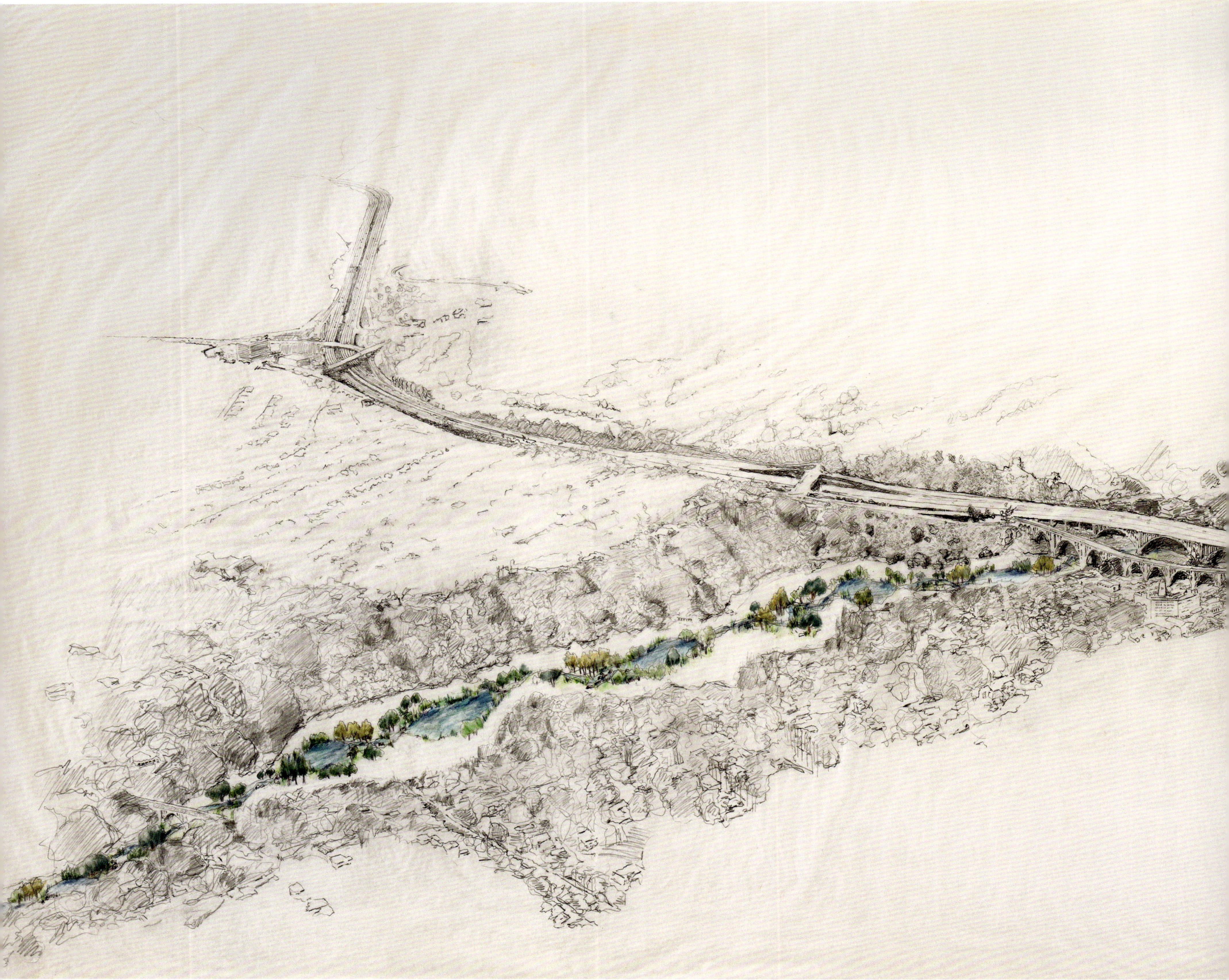

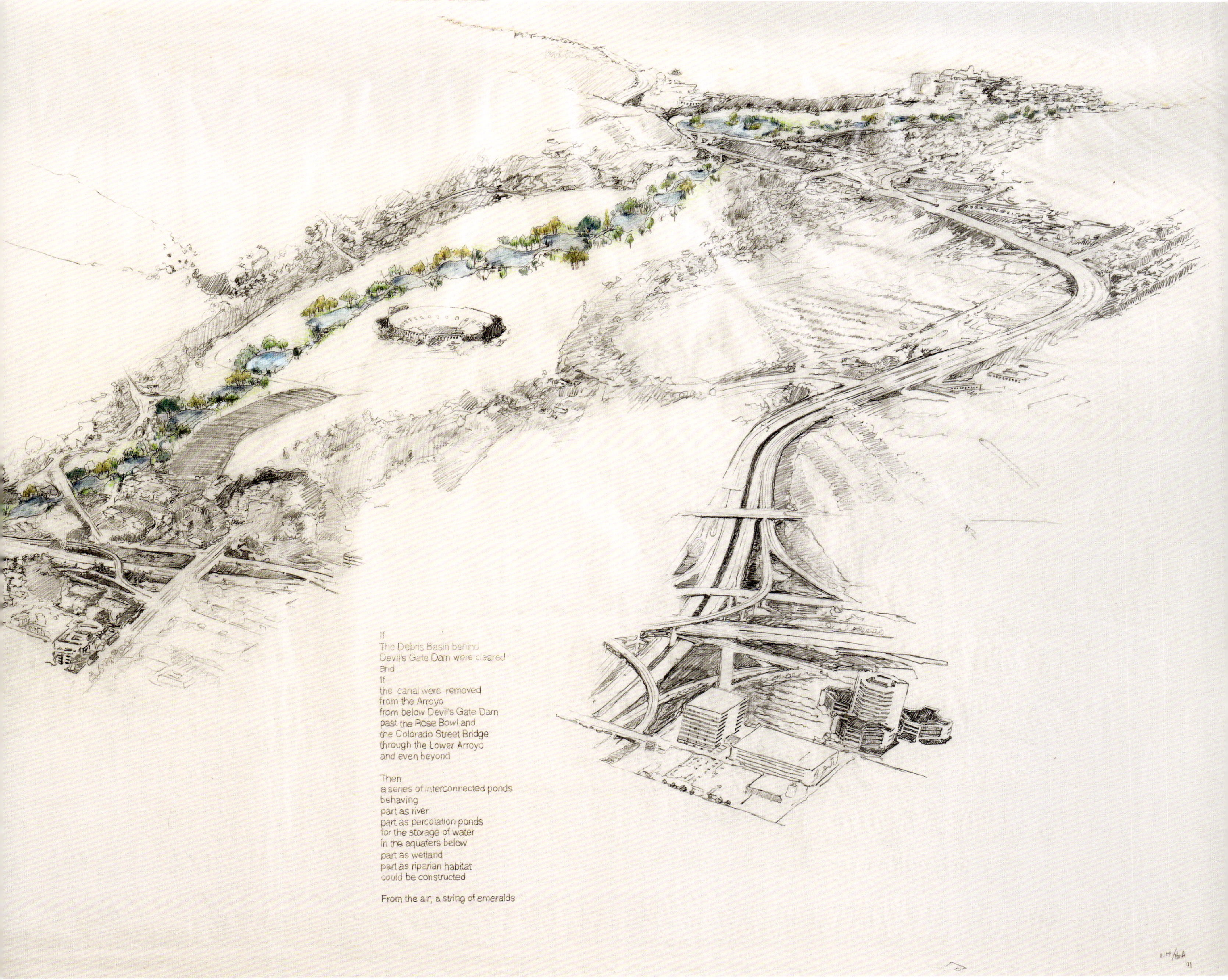
If
The Debris Basin behind
Devil's Gate Dam were cleared
and
If
the canal were removed
from the Arroyo
from below Devil's Gate Dam
past the Rose Bowl and
the Colorado Street Bridge
through the Lower Arroyo
and even beyond

Then
a series of interconnected ponds
behaving
part as river
part as percolation ponds
for the storage of water
in the aquafers below
part as wetland
part as riparian habitat
could be constructed

From the air, a string of emeralds

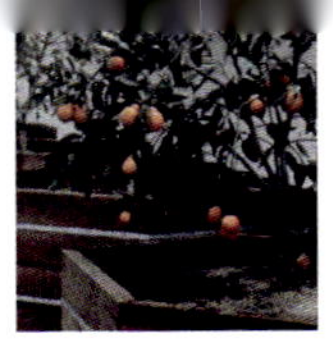

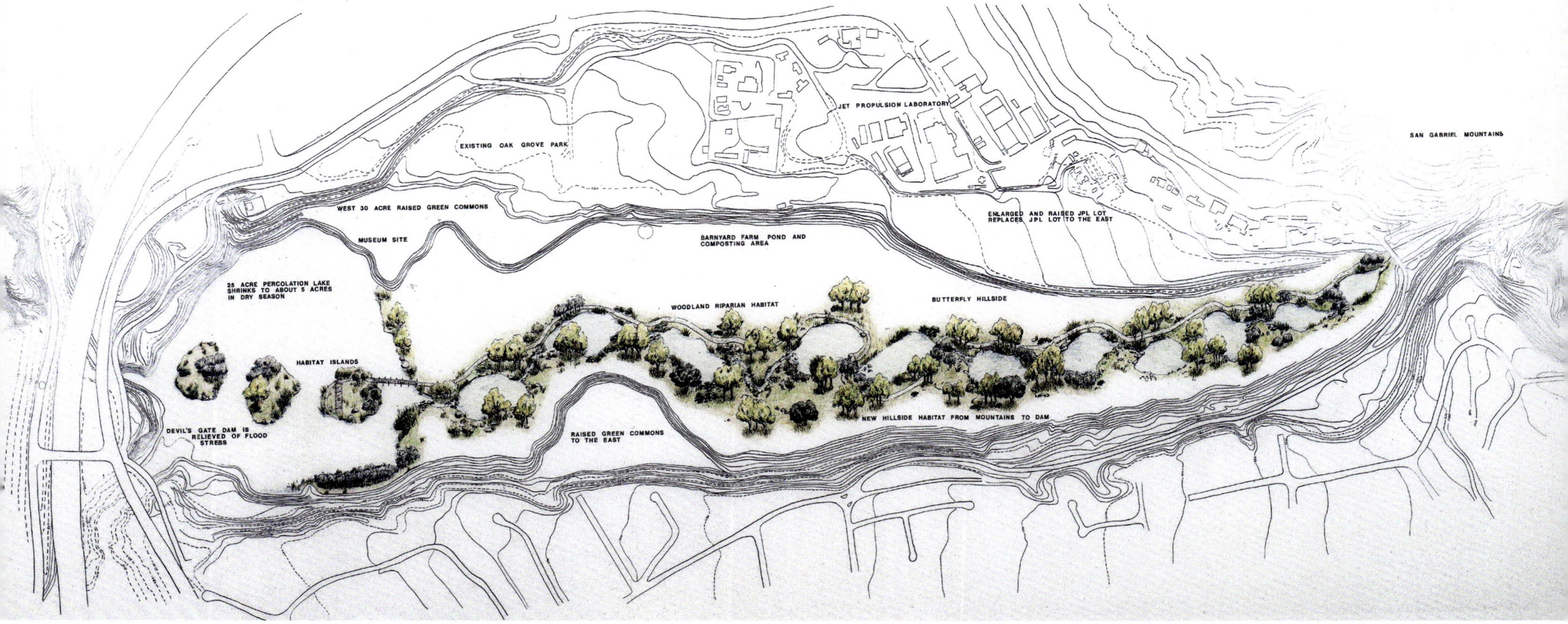

Final drawing for the Devil's Gate debris basin entitled A String of Pearls

Although the Harrisons' plan was adopted by the city in 1988, the project stalled for twenty-five years because of the inability of the city and the design firms who were awarded the project to complete it. *The Devil's Gate: A Refuge for Pasadena* was finally realized in 2003 by the master planners chosen by the city, Bob Takata and Associates, albeit under the different name of the *Hahamongna State Watershed Park*. According to the artists, the leadership of the Gabrielino Indians had seen the drawings for Devil's Gate Basin and argued that the project was calling for the restoration of a sacred site their people called *Hahamongna*, "The Place of the Laughing Waters."[71] Celebrating Newton's life after his passing on September 4 of 2022, Larry Wilson, the public editor of *Pasadena Star News*, acknowledged the artists' central artistic contribution to the design of the park: "the work of art by Helen Mayer Harrison and Newton Harrison was properly world-changing art that makes a difference." He called it " ... a grand kind of landscape architecture that was the first formal step toward creating what today we know as the Hahamongna Watershed Park."[72] In all, *Devil's Gate* captures the chief endeavor of the Harrison collaboration: to restore natural balance of compromised ecosystems and urban environments and to improve the quality of life.

It was no surprise that in 1984 the Harrisons received an invitation from San Diego to join several teams of architects to contribute ideas concerning the beautification and improvement of the community. At this point in their careers, they had already mounted public exhibitions that proposed the revision and revitalization of a three-mile section of Baltimore (*Baltimore Promenade*, 1981) and an undeveloped creek in San José (*Guadalupe Meander*, 1983), while their research was well underway for the Arroyo Seco flood control project in Pasadena (*Arroyo Seco Release*, 1985). Although *Horton Plaza* (1977–1978), *San Diego Round Through Air, On*

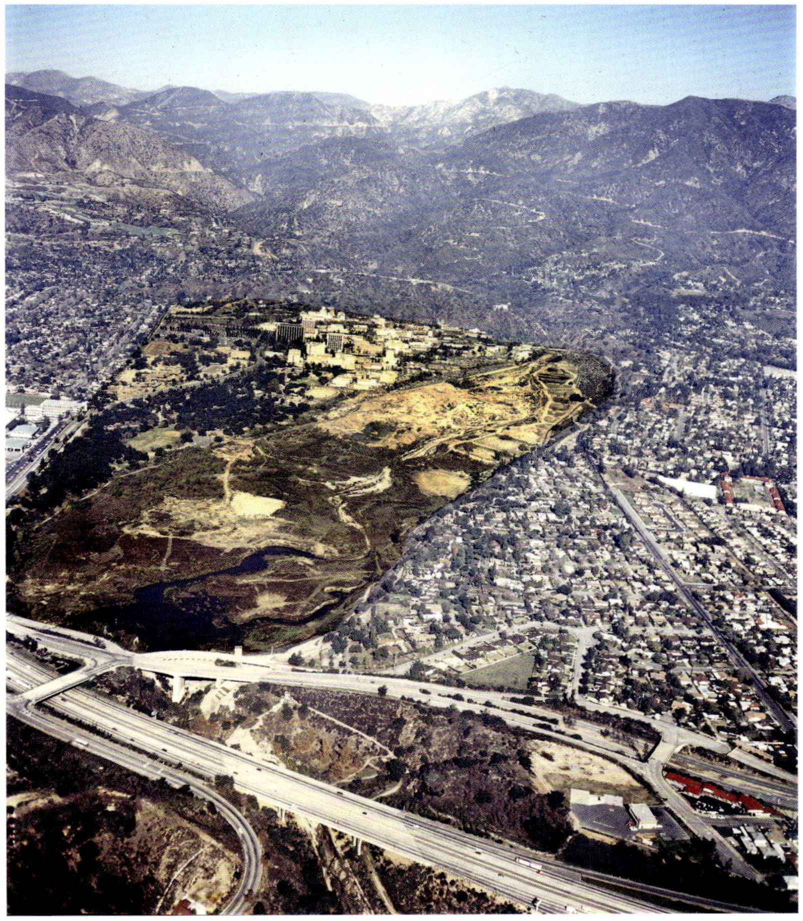

Model of the first debris basin re-design, five-by-two meters

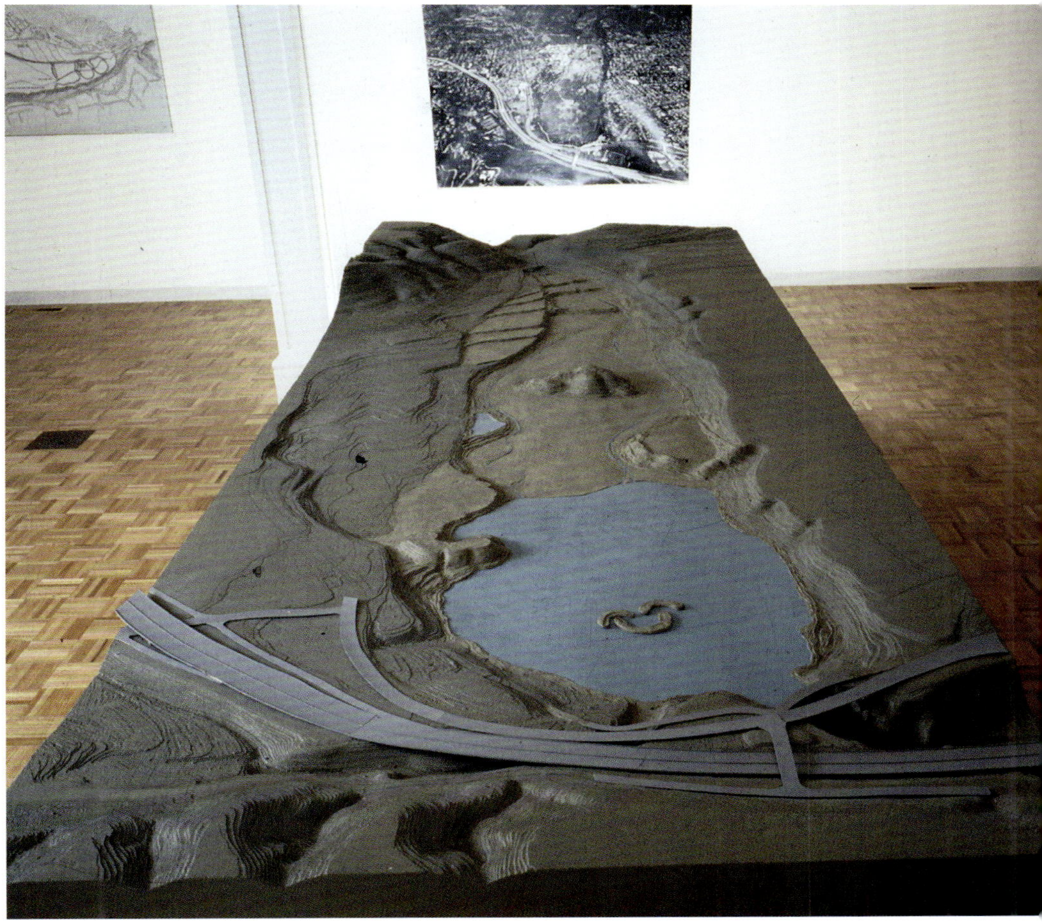

Foot, Across Waters (1984), and *Miramar Landfill* (1992) remain unrealized and were only presented in conferences, the proposals contributed to the vital dialogue about what shape the city should take as the decades unfolded, how the community could be restructured, and what public amenities could be added.

San Diego Round Through Air, On Foot, Across Waters (see pp. 56–57) was a rare proposal in which Helen and Newton formulated an alternative vision for San Diego's municipal development.[73] Sebastian "Lefty" Adler, the director of the San Diego Art Center, was instrumental in promoting their work and scheduled an exhibition concerning the revitalization of downtown San Diego at the temporary space at Horton Plaza in 1986. Although the exhibition was "stillborn," the Harrisons' proposal gained momentum and received positive critical appraisal from leading San Diego architects such as Rob Quigley, who called it "a breathtaking vision" that "won't come around again for 100 or 150 years."[74] Moreover, Quigley believed that if the artists' project were to be realized, "all questions of the civic identity would be answered." The city manager Sy Murray also showed great interest in commissioning a feasibility study through the Urban Land Institute.

The Harrisons' multifaceted plan for San Diego focused on transforming the civic core, taking into consideration the forgotten and neglected San Diego River and three desperately disconnected areas: the waterfront, Balboa Park, and Mission Valley. Combining the language of poetry with aerial photographs, they came up with an appealing narrative that was both creative and pragmatic. They proposed taking greater advantage of the proximity to the city's harbor by utilizing more of the waterfront, establishing a pedestrian link between the waterfront and Balboa Park, and extending waterways to the San Diego River and Mission Valley, thus reintegrating the river into the city. Reconsidering

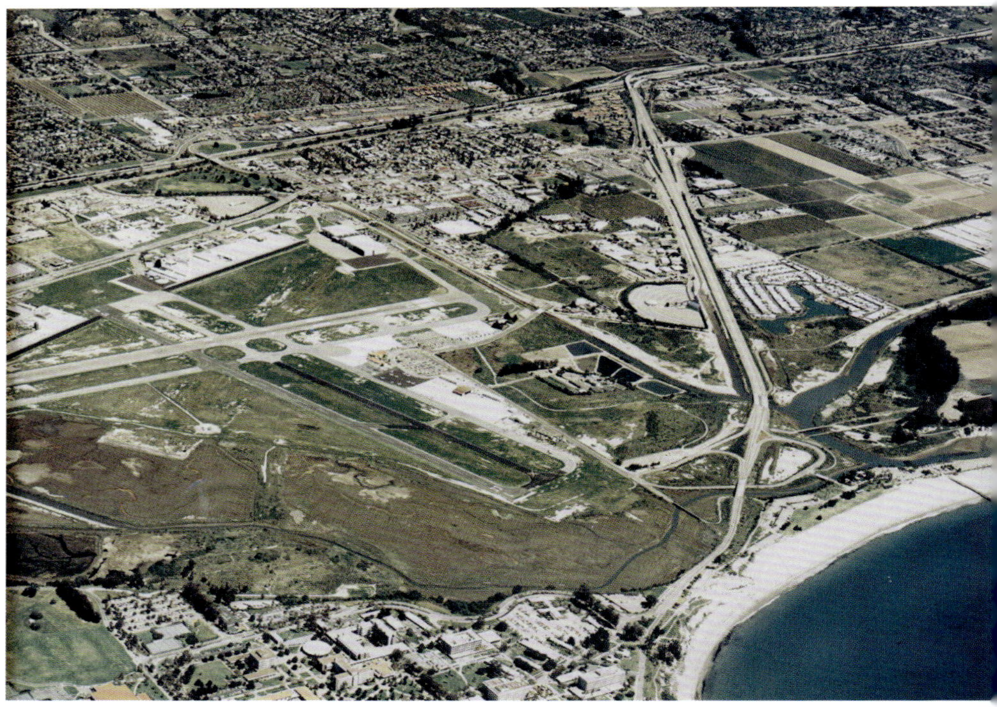

the city that had changed rapidly from a small town of 40,000–50,000 people to a region of several millions divided by freeways, the artists envisioned a new coherence by reconnecting its disparate parts through promenades, canals, and cable cars to return a humanistic perspective to the city.

Their plan described very specific elements: widening the harbor slightly to create an inlet at the end of Sixth Avenue, a "grand canal" to reach from Interstate 5 to the San Diego Jack Murphy Stadium, a smaller canal to connect Mission Valley to Mission Bay, an aerial tram from University Avenue to Mission Valley, a passenger ferry from the harbor to the Mission Valley network of channels, a promenade from the harbor up Sixth Avenue to University Avenue, and a pocket park at the Sixth Avenue bridge on the far end of the promenade. All the outlined components would provide a circular journey, as the artists stated: "One could then traverse the Park and walk down to Sixth Street, pick up the vaporetto, and do it all over again." The city was imagined as a city of inlets, canals, and trams.

**Imagine a grand canal along
Mission Valley that extends from
Route 5 in the west to the stadium
in the east that is simultaneously
an urban fantasy and a flood
control measure. Imagine the
small
canal section necessary to connect
Mission Valley to Mission Bay and
thus connect Mission Bay directly
to the San Diego harbor.**

**Imagine a promenade from the
harbor up Sixth Avenue along
Balboa Park to University Avenue
where an aerial tram would run
west of Route 163 but roughly
parallel to it, extending down the
canyon across Route 8 and part of
Mission Valley, to the Mission
Valley Canal.**

**Imagine a vaporetto moving from
a
new harbor at 6th Avenue with
stops along the way, through the
MCRD channel to its most easterly
terminus, then along a new
channel
through the present parking lots to
meet
the Mission Valley Canal, or
through
the canal extension to Mission
Bay.**

**One may begin the grand round
anywhere.**[75]

San Diego Round was designed as a public amenity, an addition to the well-being of the community as a whole, as the artists explicitly stated in public interviews and lectures. The

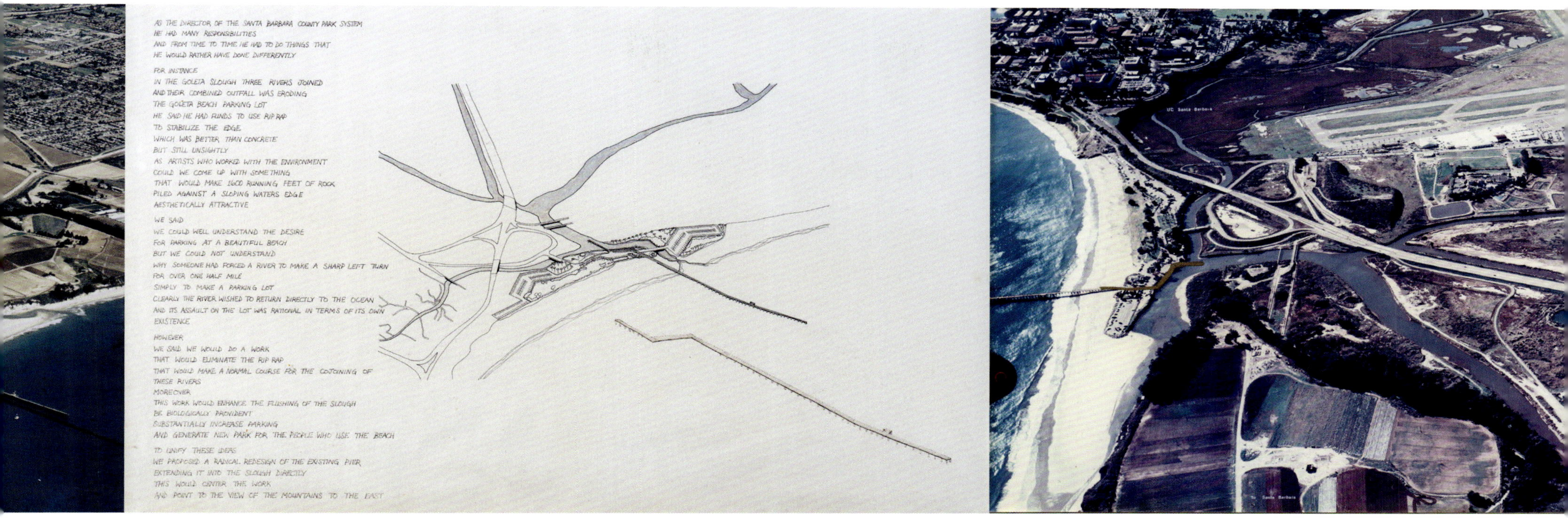

Harrisons created a breathtaking vision for the city, urging for its future to be not totally based on the automobile and proposing to reintegrate all its geographic features into a coherent whole. Even unrealized, their plan offered another perspective for a more human-centered urban landscape that entered the discussion and brought awareness about the city and its environment. Through words and pictures, the Harrisons visualized an artistically vital new unity for the city in contrast to the large-scale commercial development and suburban sprawl that was already underway. The artists explained that their project was rejected as it was not profit-generating for the local government.

The Harrisons' urban eco-critical works in San Diego also included a lesser-known proposal for land reclamation titled *Miramar Landfill* (1992). The proposal was formalized in a city document and was praised for showing "an unusual level of respect for the environment" and "sensitivity to the community of nearby residents, workers and users of the site," as well as for planning to make "the facilities more accommodating and educational for its users."[76] The artists approached the design as large-scale ecological public art and envisioned incorporating numerous sculptural and environmental elements in the future development of the Miramar landfill.

In 1991, the architectural firm of Martinez, Cutri, and McArdle invited the Harrisons to join them as artists and conceptual designers for a competition to create the master plan for the San Diego Landfill. The Harrisons created a vision statement for the proposal. Their group, comprising a team of architects, engineers, graphic designers, landscape architects, and another artist, Paul Hobson, won the competition. The plan was approved by the City of San Diego.[77] At the heart of their design was the restoration of part of the landfill to its native condition with "Ridgebacks, Saddlebacks and Muscular Hills," as Newton explained. The solution was elegant in its concern for the well-being of the area, asking for twenty million cubic yards of dirt to be removed from one part of the landfill to create space for more trash, with the same dirt to be placed atop another area of the landfill that was already at capacity. The crowning idea of the proposal was to make public art in the area by sculpting the hills and planting them with native plants to match the surrounding, natural terrain. Newton's reasoning was ecological and pragmatic: "Such folding of the earth is good ecologically, and it saves money that would be used to cart away the dirt. The shapes echo the far mountains."[78] The Harrisons offered a counterpoint to the ruthless development in greater San Diego, and more generally in Southern California, where developers brutally cut off the tops of hills and disrupt and destroy local ecosystems in the name of commercial and residential expansion.

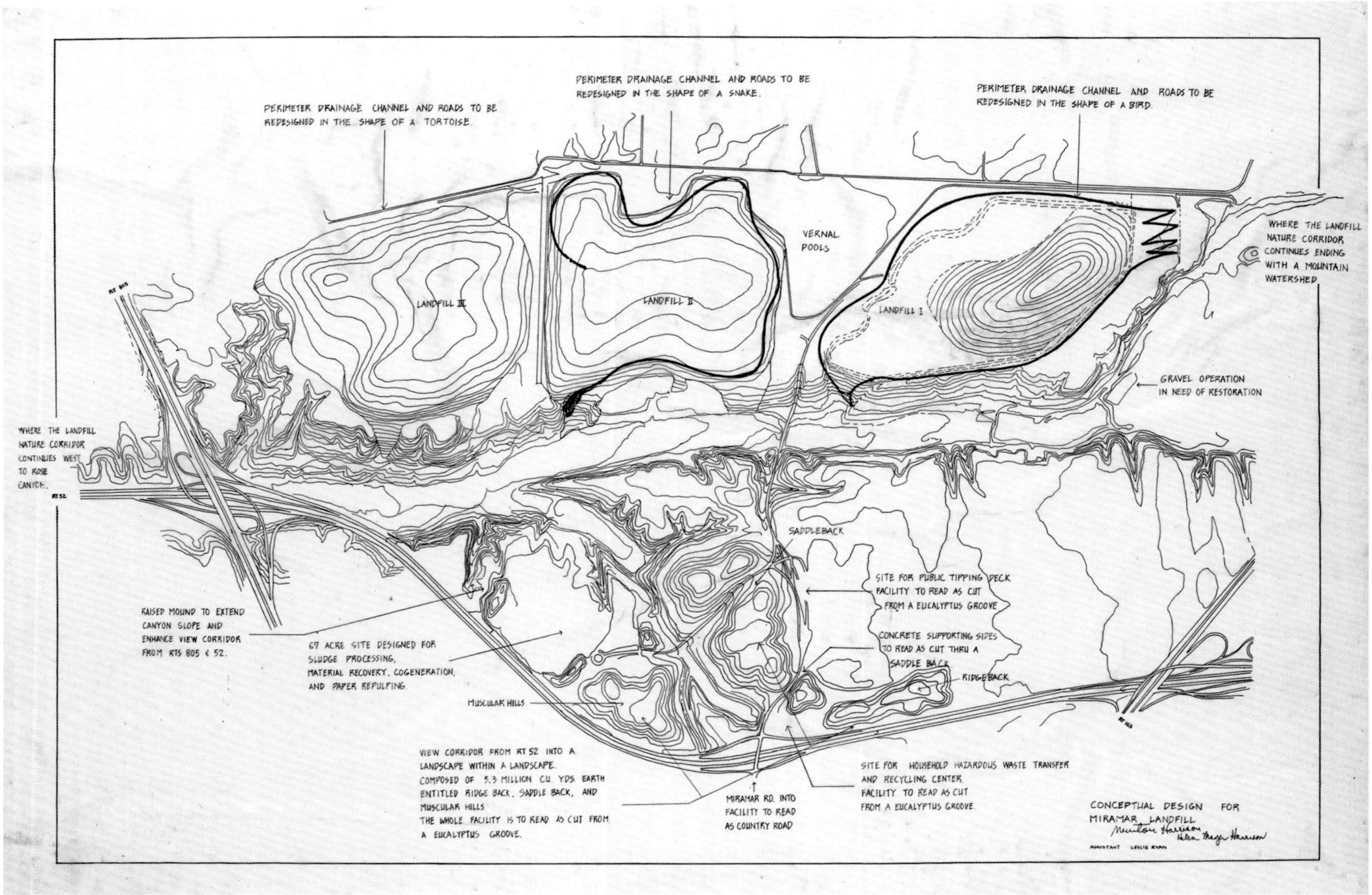

Miramar Landfill was presented in conferences and exhibited with a clay model and photographs of the area, which are preserved in the archive. The Harrisons saw this as an opportunity for the revitalization of a native ecosystem that would grow in the turned and tilled earth. The clay model showed various facilities located on the site, and accompanying photos captured views that would be available to visitors and workers. The conceptual design drawing provided the idea that the waste hills, roads, and the perimeter drainage channel could be designed in the form of a bird, snake, and tortoise. By doing so, the project drew on Newton's vision that the human species should treat the planet gently, like a sculpture, while the gigantic animal imagery was also a nod to the art and architecture of earlier Latin and Meso-American civilizations such as the Maya and the Inca, and the famous Nazca Lines of Peru. If it were fully implemented, the Harrisons would have completed the first hybrid eco-earthwork in San Diego, "part landscape, part landfill, part service facilities, part earthwork, and part reclamation," with a clear aim to restore the eco-balance in the area and bring back a nature corridor disrupted by the landfill. The unusual part of this proposal was its holistic vision of art, nature, and functional design, which would together serve for the preservation and regeneration of what Newton called the Life Web.

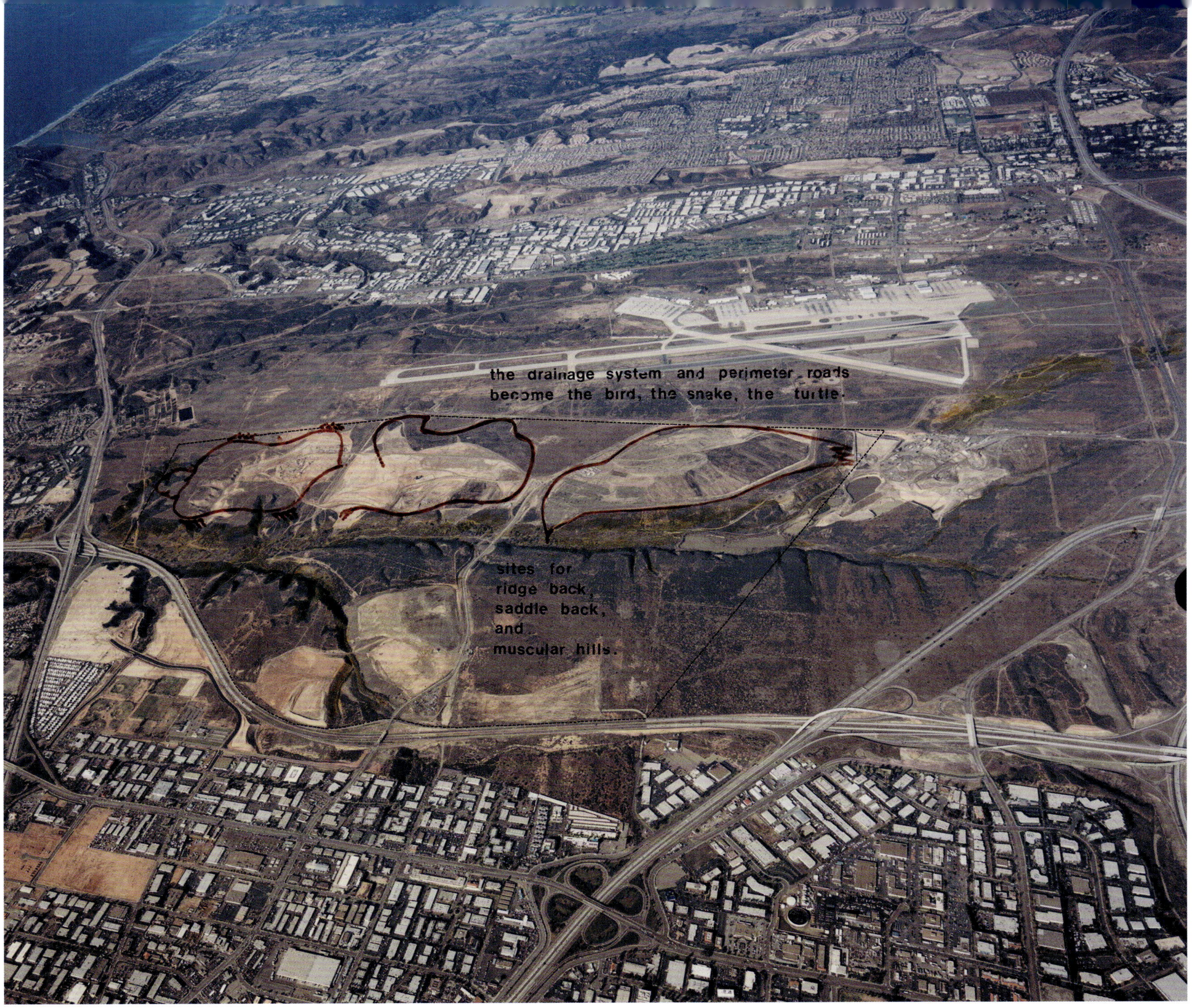

The Harrisons' commitment to a kind of urban design that leads to the restoration of native California ecologies is also visible in the fully realized *California Wash, Santa Monica Promenade* (1988–1997), an award-winning design for the city's walkway and wash garden of native California plants.[79] By this point in their career, they were internationally recognized and sought-after ecological artists, being invited to present at the Kassel *documenta*, to create a memorial forest in Dessau, and to restore ecologies around the Sava River in Croatia, to name just a few among dozens of projects that they were starting up in Europe, alongside all the others in the continental U.S. Upon their return to California, the artists were invited by Henry Korn, the head of the Public Arts Program for the City of Santa Monica, to submit a proposal for the competition to reconstruct the area at the end of Pico Boulevard as a work of art. The promenade was also to connect the city of Santa Monica to the Santa Monica Pier.[80]

The title *California Wash* was invented by the artists to tell the story of how Santa Monica's development caused the disappearance of native plants and the region's most precious resource, its water. Once on site, the Harrisons discovered that beneath the Pico promenade there was an outfall that released foul-smelling, unfiltered street runoff straight into

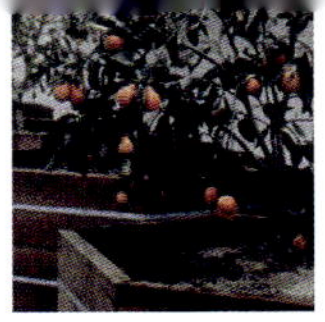

the ocean. Studying old maps of the Santa Monica Mountains watershed, the artists discovered that the natural pattern of streams and rainfall water was disrupted by urban development in the area – a familiar story of how the streams had been channelized in the city and run underground, thereby catching any debris and garbage on the surface before flowing to the bay. In their original state, before any development in Los Angeles, streams ran naturally down to the ocean and carried with them a variety of seeds from higher ground, resulting in a special "wash ecosystem," as it was described by the artists. Despite the importance of coastal ecosystems to fauna and water

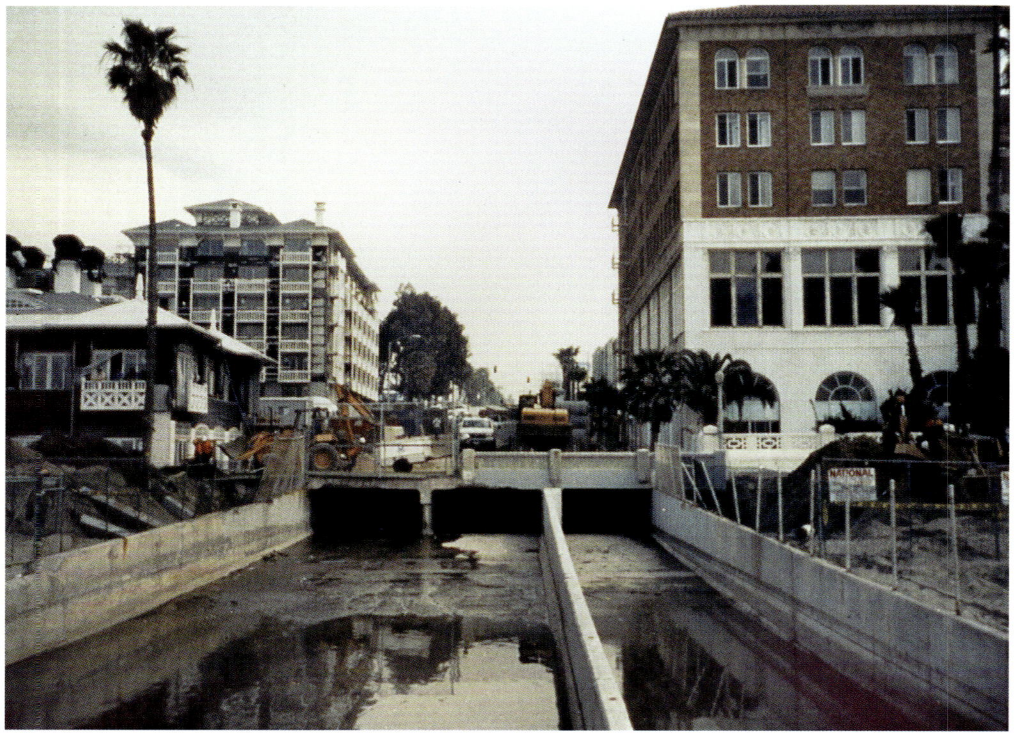

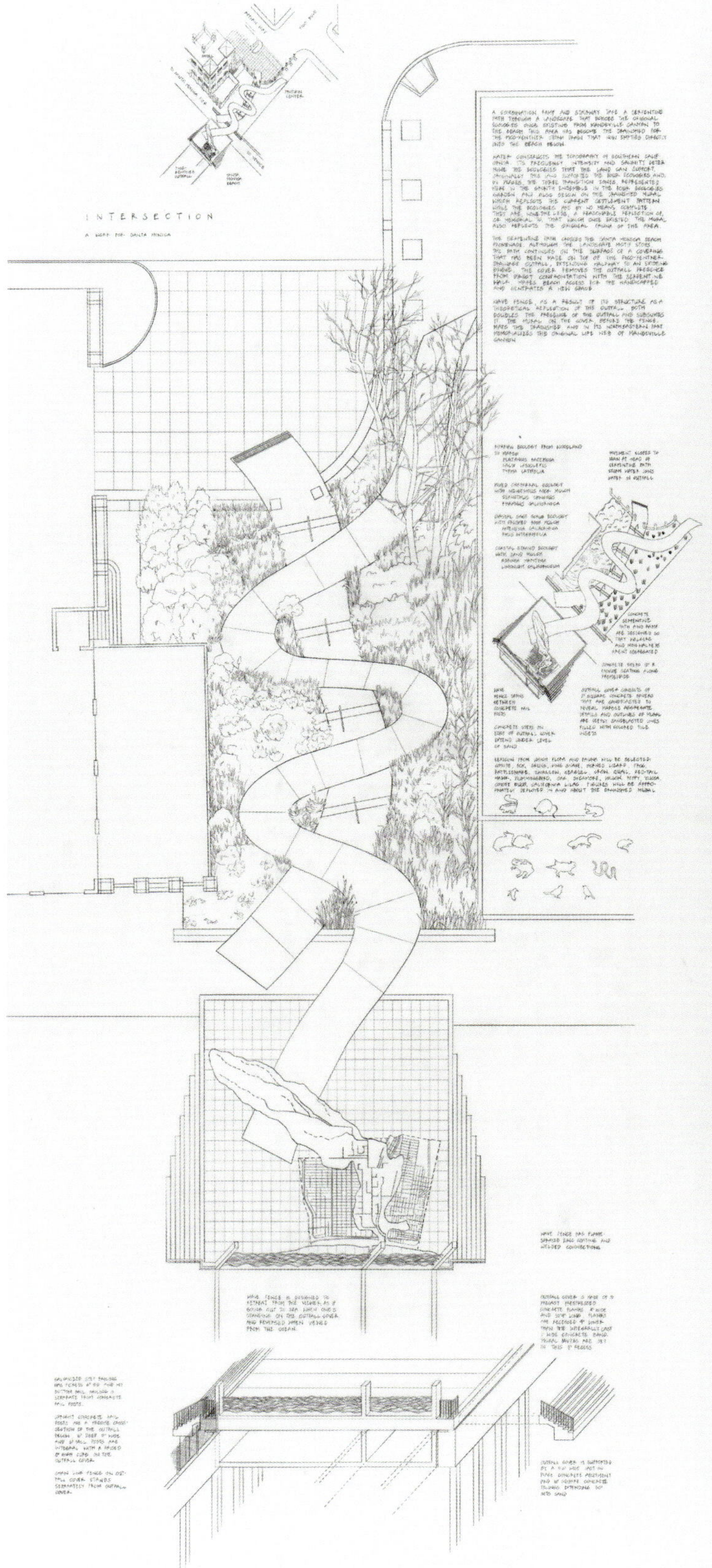

resources in Los Angeles, such systems have not been adequately studied or preserved. As the California Coastal Conservancy reports, "close to 100 percent of the original wetlands and 90 to 95 percent of in-stream riparian habitat within the Los Angeles River watershed have been lost, a consequence of urbanization and the channelization of rivers and creeks."[81] Small remnants of these coastal and riparian ecosystems continue to support a unique array of plants and animals. They also control erosion and purify water by removing contaminants. The loss of these habitats over the years negatively affected the ecological well-being of the river and its wildlife, therefore disrupting the Santa Monica watershed – thus the full spectrum of people, animals, and plants that live and grow inside the ecosystem.

California Wash reimagined the path that rainwater would have taken from the mountains to the coast before the city's development. The promenade was designed as a serpentine walk to evoke the natural state of this area. In one of many interviews Helen explained: "We translate planning ideas into visuals. We create icons, which allow a new myth of place to emerge. If it's just a matter of restoration, others can do that. We're artists and storytellers."[82] Looking at old maps and surveying the area, armed with their usual questions – "What is happening?" "What are its boundaries?" "Do we see any patterns?" – they discovered the essence of the unique landscape. Many drawings found in the archival materials and included in the exhibition show the artists' keen interest in the Santa Monica watershed. The Harrisons drew their own maps, identifying the historical flow lines that no longer exist today and had them meander downward towards the ocean. By making this watershed visible as a serpentine walk, the Harrisons hoped to etch into the public consciousness the natural state that was overcome by expanding urbanization.

California Wash comprises an 18,000-square-feet, poured-concrete section of the Pico Boulevard, a fully landscaped median strip, and sycamore-lined sidewalks. The path to the beach, along gardens of native grasses and flowers, is decorated by an inlaid mural illustrating the flora and fauna of the wash. The gardens were designed by Bob Perry and elaborated by Leslie Ryan. The *Wave Fence* marks the end of the walk and stops people from tumbling into the outfall. As Newton explained: "We had constructed *Wave Fence* such that if you stood on the path late in the afternoon or early in the morning, especially with fog coming in, the fence would visually join with the ocean. In our minds the striations, in various browns and ochres and grays, represented (in part) a dry streambed."[83] The Harrisons drew attention to the problems of disappearing native ecosystems and unhealthy urban transformations, especially in underserved communities that often lack green spaces. Thus, *California Wash* not only carried out a utilitarian task but also serves as a memorial of sorts to the continuing displacement of what once was there.

As with many public art commissions, the whole process dragged on for nearly six years. The work remained unfinished until the Harrisons discovered that there was a law stating that if the city mishandled a work of public art, the artists could ask for its return. They contacted

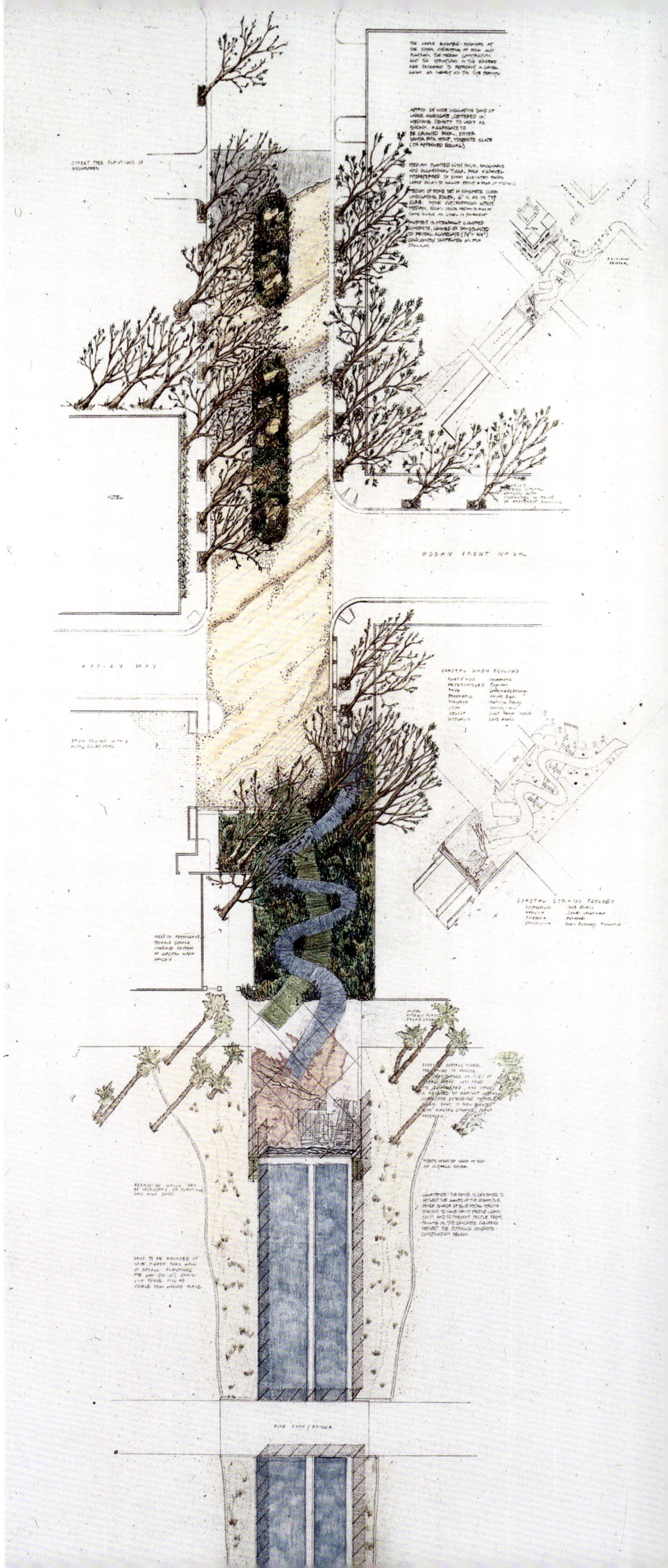

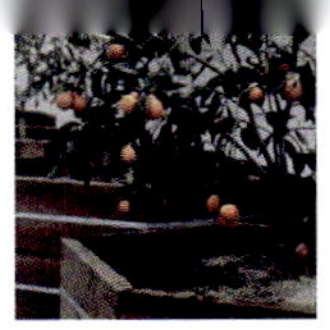

the city and requested that this work be returned – a near-impossible task and an obvious challenge to the city authorities. The ungrantable request stimulated the committee, and the work was completed within three months.

The Harrisons' urban ecological works of the 1980s and 1990s showcase an ingenious method of urban restoration and land reclamation in California. The collaboration produced work only by invitation in the form of commissioned engagements with municipalities and the managers of local ecosystems. These California works were more than site-specific think-pieces, offering sustainable interventions in urban contexts. Leslie Ryan, who worked in the Harrison Studio on various different projects, called the Harrisons' ecological approach "a caring process of bringing back from misdeeds of the past."[84] Certainly, their ethics of working with earth as a living substance rather than simply an art material played a central role in their urban reclamation projects. While art as a finite object had become increasingly irrelevant to the Harrisons, their empathy for places increased exponentially, leading them to say that the Web of Life itself was their client. Their efforts and trials with the early eco-critical urban works in California laid down a foundation for the whole-systems aesthetics required to solve whole-systems problems. Reflecting on their early works, Newton observed that their visual and narrative strategies changed after the *Survival Pieces* to reflect this direction:

> "We decided to choose a direction other than simple sculptural installations with farming systems. We began improvising ways to present whole systems by adding text, photographic and drawn or painted images and narrative to the work in a new format."[85]

Linda Weintraub, a curator and writer, emphasizes that a whole-systems approach was needed "to accommodate the enlargement of their temporal and spatial considerations."[86] Indeed, the Harrisons dramatically altered their careers to become not only artists but also ecological designers, urban planners, and researchers, as reflected in their habit of gathering voluminous amounts of information, as can be seen in their 258-linear feet research archives.

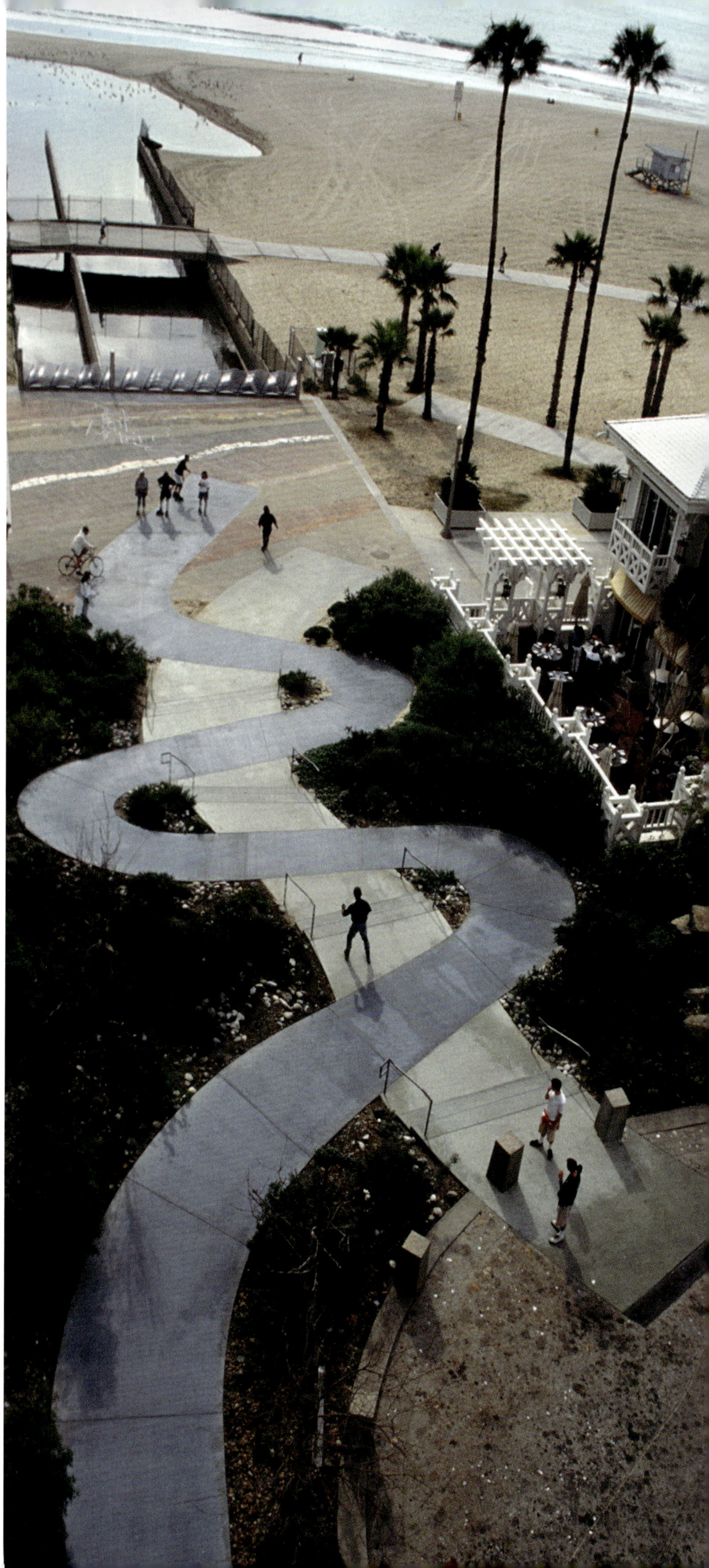

This new whole-systems direction was dictated by their own work with living and ecological systems and was a sweeping transformation of their earlier strategy of art in the expanded field. Jack Burnham, an artist and art critic, was first to apply the concept of systems aesthetics to describe art in the expanded field – artworks that were out of the frame, out of the gallery, and often not even objects.[87] According to Burnham's definition, such art practices assumed a new function to show that art resided "in relations between people and between people and the components of their environment."[88] As Leslie Ryan later suggested, "the introduction of systems into the aesthetic discourse opened up space for networks and the interdependency of ecosystems to inform art practices."[89] Theoretically, Burnham's approach provided the Harrisons with an initial scaffolding to start building their own systems art. However, their work led them to embrace strategies mirroring those that governed whole systems. The major issue was that ecological questions and problems were – and are – extremely difficult to solve even from a scientific perspective, a roadblock that the artists encountered with the unanticipated failures and shortcomings of the *Survival Pieces*. In her interview with Craig Adcock, Helen profoundly observed, "The fact is that you can never obtain total information. There are many languages of nature that we do not understand and don't even know exist. These languages are part of complex ecological interactions, and we may never understand them."[90] Therefore, one of the Harrisons' leading strategies in their urban ecological works was to show how the human species could come to use natural resources in intelligent and creative ways, to begin encountering the planet Earth artfully.

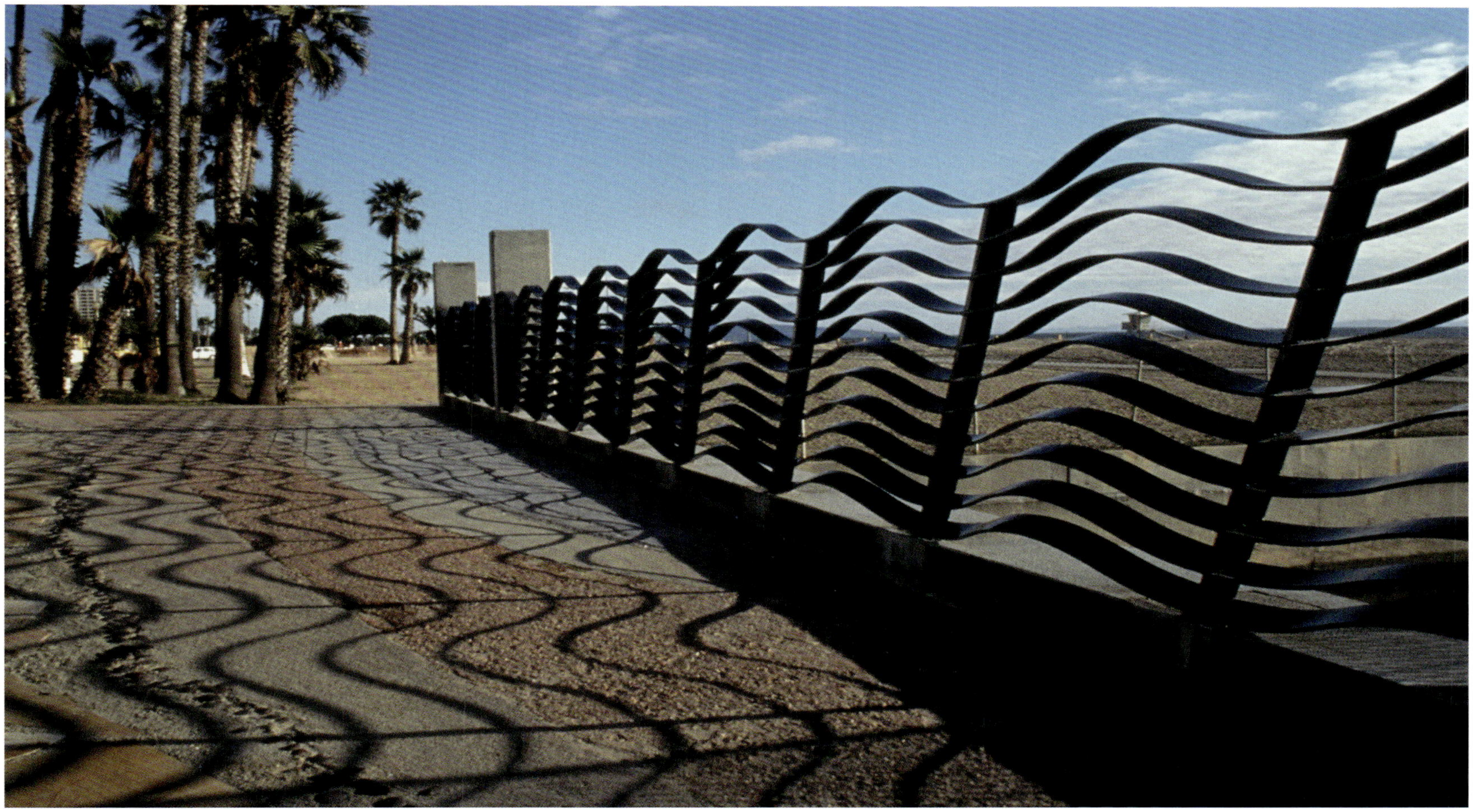

1 Harrison, Helen Mayer, and Newton Harrison, "Shifting Positions toward the Earth: Art and Environmental Awareness," *Leonardo*, Vol. 26, No. 5, 1993, pp. 371–377.

2 In several interviews with the author conducted in 2021, Newton Harrison talked about the Life Web. Also see the published interview with the artist by Oliver Kupper: Kupper, Oliver, "Force Majeure: Pioneering Eco-Artists the Harrisons Created a Survival Guide for a World Careening Toward Disaster," *Autre*, Issue 13, F/W 2021, pp. 250–257.

3 Engelstad, Janeil, "Disremembering the Harrisons," *Leonardo*, Vol. 56, No. 3, 2023, p. 299.

4 Collins, Tim, "Environmental Artworkers," *FIELD*, Issue 23, Winter 2023, https://field-journal.com/editorial/6816. Web.

5 Rogers, Laura Cassidy, "The Social and Environmental Turn in Late 20th Century Art: A Case Study of Helen and Newton Harrison After Modernism." PhD diss., Stanford University, CA, 2017.

6 The Harrisons also held five-year appointments as Arts Dean's Visiting Eminent Professors at UC Santa Cruz in 2014–2019.

7 Collins, "Environmental Artworkers," Ibid.

8 Rogers, "The Social and Environmental Turn in Late 20th Century Art: A Case Study of Helen and Newton Harrison After Modernism," Ibid.

9 This is especially visible in the sheer monumental scale and feel as well as the synergy of painting and text in many of their works, such as the *Lagoon Cycle*.

10 I am grateful to have been able to visit with Newton Harrison in Santa Cruz on several occasions in 2019–2022, including our final conversation a week before his passing on September 4, 2022. He specifically discussed the *Lagoon Cycle* and three *Meditations* as the most important works.

11 Series 7, Early Work by Newton Harrison 1960–1975. Helen and Newton Harrison Papers, M1797. Special Collections & University Archives, Stanford University, Stanford, CA, consulted in October–December 2021.

12 The beginning of their collaboration is described in Harrison, Helen Mayer, and Newton Harrison, *The Time of the Force Majeure: After 45 Years Counterforce is on the Horizon, Helen Mayer Harrison and Newton Harrison*, edited by Petra Kruse and Kai Reschke. Prestel, Munich, London, New York, 2016, pp. 19, 50, 52–53.

13 In her well-known essay "Sculpture in the Expanded Field," the art historian Rosalind Krauss called attention to new categories of art that challenged conventional definitions in the late 1960s and early 70s. As she noted, sculpture had been reinvented not only by the Duchampian Readymade and the neo-Dadaist Combine but also by rapidly developed installation art and earth or land art. Sculpture was no longer distinct three-dimensional objects on pedestals but something that was less clearly identifiable, something between architecture and not-architecture, landscape, and not-landscape, yet that belonged to neither. Krauss proposed to recognize those hybrid experiments in art, involving painting, sculpture, and photography, as "art in the expanded field." See: Rosalind Krauss, "Sculpture in the Expanded Field," *October*, Vol. 8, 1979, pp. 31–44, 37. https://doi.org/10.2307/778224.

14 Jones, Caroline A., "Caroline A. Jones on Helen Mayer Harrison (1927–2018)," *Artforum International*, April 7, 2018, retrieved August 26, 2023.

15 Billy Klüver (1927–2004), a Swedish-born electrical engineer at Bell Telephone Laboratories, began his collaborations with artists by working with the kinetic art sculptor Jean Tinguely on his *Homage to New York* (1960), which destroyed itself in the garden at Museum of Modern Art in New York (MOMA). Robert Rauschenberg also assisted on *Homage to New York*. In 1967 Klüver, together with Robert Rauschenberg, Robert Whitman, and Fred Waldhauer, founded Experiments in Art and Technology (E.A.T.), a not-for-profit service organization that established a Technical Services Program to provide artists with technical information and assistance by matching them with engineers and scientists who could collaborate with them. Klüver curated (or was curatorial adviser) for fourteen major museum exhibitions in the United States and Europe. See: W. Patrick McCray, *Making Art Work: How Cold War Engineers and Artists Forged a New Creative Culture.* MIT Press, Cambridge, MA, 2020, pp. 77–100, 129–145.

16 In 1967, Maurice Tuchman, then the brash new curator of modern art at the LACMA, introduced the Art and Technology (A&T) program, which placed artists like Robert Irwin and James Turrell at the Garrett Corporation to conduct research into perception. Tuchman spearheaded the program for five years and encouraged the region's renowned high-tech corporations to support art. The program resulted in the largest and controversial A&T exhibition at the LACMA that also traveled to Expo 1970 in Osaka, Japan. A&T served as a long-term exchange program within the institutional frameworks of museums and corporations. See: W. Patrick McCray, *Making Art Work: How Cold War Engineers and Artists Forged a New Creative Culture*, pp. 185–212, 252–263.

17 Rogers, "The Social and Environmental Turn in Late 20th Century Art: A Case Study of Helen and Newton Harrison After Modernism," pp. 114–116.

18 This series of conceptual drawings included in the exhibition is in the Harrison Family Trust. The other series of drawings is at the archive: Series 7, Early Work by Newton Harrison 1960–1975, Map Folder 382 and Box 381. Helen and Newton Harrison Papers, M1797. Special Collections & University Archives, Stanford University, Stanford, CA, consulted in October–December 2021.

19 For instance, see: Levin, Kim, "Helen and Newton Harrison: New Grounds for Art," *Arts Magazine* 52, No. 6, February 1978, pp. 126–129.

20 Interview with the artist, December 4, 2021.

21 The artwork is variously called: *Glow Discharge, Plasma Tubes, Plasma Chambers, Light Piece*, and *Encapsulated Aurora Borealis*.

22 For the detailed narrative, see: Rogers, "The Social and Environmental Turn in Late 20th Century Art: A Case Study of Helen and Newton Harrison After Modernism," pp. 120–127. Also: Scrapbook 3. Series 7, Early Work by Newton Harrison, Box 287. Helen and Newton Harrison Papers, M1797. Special Collections & University Archives, Stanford University, Stanford, CA, consulted in October–December 2021.

23 Burnham, Jack, "The 'Art and Technology' Exhibition at the Los Angeles County Museum (Two Views): Corporate Art," *Art Forum,* Vol. 10, No. 2, October 1971, https://www.artforum.com/features/the-art-and-technology-exhibition-at-the-los-angeles-county-museum-two-views-corporate-art-214271/, accessed August 1, 2022.

24 Burnham, "The 'Art and Technology' Exhibition at the Los Angeles County Museum (Two Views): Corporate Art," Ibid.

25 Tuchman, Maurice, editor, *A Report on the Art and Technology Program of the Los Angeles County Museum of Art, 1967–1971.* Los Angeles County Museum of Art, Los Angeles, CA, 1971, p. 9.

26 See Newton's claims about scientific research functions of the rocket in his correspondence with the Atlantic Research Systems Division of the Susquehanna Corporation and Secretary of Defense Melvin Laird in the Project Files, Series 2, Subseries 3, Artificial Aurora Borealis. Helen and Newton Harrison Papers Papers, M1797. Special Collections & University Archives, Stanford University, Stanford, CA, consulted in October–December 2021.

27 He repeated his conclusion about Klüver again and again in conversations we had (2019–2022) in preparation of this retrospective *California Works* exhibition.

28 Fremantle, Chris, and Anne Douglas, editors, "Paying Attention to Make Art: Twenty-nine Reflections on the Harrisons," *The Nature of Cities,* March 18, 2023, https://www.thenatureofcities.com/2023/03/18/paying-attention-to-make-art-twenty-nine-reflections-on-the-harrisons/, accessed April 1, 2023.

29 Although Max Kozloff was pleased with the overall aesthetic appeal of *Plasma Chambers*, he sustained a critical stance about all Techart, explaining that "the will to form was furthered by electro-mechanical means" and sensation and effect could not compensate for the loss of shape and structure. See: Max Kozloff, "The Multimillion Dollar Art Boondoggle," *Artforum* (October 1971), Vol. 10, No. 2, https://www.artforum.com/features/the-multimillion-dollar-art-boondoggle-2-204650/, accessed August 1, 2022. Characterization of Newton as "dangerous" is noteworthy as it refers to the fact that *Plasma Chambers* involved the real voltage-current that could potentially electrocute and kill, if out of control. Newton's demonstration was daring because of the tubes' monumental scale and long duration, unlike in a lab, where such experiments lasted a short time, and were conducted on a much smaller scale.

30 Discussion of the meaning and implications of the Harrisons' *Survival Pieces* is ongoing among scholars, and new layers of understanding of their work continue to be added. For instance, these publications offer good insights: Amanda Boetzkes, "Techniques of Survival: The Harrisons and the Environmental Counterculture," *West of Center: Art and the Counterculture Experiment in America, 1965–1977,* edited by Elissa Author and Adam Lerner. NED-New edition, University of Minnesota Press, 2012, pp. 306–323; Jill Dawsey, "The Uses of Photography: An Introduction," *The Uses of Photography: Art, Politics, and the Reinvention of a Medium*, edited by Jill Dawsey. Museum of Contemporary Art, San Diego, CA, UC Press, 2016, pp. 33–38; W. Patrick McCray, "The Art of Survival," *AEON,* October 29, 2020, https://aeon.co/essays/art-lessons-from-the-1970s-for-survival-in-an-ecologically-blighted-world, accessed August 25, 2021.

31 Bijvoet, Marga, *Art as Inquiry, Toward New Collaborations Between Art, Science, and Technology*. American University Studies, Peter Lang, New York, 1997, pp. 137–148.

32 Burnham, "The 'Art and Technology' Exhibition at the Los Angeles County Museum (Two Views): Corporate Art," Ibid.

33 Harrison, Helen Mayer, and Newton Harrison, "Making Earth, 1970." *The Harrison Studio*, https://www.theharrisonstudio.net/making-earth-1970, accessed April 1, 2020.

34 Harrison, Newton, quoted in Burnham, Jack, *Great Western Salt Works: Essays on the Meaning of Post-Formalist Art.* George Braziller, New York, 1973, p. 164.

35 Harrison, Helen Mayer, and Newton Harrison, *The Time of the Force Majeure: After 45 Years Counterforce is on the Horizon*, edited and designed by Petra Kruse and Kai Reschke. Prestel, Munich, London, New York, 2016, p. 18.

36 Boetzkes, Amanda, "Techniques of Survival: The Harrisons and the Environmental Counterculture," p. 312.

37 McCray, W. Patrick, "The Art of Survival," Ibid.

38 Cited from: Bijvoet, Marga, *Art as Inquiry, Toward New Collaborations Between Art, Science, and Technology*, p. 137.

39 Harrison, Helen Mayer, and Newton Harrison, *The Time of the Force Majeure: After 45 Years Counterforce is on the Horizon*, p. 23.

40 Green, Charles, "Memory and Ethics: Helen Mayer Harrison and Newton Harrison," *The Third Hand: Collaboration in Art from Conceptualism to Postmodernism*. University of Minnesota Press, 2001, pp. 97–122, p. 109, http://www.jstor.org/stable/10.5749/j.ctttsbj7.9, accessed July 2022.

41 Series 5, Performances and Exhibitions, Box 136. Helen and Newton Harrison Papers, M1797. Special Collections & University Archives, Stanford University,

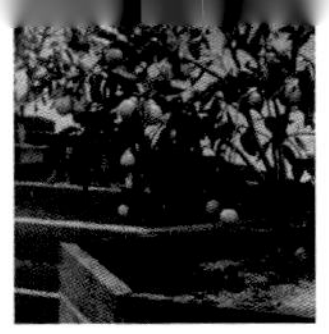

Stanford, CA. The full account is retold in Helen Mayer Harrison and Newton Harrison, *The Time of the Force Majeure: After 45 Years Counterforce is on the Horizon*, p. 22–23.

42 See video "Hog Pasture: Survival Piece I: Wilma the Pig," (2012) narrated by Helen and Newton Harrison and co-written by Nada Miljković, who served as the producer and videographer for the project, https://journal.tiltwest.org/vol4/harrison_hog_entry/, accessed August 20, 2023.

43 Harrison, Helen Mayer, and Newton Harrison, *The Time of the Force Majeure: After 45 Years Counterforce is on the Horizon*, p. 25.

44 Even though, in calculations, *Survival Piece II* could potentially yield 18000 brine shrimp per hectare, it failed in terms of the edibility of the resulting product. See: Helen Mayer Harrison and Newton Harrison, *The Time of the Force Majeure: After 45 Years Counterforce is on the Horizon*, p. 26.

45 Ibid., p. 25.

46 Burnham, "The 'Art and Technology' Exhibition at the Los Angeles County Museum (Two Views): Corporate Art," Ibid.

47 Harrison, Helen Mayer, and Newton Harrison, *The Time of the Force Majeure: After 45 Years Counterforce is on the Horizon*, p. 44.

48 Douglas, Anne, and Fremantle, Chris, "'Thinking with' the Harrisons: What Does Now Demand?" *FIELD*, Issue 23, Winter 2023, https://field-journal.com/issue-23/thinking-with-the-harrisons-what-does-now-demand, accessed December 1, 2023.

49 Details of the controversy are discussed in: A. Seidenbaum, "Hanging a Curtain is One Thing but How Can You Hang a Fish?" *Los Angeles Times*, December 26, 1971, O16; W. Wilson and A. Seidenbaum, "L.A. Artist's Fish Fry Has London Sizzling: Fishy Art." *Los Angeles Times*, October 1, 1971, A1, accessed November 2022, through ProQuest Historical Newspapers.

50 Harrison, Helen Mayer, and Newton Harrison, *The Time of the Force Majeure: After 45 Years Counterforce is on the Horizon*, p. 32. Scientists define ecosystems as dynamically interacting systems of organisms, the communities they make up, and the non-living (abiotic) components of their environment. Ecosystems are described through processes such as primary production, nutrient cycling, and niche construction that regulate the flux of energy and matter through an environment. See: D. K. Gibson-Reinemer, "A Vacant Niche: How a Central Ecological Concept Emerged in the 19th Century," *The Bulletin of the Ecological Society of America*, Vol. 96, April 1, 2015, pp. 324–335. https://doi.org/10.1890/0012-9623-96.2.324, accessed December 1, 2023.

51 Series 2, Project Files, Subseries 4, Box 22, Folders 10–16. Helen and Newton Harrison Papers, M1797. Special Collections & University Archives, Stanford University, Stanford, CA, consulted in October–December 2021.

52 Harrison, Helen Mayer, and Newton Harrison, *The Time of the Force Majeure: After 45 Years Counterforce is on the Horizon*, pp. 34–37.

53 Ibid., pp. 38–41.

54 Portable Orchard, Research 1970–1974. Series 2, Project Files, Subseries 4, Box 22, Folders 21–22. Helen and Newton Harrison Papers, M1797. Special Collections & University Archives, Stanford University, Stanford, CA, consulted in October–December 2021.

55 The United Nations report estimates that the earth has warmed one degree Celsius since the nineteenth century and cautions that even an increase of one and a half to two degrees (a limit rapidly approaching) would cause extreme weather changes, severe droughts, extinctions of terrestrial species, and other dramatic effects worldwide. See: "Global Warming of 1.5 °C," https://www.ipcc.ch/sr15/chapter/chapter-1/, accessed December 1, 2023.

56 Douglas, Anne, and Chris Fremantle, "'Thinking with' the Harrisons: What Does Now Demand?" *FIELD*, Issue 23, Winter 2023, https://field-journal.com/issue-23/thinking-with-the-harrisons-what-does-now-demand, accessed December 1, 2023.

57 Adcock, Craig, "Conversational Drift: Helen Mayer Harrison and Newton Harrison," *Art Journal*, Vol. 51, No. 2 (*Art and Ecology*), Summer, 1992, pp. 35–45, 35.

58 Ryan, Leslie, "Art + Ecology: Land Reclamation Works of Artists Robert Smithson, Robert Morris, and Helen Mayer Harrison and Newton Harrison," *Environmental Philosophy*, Vol. 4, No. 1 & 2 (Special Issue: *Environmental Aesthetics and Ecological Restoration*), Spring/Fall 2007, pp. 95–116, 97.

59 Harrison, Helen Mayer, and Newton Harrison, *The Time of the Force Majeure: After 45 Years Counterforce is on the Horizon*, pp. 176–179.

60 Series 2, Project Files, Subseries 20, Box 57, Folders 1–3, & 7–8. Helen and Newton Harrison Papers, M1797. Special Collections & University Archives, Stanford University, Stanford, CA, consulted in October–December 2021; *Arroyo Seco Release: A Serpentine for Pasadena: A Work by Helen Mayer and Newton Harrison*, exh. cat. Baxter Art Gallery, California Institute of Technology, Pasadena, CA, 1985.

61 Kaplan, Sam H., "Artists Sketch Natural Look for Arroyo Seco," *Los Angeles Times*, March 3, 1985, https://www.latimes.com/archives/la-xpm-1985-03-03-re-33075-story.html, accessed September 10, 2023.

62 Ronald Feldman Gallery, "Helen Mayer & Newton Harrison, A Tale of Three Cities." Exhibition, April 17–June 14, 1985, https://feldmangallery.com/exhibition/102-a-tale-of-3-cities, accessed August 15, 2023.

63 *Arroyo Seco Release: A Serpentine for Pasadena: A Work by Helen Mayer and Newton Harrison*, exh. cat., Ibid.

64 Series 2, Project Files, Subseries 20, Box 57, Folders 5. Helen and Newton Harrison Papers, M1797. Special Collections & University Archives, Stanford University,

Stanford, CA, consulted in October–December 2021; Helen Mayer Harrison and Newton Harrison, *The Time of the Force Majeure: After 45 Years Counterforce is on the Horizon*, p. 177.

65 Kaplan, Sam H., "Artists Sketch Natural Look for Arroyo Seco," Ibid.

66 "Devils Gate: A Refuge for Pasadena" is also called "Devil's Gate Transformation: A Refugia for Pasadena."

67 Materials related to this project can be accessed in the archive: Series 2, Project Files, Subseries 20, Box 57, Folders 9–15. Helen and Newton Harrison Papers, M1797. Special Collections & University Archives, Stanford University, Stanford, CA, consulted in October–December 2021. For discussion of the historical circumstances and the project narrative also see: Helen Mayer Harrison and Newton Harrison, *The Time of the Force Majeure: After 45 Years Counterforce is on the Horizon,* pp. 182–187; *Devil's Gate Transformation, A Refuge for Pasadena: A Work of Art by Newton and Helen Mayer Harrison*, exh. cat. Pasadena Gallery of Contemporary Art, Community Action for Parks, and Art Center College of Design, Pasadena, CA, 1987; Leslie Ryan, "Art + Ecology: Land Reclamation Works of Artists Robert Smithson, Robert Morris, and Helen Mayer Harrison and Newton Harrison," Ibid.

68 Dunn, Ashley, "Artists Sculpt Model of Costly Proposal to Renew Devils Gate," *Los Angeles Times,* December 3, 1987, https://www.latimes.com/archives/la-xpm-1987-12-03-ga-26376-story.html, accessed September 15, 2023.

69 Dunn, Ashley, "Artists Sculpt Model of Costly Proposal to Renew Devils Gate," Ibid.

70 Dunn, Ashley, "Artists Sculpt Model of Costly Proposal to Renew Devils Gate," Ibid.

71 Pasadena City, *Arroyo Seco Master Plans: Hahamongna Watershed Park Master Plan,* https://www.cityofpasadena.net/parks-and-rec/wp-content/uploads/sites/33/Hahamongna-Watershed-Park-Master-Plan.pdf, accessed November 1, 2023.

72 Wilson, Larry, "Art – fine, so far as it goes," *Pasadena Star News,* September 28, 2022, https://www.pasadenastarnews.com/2022/09/28/the-artists-who-first-drew-up-a-revitalized-hahamongna/, accessed October 1, 2022.

73 Materials related to the *San Diego Round* can be accessed in the archive: Series 2, Project Files, Subseries 19, Box 56, Folders 1–16. Helen and Newton Harrison Papers, M1797. Special Collections & University Archives, Stanford University, Stanford, CA, consulted in October–December 2021. For discussion of the historical circumstances and the project narrative also see: Helen Mayer Harrison and Newton Harrison, *The Time of the Force Majeure: After 45 Years Counterforce is on the Horizon*, pp. 172–175; and Robert Pincus, "UCSD Artists Have Grand Designs for S.D.," *The San Diego Union,* August 17, 1986, E1, 6–7.

74 Newspaper clipping, from editorials, *The San Diego Tribune* (August 25, 1986), see: Series 2, Project Files, Subseries 19, Box 56, Folders 5. Helen and Newton Harrison Papers, M1797. Special Collections & University Archives, Stanford University, Stanford, CA, consulted in October–December 2021.

75 Harrison, Helen Mayer, and Newton Harrison, *The Time of the Force Majeure: After 45 Years Counterforce is on the Horizon,* p. 175.

76 Ollman, Leah, "New Visions of Public Art in San Diego," *The Los Angeles Times,* July 1, 1992.

77 For the proposal, budget, and correspondence see: Series 2, Project Files, Subseries 37, Box 71, Folders 1–12, & Box 275, Folder 2. Helen and Newton Harrison Papers, M1797. Special Collections & University Archives, Stanford University, Stanford, CA, consulted in October–December 2021.

78 Ollman, Leah, "New Visions of Public Art in San Diego," Ibid.

79 The archival holdings are substantial and detail the proposal, grants, budget, and correspondence: Series 2, Project Files, Subseries 51, Box 89–93. Helen and Newton Harrison Papers, M1797. Special Collections & University Archives, Stanford University, Stanford, CA, consulted in October–December 2021.

80 Harrison, Helen Mayer, and Newton Harrison, *The Time of the Force Majeure: After 45 Years Counterforce is on the Horizon*, pp. 294–301.

81 "Los Angeles River Revitalization, Our River, Our Future," https://lariver.org/ecosystem, accessed December 13, 2023.

82 Emerling, Susan, "Art as Intervention," *The Los Angeles Times,* January 11, 2005, https://www.latimes.com/archives/la-xpm-2005-jan-11-et-harrisons11-story.html, accessed September 15, 2022.

83 Helen Mayer Harrison and Newton Harrison, *The Time of the Force Majeure: After 45 Years Counterforce is on the Horizon*, p. 297.

84 Ryan, Leslie, "Art + Ecology: Land Reclamation Works of Artists Robert Smithson, Robert Morris, and Helen Mayer Harrison and Newton Harrison," p. 107.

85 Harrison, Helen Mayer, and Newton Harrison, *From There to Here.* The Harrison Studio, San Diego, CA, 2001.

86 Weintraub, Linda, "Helen and Newton Harrison: Strategies to Sustain Life," *To Life! Eco Art in Pursuit of a Sustainable Planet,* Linda Weintraub. University of California Press, Berkeley, CA, 2012, pp. 74–80, 77.

87 Burnham, Jack, "Systems Esthetics," *Art Forum,* September, 1968, https://www.artforum.com/features/systems-esthetics-201372/, accessed October 1, 2023.

88 Burnham, Jack, "Systems Esthetics," Ibid.

89 Ryan, Leslie, "Art + Ecology: Land Reclamation Works of Artists Robert Smithson, Robert Morris, and Helen Mayer Harrison and Newton Harrison," p. 103

90 Adcock, Craig, "Conversational Drift: Helen Mayer Harrison and Newton Harrison," p. 39.

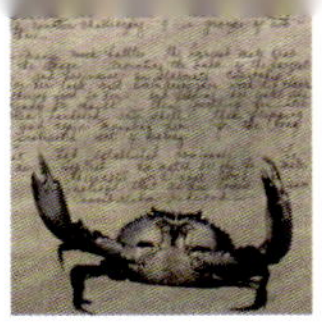

Prophetic Works TATIANA SIZONENKO

We understand the universe as a giant conversation taking place simultaneously in trillions of voices and billions of languages, most of which we could not conceive even if we knew that they existed. Of those voices whose existence has impinged upon our own to the degree that we can become aware of them, we realize that our awareness is imperfect at best. Therefore, it seems to us that the casual and wanton destruction and disruption of living systems of whose relationships we know so little requires extraordinary hubris.
Helen Mayer Harrison and Newton Harrison.[1]

After all our studying and art making, the artist between us made a prophecy and an intuitive leap that the earth would soon warm, and began to imagine what a warmed earth would be like.
Helen Mayer Harrison and Newton Harrison,
From the *Seventh Lagoon*.[2]

And in this new beginning
this continuous rebeginning
you will feed me
when my lands can no longer produce
and I will house you
when your lands are covered with water
and together we will withdraw
as the water rise.
If we achieve this
then the oceans rise gracefully
we can withdraw with co-equal grace.
Helen Mayer Harrison and Newton Harrison,
From the *Seventh Lagoon*.[3]

Following the successes and controversies of the *Survival Pieces*, Helen and Newton continued their collaboration with scientists, expanded their critique of environmental degradation, and pursued more ardently their quest for the means of survival. Throughout the 1970s and 1980s the scope of their work expanded constantly, and they shifted from closed (portable) or localized ecosystems to bioregional works, taking a greater interest in ecological restoration on an ever-larger scale. Their work also genuinely relied on scientific methods in researching ecologies by staging real-life experiments and discovering conditions necessary to sustain functioning of ecosystems. Additionally, they interrogated and critiqued techno-scientific models of the ecosystems, of industrial and capitalistic modes of production and extraction, and came to realize the political force of their work. Thus, they imagined and, prophetically, called for a radical reorientation of lifestyles. At that very busy and fertile period, the Harrisons' work emerged in increasingly complex ways, comprising scientific diagrams, photography, painting, poetics, maps, design, metaphors, narratives, politics, and written dialogues that they also performed. Shifting away from both avant-garde aesthetics and art-technology experiments, the Harrisons began exhibiting their work as large-scale installation panels that visualized multi-faceted ecological processes and deep philosophical arguments. Through their works of the 1970s, 1980s, and 1990s, the artists developed a holistic vision of a sentient universe, the Web of Life, situating their own work in relation to the central issue of survival. By engaging with deep concerns such as ecological preservation and rethinking the current uses of technology, the Harrisons produced art with equally deep implications, making concrete predictions about the future and the long-term outcomes of environmental damage. Reflecting on their fifty-year career, the artists considered their work from this period as prophetic, because more and more of their predictions began to come true.

(RE)INVENTING VISUAL LANGUAGE

From 1973, the Harrisons started working with maps, making them a central part of their artistic expression and thus marking a fundamental change to their work. Michel de Certeau, writing an introduction to the 1985 exhibition of the *Lagoon Cycle* at the Herbert F. Johnson Museum of Art at Cornell University, observed that, beginning from the Renaissance, "the founding gesture" that "created space" was map-making, which "represented reality ... in order to change it."[4] *San Diego as the Center of a World* was the first work where the artists used a series of Mercator projection maps of the entire globe, which can be understood as signaling the extent of their ambition and the domain itself. The Earth appeared as an elegant Mercator projection of the Earth, with San Diego, the locus of the artists, at its exact geometric center. They literally put San Diego, a periphery of the international art world, on the map. The map not only visualized but also re-presented a world that was being both described and invented at the same time. This perspective further meant that they did not necessarily conceptualize New York as the center of the world (as the site of artistic value). De Certeau went further to say that by implications, their map-making showed not only the movement (idea) in the present but also in the future.[5] For this artwork, the Harrisons' approach to using maps was in its embryonic stage: according to Gilbert Plass and Robert Bryce, they simply appropriated a ready-made map and juxtaposed it with texts to visualize the contradictory arguments about climate change and its implications for our planet.[6] Later in their career, they would engage in profound map-making and re-making, directly pertaining to their research projects.

According to a story recounted by the artists, Helen found a book by Gilbert Plass, who made the powerful argument that the burning of coal and oil would cause global warming (as we now define it), thus higher CO_2 levels, an accelerated greenhouse effect, melting glaciers, and a rise in temperature and sea levels. Helen also picked up a book by Robert Bryce, who argued that the planet was in an interglacial period and would in fact get colder. Employing the strategies of conceptual art, word-image play, and irony, the Harrisons visualized the implications of the arguments of both Bryce and Plass by proposing scenarios of both melting and freezing.

The resulting work comprises five photo-text images of an azimuthal world projection with San Diego at its exact geometric center.[7] Each work discusses a different scenario and set of proportions. The first three maps unpack Bryce's argument, picking a different moment from a period of glaciation and discussing the probability of changes in the depth of the world's oceans resulting from alterations in the

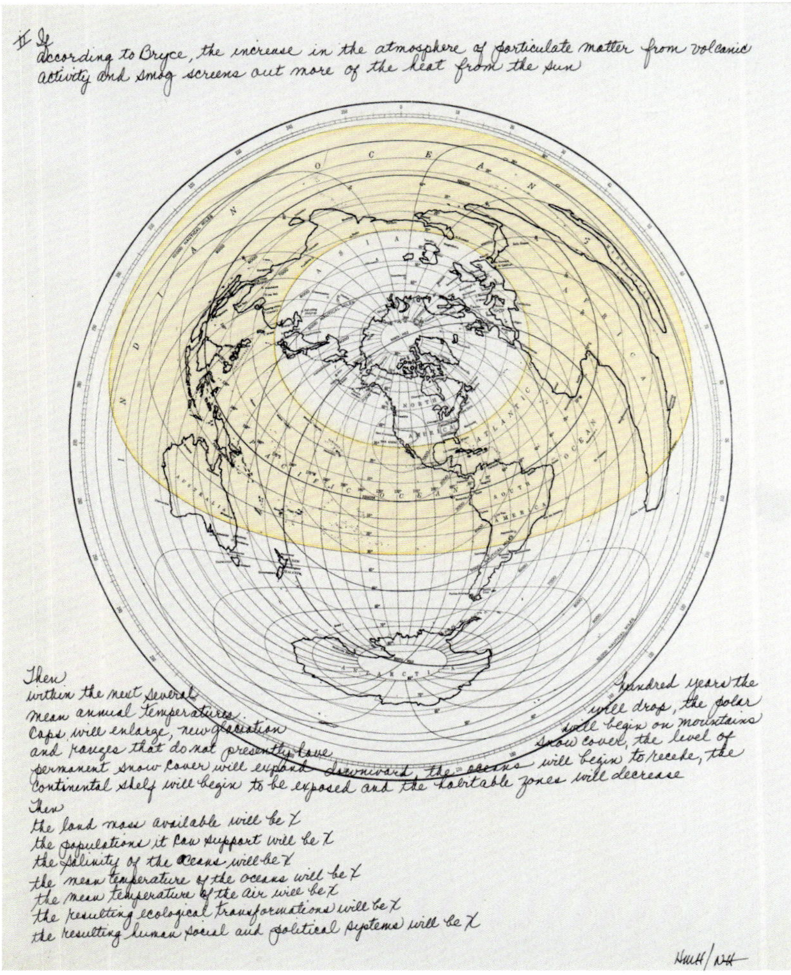

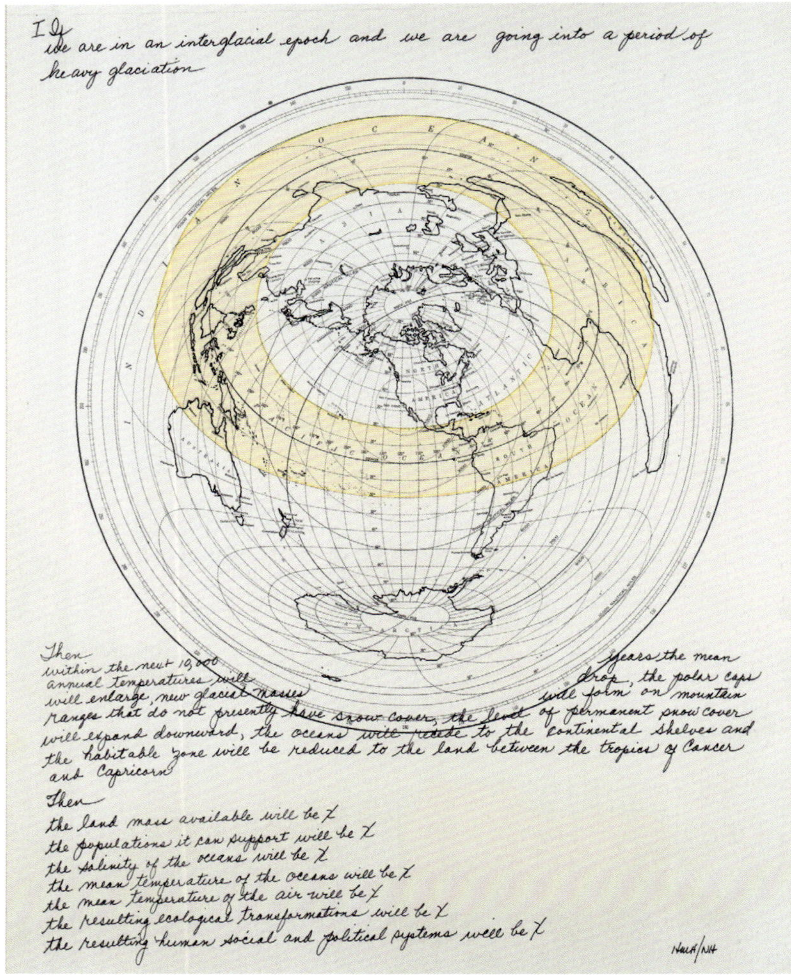

earth's climate. Map IV projects a global warming scenario based on Plass' argument, by positing a mean air temperature rise of 22 degrees Fahrenheit and an ocean level rise of at least 20–30 feet, with many coastal areas becoming uninhabitable, leading to profound ecological, social, and political transformations. Map V presents its conclusions in alternatives for remedial action by advising that if one of the proportions I through IV are true, then "begin long- or short-range planning." However, if it cannot be determined which proportion is true or which combination of proportions is true, then an accompanying text below the map advises, in Helen's words (essentially), "Begin both long- and short-range planning."

The text of *San Diego is the Center of a World* is transcribed as following:

I.
If
We are in an interglacial epoch and we are going into a period of heavy glaciation

Then
within the next 10,000 years the mean
annual temperatures will drop, the polar caps
will enlarge, new glacial masses will form on mountain
ranges that do not presently have snow cover, the level of
permanent snow cover
will expand downward, the ocean will recede to the
continental shelves and
the habitable zone will be reduced to the land between
the tropics of Cancer and Capricorn

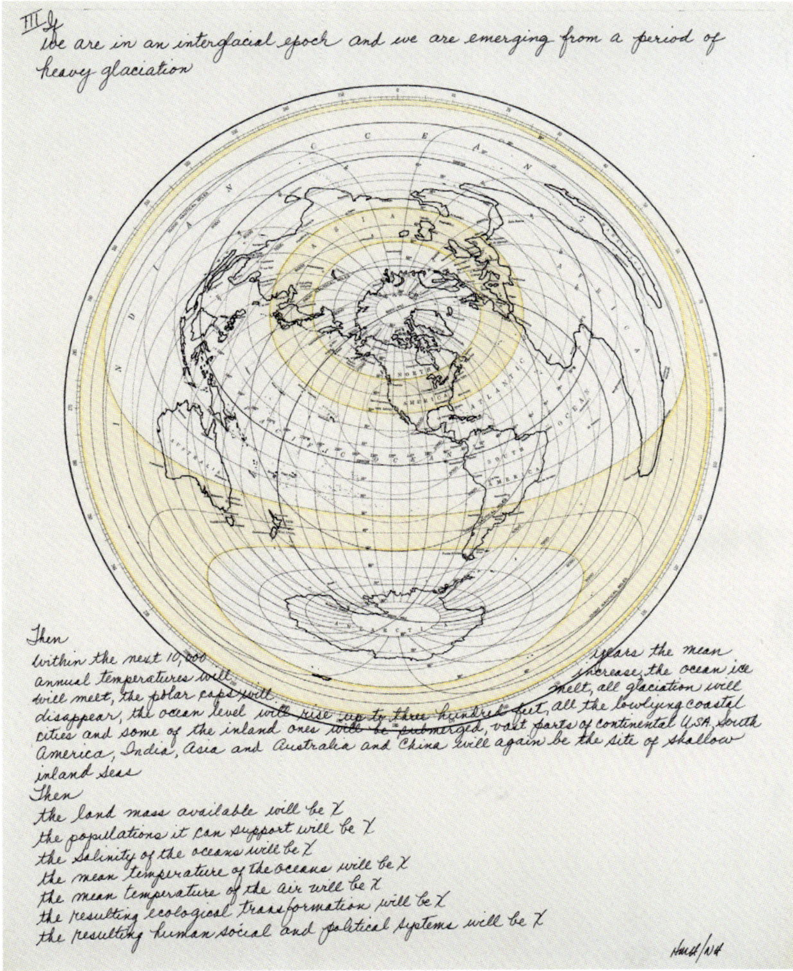

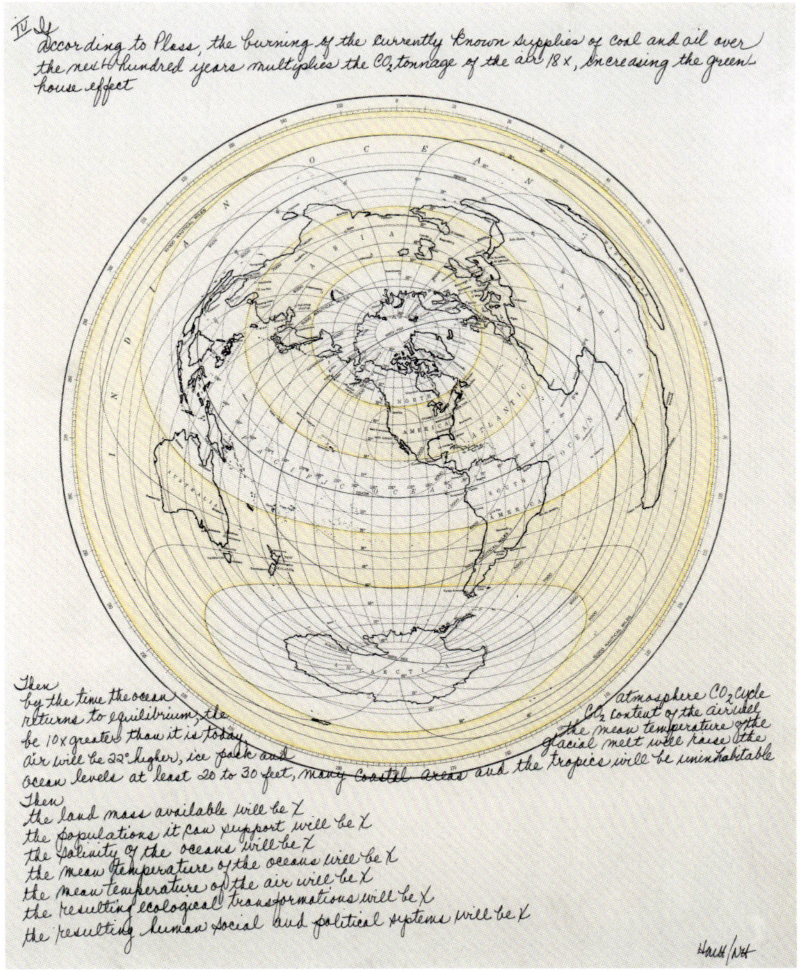

Then
the land mass available will be X
the populations it can support will be X
the salinity of the oceans will be X
the mean temperature of the oceans will be X
the mean temperature of the air will be X
the resulting ecological transformations will be X
the resulting human social and political systems will be X

II.
If
According to Bryce, the increase in the atmosphere
of the particulate matter from volcanic
activity and smog screens out more of the heat
from the sun

Then
within the next several hundred years the
mean annual temperatures will drop, the polar
Caps will enlarge, new glaciation will begin
on mountains and ranges that do not presently
have snow cover, the level of
permanent snow cover will expand downward
the oceans will begin to recede, the
continental shelf will begin to be exposed and
the habitable zones will decrease

Then
the land mass available will be X
the populations it can support will be X
the salinity of the oceans will be X

the mean temperature of the oceans will be X
the mean temperature of the air will be X
the resulting ecological transformation will be X
the resulting human social and political systems will be X

III.
If
We are in an interglacial epoch and we are emerging
from a period of heavy glaciation

Then
within the next 10,000 years the mean
annual temperatures will increase, the ocean ice
will melt, the polar caps will melt, all glaciation
will disappear, the ocean level
will rise up to three hundred feet,
all the low-lying coastal
cities and some of the inland ones will be submerged,
vast parts of the continental U.S.A.,
South America, India, Asia and Australia and China
will again be the site of shallow
inland seas

Then
the land mass available will be X
the populations it can support will be X
the salinity of the oceans will be X
the mean temperature of the oceans will be X
the mean temperature of the air will be X
the resulting ecological transformation will be X
the resulting human social and political systems will be X

IV.
If
According to Plass, the burning of currently known supplies
of coal and oil over
the next hundred years multiplies the CO_2 tonnage of the air 18X,
increasing the green-house effect

Then
by the time the ocean atmosphere CO_2 cycle
returns to equilibrium the CO_2 content of the air will
be 10X greater than it is today the mean temperature of the
air will be 22° higher, ice pack and glacial melt will raise the
ocean levels at least 20 to 30 feet, many coastal areas and the
tropics will be uninhabitable

Then
the land mass available will be X
the populations it can support will be X
the salinity of the oceans will be X
the mean temperature of the oceans will be X
the mean temperature of the air will be X
the resulting ecological transformation will be X
the resulting human social and political systems will be X

and

If
only proposition I is
true, begin long range
planning

If
only proposition II is
true, begin long range
planning

If
only proposition III is true, begin
short range planning

If only proposition IV is true
begin short range planning

If it cannot be determined which of these propositions
is true or it cannot

be determined which combination of these propositions
is true or it cannot
be determined which of these propositions is false,
either singly or in combination,
then begin both long and short range planning.

San Diego as the Center of a World was their first artwork to engage the problem of climate change. Embedded in this particular narrative, the image of a whimsically "decentered world" expressed the shocking implications of different possible climatic scenarios in a language that people could understand. Their visualization of the 200-page arguments of Bryce and Plass in compelling word-image maps was an invitation to a dialogue so that, as Newton said, "everyone could see what could potentially happen and ... become their own planner." This was an indication of their transformative thinking and steadfast commitment to the idea that the planet was their client and that they would only do work to benefit the ecosystem. This would be the last work in which the Harrisons' roles were distinct, Helen being the researcher and Newton the form-maker, with them collectively being the poet. From here on their collaboration essentially changed and became co-equal, as they began imagining that there was "a third party, a unique co-creator – the real artist," visible only to them.[8]

The Harrisons started to work on an epic scale in the 1970s by adopting the "Renaissance mural" format. Their works, in the form of photographic collages mounted on canvas and painted with Marschall's photo oils and ink, behaved as monumental painting and fresco cycles on the walls of galleries and museums. Originating from the manipulation of their original photography and their drawings and writings on vellum, and then further altered through photographic processes, these large-scale collages of images, maps, and poetic texts, complete with metaphorical thinking, began to index greater environmental imperatives.

MAPPING AS A MEANS OF DISCOVERY: FIRST BIOREGIONAL WORKS

Three monumental and philosophically consequential artworks were the first by the Harrisons to address the themes of social and environmental justice from a bioregional perspective: the *Meditation on the Gabrielino, Whose Name for Themselves is No Longer Remembered Although We Know that They Farmed with Fire and Fought Wars by Singing* (1976); the *Meditation on the Great Lakes of North America* (1977); and *the Meditations on the Sacramento River, the Delta, and Bays of San Francisco* (1976–77). These intellectually and visually complex installations spoke about natural resource management, starting with the ecological intelligence of native peoples such as the Gabrielino, whose near-genocide led to ecocide by their Spanish colonial rulers, and the development of modern exploitative agricultural practices in California. The Harrisons' works also eloquently exposed the extent of state and federal agricultural subsidies for California's Central Valley that reinforced intensive irrigation for maximum corporate profits, another form of ecocide, on a massive scale, of the region's natural watersheds. Made in the mid-1970s, the artworks have even stronger resonance today as we grapple with depleting topsoil, rapidly diminishing biodiversity, and the effects of climate change expressed through rising temperatures, severe weather patterns, prolonged droughts, and increasingly horrific wildfires in California.[9] The Harrisons' research and findings presented an argument for the restoration of natural ecosystems and watersheds, reductions in irrigated farming, advancements in water recycling, and improvements in outreach and public participation in setting water management policy.

The *Meditation on the Gabrielino* appropriates historical photographs and texts to trace the human impact, both ecological and political, on the existing ecosystem of the greater Los Angeles River watershed. Originally titled *Survival Piece No. 10*, the work was commissioned by California State University Long Beach for the exhibition *Beyond the Artist's Hand*.[10] Based on what could be reconstructed by the artists, this project explored the Gabrielino Indians' way of life and speculated about their relationship to the land. Upon arriving in Long Beach, the Harrisons studied the place as it was before the development of oil wells. The work became an observation on the ecological practices of the Gabrielino Indians, whose history was visualized through excerpts from a series of letters written to the *Los Angeles Star* in 1850 by journalist Hugo Reed, who retold the story of the Spanish invasion and conquest as it had been communicated to him by contemporary Gabrielinos. The *Meditation on the Gabrielino* made a subtle comparison of the consumption and production practices of the indigenous people with that of now, noting obvious effects of their differences in land use by looking at trees, streams, estuaries, vanished fields, diverted rivers, and filled-in marshes. In all, the work showed that so little of the original ecosystem was left in the Los Angeles and Long Beach area; both the land and the people who populated it experienced ecocide and genocide, first at the hands of Spanish missionaries, and later as a result of industrialization and urbanization throughout the area.

The work's character was that of a collage, with photographs, maps, and texts representing the successive transposition as each succeeding culture displaced the viability of the prior by destroying the ecology that had supported it. The Harrisons conceived the work as two large photographs, one with a supporting body of smaller images, the other complemented by historical printed chapters relating the history of the people. The work exists in two versions: one is a sketch in the Brooklyn Museum of Art and the other, the final version, is at the Museum of Contemporary Art San Diego. Through close examination of vintage photographs taken by the 19th-century anthropologist Roger de Sawtelles at the Black Star Canyon in the San Gabriel Mountains, the artists revealed small holes bored into rocks, the marks of past human engagement with the landscape. Handwritten text added by the artists explained that these depressions were a result of the corn-grinding processes used by the original inhabitants of the land, whose ecologically sustainable practices were disrupted by the depredations of inappropriate techniques introduced by Spanish colonists. The artists also learned about the ecological intelligence of the indigenous people, who practiced selective burning to control the undergrowth and avoid big forest fires. The Harrisons juxtaposed this native existence with that of the Spanish (and their Mexican successors), represented by a photograph of the San Gabriel Mission, who would also find their way of life overwhelmed by the arrival of new colonists and new industrial processes when California became part of the United States.

Presented as a reflection on landscapes, timescales, and social and environmental justice, the *Meditation on the Gabrielino* has poetic and melancholic undertones. The artists employed photographic images "to extend" the narrative, as Jill Dawsey describes the practice,[11] by focusing on the earth and geological time rather than on people, although the traces of human practices were made visible. The work bears apparent implications to our own time, as it suggests potent questions about the transience of cultures and systems, and of a future that can be foreseen in which humans are no longer present.

The *Meditation on the Great Lakes of North America* (1977), which is the first bio-regional and watershed work of the artists, was developed as a result of an invitation from the Center for the 20th Century Studies at the University of Wisconsin-Milwaukee (UWM). Realized as a series of four colored maps, which were preceded by design sketches, the Harrisons proposed to remove political divisions between the United States and Canada to create the Great Lakes Watershed Area.[12] Making of this work was concurrent with their decision to do only work by invitation and only when the request came from an institution or private patron that would allow the artists to integrate themselves into a community, as well as to provide needed time to think and research as part of the commission. UWM offered exactly that: it offered the university setting on Lake Michigan, time in the libraries examining maps of the Great Lakes Watershed and its ecologies, and an opportunity to engage students in research and discussion of the environmental history of the region during a summer workshop conducted by the artists.

Meditation on the Great Lakes of North America, 1977

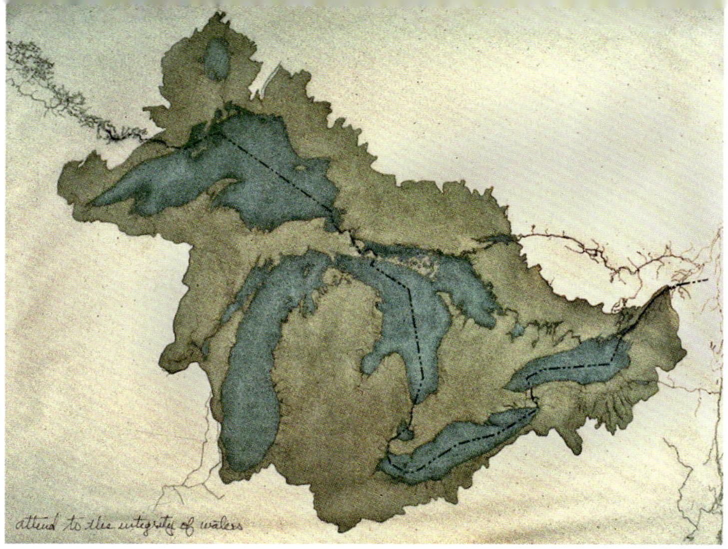

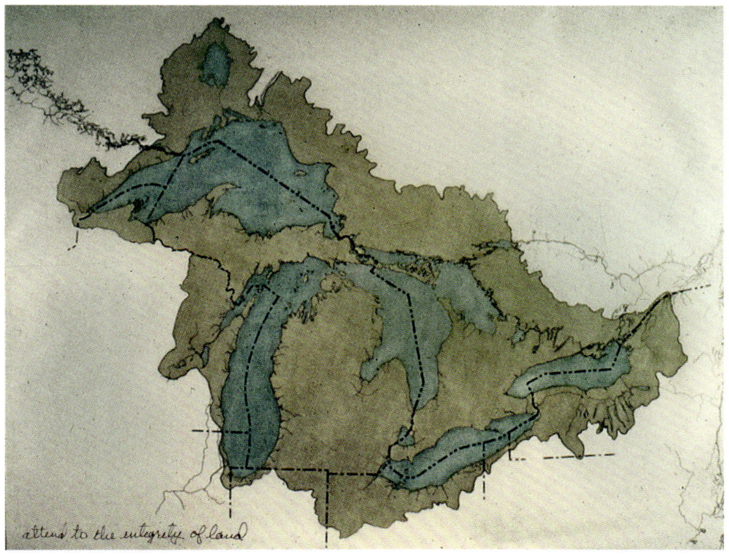

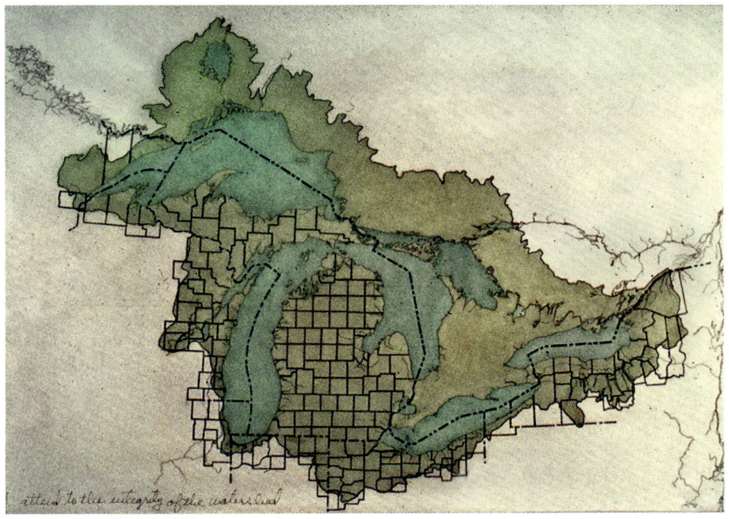

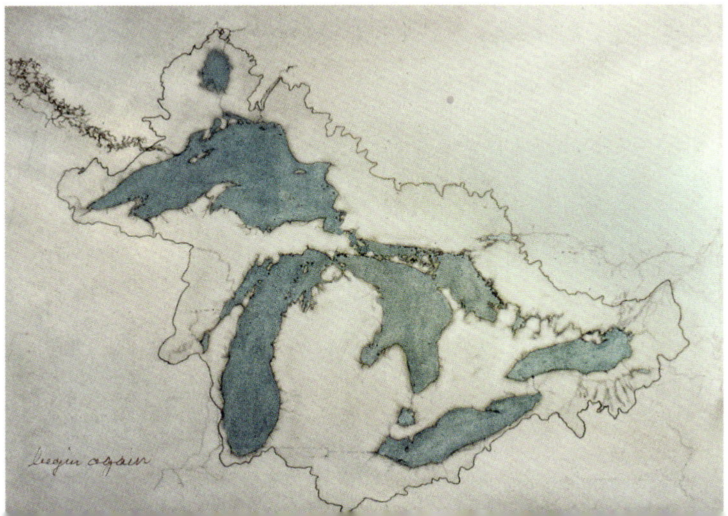

During their short tenure at UWM, the Harrisons realized that the regional and international borders were literally drawn on water, if such a thing were possible, as Newton would ask his host, Michel Benamou. The artists also discovered that, contrary to the widespread belief that it was potable, the water of Lake Michigan was polluted by chemical and industrial waste that came from Chicago. The artists proposed a utopian idea, emerging from maps, drawings, text, and performances, that people residing in the Great Lakes Watershed, on both sides of the border – Canada and the United States – would collectively withdraw from these countries to form a new ecologically conscious nation that they called "a Dictatorship of the Ecology."[13] The artists' vision made a nod to historically conceptualized dreamlands such as Thomas More's *Utopia* (1516) and Francis Bacon's *New Atlantis* (1626). In his interview with Craig Adcock, Newton further explained: "Our Great Lakes proposal, for example, suggests that the North American continent should balkanize into bioregional entities with supernational powers. Above all, such bioregional entities would be able to control their own taxes, their own industries and inputs into the environment. Bioregionalists have been suggesting something like this for well over a decade."[14] Building on the utopian metaphor, the artists even began to outline the dictates of the ecology that could sustain both ecosystems and cultural systems.

The *Meditation on the Great Lakes of North America* was one of the first series of maps where the Harrisons employed symbolic (or iconic) language for representation of an ecological process. The four colored charts, visualizing in various ways the Great Lakes Watershed, also directed the viewers' attention to the argument through commanding texts: "Attend to the integrity of waters," "Attend to the integrity of land," "Attend to the integrity of the watershed," "Begin again." The addition of color to the maps not only amplified the message visually but also communicated the idea of unity across the watershed, presenting the area as organically shaped, a living body. The artists repeated the

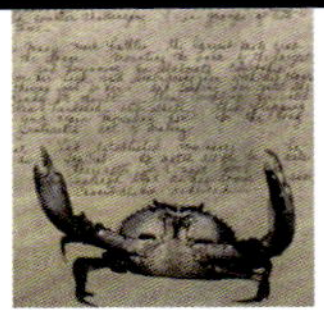

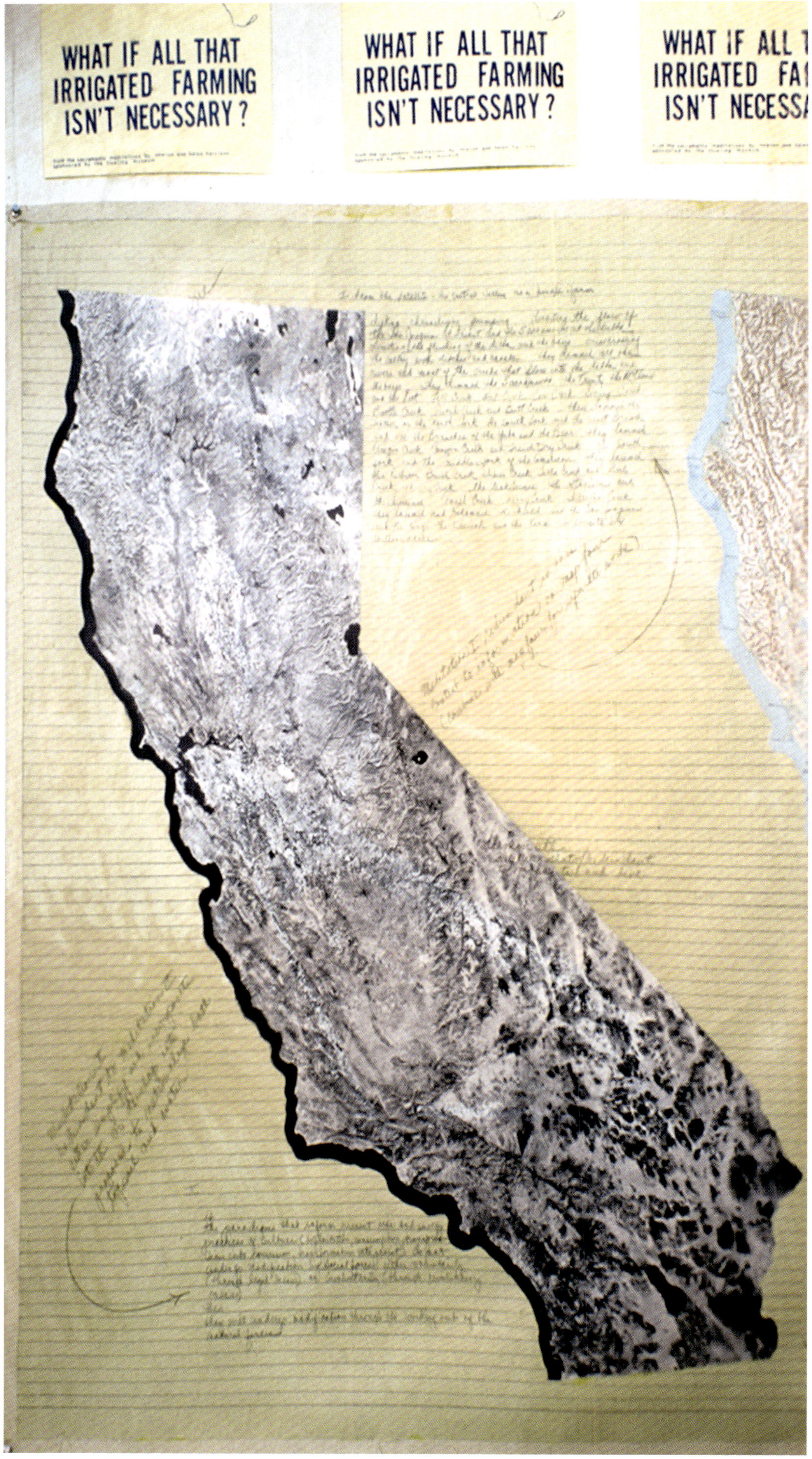

These posters were put up on San Francisco street corners and in public restrooms, graffiti added by the public in the course of time
From Meditations on the Sacramento River, the Delta, and the Bays of San Francisco
1976–1977

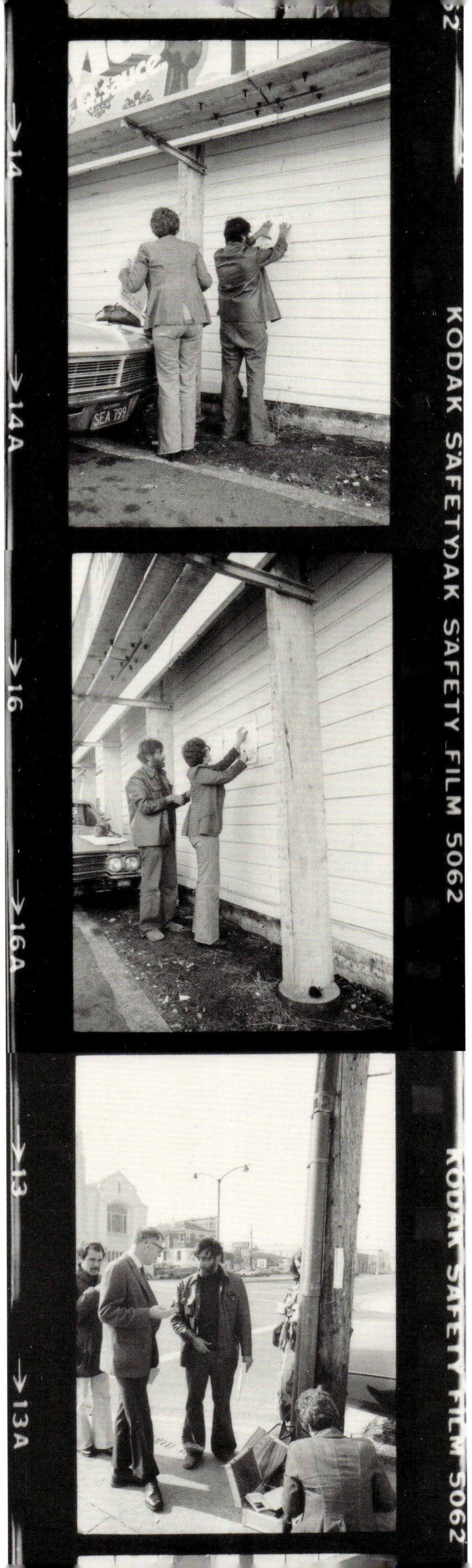
KODAK SAFETY FILM 5062

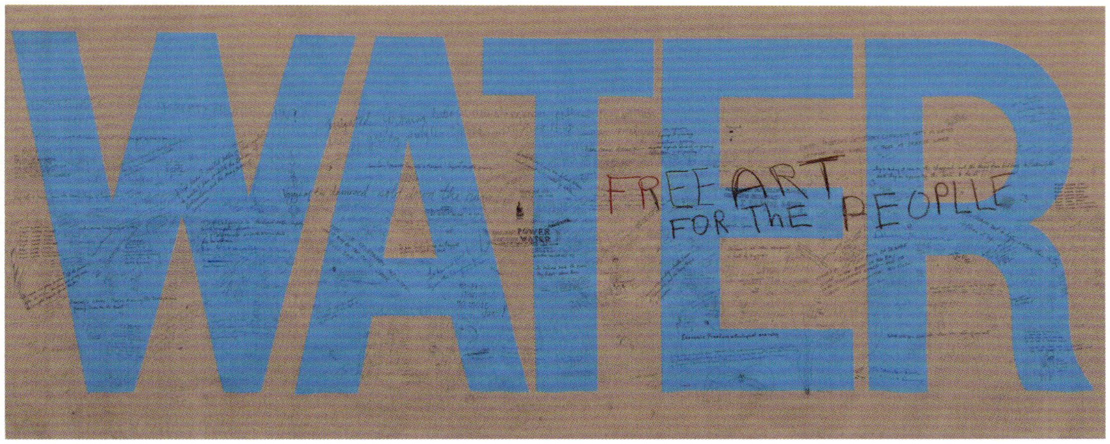
WATER
FREE ART
FOR THE PEOPLE

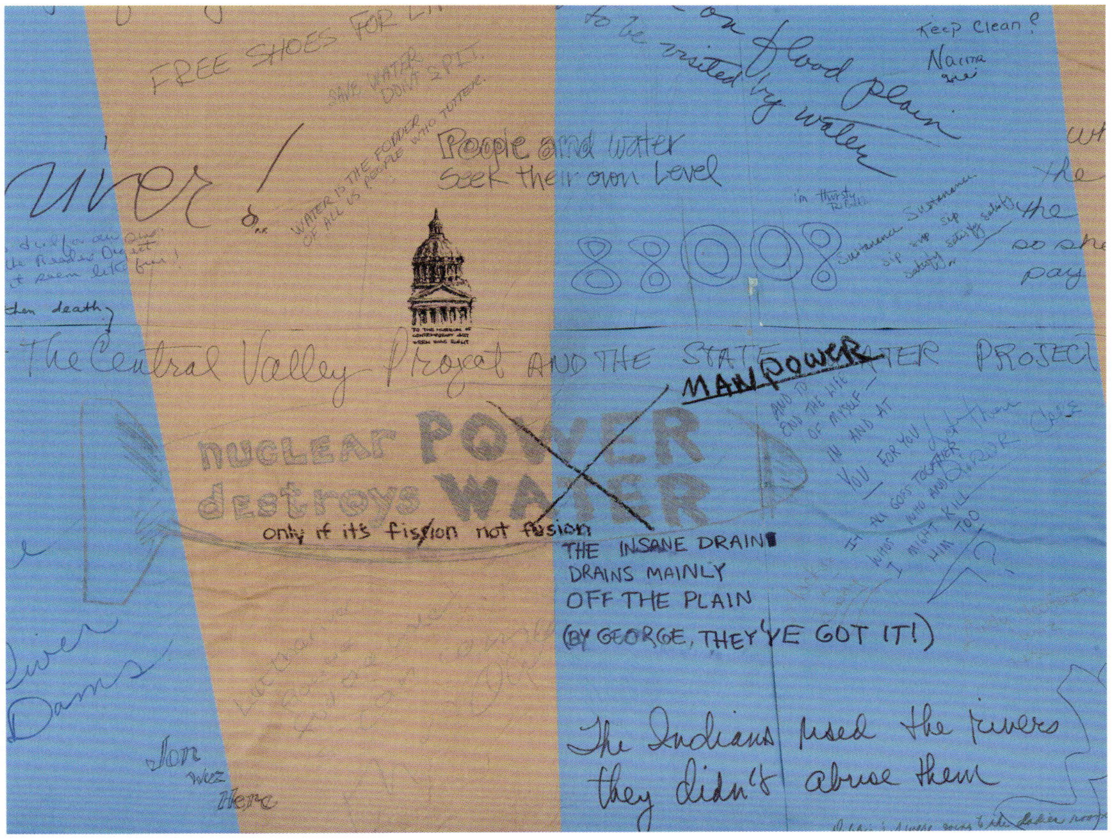
Keep Clean!
People and water
seek their own level
88008
The Central Valley Project AND THE STATE
MANPOWER
nuclear POWER
destroys WATER
only if it's fission not fusion
THE INSANE DRAIN
DRAINS MAINLY
OFF THE PLAIN
(BY GEORGE, THEY'VE GOT IT!)
The Indians used the rivers
they didn't abuse them

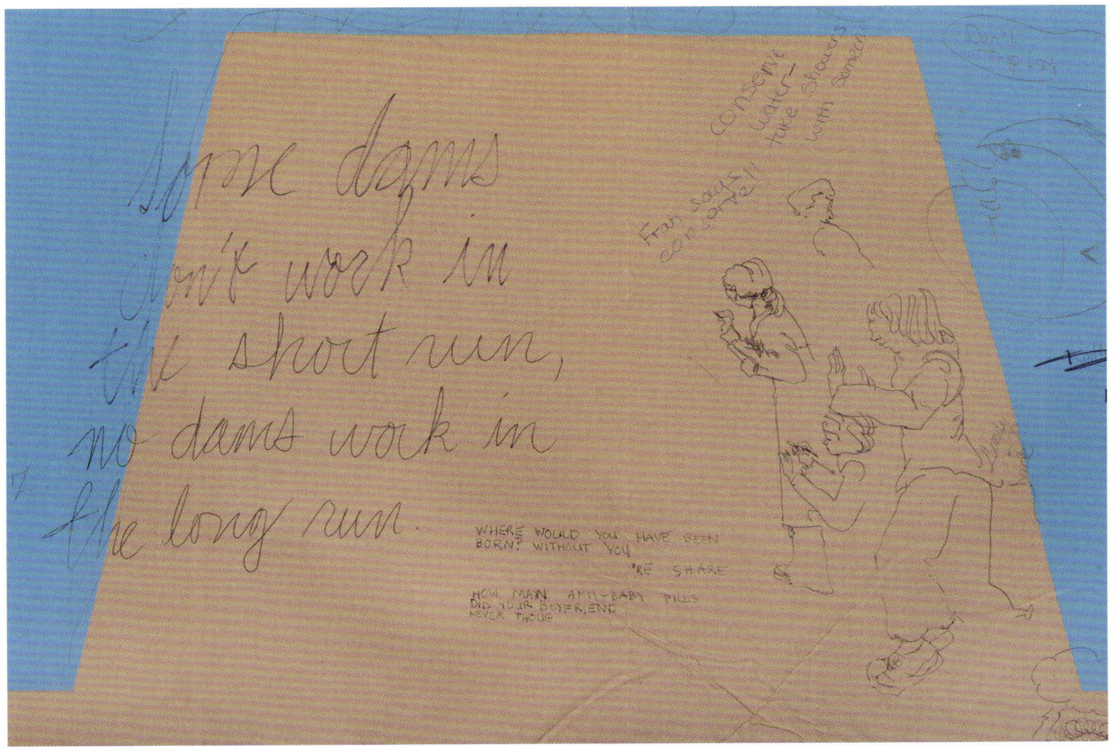
Some dams
don't work in
the short run,
no dams work in
the long run.

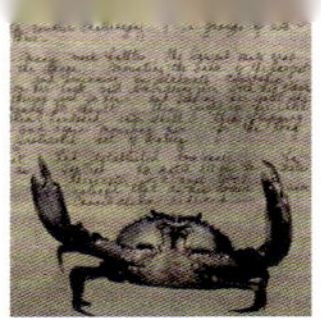

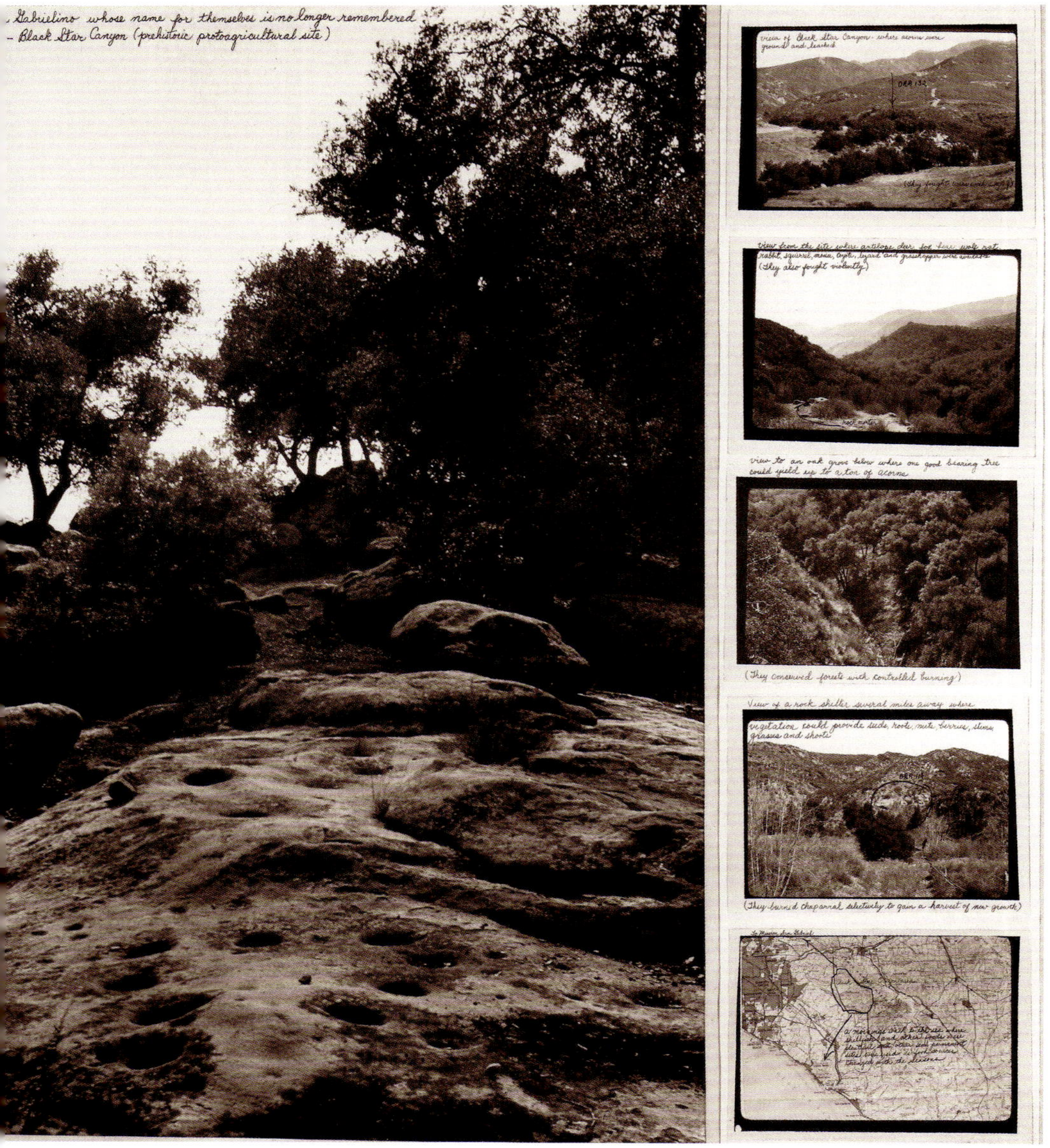

Meditation on the Gabrielino Whose Name for Themselves Is No Longer Remembered Although We Know They Farmed with Fire and Fought Wars by Singing, 1976 Long Beach Museum of Art, CA

image of the watershed in this series, using its iconic form as a mnemonic device to activate the audience's imagination and consciousness. Thus, the Harrisons attempted to persuade spectators of the possibility of a different reality by making them aware of the actual disturbing condition. Charles Green theorized that the Harrisons' proposals assigned great importance to the icons used as "a conceptual tool mediating between information and action, reducing ecological proposals to iconic logos," and therefore utilizing this visual method to help the viewer to grasp "a complex abstraction – the ecology of a particular environment – without being overwhelmed by it."[15] Consequently, the *Meditation* presented an imagined alternative reality, both feasible and less likely, of a particular fictive or utopian type. This work opened up the possibility of a new field of visual play that the artists would employ in all later works: they began to use iconic map-forms abstracted from the shapes of watersheds and green corridors to encode a complex array of ecological functions, processes, and concerns.

In many conversations, Newton underscored that "our first watershed piece was Sacramento in 1977,"[16] and in the triptych of meditations, the *Sacramento Meditations*, also known as the *Meditations on the Sacramento River, the Delta, and Bays of San Francisco*, stands out as the pivotal work in its examination of the elements, processes, and functions associated with a watershed. The Harrisons focused their research on California's two largest rivers, the Sacramento and the San Joaquin, and addressed the conditions and usage of river water, subsurface water, and surface runoff, thus essentially drawing attention to officially endorsed yet disastrous water policies and the horrific mismanagement of natural resources. They amassed data concerning all of the components of the watersheds and created an exhibition, billboards, radio and TV performances, and graffiti, poster, and media campaigns to convey how the current practices create water crises. Original press clippings preserved in the archives suggest that the work was received with criticism and hostility even by people within "the so-called ecological community," who thought they "had gone a bit too far."[17]

The work originated from the invitation of Lynn Hershman, the director of the Floating Museum in San Francisco, who visited the Harrisons' studio at UCSD and was immensely impressed with their work on the *Lagoon Cycle* and the *Salton Sea*. The *Sacramento Meditations* comprises the first sketch, a series of ten California maps accompanied by handwritten texts, eleven posters, a water billboard with graffiti generated by audience participants, and other ephemera related to the original exhibitions held at the Floating Museum, the San Francisco Art Institute, and San Francisco Museum of

▶ Meditations on the Sacramento River, the Delta, and the Bays of San Francisco

1977 San Francisco Art Institute, San Francisco Museum of Modern Art, CA ▶▶

Modern Art (SF MoMA)[18]. As the archival documentation shows, the original nine texts commissioned by the Floating Museum underwent some revision for a later exhibition at Ronald Feldman's gallery in New York and the Chicago Museum of Contemporary Art (1980). Based on research conducted over a period of six months at the Berkeley Water Resources Library, the work referenced nearly seventy scholarly articles on the condition of water and irrigation in California and contained considerable data that was not public knowledge.[19]

Each of the ten iconic mappings visualized the state of California differently: as a satellite image of the Central Valley in the form of a single mega-farm, as a web of political boundaries and water districts, and as maps of water resources, irrigable land, and topology. The work was designed in such a way that each map presented a unique perspective on the watersheds: the bird's-eye view of the state allowed a viewer to grasp the watersheds in their entirety, the topography of the land reflected the cultural perspective of native people, with dams and pumping stations revealed through a technocratic and engineering lens, while the various political divisions reflected the interests of government, big money corporations, and the military. The purpose of the presentation was to guide viewers to discover that the agricultural lands of California's Central Valley were beset with ill-conceived dams, ill-advised irrigation systems, and ill-managed agricultural practices. From the artists' research, it became clear that all but a few rivers were dammed, with irrigated farming receiving 90 percent of the water. Moreover, the Harrisons discovered that 10 percent of all irrigated farmland became too saturated with salt to farm, and the wetlands were substantially damaged by the reversed flow of the San Joaquin, which became deadly from pesticides and other agricultural pollution. A disturbing narrative, written as a poetic text for two voices (male and female), hung next to hand-worked maps and invited audiences to reconsider all Central Valley operations – farming, water usage, and damming.

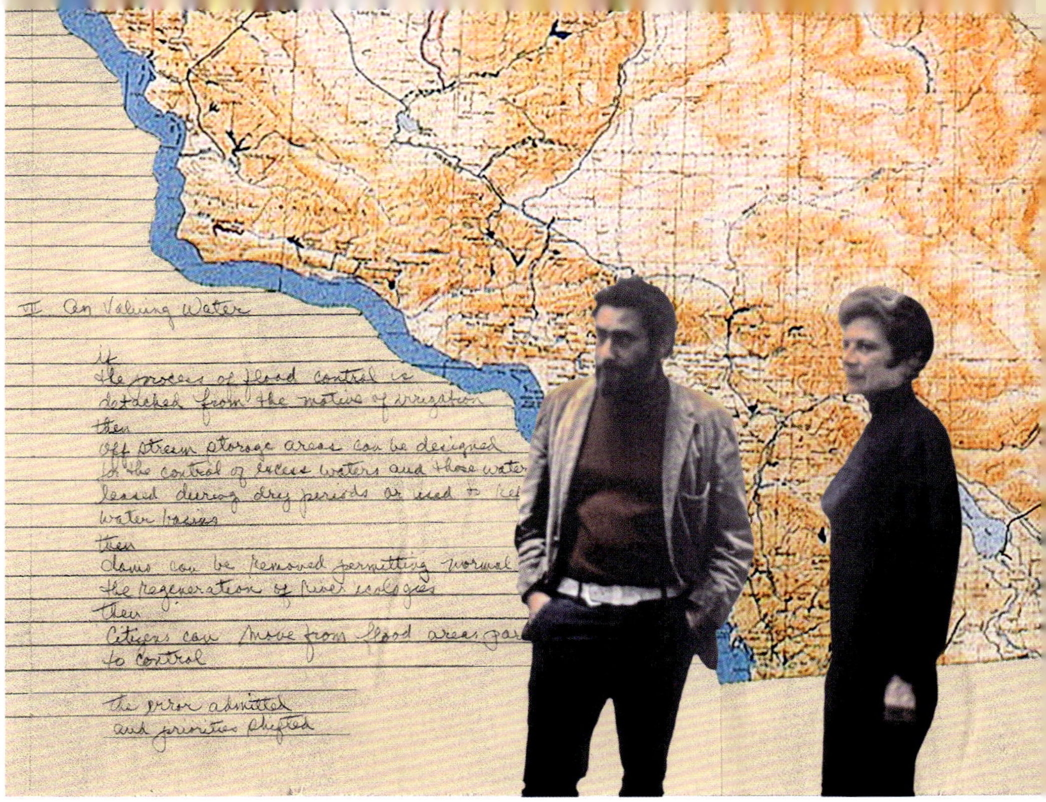

I. From the Satellite the Central Valley Is One Farm:

Diking, channelizing, pumping
Diverting the flow of the San Joaquin River at Friant
and the Sacramento River at the delta
Limiting the flushing of the delta and the bays
Crisscrossing the valley with ditches and canals
They dammed all the rivers and most of the streams that
Flow into the delta and the bays
They dammed the Sacramento River, the Trinity River,
the McCloud River and the Pitt River
Fall Creek, Hat Creek, Cow Creek, Stony Creek, Battle Creek
Putah Creek and Butte Creek
They dammed the Feather on the North Fork, the South Fork,
and the West Branch,
and all the branches of the Yuba River and the Bear River
They dammed Oregon Creek, Canyon Creek,
and French Dry Creek
The South Fork and the Middle Fork of the American
They dammed the Rubicon River, Brush Creek, Silver Creek,
Tells Creek, Gerle Creek, and Dry Creek
The Mokelumne River, the Stanislaus River, the Tuolumne River
Angel Creek, Cherry Creek, Sullivan Creek
They dammed and re-dammed the Merced River and
the San Joaquin River
The Kings, the Kaweah, and the Kern
To irrigate over 2 632 000 hectares

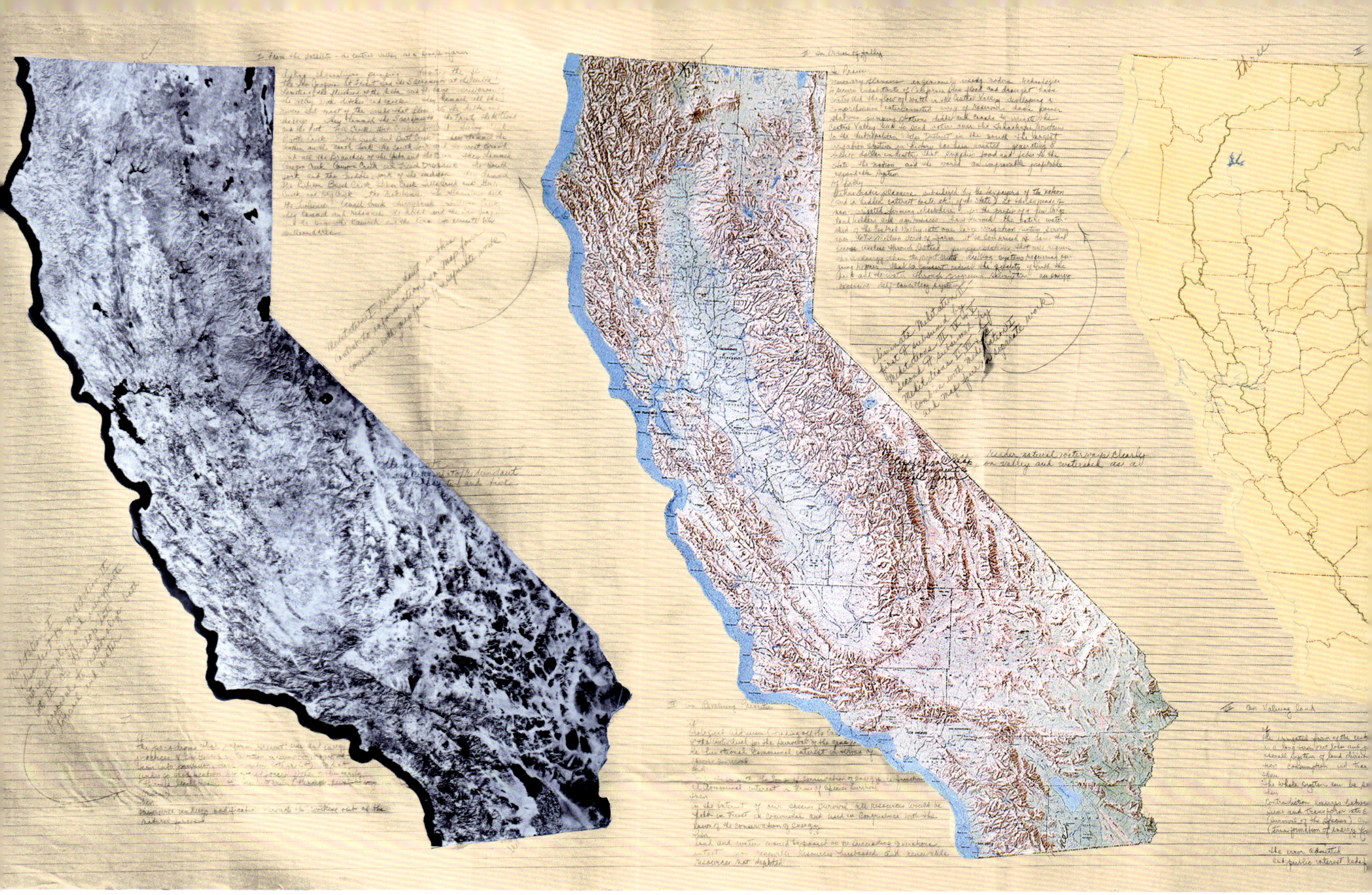

II. In Praise of Folly

Visionary planners ingeniously using modern technologies
to secure inhabitants of California
from flood and drought
have controlled the flow of water
in the Central Valley,
developing a comprehensive, interconnected array
of reservoirs, dams, power stations, pumping stations,
ditches and canals, to irrigate the Central Valley
and to send waters over the Tehachapi Mountains
to the metropolitan water district in the south
The largest irrigation system in history has been created
generating an eight billion dollar industry
that supplies food and fiber to the state, the nation,
and the world
an improvable, profitable, expandable system of folly
Technocratic planners subsidized by the taxpayers
of the nation (and in hidden interest gifts by the state)
at the expense of non-irrigated farming elsewhere
For the profit of a few large landholders
and agri-business
have turned the entire watershed of the Central Valley
into one large irrigation system serving
over 2 632 000 hectares of farmland
It is composed of dams that become useless thru silting,
a pumping system that will use more

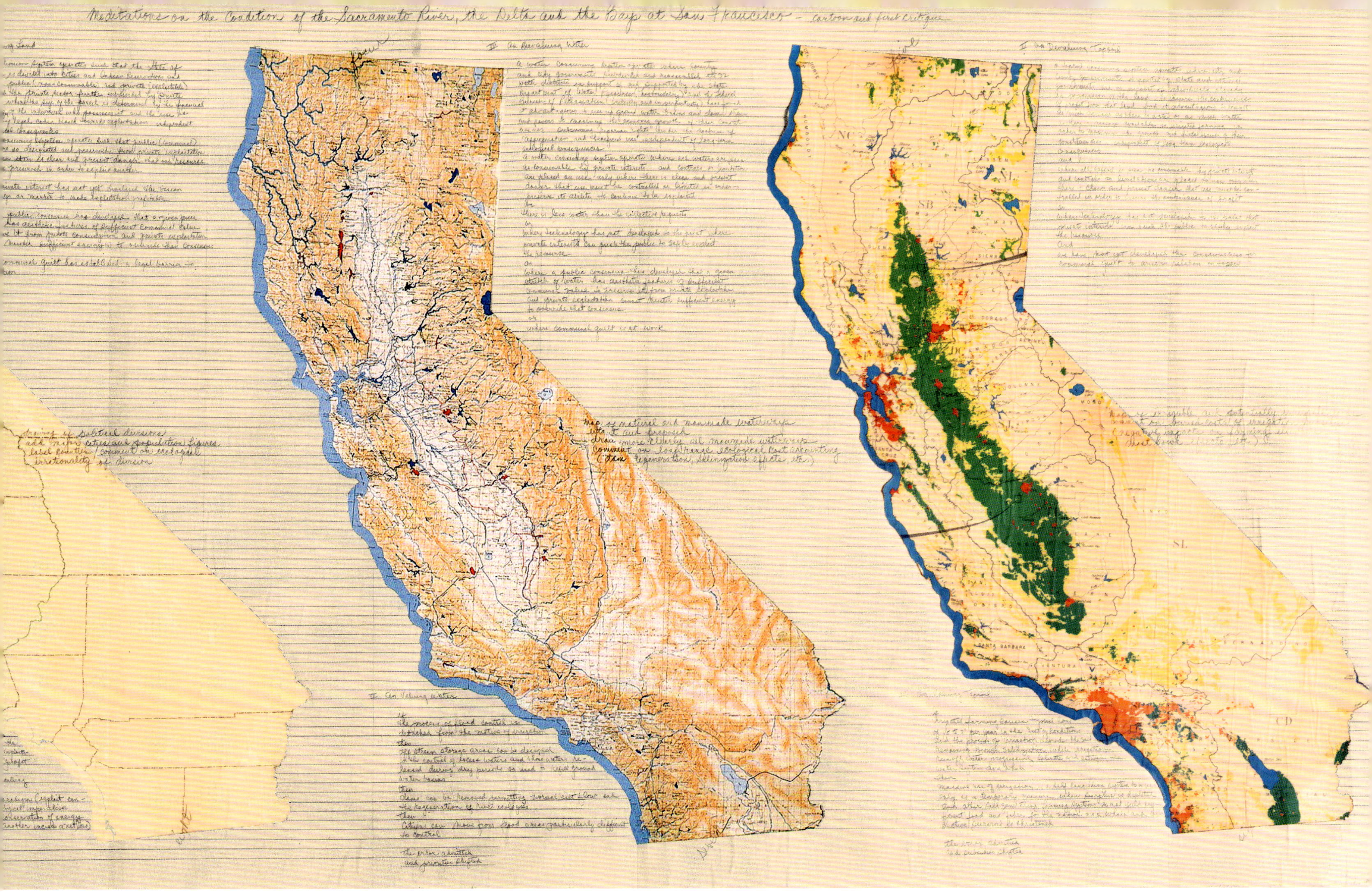

energy than the project creates,
a diking system requiring ongoing repair,
that in concert
reduce the quality of both the land and the water
through progressive salinization
and anenergy-expensive self-canceling system

III. On Devaluing Land
A land-division system operates such
that the State of California is divided into cities and Indian
reservations, counties, public (nonconsumable)
and private (exploitable) land and the private
sector further subdivided by private ownership,
where the size of the parcel is determined
by the financial capability of the individual who possesses it
and the use is limited by legal codes
biased toward exploitation, independent
of long-term ecological consequences
A land-consuming system operates such
that public (communal) lands are so designated and
preserved from private exploitation only
when there is clear and present danger that
one resource must be preserved in order to exploit another
Or
When private interest has not yet developed the vision,
technology, or market to make exploitation profitable

Or
Where a public consensus has developed that
a given piece of land has aesthetic features
of sufficient communal value to preserve it from
private consumption, and private exploitation
cannot muster sufficient energies to override that consensus
Or
When communal guilt has established legal barriers
to consumption
to meditate upon constructive alternatives:
creating nature reserves, planting forests,
installing vegetative flood controls, and so on.
Hopeful solutions accompanied alarming messages.

IV. On Devaluing Water

A water-consuming system operates where county
and city governments, subdivided and
reassembled into 32 water districts, in support of and
supported by the State Department of Water
Resources (historically) and the federal Bureau of Reclamation
(initially and in perpetuity), have
found it advantageous to use up groundwater basins
and dam streams and rivers to
maximize the economic growth of their constituencies,
subsuming "riparian rights" under the
doctrine of "appropriation and beneficial use," independent of
long-term ecological consequences
Where all waters are seen as consumable by private interest,
and controls or limitations are
placed on use only when there is clear and present danger
that use must be controlled or limited
in order to preserve its ability to continue to be exploited
Or
There is less water than the collective requests
Or
Where technology has not developed to the point where
private interests can push the public
to safely exploit the resource
Or
Where a public consensus has developed that a given stretch
of water has aesthetic features of
sufficient communal value to preserve it
from private exploitation and private exploitation
cannot muster sufficient energy to override that consensus
Or
Where communal guilt is at work

V. On Devaluing Topsoil

A topsoil-consuming system operates where city
and county governments, in support of
individuals already in possession of the land,
to insure the continuance of profit from that land,
find it advantageous to commit as much acreage
as there is water available or as much water
as there is acreage available in order to maximize
the growth and fiscal power of their constituencies,
independent of long-term ecological consequences
And
Where all topsoil is seen as consumable by private interests
and controls or limitations are placed
on use only when there is clear and present danger
that use must be controlled
in order to insure the continuance of profit
Or
Where technology has not developed to the point that
private interests can push the public to safely exploit the resource
And
We have not yet developed the consciousness for
communal guilt to arise in relationship to topsoil

Not content with these alarming reflections, the artists also spoke about creative responses to problems that would be based on the law of conservation of energy. The artwork concluded by presenting an alternative to the water-consuming system that operated in the Central Valley. The poster sketch that was exhibited with the ten meditation mappings began with the prompt "For instance ... if ..." and ended with the question, "What if all irrigated farming isn't necessary?"

VI. On Valuing Topsoil

If
Irrigated farming causes topsoil loss of 0.5 centimeters
to five centimeters per year in the best of
conditions and the process of irrigation degrades the soil
remaining through salinization
While irrigation runoff waters progressively salinate
and entropy the water system as a whole
Then
Massive use of irrigation is a self-canceling system to be used
only as a temporary measure
Then
surplus is depleted and other soil-generating farming systems
do not yield sufficient food and
fiber for the nation as a whole and collective survival
is threatened

The error admitted
and subsidies shifted

VII. On Valuing Water

If
the process of flood control is detached
from the motive of irrigation
then
Off-stream storage areas can be designed for the
control of excess waters and those waters released
during dry periods or used to refill ground water basins
Then dams can be removed permitting normal silt flow
and the regeneration of river ecologies
Then citizens can move from flood areas particularly difficult
to control

The error admitted
And priorities shifted

VIII. On Valuing Land

If
The irrigated farm of the Central Valley is seen as a
long-term net loss and paradigmatic of the overall system
of land division, sub-division, exploitation, consumption
and transformation into profit
Then
The whole system can be seen as self-canceling
Then
Contradiction emerges between socio-economic paradigm
(exploit, consume,
and transform into capital), biological imperative
(survival of the species),
and the laws of the conservation of energy
(transfer of energy from one form to another always incurs
a net loss)

The error admitted
And public interest redefined

IX. On Revaluing Priorities

If
Biological altruism (trading off the interest of the individual
for the survival of the gene pool)
is functional communal interest
in terms of species survival
and
Congruence with the laws of conservation of energy
is functional communal interest
in terms of species survival
Then
In the interest of our species survival all resources
would be held in trust as communal and used in congruence
with the laws of the conservation of energy
Then
Land and water would be passed on to succeeding generations
intact, nonrenewable resources
husbanded, and renewable resources not depleted

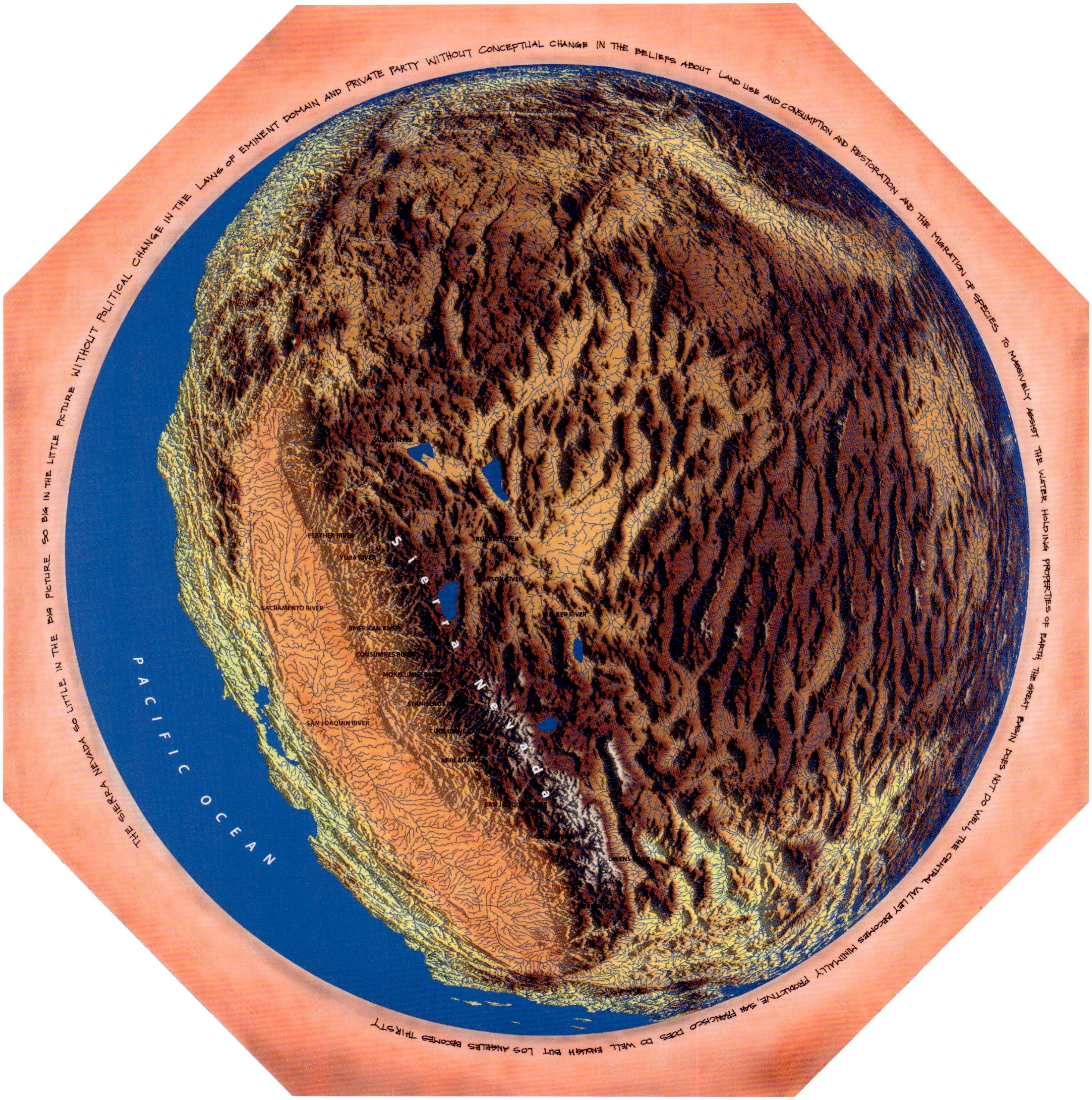
THE SIERRA NEVADA SO LITTLE IN THE BIG PICTURE SO BIG IN THE LITTLE PICTURE WITHOUT POLITICAL CHANGE IN THE LAWS OF EMINENT DOMAIN AND PRIVATE PARTY WITHOUT CONCEPTUAL CHANGE IN THE BELIEFS ABOUT LAND USE AND CONSUMPTION AND RESTORATION AND THE MIGRATION OF SPECIES TO MASSIVELY ASSIST THE WATER HOLDING PROPERTIES OF EARTH, THE GREAT BASIN DOES NOT DO WELL, THE CENTRAL VALLEY BECOMES MINIMALLY PRODUCTIVE, SAN FRANCISCO DOES DO WELL ENOUGH BUT LOS ANGELES BECOMES THIRSTY
PACIFIC OCEAN
Sierra Nevada
FEATHER RIVER
YUBA RIVER
SACRAMENTO RIVER
AMERICAN RIVER
SAN JOAQUIN RIVER
TRUCKEE RIVER
CARSON RIVER

Three parts of Meditations on the Sacramento River, the Delta, and the Bays of San Francisco, 1976–1977

▶ The original images overlaid on a Google map of farming of the Central Valley

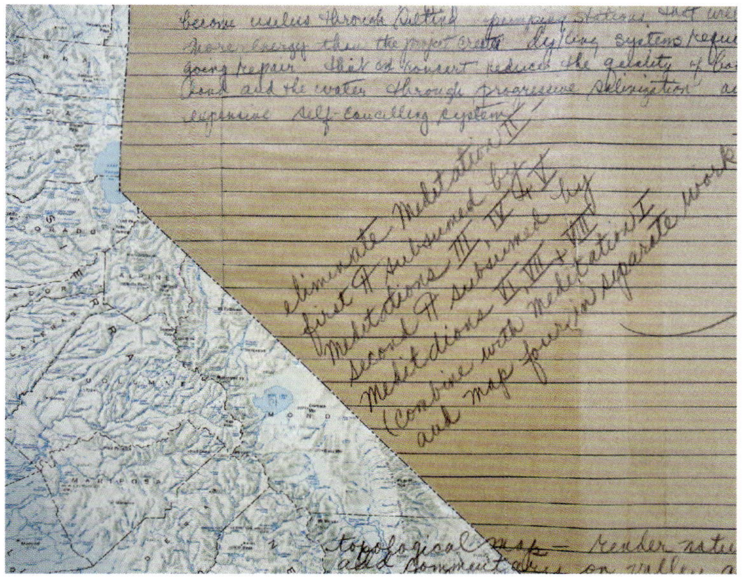

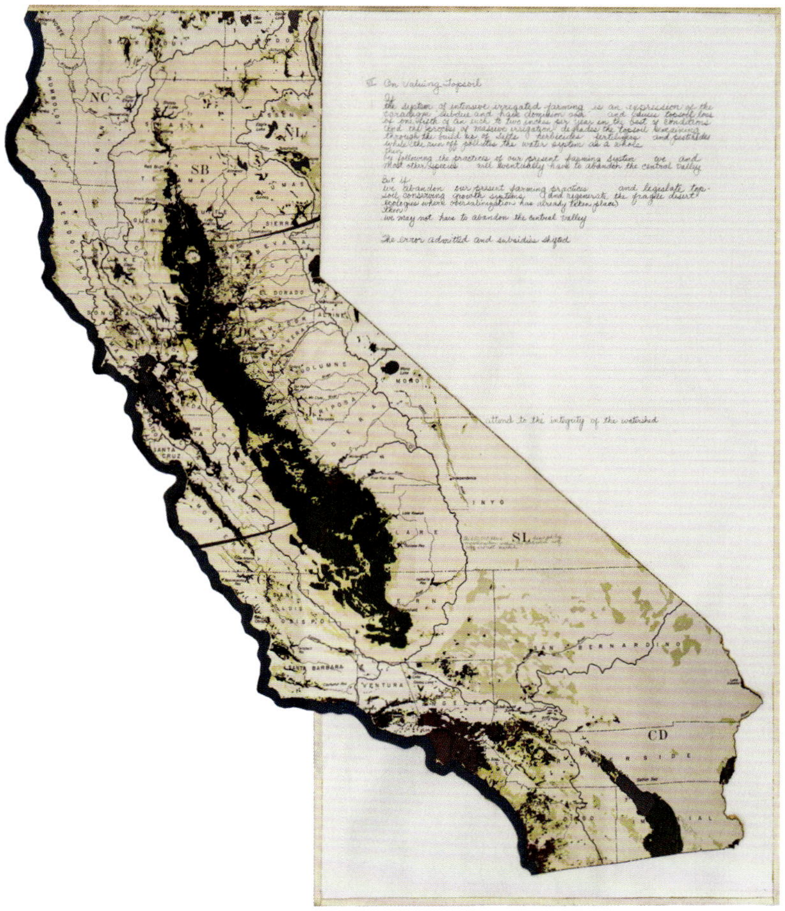

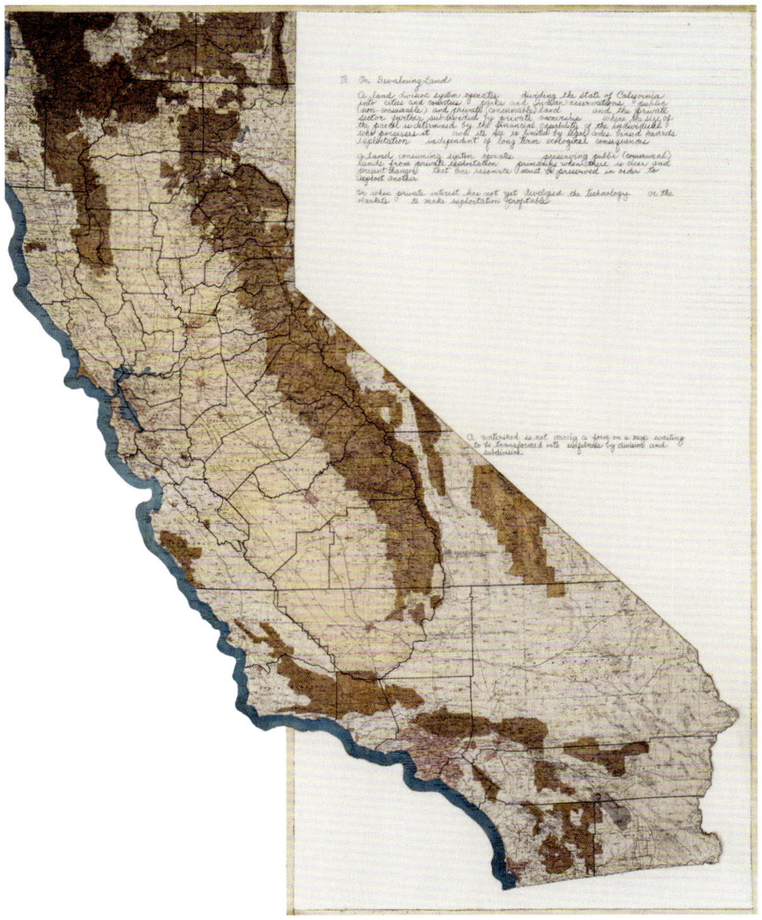

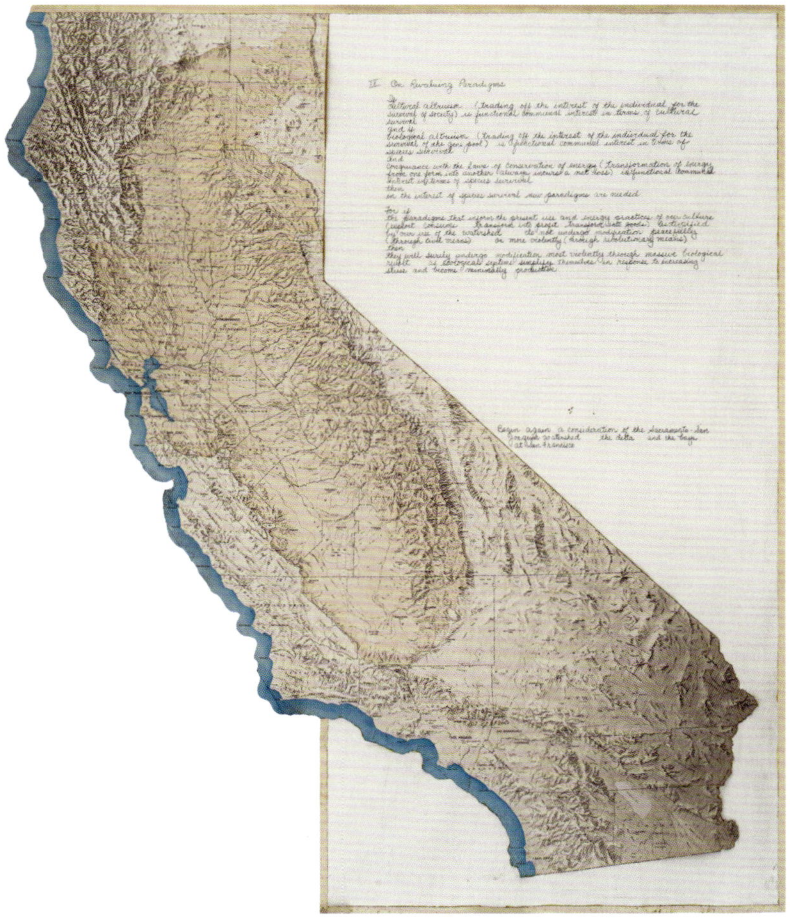

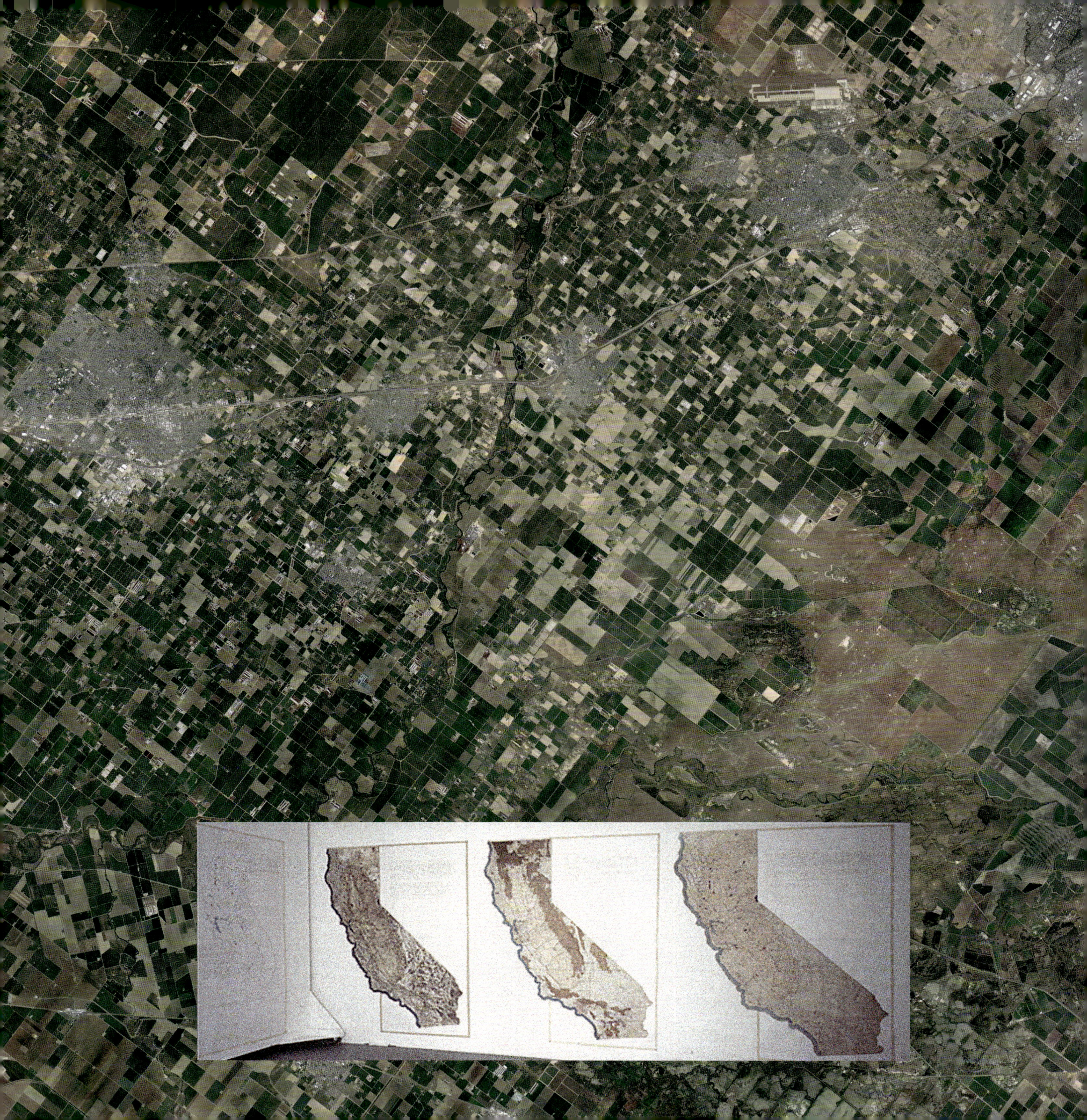

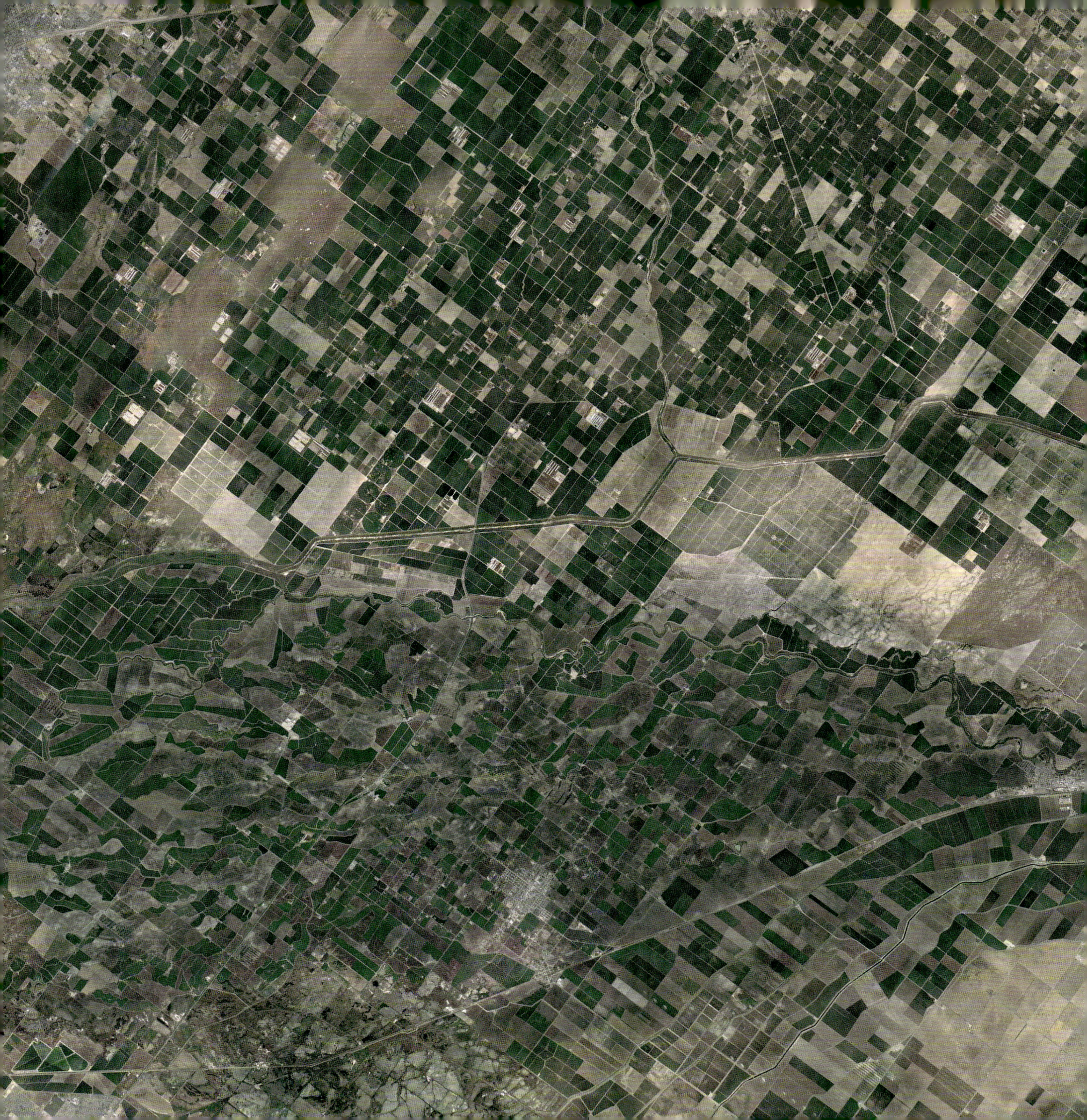

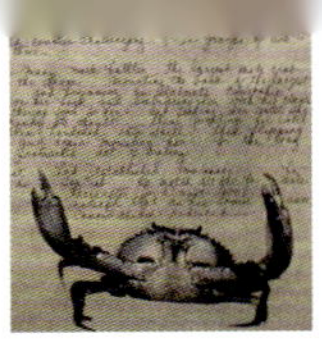

X.
If
The paradigms that inform the present use and energy practices of culture (exploitation, consumption, transformation into possession, transformation into profit) do not undergo modification by social forces either voluntarily (through legal means) or involuntarily (through revolutionary means)
Then
They will undergo modification through the working out of the natural forces (read entropy)

In the ideas emerging from its mappings and poetic texts, the *Sacramento Meditations* offers complex eco-political observations on all Central Valley agrobusiness operations, which exist against the laws of the conservation of energy. The artists prophesied that this state of affairs was doomed as it was self-cancelling, with the signs of extreme drought and shortages of resources already underway.

The monumental implications of this artwork relate to philosophical questions of survival of ecosystems that are not confined to the Sacramento/San Joaquin River watersheds. For the artists, the *Sacramento Meditations* served as "a guiding metaphor, a lens through which [they saw] many existing cultural landscapes in the process of being transformed into industrial landscapes" that could be dealt with by artists like themselves, "with the idea that new and different possible histories could become available and open for exploration and criticism."[20]

Forty years later, the Harrisons realized that the *Meditations*, along with other prophetic works from this period, had been addressing the great forces of entropy set in motion by "runaway economic development" and the "energy-consuming" exploitation of nature, as well as the accelerated pressure of global warming on all planetary systems.[21] They named this collective great force the Force Majeure and held the human race responsible for bringing it into being. Their survival-driven question from the *Sacramento Meditations* – "What if all irrigated farming isn't necessary?" – would be rephrased into a new question: "Would it be enough for life to continue, by reducing local entropy system by system?"[22]

Many scholars recognized the *Sacramento Meditations* as a foundational work for ecological activism because of its multilayered presentation: as exhibition, performance, media campaign, and call for political action. For instance, Charles Green considered the work "a reasoned, researched critique of the green revolution and industrialized agrobusiness" by which the Harrisons "used 'art' as a discursive site within which they could situate real time demonstrations and futures modeling."[23] Indeed, the work was very successful in staging actual political campaigns from San Francisco to Sacramento. In the proposal to the Floating Museum the artists outlined three parts: 1) the exhibition would open with a series of billboards, posters, graffiti, videos, and radio broadcasts, all presenting commentaries on water codes, water management, and the political and ecological implications of one course of action as opposed to another, with all elements planned in collaboration with the Floating Museum and the Art Institute; 2) the exhibition at SF MoMA, designed in collaboration with the Floating Museum, would function "as an outline for master planning," weighing arguments against one another and with conclusions presented as suggestions for change; 3) "the exemplar proposal for the grounds of the Capitol Building at Sacramento" would outline water recycling programs and be exhibited at SF MoMA.

The artists' performances were a success, agitating San Francisco from street corners, billboards, and radio and TV programs, relating the message: "Somebody's crazy, they are draining the swamps and growing rice in the desert" or "Dear Jerry Brown: Right water action."[24] The *Sacramento Meditations* played a considerable role in the assertion of the Harrisons' aesthetic agenda. Describing their position as post-modern and post-conceptual, they took advantage of the roles of textual discourse and social context to present their ideas as dialogues or conversations rather than as adversarial confrontation, and began to employ metaphors that indexed larger

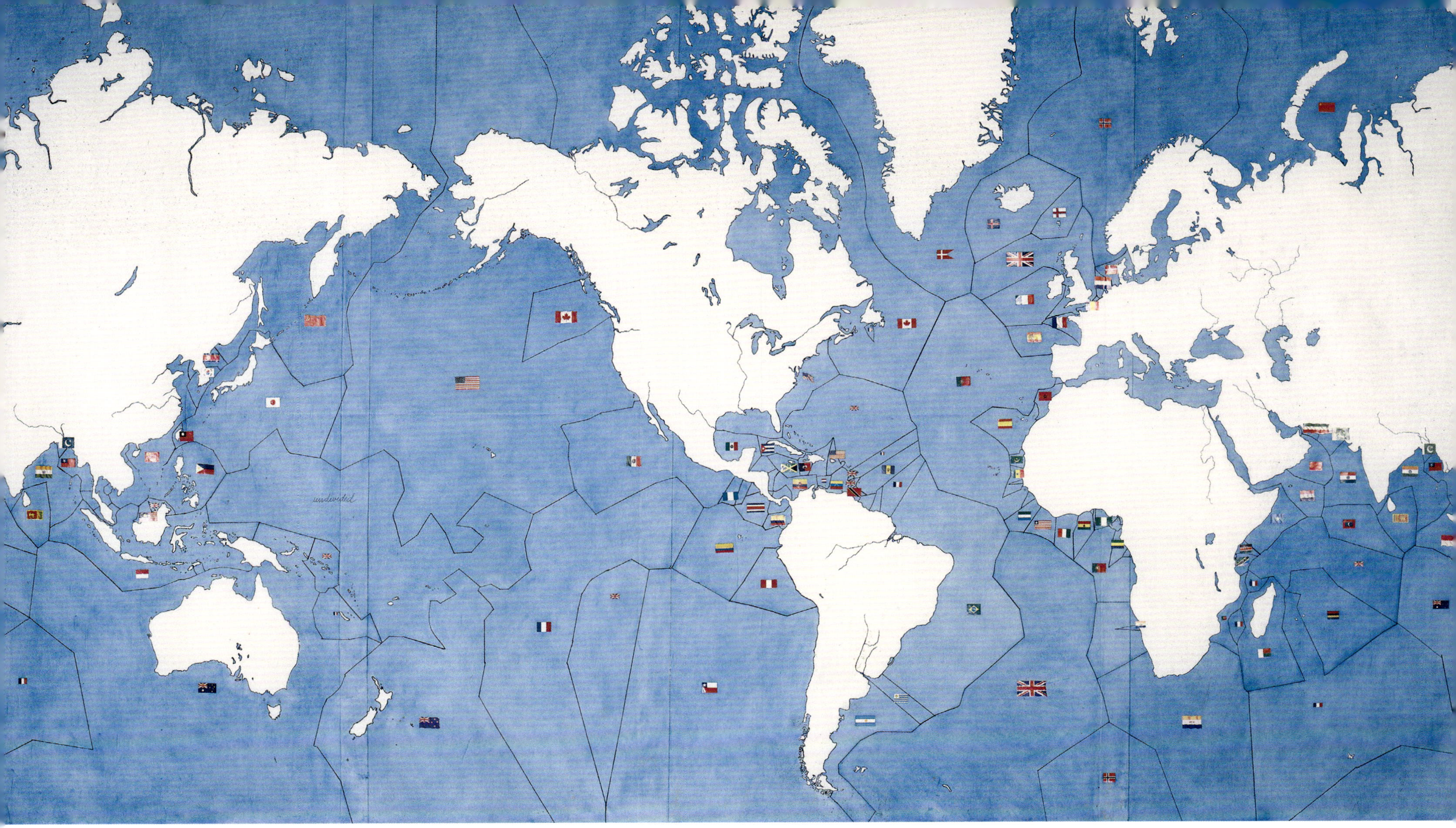

environmental issues with a worldwide or continental frame of reference. In his explanatory statement to the press, Phil Linhares, the Director of Exhibitions at San Francisco Art Institute, summed up the Harrisons' artistic position:

"The Harrisons described their position as post-conceptual; their interest in concept extends beyond the idea stage through the implementation of their ideas in the form of objects, drawings, maps, systems, demonstrations, text, ct. Their concern with the object and interest in the outcome of the various projects places their work beyond the framework of strictly 'conceptual' art; indeed, their overriding concern for human survival through a new understanding of the planet Earth takes their work beyond a strictly 'art' context: it deals with ecology, economics, politics, agriculture, and law on global scale. The content of this cooperative city-wide explosion is directed to the entire populace: its implications are visionary [prophetic] and its attitude is humanistic."[25]

At this point of their career, the Harrisons insisted on embedding visual art within textual discourse: the *Sacramento Meditations* mappings appeared within the framework of text in the installation combined with the wider context of conversations that started outside the art museum in the form of billboards, posters, media broadcasts, and the viewers' graffiti. The artists' poetic dialogues offered narratives about the place, and its future development that were informed by cultural tradition, modernization, politics, climate change, and other forces that have given rise to specific environmental challenges.

The Harrisons' increasingly conceptual play with maps can be seen in another significant work from this period entitled the *Law of the Sea Conference*, also called *Wherein the Appetite is Discovered to be Endless*.[26] Helen and Newton developed a room-sized installation as their contribution to the 1976 Venice Biennale, on invitation from Pierre Restany, the prominent French art critic who had visited San Diego the prior year to explore the local conceptual art phenomenon.[27] The *Law of the Sea* comprises a huge wall map and a dozen smaller mappings challenging the maritime law propositions of the Third Conference on the Law of Sea, held over several sessions between New York, Caracas, and Geneva in 1973–1975, during which no agreement was reached. The artists appropriated the map created for the Second Conference on the Law of Sea in 1967. Given the international context of the Venice Biennale, the *Law of the Sea* was a timely topic, especially as the artwork drew attention to the conflicting demands and sovereign interests of international states over such issues as the sharing of the high seas, exclusive control of coastal waters, and industrial development of seabed minerals and other submarine resources. Attention was drawn to the discussion by a number of major newspaper headlines.

In particular, the Harrisons critiqued the proceedings of the Second and Third Conference on the Law of the Sea that discussed fundamental changes to maritime law in the uses of territorial waters and free economic zones. *Wherein the Appetite Is Discovered to Be Endless* is an attempt to visualize the implications of these changes so they could become accessible to the public. The ensemble of maps showed a hypothetical sectioning of the oceans among nations. Considerable attention was devoted to color interactions on the map, while texts written across smaller mappings helped to pinpoint critical issues, with the corresponding country's flag posted in each section of the ocean.

Utilizing the symbolic language of maps, *Wherein the Appetite Is Discovered to Be Endless* represented the tangled histories and unresolved issues of the various Law of the Sea conferences. Initiated after World War II by the United Nations, the First Conference on the Law of the Sea in 1958 incorporated new exclusive economic zone rights beyond the territorial seas of all developed countries, established straits for international navigation, and guaranteed free access for land-locked countries to and from the sea. The Second Conference of 1967 attempted to address the peaceful uses of seabed resources beyond the limits of national jurisdiction, albeit failing to achieve any resolution. The Third Conference in 1973–1975 dealt with the outstanding problems of the Law of the Sea, since intensified by rapid technological progress and the diversity of interests among the participants, along with claims by new nation-states to equitable sharing of submarine resources. The Third Conference aimed to find a compromise between the opposing interests of developed and developing countries about income redistribution, including the wish of land-locked and shelf-locked states to enjoy benefits from the living and nonliving resources of the sea. As Milenko Milic reported, "Some African and Latin American countries believed that it would be better simply to demand a 200 nautical mile territorial sea. Other countries opposed the zone because they believed it might endanger freedom of navigation and therefore become a source of disputes."[28]

Wherein the Appetite Is Discovered to Be Endless pictured the hypothetical division of the world's oceans among coastal states and islands using four guiding metaphors: 1) "wherein the appetite is discovered to be endless," 2) "wherein the argument is discovered to be endless," 3) "wherein the conflict is discovered to be endless," and 4) "wherein possibilities are discovered to be endless."[29] Texts written across the maps amplified the artists' critique of the conference in various ways, as the following examples show:

It is an illustration of how the sea floor might look if it were divided doing lines equidistant from the closest points of adjacent or opposite coastal states and islands as a basis for the establishment of exclusive rights to the exploitation of deep sea minerals
Cutting up the whole pie and giving it to those who already have some
Cutting the pie at the edges and giving pieces to those who already have some
Leaving the rest to the endless argument (200 mile limit)
One of the many attempts to divide the world ocean for the benefit of coastal states, presumably

The Harrisons mocked the overall logic of such divisions, teasing out problems about which countries gained and which did poorly, as illustrated by these further example inscriptions:

Chile does well, Bolivia gets nothing at all
The Unites States territory is abundantly expanded and inherently protected
Somalia does well, Kenya modestly and Ethiopia poorly and Uganda gets nothing
Clearly new conditions for conflict have been generated
The Mediterranean is undivided
Therefore new conditions for conflict do not apply

Another set of maps prophetically anticipated future geopolitical conflicts resulting from impending climate change, which would create new coastlines, whether due to glaciation or to global melting of the ice, according to Bryce's and Plass' arguments. Thus, the artwork raised questions about how the political globe would have to change to accommodate the various scenarios of global warming, as the inscriptions declared:

It is odd to spend time planning the discussion of the seabed, extending the concept of national sovereignty over the ocean floor
Better to spend time planning the movement of populations as the coastlines change in response to increases or decreases in glaciation

In all, *Wherein the Appetite Is Discovered to Be Endless* created imaginary projections of new geopolitical divisions, relying on the irony and fiction that always played a role in the artists' demonstrations. The Harrisons were quite clear about the message: their point was to demonstrate that "any politically based system of division that ignores the workings of the ecology" would arrive at the endless and pointless argument "embedded in the concept of this style of division."[30]

FROM MAPS TO METAPHORS: ON NATURE AND HUMAN CULTURE

Throughout the 1970s, the Harrisons continued their research and experimental work with self-contained and self-generating ecosystems as design prototypes for indoor and backyard farming. They were actively searching for solutions to surviving calamitous times and for ecological alternatives to the industrialized food system with its inherent disregard for ecosystems. Using the lessons of the *Portable Fish Farm* from 1971, with its various problems, they started to research another living creature, the Scylla serrata crab – incredibly resilient, fast-growing, and a favorite food in Sri Lanka. Quite some time passed before they discovered the conditions necessary to sustain the crab's breeding cycle. Bringing live creatures back into their research brought about the artists' most elaborate project, entitled the *Lagoon Cycle*. The story of their research on portable orchards, vegetable gardens, and fish farms that had started as intimate survival pieces installed in galleries gradually expanded into the planning of whole ecosystems. Carefully modeling their working method after the functioning of such systems in the natural world, the Harrisons hoped to solve a fundamental paradox of all food systems: how one could create a means to feed the human race without degrading the earth.

The Lagoon Cycle (1972–85) is a story in seven phases, referred to as the First Lagoon, the Second Lagoon, the Third Lagoon, and so forth. A complex 360' photo mural in 60 parts, it was originally exhibited at the Herbert F. Johnson Museum at Cornell University (1985) and the Los Angeles County Museum of Art (1987), and was later acquired by the Centre Georges Pompidou in Paris. This work has never been displayed in totality in San Diego, nor seen in public since its acquisition by France in 1997. Initiated with the *Crab Farm* (1972), the *Lagoon Cycle* was first conceived as an aquatic farming prototype that could be maintained within the conditions of a museum or art gallery as a work of art. The *Lagoon Cycle* mapped out the framework of environmental

The Lagoon Cycle, Book of the Lagoons

1985 Herbert F. Johnson Museum of Art, Cornell University, Ithaca, NY

1987 Los Angeles County Museum of Art, CA,

2011 Orange County Museum of Art, Newport Beach, CA

2012 Berkeley Art Museum and Pacific Film Archive, CA

et al.

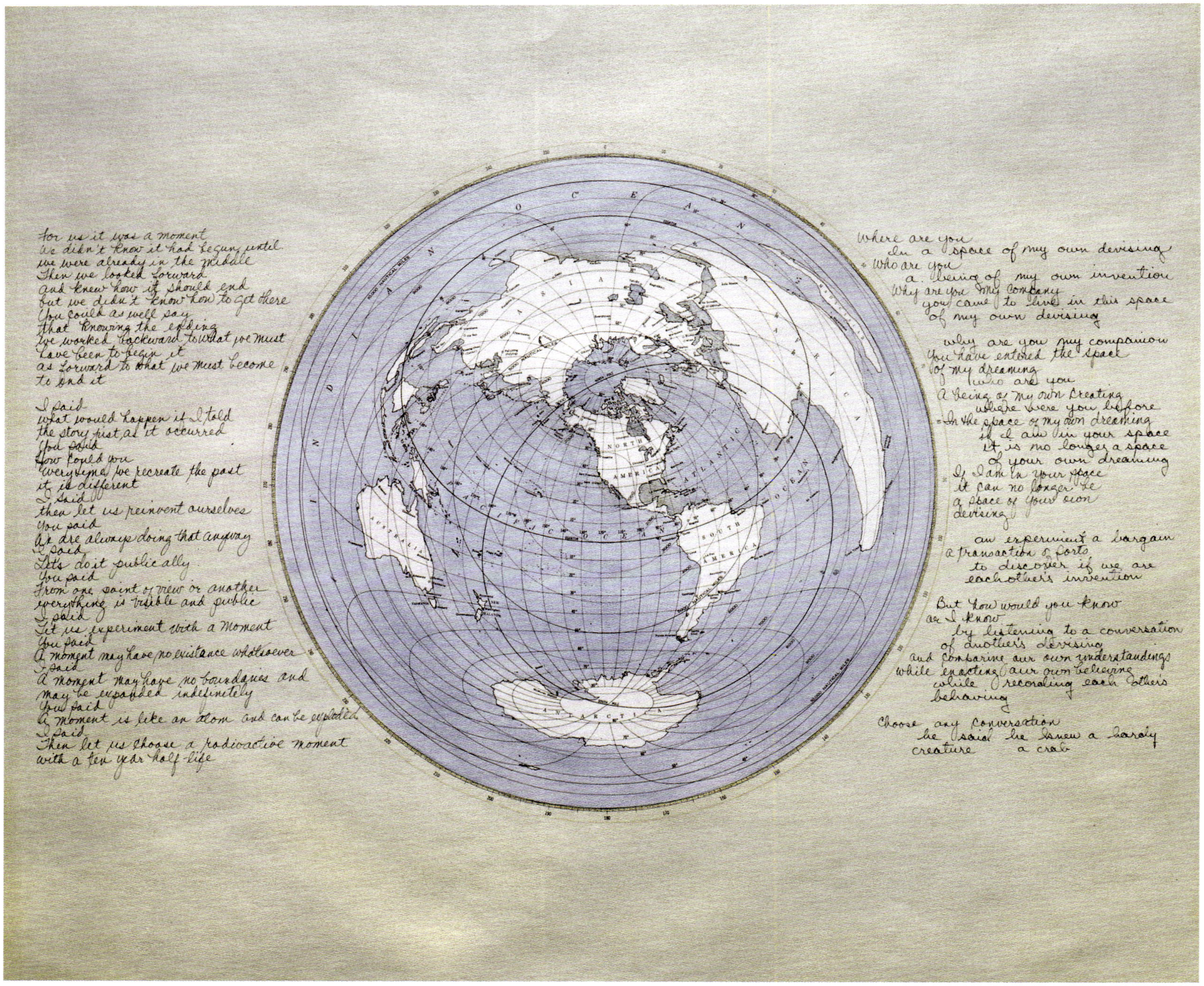

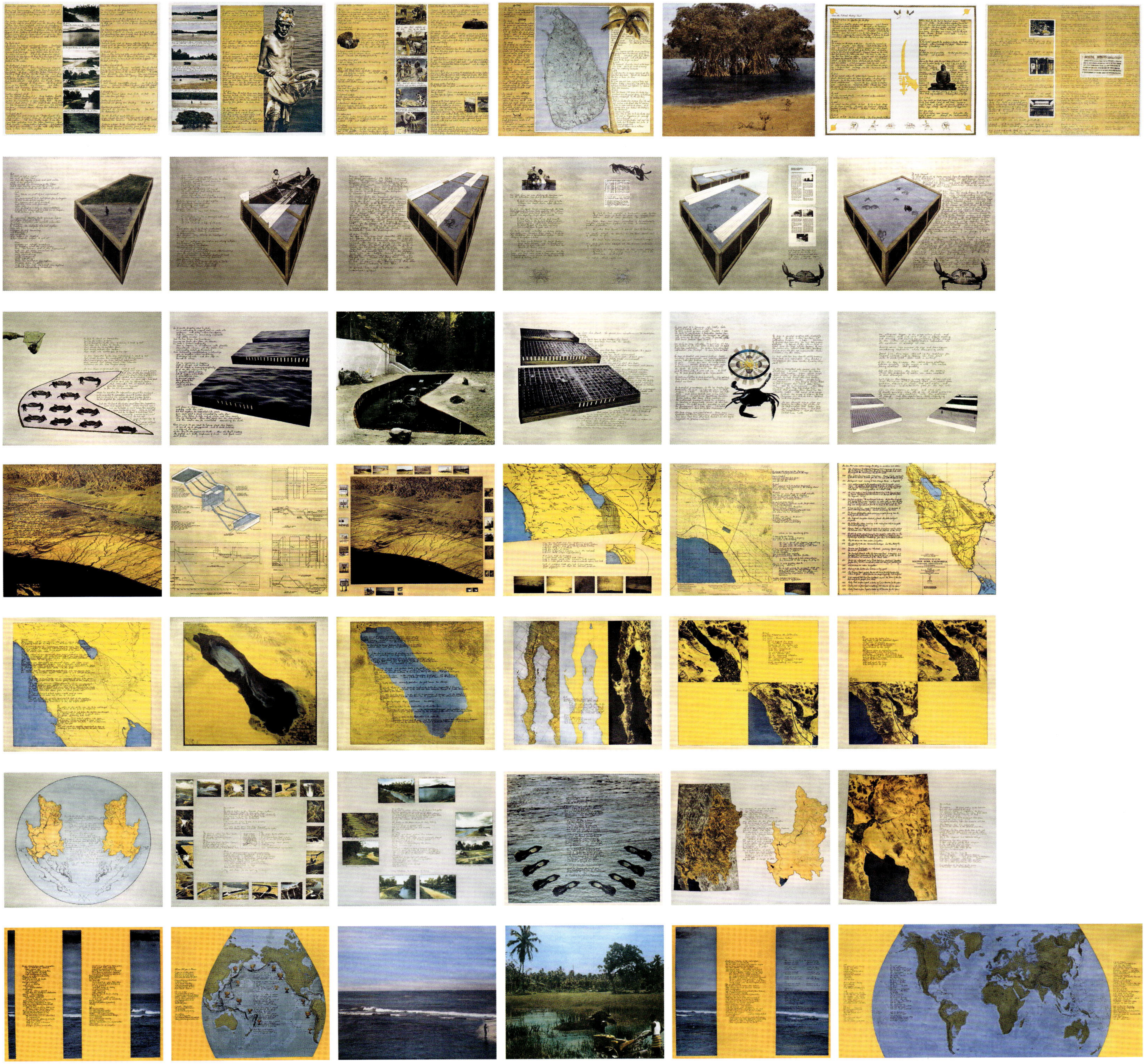

research, addressing how living organisms react to a specific environment, and was, according to the Harrisons, "the basis for a decade of work."[31]

Presented jointly as a stylized stage set, a monumental multimedia mural, and a picturesque written narrative, the *Lagoon Cycle* takes the Harrisons' real-life research investigations and frames the data in the form of poetic dialogues between two mythical alter egos, the Lagoonmaker and the Witness, the characters in some ways "exaggerations" of Newton and Helen themselves.[32] The cycles reflect both an exploration of self and the world experienced by the artists in their journey to make a productive farm. The *Lagoon Cycle* visualizes a story involving an unlikely hero, a Sri Lankan crab named Scylla serrata (*Forsskal*), who is transported to the West Coast of the United States. At the heart of the *Lagoon Cycle* are several wide-ranging themes: the consideration of lagoons and watersheds as complex self-sustaining polyculture ecosystems, the relationship of ecology and culture, the future of ecological and eco-cultural wellbeing, the delusions of experimental science, and the inadvertent harmful outcomes of mega-technology on nature. The *Lagoon Cycle* laid the methodological foundations for a work of art being a research project concerned with understanding complex ecosystems (such as lagoons and watersheds) as well as regenerative agriculture, water usage, and the reality of accelerating climate change. It ends with a prophecy about what is happening now: ocean rise, ecosystem collapse, and civilization itself is under stress.

The *Lagoon Cycle* begins with the Lagoonmaker and Witness' inquiry into a mud crab, a hardy creature that serves as a high-protein staple food source in the coastal lagoons of Sri Lanka. The *First Lagoon: The Lagoon at Uppuveli* recounts the visit to Sri Lanka and the search for the crab as a possible subject for a self-generating aquaculture system and delves deeply into the history, culture, and water politics of the post-colonial island nation.

The *Second Lagoon: Sea Grant* tells the story of how the Harrisons obtained the prestigious Sea Grant, administered by the Scripps Institution of Oceanography, to study the mating behavior of the *Scylla serrata* crab at their newly acquired Pepper Canyon laboratory. In their roles as the Lagoonmaker and Witness, Newton and Helen built a water tank to house an imported sample population of lagoon crabs. Their primary discovery was the lagoon crab's mating habits were tied to fluctuations in salinity and temperature, coinciding in Sri Lanka with seasonal monsoons. The *Second Lagoon* narrates the idea of the tank as replacement for the lagoon – the natural localized ecosystem with an elaborate chain of interdependent life cycles. The dialogue and imagery critically question the supposed objectivity of scientific methodologies yet, ironically, participate in the use of such methodologies by incorporating the Harrisons' data logs, detailed observations, and research publications.

The *Third Lagoon: The House of Crabs* recounts how the Lagoonmaker and Witness are variously approached by a businessman, scientist, journalist, and accountant, who each give advice on how to capitalize on the success story of the crab's breeding cycle. This episode is a dramatization of their experience with Ted Hartley, a Hollywood actor, producer, and investment banker, who invited the Harrisons to build an outdoor crab tank "as a work of art and science" in the backyard of his private home in the Hollywood Hills. The actual plans went askew, bringing an end to the private lagoon, and the story becomes a criticism of all existing capitalist models.

The *Fourth Lagoon: On Mixing, Mapping and Territory* entertains the prospect of transforming the Salton Sea into a giant fish farm. In the form of large-scale gravity-fed ponds, the repurposed body of water would accommodate a large population of crabs, algae, clams, and mussels, a so-called "polyculture system." Presented as a schematic design, with no physical counterpart, it proposes mixing freshwater from the Colorado River and the All-American and Coachella Canals with saltwater from the Salton Sea, which for its part is described as a disastrous example of destroyed ecological systems.

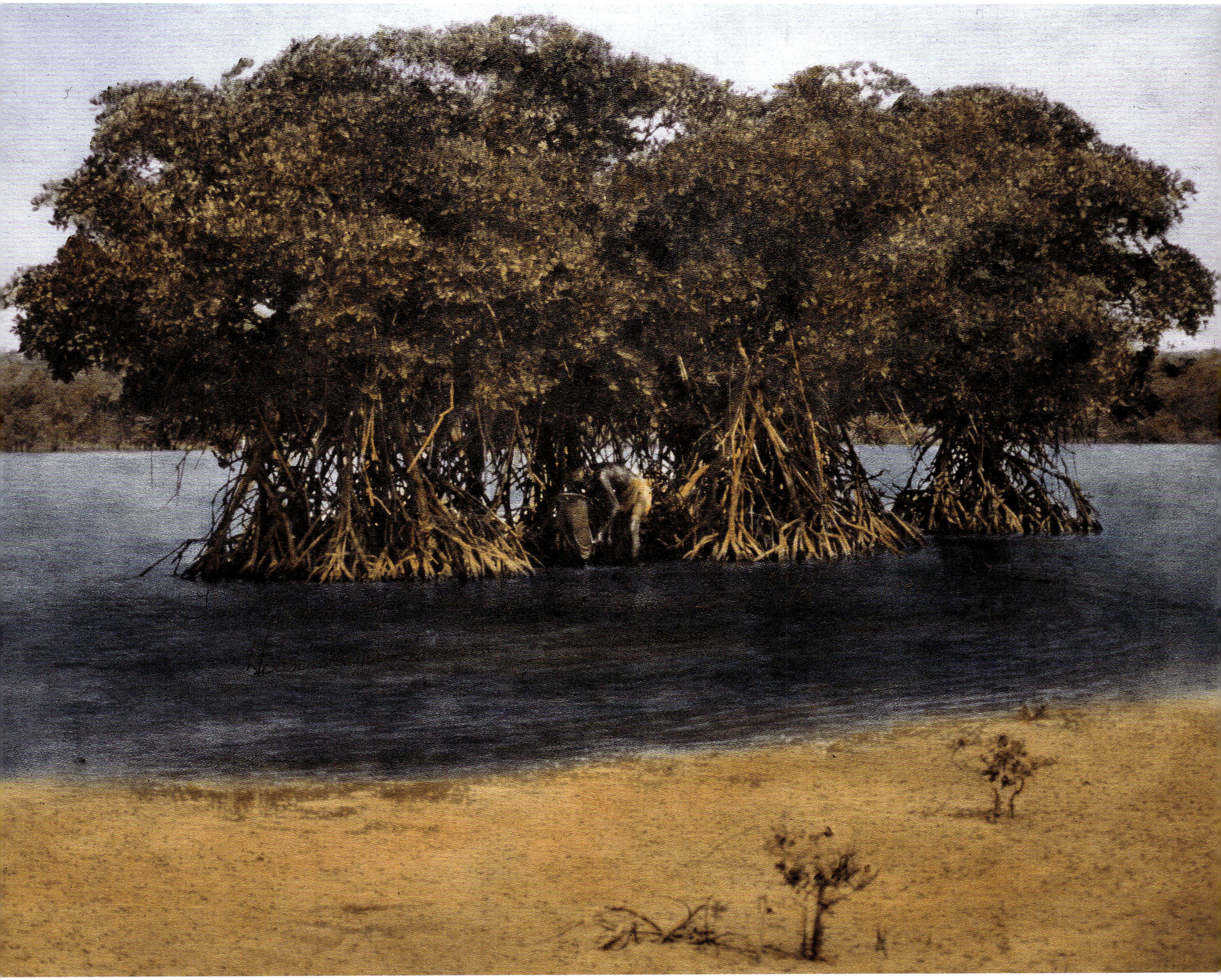

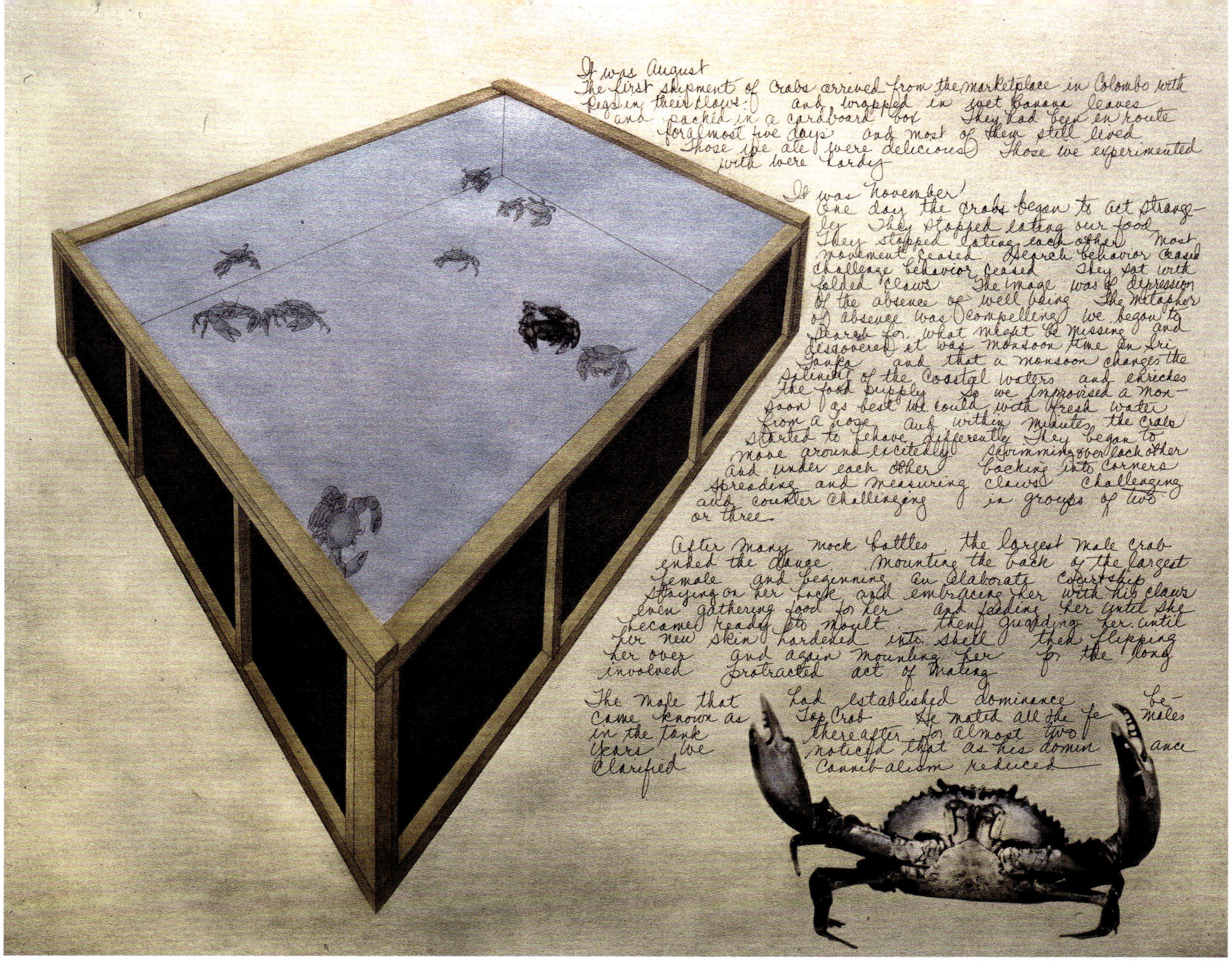

The *Fifth Lagoon: From the Salton Sea to the Pacific–From the Salton Sea to the Gulf* tells the story of several complications in this imagined food system, especially concerning pollution and organic waste. The Lagoonmaker proposes to cut a channel through the mountains to the Pacific Ocean or through the Colorado River delta to the Gulf of California so that the polluted Salton Sea will be fed and cleansed by the clean ocean waters and will turn into a productive estuarial lagoon. The Witness responds by asking, "but if the polluted waters of the Salton Sea are exchanged with the Pacific or the Gulf, who will flush the Ocean?"

The *Sixth Lagoon: On Metaphor and Discourse* takes the whole of the Colorado River basin as its subject for a discourse on how human industrial activities have completely distressed the original ecosystems. The Lagoonmaker and Witness reflect on the historical conditions of the Colorado River Watershed.

The *Seventh Lagoon: The Ring of Fire* imagines a series of aquaculture systems surrounding the Pacific Ocean that would supply sufficient food without the present industrial and technological operations. The Lagoonmaker and Witness consider the world's ocean as the ultimate lagoon, shaping the whole of the hydrological earth system. Therefore, there is a direct link between the quality of life in the oceans and the quality of life on land.

Central to the *Lagoon Cycle* is the argument about the estuarial lagoon. As a metaphor for nature meeting culture, the Harrisons describe the lagoon as a special place with a rich variety of life, yet also fragile.

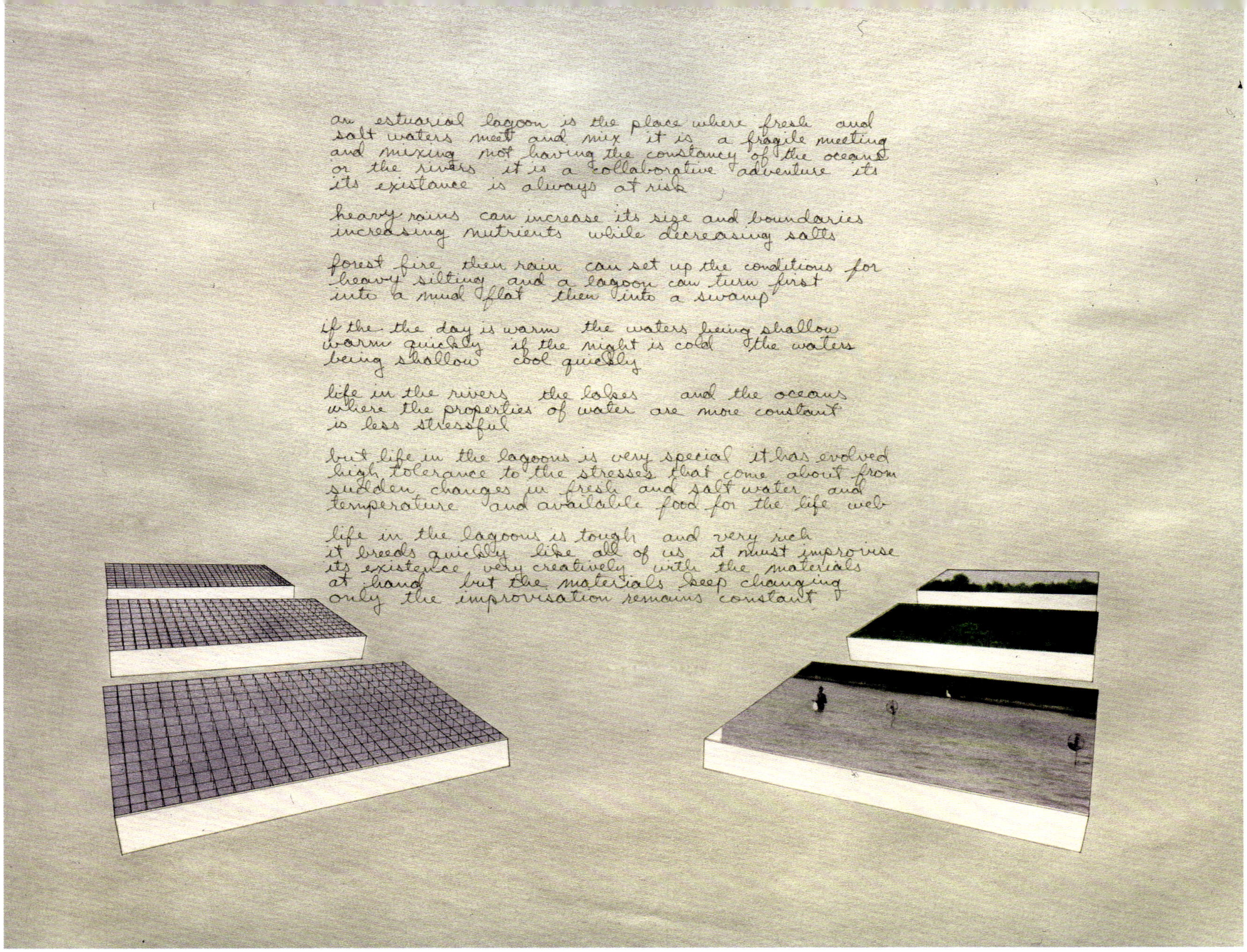

In the *Third Lagoon*, the Lagoonmaker says:

An estuarial lagoon is a place where fresh and
salt waters meet and mix it is a fragile meeting
and mixing not having the consistency of the ocean
or the rivers it is a collaborative adventure
its existence is always at risk ...

but life in the lagoon is very special it has evolved
high tolerance to the stresses that come about from
Sudden changes in fresh and salt waters and
temperature and available food for the Life Web.

Life in the lagoon is tough and very rich ...[33]

Developed as an artistic visualization of the Harrisons' experimental scientific work on how living organisms react to a specific environment, the *Lagoon Cycle* presented a firm argument against industrial exploitation of the environment leading to the depletion of ecosystems. Beginning from the *Second Lagoon*, the artists established themes challenging the accepted technological discourse through dialogues between the Lagoonmaker, the engineer of the project, an alter ego of Newton, and the Witness, performed by Helen as a poet figure who counters the hubris and presumption of the Lagoonmaker. They understand the limitations of their experiments. Therefore, the second panel of the *Second Lagoon* shows the artists represented by their crab tank in juxtaposition with the written text, clearly stating that the tank is a mere simulacrum of the Sri Lankan lagoon:

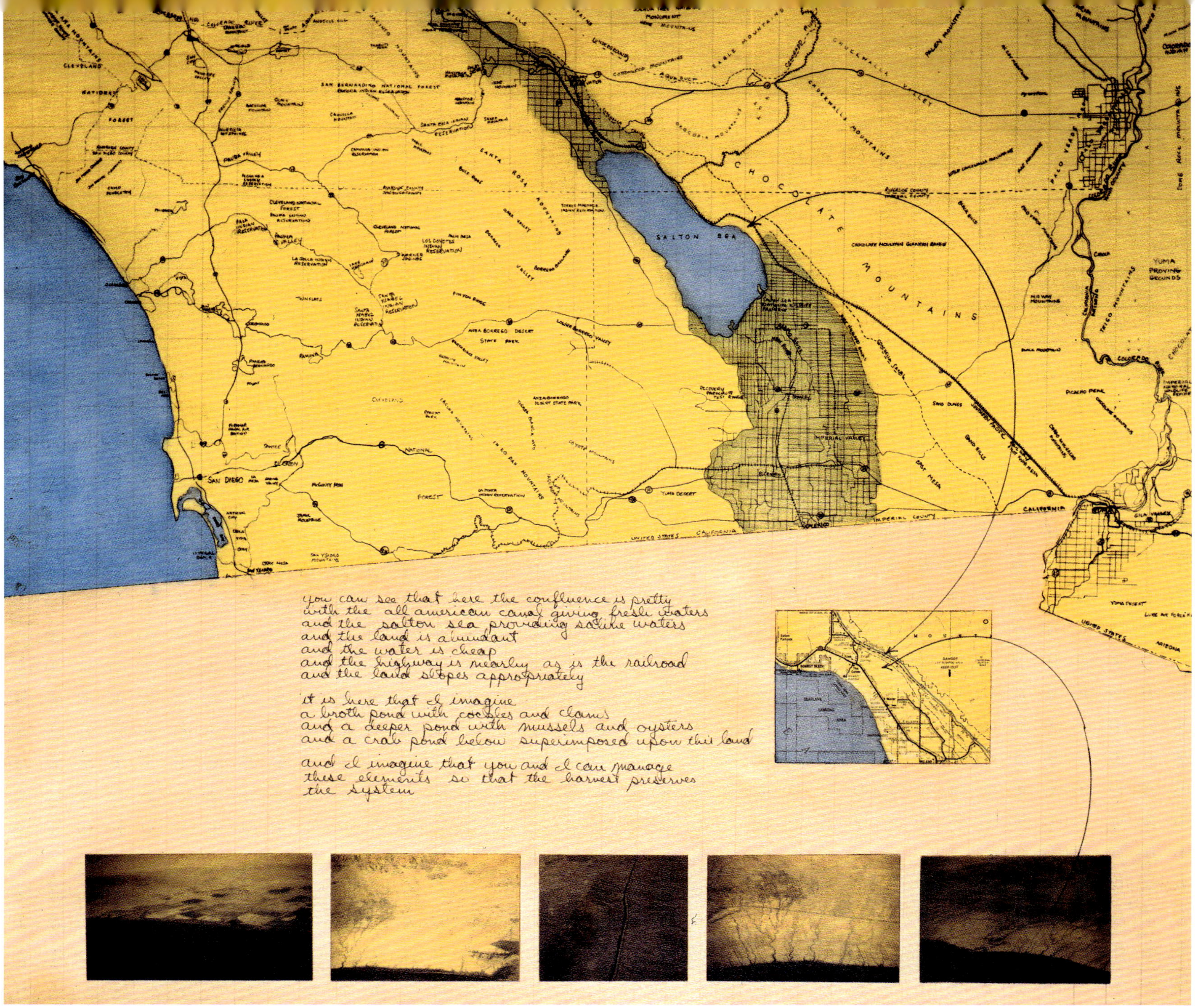

The tank is not a lagoon
nor is it a tidal pond
nor does the mixing of fresh and salt water
make it an estuary ...

But
the tank is part of an experiment
and the experiment is a metaphor for a lagoon
if the metaphor works
the experiment will succeed
and the crabs will flourish ...

But
a metaphor can be a fragile idea
an improvisation born of discourse
of observation
and anyone may change or reinterpret it
for any reason

Yet the metaphor for nature is a strong metaphor
an arrogant metaphor
a useful metaphor
an improbable metaphor
a playful metaphor

a dangerous metaphor that draws attention away
from the destruction of habitat
a valuable metaphor that will lead
to the regeneration of habitat.[34]

While making what Newton called "this megalomaniacal design" for their large-scale fish farm, the Harrisons also developed a firm argument against the monoculture paradigm extant in Southern California that dominated the Coachella Valley and had brought about the poisonous conditions of the Salton Sea. The *Fourth* and *Fifth Lagoons* imagined the transformation of the Salton Sea into an estuarial lagoon, enabling it to support a large-scale crab population, and cutting an input-output channels to the Pacific Ocean and the Gulf of California to remove excess salinity. The proposed design, including its unintended outcomes, is discussed by two voices:

The Salton Sea is not a naturally self-cleansing lagoon
the All-American Canal is not a sweetwater river
and agricultural wastewaters are not the nutrient rich waters
that run off after a monsoon ...

But in the Salton Sea there are outcomes from
another experiment alienating the condition of the waters
resulting in about 1,300,000,000 acre feet of agricultural
wastewaters entering the Sea every year ...

Why are you so certain?
When I look at the algal bloom and remember the story
of the Salton Sea then I know the condition of the waters.[35]

As noted, the artists soon discovered that this would lead inadvertently to substantial pollution of the Pacific Ocean, so they ended the hypothetical experiment, concluding that it was an unethical project to carry out, and it was never developed beyond the design stage. At the heart of the *Lagoon Cycle* lies the quintessential argument about the cost

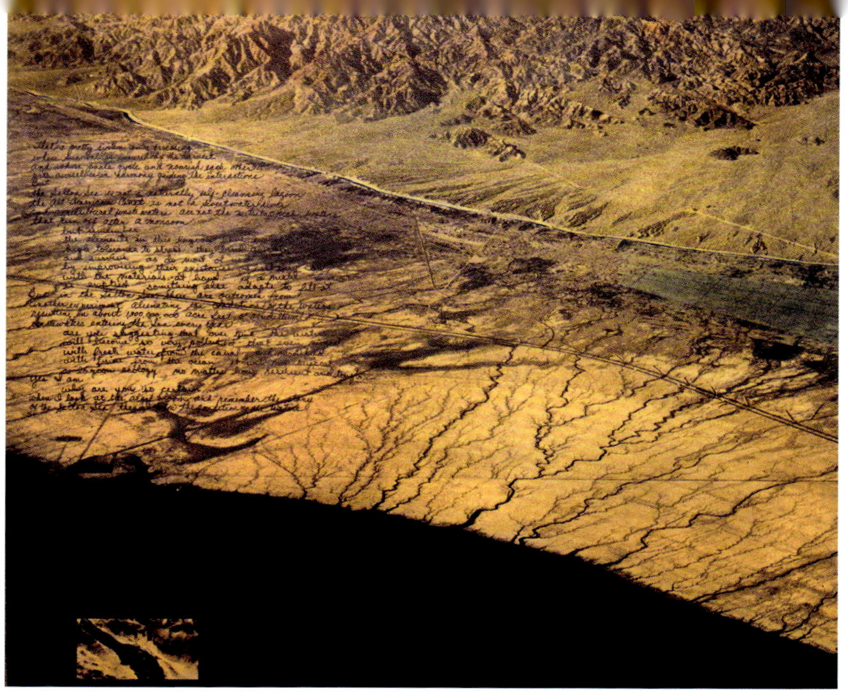

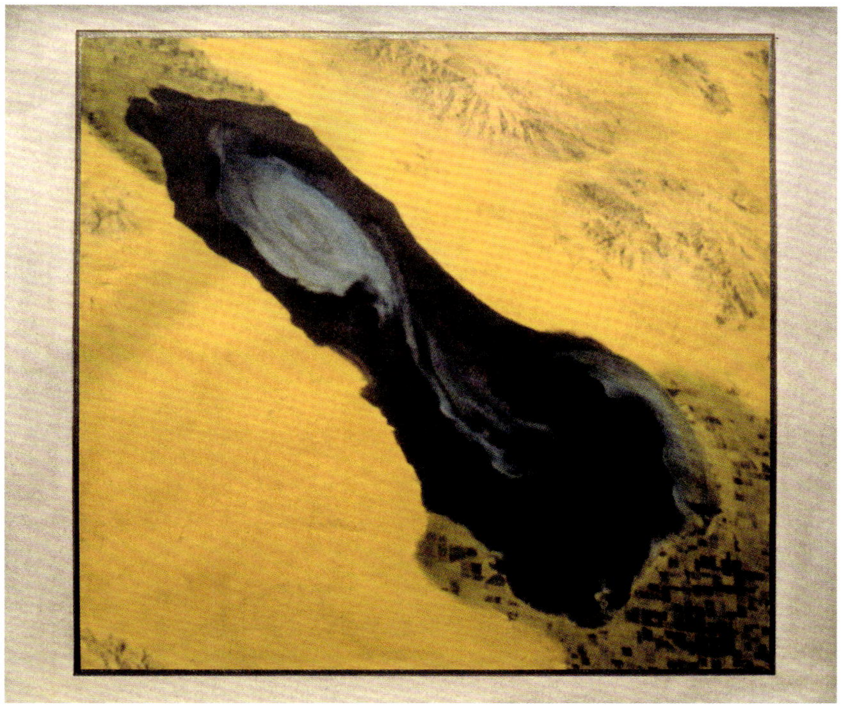

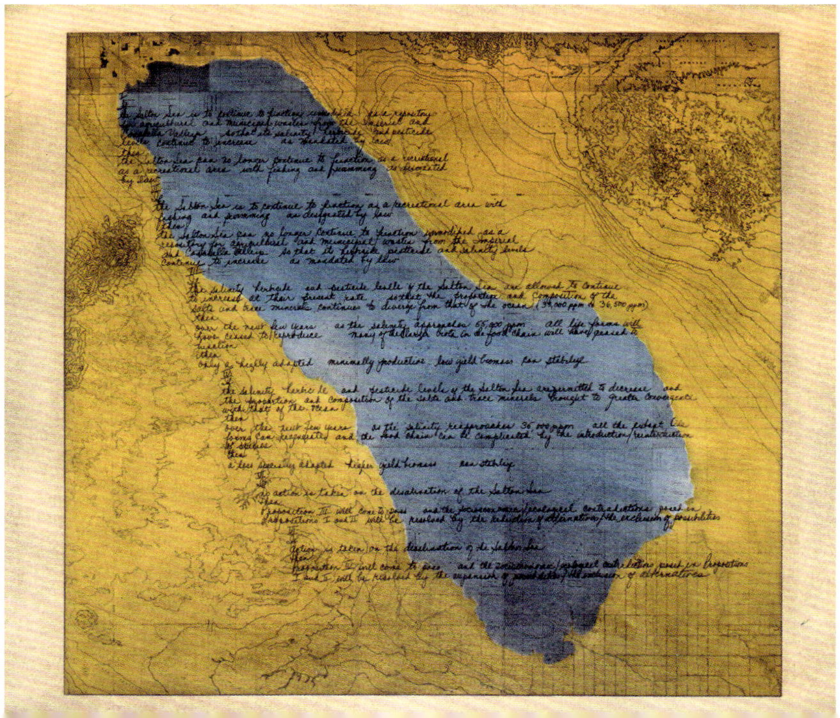

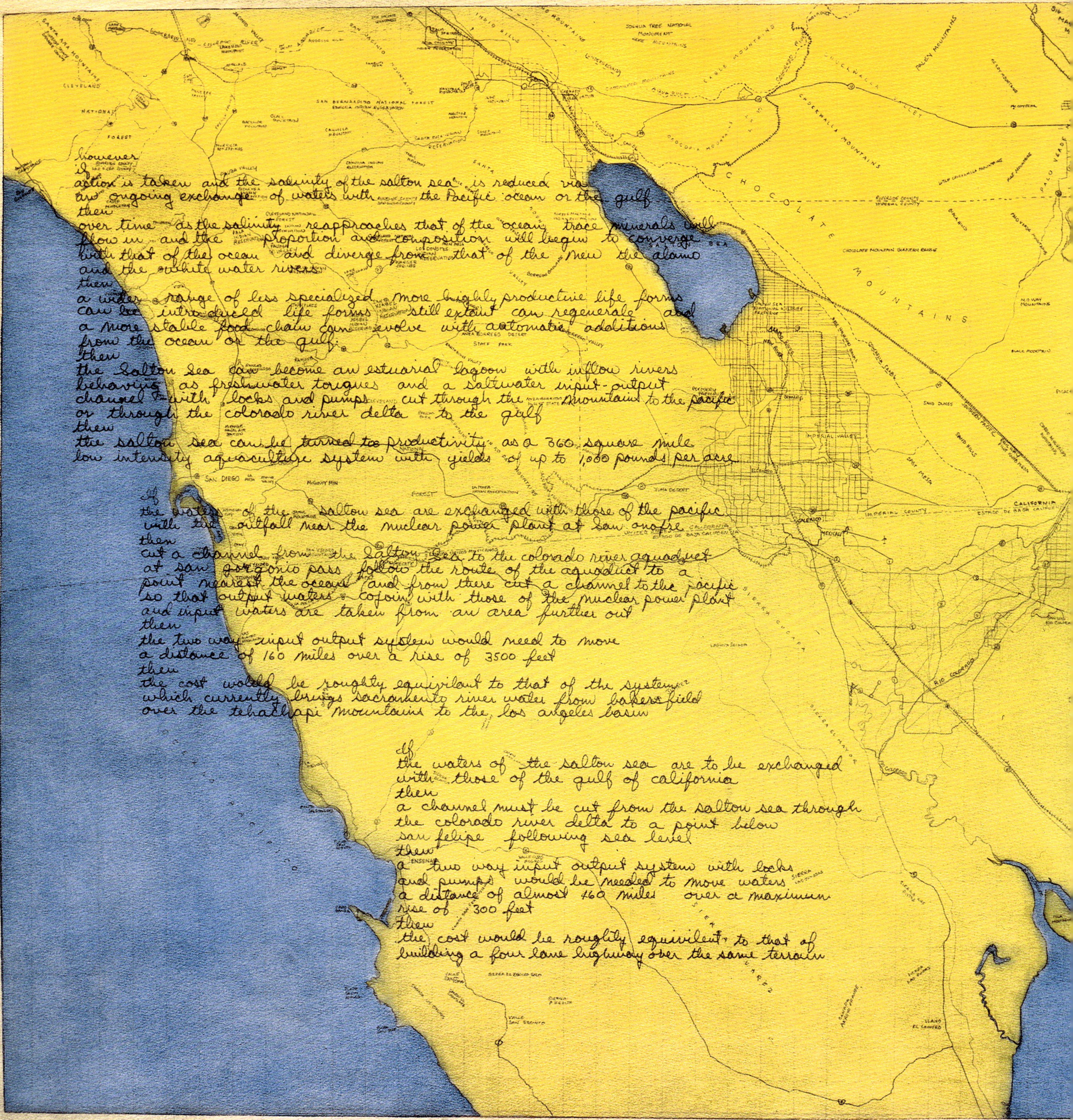
however
if
action is taken and the salinity of the salton sea is reduced via
an ongoing exchange of waters with the Pacific ocean or the gulf
then
over time as the salinity reapproaches that of the ocean trace minerals will
flow in and the proportion and composition will begin to converge
with that of the ocean and diverge from that of the new the alamo
and the white water rivers
then
a wider range of less specialized more highly productive life forms
can be introduced life forms still extant can regenerate and
a more stable food chain can evolve with automatic additions
from the ocean or the gulf
then
the Salton Sea can become an estuarial lagoon with inflow rivers
behaving as freshwater tongues and a saltwater input-output
channel with locks and pumps cut through the mountains to the pacific
or through the colorado river delta to the gulf
then
the salton sea can be turned to productivity as a 360 square mile
low intensity aquaculture system with yields of up to 1,000 pounds per acre
if
the waters of the salton sea are exchanged with those of the pacific
with the outfall near the nuclear power plant at san onofre
then
cut a channel from the Salton Sea to the colorado river aquaduct
at san gorgonio pass follow the route of the aquaduct to a
point nearest the ocean and from there cut a channel to the pacific
so that output waters cojoin with those of the nuclear power plant
and input waters are taken from an area further out
then
the two way input output system would need to move
a distance of 160 miles over a rise of 3500 feet
then
the cost would be roughly equivilant to that of the system
which currently brings sacramento river water from bakersfield
over the tehachapi mountains to the los angeles basin
if
the waters of the salton sea are to be exchanged
with those of the gulf of california
then
a channel must be cut from the salton sea through
the colorado river delta to a point below
san felipe following sea level
then
a two way input output system with locks
and pumps would be needed to move waters
a distance of almost 160 miles over a maximum
rise of 300 feet
then
the cost would be roughly equivilent to that of
building a four lane highway over the same terrain
CHOCOLATE MOUNTAINS
SAN DIEGO
CALIFORNIA

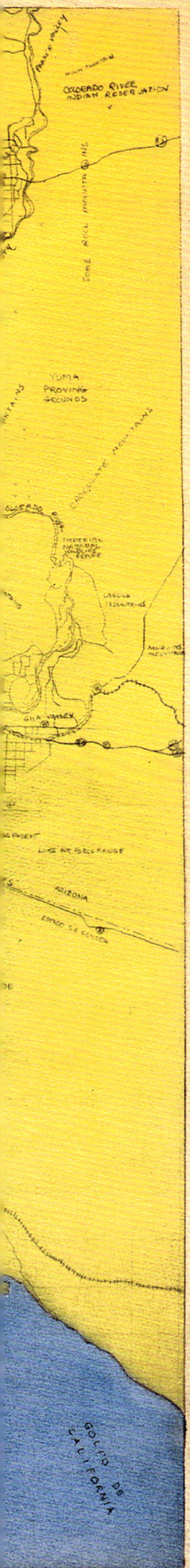

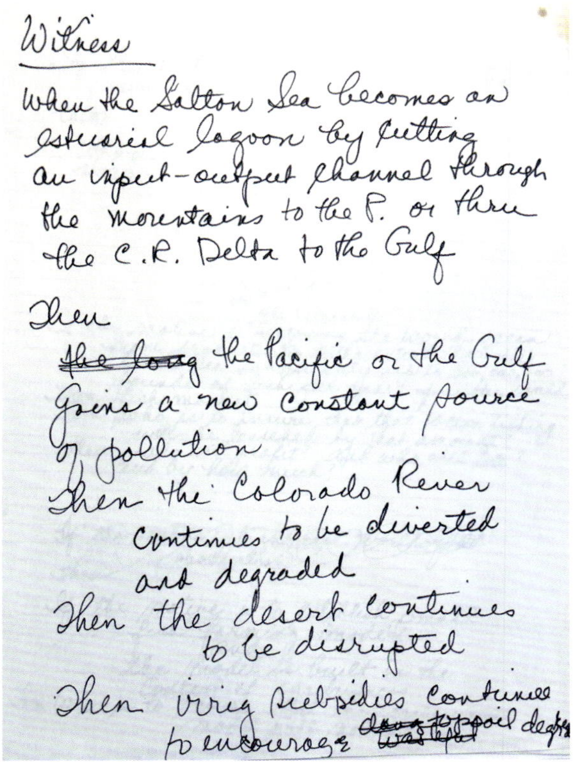
Witness

When the Salton Sea becomes an estuarial lagoon by cutting an input-output channel through the mountains to the P. or thru the C.R. Delta to the Gulf

Then
~~the long~~ the Pacific or the Gulf gains a new constant source of pollution
Then the Colorado River continues to be diverted and degraded
Then the desert continues to be disrupted
Then irrig subsidies continue to encourage ~~wasteful~~ ~~despoil~~ deg

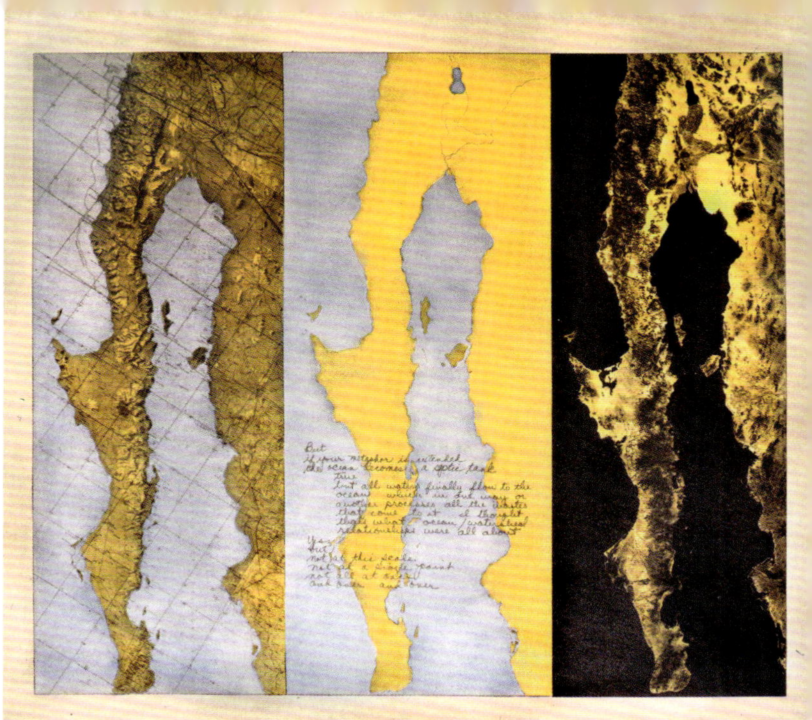

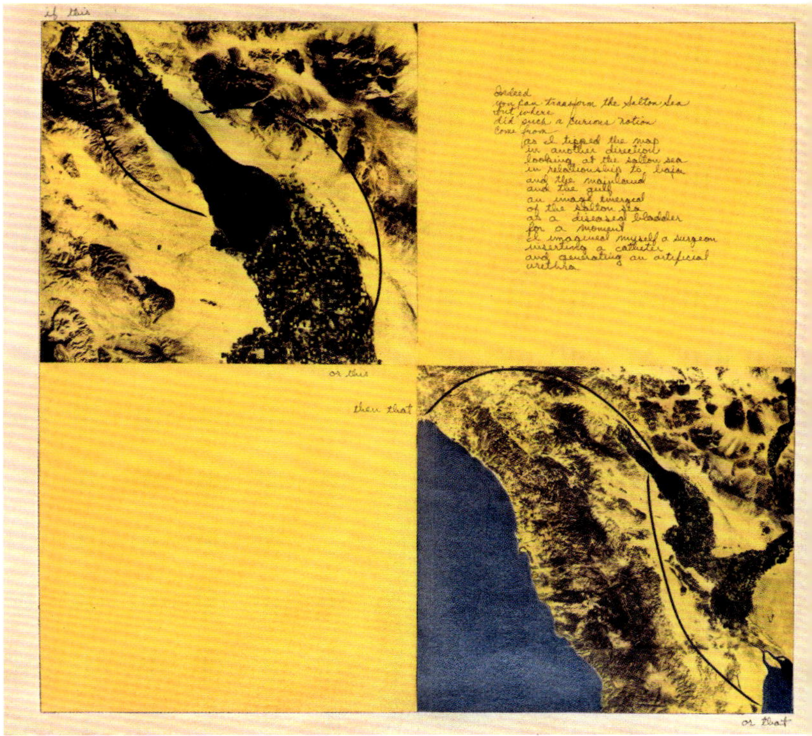

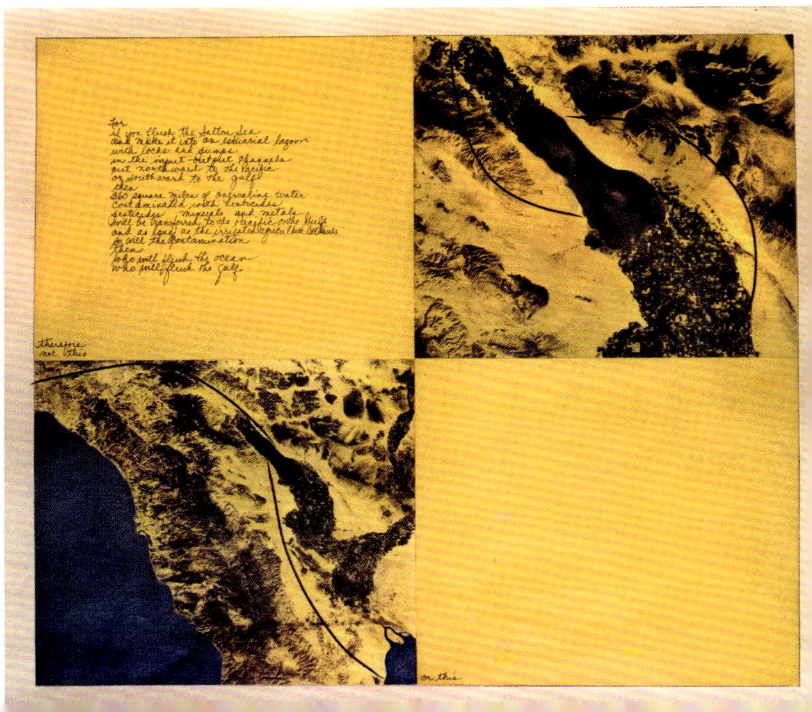

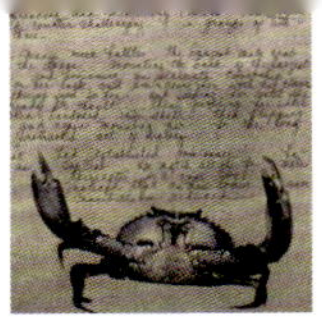

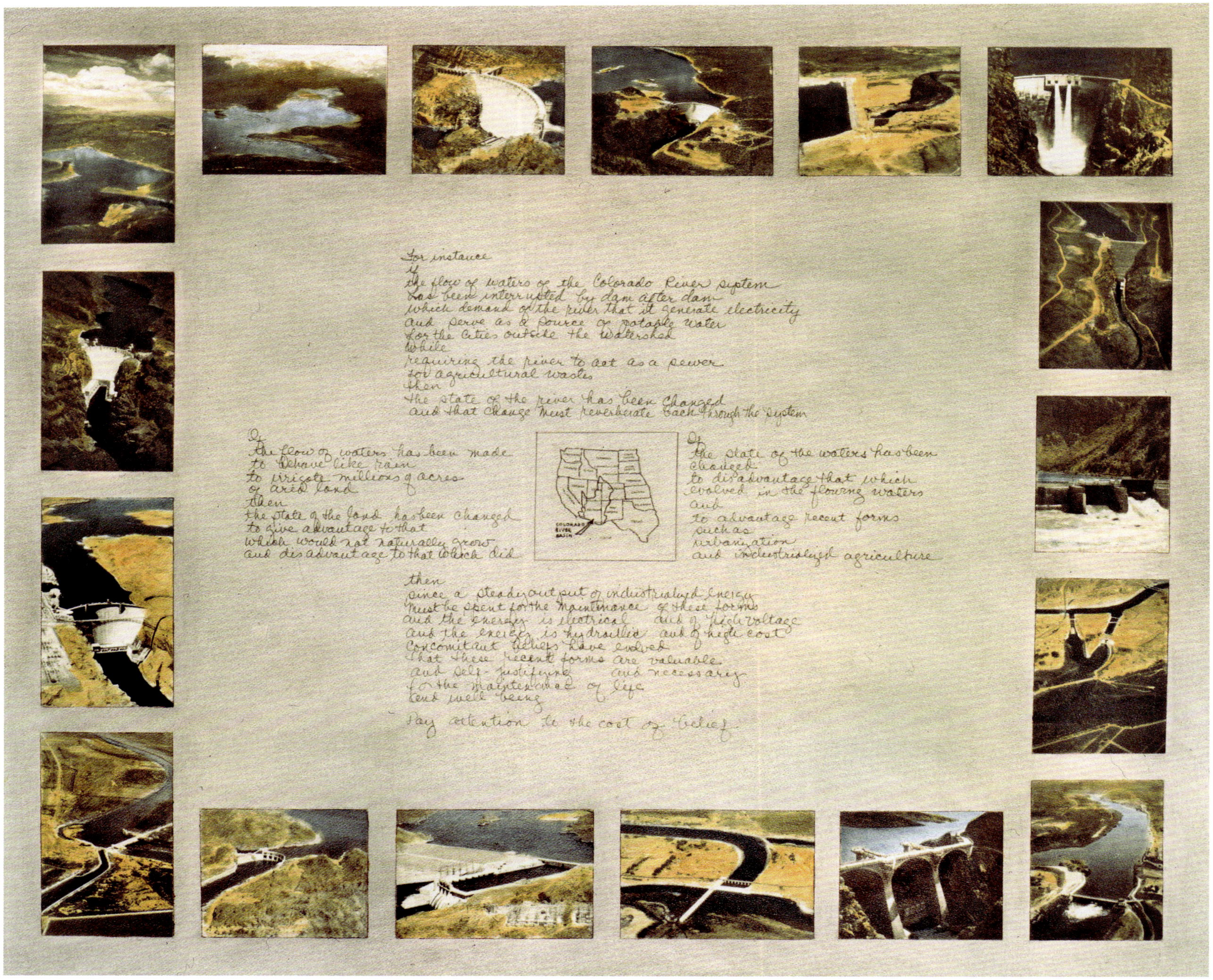

of belief. "How much does it cost to believe in something?" the artists ask. "If I believe in boundless resources, then the cost of that belief is the death of our ecosystems."[36]

The *Fifth Lagoon* raised the important question as to who would flush the ocean pollution resulting from the modification of the Salton Sea. The Lagoonmaker and Witness, speaking for the Harrisons, have come to an agreement about the catastrophic long-term outcomes of such massive technological solutions:

For
If you flush the Salton Sea
and make it an estuarial lagoon
with locks and pumps
in the input-output channels
cut northward to the Pacific
or Southward to the Gulf
then

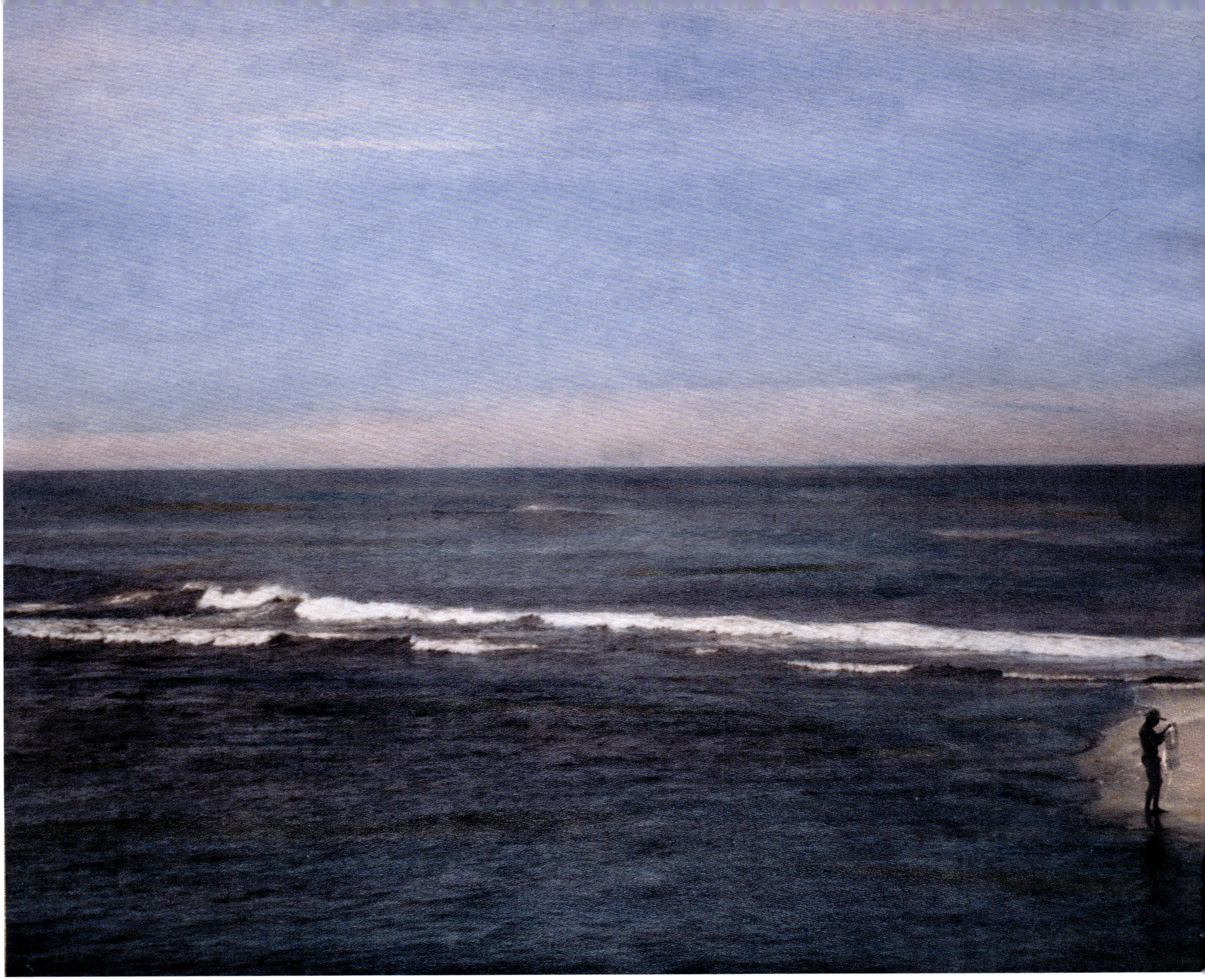

360 miles of coastline water
Contaminated with herbicides
pesticides minerals and metals
will be transferred to the Pacific or the Gulf
and as long as irrigated agriculture continues
so will the contamination
then who will flush the ocean
who will flush the gulf[37]

Through such empathy for the environment, the *Lagoon Cycle* visualized catastrophic outcomes of the vast evolving system of resource extraction that has led to environmental degradation and the climate crisis – the central theme of all the Harrisons' later investigations. Exploring the Colorado River watershed and its water uses and policies, the *Sixth Lagoon* demonstrated that the river system did not fare well, as it was dammed and re-dammed and its ecosystems

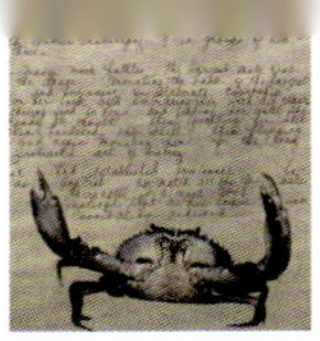

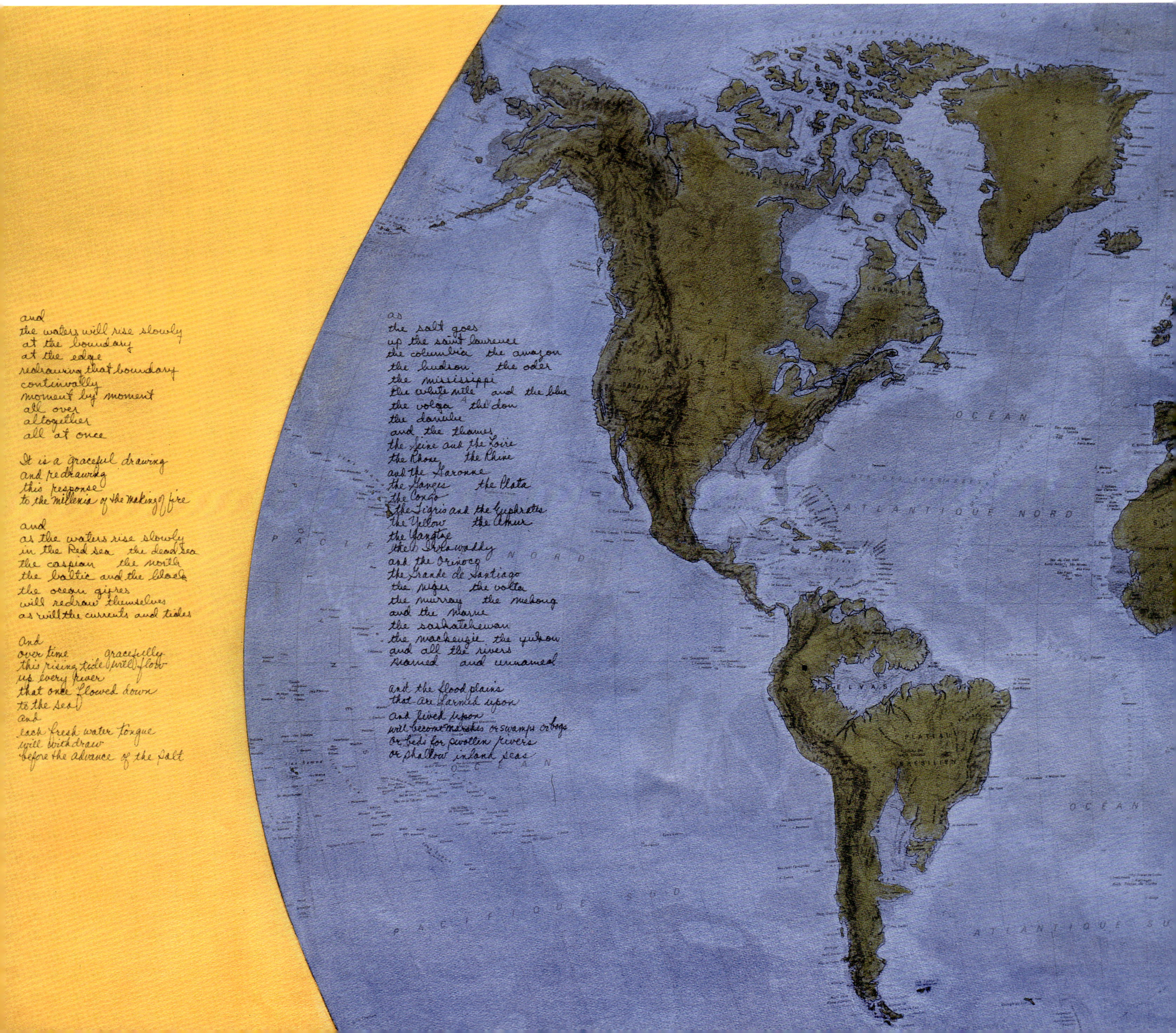
and
the waters will rise slowly
at the boundary
at the edge
redrawing that boundary
continually
moment by moment
all over
altogether
all at once

It is a graceful drawing
and redrawing
this response
to the millenia of the making of fire

and
as the waters rise slowly
in the Red sea the dead sea
the caspian the north
the baltic and the black
the ocean gyres
will redraw themselves
as will the currents and tides

And
over time gracefully
this rising tide will flow
up every river
that once flowed down
to the sea
and
each fresh water tongue
will withdraw
before the advance of the salt

as
the salt goes
up the saint laurence
the columbia the amazon
the hudson the oder
the mississippi
the white nile and the blue
the volga the don
the danube
and the thames
the Seine and the Loire
the Rhone the Rhine
and the Garonne
the Ganges the Plata
the Congo
the Tigris and the Euphrates
the Yellow the Amur
the Yangtze
the Irrawaddy
and the Orinoco
the Grande de Santiago
the niger the volta
the murray the mekong
and the marne
the saskatchewan
the mackenzie the yukon
and all the rivers
named and unnamed

and the flood plains
that are farmed upon
and lived upon
will become marshes or swamps or bogs
or beds for swollen rivers
or shallow inland seas
OCEAN
ATLANTIQUE NORD
OCEAN

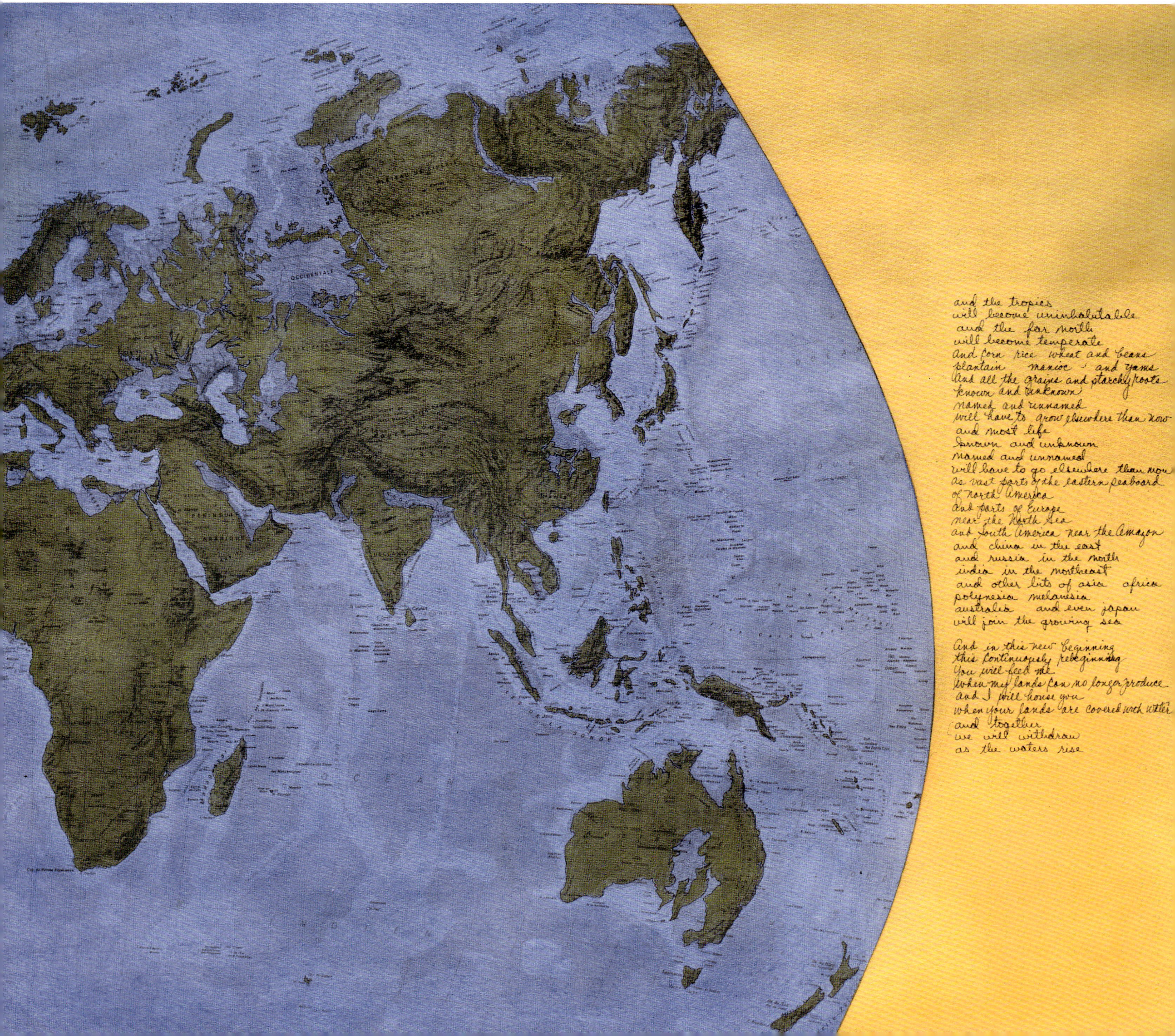
and the tropics
will become uninhabitable
and the far north
will become temperate
and corn rice wheat and beans
plantain manioc and yams
and all the grains and starchy roots
known and unknown
named and unnamed
will have to grow elsewhere than now
and most life
known and unknown
named and unnamed
will have to go elsewhere than now
as vast parts of the eastern seaboard
of North America
and parts of Europe
near the North Sea
and South America near the Amazon
and china in the east
and russia in the north
india in the northeast
and other bits of asia africa
polynesia melanesia
australia and even japan
will join the growing sea

And in this new beginning
this continuously rebeginning
You will feed me
when my lands can no longer produce
and I will house you
when your lands are covered with water
and together
we will withdraw
as the waters rise

marginalized compared to the river systems in Sri Lanka, the starting point for the *Lagoon Cycle*. As with their previous *Lagoon* phases, the Harrisons engaged satellite and bird's-eye view photography, hundreds of pages of scientific reports, and their own hand-drawn sketches of the whole river system.[38] The results were to then be presented poetically by the Lagoonmaker and Witness, once again discussing the environmental conditions:

For instance,
if
the flow of waters in the Colorado River system
has been interrupted by dam after dam
which demands of the river that it generates electricity
and serves as a source of potable water
for the cities outside of the watershed
while
requiring the river to act as sewer
for agricultural wastes
then
the state of the river has been changed
and that change must reverberate back
through the system ...

Pay attention to the cost of belief.[39]

With its large-scale painted murals combining maps, designs, photography, and poetic texts, the *Lagoon Cycle* developed a completely new understanding of lagoons and watersheds as highly endangered ecosystems. The cycle concludes with a prophecy of the future existence laid out in the *Seventh Lagoon*. After decoding lagoons and watersheds and their reduced state of existence, the Lagoonmaker and Witness recount a dream they saw: Earth has warmed, all ice has melted, the oceans have risen, and ecosystems and civilization alike are under stress. Like before, the Lagoonmaker and Witness speak with a single voice:

Upon hearing this
we took a present world map and
drew a probable world

It is said that if all the ice melted
the oceans would rise about 300 feet
So we drew line as best we could
at the 300-foot level
and thought about how the land would shrink
as the oceans grew

And the waters will rise slowly
at the boundary
at the edge.[40]

Finished in 1984, after a series of intuitive and imaginative leaps by the artists, the *Lagoon Cycle* envisions future ecologies while prophetically concluding that climate change and global warming are inevitable:

And the flood plains that are farmed upon and lived upon
will become marshes or swamps or bogs
or beds for swollen rivers
or shallow inland seas
and the tropics will become uninhabitable
and the far north will become temperate
and corn and rice and wheat and beans
and plantain manioc and yams
and all the grains and starchy roots
known and unknown named and unnamed
will have to grow elsewhere than now and most life
known and unknown
will have to go elsewhere than now
as vast parts of the eastern seaboard
of the United States, and parts of Europe
near the North Sea
and much of South America near the Amazon
and China somewhere ... [41]

The *Lagoon Cycle* remains one of the most important and well-known works by the Harrisons. Its recognition stems from a decade of both solo and group exhibitions, until the Centre Georges Pompidou in Paris decided to acquire the work for its permanent collection. The Harrisons' archives preserve a saga of the lengthy negotiations between the artists and the museum leadership. It was finally transferred to Paris in 1997, valued at $1,050,000.[42] However, the work has not been displayed in its entirety since that time period and is mostly known today through the *Book of the Seven Lagoons* that was handmade by the Harrisons and occasionally circulates in museum exhibitions and collections.

The *Book of the Seven Lagoons*, a smaller-format set of 45 hand-colored pages, transformed the *Lagoon Cycle* into a comfortably portable work of art. The Harrisons produced the book in a limited edition, which was published by Laurence McGilvery's publishing house in La Jolla. The work started in 1987 with the artists' phone call to the owner, asking him to come to their studio at UCSD. Laurence recruited his daughter Erin McGilvery and her friend Allwyn O'Mara to prepare the publication.[43] The crucial element was a sequence of large Mylar sleeves that could be bound at one edge and left open at the outside edge, so the individual photographs could be removed and replaced. Twenty of the bindings were produced overall in 1987, with three additional bindings in 2012.[44]

MAPPING A NEW ECO-CONSCIOUS CULTURE

The monumental, 49-meter-long mural in 60 parts and the *Book of the Seven Lagoons* laid out the Harrisons' argument about the interconnectedness of ecology and the economy. After the *Lagoon Cycle*, they began to work on an even larger scale, introducing bio-regional thinking and planning while discussing honestly the consequences of vast, technologically-enabled exploitation of natural resources, leading in the end to widespread ecocide. Working for over a decade on the *Lagoon Cycle* had enabled them to move part of their activities into the real world by offering their expertise outside the museum or gallery context as organizers and planners dealing with difficult environmental issues. Visually striking and particularly noteworthy among such projects was the 80-feet urban ecology multi-media piece, the *Guadalupe Meander, A Refugia for San José* (1983), that proposed the reclamation of the Guadalupe River in San José, California. As in many of their projects, the Harrisons made use of their skills as researchers and collaborated with San José city planners, scientists, and engineers. Through coming to understand the workings of small ecosystems in the *Survival Pieces* and the *Lagoon Cycle*, they were able to tackle larger, more complex urban ecologies. The *Guadalupe Meander, A Refugia for San José* embodied the Harrisons' growing concern about river and watershed restoration and the need for policy changes in natural resource use and management in California. This installation, exhibited originally at the San José Museum of Art and later at the University Art Gallery, University of California Irvine, included large-scale elaborate photomurals, specially designed maps, photo-text panels, conceptual drawings, and textual discourses.[45] The work was supported by the National Endowment for the Arts (NEA) grant and the Arts Council of the City of San José.

The Harrisons' creativity was always inspired by local conditions. They were invited by the San José University and the City Council of the Arts to make a proposal. The *Guadalupe Meander, A Refugia for San José* began with their exploration of the city, including walks across the bridges in the center of town. They noticed herons and a small river that was still alive, albeit overpowered by the surrounding urban development and the network of concrete bridges and highways. Their proposal developed around the idea of a promenade that would restore the integrity of the river and its watershed, as recalled later by the artists:

"We said, 'Let a riverbank be built such that the cityscape disappears for the walker and city time dissolves into wander time. Let a riverbank be built that meanders along the Guadalupe River and serves as a green spine for the city and serves as a refugia for plants and animals and a refuge for

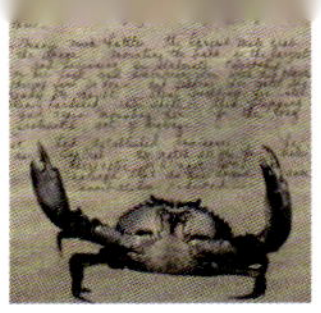

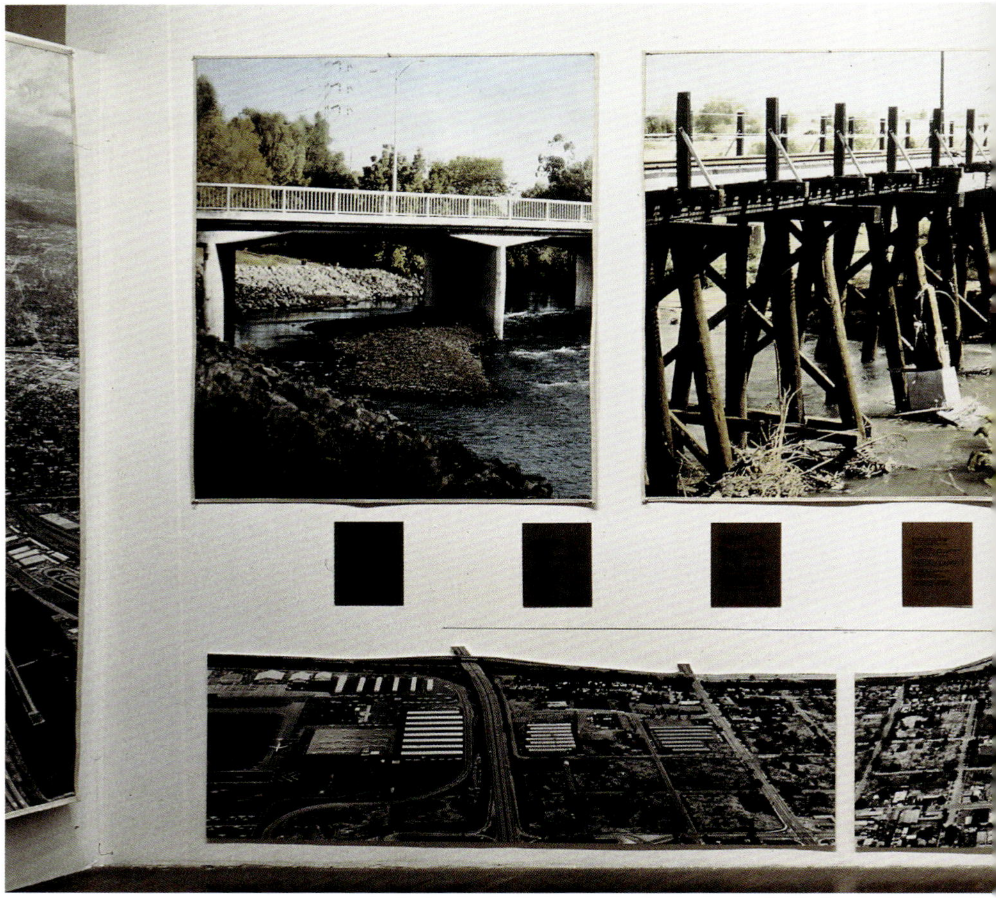

the water.' And so we proposed a walk, *The Guadalupe Meander*, which would echo the meander of the river and follow its banks through the city, moving along and across the banks from Highway 17 at the airport to the Highway 280 interchange."[46]

The intent of the *Guadalupe Meander* was to make the city council and the community members aware of the disastrous consequences of channelization of the river and construction of water-controlling dams that damaged the natural conditions of the watershed and its biodiversity. The Harrisons' proposal started not with a presentation of solutions but, more importantly, as a new way of thinking, a call to change the attitude that had led to the problems in the first place. The *Guadalupe Meander* began with asking questions and staging a dialogue with the city council members, museum staff, and business leaders of the community.

We said,
Let there be access to the river at every bridge.

Let the riverbanks be extended by 15 meters on each side wherever possible and as redevelopment occurs.

Let additional space accrue to the banks here and there and where exigencies of the situation dictate less.

Let the equivalent of the space lost accrue to the river elsewhere.

Let the dams that withhold the waters make controlled releases throughout the dry months and let the water district add such waters as might be needed to keep the flow going for a large part of the year.

The proposal's texts described how industrial construction had impacted the flow of the Guadalupe River, with ecological consequences for the flora and fauna surrounding its original course. Their solution was to reverse what had been done. On monumental canvases showing the natural bend of the river and presenting its fauna and flora, the artists imagined and described possibilities for a revitalized city around the natural banks of the river:

We said,
Let a floodplain for the floodflow of the Guadalupe
be established.

Let it be a park and ecological preserve bounded
by the Guadalupe Expressway to the East,
Coleman Avenue to the West,
Highway 17 to the north, and the railroad to the south.

Let the perimeter of the floodplain be raised.

Let it be patterned with hillocks and valleys and ridges,
highs and lows so at floodtime the hills would appear as islands,
and the ridges as pathways between them.

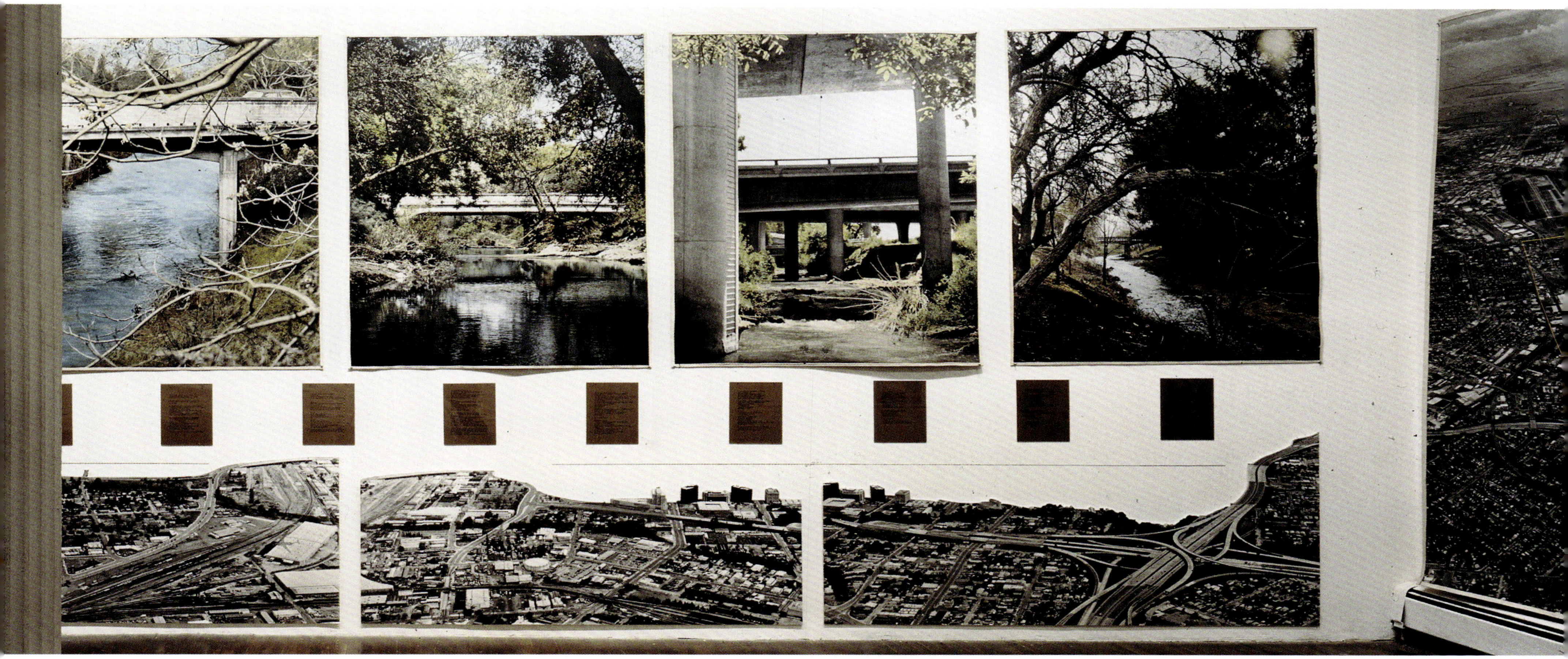

Let the landscape become a preserve planted with oak and other natives of the floodplain. Let the excess waters of the Guadalupe enter, channeled by dam diversion levee and stormdrain. Let there be such other plantings as to encourage percolation.

Despite the positive reception of the artists' proposal by the museum staff and the Art Council of San José, the city council members decided to put the river in more conventional concrete banks according to practices widely applied in California. Trees were planted in neat holes and birds had to adapt to the new diminishing state of the natural environment.

The *Guadalupe Meander* was an attempt to introduce a new eco-conscious attitude and to positively transform the city, which was portrayed in their monumental photographic murals as an unattractive concrete grid chopped up by a network of busy freeways. By proposing to create a river walk and to bring nature back to the city, this work anticipated many of the problems that California faces today in the context of global warming, when greening cities has become a pressing concern. The artists were painfully aware that nothing would happen if our thinking did not change. The *Guadalupe Meander*'s main message overlapped with that of the *Sacramento Meditations*:

Congruence with the laws of conservation of energy
is functional communal interest
in terms of species survival
Then
In the interest of our species survival all resources
would be held in trust as communal and used in congruence
with the laws of the conservation of energy

Then
Land and water would be passed on to succeeding generations
intact, nonrenewable resources
husbanded, and renewable resources not depleted

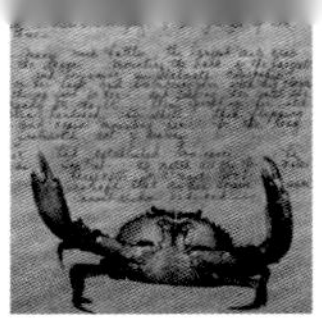

If
The paradigms that inform the present use and energy practices of culture (exploitation, consumption, transformation into possession, transformation
into profit) do not undergo modification by social forces either voluntarily (through legal means) or involuntarily (through revolutionary means)
Then
They will undergo modification through the working out of the natural forces (read entropy)

Marga Bijvoet interpreted the work of the Harrisons as "embodying an unmistakable concern about current and future ecological disasters, using metaphors as a strategy to voice their warnings and suggestions for change."[47] The Harrisons layered their work visually, using photography, painting, scientific data, historical documents, and information about natural landscape conditions and human involvement, presenting the interrelated histories of human culture and the environment. Their message was about the need for everyone to generate an ethical force and to take responsibility for their collective future and for the ecology.

The Harrisons have been celebrated as pioneers of ecological art not only for their ability to reflect on the complexities of ecosystems and watersheds and to intervene in issues of environmental degradation but also for their capacity to foresee the complex ecological issues of the future.[48] Many of their themes developed and recurred across different works and were addressed in various ways throughout their fifty-year collaboration. For instance, the methods of exploration and imagination tested in the *Lagoon Cycle* and the *Sacramento Meditations* are evident in their later work. In 2012, for example, they were invited by Laura Rogers to contribute to a show called *The Blue Line*, organized in San Francisco in conjunction with a local boat race. The artists drew on their earlier work focusing on how the city of San Francisco and its adjacent bay might respond to climate-change forecasts of rising ocean levels, drought, and glacial melt. The artists initiated their exploration with four maps.

The Bays of San Francisco Become a 162000-hectare Estuarial Lagoon When The Ocean Rises Three Meters (2007–2013) picked up thematically and stylistically from where the Harrisons had left off with the *Sacramento Meditations*. However, instead of focusing on the issues in California of farmland irrigation and agricultural pollution, *The Bays of San Francisco* explored a scenario of global warming in which local waters were set in motion, turning dry land into kilometers of fringing marshes.[49] The artists envisioned that, as the sea level rose, tides and tidal surges would activate, causing San Francisco Bay to expand and flow through the Central Valley, reaching Sacramento within 100 years. The Harrisons said that this three-meter ocean rise would generate a massive estuarial lagoon. "Who was going to take responsibility for assisting a viable ecosystem to form?" they asked, arguing that an active method of re-terraforming was needed rather than leaving this vast occurrence to chance. The *Lagoon Cycle* posits that such places are rich in life yet fragile, so a scientific team could, in the Harrisons' words, assist in "giving birth to the estuarial lagoon" of a future San Francisco. The Harrisons asserted that a rise in sea level of three meters, alongside rising temperatures of three to four degrees Celsius, would result in a productive ecosystem: polyculture on the shores of the lagoon could be established with the economic opportunity to produce an abundance of seafood in a low-intensity fish-farm scenario. The Harrisons maintained that paleo-botanical research could reveal what had thrived in the distant past, when both temperature and sea level were higher, and could thus assist in determining how to form the lagoon as a "self-continuing, self-complicating and self-growing" environment.

The Bays at San Francisco offers an unexpected look at the incredible pressure climate change puts on all ecosystems and how it threatens human existence in particular. It also considers the possibilities for our survival, the Harrisons posing the question, "Can we adapt to this scale of change in a way that benefits a changing culture while collaborating with an

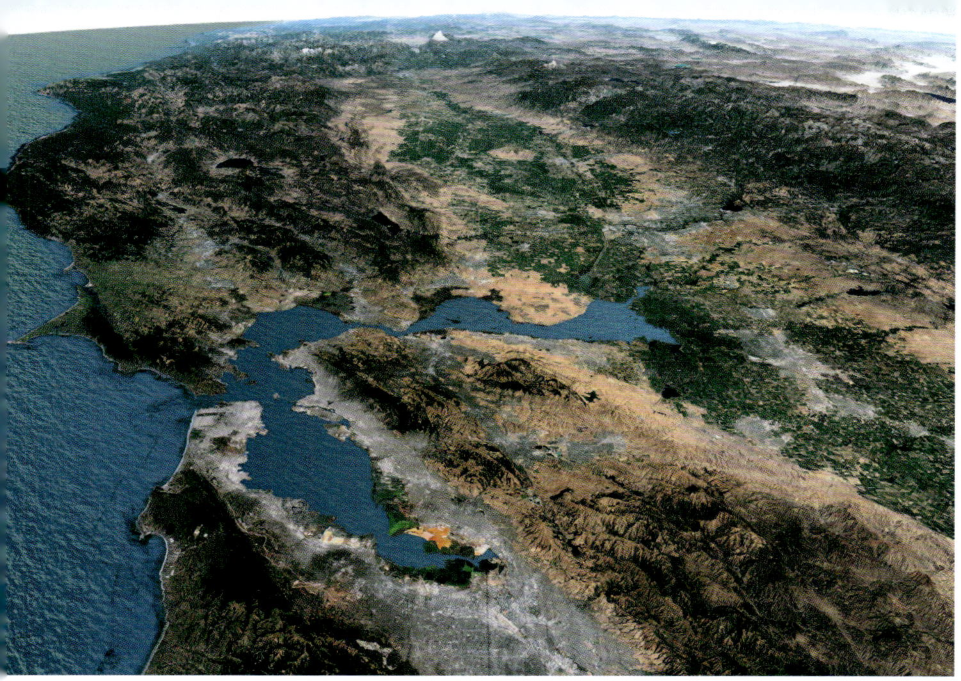

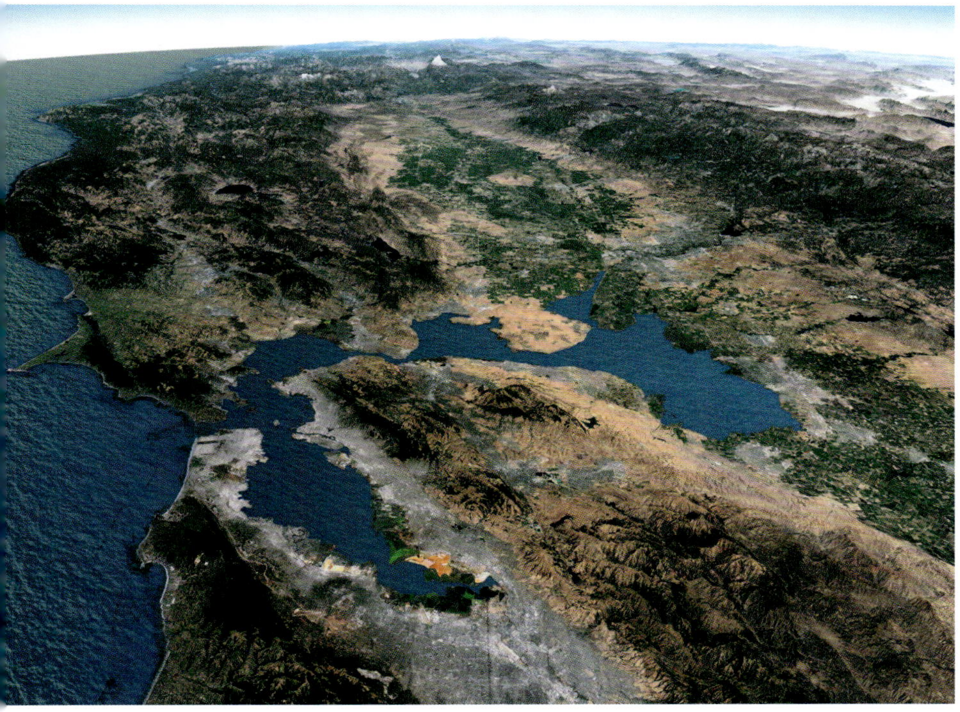

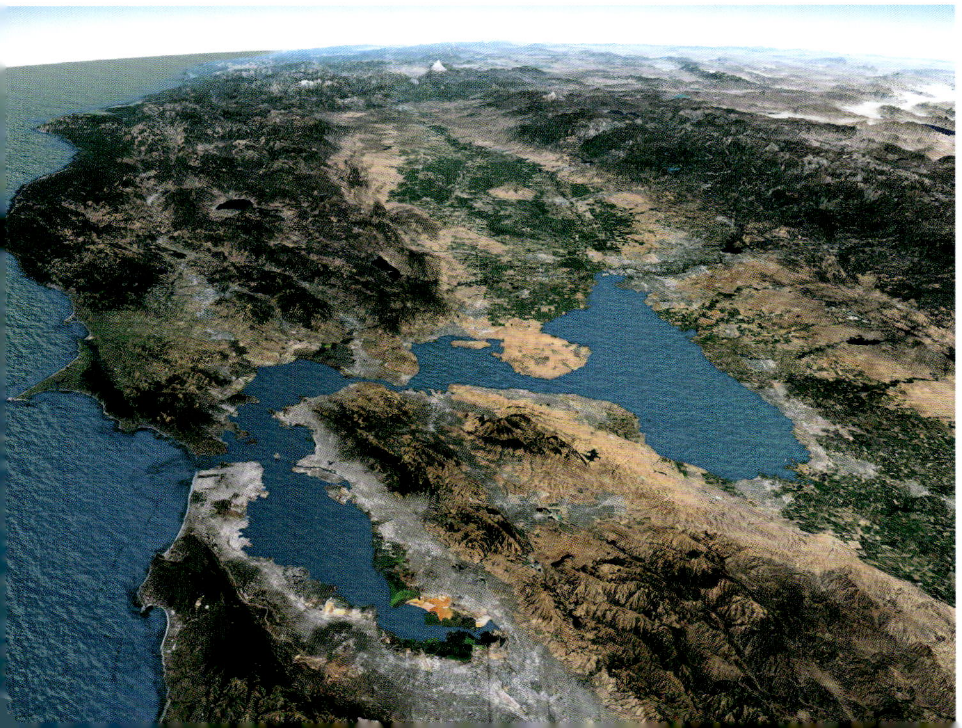

evolving ecosystem?" The answer was surprising: *exergy*, defined by the Harrisons as the raising of the available energy in a system to do necessary work.[50] If *exergy* were combined with human creativity, the resilience of ecosystems could be restored, and entropy and energy could be regulated and re-balanced in collaboration with the Web of Life.

The Bays at San Francisco falls into the category of works that Newton referred to as "preemptive planning."[51] It not only comments on the calamitous effects of climate change but also suggests scenarios to ameliorate the consequences locally, as well as ways to enact short- and long-range planning for life adaptation – a recurring theme in the Harrisons' work since *San Diego as the Center of a World* (1974). Visualization of research data was central to many of the artists' investigations, but they were always driven by the audacity to practice eco-conscious imagining beyond scientifically controlled experiments, as became clear to them while working on the *Second Lagoon*. *The Bays at San Francisco* takes liberties to illuminate the meaning of climate-data research and to understand the possible ways of nature, employing the artists' imagination and intuitive insights. Roger Malina observes that through their process of appropriation, reconfiguration, and reinterpretation of scientific data, the Harrisons' work adds a fresh dimension to our understanding of the environment, and "new knowledge is co-created."[52]

The ideas of the *Law of the Sea Conference*, the *Lagoon Cycle*, and the *Bays of San Francisco Become a 162000-hectare Estuarial Lagoon When The Ocean Rises Three Meters* took an unexpected turn in two later works. *Apologia Mediterraneo* (2019) and *A Sensorium for the World Ocean* (2019–2024) were proposed and completed by Newton in the final years of his life, after Helen, his collaborator and wife of 45 years, passed away in 2018. *Apologia Mediterraneo* is, as the name declares, an apology to the sea and a call to the coastal nations and industrialized countries to give back more than they take out. The ten-minute video combines found footage and Newton's voice-over

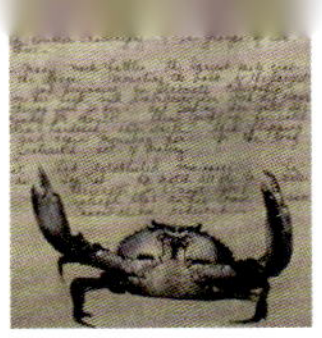

reciting a poetic letter addressed to the Mediterranean. Newton, embodying the deeply concerned voice of the sea itself, speaks of the troubles and pains that it has had to endure. Newton passionately invites his listeners to side with the beleaguered Mediterranean, which he imagines as a sentient being, more than human. In this work, he returns to his earlier call for environmental justice, first examined at the 1976 Venice Biennale with the *Law of Sea Conference* (1976), which drew attention to the conflicting demands of international states over the industrial use of coastal shores and high seas, resulting in ever-increasing levels of industrial pollution in the waters. Like that earlier project, *Apologia Mediterraneo* was presented in exhibition events.[53] However, Newton enlarged the ethical dimension of his work by expressing the concept of the Life Web. Recalling her conversations with him, the artist Terike Haapoja concludes that this work was developed from a place of extreme empathy with nature and the environment:

"We discussed empathy and what awakens it in people. We agreed that it had to be an embodied, particular experience because one cannot convince another to feel for an animal, or an earthworm, or earth itself by rational arguments. For Newton, this kind of awakening had happened early in life, when he was driving along a highway in California, seeing the broken landscapes under constant, violent human excavation. Suddenly, he said, he could hear the earth screaming. From then on, earth was someone, not something."[54]

Themes of empathy, environmental justice, and whole-systems thinking further unfold in *A Sensorium for the World Ocean*, the artist's final work-in-progress, which proposes a performative and immersive environment with the world's seas personified by an AI-generated voice. The aim of the exhibition is to allow the visitor to experience viscerally how no part of the world ocean has been left undamaged. The prototype for the *Sensorium* is currently being developed by the Center for the Force Majeure at UC Santa Cruz in collaboration with JoAnn Kuchera-Morin, creator of the Allosphere at UC Santa Barbara. The original design envisioned a map of the world ocean on the floor and scientific information on the walls surrounding the audience. Newton proposed to build an interactive environment, where visitors would have conversations with the world oceans enacted by AI. Most significantly, Newton imagined the *Sensorium* as a pre-emptive planning tool where oceanic problems, which are mostly of human creation, can be seen and acted upon though a lens of interconnectivity rather than viewed as simple cause-and-effect scenarios.

When fully realized, the *Sensorium* installation will address a series of topics related to acidity, dead zones, core samples, nurseries, wetlands, watersheds, and environmental conditions around the world, suggesting various scenarios of how the pressing ecological problems can be addressed and solved. The Ocean voice will explain how the rest of our planet's life would be at risk if the world ocean were to simplify itself and become minimally productive. Kuchera-Morin, who met Newton during the National Academy of Sciences Fall 2021 Salons (organized in conjunction with, and preparation for, the Pacific Standard Time 2024, Art and Science Collide Biennale), explained what he had achieved towards his final artwork's completion: "The project had gathered a vast amount of information concerning the world's oceans and the condition that our current environment is in due to the pollution from the land into ocean runoff as well as from the thousands of ships on the ocean floor polluting the waters and the plastics and other pollutants in the sea. The project's current state at that time was an art installation that also had much science involved due to the tremendous amounts of scientific data that they [the Harrisons] had collected over many years."[55]

The *Sensorium* builds on the metaphors and earlier empirical investigations that the artists developed working on the *Lagoon Cycle*. In the *Seventh Lagoon*, the Ocean is described as a sentient being whose language they can understand:

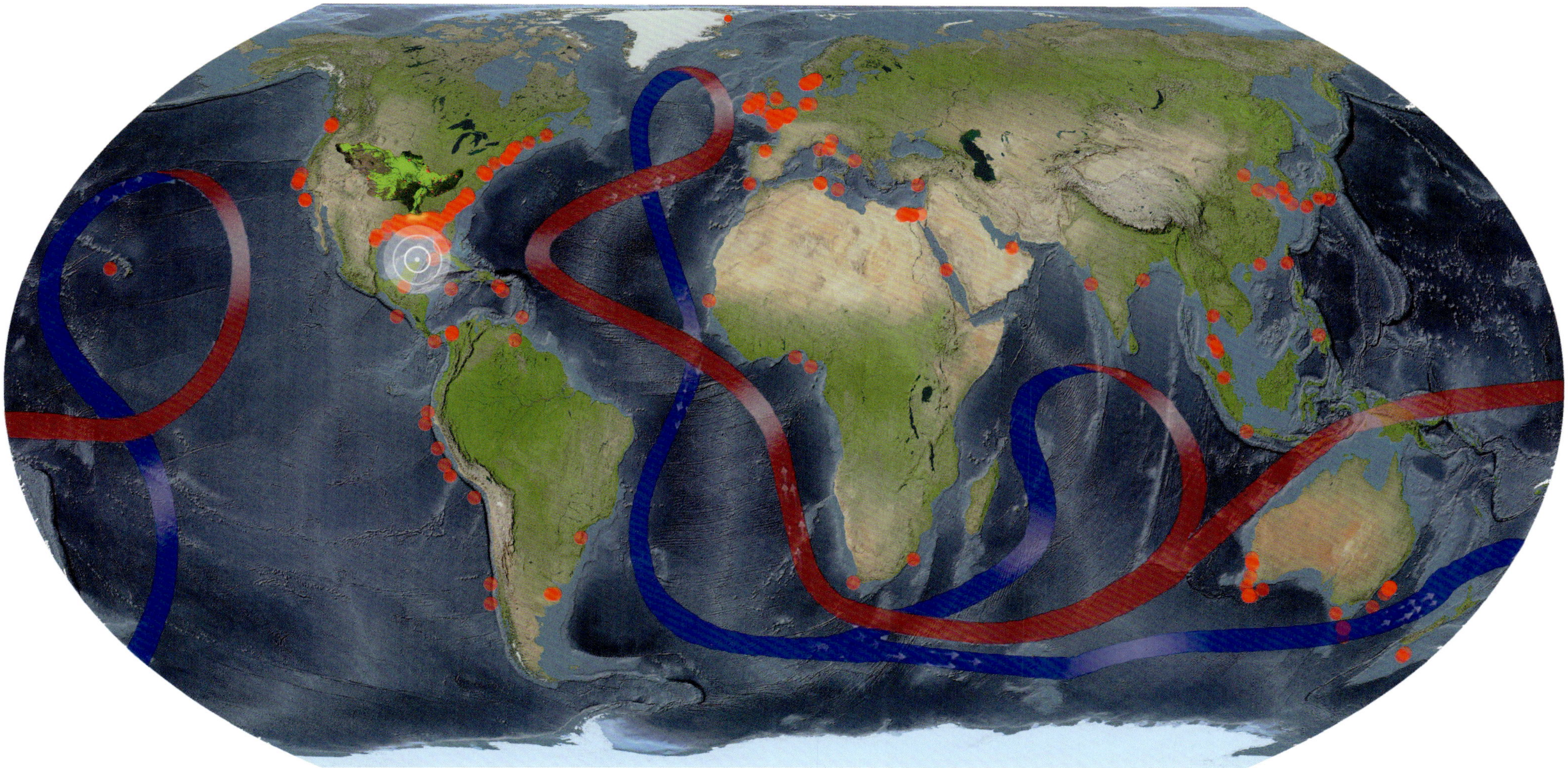

One morning we heard the ocean singing

Increase in heat decrease in ice
Increase in water decrease in land
Ice into water water to ice
Stated changes changes of state ....

After all the ocean whispered
I am the beneficiary of your garbage can
as you are the beneficiary of my abundance
and everybody knows that ice into water
and water to ice are changes of state

Upon hearing this
we took a present world map and
drew a probable world.[56]

The *Sensorium* continues the Harrisons' commitment to investigating the Life Web, using their imagination, intuition, poetry, empirical research, scientific inquiry, and expert artistry. By the end of the *Lagoon Cycle*, they had begun to approach ecosystems holistically, which paved the way for systems-thinking rather than problem-solving. The *Bays of San Francisco* and *Apologia Mediterraneo* inspired Newton to create a whole new research system and way of thinking to address the environmental conditions of our planet's oceans. The project is another exciting experiment in bridging art and science by collaborating with physicists, chemists, biologists, and other scientists to explore complex systems through visualization, sonification, and interactive computation. The *Sensorium* is an attempt to further illuminate the workings of our planet's diverse ecologies and the condition of its oceans through the integration of experimental models and simulations.

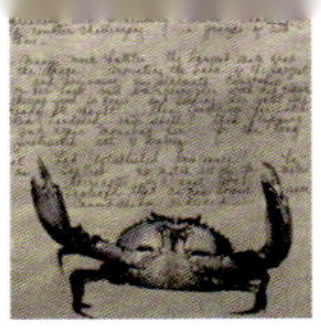

Sensorium 2024: Installation drawing and test at the Allosphere, UC Santa Barbara, CA

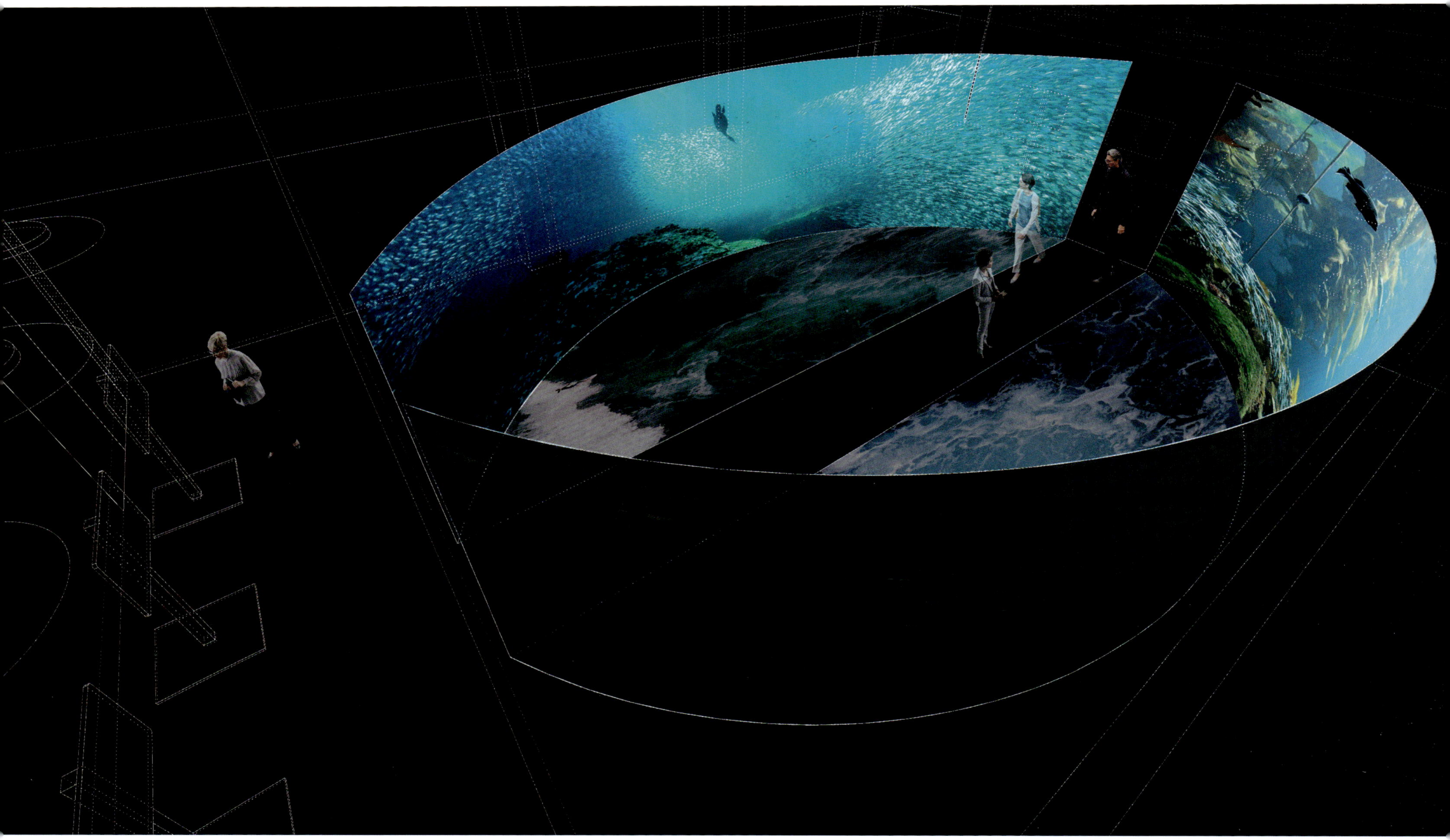

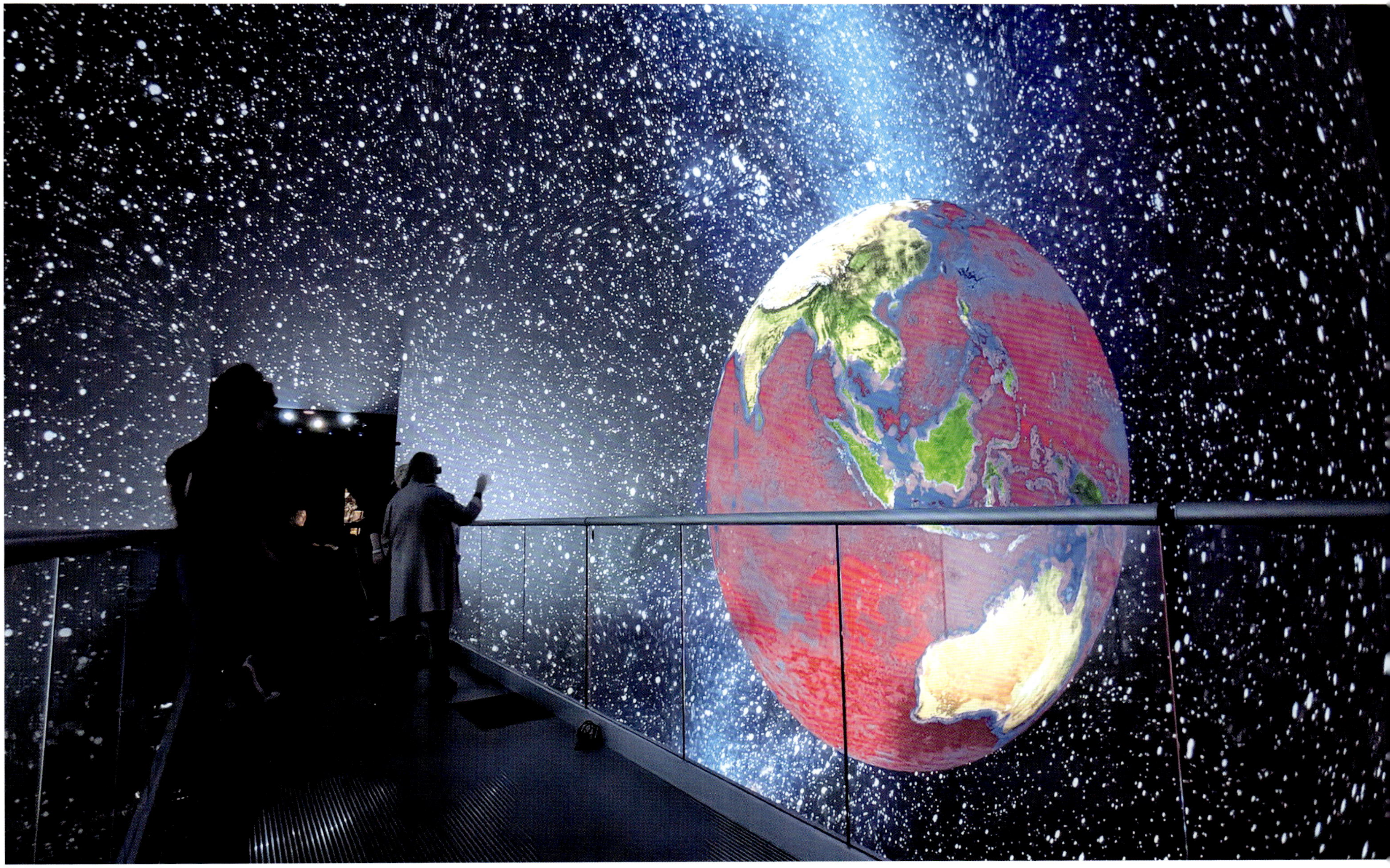

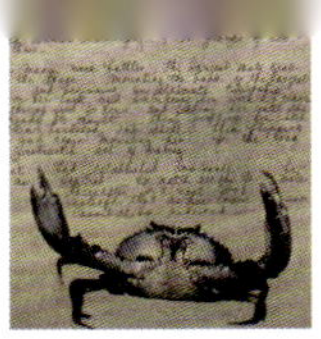

However, Newton's final work should not be understood as handing over responsibility to machines to find solutions in our current ecological plight. Newton remained resolute throughout his entire career that only cultural changes can produce a positive transformation and ameliorate the planet's ecological state. In his interview with Craig Adcock in 1992, he clearly stated: "We've been very alienated from our resources, but our time of grace is over. The idea that technology is able to buy us out of our problems is an illusion. We are going to have to make vast changes in our consciousness and behavioral patterns, because if we don't, we won't be here."[57]

Beginning from the mid-1970s, the Harrisons' proposals and designs began to address not only the consequences of industrial pollution, over-exploitation of natural resources, and the constant mismanagement of lands, waters, and watersheds, but also the issue of global warming. Their work not only started to educate audiences about its horrific implications for our species' survival – "because news is not good and only getting worse" – but also invited and ignited transformative thinking about human adaptation at great scale. The Harrisons insisted that art could change the world for the better – not just by enriching the life and spirit of those who love it but by proposing new solutions to problems revealed through an artist's way of seeing combined with science, engineering, and social critique. These ideas about the agency of art overlapped with a position held by British social anthropologist Alfred Gell, namely that "visual art objects are not a part of language ... nor do they constitute an alternative language" and thus should not be treated simply as illustrations or visual texts. Instead, Gell argued that artworks were tangible indices of social interactions and acted as "social agents."[58] Newton himself said that transformative thinking was exciting and that works of art were inherently transformative, and the Harrisons' commitment to the Web of Life – which they labelled, rather bluntly, a Dictatorship of the Ecology[59] – led them to produce works of art that could act as just such social agents to reshape the world in which we live.

1 Harrison, Helen Mayer, and Newton Harrison, "Shifting Positions toward the Earth: Art and Environmental Awareness," *Leonardo*, Vol. 26, No. 5, 1993, pp. 371–377, 371, https://doi.org/10.2307/1576031, accessed November 1, 2022.

2 Harrison, Helen Mayer, and Newton Harrison, *The Time of the Force Majeure: After 45 Years Counterforce is on the Horizon*, edited by Petra Kruse and Kai Reschke. Prestel, Munich, London, New York, 2016, p. 93.

3 Ibid., p. 143.

4 Certeau, Michel de, "Pay Attention: To Make Art," *The Lagoon Cycle: March 23 through June 2, 1985*, Harrison, Helen Mayer, and Newton Harrison, exh. cat. Herbert F. Johnson Museum of Art, Cornell University, Ithaca, NY, 1985, pp. 17–23, 17.

5 Ibid.

6 Harrison, Helen Mayer, and Newton Harrison, *The Time of the Force Majeure: After 45 Years Counterforce is on the Horizon*, pp. 50–53.

7 The original series of five maps was found in the Harrison Studio archive in the process of preparation for this exhibition and is included in the exhibition display. Sometime later, the artists made another photographic version of the series. The archival files document the progression of their ideas, variations of the maps, and typescripts of the text. See: Project Files, Series 2, Subseries 7, Center of the World, Box 34, Folder 1–4. Helen and Newton Harrison Papers, M1797. Special Collections & University Archives, Stanford University, Stanford, CA, consulted in October–December 2021.

8 Harrison, Helen Mayer, and Newton Harrison, *The Time of the Force Majeure: After 45 Years Counterforce is on the Horizon*, p. 53.

9 Statewide and regional climate assessments reports are readily available through various state agencies. For example: https://www.climateassessment.ca.gov/state/overview/, accessed December 1, 2023.

10 Project Files, Series 2, Subseries 9, Gabrielino Indians, Box 34–35. Helen and Newton Harrison Papers, M1797. Special Collections & University Archives, Stanford University, Stanford, CA, consulted in October–December 2021.

11 Jill Dawsey makes an important argument about the photo-conceptual art practices to which the Harrisons greatly contributed as founding members of the Visual Arts Department at UCSD. In that sense, the *Meditation on the Gabrielino* was one of the early iconic text-and-image installations that closely aligned with late-1960s conceptual art practices. See: Jill Dawsey, "The Uses of Photography: An Introduction," *The Uses of Photography: Art, Politics, and the Reinvention of a Medium*, edited by Jill Dawsey. Museum of Contemporary Art, San Diego, CA, UC Press, 2016, pp. 38, 107–108.

12 The original work was sold to a private collection and cannot be traced. Design sketches included in the current exhibition were rediscovered at the Harrison Studio in

Santa Cruz during preparation for this exhibition. Project files in the archive document the circumstance of the commission, planning notes, research, and performances. See: Project Files, Series 2, Subseries 37, Gabrielino Indians, Box 37–39. Helen and Newton Harrison Papers, M1797. Special Collections & University Archives, Stanford University, Stanford, CA, consulted in October–December 2021. The essence of the work is distilled by the artists in their final book: Harrison, Helen Mayer, and Newton Harrison, *The Time of the Force Majeure: After 45 Years Counterforce is on the Horizon*, pp. 64–65.

13 Ibid., p. 65.

14 Adcock, Craig, "Conversational Drift: Helen Mayer Harrison and Newton Harrison," *Art Journal*, Vol. 51, No. 2 (*Art and Ecology*), Summer, 1992, pp. 35–45, 37–38.

15 Green, Charles, "Memory and Ethics: Helen Mayer Harrison and Newton Harrison," *The Third Hand: Collaboration in Art from Conceptualism to Postmodernism*, University of Minnesota Press, 2001, pp. 97–122, 114, http://www.jstor.org/stable/10.5749/j.ctttsbj7.9, accessed July 2022.

16 Project files in the archive document the circumstance of the commission, planning notes, research, exhibition history, and performances. See: Project Files, Series 2, Subseries 14, Sacramento Meditations, Box 42–45. Helen and Newton Harrison Papers, M1797. Special Collections & University Archives, Stanford University, Stanford, CA, consulted in October–December 2021. The essence of the work is distilled by the artists in their final book: Harrison, Helen Mayer, and Newton Harrison, *The Time of the Force Majeure: After 45 Years Counterforce is on the Horizon*, pp. 66–78.

17 Statements by the artists dating to 1977 can be viewed in Box # 42, Folder # 4: Project Files, Series 2, Subseries 14, Sacramento Meditations, Box 42–45. Helen and Newton Harrison Papers, M1797. Special Collections & University Archives, Stanford University, Stanford, CA, consulted in October–December 2021.

18 This work is part of the Harrison Family Trust Collection.

19 Photocopies of all research articles consulted by the artists are all conserved in project files of the archive, Box # 42, Folder # 4: Project Files, Series 2, Subseries 14, Sacramento Meditations, Box 42–45. Helen and Newton Harrison Papers, M1797. Special Collections & University Archives, Stanford University, Stanford, CA, consulted in October–December 2021.

20 Cited from: Weintraub, Linda, "Helen and Newton Harrison. Strategies to Sustain Life," *To Life! Eco Art in Pursuit of a Sustainable Planet,* Linda Weintraub, University of California Press, Berkeley, CA, 2012, pp. 74–80, 79.

21 Harrison, Helen Mayer, and Newton Harrison, *The Time of the Force Majeure: After 45 Years Counterforce is on the Horizon*, pp. 376–377.

22 Ibid.

23 Green, Charles, "Memory and Ethics: Helen Mayer Harrison and Newton Harrison," p. 110.

24 Planning notes can be viewed in Box # 42, Folder # 12, 14, 16: Project Files, Series 2, Subseries 14, Sacramento Meditations, Box 42–45. Helen and Newton Harrison Papers, M1797. Special Collections & University Archives, Stanford University, Stanford, CA, consulted in October–December 2021.

25 See: Box # 42, Folder # 7: Project Files, Series 2, Subseries 14, Sacramento Meditations, Box 42–45. Helen and Newton Harrison Papers, M1797. Special Collections & University Archives, Stanford University, Stanford, CA, consulted in October–December 2021.

26 This work is fully preserved in the Harrison Family Trust Collection and is entirely included in the exhibition.

27 Harrison, Helen Mayer, and Newton Harrison, *The Time of the Force Majeure: After 45 Years Counterforce is on the Horizon*, pp. 60–63. Archival materials, including correspondence, outlines, research, newspaper clippings, and installation notes offer additional insight into the artists' proposal and concept development, see: Project Files, Series 2, Subseries 10, Venice Biennale, Box 35–36. Helen and Newton Harrison Papers, M1797. Special Collections & University Archives, Stanford University, Stanford, CA, consulted in October–December 2021.

28 Milic, Milenko, "Third United Nations Conference on the Law of the Sea," *Case Western Reserve Journal of International Law*, Vol. 8, Issue 1, 1976, pp. 168–186, https://scholarlycommons.law.case.edu/jil/vol8/iss1/11, accessed November 21, 2023.

29 Project files contain handwritten notes explaining the layout of the Venice Biennale installation and its logic. See: Box # 36, Folder # 7, Project Files, Series 2, Subseries 10, Venice Biennale, Box 35–36. Helen and Newton Harrison Papers, M1797. Special Collections & University Archives, Stanford University, Stanford, CA, consulted in October–December 2021.

30 Harrison, Helen Mayer, and Newton Harrison, *The Time of the Force Majeure: After 45 Years Counterforce is on the Horizon*, p. 61.

31 Ibid., pp. 84–93. Several descriptions of the *Lagoon Cycle* can be seen in the archives: Box # 23, Folder # 17, Series 2, Project Files, Subseries 5, Lagoon Cycle, Box 22–33. Helen and Newton Harrison Papers, M1797. Special Collections & University Archives, Stanford University, Stanford, CA, consulted in October–December 2021.

32 The striking aesthetic character of the *Lagoon Cycle* has garnered considerable attention from art critics and scholars since its first monographic publication in 1985 in the exhibition catalogue. The essays included there by Michel de Certeau ("Pay Attention: To Make Art") and Carter Ratcliff ("Compendium") paved the way in discussing many of the unusual artistic features of the cycle. See: Leavitt, Thomas W., Bealle, Penny, editors, *The Lagoon Cycle*: *March 23 through June 2, 1985*, Harrison, Helen Mayer, and Newton Harrison, exh. cat. Herbert F. Johnson Museum of Art, Cornell University, Ithaca, NY, 1985.

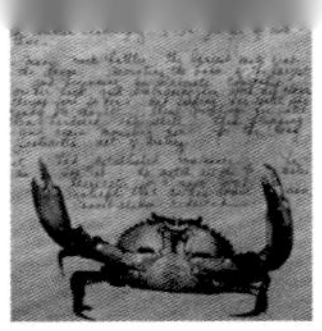

33 Harrison, Helen Mayer, and Newton Harrison, *The Time of the Force Majeure: After 45 Years Counterforce is on the Horizon*, pp. 117.

34 Ibid., pp. 105–106.

35 Ibid., p. 124.

36 Also see Oliver Kupper's published interview with the artist: Oliver Kupper, "Force Majeure: Pioneering Eco-Artists the Harrisons Created a Survival Guide for a World Careening Toward Disaster," *Autre*, Issue 13, F/W, 2021, pp. 250–257, 254.

37 Harrison, Helen Mayer, and Newton Harrison, *The Time of the Force Majeure: After 45 Years Counterforce is on the Horizon*, p. 131.

38 Materials documenting the Harrisons' research in the archive are abundant and include their detailed observations of the crab, their scholarly publication about its mating behavior, data logs of salinity and temperature, correspondence with scientists, reprints of scholarly articles by scientists, grant applications and proposals, and conceptual and engineering design sketches. Hundreds of articles that they consulted are gathered in the archive: Box # 23-26, Series 2, Project Files, Subseries 5, Lagoon Cycle, Box 22–33. Helen and Newton Harrison Papers, M1797. Special Collections & University Archives, Stanford University, Stanford, CA, consulted in October–December 2021.

39 Harrison, Helen Mayer, and Newton Harrison, *The Time of the Force Majeure: After 45 Years Counterforce is on the Horizon*, p. 147.

40 Ibid., p. 156.

41 Ibid., pp. 154–155.

42 Donation to the Centre Georges Pompidou in Paris, France, was discussed in correspondence in 1996–1997, see: Box # 23, Folder # 18. Series 2, Project Files, Subseries 5, Lagoon Cycle, Box 23. Helen and Newton Harrison Papers, M1797. Special Collections & University Archives, Stanford University, Stanford, CA, consulted in October–December 2021.

43 The book colophon recognizes the contributions of David Behlke, Gabriel Harrison, Joy Harrison, John Hudak, Michel Greenstein, Virginia Maksymowicz, Dwaraka Rao, Blaise Tobia, Vera Westergaard, Karen Wirth, and Minori Yata, who helped in the book's execution. See materials in the archive: Series 2, Project Files, Subseries 5, Lagoon Cycle, Box 23, Folders 4–10. Helen and Newton Harrison Papers, M1797. Special Collections & University Archives, Stanford University, Stanford, CA, consulted in October–December 2021.

44 Ten of the early bindings went to John Kluge of Metromedia. He was a philanthropist who had been supporting the Harrisons' projects for years, and the bindings were a partial repayment of his investment in their work. He in turn donated copies to other individuals and institutions, including Prince Charles (now King Charles III), who was already known as a conservationist, and the Museum of Modern Art in New York. These details of the Harrisons' story were related to me in writing and photographs by Laurence and Erin McGilvery, whom I met and corresponded with via email while working on this exhibition. I express my sincere gratitude to Laurence and Erin.

45 Materials documenting the grant, proposal, and workshops conducted by the artists in San José are abundant in the archives: Series 2, Project Files, Subseries 18, Lagoon Cycle, Box 53–56. Helen and Newton Harrison Papers, M1797. Special Collections & University Archives, Stanford University, Stanford, CA, consulted in October–December 2021.

46 Harrison, Helen Mayer, and Newton Harrison, *The Time of the Force Majeure: After 45 Years Counterforce is on the Horizon*, pp. 166.

47 Bijvoet, Marga, *Art as Inquiry, Toward New Collaborations Between Art, Science, and Technology*. American University Studies, Peter Lang, New York, 1997, pp. 137–148, 148.

48 Ingram, Mrill, "Ecopolitics and Aesthetics: The Art of Helen Mayer and Newton Harrison," *Geographical Review*, Vol. 103, No. 2, April, 2013, pp. 260–274, https://www.jstor.org/stable/43915991, accessed October 20, 2021.

49 The history of its commission and the governing metaphor are described in the book. See: Helen Mayer Harrison and Newton Harrison, *The Time of the Force Majeure: After 45 Years Counterforce is on the Horizon*, pp. 406–409. Archival materials show the development of the proposal in many drafts, contain explanations of the guiding metaphor, and also discuss how the artists' inspiration was grounded in the *Lagoon Cycle* and the *Sacramento Meditations*, see: Series 2, Project Files, Subseries 63, Bay Area Project 2005–2009, Box 111–112. Helen and Newton Harrison Papers, M1797. Special Collections & University Archives, Stanford University, Stanford, CA, consulted in October–December 2021.

50 Harrison, Helen Mayer, and Newton Harrison, *The Time of the Force Majeure: After 45 Years Counterforce is on the Horizon*, p. 409.

51 The Harrison Family Trust, which maintains the Wikipedia page, traces the beginning of this body of work to 2015, when Helen began to withdraw due to dementia. See: https://en.wikipedia.org/wiki/The_Harrison_Studio, accessed February 2024.

52 Malina, Roger, "Force Majeure: Performing the Data of Climate Change," in Harrison, Helen Mayer, and Newton Harrison, *The Time of the Force Majeure: After 45 Years Counterforce is on the Horizon*, pp. 447–450.

53 *Apologia Mediterraneo* was included in the Collateral events of the 58th Venice Biennale, as part of *Artists Need to Create on the Same Scale that Society Has the Capacity to Destroy: Mare Nostrum* at the Complesso della Chiesa di Santa Maria delle Penitenti, Fondamenta di Cannaregio, 910, from 8 May–24 November, 2019.

54 Haapoja, Terike, https://www.thenatureofcities.com/2023/03/18/paying-attention-to-make-art-twenty-nine-voices-on-the-legacy-of-newton-and-helen-mayer-harrison/, accessed March 2023.

55 Kuchera-Morin, JoAnn, https://www.thenatureofcities.com/2023/03/18/paying-attention-to-make-art-twenty-nine-voices-on-the-legacy-of-newton-and-helen-mayer-harrison/, accessed March 2023.

56 Harrison, Helen Mayer, and Newton Harrison, *The Time of the Force Majeure: After 45 Years Counterforce is on the Horizon*, p. 143.

57 Adcock, Craig, "Conversational Drift: Helen Mayer Harrison and Newton Harrison," *Art Journal*, Vol. 51, No. 2 (*Art and Ecology),* Summer, 1992, pp. 35–45, 45.

58 Gell, Alfred, *Art and Agency. An Anthropological Theory*. Clarendon Press, Oxford, 1998, p. 6.

59 The idea of the "dictatorship of the ecology" first appears in the Harrisons' thinking during their work on the *Meditations on the Great Lakes of North America* (1977). They wrote a semi-poetic text in which they urged "the citizens of the watersheds of the Great Lakes of North America to withdraw from Canada and the United States and generate a Dictatorship of the Ecology, for reasons of survival (of both ecosystems and cultural systems)." Harrison, Newton and Helen Mayer Harrison, *The Time of the Force Majeure: After 45 Years Counterforce is on the Horizon*, p. 65.

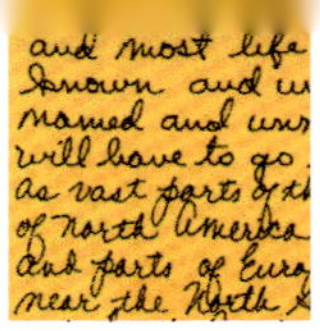

Poetry, Poetics, and Policymaking in the Harrisons' Artistic Practice

MONICA MANOLESCU

Helen Mayer Harrison and Newton Harrison are usually presented as interdisciplinary ecological artists. While the various strands of their multifaceted art should be considered together and in interaction, my reading offers a sustained focus on a specific dimension emblematic of their practice: that of writing and performing poetry. Throughout their long, collaborative career that lasted five decades, the Harrisons developed a multimedia discourse that combined poetry, performance, maps, photographs, documentation, site-specific installations, and scientific experimentation. Poetry is key to their artistic expression in two forms: handwritten or printed texts in free verse and reading performances of their continuously revised texts, in conjunction with other media and within specific projects.

In Marjorie Perloff's study of David Antin's poetry included in *The Poetics of Indeterminacy*, she articulates a theoretical model meant to do justice to poetic performativity. She starts from Aristotle's six constituent parts of tragedy (the supreme form of poetry according to him) in *The Poetics*: *mythos* (plot), *ethos* (character), *dianoia* (thought), *lexis* (diction), *melopoeia* (rhythm and song), and *opsis* (spectacle). Perloff reminds us that romanticism and modernism emphasized the second, fourth and fifth of these elements.[1] Performance poetry insists rather on spectacle, but also on plot, exemplified by poets and artists such as John Cage, Jackson Mac Low, Jerome Rothenberg, and David Antin. This parsing is very useful for Perloff's argument because one of her assumptions is that "*poiesis* can be many different things."[2] The simplicity and obviousness of this assertion does not prevent it from being a particularly complex and far-ranging hypothesis that foregrounds a non-normative understanding of poetic discourses as adopting selected series of coordinates in varying configurations. It is significant that Helen Mayer Harrison and Newton Harrison, David Antin, Eleanor Antin, and Jerome Rothenberg were colleagues at the Department of Visual Arts of the University of California, San Diego. Their respective bodies of work took distinct directions, but shared an interest in experimenting with poetic form, especially with performance and orality, throughout their careers.[3] The notion of influence is not useful or productive here. Rather, it is more fruitful to talk about a conversation among members of an artistic community with original individual voices.

Helen and Newton's combined educational backgrounds were extremely varied: English, educational philosophy, language, learning, psychology, painting, and sculpture. Their high regard for poetry (and discourse more generally) can be traced back to several sources: literary traditions from various cultures, teaching, the linguistic turn in conceptual art and in land art at the end of the 1960s, and performance art. Helen was an English major, and had degrees in pedagogy and psychology as well. In 1957, she co-founded a Montessori school in Florence. Helen and Newton shared their skills and knowledge to become "a unique co-creator:"

"One of us – who had been an artist from early adolescence on – had to change completely to do this. The other of us – who had been a lifelong teacher, researcher, educational philosopher, and student of psychology and literature – had to change completely to do this. We were convinced that neither of us had the capability to become ecosystemically empowered without the help, encouragement, and dramatically different talents, experience, and tolerance for ambiguity of the other."[4]

In this process of co-creation, references to literature abound: the Harrisons compared *The Lagoon Cycle* to a picaresque novel;[5] the figure of the bard is often mentioned as a model of poet and policymaker; ancient epics like *Gilgamesh* are major landmarks for their thinking about time and poetic diction.[6] Before embracing ecology as a significant direction in their art-making, the Harrisons had affinities with land art, with which they shared an unsettled relationship with the gallery and museum, and a deep interest in language and discourse. Robert Smithson, whom Newton met in New York in 1970, advocated a new relationship between the site and the non-site, with texts, photographs and maps supplementing the site rather than representing it. Smithson was also a poet and an avid reader, whose *Collected Writings* are densely abstract and richly intertextual. Nancy Holt, Walter De Maria and Robert Morris included writing (sometimes poetry) in their work. Performance art was very close to the Harrisons in the version it took as "environments" and "happenings" through the figure of Allan Kaprow, who was the Harrisons' colleague at the University of California, San Diego from 1974 to 1993.[7]

While many readings of the Harrisons discuss their ecological and activist ideas, the question of poetic form and its significance has received less attention. Anne Douglas and Chris Fremantle in particular have examined major literary aspects of the Harrisons' work, notably their interest in conversational drift, performance, improvisation, and contradiction.[8] Focusing on form in ecological art (both by artists and critics) goes back to Adorno's argument in *Aesthetic Theory* that art should develop a distinctive identity in order to be meaningful for social issues. Mark Cheetham starts from Adorno to inquire about the "difference" of art in the context of ecology and ecological activism.[9] Suzaan Boettger has criticized an imbalance in recent ecological art between an "enlarged subject matter" and a "slighting of the persuasive powers of artistic form itself."[10] The question of the blurred boundaries between art and activism, and the possible "difference" of art in the context of activism forces us to reconsider conventional artistic categories such as aesthetic autonomy, medium specificity and, ultimately, the definition and status of art. Grant Kester has pointed out the confluence of art, community, and conversation by looking at artists who seek alternative forms of art-making that blend with other cultural practices and adopt alternative circuits. While the debate revisits the lingering traditional coupling of form and content, it is worth going beyond the question of how content and form are articulated in order to think about the persuasive power of the Harrisons' art and the ways in which poetry as artistic expression contributes to this persuasiveness. The argument I would like to develop here is that by writing and performing poetry, the Harrisons aspired to influence policymaking and to act as policymakers on a par with administrators, mayors, governors, and other decision-makers. They placed the articulation of poetry and policymaking in the tradition of the Celtic bards, thus revisiting the venerable figure from the perspective of ecological discourses on reversing the effects of global warming and environmental destruction.

THE LAGOON CYCLE: MYTH, EPIC AND DIALOGUE

The Harrisons' poetry celebrates and gives rise to voice, dialogue, storytelling, myth, and metaphor, which are key features and procedures of their poetic art. These are richly layered in *The Lagoon Cycle*, which is among the Harrisons' most impressive and complex works taking the form of a 360-foot long and 8-foot tall mural that combines poetry, maps, photographs, and paintings, presented in several exhibitions, with a double conceptual and performative dimension. It tells a story in poetic form, and is founded on documentary and scientific practices. An anthropological trip to Sri Lanka to visit the mangroves and find out about the country's culture and a laboratory experiment with the crab *Scylla serrata* are part and parcel of the project. The combination of narrative and poetry brings it close to the epic poem and to the tradition of bards telling stories whose performances can be reproduced for various audiences. Although orality and performance are crucial dimensions of the work, its material form is also important. The printed pages of the eponymously titled exhibition catalogue present various types of fonts, with the use of italics, line breaks, and extra spaces within lines immediately manifest. *The Book of the Lagoons* contains only handwritten text which gives the reading experience a very personal and subjective feel. There is a large amount of reading involved, which is why some reviewers found the exhibition "boring."[11] In the exhibition, it is unlikely that continuous, linear reading was privileged by individual visitors, given the variety of media and the sheer size. A general feel of the exhibition environment was most likely obtained by grasping snippets of text and images, not necessarily in linear fashion. Michel de Certeau called *The Lagoon Cycle* a book that "stands up" and that "becomes a mural book, covered with drawings and graffiti. It moves. It's a cinema-book, a forest-book."[12] In this exhibition-book or book-exhibition, reading and listening become hermeneutic experiences that allow one to extract meaning at various levels, by reading in fragments, by looking at pictures and maps, and by attending readings by the Harrisons.

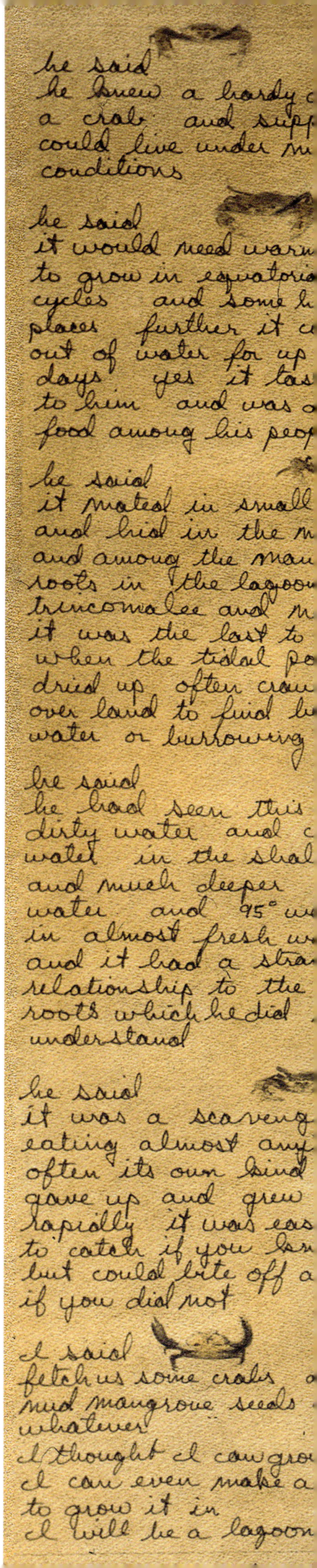

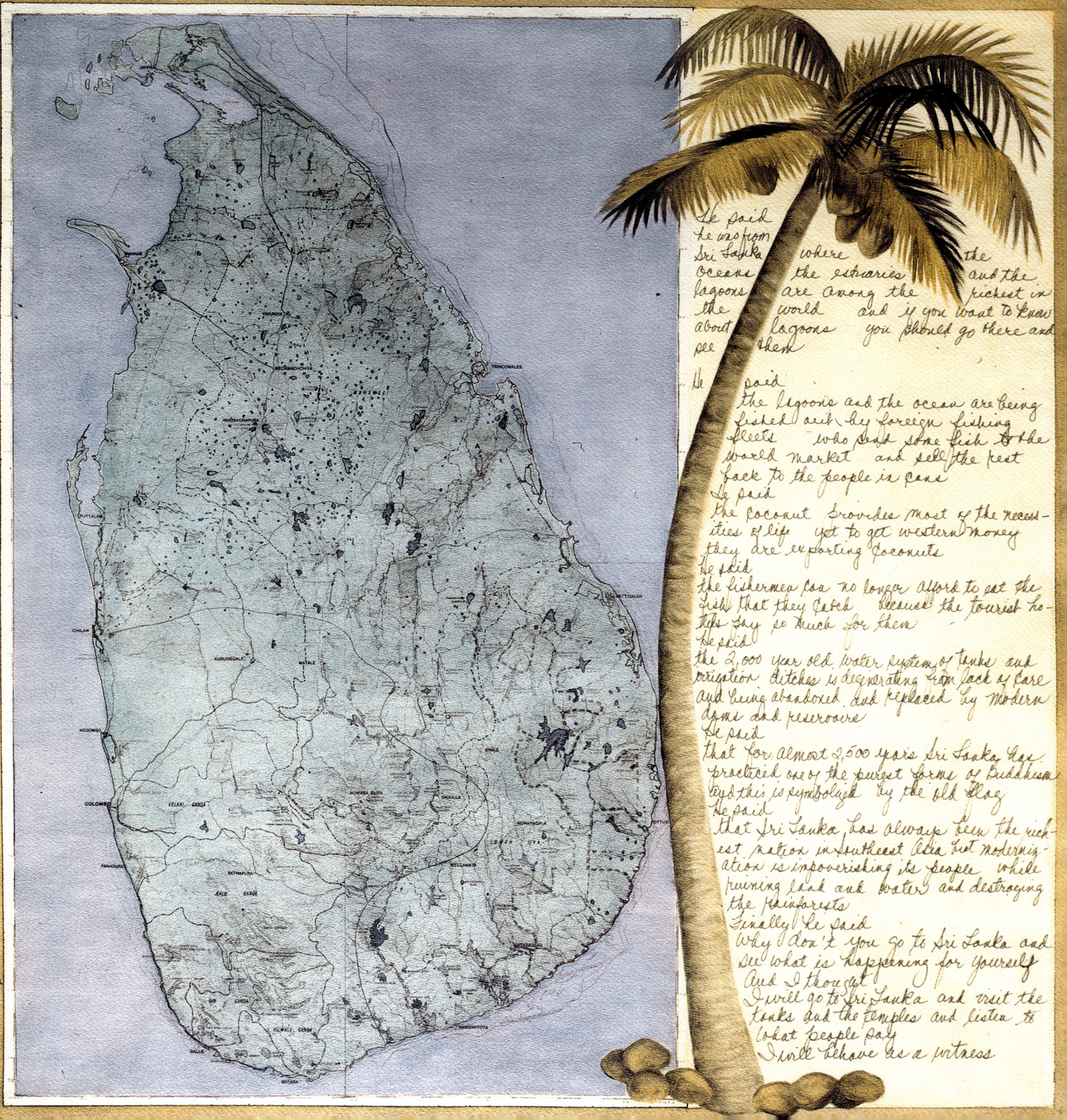
He said
he was from
Sri Lanka where the
oceans the estuaries and the
lagoons are among the richest in
the world and if you want to know
about lagoons you should go there and
see them
He said
the lagoons and the ocean are being
fished out by foreign fishing
fleets who send some fish to the
world market and sell the rest
back to the people in cans
He said
the coconut provides most of the necess-
ities of life yet to get western money
they are exporting coconuts
He said
the fishermen can no longer afford to eat the
fish that they catch because the tourist ho-
tels pay so much for them
He said
the 2,000 year old water system of tanks and
irrigation ditches is degenerating from lack of care
and being abandoned and replaced by modern
dams and reservoirs
He said
that for almost 2,500 years Sri Lanka has
practiced one of the purest forms of Buddhism
and this is symbolized by the old flag
He said
that Sri Lanka has always been the rich-
est nation in Southeast Asia but moderniz-
ation is impoverishing its people while
ruining land and water and destroying
the rainforests
Finally he said
Why don't you go to Sri Lanka and
see what is happening for yourself
And I thought
I will go to Sri Lanka and visit the
tanks and the temples and listen to
what people say
I will behave as a witness

Storytelling is a cherished practice in all of the Harrisons' projects. Their works tell stories of places and ecosystems, and imagine new stories about their potential future. Places are represented as palimpsests of stories created on the combined scales of deep time and recent history, whose calcified layering does not prevent the belief in change driven precisely by the force of storytelling. The epic poem is the privileged form adopted by the Harrisons in *The Lagoon Cycle* to capture both mythical origins and possible futures, offering what de Certeau calls "the unfolding of a narration in the space created by a myth."[13] The conjunction between myth and space is crucial here, on several levels: the space of the exhibition, the space of the page and the various narrated spaces (Sri Lanka, California). However, *The Lagoon Cycle* is by no means a conventional replay of the traditional epic poem: it revisits the genre to destabilize its monolithic framework of storytelling, to introduce the hesitations of a heuristic progress in the narrative, and to suggest that dialogue is a privileged way of speaking and thinking about the world. *The Lagoon Cycle* unsettles Bakhtin's famous distinction between the epic and the novel articulated in his 1941 essay "Epic and Novel: Towards a Methodology for the Study of the Novel," according to which the epic is endowed with marble-like finality, does not engage with contemporary events and presents a remote, enclosed and absolute past which does not allow the individual to develop a subjectivity and independence outside of this framework, while the novel enjoys the plasticity of clay, confronts present contexts and reconceptualizes the character as an evolving figure. If the Harrisons adopt the solemn modes of diction and the long temporal perspective of the epic, their revisiting of the genre involves confrontations with the present seen in connection to past and future, an absence of finality and an embrace of fluctuation. The course of events can be changed, positions can be shifted and strategies amended. The Harrisons mentioned *Gilgamesh*, *The Odyssey*, *The Aeneid*, *Popol Vuh*, *Mahabharata*, *Ramayana* as important sources for their work.[14] *The Lagoon Cycle* defines itself from the beginning as an "experiment with a moment" "that may have no boundaries/and may be expanded indefinitely."[15] Time includes both the present moment and the Lagoonmaker's myth of creation: "and/I thought/I can grow a crab/I can make a lagoon to/grow it in/I can be a lagoonmaker."[16] *The Lagoon Cycle* conjoins the present of documentary and scientific research, the ahistorical temporality of myth and an open future. The mythical animal of the epic poem is the crab, "a hardy creature"[17] that the Lagoonmaker chooses to experiment with. The latter's voice and grammatical persona is regal if not demiurgic: "I said/fetch us some crabs and some bottom mud/and some mangrove seeds and whatever."[18] Transplanting the crab from Sri Lanka in a laboratory in San Diego is not a mere repetition of a myth of origins, it is also an experiment marked by variation: "but the materials keep changing/Only the improvisation remains constant."[19] Instead of displaying the confidence of divine or heroic creators, *The Lagoon Cycle* shows awareness not only of the improvisatory nature of the task, but also of the fragility of the ecosystem transferred to the laboratory, which is defined as "a culture," that is "a cooperative adventure a complex system/of shared interrelated beliefs about the nature of reality."[20] *The Lagoon Cycle* is thus an experimental and improvised epic that openly acknowledges the failures and hubris of the Lagoonmaker by the end of the experiment with the tank as "playground."[21] The creator behaves like an arrogant child forgetting to "pay attention."[22] Moving away from the tank in the laboratory to the grandiose and unrealistic plan of transforming the Salton Sea into an estuarial lagoon, the Lagoonmaker adopts a quasi-divine authorial posture, but also parodies the procedures of earthwork artists such as Robert Smithson, Michael Heizer and Walter De Maria, whose monumental site-specific works involved massive displacements of material and huge labor efforts.[23]

Voices in dialogue carry the storytelling forward, with occasional pauses meant to look back and take stock. Poetic dialogue becomes a creative trigger, an intersubjective exchange that allows for a confrontation of ideas and makes it possible to change course. Conversational poetry constitutes the distinctive conceptual and vocal matrix of *The Lagoon Cycle*. Identity, authorship, and voice are redefined as collaborative and dialogic, emerging out of encounters with difference, and engaged in a process of becoming. While the dialogue of the Lagoonmaker and the Witness seem to be confined to the page, they actually unframe the latter to reflect on dialogue as a mode of existing and living that involves more than two voices to include other creatures and institutions. This is an instance of what Stephen Fredman calls "poetry as transactional art" underlying "poetry's existential interaction with the outside world,"[24] intent as it is on pursuing conversation and exchanges with its contexts and historical moment. The dialogic poetry of the Harrisons also functions along the lines of what Hoffman, quoting Bakhtin, identifies as "second culture," an alternative discourse to dominant discourses. The poetics of voice thus becomes a politics and an ecology of voice. Voices in dialogue create friction and become sites of confrontation, not consensus, which generate readjustments and unexpected points of view. It is through them that distinct perspectives, cultures, and ideologies are articulated and sounded out in the attempt to address specific disturbances or problems.

The First Lagoon is emblematic in this respect, since it presents the culture and history of Sri Lanka through polyphony. Opinions expressed by different speakers are listed: a merchant, a taxi driver, a stranger, a wealthy friend, a guide, a second guide, a diplomat, a historian, a young student, his mother, a traditional dancer, an actor, a shopkeeper, a priest, a farming village, a doctor, another priest, an intellectual, the people of the trust, a hotel guest, a tourist guide.[25] Between the list and the collage, these discourses make sense together, in their concomitance and in their contradictions. We read for instance that "one friend said/Tourism is saving our country We need to encourage it" and "another friend said/Tourism is ruining the country We need to discourage it."[26] These dissonant opinions are placed one after the other, in a non-hierarchical and cumulative sequence. The multiplicity of voices suggests that "a culture is a cooperative adventure"[27] and this is precisely the kind of adventure that the Lagoonmaker and the Witness will perform. The discourses of the various speakers lack quotation marks and are presented as originating in individuals whom the "witness" speaking in the first person has met and listened to: "And I thought/I will go to Sri Lanka/and behave as a witness."[28] The Harrisons' documentary and anthropological practice took them to Sri Lanka to become acquainted with its mangrove system. Since the mangrove is embedded in larger economic patterns and cultural practices, it cannot be suspended from its surrounding fabric without damaging consequences. The question of voice is a poetic, but also an anthropological question for the Harrisons. Listening to a plurality of voices leads to an enlarged understanding of the present experienced as a consequence of past events, of social and economic structures as perceived by citizens. This whole universe of polyphony orbits around a single creature, the crab, which has no voice, and whose transplanted life (real and imaginary) we will follow throughout the rest of the book, in a tank in San Diego and in larger, abandoned, California prospects.

As Lytle Shaw has shown in *Fieldworks*, studying and researching a given site's history was an enterprise that many American poets and artists were interested in after World War II, conducive to various poetic and artistic strategies. In the crab experiment, the voices of the artists become "we" and also a couple of "you" and "I" choreographing their arguments in exchanges of opinions:

Are you suggesting that over time
the water will become so very
polluted that even mixed with
fresh water from the canal and
modified with brine from the
ocean it will not support a lagoon
ecology no matter how tough and resilient
Yes   I am
Why are you so certain
When I look at the algal bloom
I know the conditions of the waters[29]

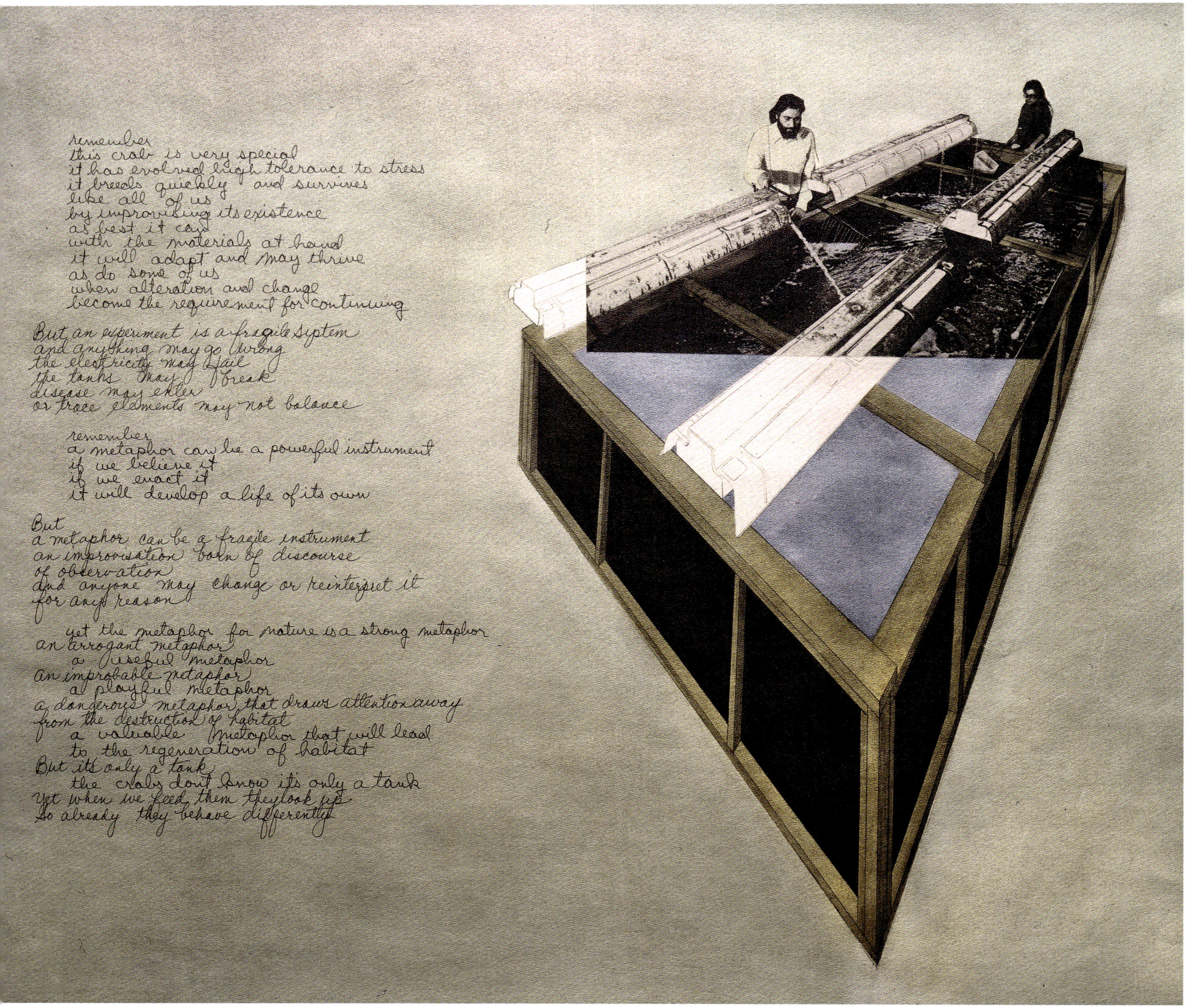
remember
this crab is very special
it has evolved high tolerance to stress
it breeds quickly and survives
like all of us
by improvising its existence
as best it can
with the materials at hand
it will adapt and may thrive
as do some of us
when alteration and change
become the requirement for continuing

But an experiment is a fragile system
and anything may go wrong
the electricity may fail
the tanks may break
disease may enter
or trace elements may not balance

remember
a metaphor can be a powerful instrument
if we believe it
if we enact it
it will develop a life of its own

But
a metaphor can be a fragile instrument
an improvisation born of discourse
of observation
and anyone may change or reinterpret it
for any reason

yet the metaphor for nature is a strong metaphor
an arrogant metaphor
a useful metaphor
an improbable metaphor
a playful metaphor
a dangerous metaphor that draws attention away
from the destruction of habitat
a valuable metaphor that will lead
to the regeneration of habitat
But its only a tank
the crabs dont know its only a tank
Yet when we feed them they look up
So already they behave differently

The material aspects of the poetics of voice come to the fore in such instances that reveal the use of specific typeface (italics) or not, the absence of punctuation (no question mark although the syntax of the interrogation is expecting it), the additional white spaces between words ("Yes   I am") to suggest a pause or an emphasis on the silence between words. The material grounding of voices is also made possible by the use of maps (maps of the globe, of Sri Lanka, of the Salton Sea, the map of the *Ring of Fire*). Poetry and cartography work together to tell the story of the lagoon and to anchor the voice firmly in place.

THE BARD'S POWER: PERFORMANCE AND POLICYMAKING

How are the Harrisons' texts supposed to be performed? The Harrisons read their texts in public and performed them as a duo responding to each other in male and female voices, as they called them. In the preliminary remarks to *San Diego As the Center of the World* and *Meditations on the Sacramento River* published in Jerome Rothenberg's *New Wilderness Letter* of December 1977–January 1978, the Harrisons specify (without using punctuation marks) that the first work "is scored for alternate reading by male and female voice in the final four lines two second pauses are required between phrases" and the second work "was done simultaneously in three San Francisco museums on billboards radio and TV and at readings and street corner performances to explore the campaign form it is scored for alternate readings for instance and the refrain in male voice the verse in female voice."[30] The notion of the poem as a "score"[31] denotes a musical and performative dimension that resonates with the principles that guide Rothenberg's journal. The "street corner performances" suggest the public and democratic venue where the artists choose to perform their texts in order to share them with the community.

If we try to address the ways in which the Harrisons' texts can be performed by examining the texts themselves and the stylistic features they display, it can be argued that reading aloud is not the only option. The many repetitions and anaphora we find in their texts, their orality, their aphoristic nature as well as their visionary drive encourage a comparison with religious discourses beyond specific denomination. Aphorisms and wise directives abound: "Only the improvisation remains constant,"[32] "paying attention to paying attention."[33] Visionary and prophetic moments are particularly striking in *The Lagoon Cycle*, both in the image of the *Ring of Fire* ("I see the Ring of Fire/as a discourse between fire and rock/taking place mainly at the water's edge,"[34]) and in the related image of the rising water: "and the tropics will become uninhabitable."[35] However, these moments that convey the content of a vision or the certainty of future events are not channeled by irrational powers of transcendent seeing, but are rather supported by sound scientific arguments. It is their expression that takes the form of visionary diction, but their sources lie in the verifiable predictions of scientific research. This combination of scientific data and visionary expression bridges the gap between distinct registers and temporalities, where state-of-the-art science and technology synchronous with the creation of the work (in the late 1970s and early 1980s) meet literary forms usually associated with religious belief, wisdom, and practice.

A significant mode of performing religious texts is chanting, and its relevance for the Harrisons has been signaled by Anne Douglas and Chris Fremantle, who performed the Harrisons' texts at the University of Glasgow in 2020: "The work is a chant and was made to be read aloud."[36] The storytelling of myths and ancient epics thus crosses paths with the cadences and prophetic tones of sacred texts. The Harrisons' poetry invites chanting as a suitable adjustment of human voice to specific registers and styles in the text inscribed in a constellation of sacred traditions. In the Harrison team, despite the fusion of their artistic personalities, Helen was more associated with the literary aspects of their work and Newton with the visual. Jerome Rothenberg appears as a highly significant reference as far as oral religious literature from many traditions is concerned, and also the mapping of poetry from various parts of the world, across a variety of cultures. Jerome

Rothenberg and the Harrisons worked in the same Department of Visual Arts at the University of California, San Diego for a few years. Helen and Newton Harrison published two texts in the *New Wilderness Letter* that was edited by Jerome Rothenberg: "Two Meditations, Two Commentaries and Eight Questions on the Great Lakes of North America," accompanied by maps (Summer 1979), and "One Full Work and Part of Another" (December 1977–January 1978). The two works referred to in the latter are *San Diego as the Center of the World* and *Meditations on the Sacramento River*. Helen Mayer Harrison and Newton Harrison were on the advisory board of the *New Wilderness Letter*, together with David Antin, Eleanor Antin, Dick Higgins, Allan Kaprow, Steve McCaffery, Linda Montano, Charlie Morrow and Pauline Oliveros.

In the "Editor's notes" to volume 1, numbers 2–3 of *New Wilderness Letter*, in which the Harrisons published their texts, Rothenberg asserts the ambition of the issue:

> The present double number of *New Wilderness Letter* again takes up the role of poets/artists as "technicians of the sacred." Here in the image of the "First Poet" as defender of the earth herself as sacred, they recall us to a sense of natural orders, even or especially in the face of those disasters we create and have always created in our human state (that the ecological strategy of tribal people, say, may itself be a response to earlier wipeouts…). The theme of a virtual ArtEcology underlies much said in previous numbers of *New Wilderness Letter* and in those to come; and it does so in spite of shifts in fashion and of the desire, also with us, "to make things new." The thrust of the performance forms that dominate these pages is toward a public viewing.[37]

Rothenberg and the Harrisons meet on common ground, although the concepts they use are not identical. Rothenberg puts forth his signature notion of the poet as "technician of the sacred" whose task is to rekindle an awareness of nature and its workings in the context of repeated disasters. As Fredman shows, Rothenberg's anthology *Technicians of the Sacred* "expanded the scope of American literature in 1968" and connected American avant-garde poetry with shamanistic rituals, various creation myths from around the world and divinatory incantations.[38]

The portmanteau word "ArtEcology" signals a fusion between artistic and ecological concerns. Art and ecology share the same lexical space and work towards a single project and ambition. Ezra Pound's injunction to "make it new" is explicitly mentioned, but the journal ambiguously quotes it and works against it by continuing to publish pieces on the theme of the "new wilderness." Pound's imperative, which has been famously read as presiding over modernist poetry, surfaces in Rothenberg's remarks as an invitation to novelty that the contributors to *New Wilderness Letter* conform to, although they choose to go back to the same topic over again.[39] The combination of repetition and renewal is central to "ArtEcology" and also to the Harrisons' art. In a talk Rothenberg gave in 1994, "Ethnopoetics at the Millennium," he celebrates the nexus of modernism, experimentation, and ethnopoetics. The latter was born "during the great wave of experimental twentieth-century modernism from the mid-1950s to the mid-1970s." However, ethnopoetics cannot be reduced to the traditional category of "literature." It carries with it a spiritual and redeeming charge; it is a "counter-language" that seeks social and ecological justice. Rothenberg explicitly endows ethnopoetics with the goal of doing away with racism and social ranking, and proposing a "more sane relation to the natural world and its other-than-humans as well as human inhabitants" which is at the heart of the cultures outside the Western traditions whose poetry ethnopoetics promotes. On the margins of more conventional literature, poetry, and ethnopoetics are inextricable from public performance and from alternative ways of thinking about and with the Web of Life.

The Harrisons' version of the poet as "technician of the sacred" is the Celtic bard seen not only as poet and performer, but also as policymaker with influence over authorities and institutions:

> "I am influenced – and Helen was, too – by the work of the ancient bards, particularly in Ireland and Scotland. In those

times, nothing was written down, everything was an oral tradition. The poets in their poetry were policymakers and were listened to by the leadership and policymakers of those countries. So, we took lessons from them as well as Heraclitus, Socrates, the Noble Eight-Fold Path of the Buddha, with a little help from Gandhi. Our work is meant to be read but often does best as a performance where Helen and I did alternate reading. If you go to our book and review *The Lagoon Cycle* you will find much of it is written by both of us and you can understand this by looking at the difference in our handwriting—mine being a little bit awkward and Helen's being elegant. When others read the work, we tell them, let the male voice speak the words that are written awkwardly, let the female voice read the words that are written elegantly. Where influencing policymakers is concerned, the last works in our poem *Urgency of the Moment* did the work for us and affected the planners considerably."[40]

This understanding of the bard and his public recognition is a projection of the artists' objectives in a specific context rather than an entirely accurate historical perspective on the Celtic bard. The Harrisons' interest in the figure of the bard and in the power of orality is best understood against the backdrop of post-1960 fascination with "the psychedelic, oracular, tribal, and improvisatory decade that brought us the Beat Poets and the Beatles, Bob Dylan and Elvis in Hollywood."[41] The 1960s also witnessed the acceleration of communications technology which gave rise to a nostalgia for a pre-bookish past, combined with an interest in orality that led to a proliferation of studies of orality and oral poetry.[42] As Lerner points out, the figure of the bard stands for "the lost unifying power that poetry supposedly formerly had," and Lerner questions the existence of this power of poetry in the past (he examines Whitman in particular) and in the present.[43]

According to the accounts of historians and literary scholars, Celtic bards were court poets dependent on the patronage of the nobility, who dispensed both praise and satire. They belonged to a full-time and highly codified profession that required specialized training in Wales and Ireland until as late as the 16th century.[44] The bards recorded the heroic deeds of rulers and warriors and sometimes composed prophetic poems about a national deliverer in the face of adversity.[45] Their craft was a "social institution" of "vital importance to the social fabric."[46] They enjoyed high status and dignity, and were part of a well-organized bardic order. They celebrated and entertained patrons and their courts with their verse, music, and storytelling. A particularly fascinating figure for European culture, the bard as poetic-druidic visionary and repository of a heroic past has attracted great fascination and versatile reworkings across time.[47] The Harrisons imagine the bard as a policymaker whom rulers and administrators listen to. However, it can be argued that the bard, although invited and appreciated in court, was not a policymaker *per se*. He was the voice of the existing social and political order, expressing the beliefs and values of the higher ranks, and crystallizing shared community feelings and hopes of victory in the face of inimical forces. The bard's prerogatives did not include independent and critical strategies of policymaking, although he was fantasized as a parallel authority by later poets. He had to strike a difficult balance between satire and eulogy, and was subservient to patrons and institutions. The institutional constraints and dependency of bardic guilds in the Middle Ages do not apply to the Harrisons' version of the bard, which emerges out of a desire to reinstate the artist and poet as an influential public figure and interlocutor. The adoption of certain features associated with bardic expression (verse, storytelling, orality, performance) is inscribed in the deeper urge to recover a long-lost social and public status for the poet and artist, on a par with the status of decision-makers and official figures. Speaking like a bard means aspiring to the social relevance of the bard within a larger political and social dialogue. Poetry is not simply an activity of creation and expression, but rather a profession that deserves recognition and influence in policymaking. In the Harrisons' view, poets create, but also act on and in the world as agents of change.

The Endangered Meadows of Europe, 1994 Kunst- und Ausstellungshalle der Bundesrepublik Deutschland, Bonn

Poetics is thus equated with policymaking, endowed with a performativity that sways policymakers and has an impact on decision at high levels. The Harrisons' understanding of the bard revisits the figure to endow it with critical power and with the prestige of a public intellectual whose opinions on issues of importance to society and public life (the environment in particular) should be heeded.

The Harrisons' ambition of reinserting the poet and artist in the fabric of social conversation and decision-making is not isolated in the landscape of the 1960s and the 1970s. Robert Smithson's vision of the artist as active participant and agent in natural environments, as intermediary between ecology and industry, illustrates his ambition to promote the artist to the status of significant interlocutor in the larger conversation about the transformations of the environment. Smithson claimed that "art can become a physical resource that mediates between the ecologist and the industrialist," that "the artist, ecologist and industrialist must develop in relation to each other, rather than continue to work and to produce in isolation" and called for the artist's embrace of the concreteness of the present: "The artist must come out of the isolation of galleries and museums and provide a concrete consciousness for the present as it really exists, and not simply present abstractions or utopias."[48] Although Smithson's philosophy of reclamation and the Harrisons' ecological thinking are extremely different in approach and concept, and the Harrisons were critical of the early earthworks, including Smithson's, which they considered "environmentally destructive,"[49] they do share a similar belief in the central role of the artist in social and environmental exchanges and decisions. The Harrisons' admiration for the bard should also be linked to the literary landscape of 1960s and 1970s American poetry and fiction, with its emphasis on poetry readings, on a poetics of presence, on voice, orality and spontaneity, and on poetic performance in political and countercultural contexts, breaking away from the tradition of print-based modernism and modernist impersonality.[50]

Some of the Harrisons' projects did gain support from politicians and public figures, leading to successful policymaking. *The Endangered Meadows of Europe* (1996, Bonn) is a case in point. It started out as a plant installation on the rooftop of the Kunst- und Ausstellungshalle in Bonn which celebrated meadows as an important element of biologically diverse European landscapes and of successful plant-human-animal collaboration, which thrives because of practices like harvesting and grazing. The rooftop meadow was then transplanted in the Great Rhine Park of Bonn, retitled a "Mother Meadow for Bonn," and seeds from this meadow were used to produce further meadows in the parks of Bonn and elsewhere.

It is interesting to note that although the Harrisons presented themselves as artists and storytellers, some of the policymakers they interacted with were baffled by the fact that artists should extend their prerogatives to public spaces and the environment. For these policymakers, there is an incompatibility at work between the conventional domain of art and the Harrisons' projects of public relevance, for instance in *Baltimore Promenade*:

"Finally, though we considered ourselves storytellers of a specialized kind who were generating a new urban narrative that would underpin more humane urban design, we were treated by most, particularly the Baltimore Planning Department, as an odd species of urban planner, one part Jane Jacobs and another part too eccentric to categorize."[51]

Thus, the Harrisons enact an expansion of art, not only through an exploration of sites outside the gallery and museum which had been conducted by artists since the 1960s (and even before in the contexts of Surrealism and Situationism), but also through an extension of art to activism, urban planning and environmental action.

POETIC VISION IN *THE LAGOON CYCLE*

How do the Harrisons as 20th and 21st century bards communicate with their audience and what is the tenor of their arguments? Between *The Lagoon Cycle* (1985) and the Force Majeure manifesto (2007), the Harrisons' vision was

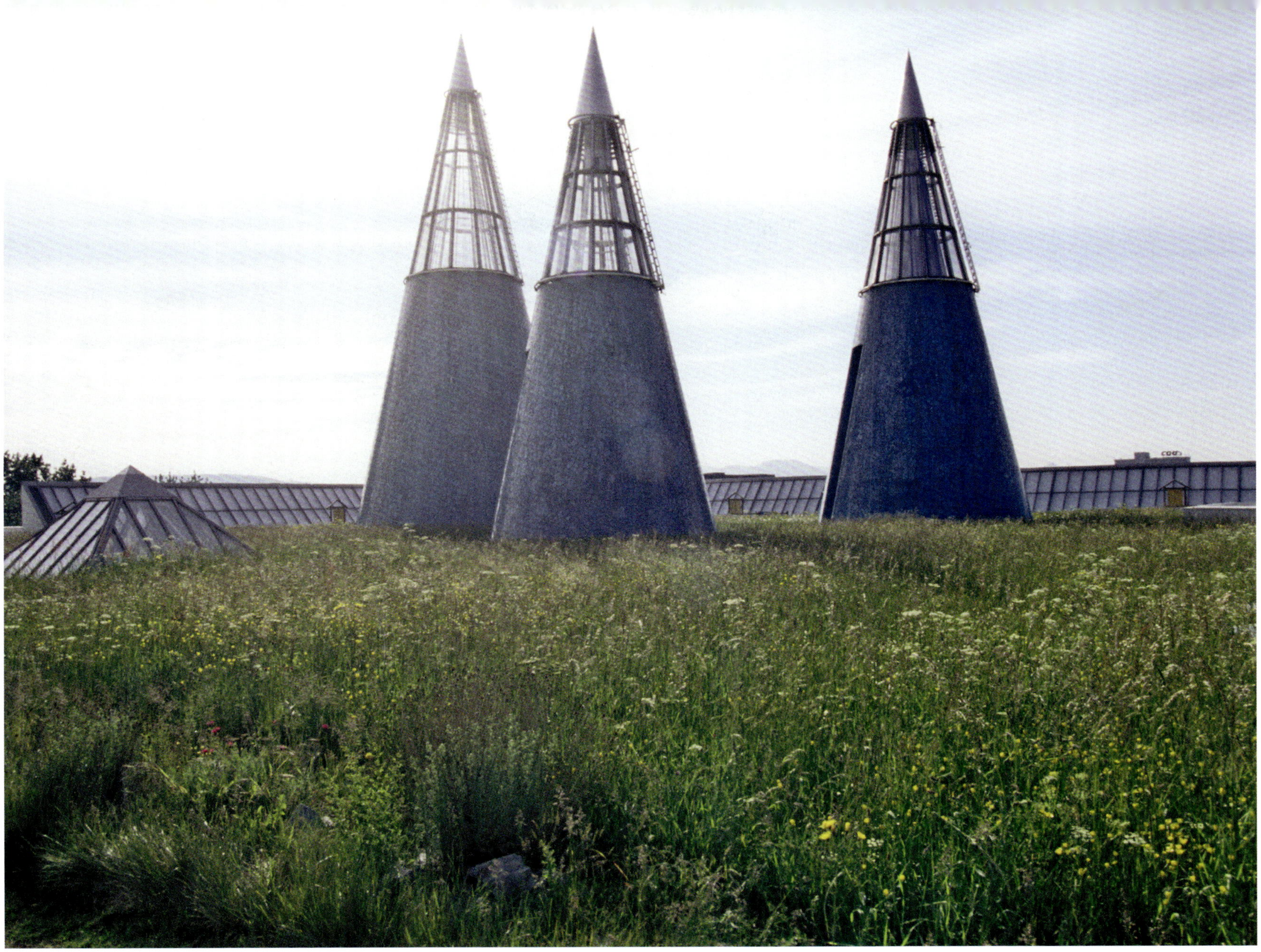

tested and proved by time. The circles of fire and water in the *Seventh Lagoon* announced global warming and the rise of oceans.

What looked like a hypothetical future in 1985 turned out to be a demonstrated and directly experienced certainty at the beginning of the 21st century. For the Harrisons, poetry provided a key mode of expression of their visionary ideas in the 1980s and of their artistic and ecological program in 2007, when they wrote the *Manifesto for the Twenty-First Century* for the Center for the Study of the Force Majeure at the University of California, Santa Cruz.[52] Instead of expressing ideas in essay or prose form, the Harrisons chose to couch them in free verse. Undoubtedly considered more persuasive than an essay or an article, poetry introduces linguistic difference into the fabric of everyday communication and functions as a verbal regime whose insistence on voice favors performance, presence and, in its performative version, a direct link between the poets/artists and the audience. The Harrisons' texts convey ecological ideas and arguments, but it would be more accurate to say that they offer a poetic and vocal vision of ecology and the Life Web. Their poetry is particularly powerful at the level of vision. It remains perfectly legible and comprehensible (far from modernist unreadability), and it invites close reading and close listening because otherwise all of its subtle details will not be grasped. The Harrisons' poetic choices in *The Lagoon Cycle* reflect ethical values and larger concerns about our relationship with ecosystems and inhabiting the Earth, by favoring voices in dialogue, open-endedness, and collaboration.

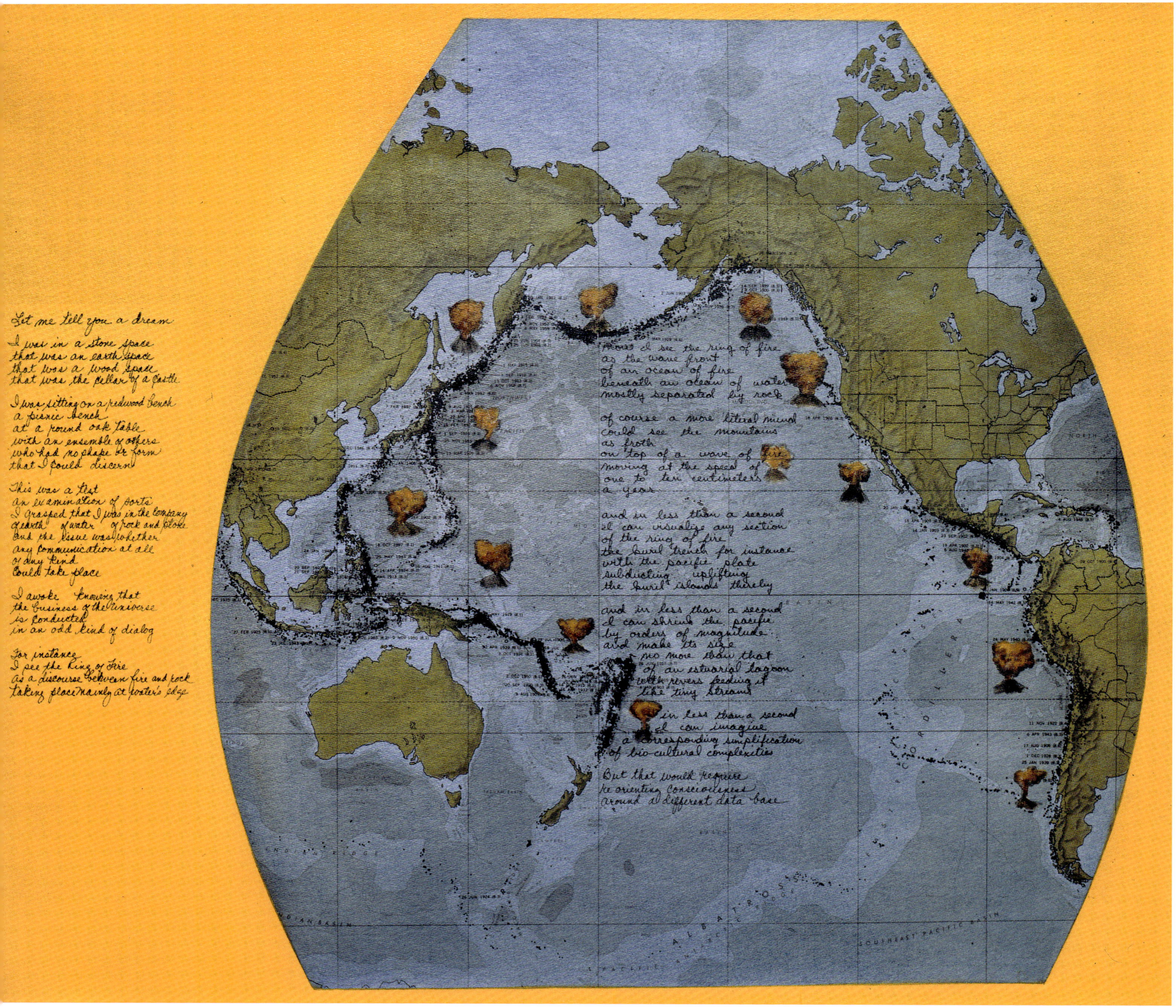
Let me tell you a dream
I was in a stone space
that was an earth space
that was a wood space
that was the cellar of a castle
I was sitting on a redwood bench
a picnic bench
at a round oak table
with an ensemble of others
who had no shape or form
that I could discern
This was a test
an examination of sorts
I grasped that I was in the company
of earth of water of rock and stone
and the issue was whether
any communication at all
of any kind
could take place
I awoke knowing that
the business of the universe
is conducted
in an odd kind of dialog
For instance
I see the Ring of Fire
as a discourse between fire and rock
taking place mainly at water's edge
Now I see the ring of fire
as the wave front
of an ocean of fire
beneath an ocean of water
mostly separated by rock
of course a more literal mind
could see the mountains
as froth
on top of a wave of fire
moving at the speed of
one to ten centimeters
a year
and in less than a second
I can visualize any section
of the ring of fire
the kuril trench for instance
with the pacific plate
subducting uplifting
the kuril islands thereby
and in less than a second
I can shrink the pacific
by orders of magnitude
and make its size
no more than that
of an estuarial lagoon
with rivers feeding it
like tiny streams
in less than a second
I can imagine
a corresponding simplification
of bio-cultural complexities
But that would require
re-orienting consciousness
around a different data base

The *Ring of Water* in the *Seventh Lagoon* is a case in point. It reads like a prophecy of rising oceans, depicting a series of phenomena projected in the future. Based on rigorous scientific data and models, it does not adopt the language and style of scientific discourse but condenses their information in vivid imagery, in an attempt to envision a future of rising oceans: "We took a present world map/and drew a probable world."[53] Starting by conjuring what is generally considered an objective representation of the world ("a present world map"), the Harrisons invite readers and listeners to imagine the transformation of the map and, implicitly, of the territory that the map encompasses and schematizes. The map is not an objective representation, but rather a construct that results from certain scientific choices and ideological biases. The map chosen by the Harrisons in the *Seventh Lagoon* is a French (rather than an American) map that features the Pacific Ocean at its center.[54] The conceptual dimension of the Harrisons' work is foregrounded in their insistence on various types of representations and models: the map as cartographic representation, their own poetry as representation of a probable global outcome, and scientific representations of climate change. This conceptual dimension that highlights the rigorous basis of their prediction and its anchorage in the world is fused with a poetic mode of vision and prophecy:

It is said that if all the ice melted
The oceans would rise about 300 feet
So we drew line as best we could
At the 300-foot level
And thought about how the land would shrink
As the oceans grew[55]

Logic infuses the parallelism between melting ice and rising oceans, in interlocking and inescapable consequence. The Harrisons' vision relies on simple gestures, verified data, impeccable logic: drawing a line on a map to show the water level, making geographic interconnections, coordinating geographic points and scales: "Melt at the South Pole rise in LA."[56] This laconic and elliptic verse brings together distant locations bound together by identical mutations. While it might seem that humans are the primary victims of rising waters, the Harrisons quickly nuance this reductive understanding by introducing the voice of the ocean in the poem. The ocean is "singing" the song of its own rise and addressing human interlocutors to explain upcoming evolutions. Giving voice to the ocean is the result of the time-honored device of personification, which has the merit of introducing imagined non-human speakers in the text. It takes an effort of imagination and a poetic perspective to hear the ocean speak, even if its speech is a human invention. By becoming "I," the ocean acquires an identity, a point of view, a subjectivity that enters the conversation:

After all   the ocean whispered
I am the beneficiary of your garbage can
as you are the beneficiary of my abundance
and everybody knows that ice into water
and water to ice are changes of state[57]

The personal pronouns "I" and "you" become unequal partners in a transaction that pits humanity's garbage can against the ocean's abundance. The two entities are connected in a massively unbalanced way, one dominating the other in a circuit of consumption and production that lies at the origin of global warming itself. The ocean becomes the dominant speaking voice in the *Seventh Lagoon*, in the future tense, offering a vision of its own evolving nature which necessarily affects human and animal habitats, and ultimately life itself.

This poetic vision of the future is grounded in toponymy, in a mapping of the rivers of the world that, collectively, start behaving strangely: invaded by ocean water, fresh water alters and diminishes, leading to a tremendous upheaval of ecosystems. The ample use of cartography in *The Lagoon Cycle* and elsewhere in the Harrisons' work anchors this vision in place, more precisely in a constellation of place names that suggest a shared, diffuse, large-scale transformation:

Up the Saint Lawrence the Columbia
the Amazon the Hudson the Mississippi
the White Nile and the Blue
the Volga the Don the Danube
and the Thames
the Seine and the Loire
the Rhone and the Rhine
the Garonne
the Ganges the Congo
the Tigris and the Euphrates
the Yellow the Amur the Irrawaddy
the Lena the Potomac and the Snake
and all rivers named and unnamed
And the flood plains that are farmed upon
And lived upon
will become marshes or swamps or bogs
or beds for swollen rivers
or shallow inland seas[58]

The emphasis on water under the guise of oceans and rivers gives rise to the metaphor of flow, circulation, and inter-connectedness. In *Guadalupe Meander* we are told that "a river is a medium for a discourse between life forms which exist in mutual support."[59] Individual waterways and individual oceans form a system to which all life forms belong. A perturbation in a given point of the system necessarily affects the rest. Rivers are, for the Harrisons, metaphors for exchange and conversation, which lie at the heart of their poetic and ecological strategy. By placing disrupted rivers and oceans at the end of *The Lagoon Cycle*, by letting the ocean sing and whisper its own vision of change, the Harrisons suggest that the conversation needs to be recalibrated and reconsidered in order to bring balance in the Life Web. The poem flows and carries the readers along to make them see and experience the vision of the unsettled future of water and the probable extinction of certain life forms, including the human one. Similar to a slow apocalypse giving rise to a new myth of origins, the end of the *Seventh Lagoon* prophesies, with scientific arguments, the end of our world and the beginning of another. This conflation of our own ending and a new beginning is marked by a shifting pronoun "I" which seems to designate multiple entities – the artist, the ocean or the human species:

And in this new beginning
This continuous rebeginning
you feed me when my lands
Can no longer produce
And I will house you
When your lands are covered with water?
And together
We will withdraw
As the waters rise[60]

This togetherness is central to the ethics and poetics of *The Lagoon Cycle*, and to its consideration of a shared subjectivity between humans and more-than-humans. Collaboration, conversation, and joint action are poetically expressed in this evolving "I" whose pronominal territory moves between creatures, and in the use of the collective "we" with its future promise of community.

The Harrisons' poetic practice is thus crucial to their interdisciplinary artistic endeavor and to their philosophy of the artist as significant interlocutor and agent at the highest social and political levels. As activists and poets, the Harrisons develop a conjoined and sustained reflection on poetic form and activist expression. Their aspiration to act as bards performing works about perturbed ecosystems and imagining ways of redeeming them shows their ambition to bring about change through poetry and art, as poets and artists taking environmental decisions and conjuring visions of the future. Going back to premodern traditions of poetic performance in which poets mattered, inspired by 1960s poetics of voice and performance, and by 1970s discourses about artists as mediators, the Harrisons have proved that policymaking is not the exclusive domain of politicians and administrators, but is also the rightful domain of poets and artists.

1 Perloff, Marjorie, *The Poetics of Indeterminacy. Rimbaud to Cage*. Princeton University Press, Princeton, 1981, p. 288.

2 Ibid., p. 289.

3 They participated in exhibitions together, for instance in *Dialogue, discourse, research* at the Santa Barbara Museum of Art in 1979. Participants included David Antin, Eleanor Antin, Helen Mayer Harrison, Newton Harrison, Fred Lonidier, Barbara Strasen.

4 Harrison, Helen Mayer, and Newton Harrison, *The Time of the Force Majeure. After 45 Years Counterforce is on the Horizon,* edited by Petra Kruse and Kai Reschke. Prestel, Munich, London, New York, 2016, p. 53.

5 Ibid., p. 82.

6 Rogers calls *The Lagoon Cycle* a "contemporary epic" that does not embrace the totalizing vision of ancient epics. Rogers, Laura Cassidy, "The Social and Environmental Turn in Late 20th Century Art: A Case Study of Helen and Newton Harrison After Modernism." PhD diss., Stanford University, CA, 2017, p. 264.

7 Newton Harrison and Allan Kaprow participated in the exhibition *Earth, Air, Fire, Water: Elements of Art*, at the Boston Museum of Fine Arts in 1971. David Antin, Robert Smithson, Dennis Oppenheim, Michael Heizer, Douglas Huebler, Richard Serra, Dan Graham also participated.

8 Douglas, Anne, and Chris Fremantle, "Inconsistency and Contradiction: Lessons in Improvisation in the Work of Helen Mayer Harrison and Newton Harrison," *Elemental: An Arts and Ecology Reader*, edited by James Brady. Gaia Project Press, Manchester, https://rgu-repository.worktribe.com/output/246162/inconsistency-and-contradiction-lessons-in-improvisation-in-the-work-of-helen-mayer-harrison-and-newton-harrison, 2016b, accessed July 25, 2023.

9 Cheetham, Mark A., *Landscape into Eco Art. Articulations of Nature Since the '60s*. Penn State University Press, University Park 2018, p. 11.

10 Boettger, Suzaan, "Ways of Saying. Rhetorical Strategies of Environmentalist Imagining," *The Routledge Companion to Contemporary Art, Visual Culture, and Climate Change*, edited by T. J. Demos, Subhankar Banerjee, and Emily Eliza Scott. Routledge, London, 2021, p. 252.

11 Harrison, Helen Mayer, and Newton Harrison, *The Time of the Force Majeure. After 45 Years Counterforce is on the Horizon*, p. 147.

12 Harrison, Helen Mayer, and Newton Harrison, *The Lagoon Cycle*. Herbert F. Johnson Museum of Art, Cornell University, Ithaka, NY, 1985, p. 17.

13 Ibid., p. 20.

14 Rogers, Laura Cassidy, "The Social and Environmental Turn in Late 20th Century Art: A Case Study of Helen and Newton Harrison After Modernism." PhD diss., Stanford University, CA, 2017, p. 264.

15 Harrison, Helen Mayer, and Newton Harrison, *The Lagoon Cycle*. Herbert F. Johnson Museum of Art, Cornell University, Ithaka, NY, 1985, p. 26.

16 Ibid., p. 31.

17 Ibid., p. 31.

18 Ibid., p. 31.

19 Ibid., p. 37.

20 Ibid., p. 37.

21 Ibid., p. 61.

22 Ibid., p. 80.

23 For a discussion of Smithson and the Harrisons which contests the latter's reading of *The Spiral Jetty* see Raskin, David, "Jetties and Lagoons: The Art of Robert Smithson and Newton and Helen Mayer Harrison," *Tracing Cultures: Art History, Criticism, Critical Fiction*. Whitney Museum of American Art, New York, NY, 1994, pp. 139–159.

24 Fredman, Stephen, *American Poetry as Transactional Art. Modern and Contemporary Poetics*. Alabama University Press, Tuscaloosa, AL, 2020, xi.

25 Harrison, Helen Mayer, and Newton Harrison, *The Lagoon Cycle*. Herbert F. Johnson Museum of Art, Cornell University, Ithaka, NY, 1985, pp. 35–37.

26 Ibid., p. 37.

27 Ibid., p. 37.

28 Ibid., p. 31.

29 Ibid., p. 71.

30 Harrison, Helen Mayer, and Newton Harrison, "One Full Work and Part of Another," *New Wilderness Letter*, edited by Jerome Rothenberg, December 1977–January 1978, p. 24.

31 Already pointed out by Douglas, Anne, and Chris Fremantle, "What Poetry Does Best. The Harrisons' Poetics of Being and Acting in the World," *The Time of the Force Majeure: After 45 Years Counterforce is on the Horizon*, Harrison, Helen Mayer, and Newton Harrison, p. 459.

32 Harrison, Helen Mayer, and Newton Harrison, *The Lagoon Cycle*. Herbert F. Johnson Museum of Art, Cornell University, Ithaka, NY, 1985, p. 60.

33 Ibid., p. 80.

34 Ibid., p. 91.

35 Ibid., p. 96.

36 Douglas, Anne, and Chris Fremantle, "The work is a chant and was made to be read aloud," 2020, https://glasgowtheatreseminar.wordpress.com/2020/01/02/anne-douglas-and-chris-fremantle-the-work-is-a-chant-and-was-made-to-be-read-aloud-23-01-2020/, accessed July 25, 2023.

37 Rothenberg, Jerome, "Editor's notes," *New Wilderness Letter*, Vol. 1, Nos. 2–3, December 1977–January 1978, inside cover, n. p.

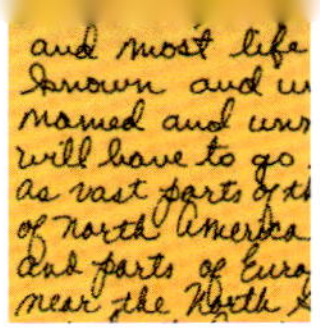

Cover of *The Time of the Force Majeure. After 45 Years Counterforce is on the Horizon* (detail)

38 Fredman, Stephen, *American Poetry as Transactional Art. Modern and Contemporary Poetics*. Alabama University Press, Tuscaloosa, AL, 2020, p. 30.

39 On Rothenberg's reverence for Pound, see Fredman, Stephen, *American Poetry as Transactional Art. Modern and Contemporary Poetics*. Alabama University Press, Tuscaloosa, AL, 2020, pp. 33–34.

40 Kopytin, Alexander I., and Stephen K. Levine, "An interview with Newton Harrison," *Ecopoiesis: Eco-Human Theory and Practice*, Vol. 2, No. 1, 2021, https://en.ecopoiesis.ru/interviews/article_post/an-interview-with-newton-harrison, accessed July 25, 2023.

41 Frank, Roberta, "The Search for the Anglo-Saxon Oral Poet," *Bulletin of the John Rylands Library*, Manchester, 1993, p. 12.

42 Ibid, p. 12–13.

43 Lerner, Ben, *The Hatred of Poetry*. Fitzcarraldo, London, 2016, p. 61.

44 Koch, John T., editor, *Celtic Culture: A Historical Encyclopedia*. 5 Vols. ABC-Clio, Santa Barbara, 2006, pp. 169–173; 174–183.

45 Ibid., p. 173.

46 Ibid., p. 171.

47 Karlin, Daniel, *The Figure of the Singer*. Oxford University Press, Oxford, 2013, pp. 15–40.

48 Smithson, Robert, *The Collected Writings*, edited by Jack Flam. California University Press, Berkeley, CA, 1996, p. 379.

49 Harrison, Helen Mayer, and Newton Harrison, "On *The Endangered Meadows of Europe*," *Kongreßdokumentation. Wiesen und Weiden – ein gefährdetes Kulturerbe Europas*, Forum der Kunst- und Ausstellungshalle der Bundesrepublik Deutschland, Bonn, 1996, pp. 15–16.

50 See Allison, Raphael, *Bodies on the Line. Performance and the Sixties Poetry Reading*. University of Iowa Press, Iowa City, 2014, pp. xi–xvii, and Davidson, Michael, *Ghostlier Demarcations. Modern Poetry and the Material Word*. University of California Press, Berkeley, CA, 1997, pp. 196–197. For a larger historical perspective on poetic performance in American poetry from the 1920s up to today, see Wheeler, Lesley, *Voicing American Poetry. Sound and Performance from the 1920s to the Present*. Cornell University Press, Ithaca, NY, 2020.

51 Harrison, Helen Mayer, and Newton Harrison, *The Time of the Force Majeure. After 45 Years Counterforce is on the Horizon*, p. 155.

52 Ibid., pp. 378–379.

53 Harrison, Helen Mayer, and Newton Harrison, *The Lagoon Cycle*. Herbert F. Johnson Museum of Art, Cornell University, Ithaka, NY, 1985, p. 96.

54 Ibid., p. 97.

55 Ibid., p. 96.

56 Ibid., p. 96.

57 Ibid., p. 96.

58 Ibid., p. 96.

59 Harrison, Helen Mayer, and Newton Harrison, *The Time of the Force Majeure. After 45 Years Counterforce is on the Horizon*, p. 170.

60 Harrison, Helen Mayer, and Newton Harrison, *The Lagoon Cycle*. Herbert F. Johnson Museum of Art, Cornell University, Ithaka, NY, 1985, p. 96.

and the tropics
will become uninhabitable
and the far north
will become temperate
and corn rice wheat and beans
plantain manioc and yams
and all the grains and starchy roots
known and unknown
named and unnamed
will have to grow elsewhere than now
and most life
known and unknown
named and unnamed
will have to go elsewhere than now
as vast parts of the eastern seaboard
of North America
and parts of Europe
near the North Sea
and South America near the Amazon
and china in the east
and russia in the north
india in the northeast
and other bits of asia africa
polynesia melanesia
australia and even japan
will join the growing sea

And in this new beginning
this continuously rebeginning
You will feed me
when my lands can no longer produce
and I will house you
when your lands are covered with water
and together
we will withdraw
as the waters rise

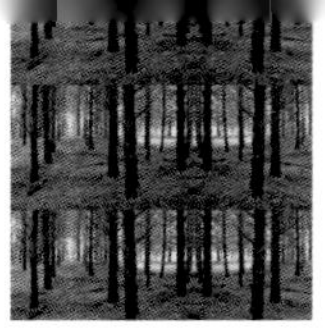

Saving the West TATIANA SIZONENKO

Fundamentally, we have a non-possessive attitude about our work – we make what has been called 'art in the public interest' as best as we can define what that interest is in the moment we are in. When our work is presented, it is obvious that its place is in the public domain ... If we were to do a work here, it would, like all of our works, emerge from our whole life experience, which is with rivers and watersheds, social systems, and global warming. Furthermore, it would have core questions embedded in it: What's farming doing to the topsoil? What's over foresting doing to the rivers and the watersheds? What is the overproduction of sameness doing to the psyche? All of these problems are related to seeing the world as a whole interacting system, which is where we begin.
Helen Harrison[1]

Who will pay this eco-debt
and where will we find eco-credits
to put against it
as ecosystems simplify
and become minimally productive?
From the *Serpentine Lattice*[2]

Throughout their prolific collaborations, Helen and Newton Harrison's work has demonstrated a powerful multidisciplinary engagement with the innermost workings of California's natural landscapes. The urban "backyard farming" experiments of the *Survival Pieces* involved closed ecosystems in response to Southern California's disappearing orchards. The *Lagoon Cycle*, their decade-long research project, considered geographical themes of the Pacific Gulf, the Salton Sea, the Colorado River Watershed, and the ecologies of estuarial lagoons. The *Sacramento Meditations*, *Arroyo Seco Release*, and *Devil's Gate* addressed environmentally threatened conditions in the various terrains, from bays to deserts, between Sacramento and Los Angeles, considering urban canyons, arroyos, rivers and watersheds, and agricultural valleys. At the beginning of the 1990s, the Harrisons were fully ready to work with complex ecologies on an increasingly larger bioregional scale, so they turned their attention to higher altitudes. *Saving the West*, as it was later called, is a series of works, including *Serpentine Lattice* (1993) and *Sierra Nevada* (1998), that made persuasive arguments about how the fragile and vanishing ecosystems of the North American fog forests and the Sierra Nevada mountains might be restored. The Harrisons' bioregional works mapped out the impacts of overexploitation and mismanagement of natural resources and the effects of global warming on the forests' complex bionetworks and watersheds – the focus of their work from the 1990s through 2000s.

The development of this body of work coincided with a new phase of the Harrisons' career and an extremely productive and formative period in their lives. In 1993 their early retirement from the joint professorship at UC San Diego, prompted by economic recession and corresponding budget cuts, enabled them to move their activities from the ivory tower of the university into the real world. In the same year, Newton formed the Harrison Studio, recruiting youngest son Gabriel and artist Vera Westergaard. Over the next decade, Gabriel and Vera helped to fully establish the studio while also aiding in revitalizing the Harrisons' reputation as internationally acclaimed contemporary artists. As experts and planners dealing with land reclamation and difficult environmental issues, Newton and Helen were commissioned for complex large-scale projects not only in the US but also in Europe, such as *A Vision for the Green Heart of Holland* (1994), *A Brown Coal Park for Südraum Leipzig* (1994), and *Endangered Meadows of Europe* (1996), among many other works.

THE SERPENTINE LATTICE PROPOSAL

Saving the West began with the *Serpentine Lattice* in 1991. Susan Fillin-Yeh, director of the Douglas F. Cooley Memorial Art Gallery, invited the Harrisons to give a talk and to do a workshop or a project at Reed College in Portland, Oregon.[3] This invitation led to a detailed study of the North American fog forest stretching from the Big Sur area and San Francisco northward to Yakutat Bay, Alaska – a little over 3,220 kilometers. The trees in this zone are known for getting most of their water moisture via their pine needles, which are saturated by the fog that rolls in daily from the Pacific Ocean.

The work took shape during their visit in June 1992, after the artists first walked and flew over forest land near Oxbow Park and Forest Park, Oregon, along Oregon's Salmon River, and over the northern Oregon Coast Range and the Nehalem River basin. They then engaged in conversations with local residents, tree loggers, biologists, ecologists, foresters, and simply "anyone who would listen" to them.[4] During that visit the Harrisons discovered that, since the 1880s, almost 95 percent of the old-growth forest, that is about 130,000 square kilometers of old-growth forest within an area of 143,000 square kilometers, had been mostly clear-cut. This clearcutting had subsequently destroyed the forest ecosystems of over 3,800 rivers, disturbing more than 70 percent of the 161,000 kilometers of rivers, streams, and creeks that flow through the region.

With the help of Susan's daughter and Reed Noss, a conservation biologist, the artists calculated more precisely the extent of such damage, documenting that "the wreckage of the water system was massive, and its ability to revive itself at that scale was practically nonexistent."[5] The removal of the trees had disrupted not only the biodiversity of local ecologies, severely reducing the number of resident species in them, but also their productivity: for instance, the salmon, which relied on shaded cool waters, died off as the sun warmed the streams and the resident stream life. The Harrisons also learned from foresters that ozone and oxygen levels were negatively impacted from the loss of trees. The artists experienced a great sadness from observing the death of the North American fog forest and, in *Serpentine Lattice*, lamented that what was left was just "a pathetic remnant:"

From Southern Alaska
to Northern California
North America's last great temperate rain forest is dying
everybody knows there's less than 10 percent
of the old growth left
between
San Francisco and Vancouver Island
perhaps 40 percent in British Columbia
and nobody can agree about Alaska

By now
everybody knows that a tree farm is not a forest
that is, everybody knows
who thinks about such things

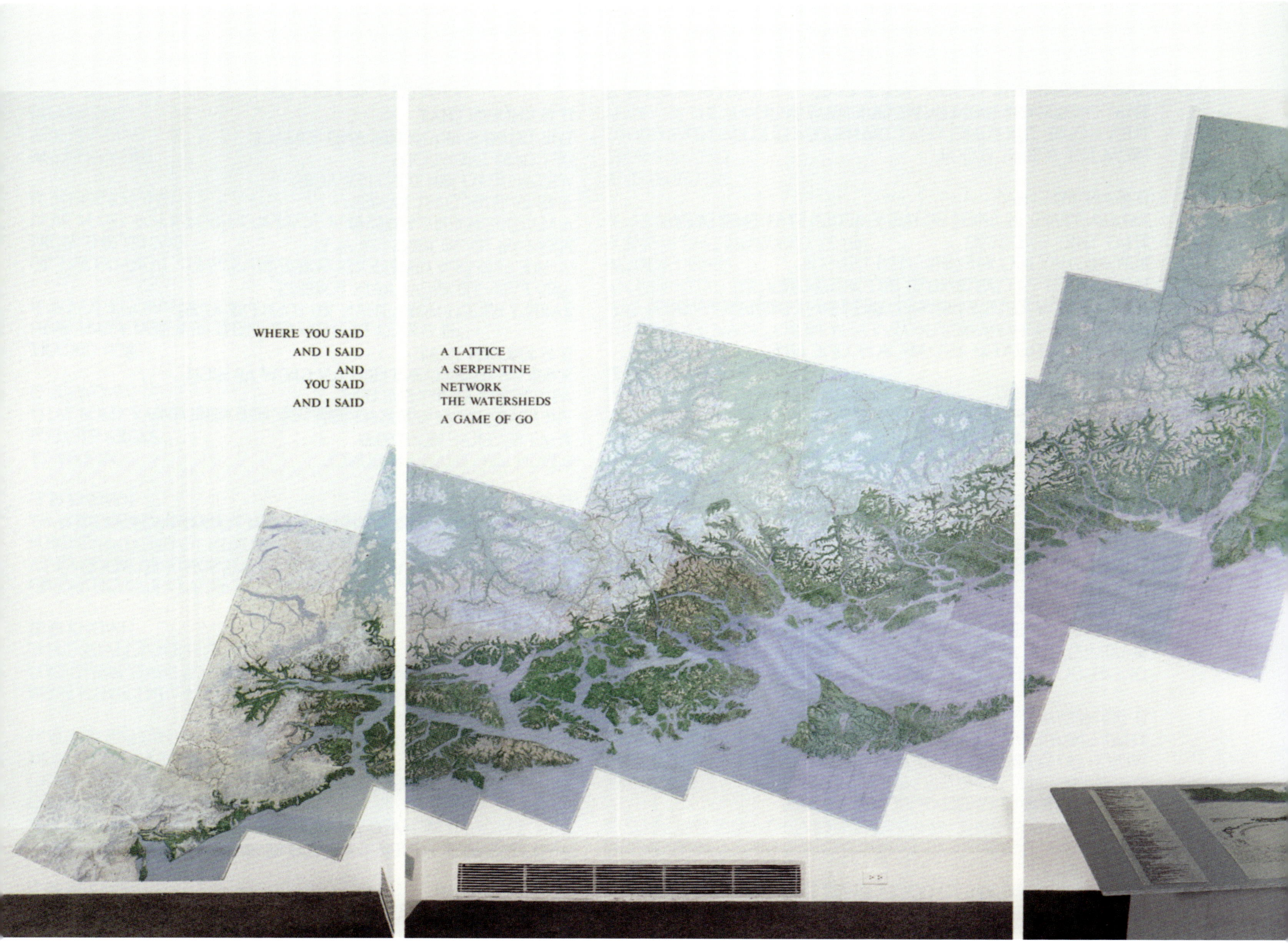
WHERE YOU SAID
AND I SAID
AND
YOU SAID
AND I SAID
A LATTICE
A SERPENTINE
NETWORK
THE WATERSHEDS
A GAME OF GO

Serpentine Lattice: Installation view

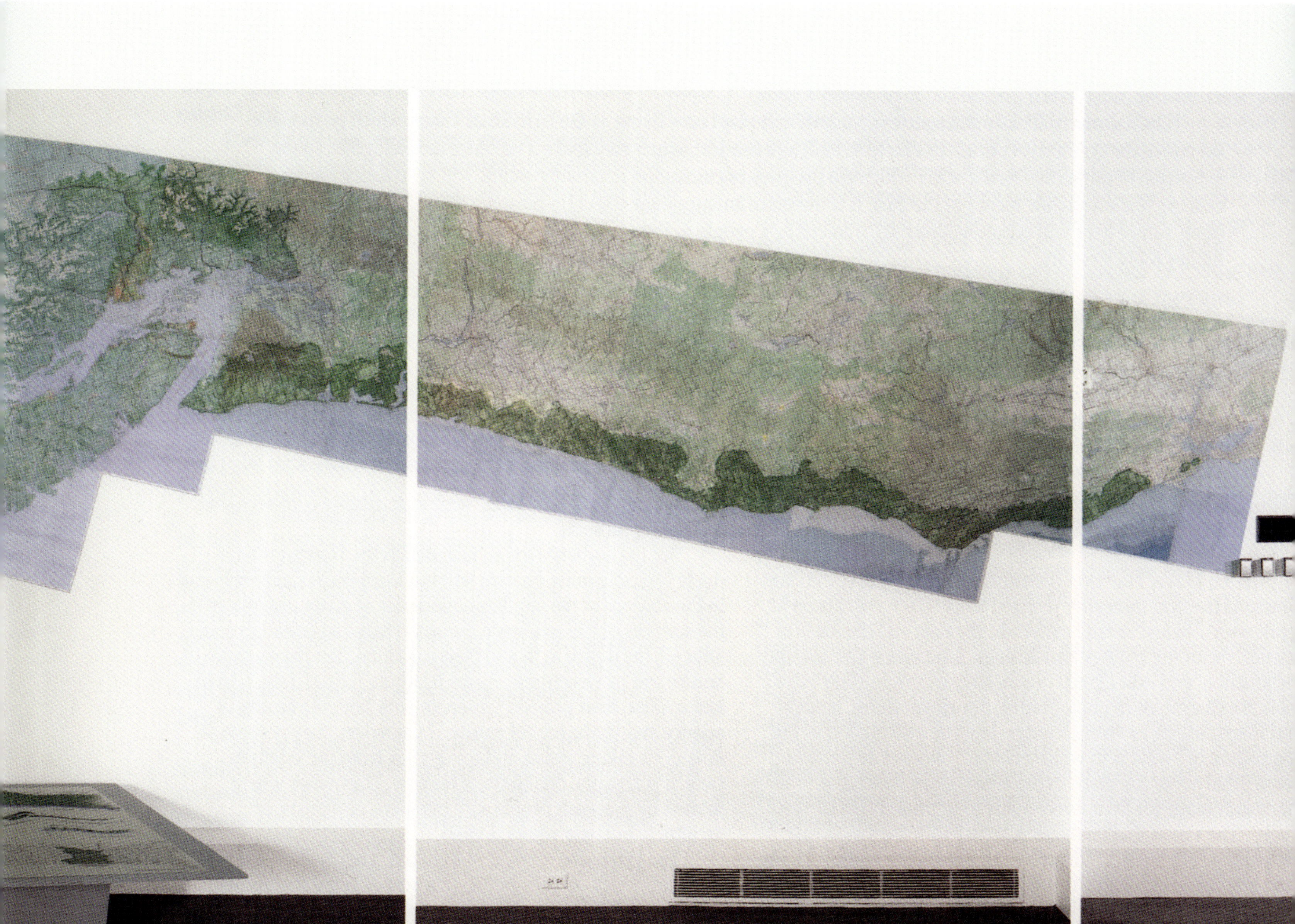

There is enough new information about
and enough old wisdom around
for anybody who thinks about these things
to know that the death of a great forest
is a global tragedy

Thinking about this forest
stretching along the coast
from the Western Hemlock of Southern Alaska
downward through Sitka Spruce
Western Red Cedar
and Douglas Fir
to Northern California
where the Coast Redwoods carry on

Knowing that embedded
in this terrain this once great
Pacific coastal fog forest
is the whole North American

Rain Forest
then who can seriously value
its total destruction …[6]

Developed over the summer and fall of 1992 and presented in the form of a conceptual design and installation, the *Serpentine Lattice* research proposed a plan for topological reclamation and restoration of the forests in the Pacific Northwest. First displayed at the Douglas F. Cooley Memorial Art Gallery from February 2 to March 15, 1993, the exhibition featured three interconnected parts: descriptive text, a 12′ × 36′ hand drawn map, and a 10′ × 36′ dissolving slide mural that showed the disappearing North American Pacific Coast Temperate Rain Forest together with forest image murals.

At the heart of *the Serpentine Lattice* is an embedded visual narrative juxtaposing the past and the possible future for the North American Pacific Coast temperate rainforest. The ten-minute loop of some 300 slides told the history of devastation involving California's destroyed redwoods and the cedar, fir, spruce, and hemlock forests of Oregon, Washington, British Columbia, and Alaska, with the clear-cuts taking over the screens.[7] A large, semitransparent parchment map was shown as a visual counterweight, presenting a redrawn Pacific Northwest Forest with its watersheds laid over a recent Geological Survey map of the same region. On the one hand, the map depicted in green color the great vanished forest, showing the appalling scope of its loss from logging, mining, urbanization, and agriculture. On the other hand, it indicated some areas that retained nearly 90 percent of their original canopy, but these existed only as patches of green rather than as a continuous expanse. The Harrisons proposed that the remaining areas of green patches, together with the cleared land, be seen as a lattice that would act as a scaffolding for the rainforest's sustainable reclamation. Therefore, the map suggested to preserve not only the seven percent remnant of old growth forest – already the focus of conservation biologists – but also to reclaim the other 93 percent, of the clear-cut areas, which would become healthy succession forest if left alone for a hundred years, without any building or development.

Bringing in photographic installations, maps, and poetry, the artists visualized practical ways to reverse the damage to Pacific Northwest Forest ecosystems. Based on their collation of scientific and sociological fieldwork, the *Serpentine Lattice* presented critiques and solutions, effectively warning the viewers that without a change in culture, forests would become only a memory. The project's title *Serpentine Lattice* described the Harrisons' visual metaphor for forest reclamation: literally, the "serpent" was the shape of the forest ridge seen in concert with the shoreline, running from Northern California up to the bottom of Alaska. Bound by coastal temperate rainforest watersheds to the east, the Pacific Ocean to the west, the Yukutat Bay in Alaska to the north, and San Francisco Bay

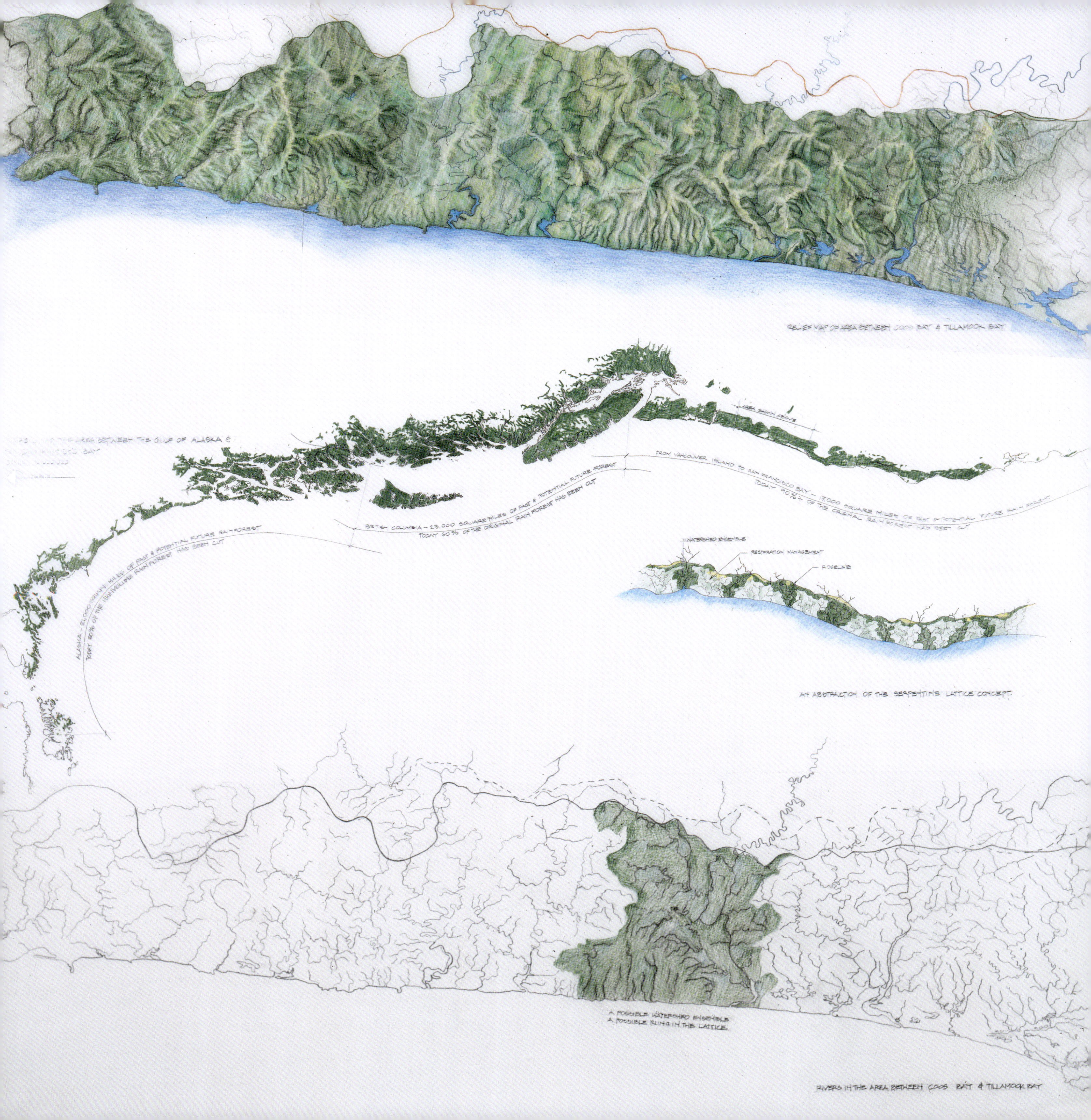

RELIEF MAP OF AREA BETWEEN COOS BAY & TILLAMOOK BAY
AREA SHOWN ABOVE
FROM VANCOUVER ISLAND TO SAN FRANCISCO BAY – 17,000 SQUARE MILES OF PAST & POTENTIAL FUTURE RAIN FOREST
TODAY 90%+ OF THE ORIGINAL RAIN FOREST HAS BEEN CUT
BRITISH COLUMBIA – 23,000 SQUARE MILES OF PAST & POTENTIAL FUTURE FOREST
TODAY 60% OF THE ORIGINAL RAIN FOREST HAS BEEN CUT
WATERSHED ENSEMBLE
RESTORATION MANAGEMENT
RIDGELINE
AN ABSTRACTION OF THE SERPENTINE LATTICE CONCEPT
A POSSIBLE WATERSHED ENSEMBLE
A POSSIBLE RUNG IN THE LATTICE
RIVERS IN THE AREA BETWEEN COOS BAY & TILLAMOOK BAY

to the south, the area of dark and light green markings on the map, representing the fragile remnants of the largest coastal temperate rainforest in the world, "was proposed to be seen as a connective 'lattice,' a tissue of watershed ensembles" – thus modules of future forest ecosystems from which large-scale forests could spring back to life.[8] This vision was clearly captured by their poetic discourse displayed next to the map:

We being grateful
for the invitation to join this perilous conversation
began to imagine an act of restitution
you seeing a serpentine
I seeing a lattice
we began to imagine North/South continuities from the
Yakutat Bay
to San Francisco
continuities that would bespeak
the eco-poetics of the whole

Now looking at healthy succession
looking at old growth remaining
wondering about a matrix in which to insert a new vision
suddenly
you said a lattice
and I said serpentine
and you said network the watersheds

I said a game of go
Imagine the serpentine form
of the crest of the coastal mountains
imagine the serpentine form of the Pacific Coast
imagine some of the rivers
really watershed ensembles
extending from crest to coast
connecting the serpentines
as nearly leaf shaped rungs
or cross members of the lattice

Then
within this lattice could begin
the restoration of the more pristine environments
by leaving them alone
by engaging in a more active restoration
only where clear-cutting has been most severe
by closing off entry roads
when finished

A willful getting out of the way
A felicitous withdrawal

Then within these cross members a minimally mitigated
environment
moving towards the pristine
would exist and could flourish
and expand

Then
a new reversal of ground can come into being
where human activity becomes a figure
within an ecological field
as simultaneously the ecology ceases being an ever-shrinking
figure
within the field of human activity[9]

As in their other works, the Harrisons employed here a series of metaphors expressed in multiple views, with overlays of hand drawn and colored maps operating as iconic forms. A network of interlinked watersheds, sampling the entire 1,800 miles of forest ecosystems from California to Alaska, produced a convincing conceptual design and a planning document that emphasized different perspectives. Highlighting the Harrisons' special use of maps, Charles Green argued that the repeated serpentine image in the installation, "hanging in darkness, resembled a brain set inside a skull," acting "as a mnemonic device that would refer viewers to plans for the forests' regeneration."[10] Their proposal was further accentuated by the authoritative use of projected photographs presented as a cinematic spectacle, creating a visual and emotional overload of information while offering many entrance points into the poetically narrated proposal.

Furthermore, the *Serpentine Lattice* was one of the initial works in which the Harrisons laid out a new framework for the assisted migration of species. Following the exhibition, Sana Krusoe, the Chair of the Fine Arts Department at the University of Oregon, invited Helen and Newton to teach a master class in October 1993. Preserved in the artists' archives, the class syllabus describes assisted migration "as an artistic and visionary approach to restoration of part of the damaged coast range that would involve aerial and terrestrial mapping of one or two selected areas of the local coast range and a week of intensive restoration: planting, reseeding, repopulating the damaged areas."[11] The proposed one-week intensive interdisciplinary workshop was conceived as part of a master plan intended to restore the coastal region to a life and vitality that has been severely threatened by clearcutting.

AN ECO-SECURITY SYSTEM

Sponsored by the Lectures and Exhibition Committee, the Dean's Office, and the Fine Arts Department, the workshop was held in the community of Deadwood Zoom, an hour-and-a-half drive from Eugene, Oregon. The artists chose Deadwood as representative of the bulk of the Pacific Northwest, with no old growth left, everything having been cut twice, resulting in troubled rivers, perilous fires, and land erosion. The artists envisioned taking all cutting out of Deadwood, setting a new kind of forestry for the whole Deadwood Creek Watershed. They hoped to implement non-invasive cutting, emergency planting where necessary, and emergency healing of the streams and fish life by inventing new and temporary solutions like shelters and shade zones. They proposed to set up the watershed as a study area for developing and testing ideal forestry practices: selective logging and reforestation, uneven thinning, density variation, understory planting of multiple species, and promotion of ecosystem diversity. The

AN ASSISTED MIGRATION WITH NEWTON & HELEN HARRISON

Syllabus
ART 408-508

A one-week intensive interdisciplinary workshop
October 25- Nov. 1
9-5
1 credit P/N

Sana Krusoe
202 B Northsite
3629 3610

(Because the Harrisons are out of the country as we write this we cannot list dates and times more precisely; any changes will be minor & all activities will fall within this week.)

Required reading: The Serpentine Lattice, Newton and Helen Harrison (bookstore)
Suggested reading: The Lagoon Cycles, Newton and Helen Harrison (AAA library)

Class Requirements:

The class will function as a core group, helping to design and implement an assisted migration, which involves the total restoring of a part of the ecologically damaged coast range. Students will meet with faculty this spring to help plan the project, and will meet Oct 5 at 5:30 in the Dean's Conference Room for an orientation meeting. The week of Oct 25-Nov 1 will involve days of, as the Harrisons put it, "running around from dawn to dusk." The work will be in clear-cut areas, will involve planting, and will be dirty, physical, and possibly wet. If we involve larger numbers, each of the core group may be responsible for a team of as many as ten. The sole class requirement is total and whole-hearted participation.

First meeting: Orientation meeting Tuesday October 5 Dean's Conference Room.

Lecture: Monday October 25, 7:30 pm, LA 177
Class begins: 9 a.m. Tuesday October 26, 9 a.m. Dean's Conference Room
Class ends: after wrap session, Monday November 1: TBA

Class Description

Assisted Migration

An artistic and visionary approach to restoration of part of the damaged coast range, this workshop with internationally recognized artists and ecologists Newton and Helen Harrison will involve aerial and terrestrial mapping of one or two selected areas of the local coast range and a week of intensive restoration: planting, reseeding, repopulating the damaged area. This is part of a master plan to restore the coast range to a life and vitality that has been severely threatened by clearcutting. This will be hands-on and will involve long days: faculty will be asked to excuse students participating in this workshop from classes during that week. Information on the work of the Harrisons will be distributed to the departments as we receive it.

This event is sponsored by the AAA lectures & Exhibition Committee in conjunction with the Dean's Office and the Fine Arts Department. Members of the Lectures and Exhibition Committee are Al Acres, Chris Luebkamen, Sana Krusoe, and Jenny Young, faculty; and Rebecca Nolan, Natalie Whitson (MFA 93), and Lisa McClellan, students. Any of us may be contacted for information. sk

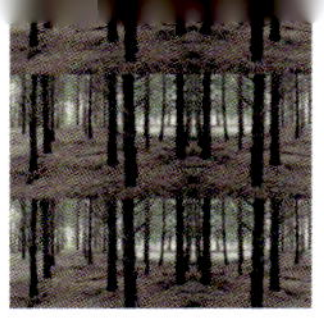

Harrisons saw one of the major aims to be a duplication of the natural pattern of forest rehabilitation, with timber harvest from the area occurring on a 250-year cycle, with the intention of providing high-grade lumber for commercial purposes. To achieve this, the Harrisons projected the development of an "ecological corporation" with rules and regulations for managing the watershed. This corporation would be financed by grants, the profits from green industries, and carbon credits paid by carbon producers such as utilities companies and automobile users. Although the Deadwood proposal was not supported by further grants, the Harrisons used it to expand the *Serpentine Lattice*, adding poetic texts from the Deadwood workshop in subsequent exhibitions. The elaborated text introduced the ideas of *eco-debt*, *eco-security*, and *gross national ecosystem*, imagined like the Social Security system:

For instance
if
according to the laws of the conservation of energy
the transfer of energy
from one form to another
generates a net loss
then the clear-cutting of old growth forest
must involve a net loss equal to more
than the energy gained
from transforming it into profit

Who will pay the costs of the loss of plants and herbs
whose medicinal values
are as yet unknown
and the price
when sequestering of carbon
by succession of ecologies diminishes
and who will pay the costs
of apparently unsupervised
aggressive clear-cutting on private lands
after all this long-term energy debt
comes due in the next generation

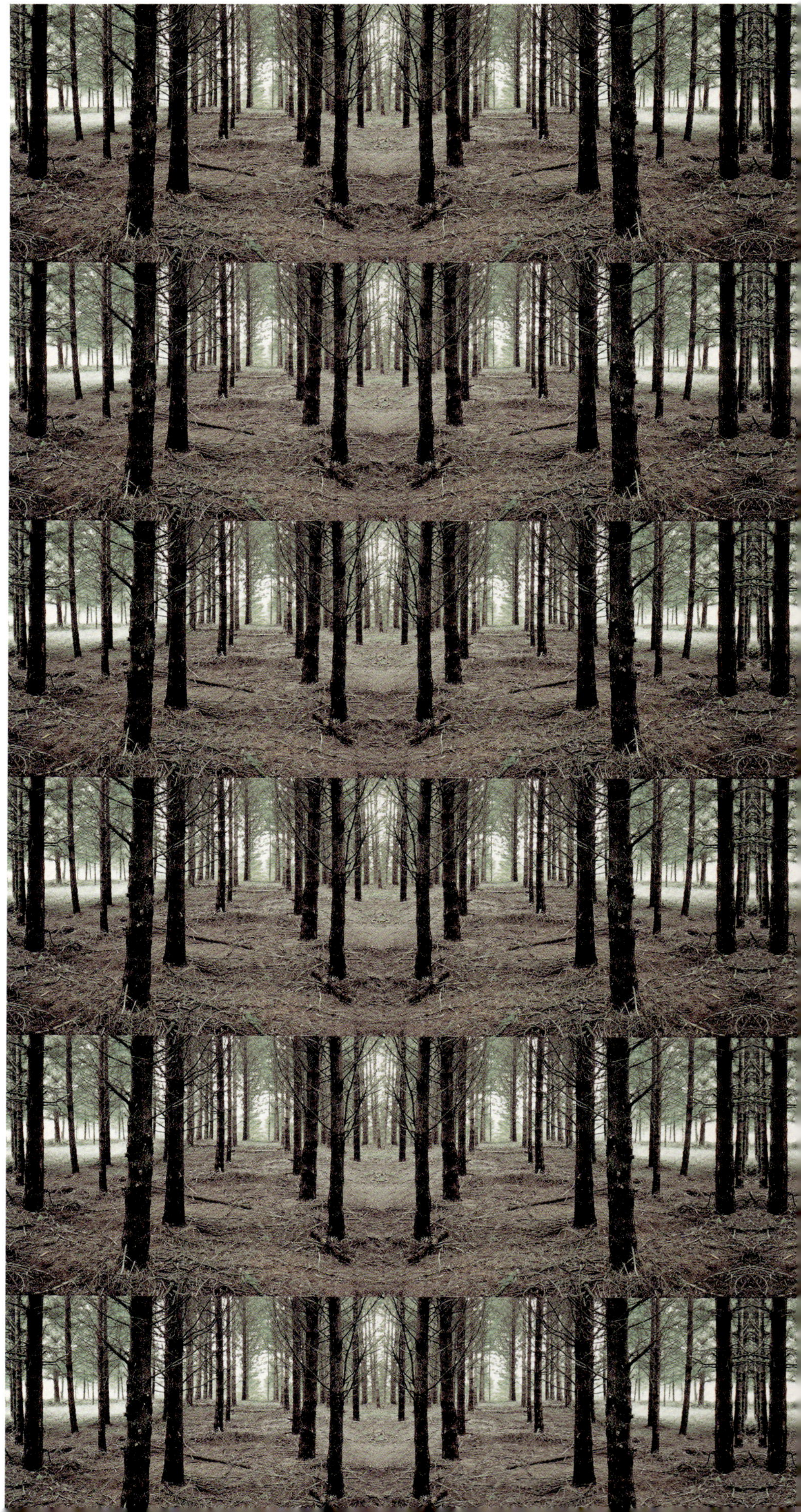

Where it can be seen that a tree farm is not a forest

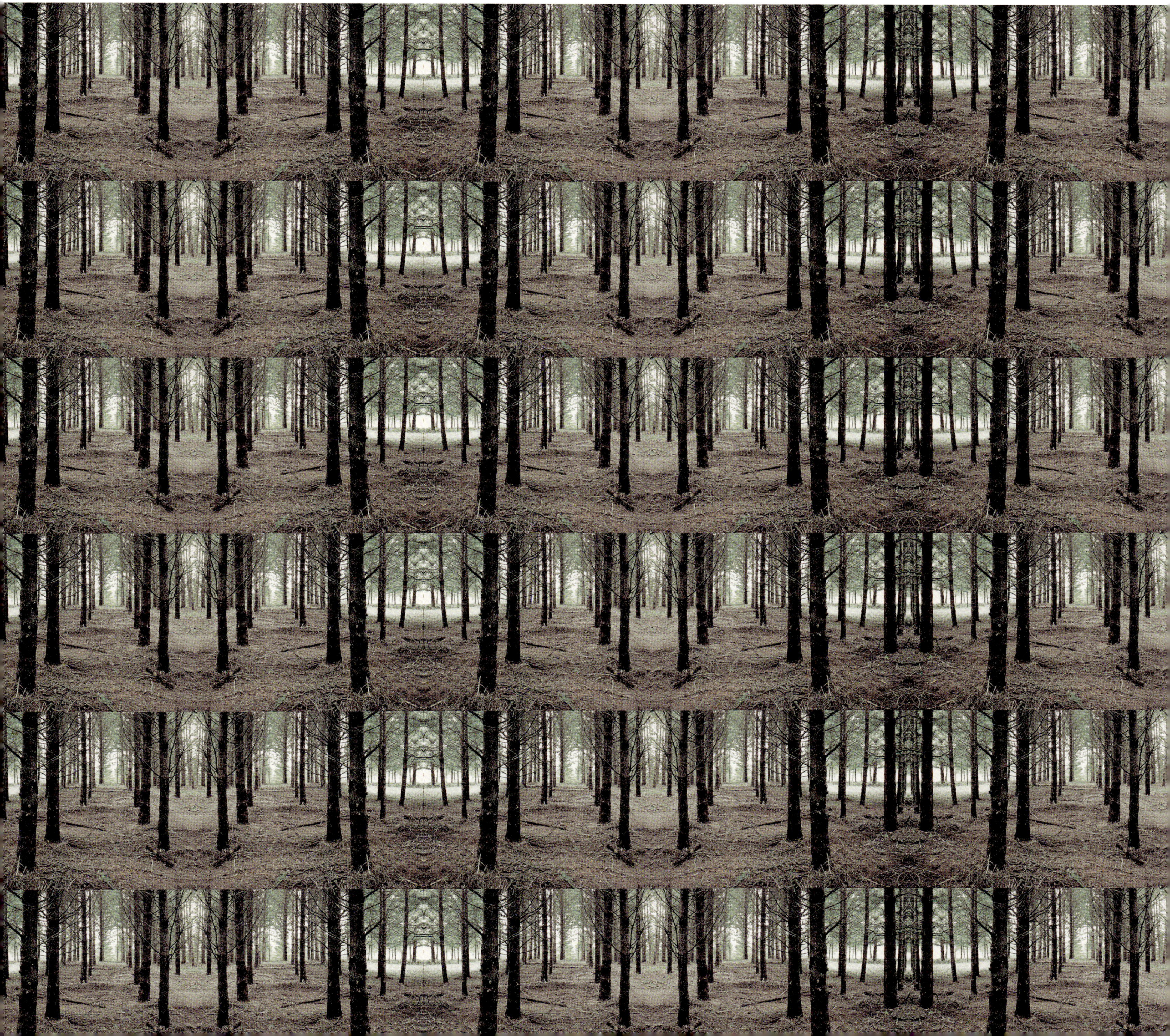

With the turning of 130 000 square kilometers
of biologically productive lands
into functional deserts
and the elimination
of productive ecosystems
from over 161 000 kilometers
of river-stream habitat
the water-purifying properties
of the wetlands
disappear

Who will pay this eco-debt
and where will we find eco-credits
to put against it
as ecosystems simplify
and become minimally productive

For instance
if the gross national product
is 5.7 trillion dollars
and
producing the gross national product
is the outcome of exploiting
the gross national ecosystem
and the gross national ecosystem
is not infinitely renewable
then it is not difficult to imagine
the gross national product shrinking
in concert with an overexploited
less-productive
gross national ecosystem

However
if as a form of recycling
we take one percent
of our gross national product
and establish an eco-security system
not unlike
our social security system
then
roughly 57 billion dollars
become available yearly
for restoration/reclamation

Finally
ground would be reversed
so that the ecosystem
becomes the field
and human use
the figure within it

Then
the gross national ecosystem
would take its place
privileged appropriately
as the field within which
the political systems
social systems
and business systems
that constitute
our eco-cultural entity
can exist[12]

From the poetry emerges the concept of an *environmental* security system, not so different from the social security pension system, proposing to use one percent of the Gross National Product to fight against the seemingly endless destruction of our environment and fund acts of environmental restitution. As in the *Meditation on the Great Lakes of North America* (1977), the artists envisioned a world in which ecological necessity was not subjugated by human activity. In her introduction to the exhibition of the *Serpentine Lattice*, Eleanor Hartney called the proposal "eminently practical" because the artists insisted on long-range planning that included reclamation and restoration and in which "jobs and homes were not irreconcilable with environmentalism."[13]

The trajectory of the Harrisons' work showed their increasing concern with the issues of environmental degradation, industrial exploitation of natural resources, and mismanagement of lands, waters, and watersheds. Taking as a point of departure the earlier *Sacramento Meditations* (1977), which critiqued the irrigation policies of the Sacramento-San Joaquin watershed in Northern California that led to unforeseen side effects as deadly wetlands, salt contaminated land, and severe droughts, the *Serpentine Lattice* countered just such backwards thinking. The artists insisted on a paradigm shift from "exploitation and consumption" to "appropriation and beneficial use."

Like the *Sacramento Meditations*, the *Serpentine Lattice* expressed a call to action, a call that was often resisted and opposed. Lumber companies pressured politicians to refrain from attending the exhibition. The artists offered to debate representatives from the lumber companies on a local public radio station and tried to enlist support from Bill Clinton's political campaign. Not unexpectedly, the radio broadcast was cancelled at the last minute, and President Clinton never showed up at the Harrisons' exhibition, which they mounted in proximity to political meetings that he held in the region with other environmentalist groups.[14] Moreover, the lumber companies, which had generously funded the Clinton campaign, succeeded in introducing a law to protect the American forest elsewhere – but not in the Pacific Northwest.

Concluding with the refrain, "A tree farm is not a forest," the *Serpentine Lattice* prompts the viewer to engage in a form of eco-politics. Through the map that shows the coast from San Francisco to Alaska, the artists invited the viewer to imagine the forests crossing state lines and national borders, to reinvent them as bioregions rather than political constructs. The Harrisons insisted that the lumber business would always protect its own economic gains rather than act in the interest of ecology; therefore, it was not capable of stopping environmental destruction or the mass extinction of species.

Over the years, art historians, art critics, and artists have underscored the importance of the generative and compelling metaphors in the Harrisons' activist poetics. During the period of their work on the *Serpentine Lattice*, the art critic Rebecca Solnit wrote that "the most distinctive – and exhilarating – aspect of their work is the way it acknowledges metaphor," making it basic to the success of their art.[15] The *Serpentine Lattice*'s poetic discourse stands out in the way that the artists employed "serpentine" and "lattice" both visually and verbally to describe their plan for forest and watershed reclamation. Susan Fillen-Yeh correctly observed that the choice of "lattice" rather than the more rigid "grid" implied "support for growth (a vine)" and "ad hoc irregularity and flexibility," thus a possibility to generate motion and change direction, or as Newton put it, to "wiggle."[16] In other words, the Harrisons employed the organic language of nature to describe the dense network of interconnected watersheds and forest ecologies on the map, providing a visual metaphor for transformation.

MAPPING ENTROPY

Beginning from the 1990s, the Harrisons' proposals and designs began to seriously engage with the concept of entropy to describe the condition of ecosystems and identify the direction of consequent action. They realized that when entropy was raised in a system, it meant that the system had lost the energy needed to maintain itself in its former state, or "in other words, it has become more uniform, with less usable energy."[17] According to their thinking, logging in a watershed resulted in the degradation of matter and scattering of energy, thus serving as a textbook example of entropy. They understood that the industrial destruction of nature by humans dispersed its energy, created waste, and put entire ecosystems out of balance. Reflecting on the laws of conservation of energy in 2016, they presented their conclusions about ecological exploitation and the replacement of a natural balance by highly entropic systems:

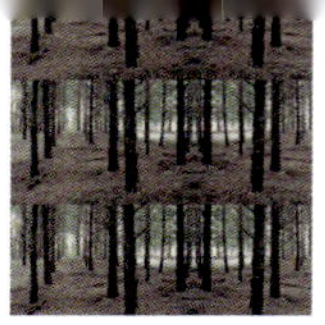

Matter/energy can be transformed from one form to another.
Matter/energy can be neither created nor destroyed.
When matter/energy is transformed from one form to another,
there is a net loss of available energy to perform work.
This loss is called entropy.
A system that has been so transformed and has lost energy
moves towards higher local entropy.
A system that maintains its ability to take useful energy
into itself
and dissipate unuseful energy
tends to be a healthy, low-entropy system.

If a forest in a watershed is clear-cut
all the useful energies in the forest
are transformed and dispersed.
The energies within topsoil
supporting a multiplicity of lives
as a consequence of erosion, in part are dispersed.
The entropy of the watershed has been increased
by the dispersal of these energies.
The energies so dispersed cannot be retrieved.

What then, watershed, what then.[18]

By the late 1990s, the Harrisons had become even more concerned about the difficulty "for life to continue" as they realized the whole planet and the lives on it were becoming increasingly affected by global warming. Their Survival Art shifted its focus to methods of large-scale adaptation to the extreme environmental changes being caused by intensifying heat and the corresponding pressures on all ecosystems. Their work not only started to educate audiences about the horrific implications for our species' survival but also proposed certain strategies for lowering entropy within living systems so that such systems could continue. The artists called for "the elimination or transformation of all economic systems based on exploitation, and their regeneration into systems of exchange."[19]

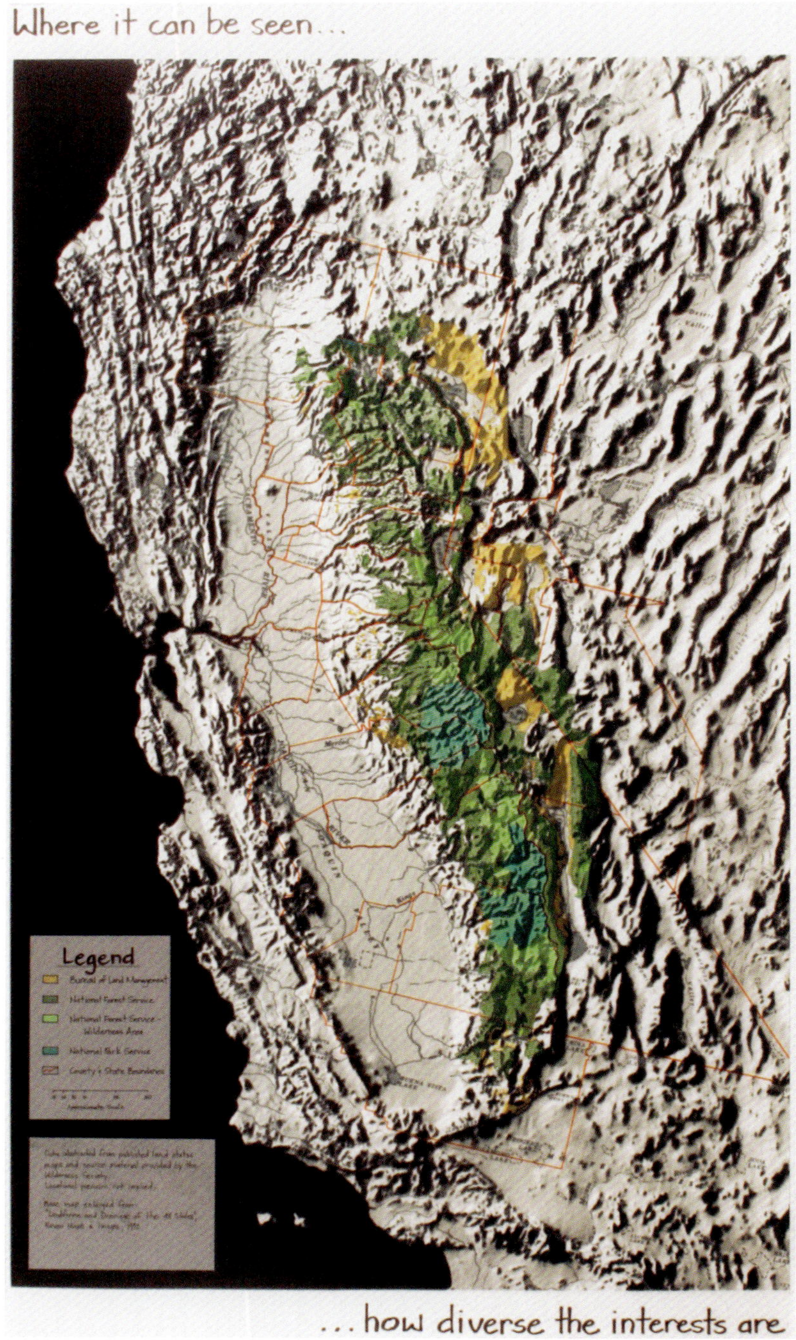

AN ADAPTATION AT GREAT SCALE

In 1998, as part of what Newton later labelled the *Saving the West* series, the Harrisons began a set of works entitled *Sierra Nevada, An Adaptation*, which evolved over the course of a decade while the Harrisons pursued the concept of ecological adaptation on a grander scale. Their initial proposal comprised seven large photo-text and map panels of

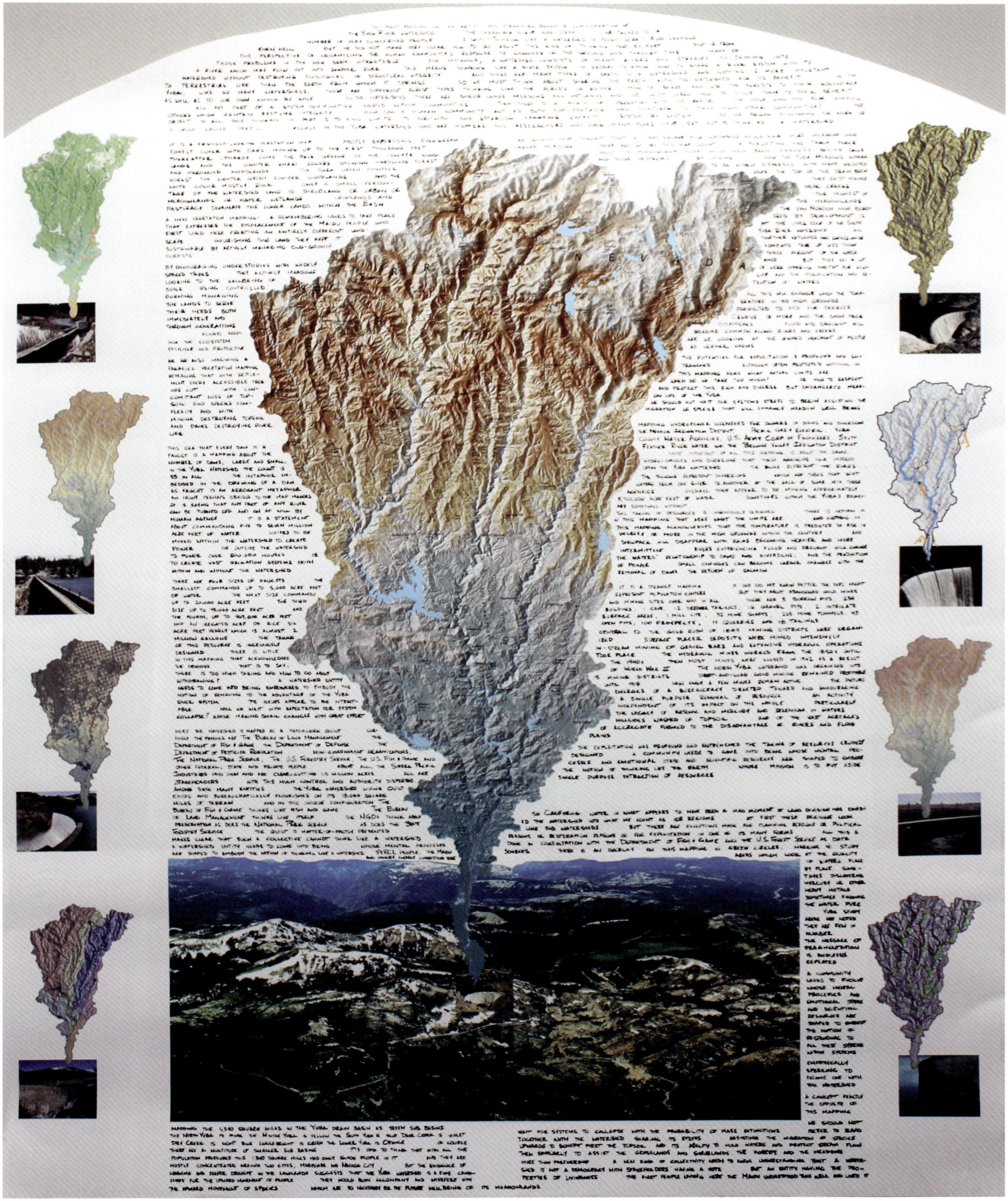

The Sierra Nevada: An Adaptation, 2011 installation view in the Nevada Museum of Art, Reno, NV

the Sierra Nevada mountains and the Truckee and Yuba watersheds; this was later expanded with a 36-foot floor map of its mountain range (2011), topographical sketches of its seventeen principal watersheds printed on canvas (2011), and a video work entitled *Saving the West* (2016).[20] *Sierra Nevada: An Adaptation* was funded in its first expanded phase (2011) by the Center for Art + Environment (CA+E) at the Nevada Museum of Art.

Exhibited in 2011 at the Feldman Art Gallery, New York, and then at the Nevada Museum of Art, Reno, *Sierra Nevada: An Adaptation* addressed the effects of global warming on one of the world's great mountain chains, a range covering 28,000 square miles. The artists, whose work had already influenced long-term public policy planning, visually explored methodologies for buffering drought and erratic weather, conditions that would distress the Central Valley of California as well as the high grounds of the Sierra Nevada. The artists wrote in their exhibition proposal: "We believe that a Sierra Nevada response in the 'now,' of the kind we propose, can forestall the great social and economic difficulties that the predicted rise in temperatures will cause, while at the same time generate a badly needed new botanically based industry. Essentially, we're arguing for design from a highly probable future, backward to the immediately knowable present."[21]

Sierra Nevada: An Adaptation considered the impact on ecosystems of a predicted temperature rise in the range of 5° centigrade in the high ground of the Sierra Nevada. The artists described that such a temperature increase would generate, in varying degrees, drought, flood, and species die-off, with probable unfortunate outcomes for the four rivers that flow down into the Great Basin on the eastern side of the Sierra Nevada. That same negative outcome would be applicable for the thirteen rivers that flow into the Central Valley of California on the western side as well. The Harrison Studio examined the high ground areas where the rivers and watersheds began and identified approximately seventeen sites of the thirteen principal watersheds for the west side and the four principal watersheds for the east.

Sierra Nevada, An Adaptation used colorful large-scale maps like matte paintings and special effects on the sets of vintage Hollywood science fiction films. Wall panels of watershed maps and photographs expressed current and future ecosystems visually, while a 36-foot aerial image of the Sierra Nevada, enhanced with drawings and text on the floor, allowed viewers to "walk" the mountain range. With feet or fingers tracing colors shades, boundaries, and ridgelines of watershed ensembles, visitors not only tangibly perceived the map but even experienced a sensation of flying over the range. As with the earlier *Serpentine Lattice*, the artists presented their maps as visual metaphors for transformation. By accentuating Independence Lake, the Truckee watershed, and the adjacent Yuba River watershed, collectively comprising a pair of drain basins, the map depicted the beauty and abundance that could be lost. It also proposed sites for adaptive responses. A colorful watershed ensemble – printed on canvases and displayed on the walls – framed the artists' vision for land restoration and adaptation. Each map included notes on the work already being done in them, principally existing restoration efforts. The primary intention behind the installation was to prepare the necessary scale of thinking and action. In the exhibition documents, the artists wrote that they considered "the *Sierra Nevada* work of greatest importance, since it has the possibility of being validated on the ground and re-validated, watershed by watershed. If so, it would have performed its function as a work of art."[22]

The joint effect of maps as seen from space and tracked in the viewer's imagination were complemented by narrative text panels using Socratic questioning to encourage public discourse. The artists presented a debate over contrasting possible futures in the next fifty years: a landscape that has been overgrazed and overcut with minimum intervention versus a world where assisted migration of beneficial species had achieved the objective of regenerating topsoil. The complexity of the artists' thinking is best captured in their final text for *Sierra Nevada*, situating it as the primary work within the *Force Majeure* series:

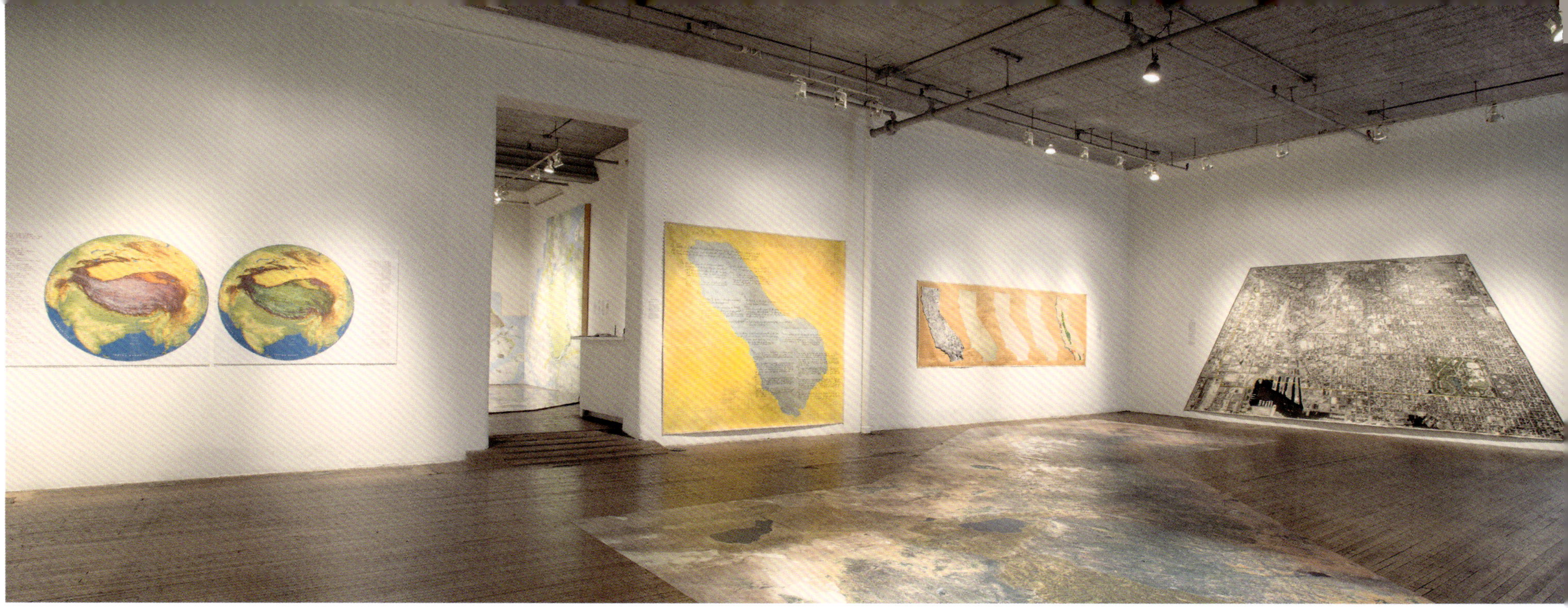

Sierra Nevada:
The Force Majeure: On the Ground

Adaptation at great scale
Requires an unorthodox knowledge base
For instance within 100 years
Temperatures rise six degrees Celsius
In the high grounds of the Sierra Nevada
Glaciers and snowpack disappear
Intense rainfall happens a few months yearly
Rivers function erratically, drought increases
Then assisting the migration of species
Especially in the high grounds
To help create the new ecosystems
Adapted to climate shock
To again produce on a more constant basis
The water-holding earths
The carbon-sequestering earths
For the forests, the grasslands
And river systems that are threatened

First studying the west side of the Sierras
Where almost all the rivers are dammed
90 percent used for irrigated farming
A bit for and industry
And the rest for urbanity
It's just possible to cognize
The depletion of available systems energies
That happens with this kind of transformation

From the perspective of the laws of the conservation of energy
The river systems that spring from watersheds
That collectively constitute the 62 400-square-kilometer
footprint
Of the Sierra Nevada
Have experienced over the last 100 years
A profound transformation
Moving from high energy but self-sustaining systems
To far more tenuous, high local entropy,
low overall available energy systems
Whose continuous flows of water are in doubt
Due to the accelerating presence
Of the Force Majeure

Flying over this terrain,
Then making a 14-meter-long, two-and-a-half-meter-wide
Aerial photo of the whole, able to be walked upon
The power of the mapping
Reveals a 62 400-square-kilometer, mostly exhausted
landscape
That energies embedded in much of its once rich forests
Transformed into short-term cultural production
Revealing a treescape pattern of thousands of square kilometers
Of lumber extraction

The Sierra Nevada: An Adaptation, 2011 installation view of sixteen watersheds in the Feldman Gallery, New York, NY

From the perspective of the laws of the conservation of energy
The forest systems that spring from watersheds
That collectively constitute the footprint of the Sierra Nevada
Have experienced over the last 100 years
A profound transformation made manifest by clear-cutting
Moving from a low-entropy, high-energy,
self-sustaining system
To a high-entropy, low-energy system
Whose continuous self-regeneration is in doubt
Due to the accelerating presence of the Force Majeure

Then looking at a tree stump
Seeing the mark of topsoil before cutting
Seeing the mark of topsoil 50 years later
Looking at a 10-centimeter topsoil loss and knowing
That 2.5 centimeters of topsoil takes 1 000 years to produce
It becomes clear that a 4 000-year energy debt is the outcome
From the transaction between clear-cutting and erosion
A topsoil loss of uncountable millions of cubic meters
And billions upon billions of microorganisms
That constitute the topsoil eco-net
That collectively participate in the Sierra Nevada Life Web
Have experienced a profound transformation
Moving from a low-entropy, high-energy, self-sustaining
system
To a high-entropy, low-energy system
Whose ability to regenerate over time
Is no longer congruent
With the way such systems regenerate
Due to the accelerating presence
Of the Force Majeure

Recreating carrying capacity requires
Assisting the migration of species
Reenergizing stressed ecosystems
Of whole mountain ranges
Increasing the resilience thereby
What amounts to be an Eco-Security system is required
Supported by a quantum of the gross transnational production
In which nature and the protection and well-being of systems
Are given co-equal agency and protections
Under the law typically afforded to human populations
Done at large enough scale
Such an effort
Would re-energize planetary ecosystems
Reestablishing continuing resilience
A counterforce to the Force Majeure

Through these poetic texts and the immersive visual displays, the Harrisons' preliminary proposal concluded that no single approach to a complex system like the high grounds of the Sierra Nevada was sufficient to meet all exigencies. However, the artists believed that with available research, conservation methods, and useful models on the ground, adaptation work could succeed concerning both shrublands and open-canopy forest. Such efforts could mitigate drought and desertification, reduce erosion, encourage biodiversity, and increase the productivity of land for water generation and herding. Engaging with complex currents of environmental and ecological science, the Harrisons presented a bold new vision and a call for transformation in addressing environmental issues of planetary importance.

The prophetic ideas of *Serpentine Lattice* and *Sierra Nevada* were synthesized in the *Saving the West* video produced by the artists in 2016. Here the Harrisons brought together their nearly fifty-year research on the California landscape, proposing a whole systems thinking approach as a means to combat increasingly devastating fires in the West and adapt to potential mass extinction caused by the accelerated rate of global warming. In this work, the Harrisons return to their earlier call for environmental justice, first presented in the *Meditation on the Gabrielinos* and developed over the series of works surveying the health of California's high grounds, but now they apply their vision not only to the state of California but also to a total of eleven states on the western side of the USA. The thirteen-minute video combines imagery

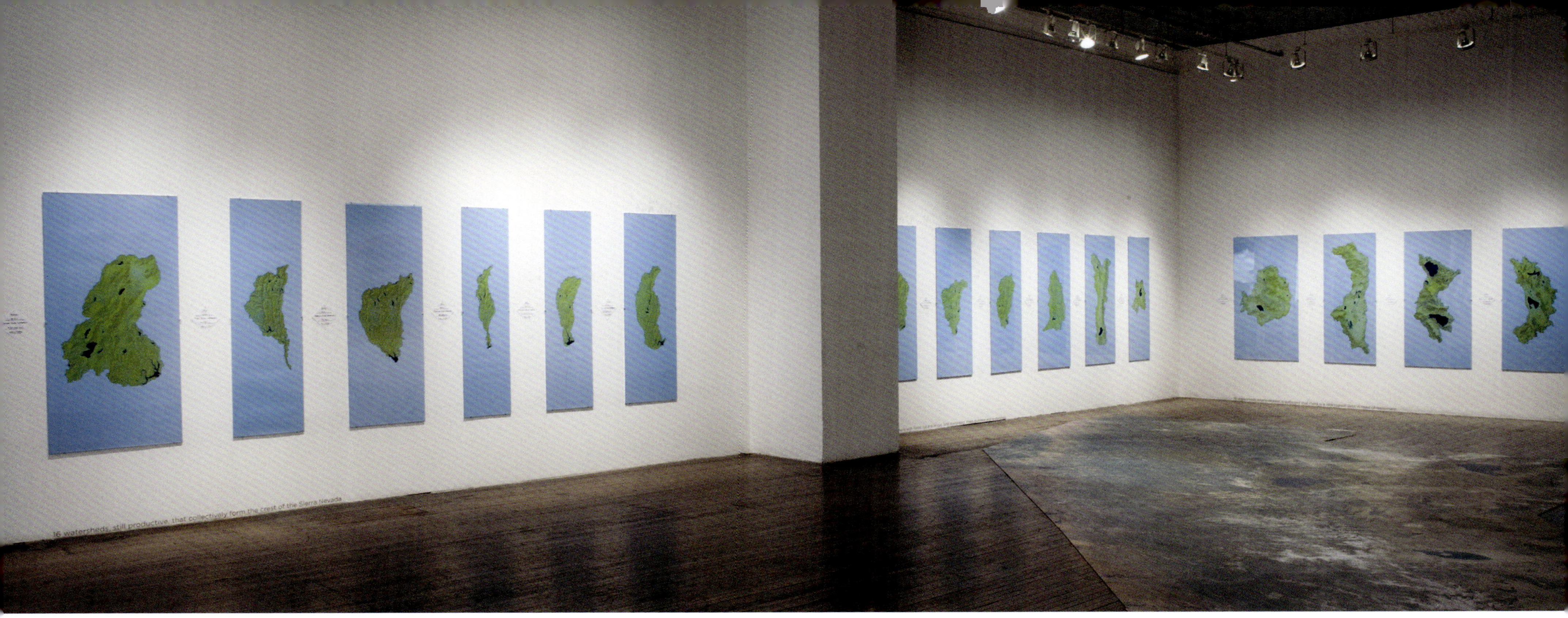

from across the Pacific Northwest, including from Sagehen Creek Field Station in the Sierra Nevada, with the Harrisons' digitally enhanced maps and Newton's voice-over reciting a poetic proposal.[23] His voice conveying a mood of deep concern, he speaks of fire and water as the major issues facing the entire Mountain West. The video invites listeners to consider a whole systems approach, in collaboration with the Web of Life, as the only strategy for survival:

Saving the West

In many places the West is afire
as drought continues
temperatures rise
species vanish
forests clear cut
work for many lost
as is infrastructure
lives endangered
top soil eroded
and ecosystems simplified
These altogether
become a serious contribution to
the sixth mass extinction
which is now upon us

We came,
we dismissed the First Peoples
and their knowledge of place
We consumed the forest
and the meadowlands

The West covers 11 states
and is a physical presence of
1.3 million square miles
The West is not small
taking up about a third of the United States occupied by 72 million people.
Within this terrain are 160 million
now fire-endangered acres of forest

A wave front of heat
moving through the west,
an invitation to crown fire

The West was harvested from a monocultural perspective
The waste profound and pervasive
The Life Web ignored
Capacity to regenerate impaired
Erosion becomes a norm
Biodiversity loss incalculable

Trees return after clear cutting or crown fire thin, crowded, very dense
Trees return after clear cutting or crown fire
thin, crowded, very dense
Density combined with drought invites fire
Crown fire becomes uncontrollable
Vast amounts of CO_2 enter the atmosphere
A tsunami of fire
unstoppable
until all energy is exhausted

Counter forces are available
For instance
15 million acres in California alone are at risk of catastrophic fire
at a containment cost of
1.5 billion dollars a year

If
one million acres of overgrown forest were thinned yearly
at an average cost of 1000 dollars per acre
and an annual cost of 1 billion dollars

Then
we are looking at 1 billion dollars allocated yearly for 15 years.
Fire risk is reduced by 7% each year
mostly eliminating catastrophic fire in California
co-equally reducing the cost of fire-fighting.

Then
these lands become
over the long term
ecologically sustainable
adapting to climate change as it happens
creating jobs
often in small industry
often for the indigenous people who have historic knowledge
in assisting the forests to continue

Imagine a response
to these 160 million acres of forests
some intact but many overcrowded and stressed
where over the long run by design
catastrophe can be flipped into opportunity

The 8,000 acre Sagehen Project
designed by people at the UC Berkeley
Sagehen Creek Field Station is deceptively simple

Through 10 years of experimentation
the Sagehen group has discovered
that fire-endangered forests transform
when thinned to 40-60 trees per acre
in groupings disbursed variously
according to the needs of the topology

the ground plane ecosystem
emerges as fire tolerant
and catastrophic fire disappears

When
the risks of catastrophic fires disappear
and ground fires self-extinguish

Then
the ecosystem is transformed
into an open canopy forest
with meadowlands randomly appearing
and carbon is sequestered
wood products are abundant

Then
the act of harvesting trees nourishes the ecosystem
providing renewable source material
that revitalizes the economy
while simultaneously storing massive amounts of carbon
in the built environment

Excess growth is thinned by hand and by machine
After thinning, before first growth
Soon, ground cover returns rich and resilient.
And managed fire benefits the whole
Chipping continues acre by acre
The results of all this thinning are turned into building materials
Turning into profit twice becoming both
building materials and carbon credits

If
one cubic meter of wood in a building
effectively sequesters one ton of CO_2

Then
one 20-story building will act
as a carbon sink for 3100 tons of CO_2

and
1200 tons of CO_2 emitted in the construction
of a 20-story concrete building is prevented

Then
a net difference of 4300 tons of CO_2 result.

The reasons for extending the Sagehen project
over the fire-endangered Western forests
and others like it are compelling.
The multiplier effect is profound.

If
large-scale building with wood
is developed city by city
creating thousands of local jobs and businesses

then
giga-tons of CO_2 are retained
reducing greenhouse gases
at close to planetary scale

A grand synthesis needs to be designed
and put on the ground
Many parts are in place
Industry, knowledge, science
with the exception of a viable market
yet all are separate
each happening in a different place

We propose a new category entitled
Whole Systems Sites
where a grand synthesis can occur

A guiding metaphor appears
Assisting adaptation
is
collaboration with nature
and business as usual
becomes finding a niche in the Life Web

Such a site, 20,000 acres or much larger
with a scientific community ensuring
the health of the forest, its ground plane
and all dependent species

twinned with the ecological imperative
are production, manufacturing,
and distribution facilities
for forest products

And it is clear to all participants
that all aspects of this work
contribute to the continuing
of the whole systems site
while conferring benefit on those
who work there

Taking a 50-year view, the 1.5 billion dollars a year
spent for fire control adds up to 75 billion dollars.

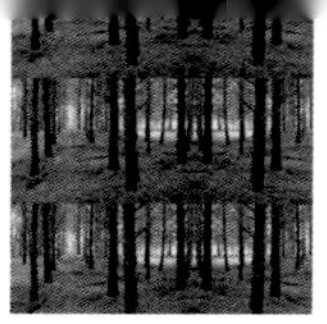

**If one billion extra is spent yearly for 15 years to thin forests
causing the fire costs to normalize over 15 million acres
then after these 15 years the cost of fire repression
reduces drastically and the majority of California forests are
saved**

**Taking this larger view,
the savings come to about 37.5 billion dollars.
Yet, we discover that no one wants to spend the extra
15 billion**

**Finally, in the prior year, the hottest year in this state's history,
over 500,000 acres burned.
Not accounting for increasing heat and drought,
in 10 years, at least 3 million acres will burn
and in 50 years,
all 15 million fire-endangered acres
in the state of California will burn
Saving 15 billion dollars but at a cost of 75 billion dollars,
and for what?**

And let us remember

**Before second settlement
redundancy and diversity were the norm
with millions of square miles as the field of play**

And let us remember

the forest floor acted as a carbon sink

and let us remember

the forest floor was a habitat for many

and let us remember

that waters were abundant but not everywhere

and let us remember

the meadow life was abundant as well

**In the largest sense
taking responsibility at this scale
which finally reaches whole systems status
is imperative
as it is the only way
to virtually eliminate the threat
of catastrophic fires,
to reduce greenhouse gases
in large amounts
reducing the intensity of the
changing climate's curve
while increasing biodiversity
and the availability of water
and mediating at the million square mile scale
the effects of a sixth mass extinction
which is now upon us[24]**

Outlined in poetic form, the Harrisons' practical plan envisions how to reduce fires throughout the western states, preserve water supplies and wildlife habitat, create new industries, bring jobs to revitalize dying communities, and build tourism, among other optimistic possibilities. The *Saving the West* works demonstrated an ecological artistic practice suitable for the Anthropocene, the modern era where pressure on all planetary systems from global warming, caused directly by human industrial activity, is alarming and frightening. The Harrisons showed that concerted efforts and vast research must be invested in the design of future ecologies that could be able to function in such new temperature regimes and ecosystem conditions.

1 Allen, Jane Ingram, "How Big is Here: A Conversation with Helen Mayer Harrison and Newton Harrison," *Sculpture magazine*, Vol. 26, No. 10, December 2007, pp. 48–53.

2 Harrison, Helen Mayer, and Newton Harrison, *The Time of the Force Majeure: After 45 Years Counterforce is on the Horizon*, edited and designed by Petra Kruse and Kai Reschke. Prestel, Munich, London, New York, 2016, p. 235.

3 Ibid., pp. 230–243.

4 Materials in the archive document the progression of the project in detail: files contain exhibition catalogues, correspondence, proposed project descriptions, exhibition information, maps, meeting notes, posters, photographic material, press, research, schedules, and text for this project. See: Series 2, Project Files, Subseries 40, Serpentine Lattice, Box 73–76. Helen and Newton Harrison Papers, M1797. Special Collections & University Archives, Stanford University, Stanford, CA, consulted in October–December 2021.

5 Harrison, Helen Mayer, and Newton Harrison, *The Time of the Force Majeure: After 45 Years Counterforce is on the Horizon*, p. 232.

6 Ibid., pp. 232–233.

7 Most of the slides came from Professor Trygve Steen, who was credited as co-producer with the Harrisons of the photomural. Steen assembled and allowed the artists to access his archive of more than 20,000 aerial images of Pacific Northwest Forest. The Alaskan photographs were taken by Robert Glen Ketchum.

8 The experience of viewing the original installation is narrated by the exhibition curator in her catalogue essay: Susan Fillen-Yeh, "The Serpentine Lattice: Where You Said a Lattice and I Said a Serpentine and You Said Network the Watersheds and I Said a Game of Go," *The Serpentine Lattice,* exh. cat. Douglas F. Cooley Memorial Art Gallery, Reed College, Portland, OR, 1993, pp. 16–23, 23. The catalogue and its typescript are preserved in the archive, see: Box 73, Folder 15, Series 2, Project Files, Subseries 40, Serpentine Lattice, Box 73–76. Helen and Newton Harrison Papers, M1797. Special Collections & University Archives, Stanford University, Stanford, CA, consulted in October–December 2021.

9 Harrison, Helen Mayer, and Newton Harrison, *The Time of the Force Majeure: After 45 Years Counterforce is on the Horizon*, p. 233.

10 Green, Charles, "Memory and Ethics: Helen Mayer Harrison and Newton Harrison," *The Third Hand: Collaboration in Art from Conceptualism to Postmodernism*, University of Minnesota Press, 2001, pp. 97–122, 114, http://www.jstor.org/stable/10.5749/j.ctttsbj7.9, accessed July 2022.

11 See: Box 73, Folder 15, Series 2, Project Files, Subseries 40, Serpentine Lattice, Box 73–76. Helen and Newton Harrison Papers, M1797. Special Collections & University Archives, Stanford University, Stanford, CA, consulted in October–December 2021.

12 Harrison, Helen Mayer, and Newton Harrison, *The Time of the Force Majeure: After 45 Years Counterforce is on the Horizon*, pp. 234–235.

13 Hartney, Eleanor, "Helen and Newton Harrison's Serpentine Lattice." Exhibition brochure, Hutton Gallery, Colorado State University, January 31–March 3, 2000. See: Box 73, Folder 15, Series 2, Project Files, Subseries 40, Serpentine Lattice, Box 73–76. Helen and Newton Harrison Papers, M1797. Special Collections & University Archives, Stanford University, Stanford, CA, consulted in October–December 2021.

14 The letter to Ricki Seidman, the Policy Adviser to President Clinton, is preserved in the archives, see Box 76, Folder 8. The story is also recounted in the book by Helen Mayer Harrison and Newton Harrison, *The Time of the Force Majeure: After 45 Years Counterforce is on the Horizon*, p. 241.

15 Solnit, Rebecca, "Art in Its Ecological Context," *Artweek Focus*, 21, No. 3, 5 April 1980, p. 20. See: Box 73, Folder 15, Series 2, Project Files, Subseries 40, Serpentine Lattice, Box 73–76. Helen and Newton Harrison Papers, M1797. Special Collections & University Archives, Stanford University, Stanford, CA, consulted in October–December 2021.

16 Fillen-Yeh, Susan, "The Serpentine Lattice: Where You Said a Lattice and I Said a Serpentine and You Said Network the Watersheds and I Said a Game of Go," p. 22.

17 Harrison, Helen Mayer, and Newton Harrison, *The Time of the Force Majeure: After 45 Years Counterforce is on the Horizon*, p. 374.

18 Ibid.

19 Ibid., p. 377.

20 The *Saving the West* video work eventually furnished the title for the entire series and for the current exhibition at the San Diego Central Library Art Gallery, a part of *Helen and Newton Harrison: California Work*.

21 The proposal is in the Harrison personal digital archive that was shared with the author; all documents are dated to July 2010.

22 The proposal is in the Harrison personal digital archive that was shared with the author; all documents are dated to July 2010. Map imagery in the exhibition was generated with the assistance of the Nevada-based Desert Research Institute (DRI).

23 Mapping for the video was developed by the Harrisons' studio associates, including Leslie Ryan, Matthew Jamieson, and Heidi Cramer; Pacific Northwest imagery was provided by Trygve Steen; Sagehen imagery was provided by Jeff Brown, Sagehen Creek Field Station Director, and Faerthen Felix, Sagehen Station Manager.

24 The text is provided by the Harrison Family Trust, accessed by the author in the digital archive as part of this research. The text file is dated to August 2016. Accessed August 22, 2022.

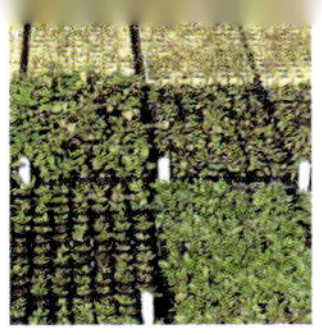

Future Gardens TATIANA SIZONENKO

For the Force Majeure is at work
With accelerated global warming
Working in collaboration
With accelerated industrial processes
Co-entangled over
The past 100 years
And beginning
To experience exponential growth.
From *Tibet the High Ground*[1]

We're most interested in bringing forth a new state of mind, first in ourselves, then hopefully in others – that is what our work is about. But this is difficult to measure: sometimes it happens slowly and takes a long time.
Helen Mayer Harrison.[2]

"The greatest difficulty in this new beginning
Is not so much the research required
Or the science or the experimental design
In which concept and design can be tested in small patches
Rather it is overcoming the inertial properties
Embedded in the major cultural forces that define
Most human behavior toward our life-support systems
They are
Democracy and capitalism
Technocracy and some religions
For this level of experimentation to succeed
All must yield agency enforceable by law
To the lives that are not ourselves
Dare we say Nature or better yet, the Life Web."
From *Peninsula Europe: Part II, III, and IV* (2007–2008).[3]

Beginning in the 2000s, propelled by a prophetic vision of rising sea levels and global emergencies associated with climate change, Helen and Newton Harrison started to work on a planetary scale. First introduced in *San Diego as the Center of a World* (1974), the theme of accelerating global warming and its potential catastrophic impact on ecosystems was expanded in the ending of the *Lagoon Cycle* (1972–1984). In subsequent works, the Harrisons raised major metaphysical questions in their accompanying poetic dialogues, conjuring up new possibilities for saving the planet during threatening times. Advocating for various forms of restoration and reclamation, the Harrisons developed a graceful philosophy urging humanity to get back into synchronism with natural processes – what they called the Web of Life. The artists would create what would be their final set of works, which they conceived as part of the Force Majeure series and entitled *Future Gardens*. Viewing *Future Gardens* as fundamental to their Survival Art, the Harrisons expressed their hope of saving the planet in the face of the threat that climate change posed to Earth's many ecosystems. At the heart of this final proposal lies the belief that the human race must abandon the unsustainable economic model and retreat into a new world based on the supportable uses of land and resources. In different works from this late period, the artists variously describe a new culture of so-called "eco-civility" based on "ecosystemic thinking as opposed to typical development models."[4]

The final arc of their career is anchored by the 2004 relocation of the Harrison Studio from La Jolla to Santa Cruz. In 2010, UC Santa Cruz appointed them as research professors, creating the possibility of establishing the Center for the Study of the Force Majeure (2012–current), which would bring artists and scientists together to design ecosystem-adaptation projects in response to climate change in critical regions around the world. Two major internationally exhibited works from this period – the *Peninsula Europe* (2001–2007 & 2012) and the *Greenhouse Britain* (2007–2009) – advanced the Harrisons' discourse on global warming and preemptive adaptation or, as they put it, "how we go about the business of adjusting to change."[5] Addressing catastrophic environmental impacts, these two bioregional examples laid out both philosophical and practical thinking to ameliorate such consequences locally, as well as to enact short- and long-range planning for life adaptation.[6] Engaged in finding ecological solutions to complex, politically charged problems, the Harrisons started to realize the full scope of their ambitions.

A monumental, multi-part work exhibited internationally in Germany, France, Holland, and the United States, *Peninsula Europe* proposed a large-scale transformation of the entire European landscape by means of re-terraforming the land to hold water as it once did naturally. Revised several times, the work addressed a range of possibilities, from the upward migration of species and people and the regeneration of forest ecosystems to predictions of the loss of coastal land due to ocean rise and the loss of farmland due to extreme drought. *Greenhouse Britain* offered yet another vision, in this case how the United Kingdom itself would be uniquely affected by accelerated global warming. Three different scenarios of five-meter ocean water rise, 10-meter ocean water rise, and 15-meter ocean water rise showed how long-range planning would assist in managing the inevitable upward migration of the population. The artists' projections and accompanying texts educated the audience about the implications of water rise, storm surges, and the need for just such long-term strategies.

While working on *Peninsula Europe* and *Greenhouse Britain*, the Harrisons considered planetary ecosystems and concluded that "an energy-consuming explosion and the runaway economic development" had unleashed a great force previously invisible to them.[7] They named this the *Force Majeure* and held the human race responsible for bringing it into being. They adopted the legal term, which refers to circumstances (often natural disasters) beyond the control of the parties involved, to describe the state of our planet. With mass extinction now a real possibility, the *Force Majeure* works laid out a framework for a new ecological art practice in the Anthropocene, exploring how humanity might cope with the probability of extreme stress on ecosystems worldwide. Helen and Newton proposed that artists be involved in collaborations with teams of biologists, climate scientists, urban planners, and other experts to redesign culture in anticipation of global environmental impacts that would set off corresponding human disasters. In *A Manifesto for the Twenty First Century*, commissioned as an outcome of the CIWEM Prize for *Greenhouse Britain*,[8] the Harrisons called for the concerted efforts and vast investment in research that would be needed to design future ecologies that could sustain life in the new temperature regimes and ecosystem conditions.

... We at the Center assert
That the Force Majeure, framed ecologically
Enacts, in physical terms, outcomes on the ground
All that we have created in the global landscape
Bringing together the conditions that have accelerated
global warming

THE GARDEN OF HOT WINDS AND WARM RAINS

IT IS A MULTI-LAYERED STORY TOLD WITH ARTIFACTS, MEDIA EVENTS, TEXTS, AND LIVING MATERIALS, WHICH ALL TOGETHER ENGAGE THE PROBABLE GREENHOUSE FUTURE DIRECTLY. IT IS A WORK OF ART THAT WILL BE GARDEN, PREDICTION, AND PROMENADE, A VOYAGE OF SORTS, MAINLY ENCLOSED IN A GLASS "GREEN HOUSE" TO MAINTAIN A CLIMATE CONSISTENT WITH THE SUPPOSED 5 TO 6 DEGREE CENTIGRADE RISE IN TEMPERATURE OVER THE NEXT 100-150 YEARS. THUS, THE GLASS HOUSE BECOMES THE VEHICLE FOR MAKING THE PHENOMENON OF THE GREENHOUSE EFFECT AND CERTAIN OF THE POSSIBLE FUTURES, THAT IT WILL ENGENDER, DIRECTLY ACCESSIBLE TO THE HUMAN SENSES.
THE VISITOR IS TAKEN THROUGH A NUMBER OF INSTALLATIONS THAT COMPRISE THE NARRATIVE. THE STAGE SET FOR THIS IS A SERIES OF POSSIBLE FUTURES THAT HAVE THEIR SOURCES IN SUCH CONCERNS AS: THE GREENHOUSE EFFECT, THE ENDANGERING OF THE FORESTS OF THE WORLD, THE REPLACEMENT OF FORESTS AND MEADOWS BY A MONOLITHIC MONO-CULTURAL AGRICULTURE AND THE VAST LOSS OF BIO-DIVERSITY IN THE OCEANIC AND TERRESTRIAL ECO-SYSTEMS.

THE TWO MAIN INSTALLATIONS WILL SHOW A SUBTROPICAL FUTURE CLIMATE SUCH AS MIGHT EXIST IN ANY TEMPERATE CLIMATE, AS THE GREENHOUSE EFFECT BECOMES MORE EVIDENT. BOTH THESE FUTURES ASSUME THAT THE WEATHER HAS WARMED AND THE OCEANS HAVE RISEN. HOWEVER, ONE FUTURE REPRESENTS AN ARID WORLD AND THE OTHER A HUMID ONE WITH HEAVY RAINFALL. IN BOTH FUTURES THE INTRINSIC VALUE OF BIO-DIVERSITY IS RECOGNIZED.

THESE FUTURES WILL LOOK TO THE PAST AS WELL AS THE PRESENT FOR INFORMATION. THAT IS TO SAY THE FLORA WILL BE DRAWN FROM THE MEMBERS, OR THEIR EXISTING RELATIVES, OF THE LIFE WEB THAT PREVAILED DURING PERIODS OF EQUIVALENT TEMPERATURE IN THE PLIOCENE ERA, THE TIME BEFORE THE LAST GREAT GLACIATON THAT RESULTED IN A MASSIVE LOSS OF SPECIES. AND SPECIES WILL BE DRAWN FROM PLACES THAT ARE NOW EXPERIENCING CLIMATE CONDITIONS EQUIVALENT TO THOSE THAT ARE PREDICTED.

THE TASK WE SET FOR THIS WORK IS THE EXPLORATION OF ECO-CULTURAL COLLABORATIONS THAT WOULD MAKE FOR A FUTURE NO LONGER BASED ON EXTRACTION. THUS, BOTH HUMID AND ARID GARDENS WILL MODEL THE PRODUCTION OF FOOD FOR HUMAN CONSUMPTION, WHILE SIMULTANEOUSLY CREATING, ENHANCING AND SUSTAINING A COMPLEX INTERDEPENDENT ECOSYSTEM. THE PRIMARY OBJECTIVE BEING THAT THE HARVEST WILL PRESERVE THE SYSTEM RATHER THAN DEPLETE IT.

THEREFORE THESE GARDENS LOOK AT WHAT A FUTURE COULD BE LIKE IF CONSCIOUS, MUTUALLY BENEFICIAL COLLABORATIONS BETWEEN HUMAN CULTURES (CIVILIZATIONS IN ALL THEIR COMPLEXITY) AND THE CULTURES OF NATURE (THE LIFE WEBS COMPLICATING AND DIVERSIFYING UP TO THE SPACE AND ENERGY AVAILABLE) BECAME A NORM.

HOWEVER, WITHIN THESE POSITIVE FUTURES, A SERIES OF UNCOMFORTABLE, SOMETIMES SHOCKING GLIMPSES OF OTHER POSSIBLE FUTURES WILL APPEAR IN SMALL GREENHOUSES. IN SUM, THIS WILL BE A PHYSICAL AND METAPHORICAL EXCURSION THROUGH POSSIBLE FUTURES WHERE THE VISITORS WILL EXPERIENCE THE EXPECTED AND THE TOTALLY SURPRISING, THE HUMOROUS, THE TRAGIC AND EMPIRICAL AS WELL AS THE PLAYFULL.

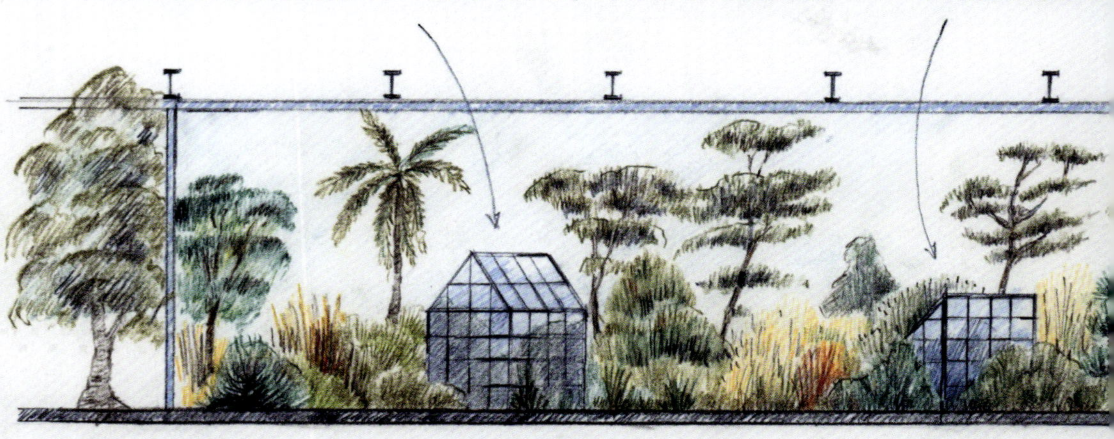

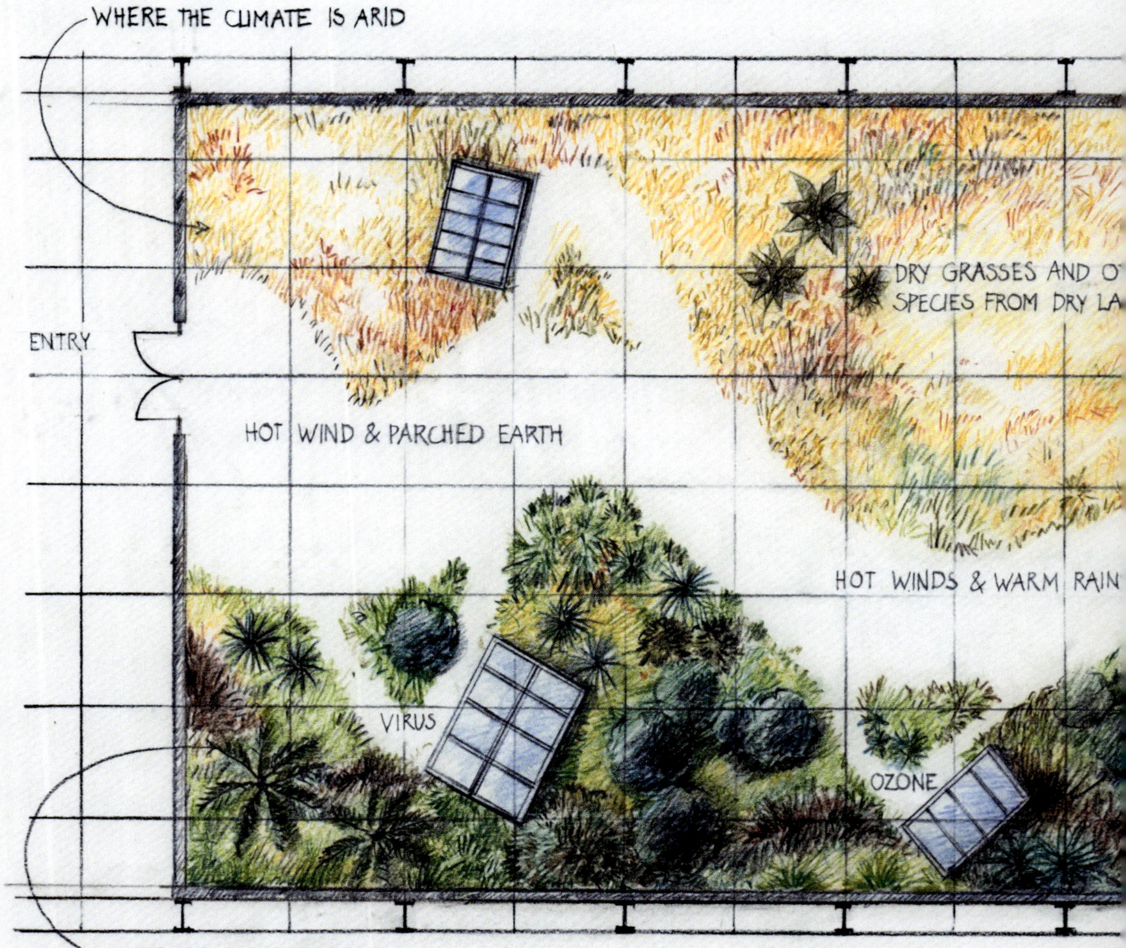

A COMMISSIONED PROPOSAL BY THE KUN

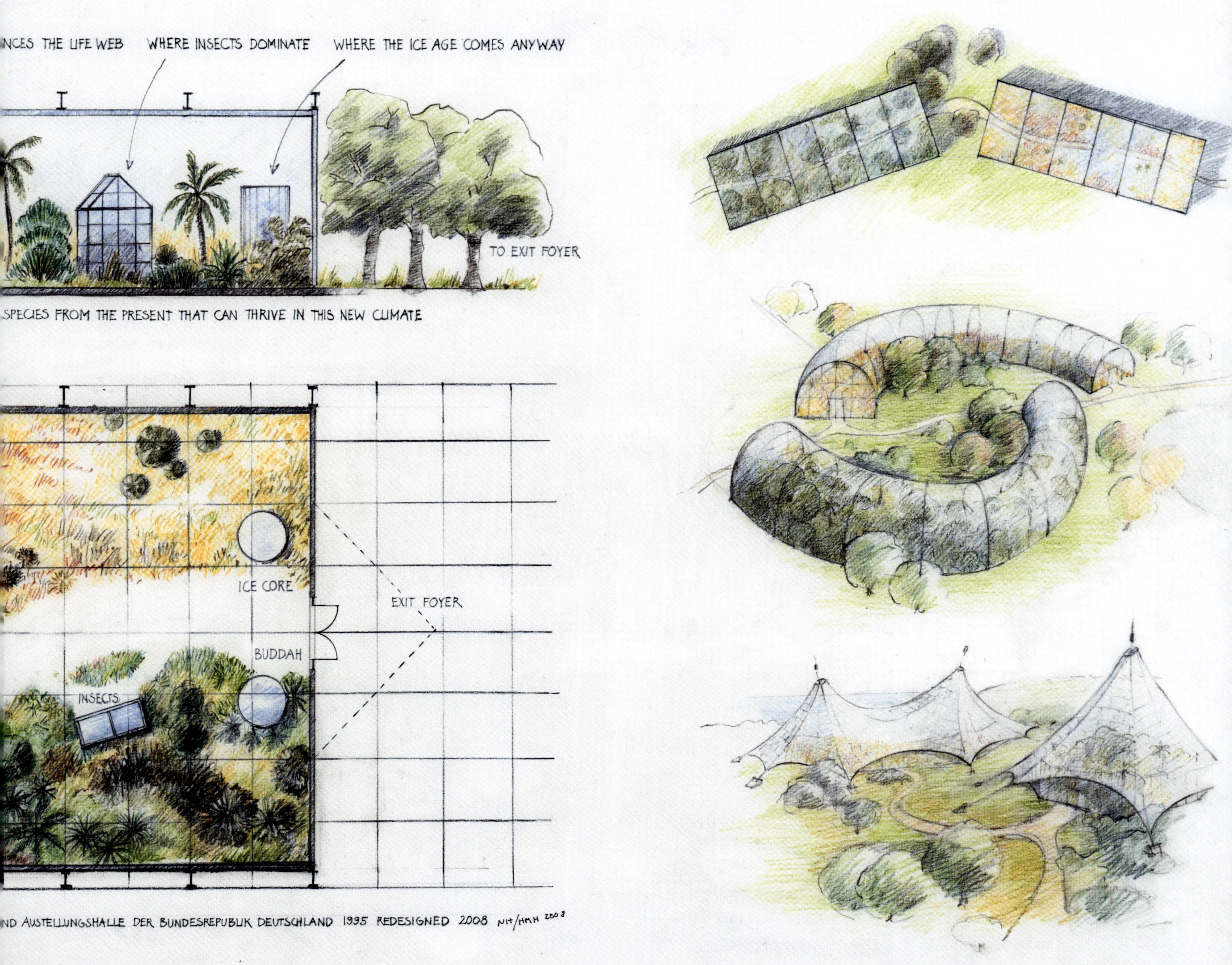
NCES THE LIFE WEB
WHERE INSECTS DOMINATE
WHERE THE ICE AGE COMES ANYWAY
TO EXIT FOYER
SPECIES FROM THE PRESENT THAT CAN THRIVE IN THIS NEW CLIMATE
ICE CORE
EXIT FOYER
BUDDAH
INSECTS
ND AUSTELLUNGSHALLE DER BUNDESREPUBLIK DEUTSCHLAND 1995 REDESIGNED 2008 NH/HMH 2008

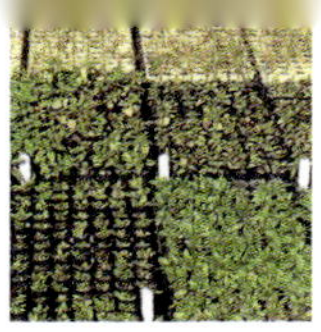

Acting in concert with the massive industrial processes
of extraction, production, and consumption
That have subtracted forests, and depleted topsoil
And profoundly reduced ocean productivity
While creating a vast chemical outpouring into the atmosphere
Onto the lands and within the waters
That all together constitute this Force Majeure
Initiating what might become the sixth mass extinction …

Look to the advancing of glaciers
The yielding of ecosystems
The increasing of uniformity over millions of square kilometers
Then look to the retreating of glaciers
The advancing of succession ecosystems
more able in warmer environments
to increase local energies available for emergent systems
to do work
over millions of square kilometers
Yes, counterforces can be found easily enough
Harnessing them and co-creating with them
For the common good is the urgency at hand

So we at the Center conclude
That counterforces are available
That can in some measure mitigate a possible 6th mass extinction
But unless created over the next 50 years
or much less
Civil society in many places will experience perturbation,
then collapse
Keeping company with ecosystems
Experiencing perturbation and then simplification.[9]

ART AS A CROSS-DISCIPLINARY RE-TERRAFORMING PRACTICE

On the deep timescale of evolution, the Harrisons recognized, humans were a relatively recent phenomenon and "our species' reign on Earth inevitably had an expiration date, just like all other dominant species that had come and gone before us."[10] Therefore, better adaptation strategies were needed than those previously outlined in the *Survival Pieces* (1971–1972). *Future Gardens* is a series of systems-thinking solutions that anticipates global impacts and demands corresponding adaptation.[11] Using drawings, large-scale maps, poetic texts, and living ensembles of plants, *The Garden of Hot Winds and Warm Rains* (1994–2008), *Tibet as a High Ground* (2007–2012), *Sagehen: A Proving Ground* (2011–ongoing, in the High Sierras near Tahoe), and *Future Garden for the Central Coast of California* (2018–ongoing, at the Arboretum at UC Santa Cruz) outlined a sequence of counterproposals to the projected impacts of rising temperatures, the loss of snowpack causing extreme drought, and other abrupt environmental changes. As described in the accompanying poetic narratives, these proposals involved re-terraforming, through the assisted migration of species to higher altitudes and latitudes and through experimentation with species better able to adapt to hotter temperatures:

The Future Gardens
A growing body of work
addressing a new frontier
A heat wave touching all surfaces
Everyplace, everywhere, everything
That is growing is changing
As temperatures warm
That which grows must move elsewhere
Or fade from existence
Yet everyplace, everywhere
At one time or another
has warmed or cooled or burned
Always there is opportunity
In fact, Every place
is the story of its own becoming.

Where Every Place is the Story of its Own Becoming
Simply put
Where ecosystems fade

unable to continue
Unable to maintain coherence
In the face of rapidly rising temperatures
A question is asked and then answered
Is it possible to propagate the future ecosystem
The future grouping of species that will self-complicate
And introduce it
Even as the existing system fades from stress
So rapidly assisting migration
That hundreds, even thousands of years
Work by the Life Web to reassert itself
are collapsed into decades.[12]

Early prototypes of *Future Gardens* first appeared in 1994–1995 as sketches, drawings, and blueprints of their proposed greenhouse in Frankfurt/Main, when the Harrisons were invited to work in the Kunst- und Ausstellungshalle der Bundesrepublik Deutschland in Bonn. The Harrison Studio developed an elaborate design for a quite tall greenhouse, approximately 3.7 to 4.3 meters in height, which would cover the museum's perimeter walk, six meters wide. The artists collaborated with the paleobotanist Wilhelm Barthlott, director of the Botanical Institute and Botanical Gardens at the University of Bonn, and two of his graduate students to investigate what could live in the region if the temperature rose approximately three degrees Celsius. The proposal outlined three possible futures – *The Sisyphus Garden*, *The Garden of Extreme Measures*, and *The Garden of Hot Winds and Warm Rains* – to describe the expected climate and to create an experience that would "help others picture the outcome of these complex events" by letting visitors walk through the structure in a climate consistent with the supposed rise in temperature.[13] Given the exorbitant price tag of several million deutschmarks, the museum director Wenzel Jacob cancelled the greenhouse plan, deeming it unattainable. However, this work exists today as a beautiful color drawing, *The Garden of Hot Winds and Warm Rains* (1995/2008), completed by Vera Westergaard and Gabriel Harrison, then artist-associates of the Harrison Studio. This drawing depicts just two possible futures: one ecosystem based upon a warm, dry landscape, the other on a warm, wet landscape, and both imagined in the next 100 years, when the weather has heated up and the oceans have risen. The idea of this future garden was to explore "an eco-cultural collaboration," in which "the garden produced food for human consumption in a complex interdependent ecosystem."[14] *The Garden of Hot Winds and Warm Rains* was envisioned next to the companion art work *The Endangered Meadows of Europe* (1994–1998), a so-called representational field sculpture exhibiting wet, dry, and stone meadows that would speak to the changes in agricultural practices associated with the loss of biodiversity and the tradition of meadows.

The Endangered Meadows of Europe became the sole installation of the German endeavor, taking up over 40,000 square feet at the center of the museum rooftop. Although the meadowlands of Europe are a comparatively recent phenomenon, the Harrisons became very interested in this kind of agriculture as a model for profitable and spontaneous collaboration between people and nature. In consultation with Martin Schneider-Jacoby, who had previously worked with the Harrisons on the Sava River project, the artists designed a series of narratives about European meadows, displayed as a living, continuously changing color field. In the process of working on this installation, the Harrisons were introduced to Wolfgang Schumacher, a professor of geobotany and specialist in meadows. He knew of a 400-year-old meadow, a little more than hundred kilometers away in the Eifel region, that was slated to be lost to a major road development. Instead of letting it be destroyed, the artists decided to save this green space and had it transplanted it to the museum roof. The resulting living meadow exhibition was accompanied by structures erected on the path of the surrounding grassland to display a series of many-layered stories showing tile images of 15 meadows from other parts of Europe, complemented with poetic texts narrating conversations between the artists, scientists, and meadow masters, as well as

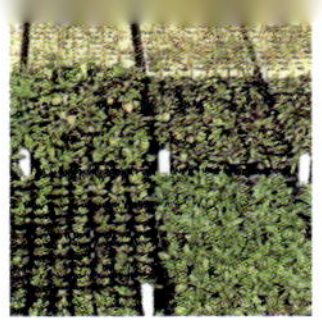

the history and cultural function of meadows.[15] *The Endangered Meadows of Europe* was extremely successful and gave voice to a unique element of the continent's cultural landscape. By transplanting and saving this 400-year-old green space, the Harrison Studio told the story of the meadows and their value as models of cooperation between human needs and a biologically diverse habitat.[16]

The completed parts of *The Endangered Meadows of Europe* brought to life issues of biodiversity and inspired the planting of *A Mother Meadow for Bonn*, which was created from the transplanted Eifel meadow and seeds from the rooftop garden. When the original exhibition ran its course, the living rooftop was transferred to the park along the Rhine River in Bonn, while seeds were also spread in other local parks, thus impacting the green infrastructure of the entire city, increasing biodiversity while reducing the use and cost of mowing, fertilizer, and weed killer. This happened two years after the work was installed on the rooftop, and the director of the parks of Bonn himself made the request that led to these positive environmental outcomes, which embodied the greater design and intent of the Harrisons' work: *The Garden of Hot Winds and Warm Rains* and *The Endangered Meadows of Europe* modelled an interdependent system of ecologies radically different from modern-day industrial practices. The Harrisons realized a harmonious eco-cultural collaboration between human cultures (civilization) and the cultures of nature (the Life Web), presenting a future that was no longer based on extraction but on practices of production that sustained rather than depleted interdependent ecosystems.

Newton Harrison called *The Endangered Meadows of Europe* the first step in developing the body of work he dubbed *Future Gardens* and, in his interviews, he often reflected that it was "an esthetic experience and a scientific product as well." In the catalogue for *The Endangered Meadows of Europe*, he wrote that "artists do, in fact, mainly work intuitively, often in a state of not knowing, or almost knowing. Therefore, it is not possible or even desirable to know the full implications

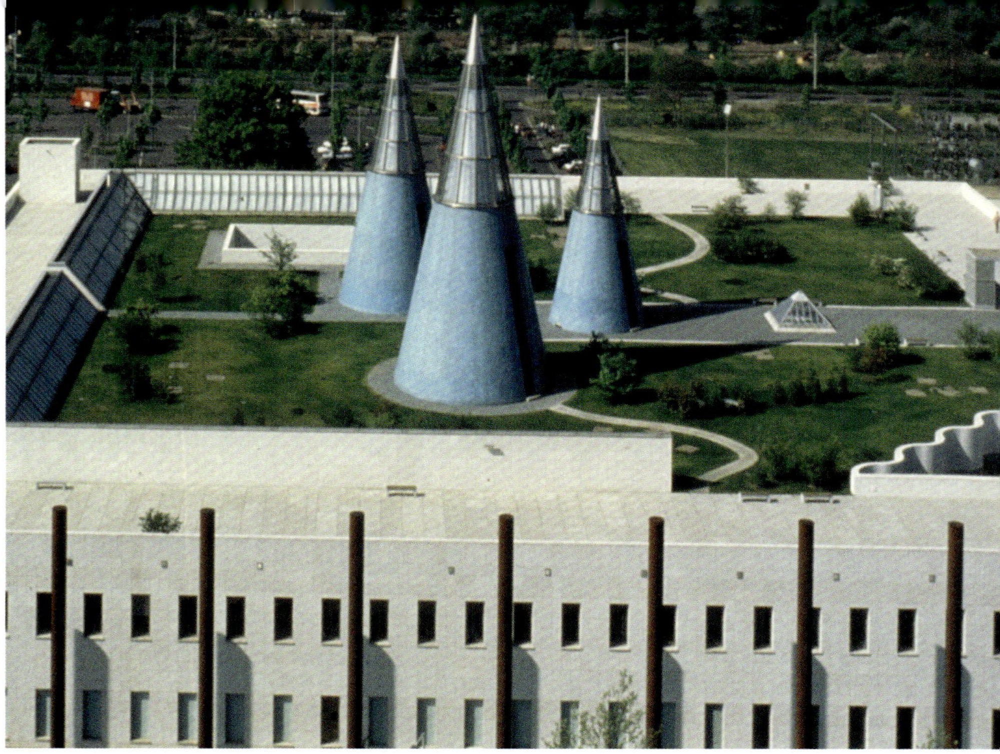

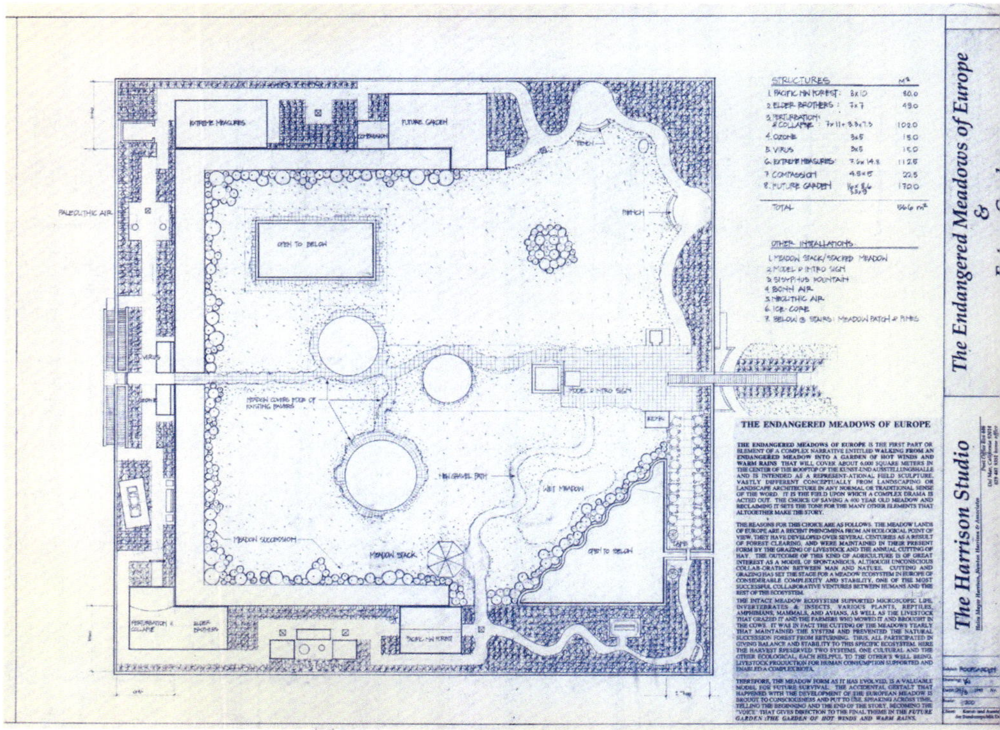

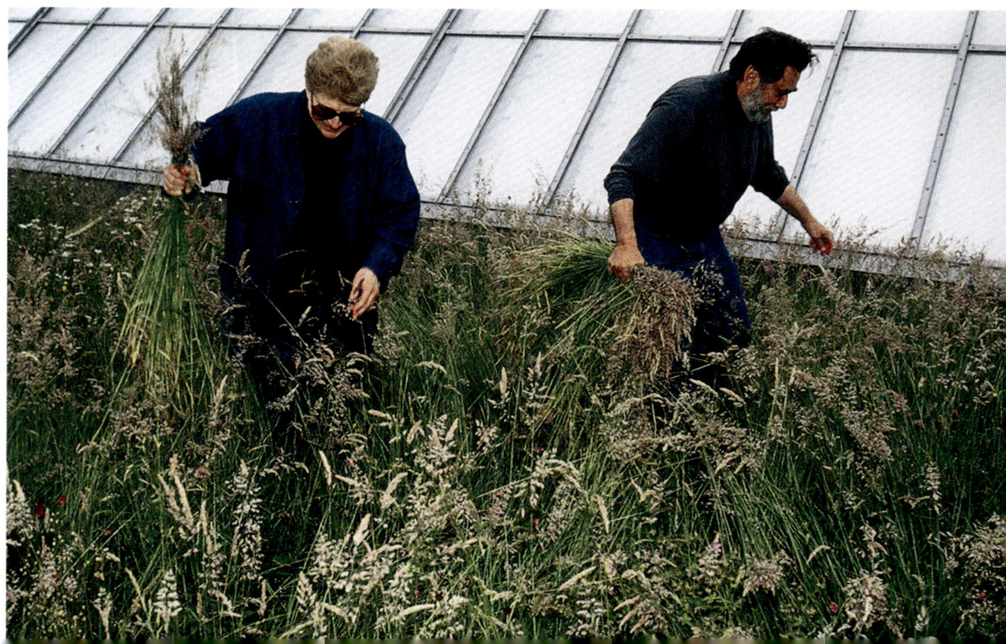

of a work until considerable time has passed. In other words, the process of art making guarantees that the artist will not know the full content of what he or she has done. This is what is meant by working at the edge of awareness. Therefore, retrospective analysis often enriches future work."[17]

Tibet is the High Ground (1991/1993 & 2007–2012) is another work with a complex backstory that Newton Harrison later viewed as an important example of a *Future Garden* dealing with preemptive planning and the assisted migration of species. Commissioned and first shown in 1993, *Tibet is the High Ground* is a response to the Dalai Lama's personal request to help him design a Peace Park on the Tibetan Plateau.[18] Studying watersheds of seven major rivers – the Indus, Yellow, Yangtze, Salween, Mekong, Brahma Putra and Ganges – that nourish much of China and Asia, the Harrisons discovered that the mass cutting of forests in the Himalayas had caused erosion and dramatically reduced the purity of the rivers and their ecological well-being. In response to this, the Harrisons chose not to develop the Peace Park but instead advocated for a transnational group to be formed to save the rivers and then proposed an entirely new work exploring the idea of an "analogue" forest to replace the over-cut woodlands. Even though the analogue forest would be only 20 percent as complex as the original depleted ecosystem, it would behave in much the same way. Its future survival would be aided by the presence of species most useful to man if harvested selectively:

"To develop a conceptual model that envisions a probable Life Web for the deforested area of Tibet. This ecological model, working with the idea of an analog forest, or a simplified wood-land-rainforest ecosystem, would also have yields of recognizable value to those who inhabit the surrounds. The process would suggest an analog for the forest that once existed, less complex than the original, but nonetheless with overstory, understory, canopy, and appropriate niches. This forest would also serve to conserve existing or replaced topsoil and protect riverine and wetland ecologies – first in Tibet proper, and then in the countries below."[19]

The final artwork created for *Tibet is the High Ground* in 1993, today referred to as Part I, was completed in the form of a world map on canvas showing Tibet, the "Roof of the World," renowned for its stunning snow-covered mountains, and an exquisite large pencil drawing of Tibet's glaciers and rivers, offering a lyrical meditation on the effects of global warming on snow-covered regions of Tibet.

In 2006 the Harrisons were invited to revisit their Tibet work and to contribute to a traveling exhibition titled *The Missing Peace: Artists Consider the Dalai Lama*. After complex negotiations with the curators, the Harrisons did a new Tibet work in three images and accompanying poetic text that was shown in seven exhibition venues across the country in 2007–2011.[20] This three-part work was further modified for *The Vanishing Ice Exhibition: Alpine and Polar Landscapes in Art, 1775–2012*, which appeared in three venues in the USA.[21] The final version of the triptych was published in 2016 in the Harrisons' book titled *The Time of the Force Majeure*.

Examining the effects of climate change in the Himalayas, the new Tibet work, or *Tibet Is the High Ground, Part II, III, and IV*, depicted the regions without political borders, proposing that the regional and national states in the area put aside political differences and unite their resources to counter the drastic deterioration of glacial melt. As a result of this rapid glacier reduction, rivers originating in the Tibet region will become much more erratic in their flow, since rainwater is much less predictable than slow and constant glacial melt.[22]

Freshwater shortages have been identified as potential sources of future conflict in the region. The artists drew attention to this well-documented diminishing glacial melt through a display of colorful, large-scale Mercator maps of the area, highlighting fifteen thousand glaciers that are the source of major rivers that provide sustenance for millions of people. The three large scale maps visualized the drastic transformation of Tibet resulting from the possible loss of snow coverage in the mountains, by depicting Tibet turning from

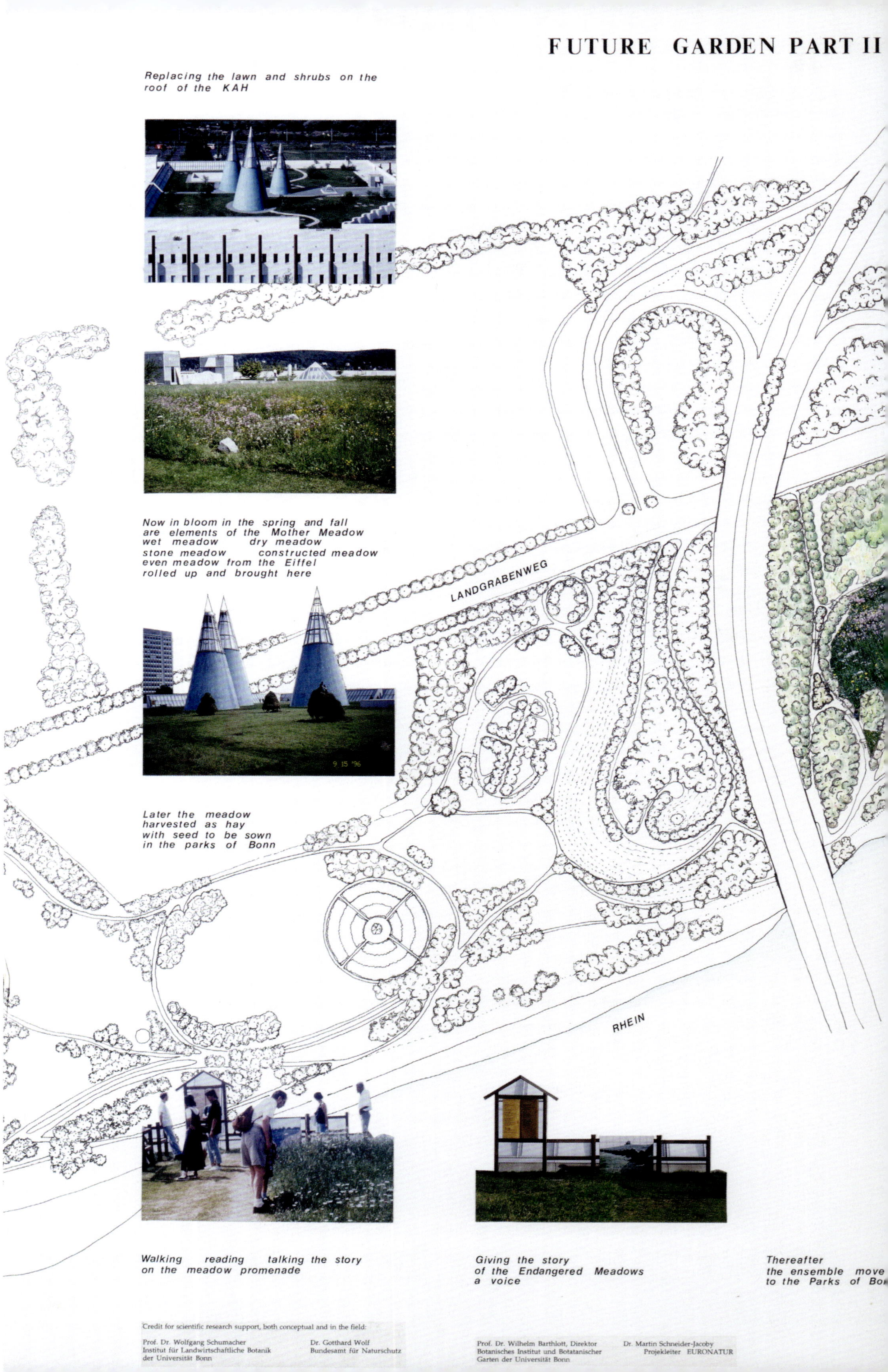
FUTURE GARDEN PART II
Replacing the lawn and shrubs on the roof of the KAH
Now in bloom in the spring and fall
are elements of the Mother Meadow
wet meadow dry meadow
stone meadow constructed meadow
even meadow from the Eiffel
rolled up and brought here
LANDGRABENWEG
Later the meadow
harvested as hay
with seed to be sown
in the parks of Bonn
RHEIN
Walking reading talking the story
on the meadow promenade
Giving the story
of the Endangered Meadows
a voice
Thereafter
the ensemble move
to the Parks of Bo
Credit for scientific research support, both conceptual and in the field:
Prof. Dr. Wolfgang Schumacher
Institut für Landwirtschaftliche Botanik
der Universität Bonn
Dr. Gotthard Wolf
Bundesamt für Naturschutz
Prof. Dr. Wilhelm Barthlott, Direktor
Botanisches Institut und Botatanischer
Garten der Universität Bonn
Dr. Martin Schneider-Jacoby
Projekleiter EURONATUR

MOTHER MEADOW FOR THE PARKS OF BONN

BY

NEWTON HARRISON

HELEN MAYER HARRISON

AND THE HARRISON STUDIO

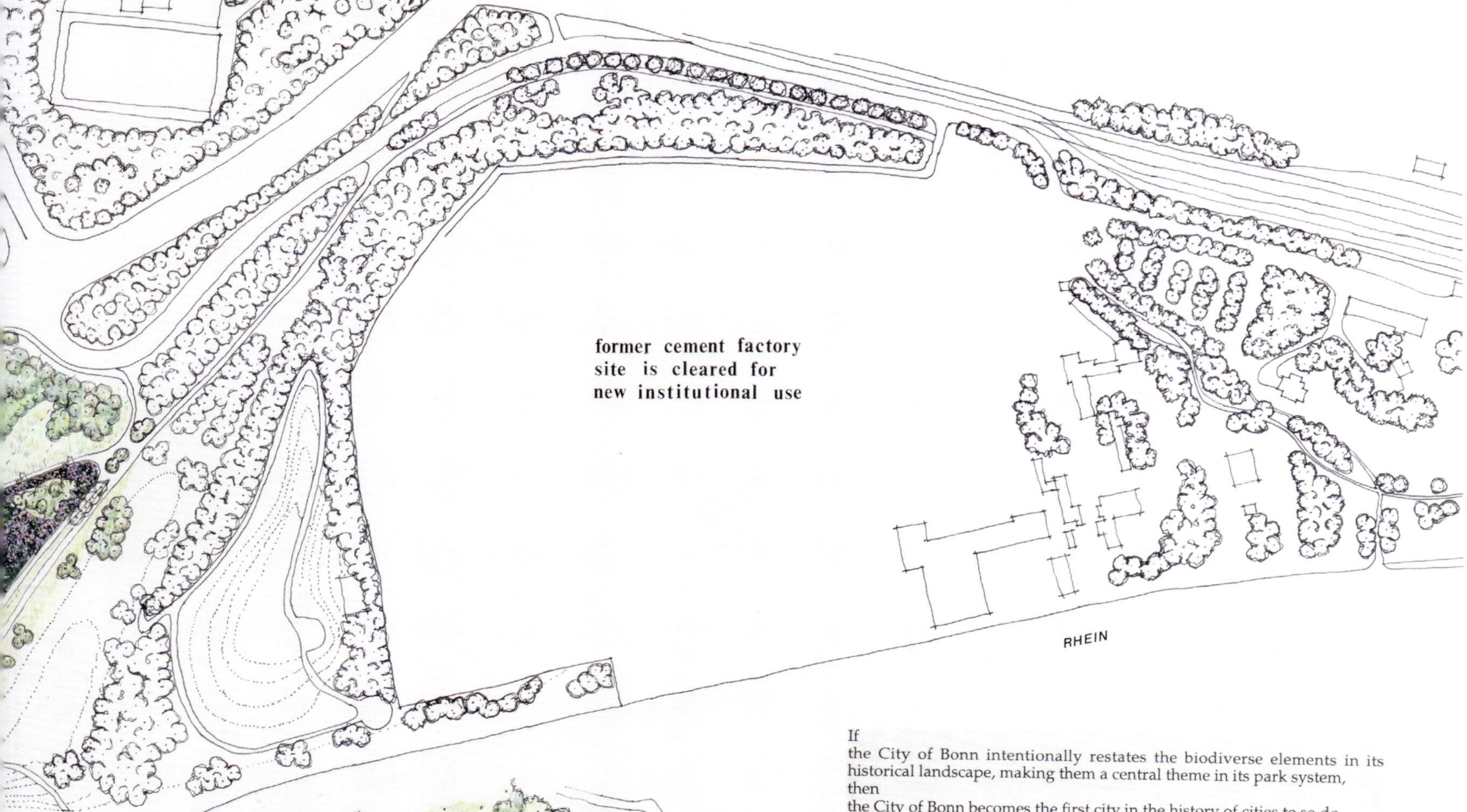

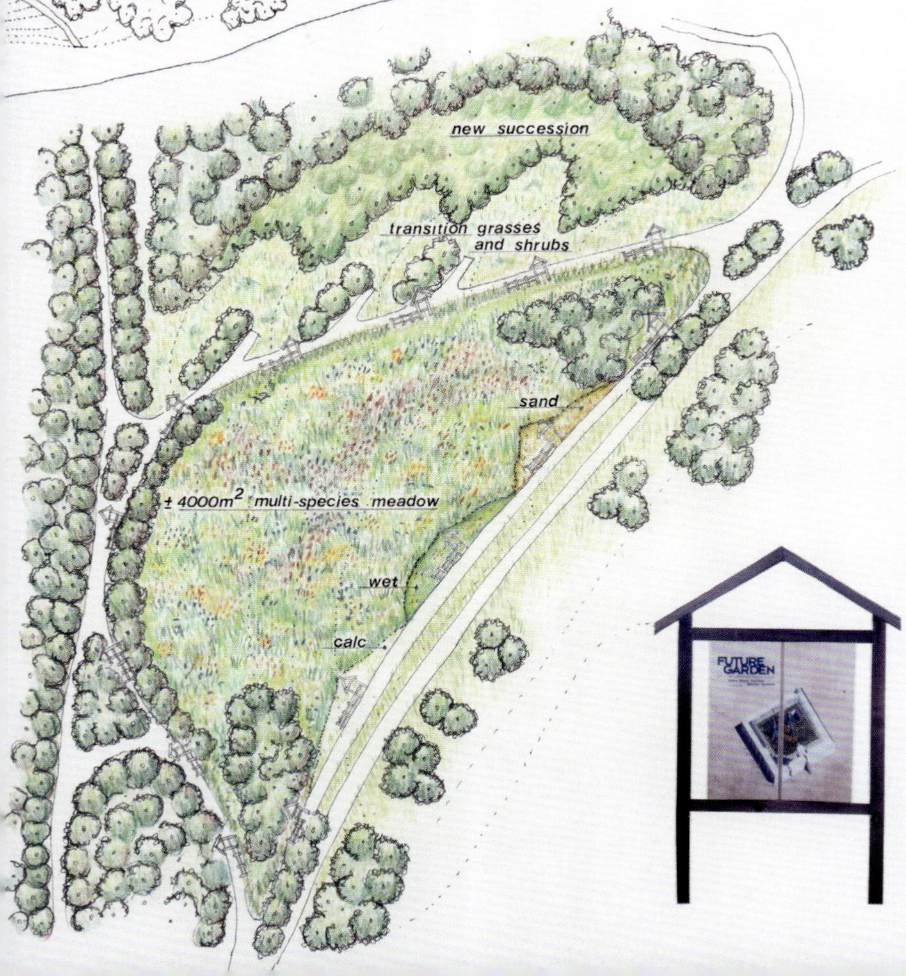

If
the City of Bonn intentionally restates the biodiverse elements in its historical landscape, making them a central theme in its park system,
then
the City of Bonn becomes the first city in the history of cities to so do.
And
this event comes to pass when the meadow on the roof of the Kunst-und Ausstellungshalle der Bundesrepublik Deutschland, entitled "Future Garden, Part 1: The Endangered Meadows of Europe" is both recycled and transformed into a new work, "Future Garden, Part 2: A Mother Meadow for the Parks of Bonn" situated in the park on the flood plain of the Rhine.

The work of art on the roof of the KAH became a collage of sorts, when four different meadow types were put together making one meadow, having a total count of about 180 different species. Thus, the garden meadow on the roof can be called a "Mother Meadow". The mother metaphor is used as this combination of seed from diverse places can birth diverse 'children' under widely differing circumstances.

In the parks of Bonn, the meadow's role enlarges. It becomes the seed bank for the transformation of much of the rest of the park grasslands into meadow. In some areas the meadow can associate with succession forest. When this happens a repeatable model is put in place where diverse meadow types, transition zones and succession forest areas can be established in any configuration. Thus biodiversity is enhanced and increased and the complexity of figure-ground relationships increased as the new design includes the meadow as field, and transition zones to succession forest/woodland as well as a new relationship between biodiverse areas and high use mono-culture areas. Moreover, in this new design, park maintenance costs are reduced as meadowlands require cutting only once or twice yearly and require no fertilization. Further, as, over time, the life web grows more complex, the aesthetic experience and educational value available in the great park system of Bonn will be available to all.

Thus, the work of "Future Garden, Part II", as it is repeated through the parks, expresses the metaphor, "A park is an echo of the values of the countryside in the city. It begins as an expression of the beliefs of its founders and continues as an expression of the concerns of those who follow them and of those who are responsible for its care."

And
this expression of concern can be seen as guiding the evolutiong of biodiversity in the city of Bonn for generations.

white to dark brown in Part II and Part III – the disaster of a cosmic proportion if it were to happen. Part IV presented the greening of Tibet as a viable solution to the problem at hand posed by global warming. Therefore, the artists not only drew attention to the impact of climate change on the region's water supply but also proposed a solution based on the adaptation and upward migration of species. Their principal idea involved reintroducing the forests and grasslands that had dominated an interglacial period thousands of years in the past when the climate was warmer. The specific plan was to "assist the migration of a palette of species" and to create "a 2 million square kilometer sponge to normalize rivers and secure the lands from flood and drought."[23]

Tibet is the High Ground boldly envisioned large ecosystems transcending national boundaries and presumed the substantial cross-disciplinary collaboration and transnational research that would be needed to support the greening of Tibet. Resurrecting the prophetic spirit of the Harrisons' early work, the Tibet proposal called for a new way to look at climate change. The artists asked the key question, "How could the Life Web adapt to survive since humanity is seemingly unable, or unwilling, to reverse the damage?"[24] The Tibet series engaged with the new global theme and employed the term Force Majeure to describe the urgency of the moment. The triptych continued the Harrisons' tradition of using art as a public forum and as a catalyst for conversation:

Research indicates on the Tibetan Plateau
glaciers will shrink so much
That their melting borders will dry up
Profoundly affecting
The Salween, MeKong, Huang-Ho
Brahmaputra, Yangtze, Ganges
And Indus River systems
That traverse inner Mongolia,
China, Tibet, Autonomous-zone India
Burma, Laos, Cambodia, South Vietnam,
Bangladesh, Kashmir and Pakistan
A Force Majeure has come into being
In the form of global warming
That will work to the disadvantage
Of 1/16th of the earth's population
Or about 1.2 billion people
Who live in the 7 drain Basins
That comprise over
2.4 million square miles

Thus we make an unlikely proposal
in this highly stressed probable future
by generating

the paleoecological research
in order to locate forest
And Savannah ecosystems
Which existed in Eemian Interglacial period
When temperatures were
Similar to those predicted in the near future
And thereafter
to search to locate local similar
ecosystems that Exist in our now
And to begin designing and in part
Creating the process to Assist the
Migration of a palette of species
Able to replace or restate
Those now coming under Extreme stress
Thereby Generating new forest
And grassland
which will in good part replace
The slow water releasing
Properties of glaciers
and snowmelt by in part creating
a 2 million square kilometer sponge
To normalize rivers
and secure the lands from flood and drought.[25]

Can it be that in this hundred-year moment or less
Both our collective history and destiny
Are being spelled out by glacial icemelt
As temperatures rise ten degrees Fahrenheit
In the high grounds

For instance
By mapping the Tibetan Plateau
As most of the field
In an azimuthal equidistant projection map
And intensifying the rivers
It is not difficult to see
That these seven rivers
Flowing from the Plateau
Nourish much of continental Asia

It is not difficult to see
That the people in these seven drain basins
Totaling 2,648,000 square miles
With a total population of 1,440,000,000
Including complex agriculture

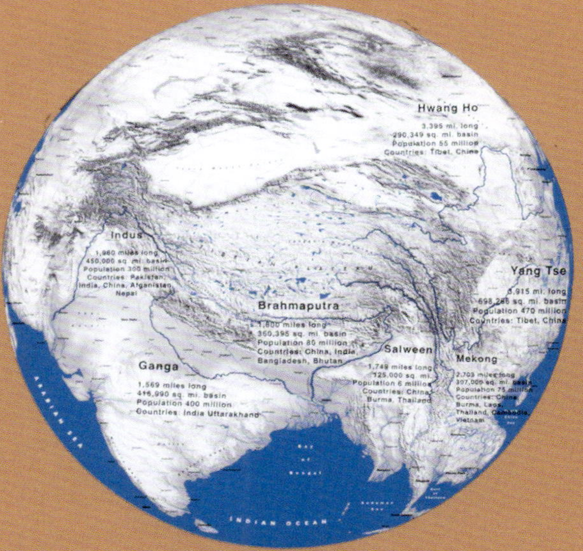

and farming systems
Are at great collective risk

For the Force Majeure is at work
With accelerated global warming
Working in collaboration
With accelerated industrial processes
Co-entangled over
The past hundred years
And beginning
To experience exponential growth

The result for Asia
As well as for the High Grounds elsewhere
Is that whole ecosystems
Are becoming erratic yet
As the Force Majeure becomes stronger
No counterforce remains visible

For instance
The research of Chinese glaciologists
As well as those from India appears to be right
And more than eighty percent
Of the glaciers in Tibet and surrounding areas
Will disappear in the next thirty-five years
As the temperatures rise
Ten degrees Fahrenheit or more

Thus producing conditions of
Flood and drought negatively affecting
The Salween, MeKong, Huang-Ho
Brahmaputra, Yangtze, Ganges
And Indus River systems
That nourish both the ecosystems and
The well-being of those living within them

The Force Majeure
Will work to the disadvantage
Of about one sixth of the earth's population
All those who live in these seven drain basins
That constitute so much of continental Asia

Thus, we make an unlikely proposal
That industry in tandem with government
Can offer a mediating role
In this highly stressed probable future
By generating the funding and initiatives

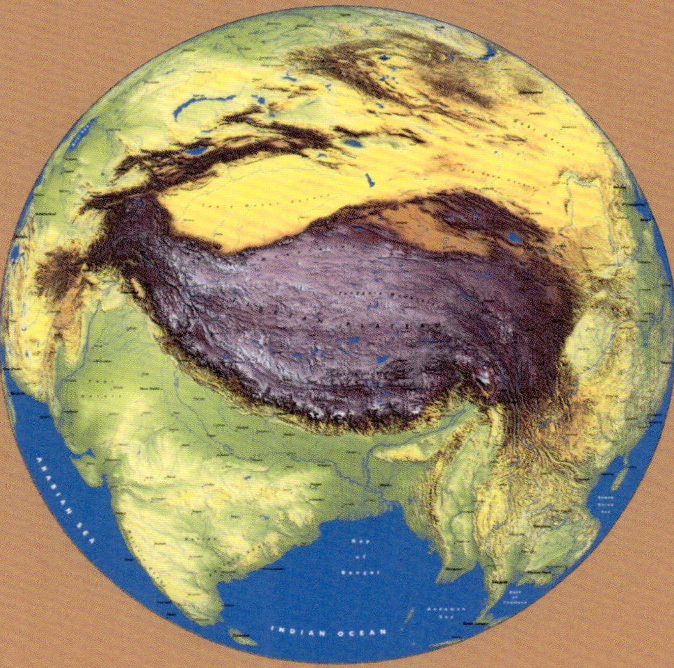

That will enable both local bioregional
And paleoecological research
To locate forest and savannah ecosystems
That existed in millennia past
When temperatures and other weather systems
Were similar to those which are in the process
Of happening in the now

And thereafter
Search to locate similar local
Ecosystems that exist in our now
Particularly at lower altitudes
And to begin designing
And in part creating through assisting the
Migration of species ensembles
Able to replace or restate
Those now coming under extreme stress

Thereby generating new forest
Where soils are sufficient
And grassland in the shallow earths
Which could replace
In part the slow water-releasing
Properties of glaciers and snowmelt
By creating a sponge mosaic where hydrology
indicated
To secure lands
From flood and drought

Thinking about the greening of Tibet
Looking at this vast, rolling partly mountainous terrain
We imagined a domain that was about eighty percent
Savannah and twenty percent open canopy forest

Not knowing the hydrology
We imagined thin soils
Over a rather large area
Specialized future biota
Moving there
As warming continues
We saw this terrain
As carefully managed pasture
With topsoils averaging
Four-to-eight inches
Capable of holding waters
And sequestering carbon
At about 320 tons per square mile
Then we imagined that about
Twenty percent of these lands
Where soils were more appropriate
And deeper as able to sustain
An open-canopy forest
Capable of sequestering about 1280 tons
Of carbon per square mile

Thus we calculate about 3.2 gigatons
Of carbon per decade
Would be the automatic sequestration for this new
772,000-square-mile potential landscape
On the Tibetan Plateau

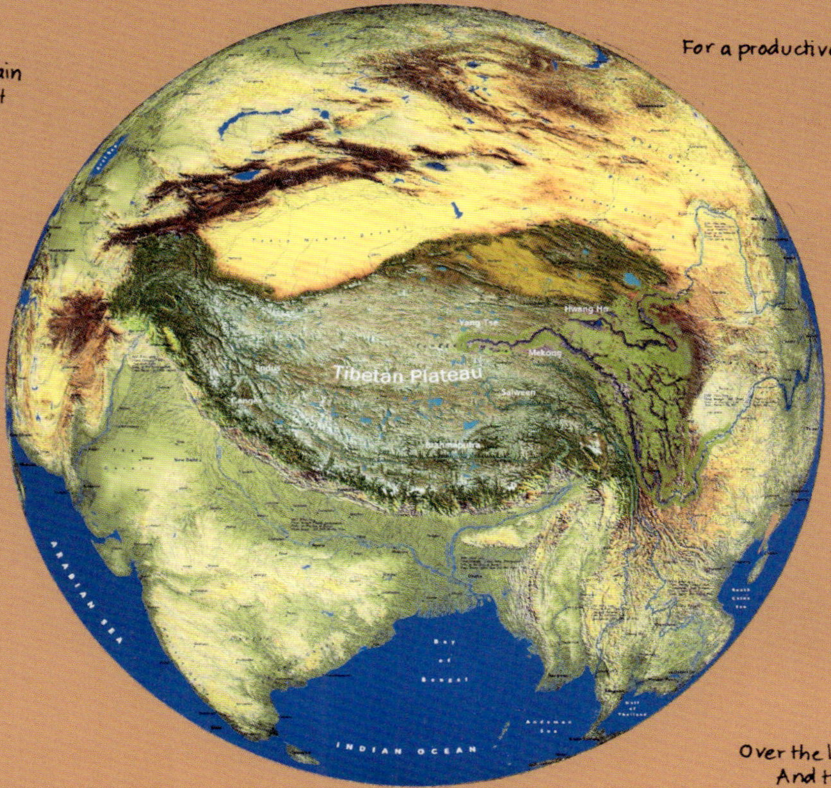

For a productive, self-sustaining self-complicating landscape
To develop bold experimentation
Becomes an absolute requirement
For instance with glaciers retreating
We imagined
Assisting the migration
Of species ensembles that form
The basis for a succession
Ecosystems to form
That follows glaciers uphill
We then imagined
A water-holding landscape
Where terrain was appropriate
And subtly terraformed
So that rains
Stayed on the lands
On which they fell

We propose
Paleobotanical exploration
Drawing botanical information
From when the weather
Was the same as that predicted
In the near future
Taking on the problem of inventing
An edible landscape
A landscape unique
In its food-producing qualities
As the harvest preserves the system
Over the long term we imagined this kind of thinking
And this kind of designing as endlessly repeatable

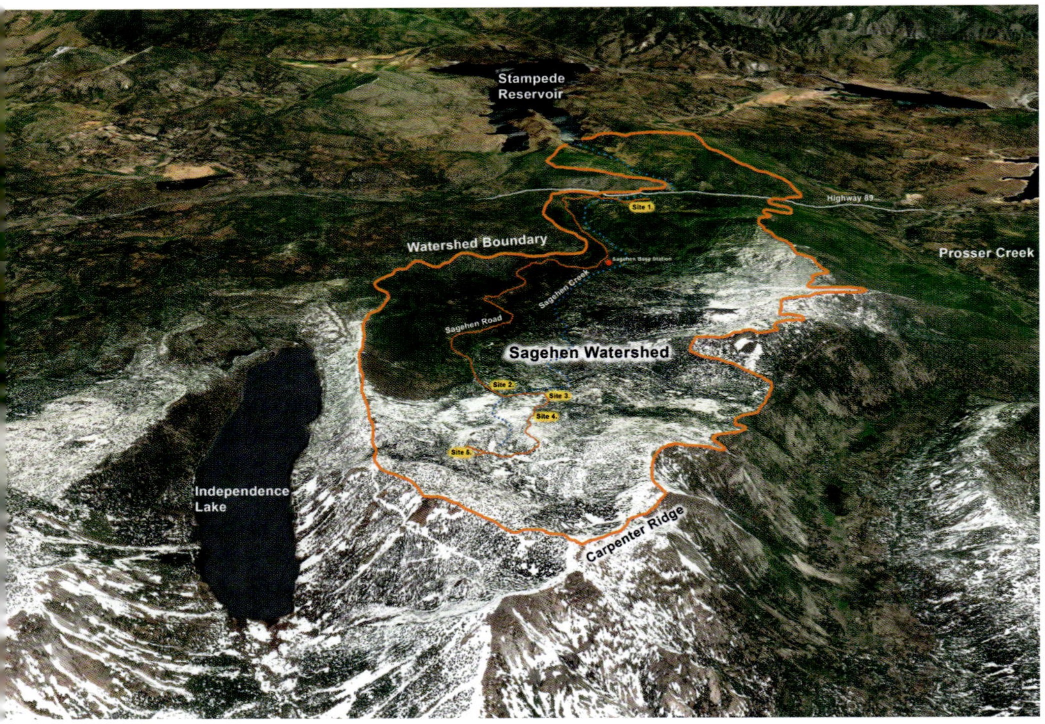

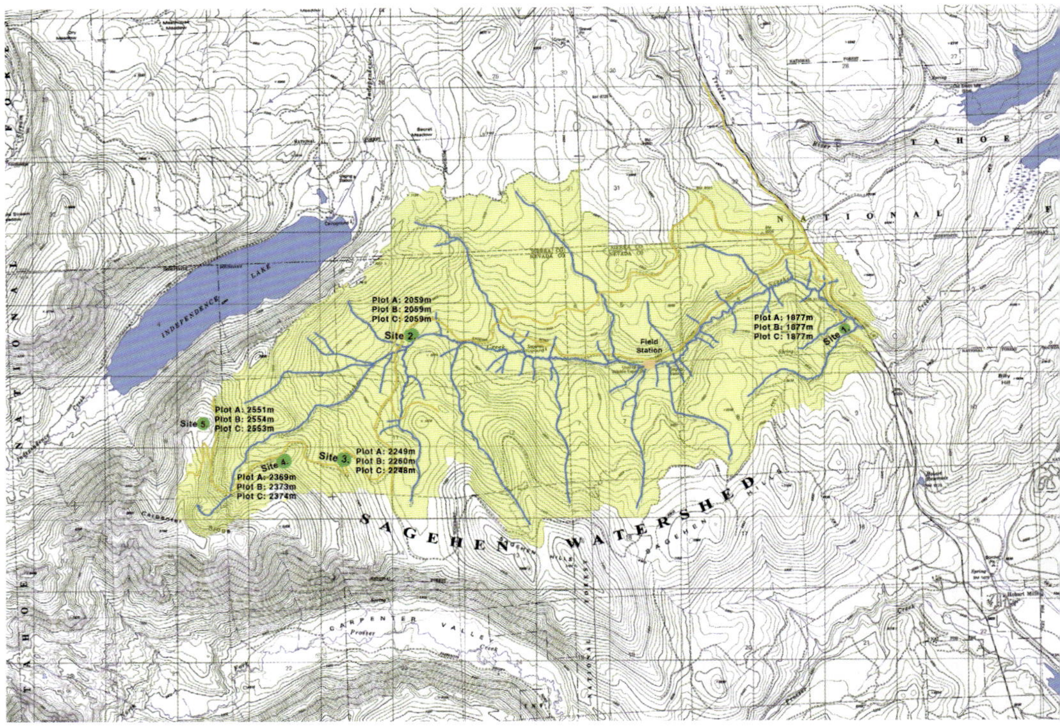

Sagehen: A Proving Ground (2011–present) exemplifies the concept of *Future Garden*, being a fully-developed art project built on the Harrisons' consistent notion of assisted migration of species in response to accelerating global warming. A multi-generational, fifty-year collaborative endeavor to conduct research in the Sagehen drain basin of the Central Sierras, the project addresses whether there are available ecological responses that will in some measure replace the value once provided by disappearing glaciers and snowmelt to river systems and dependent ecosystems and human cultures. *Sagehen: A Proving Ground* models the implementation of a simplified first-succession ecosystem intended to follow the glacier as it retreats. This involves physically moving groups of plant species like wild rose and red fir to higher ground, with the aim of helping the seedlings become adapted both to the warming effects of climate change and to growing at different altitudes. In testing the ability of a representative group of plant species (the "resilience ensemble") to survive heat, drought, flood, and altitude variation, the experiment has so far been successful, the ensemble enduring harsh conditions yet showing promising growth.

Initiated with the help of Jeff Brown, Faerthen Felix, Bill Fox, and Sara Frantz, the Director and archivist/librarian of the Center for Art + Environment at the Nevada Museum of Art, *Sagehen: A Proving Ground* is located on the grounds of the 3,240-hectare Sagehen Reserve maintained by UC Berkeley. The initial research was funded by a grant from, jointly, the Annenberg Foundation and Metabolic Studio, an independent research center and ecological art studio run by Lauren Bon in Los Angeles. With help of Brett Hall, the research director of the Arboretum at UC Santa Cruz, and his student team, 13,000 seedlings were planted in five designated plots in the summer of 2011. Each site was located approximately 165 meters above the other, at the elevation of about 1,700–1,800 meters. In the long term, the project investigates glacial succession ecosystems in order to both test the concept and answer the following question:

By following the model of assisted migration, can a simplified first-succession ecosystem be designed or otherwise enabled to follow a glacier as it retreats? The benefits of this experiment, if successful, are many.

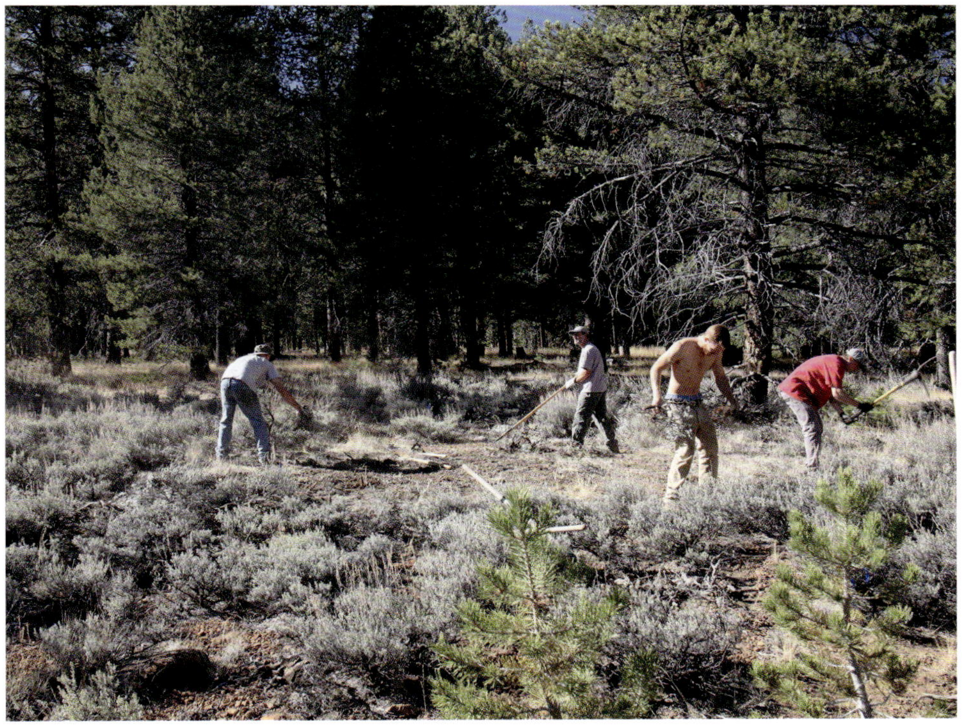

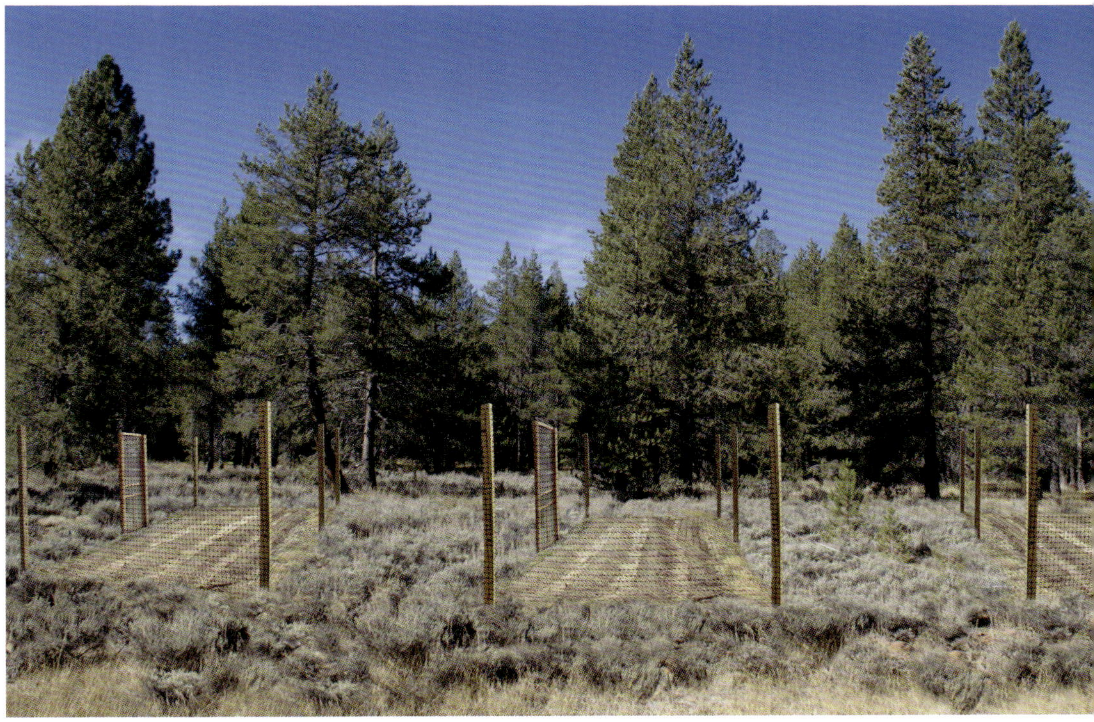

In addition, the experimental project aims to test the core research question established by the Harrison Studio for the Center of Force Majeure at UC Santa Cruz:

"Are there ecologically available responses that will replace, in some measure, the value once provided by disappearing glaciers and snowmelt to river systems and both the ecosystems and the human cultures they support?"[26]

In 2018, the Harrison Studio received additional grants from the Institute of Arts and Sciences (IAS) and the Arts division at UCSC, the Metabolic Studio, the McEvoy Family Fund of the San Francisco Community Foundation, Rowland and Pat Rebele, Kathleen Rose, and annual donors to the IAS, with the money intended to fund another *Future Garden*, this time in the Arboretum of UC Santa Cruz. Newton, with help from Brett Hall and the Arboretum staff, began to propagate plant ensembles inside three donated Buckminster Fuller domes. This research experiment was designed to test novel ensembles for heat resilience at a 50-year predicted temperature increase of 3–4 degrees Celsius. Each greenhouse maintains a unique ensemble at 3–4 degrees Celsius above the annual average. As species that cannot survive such conditions die off, they will be replaced as the experiment develops. This study focuses on testing a diverse group of plants that should ideally survive in arid and hot regions, making up a self-complicating scaffold of species that will act as replacements as others die back from rapid temperature changes. The *Future Garden* intends to make a serious contribution to the well-being of local biotic communities 50–75 years from now.[27]

Addressing the implications of climate change, the various *Future Gardens* show that concerted efforts must be invested in the design of future ecologies that would be able to function in new temperature regimes and environmental conditions. Throughout all these works, the Harrison Studio effectively showcased practical counterproposals to what was projected to happen from rising temperatures, the loss of the snowpack, and other severe and abrupt changes to environmental conditions. The concept of *Future Gardens* is "that every place that has survived heat and drought in its past has … plant species in its history and present that can survive in a heat-stressed future."[28] At its core, the artists' proposal involves their essential ideas of re-terraforming, assisting the migration of species to higher altitudes and latitudes, and experimentation with species that can adapt to hotter temperatures in the future.

Future Gardens is based on the premise that local botanists can collect such species, propagate them, and generate the scaffolding for the regeneration of local ecosystems as warming occurs more rapidly than the Life Web can accommodate unassisted. The project envisions a global network of *Future Gardens* linked to parks, botanical gardens, arboretums, zoos, churches, and other public spaces around the world, "tying people in communities large and small across the planet to a future of their own creation."[29] Today there are, along with those discussed in the chapter, several additional *Future Gardens* in the development phase: *Future Garden* at the ArtMill founded by the artist Barbara Benish in Czechia, *Future Garden* in development under the direction of Leslie Ryan at UC San Diego, and *Future Garden* in collaboration with Ya Tang of Sichuan University, in Sichuan Province on the edge of the Tibetan Plateau.

From an educational point of view, such *Future Gardens* are essential in helping to create a new eco-conscious culture. They help to translate climate change data not readily accessible to our senses into new linguistic, visual, and sensory vocabularies that are universally understood, as Roger Malina precisely observes.[30] Through an application of their complex system thinking, any ecosystem could be transformed and made capable of remaining a viable host for terrestrial life. The Harrisons proposed going beyond observation, analysis, and local initiatives aimed at alleviating the consequences of climate change. Working collaboratively with scientists, the artists would now assume a new kind of agency as "landscape artists" or "planetary gardeners," in Anne Whinston Spirn's words, as re-terraformers responsible for the mitigation of species loss, creation of succession ecosystems, and reorganization of human settlements.[31]

Future Gardens interrogate the limits of artistic agency, imagining greater possibilities for an artwork: as a work of cross-disciplinary science, a work of preemptive bioregional planning,

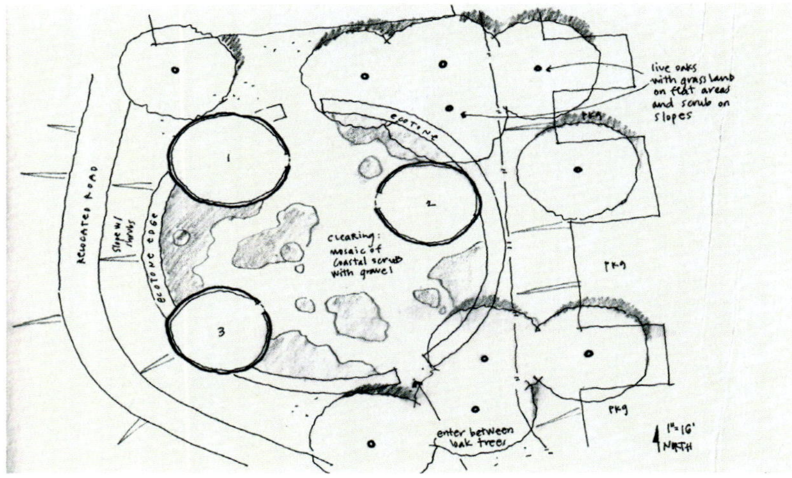

Future Garden for the Central Coast in California (2017-ongoing) at UCSC Arboretum, Santa Cruz, CA

and as a re-terraforming work that is more than simply an unrealizable metaphor in the face of ecological extinction. The Harrisons' work stretches not only the methodology but also the content of both art and science, assuming an entirely new ethical dimension while contributing to an active production of knowledge.

EXPANDED STRATEGIES IN COLLABORATION WITH THE LIFE WEB

Future Gardens, as the final series of the Harrisons' fifty-year collaboration, weaves together the key ideas from their literary and utopian worlds. It creates an arc back to the *Lagoon Cycle*, where the heroes deal with the drastic consequences of global warming in a world undergoing mass extinction:

And in this new beginning
this continuous rebeginning
will you feed me when my lands
can no longer produce
and will I house you
when your lands are covered with water?
so that together
we will withdraw
as the waters rise?

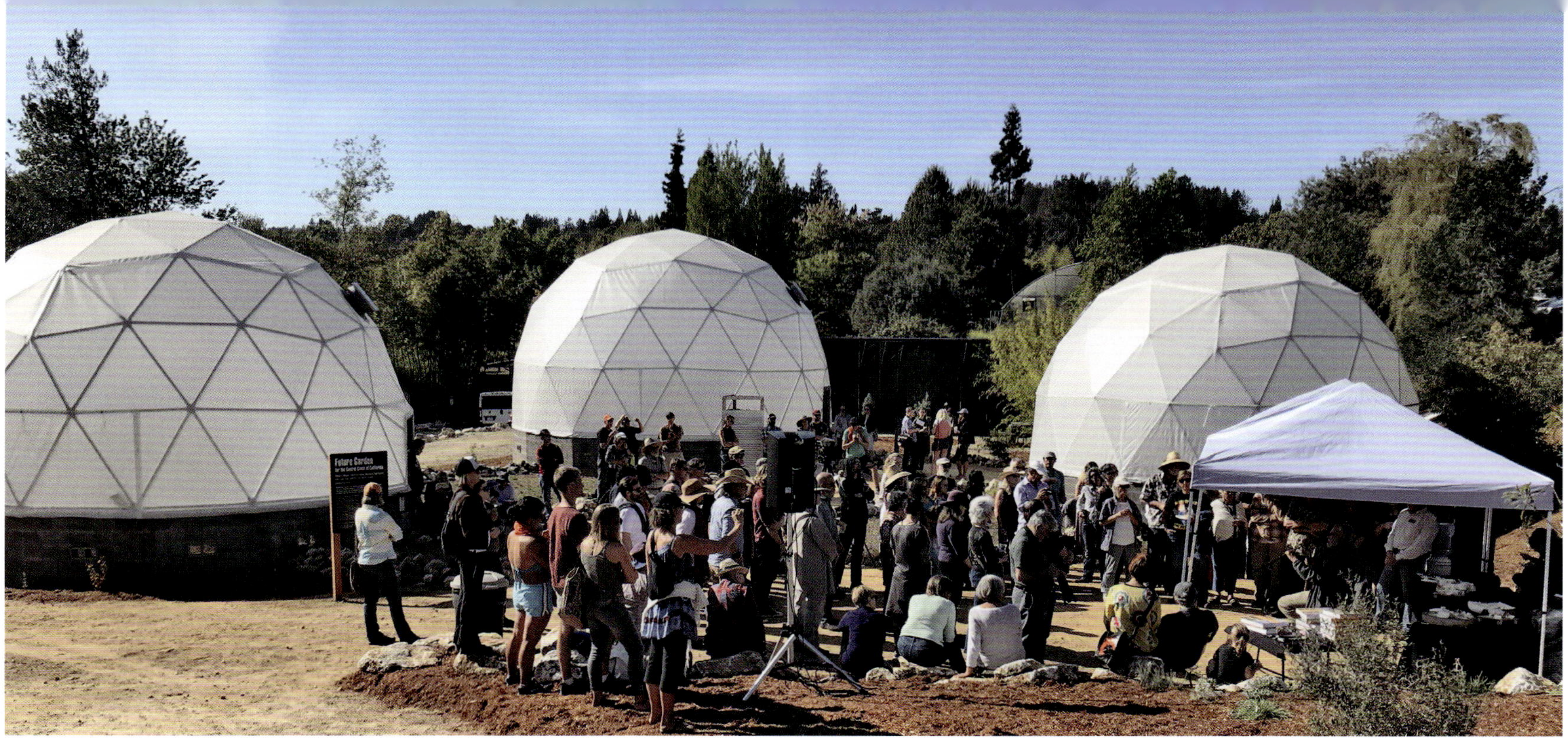

In the *Lagoon Cycle*, the Lagoon Maker and the Witness *retreat with grace* to a more sustainable community. Similarly, the *Future Gardens* imagine possibilities for the survival of humanity by joining the Web of Life, and thus forming a new culture. The poetic and critical content of *Future Gardens*, as with the transformative impact of all of Helen and Newton Harrison's creative output, urges us to imagine these new futures.

Beginning in the early 2000s, the artists frequently used "the web of life," a phrase with more than one meaning.[32] The introduction of this term in their later works suggests the transformation of their earlier thinking through new poetic metaphors. Possibly they adopted the term "Web of Life" after the publication *The Web of Life: A New Scientific Understanding of Living Systems* (1997) by the physicist, systems theorist, and ecologist Fritjof Capra. The Harrisons' ideas certainly overlapped with those proposed by Capra, who argued for a new foundation for ecological policies based collectively on the theory of complexity, Gaia theory, and chaos theory.[33]

In his conception of the Life Web, Newton Harrison came closest to Gaia theory, which describes our planet as an evolving living system.[34] The Gaia hypothesis proposes that living organisms interact with their inorganic surroundings to form a complex, synergistic, and self-regulating system that helps to maintain and perpetuate the conditions for life on the planet. Newton's notion of the Life Web also insisted on the interconnectedness of social systems and ecosystems.[35]

Both Helen and Newton advanced the idea that aggressive human interference with or destruction of the natural world posed a threat, not only to humans but to all organisms constituting the natural order, a lesson learned in Rachel Carson's seminal book *Silent Spring* (1962).

In his final vision of their Survival Art, Newton Harrison describes the need for humanity to join the web of life:

"Now, 50 years later, looking at environmental art, most of the work looks to me as if many artists are taking on local ecological problems and raising the issues at community levels. It is my opinion that our field needs to be trained in how to read the Life Web itself. After all, it continually speaks to us. And in reading this Life Web, we need to become obedient to its wishes. Its principle wish, from my perspective or my understanding, is that we the human race would do best to seek ways to join the Web, stop consuming it, but rather become niches in the Life Web which would then reinforce its evolution, but above all its ability to continue."[36]

According to Newton Harrison, the sustenance of the Web of Life requires that our society reorient all knowledge and technology towards "the wealth of our future," so that we stop the rampant consumption of nature and instead work to prevent the extinction of the human race and its planetary life-support systems.[37] Both practical and utopian, *Future Gardens* is a work of art and of love and stands as the Harrisons' final message of hope for the survival of all species on Earth, still our only home.

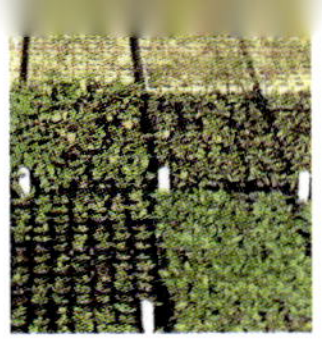

1 Harrison, Helen Mayer, and Newton Harrison, *The Time of the Force Majeure: After 45 Years Counterforce is on the Horizon*, edited and designed by Petra Kruse and Kai Reschke. Prestel, Munich, London, New York, 2016, p. 387.

2 Allen, Jane Ingram, "How Big is Here: In Conversation with Helen Mayer and Newton Harrison," *Sculpture*, Vol. 26, No. 10, December 2007, pp. 48–53, 52.

3 Harrison, Helen Mayer, and Newton Harrison, *The Time of the Force Majeure: After 45 Years Counterforce is on the Horizon*, p. 403.

4 See definition of eco-civility in *Greenhouse Britain*, 2007–2009: https://www.theharrisonstudio.net/greenhouse-britain-2007-2009, accessed September 2023.

5 Hughes, Jon, "What if Life Imitated Art?" *Ecologist,* Vol. 37, No. 10, December–January 2008, pp. 32–37.

6 I describe and analyze these two projects at greater length in my essay associated with this project: Sizonenko, Tatiana, "Helen Mayer Harrison and Newton Harrison: Meditations on Climate Change," *FIELD*, Issue 23, Winter 2023, https://field-journal.com/issue-23/helen-mayer-harrison-and-newton-harrison-meditations-on-climate-change.

7 Harrison, Helen Mayer, and Newton Harrison, *The Time of the Force Majeure: After 45 Years Counterforce is on the Horizon*, p. 377.

8 Ibid. CIWEM: The Chartered Institution of Water and Environmental Management.

9 Harrison, Helen Mayer, and Newton Harrison, *The Time of the Force Majeure: After 45 Years Counterforce is on the Horizon*, p. 378.

10 Kupper, Oliver, "Force Majeure: Pioneering Eco-Artists the Harrisons Created a Survival Guide for a World Careening Toward Disaster," *Autre*, Issue 13, F/W 2021, pp. 250–257, 252, 257.

11 In a simple definition, systems thinking refers to an approach to reasoning and treatment of real-world problems based on the fundamental notion of "system" or a purposeful assembly of components. Thus, systems thinking is aimed at understanding relationships between components and their overall impact on system outcomes (i. e. intended and unintended) and how a system of interest similarly fits in the broader context of its environment. See: Anderson, Virginia, and Lauren Johnson, *Systems Thinking Basics: From Concepts to Causal Loops,* Pegasus Comm., Inc., Waltham, Mass, 1997.

12 From the Harrison Studio's Digital Archive, accessed August 2022.

13 Ibid.

14 Ibid.

15 Petra Kruse reports: "More than 250,000 people visited the rooftop meadows over a period of two years; many of them returned frequently, experiencing the development and changing appearance of the meadows." See: Kruse, Petra, and Kai Reschke, "Chances, Limitations, and Conditions of Ecological Art: Three European Projects by Helen Mayer Harrison and Newton Harrison," *FIELD*, Issue 23, Winter 2023, https://field-journal.com/issue-23/chances-limitations-and-conditions-of-ecological-art-three-european-projects-by-helen-mayer-harrison-and-newton-harrison, accessed April 2023.

16 *The Endangered Meadows of Europe* is described on the Harrison Studio website, https://theharrisonstudio.net/endangered-meadows, accessed March 2, 2022.

17 Quoted from the interview in: Ingram, Mrill, "Ecopolitics and the Aesthetics: The Art of Helen Mayer Harrison and Newton Harrison," *Geographical Review*, Vol. 103, No. 2, April 2013, pp. 260–274, 272.

18 Harrison, Helen Mayer, and Newton Harrison, *The Time of the Force Majeure: After 45 Years Counterforce is on the Horizon*, pp. 226–229.

19 Harrison, Helen Mayer, and Newton Harrison, "Shifting Positions toward the Earth: Art and Environmental Awareness," *Leonardo*, 1993, Vol. 26, No. 5, Special Issue: *Art and Social Consciousness*, 1993, pp. 371–377.

20 See the exhibition announcement and its schedule on the website of Artworks for Change, https://www.artworksforchange.org/the-missing-peace-artists-consider-the-dalai-lama-3/, accessed September 2023. The first variation of the triptych was donated by the artists to be auctioned off.

21 The *Vanishing Ice* exhibition included only Part III, in a variation that showed the same image but with additional text placed on a dark background. This work is in the Harrison Family Trust collection and was published in the exhibition catalogue. See: Matilsky, Barbara C., *Vanishing Ice: Alpine and Polar Landscapes in Art, 1775–2012*, exh. cat. Whatcom Museum, Bellingham, WA, 2013, pp. 50–51. In the current exhibition, we are presenting an assemblage of the entire Tibet artwork: Part I (the original proposal from 1991), Part II, Part III (the final 2016 version, not the *Vanishing Ice* iteration), and Part IV.

22 Palmo, Dechen, "The World's Third Pole Is Melting. How can Asian countries survive without Tibetan glaciers and water?" *The Diplomat*, March 28, 2019, https://thediplomat.com/2019/03/the-worlds-third-pole-is-melting/, accessed November 2023.

23 Matilsky, Barbara C., *Vanishing Ice: Alpine and Polar Landscapes in Art, 1775–2012*, pp. 50–51.

24 See the Force Majeure manifesto and artworks on the Harrison Studio website: https://www.theharrisonstudio.net/art-projects-2/force-majeure-synthesis-2009-present, accessed November 2023.

25 This version of the text was published in the exhibition catalogue: Matilsky, Barbara C., *Vanishing Ice: Alpine and Polar Landscapes in Art, 1775-2012*, p. 51. The final version of the text accompanying the triptych was included in the Force Majeure book and also in the display of *Helen and Newton Harrison: California Work* at the Mandeville

Art Gallery at UC San Diego. The full text is published here: Harrison, Helen Mayer, and Newton Harrison, *The Time of the Force Majeure: After 45 Years Counterforce is on the Horizon*, pp. 390–395; and on the Harrison Studio website: https://www.theharrisonstudio.net/art-projects-2/force-majeure-synthesis-2009-present, accessed November 2023.

26 Harrison, Helen Mayer, and Newton Harrison, *The Time of the Force Majeure: After 45 Years Counterforce is on the Horizon*, p. 418.

27 *Future Gardens*, Center for the Force Majeure Brochure, https://www.centerforforcemajeure.org/publications, accessed January 2024.

28 Ibid.

29 Ibid.

30 Malina, Roger, "Force Majeure: Performing the Data of Climate Change," in Harrison, Helen Mayer, and Newton Harrison, *The Time of the Force Majeure: After 45 Years Counterforce is on the Horizon*, p. 447.

31 Spirn, Anne Whiston, "Helen and Newton Harrison: The Art of Inquiry, Manifestation, and Enactment," in Harrison, Helen Mayer, and Newton Harrison, *The Time of the Force Majeure: After 45 Years Counterforce is on the Horizon*, pp. 434–438.

32 See Cesar and Lois's response to Newton Harrison's concept of the Web of Life: Solomon, Lucy HG and Cesar Baio, "Cesar & Lois: Listening to the Web of Life," *FIELD*, Issue 23, Winter 2023, https://field-journal.com/issue-23/cesar-lois-listening-to-the-web-of-life, accessed April 2024.

33 In my email exchange with Josh Harrison, he verified that Newton corresponded with Fritjof Capra until at least 2015: "Yes, Newton was very familiar with Fritjof Capra and his work. I'm sure he had *The Web of Life* in his library and it may have been part of why he began using the term 'the Life Web' as a core description of the world system he was working to renew. He and Capra met several times; they had an intermittent correspondence with a couple of efforts to do joint projects, one at least at Schumacher College. Ruby, as I recall also took at least one of Capra's courses." Email exchange, April 23, 2024.

34 Gaia theory was independently arrived at by the bio-physicist James Lovelock and the microbiologist Lynn Margulis, as well as by the Russian biogeologist Vladimir Vernadsky.

35 Eleanor Heartney compares the Harrisons' holistic approach to nature that aims at restoring its balance to Carolyn Merchant's critique of mechanistic assumptions about the natural world stemming from the patriarchal order. Merchant, an historian of science, challenges the valorization of the Scientific Revolution and links it to the replacement of an organic female-centered vision of nature by a mechanistic, patriarchal order organized around the exploitation of natural resources. Merchant wishes to revise the paradigm of domination and exploitation of both women and nature, a common theme of activist and ecological art that relates to the Harrisons' ideal. See: Merchant, Carolyn, *The Death of Nature. Women, Ecology, and the Scientific Revolution.* HarperOne, San Francisco, CA, 1990, p. 69. See: Heartney, Eleanor, "Dancing with the Waters: Helen and Newton Harrisons' Call to Action," in Harrison, Helen Mayer, and Newton Harrison, *The Time of the Force Majeure: After 45 Years Counterforce is on the Horizon*, pp. 443–446.

36 Kopytin, Alexander I., and Stephen K. Levine, "An interview with Newton Harrison." *Ecopoiesis: Eco-Human Theory and Practice*, Vol. 2, No. 1, 2021, https://en.ecopoiesis.ru/interviews/article_post/an-interview-with-newton-harrison, accessed October 2022.

37 Ibid.

Epilogue: Reflections on Art and Science, Artists and Scientists

A ZOOM CONVERSATION BETWEEN NEWTON HARRISON AND TATIANA SIZONENKO, JULY 26, 2021
TRANSCRIBED AND EDITED BY GARETH DAVIES-MORRIS

When and how did your relationship with science begin?

I have to look at your question from two perspectives simultaneously: the first was that Billy Klüver held meetings with [Robert] Rauschenberg and others in the late 1960s. Klüver thought of himself as a physicist; I thought of him as an engineer. He liked physical engineering. He liked where electricity worked something, and you found out how. I didn't get the sense that he thought that artists themselves would deal with science. Remember, Helen and I had made the decision by those days to do no work that didn't benefit the environment, and we had to spend a couple of years finding out what we'd promised to do! And what we researched never showed up as technology or as biotechnology. It showed up as experimental research that was typical for the experimentalist in, let's say, the Scripps Institution of Oceanography, when they want to find out how an oceanographic island like kelp worked. They want to find out how things work, and this requires often very careful observation, and then requires obedience to what you observed. And that's not about politics or anything else as far as I could see at that time, except for those who would hold that every single thought was political in nature, something like that, that many of the political types thought – I didn't.

So at any rate, I got involved in the whole idea of experimentation, and that is to say, what is science? Science asks the question where the answer *is* not there. So, when we asked the question, "How do crabs mate?" – well, nobody knows. So we set out to find out, and finding out required almost a year and half of observing these crabs. And then within about eight months, when they stopped cannibalizing – we did a series of experiments to stop the cannibalizing and we found out, for instance, that it took seven hiding places a crab, on average, in various sizes, that could be invented by cinder blocks, as well as shoreline rocks or underground rocks or rocks under the ocean. And that cannibalism reduced itself to almost zero once every crab could hide. We didn't know if this was true in nature or not, because we had a controlled experiment. So this is not about engineering, and it's not about art of a design sense, it's about discovery.

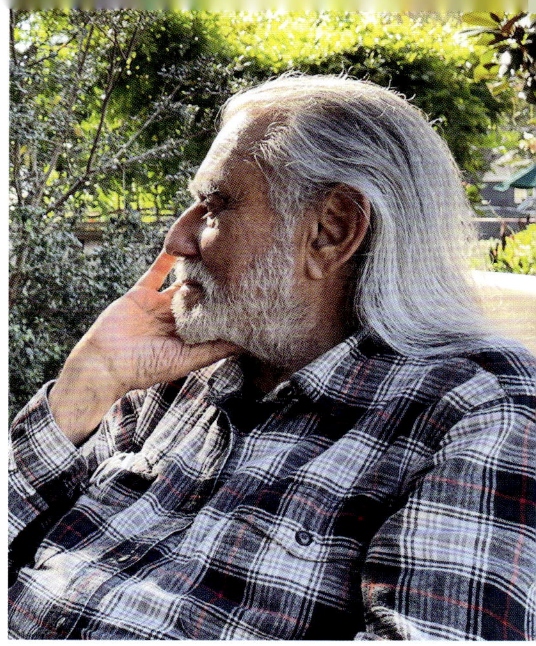

When we consider your *Aurora Borealis* or *Survival Piece II* (Brine Shrimp), which were exhibited at *The Art and Technology Exhibition* at LACMA in 1971, is it fair to say they engage with science and not technology?

So when we go to do the *Brine Shrimp* piece, one discovery is that in our little pond, if we blew it up to the size of an acre it would produce approximately 17,000 pounds a year of brine shrimp, if the algae that the brine shrimp fed on were themselves fed by Sav-On plant food, a cup every two to three weeks, and things of that sort. So these are experiments and these are processes of discovery that most art-science people don't take up. They take up often the phenomena; we were not interested in the phenomena.

Except once: I was interested in the phenomena of the glow discharge. But I was interested in it for an aesthetic question: could you make it hang in space? And so I made what amounted to be the largest glow discharge for the American Pavilion [in Japan, 1970] and then for Art and Technology [at LACMA, 1971], with one of the largest glow discharge chambers ever made, and up to a certain point it was pure technology. Why? Well, if you ask the question, "What does a neon-helium spark chamber mix look like at 10 to the .3 atmospheres?" – that's about two thirds of the way to space, to the space vacuum, which is why the phenomena starts happening with the glow stuff. What I'm getting to here is that the science stayed technological, in the sense that we knew how to do it all. I basically asked a question that a scientist might ask if he were an artist; I asked a question that [Mark] Rothko or [Josef] Albers might've asked. And that question was, "Can you get color to hang in space?" They tried it with color and color fields, but basically they didn't make color hang in space, they made color hang within color. And so I took them literally.

A student in my class, a physicist, said, "Well, you've got to look at how glow discharges work and how the aurora works." And so I went and looked at it, and then I got glow discharge chambers, injected rare gases, and started to make color hang in space. And that's how that worked. But I also found that a whole other thing was true, and that is there were five or six rare gases; if you varied their mix and you varied the amount of pressure in there – that is, closer to Earth or further away from Earth – you got different shapes, different colors, and different things. For instance, a physicist came to me 25 years later and said, "You know what? Your glow discharge chambers, which I saw, were interesting, because I went close to one and hugged it, and my magnetic field affected it, so you had a magnetic field going." And that was really interesting; I knew that but I didn't know what it was. And I didn't care, because all I cared about was hanging color in space.

Now was there any science in this? In my opinion, there was not. It was about experimentation and engineering and asking questions. You already knew what happened, you already knew the photon flow of the sun excited rare gasses at different atmospheres, on different gasses, and you got this giant aurora. We already knew all about that, so there was no science in what I did, there was only technology. But did science happen? Yes, it did, and here's how it happened. It had nothing to do with me at all; it had to do with an unintended circumstance. A couple of scientists posed the following question: if you can make a glow discharge as big as the Harrisons are (or I was) – that is, something 12 feet tall and 18 inches in diameter and all this stuff happening) – why couldn't you make a glow discharge a mile long and pumped down a rock tube that was cut into the rock for a tunnel?

And so they did this. And why did they do this? To find out something they did not know. The idea was that they had an invention, a motor, and that motor was going to drive spaceships. But what happened was it took a very long time for that motor to get up to enough speed, which would be two thirds the speed of light, to be meaningful. They wanted to find out if this was true, so they pumped it down the tunnel, and that was enough distance, a mile, for them to measure the rate of increase. That was something they didn't know, and therefore it's new information, which you can say has to do with plasma physics and experimentation and finding out information you didn't know. So the glow discharge chamber that we set up gave *permission* to do this work, but it was their association with their motor that did the science. It was our work that said, "You can, and if you do, you're going to find out stuff you didn't know before." You see, when I did the glow discharge, we did not find out stuff we didn't know before. You could know everything that I was doing by taking a couple of months and looking at how the Aurora Borealis worked, so I could only make a technological argument there.

Conversely, when we did the *Brine Shrimp* piece, there was biotechnology that emerged from just looking at the salt ponds, which told you what the algae did, and told you what the brine shrimp did, and told you what the colors were. Well, was there any original science in that? Yes, there was, and in this case it was intended. I had been collecting brine shrimp from my small pond. I weighed them and asked myself how much an acre might produce over the course of a year, since a 10-foot × 20-foot area produced over a month something like 20 pounds. I calculated up over a year and found out that we would grow brine shrimp at approximately 17,000 pounds an acre if we had sunlight, if we fed the algae that fed the brine shrimp one cup of Sav-On plant food per five square meters of growing area every two weeks. We had a little formula, we tested the formula, and that's what we found out. That is original experimental science, and it has a value. One of the reasons experimental science is interesting is that it has social and, unfortunately, political value. But above all, it has ecological value: in our case, it suggests that if you want fish food of this kind, you can grow brine shrimp in one foot of pretty salty water, feeding it the way I say, and you can get a ton of food. The original question is, can you? The answer is yes. The second question is, how much? The answer is this much: 17,000 pounds. And the third question is, what good is that? Well, pretty good!

So that is the difference between art and science and art and technology. I'm quite aware of when we do something that is technologically interesting, and when it transforms itself, by virtue of a set of questions that it raises, into the realm of experimental science. It's not clear to me that we ever entered the realm of theoretical science. I'm not sure; we may have but I'm not aware of it.

Did science matter to you more than technology, and if so, why?

The second problem I had back then was that physicists thought that the highest order of experimentation was theoretical physics, and ecology wasn't even a field. Somebody like Billy Klüver, who was such a heavy-duty fellow with all the art and science people – they weren't art and science, they were art and technology. They liked him so much, yet Klüver never worked with natural systems. Klüver worked with electricity, and things of that sort; he worked with technology. I don't think that Klüver himself made a good enough distinction between what science is and what technology is, the difference between the scientific experiment, the technological experiment, and the potential outcomes and the kind of questions that you ask. All the artists loved him too much and I think his ego got big. Klüver made personally clear to me that he though my work wasn't worth it. And I made clear to him that I not only disagreed but I thought he was wrong from the get-go. But I was a snotty young artist while he was a *serious* scientist. His science didn't seem very scientific to me, but then I was used to having talks with people like [Richard] Feynman, and [Murray] Gell-Mann who invented the charmed quark, and subatomic physicists and their theories, so I was used to talking to people who dwarfed Klüver.

But that doesn't matter because he had the power and the place. I don't think he had a position, though; I think he had a knee-jerk response that many of the physicists, and experimental physicists who were not theoretical, had, which is that the science that emerged from physics was legitimate, but it couldn't be legitimate from ecology because you didn't know it was a field and there was no guiding theory in ecology. I think there is: for instance, indeterminacy is absolutely core, since all living things improvise their existence moment by moment, so that how they existed the prior moment, you can't locate. That's exactly the definition of indeterminacy, so one finds that ecology tends to obey the physical laws, even where it appears to disobey physical laws and invent a separate system of some kind, as [Erwin] Schrödinger suggested back in the 1940s. He thought that nature disobeyed the laws of matter since it could create itself, but he happened to forget that the external energy that let it do that was called the sun, so obviously he didn't think about it till later and then admitted his mistake.

You can see the difference here. I stopped considering myself as a normal artist; I considered myself as a worker whose training and inclinations, and whose way of seeing, was that of an artist but the stuff I was producing followed my search. In a lecture once, I heard quite a useful mini-observation that turned out to have maximal responses, and that was the difference between search and research. When you research, you are finding out something already understood that you add to, while search is when you discover that which nobody thought of before and that you have brought into the realm of understanding through experimental means.

An example I use is the case of [Paul] Cezanne, who asked the original question, "How come there are no vanishing points in nature? I see vanishing points in all these paintings about cities!" When he asks this question, that leads to the real science of it. He says, "I am not seeing something, something is missing." What was missing is how you, in fact, see. So what does he do? He makes the Saint-Victoire paintings year after year, and he begins to discover that if you put something in front of something else, something else gets smaller, or if you put something bright and then something dull on the picture plane, and so on and so forth. He continues this field of experimentation and invents a half-dozen non-linear perspectives that conjoin into a new way of seeing. This is original research, and it comes from a searching-type question, which is, "What's the matter here? How come we're painting vanishing points all over the place when they don't exist in nature, yet we're painting nature as if it does?" When you unpack his question, it's really about, "What's the matter with our eyes, and what's the matter with how we're seeing, and why are we making this visual claim that is manifestly untrue in nature, yet we're acting as if it is true?" Embedded in his first question is a series of other questions, and they open up with a research question but they end up with *search*. He's searching, "What's the matter with the way we see?" And he finds out – but it was not only a matter about finding something out, it was a matter of doing something about it.

The difference between I as an artist and so many of the scientists is when they discover something, they think they're finished. My opinion is, when a scientist discovers something, that's when his real work begins, and that is, "How it's going to work out in the real world?" I mean, do I really want my DDT to poison everything just to save some crap? Yes I do, if you give me enough money. No I don't, if I'm an ethical being. And there you have the whole thing in a nutshell, and one of the fundamental flaws of capitalism, because the ethical question is removed from the action.

In yours and Helen's long career and ecological art practice, when or why did you take a different turn by engaging with science?

To me, science and art are close together. Scientific curiosity and the will to discover is common. We both ask interesting questions, something that doesn't have an immediate answer and that has embedded in it a responsibility for you to seek an answer. I don't know if this is true of other artists – I don't care. The core difference between what a physicist might do and what I as an artist might do is that a physicist might ask this question: "Can you debate indeterminacy in subatomic levels, can we find out where a subatomic particle may be even smaller than an electron is, if it's both a wave and an object, and a thing?" And the answer is the closer you get to finding the answer, the further away you get from the answer, because infinity's the answer in that case – I think. The scientist asks a question and to answer it, he needs to produce all kinds of evidence that is true, and then he needs to produce answers to all questions to what he poses. Someone says, "Well, your idea breaks down under these conditions" and you say, "Well, those conditions don't apply to what I'm talking about, or they do and therefore I have to make another theory to fit it, or I have to change my theory."

As an artist I don't take that position at all; I take a different one. When I make a work of art, I make it in such a way that I don't have to go prove a damn thing, because it's true on the face of it. I call it *prima facia*. Now what I find that's true on the face of it may add to the general knowledge, certainly in art and science, but the issue for me is that I don't make something that, in my opinion, isn't already proved; therefore it does not need a whole book of rationalizations, and it does not need key theories, and it does not need a big argument among theoretical critics about whether it's true or not. The outcomes are different. My way of working takes responsibility for what I see, whereas much of the sciences do not. Witness those bad news maps on the Mediterranean [*Apologia Mediterraneo* (2019)]; there was nothing but bad news there. Did the 30 or 40 scientists who made these maps urge us to do anything about it? No, they figured making the map was sufficient. Thanks for the bad news, buddy! I've got bad news for you; you're not going to survive if you don't do something about this stuff.

So the difference between science and art is between the preponderance of evidence and that which is true on the face of it, unless you can prove me wrong – as opposed to the reverse, which is I have to prove myself right. It's a difference in talent. We all have different talents. I have pretty powerful talents where image-making and storytelling are concerned. That's what makes me an artist. Like what made Feynman and Gell-Mann and others the scientists they were was the very powerful math talents they had, which let them see – in a series of formulaic and mathematical discoveries – how subatomic particles worked. Their talent led them to the tiniest thing; my talent led me to the biggest thing, which was the globe itself. And I made that decision when Sputnik went up in 1957. I looked at it and everybody was talking science but I was thinking that it was, in the main, a technological work, because the scientists already knew most of the answers or they wouldn't have sent it up in space in the first place. It was a high grade of technology with some science in it here and there where they would make unexpected discoveries, but the real issue was not art, not science; it was political, and it was performative. They were making a global performance by flying around the planet and saying, "We can see everything, and therefore we can organize and understand differently."

Can you think of other examples of contemporary artists whose work was imbued with science, who took environmental warnings seriously, and whose work was in any way inspirational for you?

The only thing that inspired me and Helen, Helen more than me – or me after Helen, I'd say – is the Rachel Carson book [*Silent Spring* (1962)]. It says it all. You don't have to know more, almost; everything else is details. So no, science books haven't influenced me, but art books haven't either. What interests me is: what am I seeing, what can I know from what I'm seeing and experiencing, what *gestalts* can I build, and where are my responsibilities? And not only where are they, but I will act at a fierce determination to act responsibly, and each new work tells me how to act more responsibly. I don't have a theory about responsibility, and I think the whole idea that we are individually responsible, and more so the more damage we do, is simply the name of the game, and it doesn't matter whether you are a taxi driver, or a scientist, or an artist. The reason I bring up taxi drivers is that I was riding in a taxi in Berlin in the early 1990s and I mentioned global warming, and he gave me a whole discourse on it, because that's what he learned in his third year of college. I have a high regard for European education – much better than our own.

Most scientists don't feel responsible for the consequences of their discoveries. If you discovered DDT, you discovered something so damaging that it's terrible. If you discover the way sub-atomic particles behave, like Gell-Mann did, I don't think you're going to affect negatively the life of the planet. You might reveal stuff that's ultimately useful, if sub-atomic physics and nanotechnology get married and start producing new kinds of computers, maybe. By no means am I attacking all of science, only that I raise the question, not of the experimentation, not of the discovery, but of commercialization of such and of indifference to consequences of your actions. Like if I take an action that has negative effects on half the trees in the world, I'd worry about it. There's an artist who was working with genetics, and when I met him he had spliced one of his genes into a flower. He was showing the flower, and I was saying to him, "If this flower gets out and propagates and puts your genes in all the other flowers, you don't know the outcome. Have you done experiments to show this is safe?" He said, "No, that's other people's job. I did the basic experiment." And that, in a nutshell, is why we're in trouble. It is not other people's responsibility, it is *his* – and others, if you can engage us.

A lot of artists have taken up the phenomena of something, but very few have found a way to act responsibly. Helen and I took that as a given; if we discovered something, we are responsible. The others did not. I don't even know why we took it as a given over 50 years ago. I have no idea why, but it seemed screamingly obvious. And I think you'll find lots of artists, early on at least, who got involved in the phenomena, and the phenomena are basically technological. By the time something becomes a phenomenon that you could see, it is technologically based because the science is already well established.

Could you talk about your early engagement with sciences/scientists that propelled the environmental movement, studied human extinction, and offered models of systems thinking?

No, that didn't show up in my thinking at all until I read Fritjof Capra in the early 1990s, and he pointed out very clearly stuff that was missing from Helen's and my thinking, that we weren't thinking systemically, we were thinking locally. We had no idea what systems thinking was, and extinction hadn't really come up clearly although Malthus and all that had been talked about, but all that stuff didn't become clear till the nineties. You're assuming a level of consciousness that we were in the process of discovering but we had not discovered in the full sense. You're acting as if we knew all this stuff. We did not know the answers till 20 years after we'd started, after doing work after work.

Like in working with Feynman in 1969 and spending time with him and Gell-Mann and the others, later – to understand the implications what he was trying to do took me another 15 years. I didn't think about Feynman daily and try to analyze or anything like that, but it took quite a while for it to be integrated enough in myself, and Helen to have some kind of grasp about what it was. And then the art of it astounded because it was so daring; he asked such a fundamental question, as did Einstein. And the influence on Helen and me was, could we ask and answer – they'd never answer, they'd ask – questions as fundamental as they were but from an ecological point of view? And the answer was yes but slowly, very slowly, decade after decade, and by the third decade we got good enough. You have to understand that this was almost like a calling, like a doctor gets a calling: it takes 10 years to get trained and then you work another 10 to 15 years and then you get good, and you work another 10 to15 years and you get very good. Do you see what that's like? These things do not come to you in a second. It took us a full 20 years to start thinking this way. We began from a position of really deep ignorance, and we had to retrain ourselves step by step.

For instance, I was influenced a bit by the Fluxus people – Dick Higgins and Alison Knowles and the other crew. There's a poem by Higgins where he says, "Brother Newton and Sister Helen are out in the desert growing fish/What could be more Flux?" You know, we were out there! It's, like, 1968 or 1969, and as part of all that, I'm thinking that we're really going to deal with irony and heavy-duty stuff, so I go to the head of our biology department, a guy named Herb Stern. We were friends, I liked him a lot. I was doing little things and they were used to my asking these bizarre questions, so I asked, "Herbie, can you grow a section of my liver?" He said, "We could take a section, but our experimental powers and our lab are not sophisticated enough to grow your liver. Why do you want to do it?" "Well," I answered, "If I grew my liver and we had a big pile of liver in front of us, and I sliced it up and fried it, I could serve it to all my friends and we could be discussing auto-cannibalism or the Eucharist – except where a certain famous religious figure gave bread and wine, or the loaves and the fishes, I gave liver!" He didn't think this was funny at all. Nobody thought this was funny except me. Herbie said, "Listen, why don't you grow something we can do? Let's grow a lily cell; I can do that." And that's how come I did *The Birth and the Death of a Lily Cell* [1968].

Among early books that addressed synergy, systems thinking, and entropy was Buckminster Fuller's *Operating Manual for Spaceship Earth* (1969). Can you tell me if any of Buckminster Fuller's ideas or other writers have any influence on yours and Helen's work?

I'm not influenced by anyone consciously, or rather, I think I'm unconsciously influenced all over the place. I admire Feynman so much because of his struggle to discover certain things. I think he was debating indeterminacy – pretty bold. If he was able to do that, it would be quite remarkable. Also, I think that Einstein was really interesting, because according to him his basic discoveries were outside of rational thought. He would study and learn a lot, then he would be silent, and out of his silence would come these intuitions, which then took the form of mathematics. I work the same way – not that I'm equal to him. And yes, Bucky Fuller had a real influence on my work, in the following sense: when I looked at *Spaceship Earth* and the concept of it, I thought that the metaphors in it were destructive.

A spaceship is a physical object, and the metaphor says that Earth is a spaceship, which means the nature of physical objects, as defined by Descartes early on, is that they break down and you fix them. Earth is not a physical object, it's a living system; when it breaks down, you don't fix it part by part.

I always felt that Fuller, genius that he was and wonderful questions that he asked, lacked a deep understanding about how the ecology worked, and as such, he was not able to leave engineering. For instance, he thought we could feed everybody on Earth if we were good. Well, you can't, especially since everybody on Earth could double and could become 20 billion. We could produce enough people to eat up everything that wasn't a person – maybe we should begin eating up persons! Fuller didn't ask the fundamental questions of existence and survival, which I think scientists could and should ask and do not. And we do the best we can, but I don't think we're good enough. Although if we save the Pacific, if we save the ocean or we have a voice in it, we might be approaching good enough – I'm not sure. So you can see the experimental nature of everything Fuller did, you can see the limitations, you can see the value, you can see the intellectual courage with which he approached things, and you can see what's missing. You have to take a holistic view at Fuller, instead of either an arguing look, that he's not enough of a scientist, or an adoring look like, "Oh my God, did you see what he did?" If you look at him directly, you'll see this remarkable autodidact who came at a point where his education came out of engineering and physics. Those were his lenses he looked at things through and which let him see our whole ecosystem as a mechanism. Thereafter, he was wrong in all cases, in my opinion, where *Spaceship Earth* is concerned.

When and how did you first engage with climate science? When did you first realize that global warming stress could become very intense on the planet? And can you also comment on Paul Erlich's book *The Population Bomb?* How did it influence your work or thinking, if it did?

You know, there's a very particular and explicit answer to our engagement with climate science. It begins with Helen's and my collaboration. Our collaboration begins in 1969–70. She quits her job in '71, and we work full-time ever after. Our agreement is that she'll be my assistant until she adds enough on her own to change the work so much that it doesn't look like either of our work anymore, at which point we will become co-authors. I'm expecting six or seven years. In year three of our collaboration, late 1973, Helen shows up with two books. Both are by earth scientists. One book sells itself on, "You know what? We're in an interglacial period, here are the arguments that suggest it's going to get colder!" The next book is from a guy named [Gilbert] Plass, I think, and he says, "You know what? We're in an interglacial, all the evidence suggests we are going to get warmer, and we're getting a lot warmer!"

So Helen and I did our first collective work called *San Diego as the Center of a World*, and in it we propose the basis for almost all our thinking thereafter. And that is, it doesn't matter which one is right.

Let us begin long-range planning and as we find one or the other of these positions is correct, we'll shift our energy from one to the other, so that we can plan for the future, because if the world's going to get hotter, a lot of stuff is going to change. That is the exact point in late 1973, early '74, when we made *San Diego as the Center of a World*, that it happened. Further studies and some five years later, we make an ocean map where the oceans do rise 100 feet. That was as close as I could come to a calculation back then. It turns out that 275 feet is what it'll rise when the ice melts. I was wrong by 10 percent, but I think over 40 years ago, it's okay for me to be 10 percent off. Nobody else was on either. That's when all the predictions came, and you look and they all happened in late 1979 when we wrote the last text of the *Lagoon Cycle* [paraphrasing]: "The ocean will rise, all this will change; if food can't be grown, where do you think it can be re-grown? The tropics will become uninhabitable, and the real question is, will the ocean rise gracefully and can we withdraw with equal grace? And the deep question is, am I am going to help you or you are going to help me?" And Helen and I agree to help each other, as we're two characters in this thing, in this book called the *Lagoon Cycle*. But 42 years later, a good hard look shows that we're not going to help each other very much, we're going to interfere with each other as much as we can. So there you have it.
And *The Population Bomb* added to our arguments, but our arguments were already in place. Ehrlich and his wife – I think they both did it together as a team – came to the same conclusion, for even the same reasons. But I don't know that they influenced us so much as they confirmed us. That book and Malthus and everybody else said the obvious, that we would over-populate, the act of over-populating would consume more resources, and unless we controlled our population, we were done for. Looking at the position of the Life Web, we're a very successful species. We've doubled and doubled our numbers and we've invaded every other system and taken what we wanted. It's not a dilemma, it's a set of decisions that people have made that reduce our ability to survive in the long term but increase our ability to take more. If we reduce our numbers by six or seven billion, we can probably survive, because then the planet can integrate our disturbances into itself and can force us to become a niche again in the ecosystem, which we need to do or we don't survive. Can't be divided, it just can't.

On the subject of the human race's precarious future, the Cold War and nuclear threat concerns are seemingly absent in your and Helen's work. Can you explain this?

Yes, I can, because it was intentional on our part. It was 1983 or 1984, so we're very popular and we get requests, and one request says, can we do an atomic bomb work? So we get some original pictures because we know Herb Stern and the people who worked on it way back. And we put a big picture of the bomb, with a note saying, "I can light the sun in your backyard, and you can light the sun in mine, I give you my word that I am not going to do this to you, Helen and Newton." And that was the end of it. Why? Because all this atomic bomb stuff is posturing, and if I'm paying attention to the atomic bomb and stopping people from worrying about it, why I am not paying attention to the dying ocean? The dying ocean is real and material, and before us and our fault; the atom bomb is a political instrument that we're using to intimidate each other. They are of a different order, and one sucks energy from the work and solution of the other. So in 1974, when we made this promise, we then walked away from the atomic bomb. And you notice, most people have about four or five years later. It's much like postmodernism – you know my story there, right? – which was that period in the early 80s, it was after post-structuralism and semioticians at work and all that, and Helen and I decided to skip it. Why did we skip it? Nothing we read tells us how to plant a tree; nothing we read tells how we can nurture our environment. All that we read is "What's wrong with this?" and by the time we've finished deconstructing, what have we got? A whole lot of PhDs on how to deconstruct, so where are the PhDs on how to construct? "Oh, that's not our job. And that doesn't make us money, that doesn't get us tenure." So there you have it.

The reason I ask you this question is to find out whether the *Survival Pieces* have any connection to the Cold War and the threat of the atomic bomb.

Wait a minute, that would be right. The *Survival Pieces* do have this; they were a question. It was way in the background, but it asked, if everything breaks down, how would you survive in the city? Perhaps we had done a little calculation, or we had just intuited, that cities might have to find ways to get their own food. And urban ecology, urban farming, was a way to do this, and we had done it during World War II when we had our victory gardens that produced a third of the food or whatever percentage we ate – 20 or 30 percent. So it did show that back then, everybody did have backyards and in a quarter of an acre you could damn near grow all your vegetables. And that saved canning, it saved all kinds of things. So that did influence us; it told us that urban farming can have a very positive outcome if you rethink it. There are other things that influenced us. For instance, when we were in Colombo doing the Sri Lankan work in 1979, you could walk the back streets and see the houses with the trees hanging over the walls, but all the trees were mangoes, and bananas, and fruit trees. And you could walk the streets of Colombo and get lunch by plucking fruit, and I thought, "You know what? You could harvest the city this way!" We had already done the *Survival Pieces*, but that sort of confirmed it to us, that it is possible, particularly if the population is reduced through war or other causes, for people to survive in this way. If you take a look at Detroit, which lost a third of its population or something, they're making all those little places for farming and food, so they're doing it. We showed some of our work there. I don't know if we influenced anybody or not, but I suspect not. I suspect what influences people is, "I'm hungry, and here's the next-door lot, and I'm going to grow my tomatoes there," something like that. So I don't know if you'd call it an influence, but all this certainly was part of our thought processes, part of our morning discoveries. But you want to be careful not to attribute what we've learned now back to our early work. We were learning, we didn't know. I actually didn't know what an ecosystem was!

When did you formulate for yourself what an ecosystem is?

I formulated that on October 20th 1974, when I was 37 years old. I'm kidding – how would I know when I formulated it? I just know that slowly, over time, it became part of our thinking and our understanding that we had to do our best to help whole systems. If you take a look at many of our works in the book, they attempt to do this more or less at too small a scale and, 70 percent of the time at least, unsuccessfully. You can look at it differently and say, "How marvelous their work is, they were successful 20–30 percent of the time; most architects are only successful 10 percent of the time," and so on. But I don't think that way, aside from being amused at people who do.

Perhaps we can now talk a little about making the *Lagoon Cycle*.

That's fair enough. The *Lagoon Cycle* is foundational to the whole art movement, but it was also a trip of discovery for Helen and me. I really did have a Lagoonmaker-type persona and she really did have a Witness and a reflective persona; we really could expand and elaborate our personae in such a way. We were given permission to do this – not permission, but we saw somebody else do it. We saw Vito Acconci do it one way, but we saw Eleanor Antin do it another. Eleanor Antin kept inventing new characters out of herself, like "Eleanora Antinova the ballerina." And what does Elly do? She learns how to do three or four different ballet steps and learns how to think it so she could make herself look like a ballerina for 5–10 second increments and that's enough for her film! So we learned a number of things from them, and from [Jerome] Rothenberg and from the poets. We learned that autobiography had a real place in the arts and in thinking and speaking, and one of the things we had to understand was that Freud was wrong. Eleanor had invented a theory on how the persona worked, that it did not have a nicely organized super-ego, ego, and ID. Eleanor said, "That's not how my mind works. I invent characters and I act them out. I find out about myself this way; it's a way of self-experimentation." What would she look like as the Little Match Girl, what would she look like as Eleanora Antinova the ballerina, or whatever? Then she finds out that she's Jewish. She didn't note that she knew it all the time – I think she was influenced by Jerry Rothenberg's *Big Jewish Book*, I don't know. So she makes a *schtikle* and tells us she's the Little Jewish Girl growing up, and she hires me as a rabbi to chase a *dybbuk*, a monster, out of the little girl. She was always inventing characters, and Helen and I, to extend our characters, said, "My God, look at how easily Eleanor does it – we'll do that!" It was an instant influence; we knew it within a minute of seeing what she was doing. It wasn't a carefully considered thing that you write a book about; it was, "Of course, you can extend your character any damn way you want!"
Our only problem was that it hadn't occurred to us to extend our own. But I said, "Let's do that, and I'm going to be a Lagoonmaker, and you are going to be the Witness, is that right? "Yeah, I'm going to be the Witness," Helen said, "I'm going to give you trouble." And I said, "I am going produce the trouble you can deal with." And that's how the *Lagoon Cycle* starts; Helen and I declare ourselves from the start. We begin it in a scientific way. That is, we begin it with a question: are we hearing the same thing? Ranil [Senanayake] gives us a long conversation telling us about Sri Lanka. Do we hear the same thing? No, we do not. I as the Lagoonmaker only hear about the crab and how I can make a lagoon; Helen as the Witness and cultural figure only hears about what's happening to people. Thus, we begin the *Lagoon Cycle* with misunderstanding, but also the intention to gain understanding.

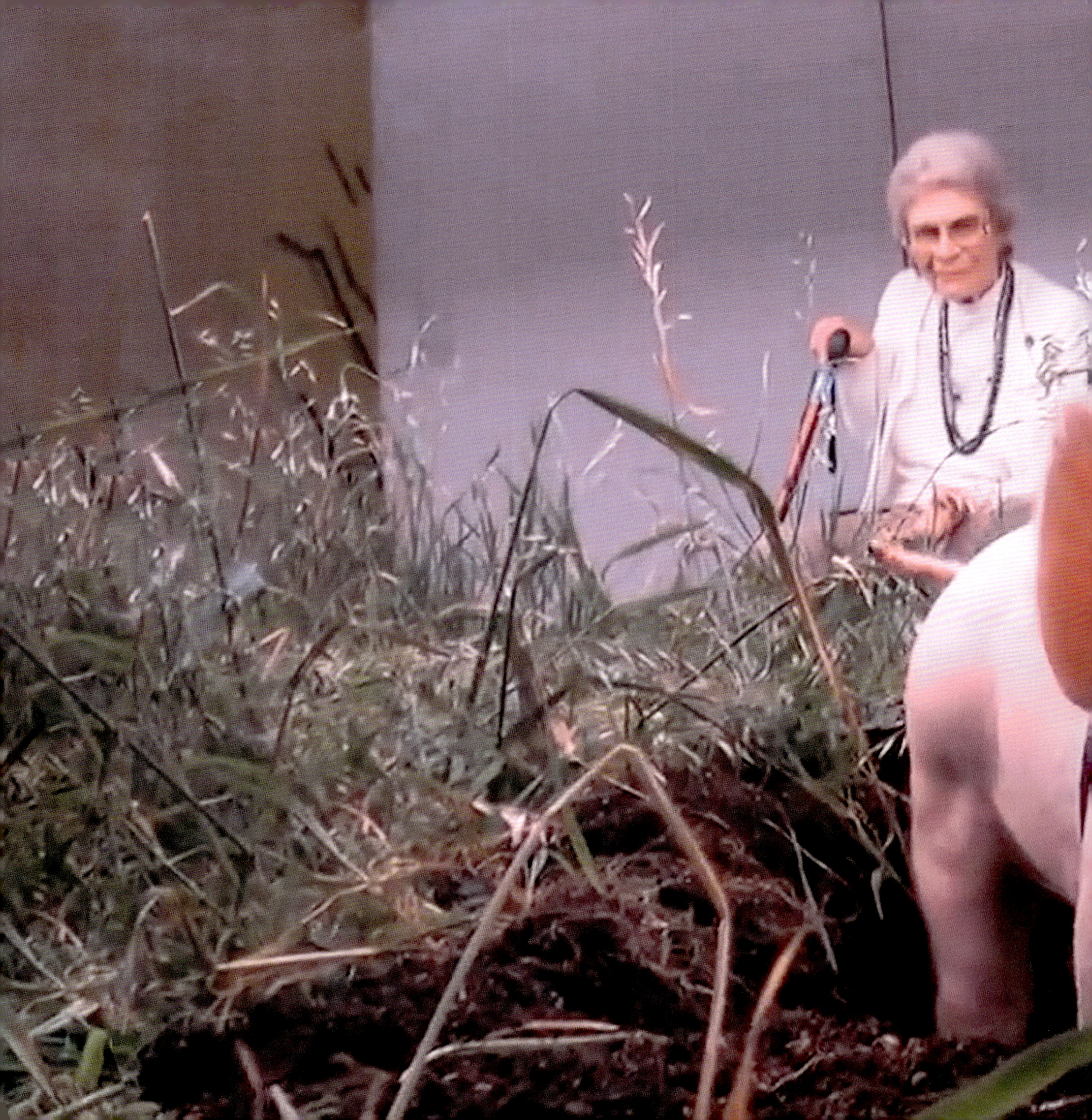

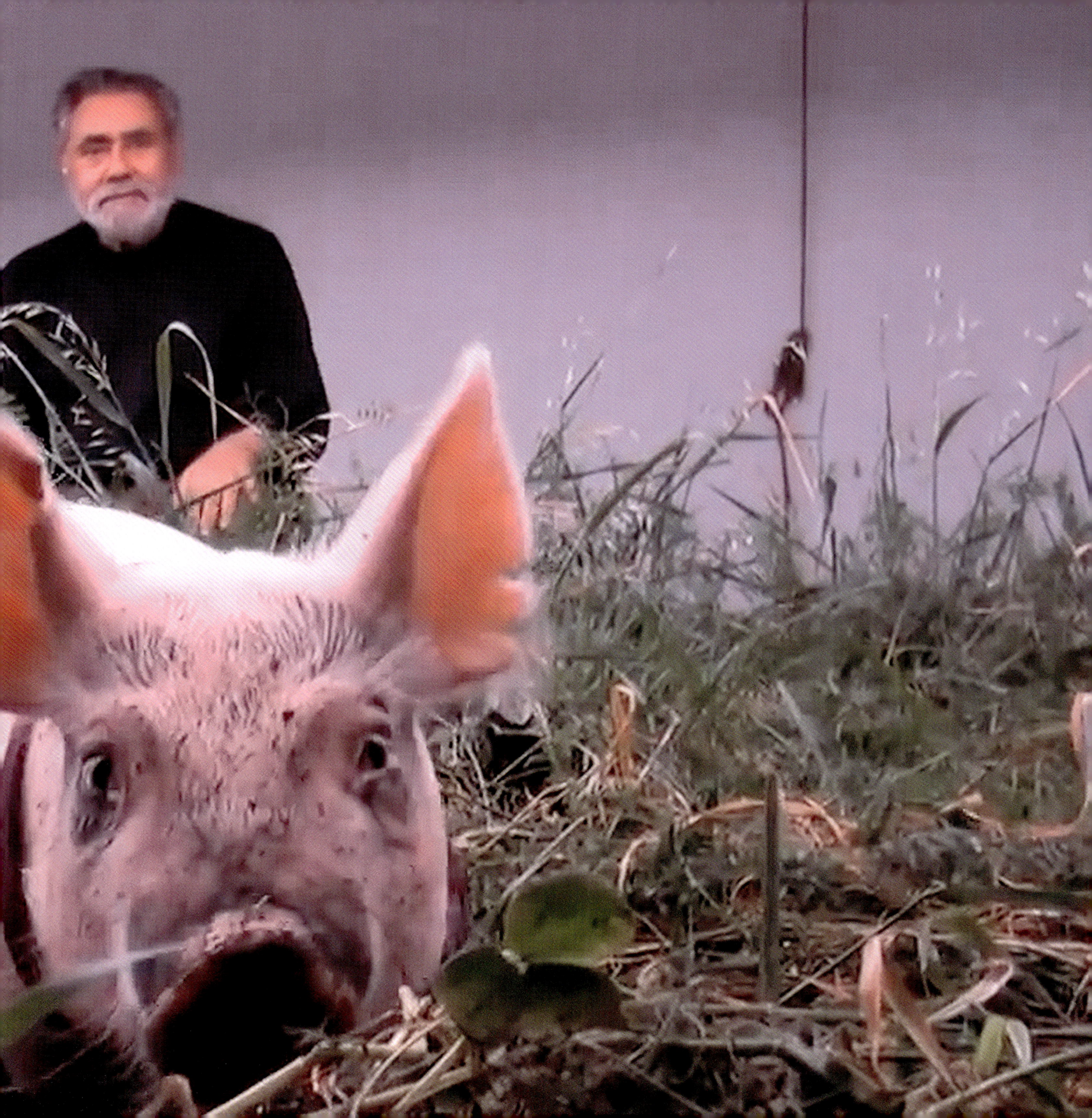

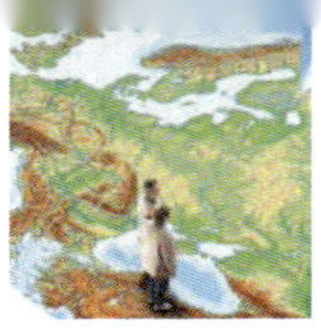

Exhibited Works

LA JOLLA HISTORICAL SOCIETY

Schematic drawing for a series of work entitled "On Growth Form and Dissolution" including *On Growth Form and Dissolution (A Time Piece), Fluorescent Seascape, Time Module, the Slow Growth and Death of a Lily Cell, Mushroom Gradient and Forest Smells (A Landscape), and Wall (A Landscape)*, c. 1969–1970
Schematic drawing on paper
25 5/8 × 38 in. (65.08 × 96.52 cm)
Courtesy of the Harrison Family Trust

***Thermal Wall and Path,* c. 1969–1970**
Schematic drawing on paper
25 5/8 × 38 in. (65.08 × 96.52 cm)
Courtesy of the Harrison Family Trust

***Soup Machine*, c. 1969–1970**
Schematic drawing on paper
25 5/8 × 38 in. (65.08 × 96.52 cm)
Courtesy of the Harrison Family Trust

***Temperature/Pressure Gradient. Participatory Water Piece*, c. 1969–1970**
Schematic drawing on paper
25 5/8 × 38 in. (65.08 × 96.52 cm)
Courtesy of the Harrison Family Trust

***Heat Gradient/Participatory Water Piece*, c. 1969–1970**
Schematic drawing on paper
25 5/8 × 38 in. (65.08 × 96.52 cm)
Courtesy of the Harrison Family Trust

***Format for Two Dances*, c. 1969–1970**
Schematic drawing on paper
25 5/8 × 38 in. (65.08 × 96.52 cm)
Courtesy of the Harrison Family Trust

***Nine Part Landscape Upon Which People Are Invited to Stroll*, c. 1969–1970**
Schematic drawing on paper
25 5/8 × 38 in. (65.08 × 96.52 cm)
Courtesy of the Harrison Family Trust

***Encapsulated Aurora Borealis*, 1969–1970**
Conceptual design drawing
Print on vellum
21 × 33 in. (53.34 × 83.82 cm)
Courtesy of the Harrison Family Trust

***Making Earth*, 1969–1970**
Six color photographs of the performance at Pepper Canyon Outdoor Studio at the University of California, San Diego, CA
Photographs and vinyl lettering on paper
51 × 68 in. (129.54 × 172.72 cm)
Courtesy of the Department of Modern Art, Los Angeles County Museum of Art, purchased with funds provided by the Modern and Contemporary Art Council

***Making Earth,* reenactment, 1969-ongoing**
Manure, soil, worms, and wood
Courtesy of the Harrison Family Trust

***Making Earth*, 1980–1981**
Video interview after Art Park, Spoils Pile Reclamation Project, 1977–1978
Duration: 34:30 min.
Courtesy of the Harrison Family Trust

Survival Piece I: *Air, Earth, Water Interface with Living Material or Annual Hog Pasture Mix*, 1971
Conceptual design drawing
Ink and graphite on paper
37 × 50 in. (93.98 × 127 cm)
Courtesy of the Harrison Family Trust

Survival Piece II: *Notations on the Ecosystem of the Great Western Salt Works with the Inclusion of Brine Shrimp*, 1971
Conceptual design drawing
Ink and graphite on paper
37 × 50 in (93.98 × 127 cm)
Courtesy of the Harrison Family Trust

Survival Piece II: *A 25-pound Bag of Harvested Salt*, 1971
Photographic print, oil, graphite, and ink on canvas
62 × 48 in. (157.48 × 121.92 cm)
Courtesy of the Harrison Family Trust

Survival Piece III: *Portable Fish Farm*, 1971
Conceptual design drawing
Ink and graphite on paper
37 × 50 in. (93.98 × 127 cm)
Courtesy of the Harrison Family Trust

Survival Piece IV: *La Jolla Promenade*, 1971
Conceptual design drawing
Ink and graphite on paper
37 × 50 in. (93.98 × 127 cm)
Courtesy of the Harrison Family Trust

Survival Piece V: *Portable Orchard*, 1972
Conceptual design drawing
Ink and graphite on paper
37 × 50 in. (93.98 × 127 cm)
Courtesy of the Harrison Family Trust

***Exterior Orchard, A Conversation with Survival Piece V*, 2024**
Outdoor installation of 12 citrus trees at the
La Jolla Historical Society's front lawn
Hexagonal planter redwood boxes
2 feet tall × 4 feet diameter;
an assortment of living citrus trees
Courtesy of the Harrison Family Trust

Survival Piece VI: *Portable Farm*, 1972
Eight Horizontal Pastures, Ten Upright Pastures,
Potato Patch, and Portable Orchard
Conceptual design drawing
Ink and graphite on paper
37 × 62 in. (93.98 × 157.48 cm)
Courtesy of the Harrison Family Trust

Survival Piece VII: *Full Farm Condensed*, 1974
Conceptual design drawing
Ink and graphite on paper
37 × 50 in. (93.98 × 127 cm)
Courtesy of the Harrison Family Trust

***Horton Plaza Proposal*, 1977–1978**
One black-and-white aerial photo and two conceptual
design prints mounted on board
32 ¾ × 32 ½ in. (83.185 × 82.55 cm), 32 ½ × 36 ½ in.
(82.55 × 92.74 cm), 32 ½ × 39 in. (82.55 × 99.06 cm)
Courtesy of the Harrison Family Trust

***San Diego Round: Through Air, On Foot, Across Waters*, 1984**
Eight conceptual design proposals, text, and map
Photographic print and ink mounted on board
24 ¼ × 36 ¾ in. (62.23 × 93.34 cm), 24 ¼ × 28 ½ in.
(62.23 × 72.39 cm), 24 × 30 in. (60.94 × 76.2 cm), 24 × 30 in.
(60.94 × 76.2 cm), 16 ½ × 24 in. (41.91 × 60.94 cm),
16 ½ × 24 in. (41.91 × 60.94 cm), 16 ½ × 24 in. (41.91 × 60.94 cm),
16 ½ × 24 in. (41.91 × 60.94 cm), 19 × 25 ¼ in. (48.26 × 64.13 cm)
Courtesy of the Harrison Family Trust

***Arroyo Seco Release: A Serpentine for Pasadena*, 1985**
Two designs of the upper dam and one watershed map
Photographic print, collage, Marshall's photo oils,
and ink on paper
48 × 54 in. (121.92 × 137.16 cm), 33 ¼ × 94 in. (84.45 × 238.76 cm),
34 × 37 ¼ in. (86.36 × 94.61 cm)
Twelve designs
Photographic print, collage, Marshall's photo oils,
and ink on paper
30 × 22 ¼ in. (76.2 × 56.51 cm), 21 ¼ × 36 3/8 in. (53.97 × 92.39 cm),
21 ¼ × 26 in. (53.97 × 66.04 cm), 21 ¼ × 27 ¼ in. (53.97 × 69.21 cm),
19 × 24 in. (48.26 × 60.96 cm), 18 ¼ × 21 ¼ (46.35 × 53.97 cm),
14 × 18 in. (35.56 × 45.72 cm), 26 × 21 ¼ in. (66.04 × 53.97 cm),
21 × 26 ½ in. (53.34 × 67.31 cm), 34 × 34 in. (86.36 × 86.36 cm),
38 ¾ × 32 ½ in. (98.42 × 82.55 cm), 44 ¼ × 34 in. (112.39 × 86.36 cm)
Courtesy of the Harrison Family Trust

***Final Conceptual Design Drawing for Devil's Gate Refugia for Pasadena: A String of Pearls (Retitled by the Gabrielino Indians Hahamongna State Watershed Park)*, 1991**
Prismacolor and graphite on paper
33 × 88 in. (83.82 × 223.52 cm)
Courtesy of the Harrison Family Trust

***Devil's Gate Refugia for Pasadena: A String of Pearls (Retitled by the Gabrielino Indians Hahamongna State Watershed Park)*, 1987**
Aerial photograph
Photographic print enhanced with ink, print, and graphite
mounted on canvas

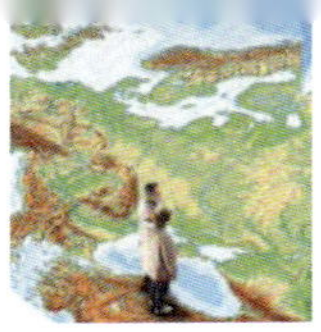

75 × 162 in. (190.50 × 411.48 cm)
Nine aerial photographs mounted on foamcore;
ink and color
40 ¼ × 91 ¼ in. (102.87 × 231.77 cm), 34 × 92 ½ in.
(86.36 × 234.95 cm), 35 ¼ × 73 ¼ in. (89.53 × 186.05 cm),
33 × 73 (83.82 × 185.42 cm), 40 ¼ × 44 ¼ in.
(102.23 × 112.39 cm), 40 ¼ × 34 in. (102.23 × 86.36 cm),
84 × 30 in. (213.36 × 76.2 cm), 39 × 27 ½ in.
(99.06 × 69.85 cm), 16 ¾ × 35 in. (42.54 × 88.9 cm),
55 × 12 in. (139.7 × 30.48 cm)
Courtesy of the Harrison Family Trust

***Santa Barbara County Park Proposal*, 1988**
Black-and-white photo text panel on paper
20 ¼ × 92 in. (51.43 × 233.68 cm)
Courtesy of the Harrison Family Trust

***Sketch for California Wash*, 1988–1997**
Four conceptual design drawings
Graphite and prismacolor on paper
32 ½ × 38 ½ in. (82.55 × 97.79 cm), 29 × 40 in.
(73.66 × 101.60 cm), 24 × 31 in. (60.96 × 78.74 cm),
70 × 34 in. (177.80 × 86.36 cm)
Courtesy of the Harrison Family Trust

***Photo of Helen and Newton Harrison*, 1980s**
Black-and-white photograph on archival paper
14 ¼ × 19 ¼ in. (36.19 × 48.89 cm) (image), 20 × 24 in.
(50.8 × 60.96 cm) (framed)
Courtesy of the Harrison Family Trust

***Miramar Landfill Proposal*, 1992**
Three aerial photographs, conceptual design drawing,
and text-panel
Photos mounted on board
23 ¼ × 33 ½ in. (59.05 × 85.09 cm), 21 × 25 in.
(53.34 × 63.5 cm), 25 × 21 in. (63.5 × 53.34 cm), 25 × 21 in.
(63.5 × 53.34 cm), 27 ¾ × 21 ½ in. (70.48 × 54.61 cm)
Courtesy of the Harrison Family Trust

CALIFORNIA CENTER FOR THE ARTS, ESCONDIDO

***San Diego as the Center of a World*, 1974**
Five photographic prints enhanced with ink, print,
and graphite; map mounted on canvas with printed
text inserts and handwritten texts
22 ¾ × 17 ½ in. (57.58 × 44.45 cm) (four prints
mounted on board); 50 × 46 ½ in. (127 × 118.11 cm)
(map on canvas)
Courtesy of the Harrison Family Trust

***The Lagoon Cycle*, 1972–1984**
Vellum paper laminated and mounted
on cotton canvas, acrylic gouache, collage,
photographic print enhanced with ink,
print, colored pencil and graphite
8 × 360 feet (243.84 × 10972.8 cm), seven lagoons,
sixty images
The major ones are 8′ tall and the minor ones are 3′ tall.
It requires approximately 360 feet of linear wall space
to be exhibited in its entirety.
Courtesy of the Centre Pompidou, Paris,
National Museum of Modern Art-Industrial Design Center:
Gift of Mr. John Kluge, 1997

***Performance of the Lagoon Cycle at List Art Gallery, Brown University*, 1979**
Video
Duration: 62:36 min.
Courtesy of Stanford University Libraries,
Department of Special Collections and
University Archives

***Book of the Seven Lagoons*, 1987**
Handmade book
Published by Laurence McGilvery in a limited edition
of 31 copies plus 8 artists' proofs.
Cloth and rope bound folio of 43 mylar-covered,
archivally processed photographs with graphite, ink,
and Marshall's photo oil on paper
26 × 28 in. (66 × 77.1 cm)
Courtesy of the Harrison Family Trust

***Untitled* (Outtake from the First Lagoon), 1974–1984, assembled 2021**
Archivally processed photographs with graphite, ink, and Marshall's photo oil on paper
14 ¾ × 44 ¾ in. (37.46 × 113.66 cm)
Courtesy of the Harrison Family Trust

***Untitled* (Outtake from the First Lagoon), 1974–1984, assembled 2021**
Archivally processed photographs with graphite, ink, and Marshall's photo oil on paper
19 ½ × 40 ¼ in. (49.53 × 102.23 cm)
Courtesy of the Harrison Family Trust

***Untitled* (Outtake from the Second Lagoon), 1974–1984, assembled 2021**
Archivally processed photographs with graphite, ink, and Marshall's photo oil on paper
20 × 69 in. (50.8 × 175.26 cm)
Courtesy of the Harrison Family Trust

***Untitled* (Outtake from the Fourth Lagoon), 1974–1984, assembled 2021**
Archivally processed photographs with graphite, ink, and Marshall's photo oil on paper
20 × 70 in. (50.80 × 177.80 cm)
Courtesy of the Harrison Family Trust

***Untitled* (Outtake from the Seventh Lagoon), 1974–1984, assembled 2021**
Archivally processed photographs with graphite, ink, and Marshall's photo oil on paper
21 × 24 ¼ in. (53.34 × 61.59 cm)
Courtesy of the Harrison Family Trust

***Untitled* (Outtake from the Seventh Lagoon), 1974–1984, assembled 2021**
Archivally processed photographs with graphite, ink, and Marshall's photo oil on paper
20 × 24 in. (50.80 × 60.96 cm)
Courtesy of the Harrison Family Trust

***Research Proposal for the Second Lagoon*, 1974**
Entitled "Hard Core Conceptual: Wherein the Transformations are Found Outside the Domain of Art in No Particular Order, in a Very Particular Order."
Photo-text panel on paper, graphite pencil, signed 1 of 15
17 × 30 ½ in. (43.18 × 77.47 cm)
Courtesy of the Harrison Family Trust

***Calculations for the Second Lagoon*, 1972-1974**
Photo-text panel on paper
32 ¾ × 44 ½ in. (83.18 × 113.03 cm)
Courtesy of the Harrison Family Trust

***Sketch for the Fourth Lagoon*, 1974–1984**
Drawing
Graphite on paper
18 ½ × 24 in. (46.99 × 60.96 cm)
Courtesy of the Harrison Family Trust

***Sketch for the Fifth Lagoon*, 1974–1984**
Drawing
Graphite on paper
27 × 30 in. (68.58 × 76.20 cm)
Courtesy of the Harrison Family Trust

***Meditation on the Gabrielino, Whose Name for Themselves is No Longer Remembered Although We Know that They Farmed with Fire and Fought Wars by Singing*, 1976**
Photographs, oil, graphite, and ink on canvas
68 1/4 × 145 in. (173.4 × 368.3 cm)
Courtesy of the Collection of the Museum of Contemporary Art San Diego, Gift of the artists and Museum purchase, 1979.2

***Sketch for Meditation on the Great Lakes of North America*, 1977**
Drawing and map
Graphite and ink on paper
39 × 46 in. (99.06 × 116.84 cm), 35 ¾ × 45 ½ in. (90.80 × 115.57 cm)
Courtesy of the Harrison Family Trust

***First Sketch for Meditations on the Sacramento River, the Delta, and the Bays of San Francisco*, 1977**
Graphite, ink, and maps on canvas
50 × 156 in. (127 × 396.24 cm)
Courtesy of the Harrison Family Trust

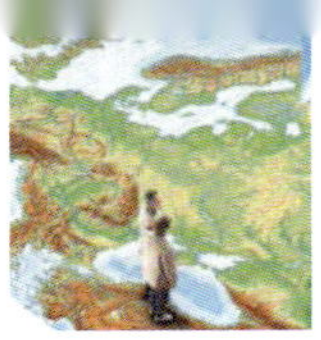

***Meditations on the Sacramento River, the Delta, and the Bays of San Francisco*, 1976–1977**

70 feet of wall space, nine large panels; eleven posters on paper; one paper billboard (with inscriptions by participants) mounted on canvas; photo of graffiti around fire hydrant on canvas; poster of "Wellbeing for the Waters of California" on canvas; "Manifesto on the Condition of Sacramento River" on canvas
Graphite, ink, Marshall's photo oils, and maps on canvas
Courtesy of the Harrison Family Trust
Part 1: From the Satellite the Central Valley is One Farm (unfinished)
90 × 79 in. (228.6 × 200.66 cm)
Part 2: In Praise of Folly or Who Dammed All the Rivers (2 parts) (unfinished)
90 × 72 ¼ in. (228.6 × 184.15 cm)
90 ¼ × 46 5/8 in. (229.23 × 118.42 cm)
Part 3: On Devaluing Land
90 ¼ × 80 ½ in. (229.23 × 204.47 cm)
Part 4: On Devaluing Water
90 ¾ × 79 ½ in. (230.50 × 201.93 cm)
Part 5: On Devaluing Topsoil
90 × 79 ¼ in. (228.6 × 201.29 cm)
Part 6: On Valuing Topsoil
89 ¾ × 78 ¾ in. (227.96 × 200.02 cm)
Part 7: On Valuing Water
90 ¾ × 79 ¼ in. (230.50 × 201.29 cm)
Part 8: On Valuing Land
90 ¼ × 80 ¾ in. (229.23 × 205.10 cm)
Part 9: On Revaluing Priorities
90 × 78 ¾ in. (228.6 × 200.02 cm)
Part 10: Water
Billboard with graffiti by the exhibition audience
Paint on paper, mounted on canvas
98 inches × 19 feet and 6 in. (248.92 × 594.24 cm)
Part 11. "For Instance, What If All That Irrigated Farming Isn't Necessary?"
Eleven posters; print on paper
11 × 17 in. (27.94 × 43.18 cm)
Part 12. Graffiti around Fire Hydrant
Photo on canvas
17 × 11 in. (43.18 × 27.94 cm)
Part 13. Wellbeing for the Waters of California
Conference poster on canvas
11 × 17 in. (27.94 × 43.18 cm)
Part 14. Manifesto on the Condition of Sacramento River
Print on canvas
30 × 21 ½ in. (76.2 × 54.61 cm)
Talking Water, Performance for Sacramento Meditations, 1977
Helen and Newton read from the texts of Sacramento Meditations at the San Francisco Art Institute
Audio file
Duration: 27:34 min.
Courtesy of Stanford University Libraries, Department of Special Collections and University Archives
Law of the Sea Conference: Where the Appetite is Discovered to be Endless, 1976
One large map and twelve smaller conceptual sketches
Photographs, ink, graphite, and colored pencil on canvas and/or on foamcore
96 ¾ × 4 feet and 3 in. (245.74 × 129.54 cm), 30 × 45 in. (76.2 × 114.3 cm)
Courtesy of the Harrison Family Trust
Guadalupe Meander, A Refugia for San José, 1983
Aerial photographs and conceptual design sketches
Collectively 80 feet, twenty-four pieces
Photographs on paper, ink, Marshall's photo oils, mounted on canvas and/or foamcore
Seven large panels: 97 × 83 in. (246.38 × 210.82 cm)
Four medium panels: 90 ¾ × 55 ¾ in. (230.50 × 141.60 cm)
Eight smaller panels: 60 × 50 in. (152.4 × 127 cm)
Four cut-outs: 24 × 77 in. (60.96 × 195.58 cm), 34 × 79 ¼ in. (86.36 × 200.66 cm), 27 ½ × 71 ¼ in. (69.85 × 180.97 cm), 29 ½ × 80 ½ in. (74.93 × 204.47 cm)
Master plan: 26 ¼ × 65 ¼ in. (66.67 × 165.73 cm)
Courtesy of the Harrison Family Trust

***The Bay Reshapes as the Ocean Rises. The San Joaquin River Watershed*, 2006**

Photographic print
35 × 67 in. (88.90 × 170.18 cm)
Courtesy of the Harrison Family Trust

***As the Temperature Rises the Sierra Nevada Does Poorly, the Central Valley Worse*, 2011**

Digital mapping, pastel, oil, and ink on archival paper
54 1/8 × 54 1/8 × 1 in. (137.79 × 137.79 × 2.54 cm)
Courtesy of the Harrison Family Trust

***The Bays at San Francisco Become a 162 000-hectare Estuarial Lagoon*, 2012–2015**

Four Panels
Archival inkjet print on archival paper
36 ½ × 56 ½ in. (92.71 × 143.51 cm)
Courtesy of the Harrison Family Trust

***Apologia Mediterraneo* (Counter Extinction Work V), 2019**

Print on vinyl and one-channel video
61 × 44 in. (154.94 × 111.76 cm)
Video duration: 10:10 min.
Courtesy of the Harrison Family Trust

***Sketches for Sensorium for the World Ocean*, 2019–2024**

Conceptual design: maps, texts, and installation views on paper
Computer and VR (Virtual Reality) visualizations and related interactive elements
42.91 × 94.88 in. (109 × 241 cm)
Courtesy of the Harrison Family Trust

***Sensorium for the World Ocean*, 2021**

Video produced by Eric Thiermann, with research and development by Dr. Ruby Barnett, Carinne Knight, Kelly Skye, and Rachel Smith
Duration: 13:40 min.
Courtesy of the Harrison Family Trust

SAN DIEGO CENTRAL LIBRARY ART GALLERY

***Serpentine Lattice*, Map, 1993**

Mixed media on paper
44-feet long × 8-10 feet wide (1341.12 × 243.84- 304.8 cm)
Courtesy of the Harrison Family Trust

***Serpentine Lattice*, 1993**

Two photomurals
Digital print on paper
6 × 4 foot (182.88 × 121.92 cm)
Courtesy of the Harrison Family Trust

***Serpentine Lattice*, 1993**

Digital projection on three projectors
Duration: 7:37 min.
Courtesy of the Harrison Family Trust

***Serpentine Lattice,* 1993–1995**

Video
Duration: 7:36 min.
Courtesy of the Harrison Family Trust

***Sierra Nevada: A Preliminary Proposal*, 1998**

Mixed media on paper
Three panels: 22 × 36 in. (55.88 cm × 91.44 cm)
Two panels: 36 × 45 in. (91.44 × 114.30 cm)
Courtesy of the Nevada Museum of Art, Robert S. and Dorothy J. Keyser Art of the Greater West Collection, Gift of the Artists

***The Yuba Watershed: Seven Maps Done Wrong – Homage to Aldo Leopold. 8 Yuba Mappings*, 2011–2012**

Digitally enhanced mapping on heavy banner vinyl photography, ink and hand in Tuscan pencil with acrylic fixative
92 × 77 in. (233.68 × 195.58 cm)
Courtesy of the Nevada Museum of Art, Robert S. and Dorothy J. Keyser Art of the Greater West Collection, Gift of the Artists

***The Sierra Nevada: An Adaptation: Floor map*, 2011**

Photographic print on linoleum laminate
36-foot long (1097.28 cm)
Courtesy of the Harrison Family Trust

***Sierra Nevada Watersheds*, 2011**

Sixteen digital prints on board
Merced – 18 × 59 ½ in. (45.72 × 151.13 cm)
Tuolumne – 20 ¼ × 59 ½ in. (51.43 × 151.13 cm)
Susan – 25 × 59 ½ in. (63.5 × 151.13 cm)
Truckee – 28 × 59 ½ in. (71.12 × 151.13 cm)
Owens – 25 ¼ × 59 ½ in. (64.13 × 151.13 cm)
Mokelumne – 15 × 59 ½ in. (38.1 × 151.13 cm)
Stanislaus – 16 ½ × 59 ½ in. (41.91 × 151.13 cm)
Walker – 32 ½ × 59 ½ in. (82.55 × 151.13 cm)
San Joaquin – 22 × 59 ½ in. (55.88 × 151.13 cm)
American – 21 ¾ × 59 ½ in. (55.24 × 151.13 cm)
Carson – 24 × 59 ½ in. (60.96 × 151.13 cm)
Mono – 19 1/8 × 59 ½ in. (48.57 × 151.13 cm)
Yuba – 18 × 59 ½ in. (45.72 × 151.13 cm)
Feather – 29 × 59 ½ in. (73.66 × 151.13 cm)
Kern – 24 ¼ × 59 ½ in. (61.59 × 151.13 cm)
Kings – 21 × 59 ½ in. (53.34 × 151.13 cm)
Courtesy of the Harrison Family Trust

***Fires in the West* or *Living Forests,* formerly *Saving the West*, video, 2016–2022**

Video duration: 13:42 min.
Courtesy of the Harrison Family Trust

MANDEVILLE ART GALLERY AT UC SAN DIEGO

***Making Earth*, 1969–1970**

Six color reproduction prints of the performance at Pepper Canyon Outdoor Studio at the University of California, San Diego, CA, mounted on foamcore
11 × 17 in. (27.24 × 43.18 cm)
Courtesy of the Harrison Family Trust

***Survival Piece V: Portable Orchard*, 1971**

Two photographs of the installation at the California State University, Fullerton, CA, on foam core
11 × 17 in. (27.24 × 43.18 cm)
The Harrison Family Trust

***Future Garden Part 1: Green House Europe, The Garden of Hot Winds and Warm Rains*, 1995**

10 blueprints and 2 conceptual design drawings
Pencil and ink on paper
24 × 33 ¾ in. (60.96 × 83.82 cm)
Courtesy of the Harrison Family Trust

***Future Garden Part 2: A Mother Meadow for the Parks of Bonn*, 1996–1997**

Conceptual design
Digital print of the photo-text panel on foam core
34 × 47 ¾ in. (86.36 × 121.28 cm)
Courtesy of the Harrison Family Trust

***The Garden of Hot Winds and Warm Rains*, 1995/2008**

Conceptual design drawing
Color pencil on paper
20 ½ × 36 in. (60.96 × 91.44 cm)
Courtesy of Roel Arkesteijn

***First Sketch for Tibet is the High Ground*, 1991–1993**

Drawing on paper and map on canvas
41 × 75 in. (104.14 × 190.5 cm)
69 ¼ × 75 in. (176.53 × 190.5 cm)
Courtesy of the Harrison Family Trust

***Proposal for the Tibetan Plateau: The Missing Peace*, 2006/2016**

Three digitally enhanced maps of Tibet
7 × 7 feet (213.36 × 213.36 cm)
Courtesy of the Harrison Family Trust

***Sketch for Tibet is the High Ground*, 2009**

Archival pigment print on canvas
54 × 44 in. (137.2 × 111.8 cm)
Courtesy of the Harrison Family Trust

***Sketch for Tibet is the High Ground*, 2011**

Digital mapping, pastel, oil, and ink on paper
48 × 48 in. (121.92 × 121.92 cm)
The Harrison Family Trust

***Sagehen: Independence Lake Watershed*, 2014**

Video animation by Derek Norpchen
Duration: 3:45 min.
Courtesy of the Harrison Family Trust

***Sagehen: A Proving Ground*, 2015**

Mixed media and digital print on paper
86 × 88 in. (218.44 cm × 223.52 cm)
Courtesy of the Nevada Museum of Art, Collection of the Nevada Museum of Art, Gift of the Artists

***Future Garden for the Central Coast of California*, 2018–ongoing**

Three photo text panels and digital projection of plants on the wall
Digital print on vinyl
3 × 4 foot (91.44 × 121.92 cm) (each)
Courtesy of the Harrison Family Trust

UCSC's Future Garden Video, produced by the UC Santa Cruz Division of Arts, 2018

Duration: 3:40 min.
Courtesy of the Harrison Family Trust

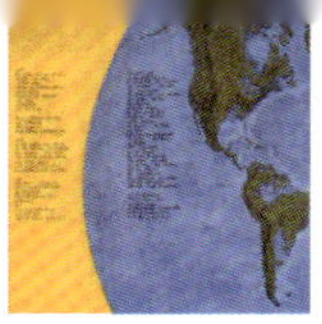

Selected Bibliography

PRIMARY SOURCES

Helen and Newton Harrison Papers, M1797. Special Collections & University Archives, Stanford University, Stanford, CA.

Harrisons Family Trust Digital Archive.

INTERVIEWS WITH THE ARTISTS

Adcock, Craig, "Conversational Drift: Helen Mayer Harrison and Newton Harrison," *Art Journal,* Vol. 51, No. 2, Summer, 1992, pp. 35–45.

Allen, Jane Ingram, "How Big is Here: A Conversation with Helen Mayer Harrison and Newton Harrison," *Sculpture magazine*, Vol. 26, No. 10, December 2007, pp. 48–53.

Harrison, Helen Mayer, Newton Harrison, and Peter Selz, "The Harrisons: Talking and Remembering," *Leonardo* 45, No. 1, 2012, pp. 9–16.

Kopytin, Alexander I., and Stephen K. Levine, "An interview with Newton Harrison," *Ecopoiesis: Eco-Human Theory and Practice*, Vol. 2, No. 1, 2021, open access peer-review internet journal. https://en.ecopoiesis.ru/interviews/article_post/an-interview-with-newton-harrison.

Kupper, Oliver, "Force Majeure: Pioneering Eco-Artists the Harrisons Created a Survival Guide for a World Careening Toward Disaster," *Autre*, Issue 13, F/W 2021, pp. 250–257.

PUBLICATIONS BY THE ARTISTS

Harrison, Helen Mayer, and Newton Harrison, *The Lagoon Cycle*. Herbert F. Johnson Museum of Art, Cornell University, Ithaca, NY, 1985.

Harrison, Helen Mayer, and Newton Harrison, "Shifting Positions toward the Earth: Art and Environmental Awareness," *Leonardo*, Vol. 26, No. 5, 1993, pp. 371–377.

Harrison, Helen Mayer, and Newton Harrison, *The Serpentine Lattice*. Douglas F. Cooley Memorial Art Gallery, Reed College, Portland, OR, 1993.

Harrison, Helen Mayer, and Newton Harrison, *Green Heart Vision*. The Harrison Studio and the Cultural Council and Province of South Holland, Den Haag, Holland and Del Mar California, 1995.

Harrison, Helen Mayer, and Newton Harrison, "Knotted Ropes, Rings, Lattices and Lace: Retrofitting Biodiversity into the Cultural Landscape," *Biodiversity: A Challenge for Development Research and Policy,* edited by Barthlott, Wilhelm, and Matthias Winiger. Springer-Verlag, Berlin, Heidelberg, New York, 1998.

Harrison, Helen Mayer, and Newton Harrison, *Peninsula Europe. The High Grounds*. Berlin, 2001.

Harrison, Helen Mayer, and Newton Harrison, *From There to Here*. Berlin, 2001.

Harrison, Helen Mayer, and Newton Harrison, "Seventh Lagoon: The Ring of Water," *Structure and Dynamics: eJournal of Anthropological and Related Sciences*, Vol. 1, Issue 4, 2006, https://escholarship.org/uc/item/45z287n2#main.

Harrison, Helen Mayer, and Newton Harrison, "Public Culture and Sustainable Practices: Peninsula Europe from an Ecodiversity Perspective, Posing Questions to Complexity Scientist," *Structure and Dynamics: eJournal of Anthropological and Related Sciences*, Vol. 2, Issue 3, 2007, Article 3, https://escholarship.org/uc/item/9hj3s753.

Harrison, Helen Mayer, and Newton Harrison, *The Time of the Force Majeure: After 45 Years Counterforce is on the Horizon,* edited and designed by Petra Kruse and Kai Reschke, essays by Anne Douglas & Chris Fremantle, William L. Fox, Eleanor Heartney, Roger F. Malina, Paul Mankiewicz & Dorion Sagan, and Anne Whiston Spirn. Prestel, Munich, London, New York, 2016.

Harrison, Newton, "Center for the Study of the Force Majeure." Center for the Study of the Force Majeure, University of Santa Cruz, CA, 2019, edited and designed by Petra Kruse and Kai Reschke.

Harrison, Newton, "Sensorium: The Voice of the World Ocean." Center for the Study of the Force Majeure, University of Santa Cruz, CA, 2022, edited and designed by Petra Kruse and Kai Reschke.

SECONDARY SOURCES

Allen, Jane Ingram, "A Marriage Made on Earth: Helen Mayer Harrison and Newton Harrison," *Public Art Review*, Issue 38, 2008, pp. 28–30.

Arroyo Seco Release: *A Serpentine for Pasadena: A Work by Helen Mayer and Newton Harrison*, introduction by Jay Belloli. Baxter Art Gallery, California Institute of Technology, Pasadena, CA, 1985.

At Home, edited by Arlene Raven. Long Beach Museum of Art, Long Beach, CA, 1983.

Beardsley, John, *Earthworks and Beyond: Contemporary Art in the Landscape*. Third Edition. Abbeville Press, New York, London, Paris, 1998.

Bijvoet, Marga, *Art as Inquiry, Toward New Collaborations Between Art, Science, and Technology*. American University Studies, Peter Lang, New York, 1997, pp. 137–148.

Bischoff, Ulrich, "Shifting Metaphors, The Creative Technique of Helen Mayer and Newton Harrison," *Atempause für den Save-Fluss*. exh. cat. Neuer Berliner Kunstverein, Berlin, Germany, and Moderna Galerija, Ljubljana, Slovenia, 1990.

Boetzkes, Amanda, "Techniques of Survival: The Harrisons and the Environmental Counterculture," *West of Center: Art and the Counterculture Experiment in America, 1965–1977*, edited by Elissa Author and Adam Lerner. NED-New edition, University of Minnesota Press, 2012, pp. 306–323.

Book of Seven Lagoons. D.A.A.D. Gallery, Berlin, Germany, 1988.

Burnham, Jack, "Systems Esthetics," *Art Forum*, September, 1968.

Burnham, Jack, "The 'Art and Technology' Exhibition at the Los Angeles County Museum (Two Views): Corporate Art," *Art Forum*, Vol. 10, No. 2, October 1971.

Burnham, Jack, *Great Western Salt Works: Essays on the Meaning of Post-Formalist Art*. George Braziller, New York, 1974.

Burnham, Jack, *Dissolve into Comprehension: Writings and Interviews, 1964–2004*, edited by Melissa Ragain. Writing Art Series, The MIT Press, Cambridge, MA, 2015.

But is It Art? *The Spirit of Art as Activism*, edited by Nina Felshin. Bay Press, Seattle, WA, 1995.

Carson, Rachel, *Silent Spring*. Houghton Mifflin, Boston, MA, 1962.

Certeau, Michel de, "Pay Attention: To Make Art," *The Lagoon Cycle*: *March 23 through June 2, 1985*, Harrison, Helen Mayer, and Newton Harrison. Herbert F. Johnson Museum of Art, Cornell University, Ithaca, NY, 1985, pp. 17–23.

Collins, Tim, "Environmental Artworkers," *FIELD*, Issue 23, Winter 2023, https://field-journal.com/editorial/6816.

Dawsey, Jill, "The Uses of Photography: An Introduction," *The Uses of Photography: Art, Politics, and the Reinvention of a Medium*, edited by Jill Dawsey. Museum of Contemporary Art, San Diego, CA, UC Press, 2016.

Douglas, Anne and Chris Fremantle, "'Thinking with' the Harrisons: What Does Now Demand?" *FIELD*, Issue 23, Winter 2023, https://field-journal.com/issue-23/thinking-with-the-harrisons-what-does-now-demand.

Engelstad, Janeil, "Disremembering the Harrisons," *Leonardo*, Vol. 56, No. 3, 2023, p. 299.

Fillen-Yeh, Susan, "The Serpentine Lattice: Where you said a Lattice and I said a Serpentine and you said Network the Watersheds and I said a Game of Go," *The Serpentine Lattice*. Douglas F. Cooley Memorial Art Gallery, Reed College, Portland, OR, 1993, pp. 16–23.

Fragile Ecologies, essay by Barbara C. Matilsky. The Queens Museum of Art, Queens, NY, 1992.

Fremantle, Chris, and Anne Douglas, editors, "Paying Attention to Make Art: Twenty-nine Reflections on the Harrisons," *The Nature of Cities*, March 18, 2023, https://www.thenatureofcities.com/2023/03/18/paying-attention-to-make-art-twenty-nine-reflections-on-the-harrisons/.

Future Garden. Kunst- und Ausstellungshalle der Bundesrepublik Deutschland, Bonn, Germany, 1996.

Gell, Alfred, *Art and Agency. An Anthropological Theory*. Clarendon Press, Oxford, 1998.

Green, Charles, "Memory and Ethics: Helen Mayer Harrison and Newton Harrison," *The Third Hand: Collaboration in Art from Conceptualism to Postmodernism*. University of Minnesota Press, 2001, pp. 97–122.

Green Heart Vision. Kunstmuseum Bonn, Bonn, Germany, 1997.

Heartney, Eleanor, "Dancing with the Waters: Helen and Newton Harrisons' Call to Action," *The Time of the Force Majeure: After 45 Years Counterforce is on the Horizon*, Harrison, Helen Mayer, and Newton Harrison, pp. 443–446.

Ingram, Mrill, "Ecopolitics and Aesthetics: The Art of Helen Mayer Harrison and Newton Harrison," *Geographical Review*, Vol. 103, No. 2, 2013, pp. 260–274.

Jones, Caroline A., "Caroline A. Jones on Helen Mayer Harrison (1927–2018)," *Artforum International*, April 7, 2018.

Juergensen, Andreas and Gertrude Koebke Sutton, *Trilogy: Art – Nature – Science*. Kunsthallen Brandts Klædefabrik, Odense, Denmark, 1996.

Kagan, Sacha, *Art and Sustainability: Connecting Patterns for a Culture of Complexity*. Second Edition. Transcript Verlag, Bielefeld, Germany, 2013.

Kastner, Jeffrey, *Land and Environmental Art*. Phaidon, London, United Kingdom, 1998.

Kester, Grant, *Conversation Pieces: Community and Communication in Modern Art*. University of California Press, Berkeley, CA, 2004.

Kruse, Petra, and Kai Reschke, "Chances, Limitations, and Conditions of Ecological Art: Three European Projects by Helen Mayer Harrison and Newton Harrison," *FIELD*, Issue 23, Winter 2023, https://field-journal.com/issue-23/chances-limitations-and-conditions-of-ecological-art-three-european-projects-by-helen-mayer-harrison-and-newton-harrison.

Lakoff, George, and Mark Johnson, *Metaphors We Live By*. University of Chicago Press, Chicago and London, 1980.

Lebowitz, Cathy, "Newton Harrison and Helen Mayer Harrison," *Art in America*, Vol. 97, No. 5, May 2009, pp. 152–154.

Levin, Kim, *Beyond Modernism*. UMI Press, Ann Arbor, MI, 1989.

Malina, Roger, "Force Majeure: Performing the Data of Climate Change," *The Time of the Force Majeure: After 45 Years Counterforce is on the Horizon*, Harrison, Helen Mayer and Newton Harrison, pp. 447–450.

***Mapping the Terrain**: New Genre Public Art*, edited by Suzanne Lacy. Bay Press, Seattle, WA, 1995.

Matilsky, Barbara C., *Vanishing Ice: Alpine and Polar Landscapes in Art, 1775–2012*. Whatcom Museum, Bellingham, WA, 2013, pp. 50–51.

McCray, W. Patrick, *Making Art Work: How Cold War Engineers and Artists Forged a New Creative Culture*. MIT Press, Cambridge, MA, 2020.

McGreevy, Linda, "Improving the Future: The Eco-Aesthetics of Newton and Helen Harrison," *Arts Magazine*, November 1987, pp. 69–72.

Ragain, Melissa Sue, "'Homeostasis Is Not Enough': Order and Survival in Early Ecological Art," *Art Journal/College Art Association of America*, Vol. 71, No. 3, 2012, pp. 78–97.

Raskin, David, "Jetties and Lagoons: The Art of Robert Smithson and Newton and Helen Mayer Harrison," *Tracing Cultures: Art History, Criticism, Critical Fiction*. Whitney Museum of American Art, New York, NY, 1994.

Ratcliff, Carter, "A Compendium of Possibilities," *Lagoon Cycle*. Cornell University Office of Publications, Ithaca, NY, 1985, pp. 11–16.

Raven, Arlene, *Art in the Public Interest*. UMI Press, Ann Arbor, MI, 1989.

Rogers, Laura Cassidy, "The Social and Environmental Turn in Late 20th Century Art: A Case Study of Helen and Newton Harrison After Modernism." PhD diss., Stanford University, CA, 2017.

Ryan, Leslie, "Art + Ecology: Land Reclamation Works of Artists Robert Smithson, Robert Morris, and Helen Mayer Harrison and Newton Harrison," *Environmental Philosophy*, Vol. 4, No. 1 & 2 (Special Issue: *Environmental Aesthetics and Ecological Restoration*), Spring/Fall 2007, pp. 95–116.
Selz, Peter, "Helen and Newton Harrison: Art as Survival Instruction," *Art in a Turbulent Era*. UMI Press, Ann Arbor, MI, 1985, chapter 35.
Sarnoff, Irving, and Suzanne, *Intimate Creativity: Partners in Love and Art*. The University of Wisconsin Press, Madison, WI, 2002, pp. 62, 101–102, 151–152, 203–204.
Shanken, Edward, "Tipping the Scales: The Harrisons and the Force Majeure," *Rydell Visual Arts Fellows 2016–2017*, exh. cat. Community Foundation Santa Cruz County, Santa Cruz, CA, 2017, pp. 24–41.
Solnit, Rebecca, "Helen Mayer Harrison/Newton Harrison: Metaphor and Habitat," *Artspace magazine*, July/August 1990, pp. 49–53.
Sonfist, Alan, editor, *Art in the Land: A Critical Anthology of Environmental Art*. E. P. Dutton, New York, 1983.
Spirn, Anne Whiston, "Helen and Newton Harrison: The Art of Inquiry, Manifestation, and Enactment," Harrison, Helen Mayer, and Newton Harrison, *The Time of the Force Majeure: After 45 Years Counterforce is on the Horizon*, pp. 434–438.
"Technology and the Great Lakes," *The Gentle Art of Survival*. Center for 20th Century Studies, Wisconsin Humanities Committee, University of Wisconsin, Milwaukee, WI, 1978.
Tuchman, Maurice, editor, *A Report on the Art and Technology Program of the Los Angeles County Museum of Art, 1967–1971*. Los Angeles County Museum of Art, Los Angeles, CA, 1971.
Wallen, Ruth, "Helen and Newton Harrison: Visionary Ecoartists," *Leonardo*, Vol. 56, No. 3, 2023, pp. 312–313.
Weintraub, Linda, "Helen and Newton Harrison: Strategies to Sustain Life," *To Life! Eco Art in Pursuit of a Sustainable Planet*, Weintraub, Linda. University of California Press, Berkeley, CA, 2012, pp. 74–80.
Winter, Michael, and Matt Lobley, *What is Land For? The Food, Fuel and Climate Change Debate*. Earthscan, London, United Kingdom, 2009.

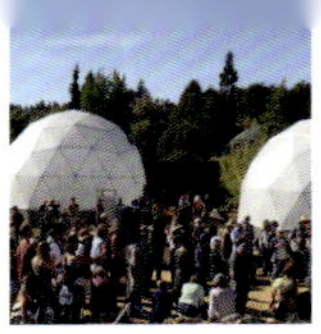

Contributors

MONICA MANOLESCU, PhD, is a Professor of American Literature and Art at the University of Strasbourg, France, and a junior member of the Institut Universitaire de France. She has written widely on 20th century and contemporary American literature and art. Her most recent publications are the *Cahier de l'Herne Nabokov* (Editions de l'Herne, 2023) and a critical edition of Véra Nabokov's previously unpublished journal (*L'Ouragan Lolita. Journal 1958–1959*, Editions de l'Herne, 2023), both edited with Yannicke Chupin. She is co-editor-in-chief of the American studies journal *Transatlantica*. She has been a visiting scholar at the Institute for Advanced Study in Princeton, an honorary research fellow at the University of Kent and a short-term visiting professor at the College of Liberal Arts of the International Christian University in Tokyo.

EDWARD SHANKEN, PhD, Professor, Arts Division at UC Santa Cruz. Since 1994, he has written on the entwinement of art, science, and technology, with a focus on interdisciplinary practices involving new media and visual culture. His scholarship has appeared in numerous journals and anthologies and has been translated into many languages. In his own words: "I believe that by opening our hearts more fully to ourselves, we can open our hearts more fully to other beings and to the Earth. To this end, my academic work seeks to create and share knowledge. I am best known for my book *Art and Electronic Media* (Phaidon, 2009). Like Jack Burnham, who thought of art as a 'psychic dress rehearsal for the future,' I've been especially interested in the ways artists create working models that allow us to get a taste of alternative futures in the present. Burnham also thought of artists as 'deviation amplifiers.' By deploying technology in a metacritical way, by 'perverting technological correctness' (Rafael Lozano-Hemmer), art becomes a 'strange tool' (Alva Noe) that offers profound insights. I believe that art, at its best, offers a type of knowledge, which Gregory Bateson likened to wisdom, that can help build a more compassionate and peaceful future. Since 2019, I have striven to integrate joy and wisdom, personally and professionally, leading to the realization that joy contains wisdom within it, and vice versa. My artistic practices as a musician and dancer have become central aspects of my work, deeply impacting my scholarship, and strengthening my commitment to serving the Earth. Into the light!"

TATIANA SIZONENKO, PhD, is an art historian and award-winning curator working across the Renaissance, Modern, and Contemporary periods. She is an art history faculty member at the Department of Art, Media, and Design, California State University San Marcos. She earned her Ph.D. in Renaissance art history from the Visual Arts Department at UC San Diego while also developing expertise in contemporary art. Tatiana was the recipient of several fellowships including the Harvard University research project "From Riverbed to Seashore," sponsored by the Getty Research Foundation's "Connecting Art Histories" program. Her chapter is included in the book *The Land Between Two Seas*, published by Brill in 2022. In 2017 she was named Environmental Fellow of John Muir College at UCSD for her curatorial work on the exhibition *Weather on Steroids: The Art of Climate Change Science,* shown at the La Jolla Historical Society. Tatiana has curated, organized, and installed several dozen exhibitions, coordinated and prepared several exhibition catalogues, and published catalogue essays and peer-reviewed articles in the United States and in Russia. Tatiana's research has also been supported by CSUSM's faculty research grants, UCSD's Dean of Art and Humanities Dissertation Research Fellowship, among others.

Exhibition Staff

LA JOLLA HISTORICAL SOCIETY

Lauren Lockhart, Executive Director
Heath Fox, Former Executive Director, Project Director for *Helen and Newton Harrison: California Work*
Tatiana Sizonenko, PhD, Project Curator for *Helen and Newton Harrison: California Work*
McKenna Clifford Yahyai, Education and Public Engagement Manager
Karla Cook, Office and Events Manager
Dana Hicks, PhD, Former Deputy Director and Collections Manager
Colette Militello, Collections Manager
Carol Olten, Historian

CALIFORNIA CENTER FOR THE ARTS ESCONDIDO

Gina Lopez, Chief Executive Officer
Beth Marino, Former Director of Museum and Visual Arts
Rokhsane Hovaida, Museum Manager
Alan Clark, Preparator
Rebecca Wright, Visitor Services Representative
Ken Hladky, Visitor Services Representative
Ernie Valverde, Facilities Director

SAN DIEGO CENTRAL LIBRARY ART GALLERY

Bonnie Domingos, Gallery Director, Library Arts & Culture
Sarah Banks, Gallery Assistant
Max Peyro-Hernandez, Gallery Assistant

THE MANDEVILLE ART GALLERY AT UC SAN DIEGO

Ceci Moss, PhD, Director and Chief Curator
Adrian Del Riego, Preparator

Lenders to the Exhibition

Roel Arkesteijn, Private Collection
Stanford University Libraries, Special Collections and Archives, Stanford, California
The Centre Georges Pompidou, Paris, National Museum of Modern Art-Industrial Design Center, Paris, France
The Harrison Family Trust, Santa Cruz, California
The Los Angeles County Museum of Art, Los Angeles, California
The Museum of Contemporary Art San Diego, San Diego, California
The Nevada Museum of Art, Robert S. and Dorothy J. Keyser Art of the Greater West Collection, Reno, Nevada
Various Small Fires Gallery, Los Angeles, California

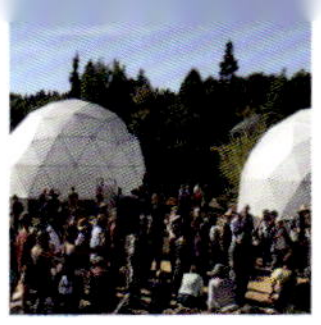

La Jolla Historical Society: Board of Directors

Acknowledgements

The Harrison Family: Steve, Josh, Gabriel, and Joy
Stanford University Archives
- Robert G Trujillo
- Tim Edward Noakes
- Leif Anderson

Department of Visual Arts, UC San Diego
- Ricardo Dominguez
- Grant Kester

Centre Georges Pompidou, Paris
- Bernard Blistene
- Raphaële Bianchi
- Karine Jonneaux
- Rania Moussa

Museum of Contemporary Art San Diego
- Kathryn Kanjo
- Jill Dawsey
- Karin Zonis-Sawrey

Los Angeles County Museum of Art
- Department of Modern Art
- Frances Lazare

Nevada Museum of Art
- Ann M. Wolfe
- Brian Eyler

Various Small Fires Gallery, Los Angeles
- Esther Kim Varet
- Ariel Pittman
- Michelle Kang

Petra Kruse
Kai Reschke
Alex Kohnke
Philipp Scholz Rittermann
Wendell Eckholm and ArtWorks San Diego
Curran Kiel
Brian Lockhart and Quint Gallery

Solomon Cohen
Ryan Campbell and Wonka Gallery
Janos Novak and JDewers Custom Framing and Fine Art Services
Lucas Coffin
Paolo Zuniga
Monica Manolescu
Edward Shanken
Anne Douglas
Chris Fremantle
Brandon Ballengée
Ruby Barnett
Barbara Benish
Lauren Bon and Metabolic Studio
Tim Collins
Ann Craig
Teddy Cruz
Betsy Damon
Gareth Davies-Morris
Alexander Gershunov
Reiko Goto
Cathy Fitzgerald
Fonna Forman
David Haley
Maureen Harrison
Judit Hersko
David Hodge
Hi-Jin Hodge
Justin Lane-Lutter
Erin McGilvery
Laurence McGilvery
Art Miller
Roger Malina
Mark Nash
Leslie Ryan
Rachel Smith
Lucy Solomon
Ruth Wallen
Anne Whiston Spirn

Partner Venues

California Center for the Arts, Escondido FOUNDATION

SD Public Library

MANDEVILLE ART GALLERY

SENSORIUM: THE BEGINNING A PARTIAL SKETCH

Sensorium is a space cathedral like sensibility created to enable anyone
to generate and experience discourse with the world ocean
Sensorium presents visually in scientific detail complex oceanic life web threats
by revealing dead zones' endless plastic input with the distributed waste from ships
from fish farming and ocean netting creating bottom dead spaces
Sensorium can give voice and image to both oceanic and land-based pollution sources
responsible for the degeneration of the oceanic life web now experiencing extinctions
Sensorium permits multisystem scanning and seeing simultaneously
similar to the envisioning developed by our ancestors to survive in their ecosystems
and become niches setting tribal life support patterns in place for long term survival
Sensorium is speculative design work that manifests complex oceanic problems
all at once and all together often requiring transdisciplinary efforts by many
Sensorium's visualizing system permits direct work on multisystem problem resolution
For instance Sensorium envisions oceanic nurseries as a network that can call forth
a transoceanic sanctuary pattern then envisioning revitalized dead zones transformed
while simultaneously revealing an unexpected resolution to global shipping pollution
simultaneously visualizing plastics and their elimination from the food chain
as fundamental to a healthy oceanic life web as imperative
Sensorium has the power to express relationships not previously
seeable therefore newly knowable thereby opening new space of mind

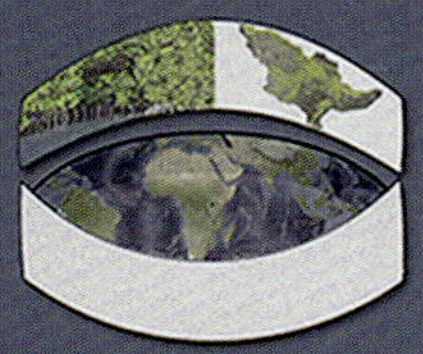

THE SENSORIUM COMPLETE
IS IN THE ROUND

SENSORIUM: DEAD ZONES TRANSFORMATION

Well-mapped dead zones over 450 in number have formed at coastlines
with oxygen depletion from the overproduction of algae as the death cause
Sensorium first maps the worst of places making clear that
most oceanic dead areas happen as a result of land-based pollution
often river inflow from agro-industrial waste urban and industrial waste
Worst is the outfall from the 1.2-million-square-mile Mississippi drain basin
pouring into the Gulf generating a 1000-mile-long 7000-square-mile dead zone
soon to be 8000-square-miles from the Mississippi outfall to the Galveston Bay
Sensorium's visualizations make clear the need for land-based purification systems
to be created on the coastline between the Mississippi outfall and Galveston Bay
Short-term solutions happen when saltwater wetland swamps are created
with pumping systems invented to exchange newly clean waters from the
wetlands and polluted Gulf waters from the dead zone newly reoxygenated
First become productive living zone or even a candidate for sanctuary
Long-term solutions require all pollution sources agro-farming in particular
need resolution at their source of creation
Complex in solving but imperative in the doing

SENSORIUM: OCEAN NURSERIES AND

Sensorium's pattern visualization proc
these diverse mothers of oceanic life
When nurseries the mangrove forest
coral reefs estuarine wetlands swam
in their entirety are conjoined and de
Sensorium can then visualize a transo
with protected nurseries acting to pro
Collectively protecting nurseries mak
Sensorium envisions cojoining a nurs
revealing a complex eco-regenerative
This envisioning further indicates that
wherein dead zones the worst of pla
cojoin in an ongoing foundational sou
And with the beginning of life protect
the invisible beneficiary is land-based

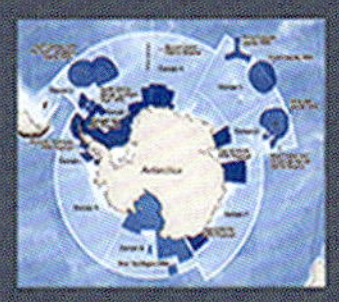

One can see that the Arctic Ocean is in
great need of sanctuary work

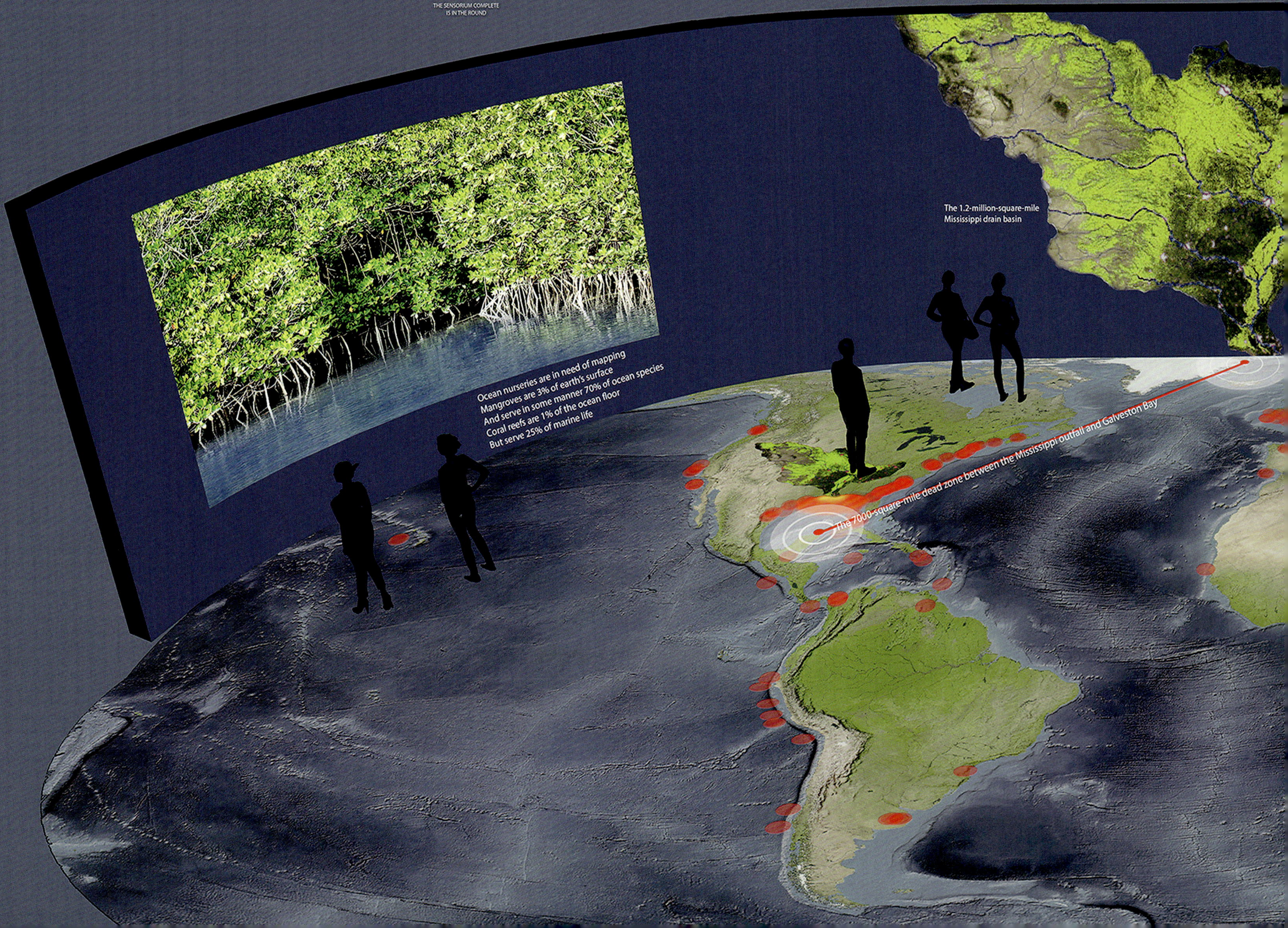

RN RECOGNITION

kes clear that oceanic nurseries
stly local places all calling for sanctuary
nouths of estuaries
rsery slicks and upwelling areas
l as sanctuaries
life support system
e beginnings of most oceanic life
valuable new pattern discovery
ctuary pattern with revitalized dead zones
ceanic sanctuary pattern
anic sanctuary pattern this complex
d nurseries the most endangered of places
oceanic life web's continuing evolution
oceanic well being guaranteed
luding our own ability to continue

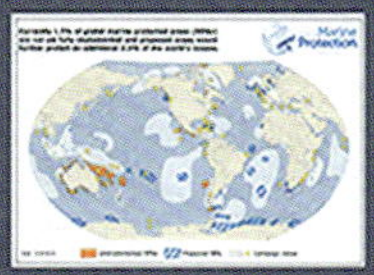

Mapping so much ocean
With so few sanctuarries

SENSORIUM: EXPRESSES A GLOBAL WETLAND PATTERN

Sensorium reveals a transoceanic pattern for wetland restoration
If saltwater and brackish water wetland purification systems are created
whose work is to receive and transform deoxygenated eutrophic waters
from the 450 land-adjacent dead zones then exchanging them with healthy
nutritious reoxygenated waters dead zone waters can be transformed
into the healthy biotope that existed before extreme extraction and pollution
Sensorium seeing a new global pattern of wetlands reveals alternative outcomes
responding with a mapping of daily oceanic vessel presence in a shocking snapshot
making clear a necessity that ships transfer waste to wetlands at nearest port of arrival
Thus relieving the ocean from yet another intractable pollution assault
all costs borne by polluters the beneficiary the world ocean's life web
with recovering fish populations and extinction reduction as outcomes
Sensorium continuing in transaction with multidisciplinary human explorers
can make clear that only the overproduction of fish populations can be harvested
envisioning the harvesting redundancy as preserving the system
protecting oceanic systems' biota population balance to stay intact
and become the life web's way of continuing while serving human need
Then criminality is associated with overharvesting and pollution creation
as are human behaviors that cause oceanic life web degeneration

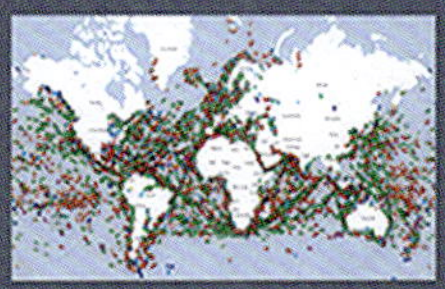

Where every ship on the whole ocean is marked
The pollution aggressive the resolution available

SENSORIUM: PLASTICS AND THE OCEAN'S LIFE WEB

Sensorium in the beginning of its development responds to the question
What is the most dangerous single element infecting the life web?
Its response now held by many is that plastic particularly micro bits
negatively affects life that ingests it first in the oceanic food chain
then infecting land-based life particularly the human food chain
So sensorium visualizes this vast plastic infection from land-based manufacture
infecting rivers oceans oceanic life and all who consume oceanic life
Sensorium sees the Benioff Clean Ocean Currents Coalition
as the most comprehensive viable approach to whole-systems plastic removal
Sensorium presents the coalition mapping oceanwide as forceful evidence
Coalition then chooses 9 of 1000 rivers to install massive plastic recovery systems
Their discovery is that 80 percent of plastic pollution
into oceans world-wide is transported by these 9 rivers
Plastic river capture removes plastic waste before ocean entry a short-term solution
This coalition simultaneously engages in eco politically land based long-term solutions
calling for recyclable alternatives dealing with plastic pollution on site
The beneficiaries are all oceanic and land-based life particularly the human food chain
Sensorium visualizes the value of the reduction of plastic production possible
only when agreement is developed to leave coal gas and oil in the ground
Sensorium's search found no better whole-systems thinking and work safeguarding
virtually all oceanic life in the doing than this coalition's work

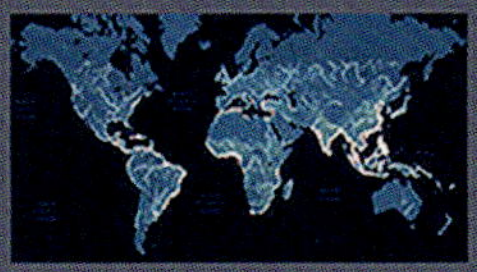

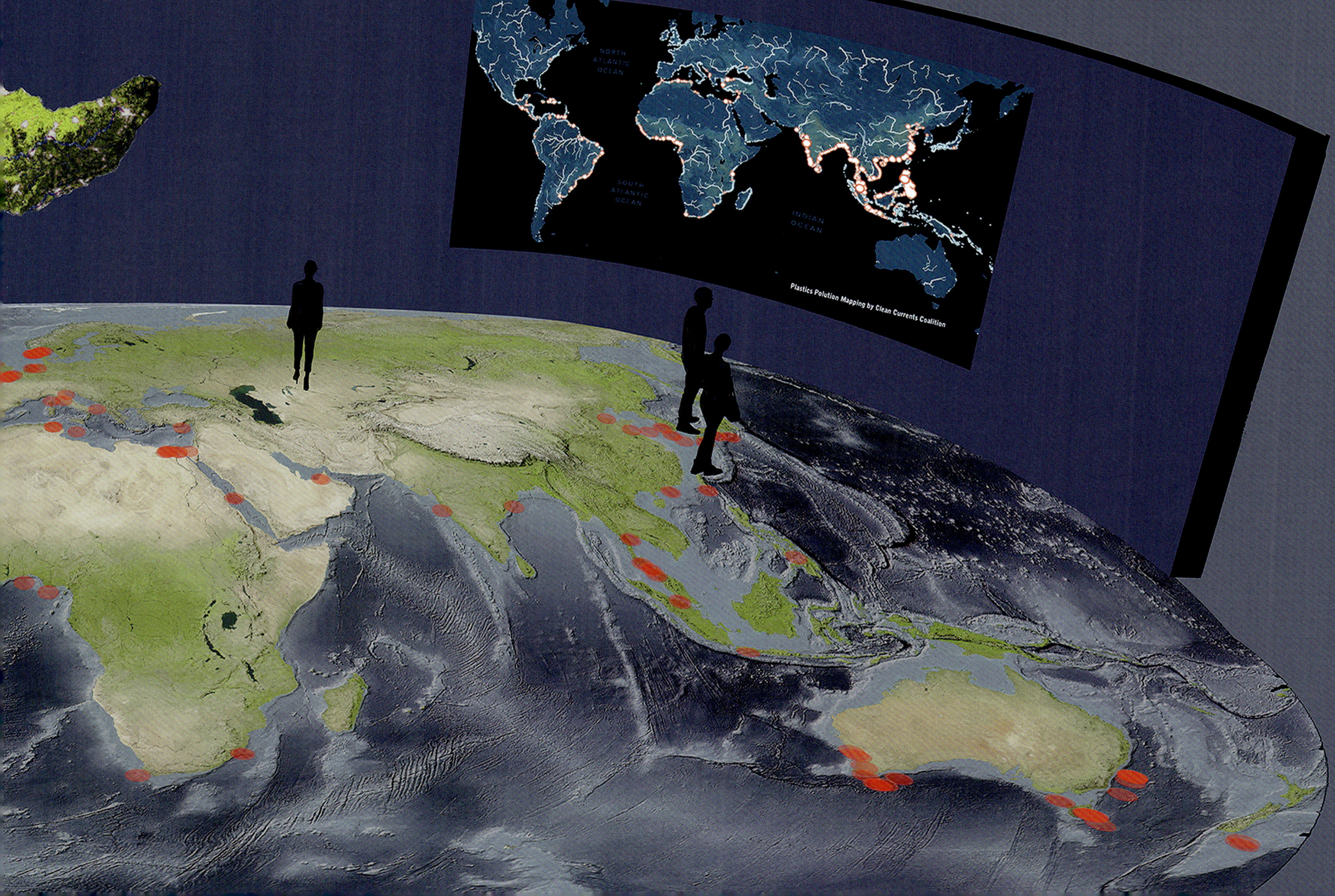

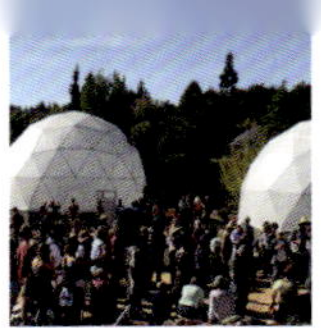

Photo Credits and Copyrights

Photo credits:
Art on Art LLC, Video Producer: Nada Miljković: pp. 202/203
AlloSphere Research Team, UC Santa Barbara: pp. 126, 127
Lennart Bourin: p. 33
Rebecca Cohen: p. 6
Matthew Jamieson: p. 123
Reschke & Kruse: pp. 149, 191

Courtesy of Art and Exhibition Hall of the Federal Republic of Germany, Bonn: pp. 143, 178 top and bottom
Courtesy of Center for the Study of the Force Majeure: pp. 125, 220/221
Courtesy of Contemporary Arts Museum Houston: p. 53
Courtesy of Museum of Contemporary Art San Diego: pp. 14, 15
Courtesy of Museum of Contemporary Art, Los Angeles: p. 37 r.
Courtesy of Nevada Museum of Art: p. 165
Courtesy of Nevada Museum of Art, Robert S. and Dorothy J. Keyser Art of the Greater West Collection: pp. 162, 163
Courtesy of Ronald Feldman Fine Arts, New York: pp. 61, 87, 167
Courtesy of Stanford University Libraries Special Collections and the Harrison Family Trust:
Cover, pp. 4 and 91 (collage Reschke & Kruse), 23, 24, 26, 27, 28, 29, 30, 31, 32, 38, 42, 43, 46, 47, 48 l., 50, 51, 52, 54, 55, 59, 62/63, 64/65, 72 r., 89 l., 113, 157
Courtesy of Various Small Fires, Los Angeles: p. 36

All other images: Courtesy of the Harrison Family Trust

The La Jolla Historical Society and the editor thank the photographers, museums, and galleries for their generous support in realization of this book. Despite careful research, it was not possible to identify every photographer or to determine every rights holder. We apologize and ask for your understanding.

This book is published on the occasion of the exhibition
Helen and Newton Harrison: California Work
at the La Jolla Historical Society in San Diego, CA,
from September 19, 2024 to January 19, 2025.
The exhibition is part of the Getty Foundation's
»Pacific Standard Time. Art and Science Collide«.

Editor Tatiana Sizonenko
Contributors Monica Manolescu | Edward Shanken | Tatiana Sizonenko
Project Management | **Design** | **Color Separation** | **Final Artwork** | **Production**
Reschke & Kruse, Berlin | Cologne (Germany)
Copyediting Logan Kennedy, Lunenburg, Nova Scotia (Canada)
Printing and Binding optimal media GmbH, Röbel/Müritz (Germany)

Typeface Mark Pro in different styles
Paper 150 g/m² Magno Volume 1.08

Part of Walter de Gruyter GmbH Berlin / Boston
www.deutscherkunstverlag.de · www.degruyter.com
Photo Credits and Copyrights p. 222

Library of Congress Control Number 2024941508

A CIP catalogue record for this book is available from the British Library.
Deutsche Nationalbibliothek holds a record of this publication
in the Deutsche Nationalbibliografie; detailed bibliographical data
can be found at: http://www.dnb.de

ISBN 978-3-422-80211-7

Cover Illustration First Sketch for Meditations on the Sacramento River, the Delta, and the Bays of San Francisco, 1977
Illustration p. 2 Helen & Newton Harrison in front of the Sixth Lagoon, ca. 1982
Illustration p. 4 Helen & Newton Harrison with the first Sketch for Meditations on the Sacramento River, the Delta, and the Bays of San Francisco performing 1977 at the San Francisco Art Institute, San Francisco Museum of Modern Art, CA
Illustration p. 6, Helen & Newton Harrison, ca. 1981/82
Illustration pp. 202 | 203 Video Still from Helen & Newton Harrison's presentation of Wilma the Pig in Hog Pasture: Survival Piece #1 (1970–1971), on September 1, 2012, at the Museum of Contemporary Art, Los Angeles, CA
Illustration pp. 202 | 203 Draft for Sensorium – The Voice of the World Ocean A Vision A New Kind of Art A New Kind of Science, 2021/22

Quote p. 224 Helen & Newton Harrison, from Greenhouse Britain, 2008

The La Jolla Historical Society thanks the photographers, museums, and galleries for their generous support in the realization of this book. Despite careful research, it was not possible to identfy every photographer or to determine every rights holder. We apologize and ask for your understanding.

Finally understanding

that the news is neither good nor bad

it is simply that great differences are upon us

that great changes are upon us as a culture

and great changes are upon all planetary life systems

and the news is about how we meet these changes

and are transformed by them or in turn transform them